Windows® 8.1
Inside Out

Tony Northrup

PUBLISHED BY
Microsoft Press
A Division of Microsoft Corporation
One Microsoft Way
Redmond, Washington 98052-6399

Library of Congress Control Number: 2013949896
ISBN: 978-0-7356-8363-1

Printed and bound in the United States of America.

Second Printing

Microsoft Press books are available through booksellers and distributors worldwide. If you need support related to this book, email Microsoft Press Book Support at mspinput@microsoft.com. Please tell us what you think of this book at http://www.microsoft.com/learning/booksurvey.

Microsoft and the trademarks listed at http://www.microsoft.com/about/legal/en-us/IntellectualProperty/Trademarks/EN-US.aspx are trademarks of the Microsoft group of companies. All other marks are property of their respective owners.

The example companies, organizations, products, domain names, email addresses, logos, people, places, and events depicted herein are fictitious. No association with any real company, organization, product, domain name, email address, logo, person, place, or event is intended or should be inferred.

This book expresses the author's views and opinions. The information contained in this book is provided without any express, statutory, or implied warranties. Neither the author, Microsoft Corporation, nor its resellers or distributors will be held liable for any damages caused or alleged to be caused either directly or indirectly by this book.

Acquisitions Editor: Rosemary Caperton
Developmental Editor: Valerie Woolley
Editorial Production: Curtis Philips, Publishing.com
Technical Reviewer: Randall Galloway; Technical Review services provided by
                Content Master, a member of CM Group, Ltd.
Copyeditor: John Pierce
Indexer: William P. Meyers
Cover: Twist Creative • Seattle

Para nana Lucy y papa José

Contents at a glance

PART 1: Getting started

Chapter 1
What's new in Windows 8.1. 3

Chapter 2
Using Windows 8.1 apps. 51

Chapter 3
Buying and installing Windows 8.1 89

Chapter 4
Upgrading and migrating to
Windows 8.1 111

Chapter 5
Personalizing Windows 8.1 123

Chapter 6
Adding, removing, and managing apps 147

Chapter 7
Using Windows 8.1 accessibility
features 173

Chapter 8
Obtaining help and support 195

PART 2: File management

Chapter 9
Organizing and protecting files 211

Chapter 10
Backing up and restoring files. 233

Chapter 11
Managing Windows search 249

Chapter 12
Managing storage 261

Chapter 13
Using SkyDrive 289

PART 3: Music, videos, TV, and movies

Chapter 14
Music and videos 307

Chapter 15
Photos 325

Chapter 16
Sharing and streaming digital media 343

Chapter 17
Creating a Home Theater PC 359

PART 4: Security and privacy

Chapter 18
Managing users and Family Safety 393

Chapter 19
Windows, application, and network
security 437

Chapter 20
Using Hyper-V 473

PART 5: Networking

Chapter 21
Setting up a home or small office
network 505

Chapter 22
Setting up ad hoc, Bluetooth, and
mobile networks 547

Chapter 23
Troubleshooting your network 563

Chapter 24
Sharing and managing files and printers. . . . 583

PART 6: Maintaining, tuning, and troubleshooting

Chapter 25
Maintaining your PC 609

Chapter 26
**Monitoring, measuring, and tuning
performance** 621

Chapter 27
**Troubleshooting startup problems,
crashes, and corruption** 653

Table of contents

Introduction xxi
    Who this book is for xxi
        Assumptions about you xxii
    How this book is organized xxii
    Supplemental videos xxiii
        List of videos xxiii
    Your companion ebook xxv
    Acknowledgments xxv
    Support and feedback xxvi
        Errata & support xxvi
        We want to hear from you xxvi
        Stay in touch xxvi

PART 1: Getting started 1

Chapter 1   **What's new in Windows 8.1 . . . . 3**
    Interacting with Windows 8.1 4
        Touch controls 4
        Mouse controls 7
        Keyboard shortcuts 8
    Windows 8.1 user interface 8
        Lock screen 9
        Start screen 10
        Charms 13
        PC Settings 14
        Autocorrect and highlight misspelled words 15
        Searching 15
        Portrait and landscape modes 16
        Language packs 17
        Accessibility 18
        Boot changes 18

What do you think of this book? We want to hear from you!

Microsoft is interested in hearing your feedback so we can improve our books and learning resources for you. To participate in a brief survey, please visit:

http://aka.ms/tellpress

Hardware 20
    Minimum hardware 21
    Display resolution. 21
    Touch hardware 21
    Sensor support 21
    Improved power efficiency. 22
    USB 3.0 support 22
    ARM support. 22
Security. 22
    Picture password 23
    PIN login 24
    SmartScreen filter. 24
    Windows Defender 25
    BitLocker 26
    Secured Boot. 26
    Microsoft accounts. 26
Networking 27
    Mobile broadband. 27
    Wi-Fi 28
Storage 29
    SkyDrive. 29
    Storage Spaces 31
Manageability, productivity, and troubleshooting 33
    Support for multiple monitors. 33
    Task Manager 33
    Refreshing and resetting your PC 35
    Client Hyper-V 36
What's new in the Windows 8.1 update 37
    Improved multitasking 37
    Boot to desktop and other navigation properties 38
    Start button on the desktop. 40
    Improved WinX menu 41
    Lock screen slide show 41
    Camera access from the lock screen. 42
    New tile sizes on the Start screen 42
    Improved Apps view 43
    More personalization options 44
    Drastically improved searching 44
    More settings available with the touch interface. 45
    Internet Explorer 11. 45
    Improved security 46
    3-D printer support 46
    Tethering 47
    New business features. 47
What's missing. 47

Chapter 2   Using Windows 8.1 apps. **51**

Common features 52
  Settings 52
  Search. 52
  Share. 53
  Printing. 53
  Resuming 54
Using apps 54
  Store 54
  Updates 56
  App commands. 58
  Snapping 58
  Live tiles 59
  Lock screen 61
How Windows 8.1 apps work 62
  Isolation 62
  Suspending Windows 8.1 apps 62
  Background tasks. 63
Changing app file associations 64
Built-in apps 67
  Internet Explorer 11. 67
  File Explorer. 71
  People. 74
  Calendar. 75
  Mail. 75
  Games. 77
  Music 77
  Video 78
  Photos. 78
  Weather 80
  Finance 80
  Reader 81
  Maps. 82
  Camera. 82
  News. 83
  Travel 84
  Sports. 84
  Food And Drink 85
  Health And Fitness 85
  Help+Tips. 86
  Reading List. 87
  Scan. 87
  Sound Recorder 87

Chapter 3	**Buying and installing Windows 8.1**............................ **89**	
	Buying Windows 8.1..	89
	Installing Windows 8.1..	91
	Making a bootable flash drive.............................	92
	Starting the installation.................................	93
	Configuring express settings.............................	97
	Selecting custom settings................................	98
	Signing in to your PC....................................	100
	Dual-booting Windows 8.1....................................	100
	Installing Windows 8.1 on a separate partition............	101
	Booting from a VHD......................................	104
	Configuring boot options................................	108
Chapter 4	**Upgrading and migrating to Windows 8.1** **111**	
	Preparing for an upgrade	111
	Upgrading from Windows XP or Windows Vista to Windows 8.1	112
	Performing the upgrade to Windows 8.1........................	113
	Migrating from an old PC to a new PC........................	116
	Post-upgrade tasks..	120
	Configuring your apps....................................	120
	Testing your apps and hardware..........................	120
	Freeing up disk space....................................	121
	Uninstalling Windows 8.1	122
Chapter 5	**Personalizing Windows 8.1**................................. **123**	
	The Start screen..	123
	Arranging tiles..	124
	Grouping apps	124
	Changing the Start screen background	125
	Showing administrative tools on the Start screen	126
	Adding restart and shutdown to the Start screen	127
	Tiles	128
	Notifications...	129
	Lock screen..	130
	Desktop...	132
	Adding the Windows 7 Start menu........................	132
	How to launch apps.....................................	132
	How to pin apps..	134
	How to add the Recycle Bin to the taskbar................	134
	Searching	135
	Power settings...	136
	Multiple monitors	139
	Configuring multiple monitors	139
	Setting up your taskbar..................................	140
	Language settings...	142
	WinX menu..	143
	Adding items to the WinX menu..........................	144

Chapter 6   **Adding, removing, and managing apps.........................147**

    Installing Windows 8.1 apps 147

    Uninstalling Windows 8.1 apps. 148

    Setting default programs. 149

    Configuring AutoPlay 151

    Managing startup apps 152

        How to examine startup apps 154

        How to remove startup apps 155

        How to add startup apps 155

    Recording app problems. 157

    Understanding app permissions. 158

    The .NET Framework. 159

    The parts of a Windows 8.1 app. 160

        Types of Windows 8.1 apps 160

        XAML app file types. 161

        HTML5 app file types. 161

        Configuration settings. 162

        File locations 162

        App manifests 164

    App compatibility settings. 165

    Managing Windows 8.1 app packages 168

        How to run Dism 169

        How to list Windows 8.1 app packages 169

        How to remove Windows 8.1 app packages. 169

    Monitoring app events. 170

Chapter 7   **Using Windows 8.1 accessibility features. 173**

    Choosing accessible hardware 174

    Configuring accessibility options 174

    Visual accessibility. 175

        Making everything bigger 175

        Increasing contrast. 177

        Magnifying the screen. 177

        Third-party screen magnification software. 183

        Narrator 183

        Third-party text-to-speech software 185

        Making the pointer easier to find 186

    User input accessibility. 187

        Using Windows 8.1 with only a keyboard 187

        Using Windows 8.1 with only a mouse. 189

        Using Windows 8.1 with speech recognition 190

        Using Windows 8.1 with touch 192

    Dyslexia and reading accessibility 192

Chapter 8   Obtaining help and support **195**

Obtaining professional support 195
Help and support 196
Determining who to contact for support 197
Searching the Internet 198
Asking for help 199
Connecting with Remote Assistance 202
    Enabling Remote Assistance.. 202
    Creating a Remote Assistance invitation 203
    Using Remote Assistance 205
Recording problems.. 206

PART 2: File management **209**

Chapter 9   Organizing and protecting files **211**

The Windows 8.1 way of organizing files 212
File system concepts.. 212
    File names 213
    Attributes... 214
Working with libraries 215
Zipping folders 218
Protecting files... 219
    Using permissions.. 219
    Using encryption 222
Advanced searching 225
Freeing up disk space.. 228
File organization tips 230

Chapter 10   Backing up and restoring files **233**

Backup concepts.. 233
Connecting a backup disk 235
Backing up and recovering files 239
    Backing up files.. 239
    Restoring files 241
Backing up and recovering apps and settings.................................. 243
Using cloud services... 244
Online backup services... 246
What if disaster strikes and you don't have a backup?.......................... 246

Chapter 11   Managing Windows search **249**

App search concepts. 249

Managing search suggestions 250

Managing file indexing 251

Managing searchable files and folders. 251

Managing the search index 254

Indexing other file types. 256

Disabling indexing 258

Chapter 12   Managing storage **261**

Storage Spaces. 261

Storage Spaces concepts. 262

Evaluating Storage Spaces 263

Configuring Storage Spaces 264

Configuring resiliency 266

BitLocker. 268

Evaluating BitLocker. 269

Drive types that can be encrypted 270

Choosing the startup mode 271

Using BitLocker without a TPM 274

Suspending and removing BitLocker 275

BitLocker recovery 276

Enabling BitLocker 279

Using BitLocker with removable drives 281

Fixing errors 283

Choosing a new drive. 286

Chapter 13   Using SkyDrive **289**

SkyDrive overview. 289

Using the SkyDrive app for Windows 8.1 290

Accessing SkyDrive from mobile devices 292

Accessing SkyDrive from a browser. 294

Using SkyDrive on the desktop 295

SkyDrive performance. 297

Handling versioning conflicts. 299

Accessing PCs through SkyDrive 300

Editing documents simultaneously with other users 302

PART 3: Music, videos, TV, and movies...........................305

Chapter 14   **Music and videos**.. 307

Using the Music app... 307
Listening to music 308
Creating and managing playlists............................. 311
Using Xbox Music... 312
Ripping CDs 313
Editing metadata.. 315
Watching videos 316
Purchasing TV and movies 317
Editing videos.. 319
Installing Movie Maker 319
Editing a video 320
Publishing a video 322
Other video editing apps 323

Chapter 15   **Photos** 325

Viewing pictures with the Photos app............................ 325
Importing photos 326
Printing photos 330
Working with RAW files 332
Selecting and sharing photos................................... 334
Sharing photos in email 334
Working with photos on the desktop 336
Organizing photos 337

Chapter 16   **Sharing and streaming digital media** 343

Xbox Music... 343
Streaming to the Xbox 344
Stereos and TVs.. 345
Smartphone 347
Car 348
Other computers.. 350
Music services 352
Video-streaming services 353
Creating media 354
CDs 354
DVDs... 355

Chapter 17   **Creating a Home Theater PC** 359

HTPC software.. 360
Media Center... 362
Media Center settings 363
Converting recorded shows 366
Configuring HTPC software to start automatically............... 369

Choosing the hardware 371
    Case 371
    Fan. 372
    Video card 373
    Processor 377
    Memory 377
    Storage. 377
    Sound card 379
    Network 380
    Cables. 381
Recording TV 382
    Encrypted digital cable with a CableCARD 383
    Using a cable box or other device that connects to a TV 384
    Analog and unencrypted digital cable. 385
    Over-the-air broadcasts 386
    Using IR blasters 386
Choosing a remote control 387

PART 4: Security and privacy 391

Chapter 18   Managing users and Family Safety 393
Logon security. 394
    Microsoft accounts. 394
    Local accounts. 397
Configuring sign-on options. 398
    Using a picture password 398
    Using a PIN 404
Password best practices 405
    Password uniqueness. 405
    Password complexity. 406
    Regularly changing your password. 412
    Using passphrases 414
Managing accounts 415
    Creating accounts for guests 416
    Deleting a user 417
    Creating groups 418
    Changing group memberships 419
Family Safety 422
    Turning on Family Safety. 422
    Web filtering 423
    Activity reporting. 428
    Time limits 431
    Curfew 432
    App restrictions. 432
    Windows Store and game restrictions 434

Chapter 19   Windows, application, and network security. 437

Malware protection 438

  User Account Control 442

  SmartScreen 442

  Windows Defender 445

Protecting your privacy 447

  Privacy while browsing the web 447

  Privacy while using Windows. 448

Removing malware. 449

  Step 1: Uninstall apps 449

  Step 2: Scan with Windows Defender. 449

  Step 3: Scan with third-party antimalware. 450

  Step 4: Perform a system restore. 451

  Step 5: Restore from backup 454

  Step 6: Refresh your system 455

  Step 7: Removing rootkits. 456

Windows Firewall. 457

  Allowing an app to listen for incoming connections. 458

  Preventing an app from listening for incoming connections. 460

  Manually configuring firewall rules. 461

  Temporarily disabling Windows Firewall 465

  Switching between public and private networks 467

Wireless security 468

Turning off security features. 469

  UAC. 469

  SmartScreen 470

  Windows Defender 471

Chapter 20   Using Hyper-V 473

Hyper-V requirements 474

Installing Hyper-V. 475

Creating your first virtual switch. 476

  Startup memory. 478

  Dynamic memory. 480

  Connection 481

  Virtual hard disk size and location 482

  Operating system. 483

Configuring VM settings 484

  Add hardware. 485

  BIOS 485

  Memory 486

  Processor 487

  IDE controllers. 488

  SCSI controllers. 489

  Network adapter 489

  Integration services 491

  Automatic stop action. 494

Starting a VM 495
Using snapshots 495
Managing virtual disks 496
    Virtual disk formats 496
    Virtual disk types 496
    Migrating physical disks 497
Hyper-V tips and tricks 499
When not to use a VM 500
Using VirtualBox 501

PART 5: Networking 503

Chapter 21   **Setting up a home or small office network 505**

Network technology overview 505
    The architecture of a home network 506
    IP addresses 508
    NAT 508
    DHCP 510
    DNS 511
Choosing an ISP 513
Connecting Windows 8.1 to your network 515
Manually configuring Windows 8.1 networking 517
Fine-tuning wireless settings 518
Routers 521
    Choosing a router 521
    Configuring a router or wireless access point 524
Choosing home networking technologies 525
    Wireless Ethernet 525
    Wired Ethernet 526
    Ethernet over coax 527
    Ethernet over phoneline 528
    Powerline networking 528
Designing a wireless network 530
    Choosing a wireless network standard 530
    Choosing a wireless access point 531
    Choosing wireless encryption 534
    Choosing a SSID 538
    Providing wireless access throughout your house 538
    Managing wireless networks 540
Web applications 541
    Email 541
    File hosting 546
    Web hosting 546

Chapter 22 **Setting up ad hoc, Bluetooth, and mobile networks** **547**

Ad hoc networking 547
Creating an ad hoc wireless network 547
Sharing an Internet connection 550
Easier ways to share an Internet connection 553
Bluetooth 554
Pairing Bluetooth accessories 555
Sending files between PCs across Bluetooth 556
3G/4G mobile broadband 559

Chapter 23 **Troubleshooting your network** **563**

Troubleshooting tools 563
Restarting 563
Network And Sharing Center 564
Network Diagnostics 566
Ping 568
PathPing 570
PortQry 572
Network Monitor 574
The home network troubleshooting process 577
Troubleshooting network performance problems 579
Measuring and optimizing Internet performance 579
Measuring and optimizing local network performance 580

Chapter 24 **Sharing and managing files and printers** **583**

Using a homegroup 583
Creating a homegroup 583
Joining a homegroup 584
Accessing shared files 586
Using folder sharing 588
Granting permissions to files 592
Using shared printers 593
Sharing a printer with a desktop PC and a homegroup 594
Sharing a printer with a desktop PC without using a homegroup 594
Sharing printers without a PC 596
Automatically connecting to shared printers 596
Manually connecting to a printer shared from a PC 600
Manually connecting to a network printer 605

PART 6: Maintaining, tuning, and troubleshooting 607

Chapter 25   Maintaining your PC 609

Updates 609
    Windows updates 610
    Windows 8.1 app updates 614
    Desktop app updates 614
    Driver and firmware updates 615
    BIOS updates 617
Backups 617
Uninstalling apps 617
Disk integrity 618
Disk space 618
Maintaining your batteries 618

Chapter 26   Monitoring, measuring, and tuning performance 621

Benchmarking your computer 621
    Benchmarking disks using HD Tune 624
    Benchmarking network performance 624
Finding and controlling a troublesome app 625
Setting priority and affinity when starting an app 627
Speeding up startup 630
    Removing startup apps 630
    Delaying automatic services 630
    Disabling unused hardware 633
    Upgrading your hard drive 634
Using Task Manager 634
    Processes tab 636
    Performance tab 639
    App History tab 640
    Startup tab 641
    Users tab 642
    Details tab 643
    Services tab 644
Using Performance Monitor 644
    Monitoring performance in real time 645
    Logging performance data 648
    Creating performance reports 651

Chapter 27   **Troubleshooting startup problems, crashes, and corruption** **653**

Troubleshooting startup problems 653
   Using Windows Recovery Environment 654
   Troubleshooting startup from a command prompt. 656
   What to do if you can see your system drive 656
   What to do if you can't see your system drive 660
Troubleshooting corruption and intermittent failures 661
   Identifying system changes and error details. 662
   Testing your hard drive. 664
   Testing your memory. 666
   Testing other hardware components 669
Refreshing your PC. 671
Resetting your PC 674

Index to troubleshooting topics **677**

Index **679**

What do you think of this book? We want to hear from you!

Microsoft is interested in hearing your feedback so we can improve our books and learning resources for you. To participate in a brief survey, please visit:

http://aka.ms/tellpress

Introduction

Windows 8 and the Windows 8.1 update include the most important changes to the Windows operating system since Windows 95. While almost everything you've come to love about earlier versions of Windows is still available, Windows 8.1 provides an infrastructure on which the next generation of PCs and apps will be built. These new PCs and apps will be powerful, fast, mobile, and touch-friendly.

Your keyboard and mouse will work fine, but you'll also be able to bring new touch-friendly PCs to your couch, kitchen, patio, or wherever you want them. Your kids, and even that technophobic family member who only knows how to use Facebook on their smartphone, will be able to use the PC with little instruction.

While anyone can use Windows 8.1, it's also one of the most full-featured operating systems ever made. By gaining a deeper understanding of Windows 8.1, you can use it to record and watch your favorite TV shows at home and while you travel, edit and share your home movies, access your files from any device anywhere in the world, get fast Internet access throughout your entire house, and so much more. That's why I wrote this book: to teach you how to use PCs to improve the lives of you and your family.

I believe books are the best way to learn. Sometimes, though, it's much easier for me to show you something in person. That's why I've recorded dozens of videos and linked to them throughout this book. You don't need to watch the videos; they're entirely optional. However, they make the process of learning about Windows 8.1 so much more fun. Often, videos can show important concepts much more clearly than text and screen shots.

If you have any questions, or you just want to keep in touch with me, I'm easy to find. On Facebook, friend me at *http://www.facebook.com/tony.northrup,* and follow my photography at *http://www.facebook.com/NorthrupPhotography*. Subscribe to my YouTube videos at *http://www.youtube.com/user/VistaClues*. Follow me on Twitter at *http://twitter.com/tonynorthrup* (@tonynorthrup). You can also just email me at tony@northrup.org.

Who this book is for

This book offers a comprehensive look at the features most people will use in Windows 8.1 and serves as an excellent reference for users who need to understand how to accomplish what they need to do. In addition, this book goes a step or two further, providing useful information to advanced users who want to get the most out of their PCs by maximizing their privacy and security, using them as Wi-Fi hotspots on the go, integrating them into their home theater system, or almost anything else you can imagine.

Assumptions about you

Windows 8.1 Inside Out is designed for readers who have some experience with earlier versions of Windows. You don't have to be a power user, IT professional, or a developer, however. While I dive deeply into how Windows 8.1 works, I always describe concepts using simple, straightforward language.

How this book is organized

This book gives you a comprehensive look at the various features you will use. This book is structured in a logical approach to all aspects of using and managing Windows 8.1.

Part 1, "Getting started," covers the most important ways in which Windows 8 and Windows 8.1 are different from earlier versions of Windows: the user interface, the touch and mouse controls, and the apps. This section also shows you how to install Windows 8.1 or upgrade to Windows 8.1 from Windows XP, Windows Vista, or Windows 7. Finally, this section shows you how to manage your apps, configure accessibility features, and get help when things go wrong.

Part 2, "File management," shows you how to manage and protect your files. You'll learn about new features, including Storage Spaces and SkyDrive, which will change how you manage your files. You'll also learn how to make sure that your important files are backed up.

Part 3, "Music, videos, TV, and movies," teaches you how to turn a PC running Windows 8.1 into a multimedia entertainment center for music, movies, and TV. You'll be able to enjoy your media whether you're in your family room, the backseat of your car, or a hotel room.

Part 4, "Security and privacy," shows you the importance of creating separate user accounts for everyone in your house. You'll be able to control and monitor everything your children do on their PCs. You'll also be able to keep your files private, even if someone steals your PC. This section also describes how to use Hyper-V to create virtual machines that can run different operating systems within a window.

Part 5, "Networking," helps you get your PCs connected to each other and the Internet at home and on the go, using wired, Wi-Fi, and wireless broadband technologies. This section also describes troubleshooting common network problems and sharing files and printers between PCs.

Part 6, "Maintaining, tuning, and troubleshooting," describes how to keep your PC running as reliably and securely as possible. Besides mastering the usual maintenance tasks, you'll learn how to tune the performance of your PC to make it as fast as it can be.

Supplemental videos

I have recorded more than two and a half hours of video training to supplement this book. These videos demonstrate Windows 8.1 and related technologies in a home environment. You'll find links to the videos in the appropriate sections throughout the book, as well as in the table below.

You can also go directly to the book's companion content page to access the videos here:

http://aka.ms/WinIO/files

List of videos

Use this table as a reference to the videos that supplement *Windows 8.1 Inside Out.*

Chapter	Video name and location
Chapter 1	Touch controls: *http://aka.ms/WinIO/touchcontrols*
	Mouse controls: *http://aka.ms/WinIO/mousecontrols*
	The Windows 8.1 user interface: *http://aka.ms/WinIO/UI*
	What's new in the Windows 8.1 update: *http://aka.ms/WinIO/new*
Chapter 2	Using charms: *http://aka.ms/WinIO/charms*
	Using apps designed for Windows 8.1: *http://aka.ms/WinIO/apps*
Chapter 3	Installing Windows 8.1: *http://aka.ms/WinIO/install*
Chapter 4	Upgrading to Windows 8.1: *http://aka.ms/WinIO/upgrade*
Chapter 5	Customizing the Start screen: *http://aka.ms/WinIO/startscreen*
	Personalizing Windows 8.1: *http://aka.ms/WinIO/personalize*
Chapter 6	Installing, updating, and removing Windows 8.1 apps: *http://aka.ms/WinIO/installupdateremove*
Chapter 7	Using Magnifier: *http://aka.ms/WinIO/magnifier*
	Using Narrator: *http://aka.ms/WinIO/narrator*
Chapter 8	Finding help online: *http://aka.ms/WinIO/help*
Chapter 9	Protecting your files: *http://aka.ms/WinIO/protect*
Chapter 10	Backing up and restoring files: *http://aka.ms/WinIO/backuprestore*
Chapter 11	Searching with Windows 8.1: *http://aka.ms/WinIO/search*
Chapter 12	Using Storage Spaces: *http://aka.ms/WinIO/storage*
	Using BitLocker: *http://aka.ms/WinIO/bitlocker*
Chapter 13	Using the SkyDrive app: *http://aka.ms/WinIO/skydriveapp*
	Using the SkyDrive website: *http://aka.ms/WinIO/skydriveweb*

Chapter	Video name and location
Chapter 14	Ripping CDs: *http://aka.ms/WinIO/ripping*
	Editing a video with touch: *http://aka.ms/WinIO/editing*
Chapter 15	Printing photos: *http://aka.ms/WinIO/printphotos*
	Transferring photos wirelessly to your PC: *http://aka.ms/WinIO/transfer*
	Sharing photos: *http://aka.ms/WinIO/sharephotos*
Chapter 16	Playing your music in your car: *http://aka.ms/WinIO/car*
	Playing your music on your stereo: *http://aka.ms/WinIO/stereo*
Chapter 17	Windows Media Center overview: *http://aka.ms/WinIO/mediacenter*
	Home Theater PC hardware: *http://aka.ms/WinIO/hardware*
Chapter 18	Creating users: *http://aka.ms/WinIO/logon*
	Using Family Safety: *http://aka.ms/WinIO/familysafety*
	Passwords, picture passwords, and PINs: *http://aka.ms/WinIO/passwords*
Chapter 19	Using Windows Defender: *http://aka.ms/WinIO/defender*
	Removing malware: *http://aka.ms/WinIO/malware*
	Allowing an app through Windows Firewall: *http://aka.ms/WinIO/firewall*
Chapter 20	Creating a virtual machine in Hyper-V: *http://aka.ms/WinIO/hyperv*
	Using snapshots in Hyper-V: *http://aka.ms/WinIO/snapshots*
Chapter 21	Creating a wired home network: *http://aka.ms/WinIO/wired*
	Creating a wireless home network: *http://aka.ms/WinIO/wireless*
Chapter 22	Creating an ad hoc network: *http://aka.ms/WinIO/adhoc*
	Pairing Bluetooth accessories: *http://aka.ms/WinIO/bluetooth*
Chapter 23	Troubleshooting a failed Internet connection: *http://aka.ms/WinIO/homenetwork*
Chapter 24	Sharing files in a homegroup: *http://aka.ms/WinIO/homegroup*
	Sharing printers: *http://aka.ms/WinIO/shareprinters*
Chapter 25	Maintaining Windows 8.1: *http://aka.ms/WinIO/maintenance*
Chapter 26	Monitoring Windows 8.1 with Task Manager: *http://aka.ms/WinIO/taskmanager*
	Monitoring Windows 8.1 with Performance Monitor: *http://aka.ms/WinIO/performance*
Chapter 27	Troubleshooting blue screens: *http://aka.ms/WinIO/bluescreen*
	Troubleshooting startup problems: *http://aka.ms/WinIO/startup*
	Testing your memory: *http://aka.ms/WinIO/memory*

Your companion ebook

With the ebook edition of this book, you can do the following:

1. Search the full text

2. Print

3. Copy and paste

To download your ebook, please see the instruction page at the back of the book.

Acknowledgments

First, I have to thank Anne Hamilton for giving me the opportunity to write this book. This isn't the first time she's given me a great opportunity; the first time was way back in 1997, when she asked me to write my very first book. I also have to thank my friend Ken Jones at O'Reilly Media for suggesting me, and for always keeping me busy writing.

My team and Microsoft Press have been amazing. First, Valerie Woolley and Rosemary Caperton, thanks so much for your patience and flexibility. Curtis Philips, you did a fantastic job, and it has been great working with you. My tech reviewer, Randall Galloway, went above and beyond and caught many of those little details that kept changing in Windows 8 and Windows 8.1 throughout the development phases.

Those are the folks I worked with most constantly, but I know there are many other people who helped with this project. For all of you working behind the scenes, thanks so much for your dedication.

I also need to thank people in my personal life who've entertained, fed, and loved me while I've been writing this book: Chelsea Northrup; Madelyn Knowles; Brian, Melissa, Tyler, Austin, and Mya Rheaume; José B. and Kristin Gonzalez; Ed and Christine Mercado; papa José and nana Lucy; Alexis Glenn; Kevin Girard; and Erkki Alvenmod.

Support and feedback

The following sections provide information on errata, book support, feedback, and contact information.

Errata & support

We've made every effort to ensure the accuracy of this book and its companion content. Any errors that have been reported since this book was published are listed here:

http://aka.ms/WinIO/errata

If you find an error that is not already listed, you can report it to us through the same page.

If you need additional support, email Microsoft Press Book Support at:

mspinput@microsoft.com.

Please note that product support for Microsoft software is not offered through the addresses above.

We want to hear from you

At Microsoft Press, your satisfaction is our top priority and your feedback our most valuable asset. Please tell us what you think of this book at:

http://www.microsoft.com/learning/booksurvey

The survey is short, and we read every one of your comments and ideas. Thanks in advance for your input!

Stay in touch

Let's keep the conversation going! We're on Twitter: *http://twitter.com/MicrosoftPress*

PART 1

Getting started

CHAPTER 1
What's new in Windows 8.1 3

CHAPTER 2
Using Windows 8.1 apps 51

CHAPTER 3
Buying and installing Windows 8.1 89

CHAPTER 4
Upgrading and migrating to
Windows 8.1 111

CHAPTER 5
Personalizing Windows 8.1 123

CHAPTER 6
Adding, removing, and managing apps 147

CHAPTER 7
Using Windows 8.1 accessibility
features 173

CHAPTER 8
Obtaining help and support 195

What's new in Windows 8.1

Interacting with Windows 8.1 4

Windows 8.1 user interface 8

Hardware 20

Security 22

Networking 27

Storage 29

Manageability, productivity, and troubleshooting 33

What's new in the Windows 8.1 update 37

What's missing 47

In the past few years, people have begun using computers in completely different ways. While many still use their computer at a desk with a keyboard and mouse, those same people step away from their desk and use mobile phones and tablets to keep in touch.

Microsoft designed Windows 8.1 to fit modern computing. The familiar Start menu is completely gone, replaced by a continuously updated Start screen. You even have the option of never touching another keyboard and mouse: Windows 8.1 is touch-friendly, allowing you to grab the latest tablet computers and navigate them with your fingers.

Windows 8.1 also integrates the cloud, allowing users to authenticate using a Microsoft account and to store and share files using SkyDrive. Social networking is deeply integrated into Windows, and Windows 8.1 connects to Twitter, Facebook, and other social networking sites just as easily as to local resources.

These changes will require those of us experienced with earlier versions of Windows to relearn some of the ways we interact with a computer. The new interface and apps are so intuitive that most people will comfortably navigate Windows 8.1 with just a few minutes of learning. The underpinnings, however, require deep examination to fully understand.

As with every version of Windows, Microsoft recognizes the importance of backward compatibility. Though Windows 8.1 is designed to be touch-friendly, it is equally usable with a keyboard and mouse. Though apps designed for Windows 8.1 provide the greatest performance, you can still run almost any app created for earlier versions of Windows, and your existing drivers will work without modification.

This first chapter gives you an overview of the most important new features of Windows 8.1. Some of these features were introduced in Windows 8 or have been updated since that release. Future chapters become increasingly more technical, providing greater detail about apps, the touch interface, documents, media, security, networking, troubleshooting, and much more.

NOTE

Because this book is focused on consumer and small business uses of Windows 8.1, it will not describe features that are exclusive to Windows 8.1 Enterprise.

Interacting with Windows 8.1

Whereas Windows 7 had a Start button that was always visible, and applications typically had menus and toolbars that remained visible, one of the design goals of Windows 8.1 is to completely immerse you in full-screen applications. Instead of wasting screen space on buttons, Windows 8.1 makes the corners and edges of the screens active, but it does not label them, so it is important for even the most experienced Windows users to learn the location of these new controls. While these new controls will not be immediately obvious to most Windows users, learning them takes just a few minutes.

Windows 8.1 is designed to be equally usable with a touch screen or a conventional mouse and keyboard. The sections that follow briefly describe the different ways you can control Windows 8.1.

Touch controls

Windows 8.1 and apps designed for Windows 8.1 are accessible using tablet computers without a mouse or keyboard. The touch controls are intuitive, especially if you have a smartphone. However, some of the controls will not be obvious the first time you use Windows 8.1. This section describes the basic touch controls.

Tap

Tapping, like clicking with a mouse, performs an action. For example, tap an app on the Start screen or a link in Internet Explorer to open it.

To select text within an app, tap it, and then use the circles to adjust the selection, as shown in Figure 1-1. Tap the selection to copy or paste it.

Figure 1-1 Select text by tapping and then adjusting your selection.

Hold

Holding your finger on an object can do one of two things, depending on the app:

- Display information about the object, much like hovering over an object with the mouse.

- Display a context menu, much like right-clicking an object.

Swipe

The edges of the screen are really important in Windows 8.1. By swiping a finger in from the edges and corners of the screen, you can perform different actions regardless of the app you have open:

- Swipe from the right side of the screen to view the charms for searching, sharing, and printing.

- Swipe from the left side of the screen to bring up a list of previously used apps.

- Swipe from the top or bottom of the screen to view app-specific commands, which function like an app's menu.

Figure 1-2 illustrates swiping from the right side of the screen.

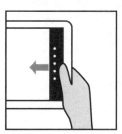

Figure 1-2 Swipe from the edges of the screen to view the charms or app commands.

Slide

Slide your finger across the screen to drag objects and scroll the screen, as shown in Figure 1-3. For example, to scroll left or right on the Start screen, just touch anywhere on the screen and slide to either side.

To view a list of recently used apps (equivalent to holding down the Alt key and repeatedly pressing Tab), tap the upper-left corner of the screen and then slide your finger down. You can then slide an app to dock it to one side of the screen, or slide it to the bottom of the screen to close it.

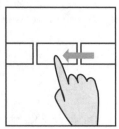

Figure 1-3 Slide your finger across the screen to scroll or drag objects.

Flick

Flick objects to select them. A flick is a short, quick, downward swipe. For example, you would tap a tile on the Start screen to open the app, but flick it to select the tile so you can change its settings.

Pinch and stretch

Some apps, including the Start screen, support pinching and stretching to zoom in and out, as illustrated by Figure 1-4. Zooming in allows you to see more detail, while zooming out shows you more context.

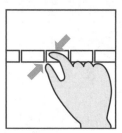

Figure 1-4 Pinch to zoom back and view more on the screen.

Rotate

In some apps, you can also use two fingers to rotate objects on the screen, as shown in Figure 1-5. For example, you might use this technique to rotate a picture from horizontal to vertical.

Figure 1-5 Rotate objects with two fingers.

▶ **Touch controls** Watch the video at *http://aka.ms/WinIO/touchcontrols*.

Mouse controls

Windows 8.1 also provides new mouse controls:

- Move your mouse to the upper-left corner to view the most recently used app. Click to open it or drag it to the side of the screen to snap it.

- Move your mouse to the lower-left corner and then click to open the Start screen.

- Move your mouse to the upper-left corner and then slide it down (without clicking) to view a list of recently used apps.

- When viewing the list of recently used apps, click an app to open it or drag it to the side of the screen to snap it.

- Move your mouse to the upper-right or lower-right corner to view the charms. Click a charm to use it.

- Right-click most apps to view the app commands. Some apps, such as Internet Explorer, provide traditional context menus when you right-click.

- Drag an app from the foreground to either side of the screen to snap it.

- Right-click the lower-left corner to open quick links.

▶ **Mouse controls** Watch the video at *http://aka.ms/WinIO/mousecontrols*.

Keyboard shortcuts

Windows 8.1 provides the keyboard shortcuts in Table 1-1 to access its features.

Table 1-1 Windows 8.1 keyboard shortcuts

Action	Key
Display the Start screen	Windows key
View charms	Windows+C
Search	Windows+Q
Search for files	Windows+F
Open Settings	Windows+I
View app commands	Windows+Z
Open quick links for power users (try it!)	Windows+X
Show the desktop	Windows+D
Lock the computer	Windows+L
Run an app	Windows+R
Snap an app to the right	Windows+Period
Snap an app to the left	Windows+Shift+Period
Switch applications	Windows+Tab

Windows 8.1 user interface

Windows 8.1 has a brand new user interface and app model. The new design theme focuses on simplicity, functionality, and touch. Gone are the beveled edges, drop shadows, and reflections that have become overused in the last decade. Instead, you interact with the simplest elements: immediately recognizable white icons and squares and rectangles designed to resemble subway tiles. Intuitive tapping and swiping controls work well with or without a mouse and keyboard.

When Windows 8.1 starts, it displays a lock screen with a picture and the time and date. Swipe up from the bottom of the screen to access the login screen. After login and every time you press the Windows key, Windows 8.1 displays the Start screen.

For more information about the apps included with Windows 8.1, read Chapter 2, "Using Windows 8.1 apps."

▶ **The Windows 8.1 user interface** Watch the video at *http://aka.ms/WinIO/UI*.

Inside OUT

Desktop apps and Windows Store apps

Windows 8 introduced a new type of full-screen, touch-friendly app. (You'll hear various names for these apps, including Windows Store apps.) Traditional apps created for earlier versions of Windows are now considered "desktop apps." These are the windowed apps with borders, menus, and toolbars. Windows 8.1, Windows 7, and earlier versions of Windows can all run desktop apps. Only Windows 8.1 can run Windows 8.1 apps. This book will refer to Windows 8.1 apps as simply "apps," and traditional apps as "desktop apps."

Lock screen

The first screen you see when you start Windows 8.1 is the lock screen, as shown in Figure 1-6. The lock screen shows a picture, the current date and time, battery life (for mobile devices), the network status, and notifications from up to seven different apps. To open the lock screen from your desk, click your mouse or press any key. To open the lock screen with touch, swipe up from the bottom.

Figure 1-6 The Windows 8.1 lock screen displays the time and date with a photo.

Inside OUT

Turning off the lock screen

While useful for preventing tablet users from accidentally entering input while carry-ing their PC, the lock screen isn't particularly useful for desktop or laptop users. Follow these steps to disable the lock screen:

1. Run **gpedit.msc** to open the Local Group Policy Editor.

2. Select Computer Configuration\Administrative Templates\Control Panel\ Personalization.

3. Double-click Do Not Display The Lock Screen. Select Enabled, and then click OK.

The next time you start the computer, Windows will display the login screen when it starts, bypassing the lock screen.

Start screen

The Start screen, shown in Figure 1-7, is always the first page Windows 8.1 displays. Like most apps designed for Windows 8.1, the Start screen scrolls horizontally, rather than vertically. Instead of scrolling, you can zoom back to see the entire Start screen. To zoom with touch, pinch or stretch the Start screen. To zoom with a mouse and keyboard, hold down the Ctrl key and either scroll the mouse wheel or press the Plus Sign or Minus Sign.

The Start screen does not show every app. If you don't see the app you need, simply type its name from the Start screen. Windows 8.1 will search for the app and display any matching results.

After you open an app, you can open the Start screen in several different ways:

- Move your mouse to the lower-left corner of the screen.

- Press the Windows key on your keyboard.

- On touch-sensitive PCs, touch the lower-left corner. You can also swipe in from the right to view the charms and then touch the Start charm.

If you press the Windows key multiple times, Windows 8.1 will switch between the Start screen and your desktop. To run a command, simply type the command name and press Enter. Alter-natively, you can open the Run dialog box from the desktop by pressing Windows+R. Press Windows+X to access the WinX menu, as shown in Figure 1-8, which contains links to com-monly used tools.

Figure 1-7 The Start screen focuses on simplicity and functionality.

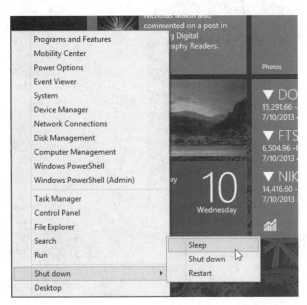

Figure 1-8 The WinX menu provides access to tools often used by power users.

Inside OUT

Getting a Windows 7–like Start menu

If you miss the Windows 7 Start menu, try giving the Windows 8.1 Start screen a few weeks. It really is better than the Windows 7 Start menu, even for traditional keyboard and mouse users. Sometimes, it's better to stick with what you know, however. While Windows 8.1 no longer has a Windows 7–like Start menu, you can download and install free alternatives. My favorite is ViStart (see Figure 1-9), available at *http://lee-soft.com/vistart/*. Another option is Start8, available at *http://www.stardock.com/products/start8/*.

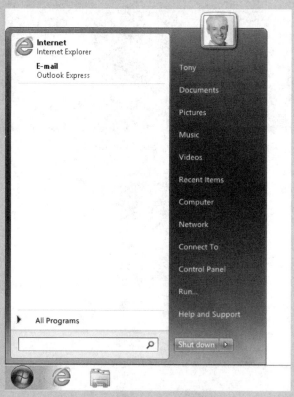

Figure 1-9 Install ViStart or Start8 if you prefer the Windows 7 Start menu.

Drag tiles to reorganize them on the Start screen. To change the size of tiles using touch, swipe up from the bottom, select a tile, and then touch an option. You can also flick tiles to select them and then open the app by swiping up from the bottom. With a mouse, right-click the tile you want to edit.

For information about live tiles and configuring apps on the Start screen, refer to Chapter 2.

Charms

Windows 8.1 introduces the idea of charms. You can use charms to perform common tasks in apps started from the Start screen, regardless of which app you're using. To view the charms with touch, swipe in the from the right. To view the charms with a mouse, move your pointer to the upper-right or lower-right corner. To view charms with a keyboard, press Windows+C.

The five standard charms are:

- **Search**   Opens the search bar to find apps, settings, and files. Some apps also use the Search charm to find content within the app. For example, to find a particular song, touch the Search charm, select the Music app, and type the name of your song. Press Windows+F to directly open the Search charm.

- **Share**   Allows you to share content within apps that support sharing. For example, to email a link to a webpage that you have open in Internet Explorer, touch the Share charm, and then touch the Mail app. Windows 8.1 will open the Mail app with a link to the current webpage in the body of the message. Press Windows+H to directly open the Share charm.

- **Start**   Opens the Start screen. You can also open the Start screen by pressing the Windows key.

- **Devices**   Allows you to print from the current app or send data to another device, if you have any supported devices installed. Press Windows+K to directly open the Devices charm.

- **Settings**   Lets you change options for the current app. Press Windows+I to directly open the Settings charm.

Charms, as shown in Figure 1-10, replace toolbar buttons and menu items that each app used to have for searching, sharing, printing, and setting options. Apps can still have unique commands for other features.

Figure 1-10 Use charms to access settings and functions you might have used menus to access in earlier versions of Windows.

PC Settings

To access PC Settings, touch the Settings charm or press Windows+I, and then select Change PC Settings in the lower-right corner. Figure 1-11 shows the new PC Settings tool that provides a touch interface to some of the Control Panel functionality you might be familiar with from Windows 7. You must still configure some settings from the Control Panel desktop app. To find a specific setting, press Windows+W, and then type words related to the setting.

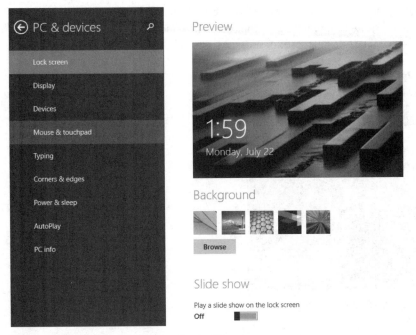

Figure 1-11 PC Settings replaces Control Panel.

Autocorrect and highlight misspelled words

Windows 8.1 can now highlight misspelled words and even autocorrect spelling errors and typos, as shown in Figure 1-12. Use the General screen within PC Settings to configure this feature.

Figure 1-12 Windows 8.1 autocorrects common typing and spelling errors and highlights others.

Searching

Windows 8.1 includes more powerful and organized search capabilities. From the Start screen, simply type to search apps, settings, files, and even webpages. Windows displays matching results, with your most commonly used resources at the top of the list.

To search only files, press Windows+F and type your search. (See Figure 1-13.) Windows 8.1 displays suggested searches below the search box, including spelling corrections. Use the Down Arrow key to select a suggestion or simply click it.

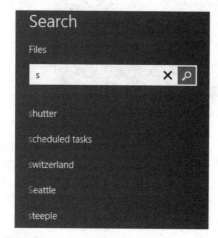

Figure 1-13 Windows 8.1 suggests searches as you type.

Results are organized based on the type of file: All (which includes every result), Documents, Pictures, Music, Videos, and Other. Hover your pointer over any result to see a larger thumbnail and more file details, as shown in Figure 1-14. You can use the Advanced Query Syntax (AQS) from Windows 7 to find files by attribute.

To search Settings, touch the Search charm and then touch Settings, or press Windows+W. Then, type words related to the setting you need to change. Windows 8.1 displays a list of settings you can modify.

Portrait and landscape modes

Windows 8.1 is designed to be used in either portrait or landscape mode, supporting the fact that users might prefer to hold tablet computers either vertically or horizontally. Most Windows 8.1 features are designed to work well no matter how the computer is held, and apps can support both horizontal and vertical displays, as well as a variety of different resolutions.

You can disable rotation, which is useful when you want to use a tablet computer lying flat or on its side.

CHAPTER 1

See all 18 photos and videos ›

Figure 1-14 Hover your pointer over a result to see more details.

Language packs

Windows 8.1 supports changing the default language. You no longer need to be concerned about the default language when you buy a computer; if you prefer to use a different language, you can change it at any time. This is particularly useful for environments where multiple users access a single computer and those users prefer different languages.

To add languages or to change the default language for your user account, use the Region & Language page in PC Settings, as shown in Figure 1-15.

Figure 1-15 Windows 8.1 supports dozens of languages.

➤ **For more information, refer to Chapter 5, "Personalizing Windows 8.1."**

Accessibility

Like previous versions of Windows, Windows 8.1 includes powerful accessibility features to make using a PC easier for users with different data input and visual needs. Windows 8.1 also makes several improvements:

- Narrator (the text-to-speech tool that audibly reads words from the screen) is now faster.

- Narrator supports more languages and voices.

- Narrator has new configuration settings that you can use to adjust the voice, speed, and other aspects of Narrator's behavior.

- Windows works better with accessibility features, making it easier for users with different needs to install and configure their PC.

- When using a Windows 8.1 tablet PC, you can hold the Windows logo key and press Volume Up to launch Narrator.

- Internet Explorer 10 and Narrator can continuously read a webpage.

➤ **For more information, refer to Chapter 7, "Using Windows 8.1 accessibility features."**

Boot changes

Windows 8.1 supports Unified Extensible Firmware Interface (UEFI) for BIOS, which allows for richer graphics using the Graphics Output Protocol (GOP) driver. UEFI also reduces the number of BIOS-related screens, allowing Windows 8.1 to provide a single visual experience from startup, instead of the computer hardware displaying BIOS screens and then switching to Windows, which provides a graphical display.

These capabilities allow Windows 8.1, when running on hardware that supports UEFI, to never display the text-based consoles that computers have used to start since before Windows existed. You can use the touch interface to select different operating systems, as shown in Figure 1-16, which shows a custom boot item (Windows 8.1 Safe Mode) added by the user with the BCDEdit tool.

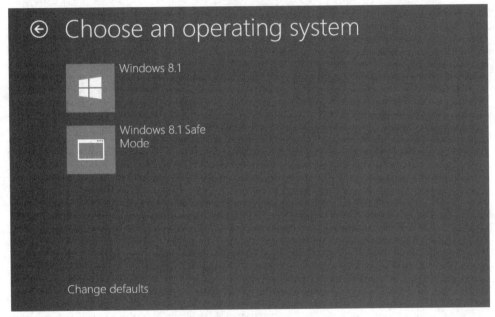

Figure 1-16 Windows 8.1 provides a graphical boot interface.

Inside OUT

Safe mode

Safe mode (also a part of earlier versions of Windows) is a special startup mode that minimizes the number of apps that run and hardware that Windows connects to. Sometimes when Windows won't start normally, you will still be able to start in safe mode. You can then use safe mode to run troubleshooting tools and recover your files. For detailed information, refer to *Troubleshoot and Optimize Windows 8 Inside Out* from Microsoft Press.

By clicking Change Defaults Or Choose Other Options, you can even change startup options before Windows starts, restore Windows, or run Windows Recovery Environment (WinRE), as shown in Figure 1-17. You never need a keyboard.

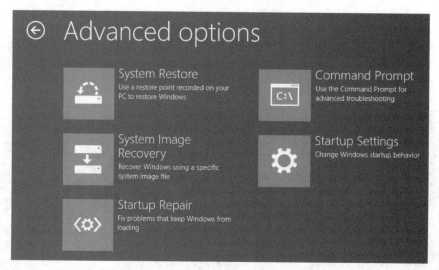

Figure 1-17 Windows 8.1 provides startup repair configuration and tools using a touch-friendly interface.

> ➤ For more information, read Chapter 27, "Troubleshooting startup problems, crashes, and corruption."

Hardware

Windows 8.1 is designed to run on almost all existing computer hardware, including desktop PCs, mobile PCs, and tablets. Most computers running Windows Vista or Windows 7 can be upgraded to Windows 8.1 and provide an even better experience.

Apps in Windows 8.1 have higher minimum screen resolution requirements than in earlier versions of Windows, but most current computers meet or exceed the screen resolution requirements.

The sections that follow describe the Windows 8.1 hardware requirements in more detail.

Minimum hardware

Hardware requirements for Windows 8.1 have not changed from Windows 7, and Windows 8.1 will perform as fast, or faster, than earlier versions of Windows on almost any recent PC. The Windows 8.1 hardware requirements are:

- **32-bit versions of Windows 8.1**   1 GHz or faster processer, 1 GB of RAM, 16 GB of free hard disk space, and a graphics card that supports DirectX 9 with WDDM 1.0 or higher

- **64-bit versions of Windows 8.1**   1 GHz or faster processer, 2 GB of RAM, 20 GB of free hard disk space, and a graphics card that supports DirectX 9 with WDDM 1.0 or higher

Display resolution

Windows 8.1, the Start screen, the desktop, and desktop apps still work at 800x600. A resolution of 1024x768 is required for apps designed for Windows 8.1. Using multitasking with snap requires a minimum resolution of 1366x768 to dock apps to either side of the screen. Windows 8.1 scales well to higher resolutions and even multiple monitors.

> ➤ **For more information about multitasking and snap, refer to Chapter 2.**

Touch hardware

Windows 8.1 supports touch-capable PCs that were designed for Windows 7. Therefore, existing Windows 7 users with tablets can upgrade to Windows 8.1. However, touch-capable PCs designed for Windows 8.1 can provide an even better experience. Microsoft's hardware certification process for touch-capable computers requires higher levels of precision that improve the accuracy of common tasks, such as tapping, swiping, and sliding.

Sensor support

Windows 8.1 provides expanded support for sensors. While Windows 7 supported using ambient light sensors (ALS) to control display brightness, a feature known as adaptive brightness, Windows 8.1 includes support for several other types of sensors:

- 3-D accelerometers that measure how the computer is moving

- 3-D gyro sensors that measure how the device is rotating

- 3-D magnetometers that measure magnetic fields, such as that from the North Pole

Windows 8.1 uses this sensor data for adaptive brightness and automatic screen rotation. More importantly, Windows 8.1 processes the information using a feature known as sensor fusion

and makes it available to apps. By using the compass, incline, and device-orientation information provided by sensor fusion, apps can determine precisely how the computer is being held,
where it is being pointed, and how it is being moved.

Improved power efficiency

When using apps, Windows 8.1 should offer increased battery life when compared to earlier
versions of Windows. For more information, refer to Chapter 2.

USB 3.0 support

Windows 8.1 natively supports USB 3.0. This does not cause existing USB 2.0 ports to support
USB 3.0; the computer must have USB 3.0 compatible hardware. Windows 7 required separate
drivers to work with USB 3.0.

ARM support

Windows RT can run on computers that use ARM processors. ARM processors are often used
in mobile devices such as smartphones, media players, and tablet computers. ARM support
means you can use Windows 8.1 on some of the smallest and most efficient touch-screen-
equipped devices, bringing the desktop experience anywhere you go.

Because ARM processors cannot run traditional Windows applications, Windows RT will
run only apps designed for Windows 8.1. In other words, you cannot run apps designed for
Windows 7 or earlier versions of Windows on Windows RT.

Security

Because security threats are constantly changing, Windows must continue to add new security
features to help protect the user's privacy and the PC's integrity. Security features are valuable
only if they do not significantly inconvenience the user, however. For example, a PC would be
more secure if it required users to type a long, complex password each time they used it. However, the inconvenience would be so great that many users would find a way to bypass the
password entry completely, nullifying the security benefits.

In Windows 8.1, Secured Boot and the improvements to Windows Defender and the Smart-
Screen filter help to improve your PC's security without further inconveniencing you. Picture
passwords, PIN logins, Windows Live integration, and BitLocker performance directly improve
Windows usability. However, by making security more convenient to users, these features can
also improve security.

The sections that follow describe these features in more detail. For detailed information about security features, read Chapter 18, "Managing users and Family Safety," and Chapter 19, "Windows, application, and network security."

Picture password

Passwords are a convenient way to log in when using a keyboard, but typing is more difficult when you're using a tablet computer. Picture passwords, a sign-in method that authenticates a user by checking gestures made on a picture, provide an easier way to log in using touch, with security that will be sufficient for many users.

To log in with a picture password, select a picture. Then, choose a sequence of three motions on the picture. Each motion can be a tap, a line, or a circle. Circles and lines can be any size or direction. Figure 1-18 shows one step of a sample picture password login: drawing a small counterclockwise circle around the nose of a fox.

Figure 1-18 Draw lines, dots, and circles (as shown around the fox's nose) to log in using a picture password.

Using the example in Figure 1-18, a user could specify any of the following sequences to log in:

- Tap the right ear, tap the nose, and then tap the left eye.

- Draw a line from the nose to the tail, draw a small clockwise circle around the right ear, and then draw a small counterclockwise circle around the left ear.

- Draw a line from the right ear to the left ear, tap the nose, and then draw a big clock-wise circle around the head.

Picture password is disabled by default. Enable it from the Account, Sign-In Options screen of PC Settings. The next time you sign in, you are automatically prompted to enter your picture password. For more information about picture passwords, refer to Chapter 18.

PIN login

You can also log in to Windows by using a four-digit numeric PIN. Pins are easy to type and remember, but they are not as secure as conventional or picture passwords. If you do decide to use a PIN, avoid common sequences such as 1111 or 1234 and important dates.

PIN login is disabled by default because it is significantly less secure than using a complex password. Enable PIN login from the Users screen of PC Settings. The next time you sign in, click Sign-In Options, and then click the keypad icon. For more information about using a PIN, refer to Chapter 18.

SmartScreen filter

Windows 8.1 integrates the SmartScreen filter from Internet Explorer into the operating system, helping to reduce the risk of users downloading and running known malware. If SmartScreen detects an application that is potentially malware or has not yet established a reputation, it warns the user as shown in Figure 1-19. The user has the option to continue on and run the application.

Figure 1-19 SmartScreen warns the user before running a potentially malicious application.

Windows Defender

As shown in Figure 1-20, Windows Defender in Windows 8.1 offers an important security improvement: improved protection from rootkits. Rootkits are a form of malware that runs below the level of the operating system and can be completely undetectable once Windows starts. On computers with UEFI-based secure boot, Windows Defender can detect potential malware attempting to load at boot and resume.

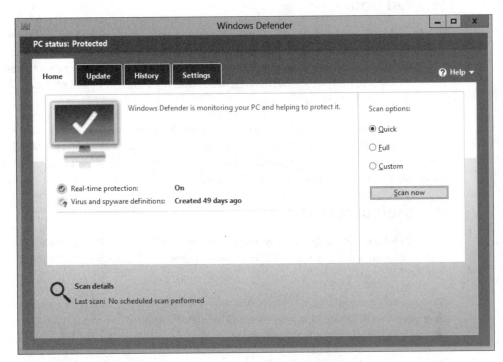

Figure 1-20 Windows Defender helps to protect your PC from malware.

When Windows Defender checks files as Windows accesses them to verify that they are not potentially malicious, Windows Defender adds some overhead, slowing your computer down just a small amount. In Windows 8.1, Windows Defender's performance is improved. Windows Defender adds only a 4-percent processing overhead to boot time. The performance improvements will also improve battery life.

Naturally, you can also choose to use third-party antimalware software or disable Windows Defender completely.

BitLocker

BitLocker is a disk encryption feature built into Windows Vista, Windows 7, and Windows 8.1. Windows 8.1 reduces the time required to initially encrypt your disk by encrypting only the portions of the disk that have data stored on them. Free space is not encrypted until the operating system writes to it.

Secured Boot

Windows 8.1 helps to reduce the risk of malware by more closely monitoring system integrity during the startup process. If Windows 8.1, working with a computer's onboard Trusted Platform Module (TPM) chip, detects any threats to system integrity, it automatically starts the Windows Recovery Environment (WinRE), which attempts to remove the malware by restoring system files and settings.

If your computer supports UEFI-based Secure Boot (as defined in the UEFI 2.3.1 specification), UEFI can help verify that all firmware and firmware updates are valid and that Windows system files are properly signed. This can make it much more difficult for a rootkit to install itself on a computer. For more information, read Chapter 27.

Microsoft accounts

Windows 8.1 supports logging in with local user accounts, just as Windows 7 and earlier versions of Windows did. For the first time, however, users have the option of logging in with a Microsoft account.

Windows and app settings work between different PCs. You can switch to a local account. Store your files in SkyDrive, and your entire Windows experience can be cloud-based. Log in to any computer, and have a familiar desktop environment and access to all your files.

This is very useful for users with multiple computers. If you use a desktop during the day, you can pick up your mobile computer, log in from a coffee shop, and continue exactly where you left off. For example, if you were in the middle of watching a video online, you can continue from that same point. If you were reading the news, Windows 8.1 will remember exactly where you were.

If you forget your password, you can use the Microsoft account website (shown in Figure 1-21) to reset your password from any device connected to the Internet. Microsoft accounts have sophisticated security features to minimize the security risks of password resets, including two-factor authentication, such as communicating with your mobile phone or a secondary email address.

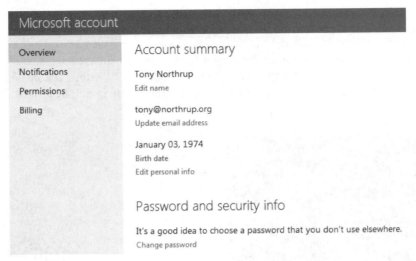

CHAPTER 1

Figure 1-21 Use a Microsoft account to synchronize settings between computers and manage your account online.

If the computer can't connect to the Internet to authenticate you, or your Microsoft account credentials are compromised, Windows 8.1 can authenticate you using cached credentials. Basically, you can log in with the same user name and password you used in the past. For detailed information, read Chapter 18.

Networking

Connecting to the Internet is one of the most important uses for a PC, and users often use Wi-Fi and mobile broadband to connect to many different networks from a variety of locations. Windows 8.1 makes mobile networking easier and more efficient by giving you better control over mobile broadband charges and by more intelligently connecting to your preferred Wi-Fi networks.

Mobile broadband

Windows 8.1 treats mobile broadband connections as metered connections. This behavior causes Windows to minimize the network traffic sent across mobile broadband connections, potentially reducing data charges. To further minimize mobile broadband usage and improve battery life, Windows 8.1 will automatically turn off your mobile broadband when a Wi-Fi hotspot is available. Wi-Fi hotspots usually have faster bandwidth, higher data caps, and lower latency. If you move away from the Wi-Fi hotspot, Windows 8.1 can automatically use your mobile broadband to reconnect to the Internet.

These improvements keep you connected while reducing your costs, maximizing your network performance, and increasing your battery life.

Windows 8.1 includes a new user interface for turning wireless interfaces on and off, as shown in Figure 1-22. If your PC is equipped with mobile broadband, Windows will show a separate option on the same screen. You can use the new airplane mode to quickly turn all wireless signals off.

Figure 1-22 You can now easily control wireless network interfaces.

➤ **For detailed information, read Chapter 22, "Setting up ad hoc, Bluetooth, and mobile networks."**

Wi-Fi

Windows 8.1 makes minor improvements to Wi-Fi behavior. If you manually disconnect from a Wi-Fi network, Windows 8.1 will stop automatically connecting to that network. If you disconnect from one Wi-Fi network and then connect to another, Windows 8.1 will configure the newly connected network at a higher priority so that Windows 8.1 automatically chooses that network in the future.

Windows 8.1 features connect more quickly to Wi-Fi networks when resuming from standby. Typically, Windows 8.1 can be connected to your preferred Wi-Fi network in about a second after resuming from standby. Windows 7 could often take more than 10 seconds.

➤ **For detailed information, read Chapter 21, "Setting up a home or small office network."**

Storage

Windows 8.1 includes two major storage innovations: SkyDrive and Storage Spaces. SkyDrive provides cloud-based storage that can be accessed from any Internet-connected PC and many different mobile devices. Storage Spaces allows you to connect just about any type of disk to your computer (including disks you have left over from older computers) and combine them into organized volumes with varying levels of protection similar to RAID (redundant array of independent disks). The sections that follow describe these features in more detail.

SkyDrive

SkyDrive stores your documents on the Internet, so they can be accessed from any device with an Internet connection. You can access files stored in SkyDrive using the SkyDrive app, shown in Figure 1-23, as well as the standard open and save tools that Windows uses to access local files.

Figure 1-23 SkyDrive provides free cloud storage.

You can even choose to allow access to files stored on your local computer through SkyDrive.

Besides Windows 8.1, some of the devices you can use to access SkyDrive include:

- Any browser using the website *https://skydrive.live.com/*

- PCs running Windows Vista and Windows 7 using SkyDrive for Windows

- Macs using SkyDrive for Mac

- Windows Phone devices

- iPhones and iPads using the SkyDrive app

- Android phones using an app that connects to SkyDrive

To download the official SkyDrive apps, visit *https://apps.live.com/skydrive*. If you install the SkyDrive for Windows desktop app, you can choose to allow access to files stored only on your local computer (as shown in Figure 1-24). This can be useful if you need to access a file that you forgot to copy to SkyDrive and your computer is turned on and connected to the Internet. Access to your local files is optional and is always protected by two-factor authentication.

Figure 1-24 Use SkyDrive to access files stored locally on computers from across the Internet.

The SkyDrive website provides browser-based tools to access common files, including Microsoft Office documents. Depending on the file type, you might need to install apps on mobile devices to view or edit documents. SkyDrive requires logging in with your Microsoft account, which has the same credentials most users use to log in to Windows.

Many apps, including the Photos and Video apps, allow you to copy files to SkyDrive by using the Share charm, as shown in Figure 1-25.

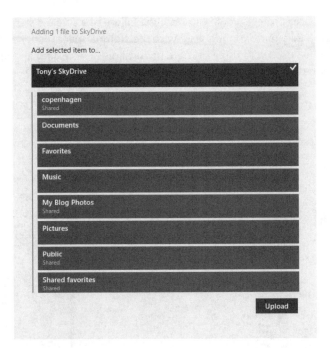

Adding 1 file to SkyDrive

Add selected item to...

Tony's SkyDrive ✓

copenhagen
Shared

Documents

Favorites

Music

My Blog Photos
Shared

Pictures

Public
Shared

Shared favorites
Shared

Upload

Figure 1-25 Use the Share charm to quickly copy files to SkyDrive.

As of September 2013, SkyDrive offers users 7 GB of free storage, with the option to buy additional storage. For more information about SkyDrive, read Chapter 13, "Using SkyDrive."

Storage Spaces

With Storage Spaces (shown in Figure 1-26), you can access hard disk storage any way you want. For example, you can connect three different disks to your computer, combine them as a storage pool, and then access them as a virtual drive (such as D:\) to store your documents. Later, you could easily add more disks to increase the space. You can even configure redundancy, protecting your data in the event a disk fails.

Disks in a storage pool can be different sizes and connected through USB, SATA (Serial ATA), or SAS (Serial Attached SCSI). Storage Spaces provides two data-resiliency options to protect your data in the event a single hard disk fails:

- **Mirroring** Storage Spaces can keep an extra copy of all data on different hard disks. If a single disk fails, Windows 8.1 will transparently access the redundant copy of the data contained on your failed disk and will even make an extra copy on the remaining disks if space is available.

CHAPTER 1

- **Parity**   Storage Spaces protects your data from the failure of a single disk by storing parity information. While mirroring requires twice the storage space, parity data requires much less space when used with three or more physical disks. Accessing and updating data protected with parity can be slower than with mirroring.

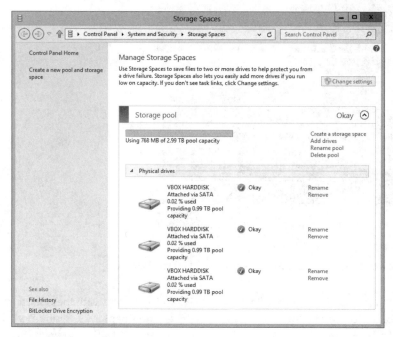

Figure 1-26 Use Storage Spaces to combine multiple drives and to provide data resiliency.

Unlike with traditional RAID mirroring and parity, you do not need to use identical partition sizes. You cannot boot from a Storage Space. Therefore, you always need a separate physical disk to use as your boot disk.

NOTE

If you have used Windows Home Server Drive Extender (a feature of Windows Home Server that is now deprecated), you might recognize some of these capabilities.

You can protect individual pools differently by using mirroring, parity, or no redundancy. For example, you could use mirroring to protect your Documents folder, parity to protect your Videos folder, and no redundancy to protect your Downloads folder.

Storage Spaces is not available with Windows RT. Chapter 12, "Managing storage," discusses Storage Spaces in more detail.

Manageability, productivity, and troubleshooting

Windows 8.1 makes several improvements that power users especially will appreciate. While many Windows 8.1 improvements will most benefit casual users, Windows 8.1 also includes features that will make power users more productive.

Improved support for using multiple monitors makes managing the extra screen space much simpler. Task Manager has been completely reworked to provide a great deal of information instantly. If you have ever had to reinstall Windows to solve problems, you will appreciate how easy Windows 8.1 makes it to refresh or reset your PC. Finally, client Hyper-V is built into Windows 8.1 and provides the ability to run almost any operating system within a virtual machine.

The sections that follow describe these features in more detail.

Support for multiple monitors

For users with two or more monitors attached to their computer, Windows 8.1 offers two improvements:

- You can use different background images for each monitor or stretch a single image across both.

- The taskbar can span both monitors, or you can have a separate taskbar for each monitor.

  ➤ **For more information about configuring multiple monitors, refer to Chapter 5, "Personalizing Windows 8.1."**

Task Manager

Task Manager gives you detailed insight into the inner workings of your computer and the power to prioritize and stop processes. The redesigned Task Manager is both easier to use and more powerful.

When you open Task Manager by pressing Ctrl+Alt+Del on a keyboard or Windows+Power on a tablet and then clicking Task Manager, Windows 8.1 starts Task Manager with a simplified interface, shown in Figure 1-27, that simply displays a list of applications and the End Task button. This interface (which replaces the Applications tab in earlier versions of Windows) is ideal for casual users, but it does not allow a user to stop the Explorer task and lacks the level of detail power users might have become accustomed to in earlier versions of Windows.

Figure 1-27 The simplified view of Task Manager lets you close running applications.

Click the More Details link to view expanded information about running applications and the operating system's state. This view of Task Manager displays seven tabs:

- **Processes**   Helps you identify which process is slowing down a computer.

- **Performance**   Displays an overview of the amount of CPU, memory, disk, and network resources Windows 8.1 and your applications are currently using.

- **App History**   Shows you the CPU and network resources applications have used, even if the application has been closed.

- **Startup**   Displays applications that start automatically.

- **Users**   Displays running and suspended applications for each logged-in user.

- **Details**   Displays in-depth information about every process running on the computer, similar to the information provided by the Processes tab in Windows 7 Task Manager.

- **Services**   Displays all services installed in Windows, whether or not they are running.

Figure 1-28 shows the new Processes tab of Task Manager.

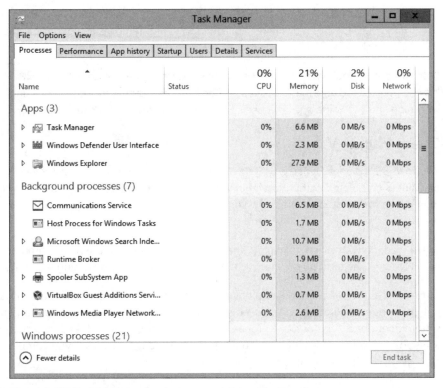

Figure 1-28 Task Manager has been completely redesigned.

➤ **For detailed information about Task Manager, refer to Chapter 26, "Monitoring, measuring, and tuning performance."**

Refreshing and resetting your PC

At times, Windows might not perform as well as it did when new. Windows might seem slow, or you might experience seemingly unexplainable problems. The cause of these types of problems varies, but often they might be caused by unreliable drivers, corrupted system files, or malware. In the past, many users resorted to reinstalling Windows to solve these problems.

Windows 8.1 gives you two easier options on the General page of PC Settings:

- **Refresh Your PC** A useful tool for solving some Windows problems that traditional troubleshooting techniques might not have fixed, refreshing your PC automatically reinstalls Windows while maintaining your documents, some system settings, and apps. You will still need to reinstall desktop applications.

- **Reset Your PC**   A useful tool for preparing your computer for a different owner, reset-ting your PC automatically reinstalls Windows and removes all your applications, files, and settings.

Both options reinstall Windows; however, the process happens automatically without prompt-ing the user for the information usually gathered during setup, including choosing a preferred language and providing a product key. For more information, refer to Chapter 27.

Client Hyper-V

Windows 8.1 includes Hyper-V, which provides the ability to run virtual machines. A virtual machine is an isolated computer within your computer that can run a second copy of Windows or many other operating systems. Essentially, it's a separate computer running inside a window.

When working with virtual machines, the term *host* refers to the physical computer that is run-ning Hyper-V. The term *guest* refers to the virtual machine that is running within Hyper-V.

Virtual machines create a simulated environment that behaves very similar to a physical com-puter. The guest operating system seems to have all the physical resources any operating system might have: one or more processors, memory, disks, network adapters, monitors, and a keyboard and mouse. However, all these resources are virtual, giving you complete control over the guest operating system.

While most users will never need to create a virtual machine, they can be very useful to advanced users. You can use virtual machines to:

- Try new software without impacting the settings on your computer, which is particularly useful if an app might be malware.

- Run an operating system other than Windows 8.1, which might be required if an app does not run properly in Windows 8.1.

- Test a variety of different configuration settings without impacting your computer.

- Undo any number of changes to a computer, instantly returning it to an earlier state.

Each running virtual machine requires dedicated memory. For example, if you want to run Windows 8.1 within a virtual machine, you need to allocate at least 2 GB of RAM to the guest operating system. This would reduce the amount of RAM available to apps running on your host. Each virtual machine also needs to store its own system files on a virtual disk. Therefore, if you plan to use virtual machines, you should consider adding extra RAM and hard disk space to your computer.

Using Hyper-V requires the 64-bit version of Windows 8.1 Pro and a computer with second level address translation (SLAT) capabilities (found in some Intel Core i7, Core i5, and Core i3 processors and in AMD processors that support Rapid Virtualization Indexing). You might need to enable SLAT by configuring your computer's BIOS settings. Hyper-V also requires an additional 2 GB of RAM, for a total of at least 4 GB of RAM.

Inside OUT

Free Hyper-V alternative

If your computer does not meet the Hyper-V requirements, consider using VirtualBox. VirtualBox, available from *www.virtualbox.org*, is free, runs on both 32-bit and 64-bit versions of Windows (including earlier versions of Windows), and requires only 512 MB of RAM.

Hyper-V is not enabled by default. To enable it, select the Hyper-V option from Turn Windows Features On Or Off in Control Panel. Then, restart your computer. You can then launch the Hyper-V Manager desktop app to configure Hyper-V.

➤ **For detailed information, read Chapter 20, "Using Hyper-V."**

What's new in the Windows 8.1 update

In October 2013, Microsoft released Windows 8.1, a free update to Windows 8. Similar to a service pack, Windows 8.1 fixes bugs, adds new features, has been more thoroughly tested than a typical update, and can be directly installed on new computers.

The sections that follow discuss the most important features added in the Windows 8.1 update.

▶ **What's new in the Windows 8.1 update** Watch the video at *http://aka.ms/WinIO/new*.

Improved multitasking

One of the biggest innovations in Windows 1 (released in 1985) was the ability to run multiple apps side by side in separate windows. That innovation was so important that an entire operating system was named after the feature.

Windows 8.1 still supports traditional windows on the desktop. However, the Windows 8.1 touch interface runs most apps full-screen.

In Windows 8, you could run two apps side by side. However, one app always ran at a resolution of 320 pixels, while the other app took up the remaining space. That worked well on most tablets, but it looked rather silly on my 30-inch monitor because the second app took up a narrow strip of only 12 percent of my screen.

The Windows 8.1 update removes the 320-pixel limitation, allowing you to resize side-by-side apps to any width. For example, you can have two apps running side by side, evenly sharing the display, or you can resize the apps, as long as each is wider than 320 pixels.

If you have a 1080p resolution screen (1920x1080 or higher), you can run three or more apps side by side in Windows 8.1. Figure 1-29 shows four apps running on a 2560x1600 pixel monitor: Photos, Weather, the desktop, and SkyDrive. If the maximum number of apps are running side by side and you launch a new app, Windows 8.1 prompts you to choose which app you want to replace.

Figure 1-29 Windows 8.1 provides more flexible multitasking.

Boot to desktop and other navigation properties

Windows 8 always showed you the Start screen after booting. Some users prefer to work on the desktop, however, or they need to automatically start a desktop app, such as Home Theater PC (HTPC) software. With the Windows 8.1 update, you can start the desktop automatically after logging in.

To go directly to the desktop when you log in, search from the Start screen for **navigation properties** and select it. Then select Go To The Desktop Instead Of Start When I Sign In, as shown in Figure 1-30.

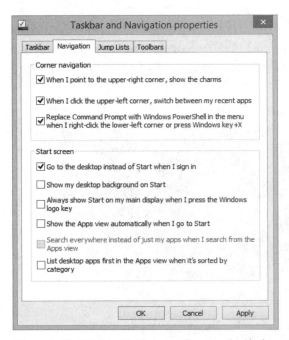

Figure 1-30 Windows 8.1 lets you boot to the desktop. Finally!

You'll find a few other useful options on the Navigation tab:

- **Show My Desktop Background On Start**   As the name indicates, you can now select your own picture as the Start screen background.

- **Always Show Start On My Main Display When I Press The Windows Logo Key**   By default, Windows shows the Start screen on whichever display you're currently using. If you'd rather have it appear always on the main display, select this check box.

- **Show The Apps View Automatically When I Go To Start**   By default, the Start screen displays the tiles that you've organized. If you'd rather see a list of all the apps, select this check box.

- **Search Everywhere Instead Of Just My Apps When I Search From The Apps View**   By default, Windows searches only your apps when searching from the Apps view; it doesn't search your files, settings, or the web. If you'd like it to search for all these, select this check box.

- **List Desktop Apps First In The Apps View When It's Sorted By Category**   If you spend most of your time on your desktop and don't use many apps designed for Windows 8.1, selecting this check box helps you find your apps faster.

Start button on the desktop

In Windows 8, users had to open the Start screen by pressing the Windows logo key on the keyboard or a tablet, or by clicking in the lower-left corner of the desktop. As shown in Figure 1-31, Windows 8.1 has added a Start button to the desktop, in the same place earlier versions of Windows had it.

Figure 1-31 The Windows 8.1 desktop has a Start button.

The desktop Start button doesn't open a Windows 7–style Start menu like you might expect; it displays the Start screen. If you've already learned how to open the Start screen without using the Start button, you can turn it off by installing the free StartKiller app from *http://www.tordex.com/startkiller/*.

If you miss your Windows 7 Start menu, get it back by installing Start8 from *http://www.stardock.com/products/start8/*.

Improved WinX menu

The WinX menu has always been my favorite power user's tool—open it by pressing Windows+X or right-clicking the lower-left corner of the screen. The WinX menu now gives you more options, including the options to sleep, restart, or shut down your PC.

Lock screen slide show

Your lock screen can now display a photo slide show. That's nice if you have a tablet displayed in a common area of your house, such as a tablet propped up in your kitchen. To set up a slide show, follow these steps:

1. From PC Settings, select PC & Devices.

2. Select Lock Screen.

3. Select Play A Slide Show On The Lock Screen.

4. Optionally, configure your slide show, as shown in Figure 1-32:

   - Select Play A Slide Show When Using Battery Power if you plan to keep your device unplugged but aren't worried about it running out of battery power.

   - Under Use Pictures From, configure the folders that have your pictures. If you keep your pictures in your Pictures folder, you don't have to configure this.

   - Select Let Windows Choose Pictures For My Slide Show to let Windows intelligently choose which pictures to show. For example, it tends to show more recent pictures from the same season, rather than embarrassing pictures of you from high school. Okay, I admit it; I have no idea how the algorithm works.

   - Configure when the slide show starts and stops by setting Show The Lock Screen After My PC Has Been Inactive For and Turn Off Screen After Slide Show Has Played For.

APP TIP

If you hate your own photos, get the free Amazing Lock Screen app from the Windows Store. It automatically displays Bing's photos on your lock screen.

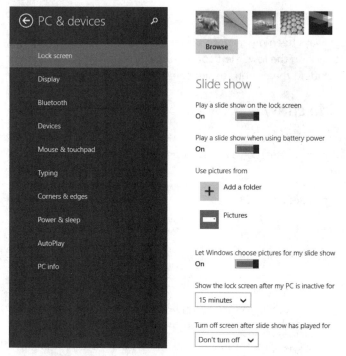

Figure 1-32 Use PC Settings to configure a slide show on the lock screen.

Camera access from the lock screen

On touch PCs, you can allow users to take pictures without unlocking the PC, similar to what you can do with most smartphones. Simply swipe down from the lock screen to open the camera without logging in. Some of the features will be limited until you log in and authenticate yourself.

Windows 8.1 enables this feature by default. To turn it off, access the lock screen settings from the PC & Devices page of PC settings, and then select Use Camera From The Lock Screen at the bottom of the page.

New tile sizes on the Start screen

You can now select larger or smaller sizes for tiles on your Start screen. The larger tile sizes allow you to get more information from live tiles without opening the associated app. The smaller tile sizes allow you to fit four times more apps on the Start screen without scrolling.

Figure 1-33 shows each of the different tile sizes: wide, large, small, and medium. To change the size of a tile, select it by flicking or by right-clicking it, and then click Resize.

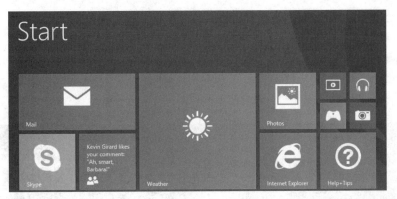

Figure 1-33 On the new Start screen, you can choose large and small tile sizes.

Improved Apps view

Just swipe up from the bottom of the screen (on touch-screen PCs) or click the down arrow in the lower-left corner of the Start screen to view all your apps, including those that don't have a tile on the Start screen. As shown in Figure 1-34, click the list at the top of the All Apps screen to change how the apps are sorted.

Figure 1-34 The All Apps screen makes it easier to find the app you need.

More personalization options

You're no longer limited to the handful of colors Windows 8 supported for the Start screen. As shown in Figure 1-35, you can select almost any color you want by opening the Settings charm and then selecting Personalize. You can also select your own desktop wallpaper, though you can't select a different image as your wallpaper.

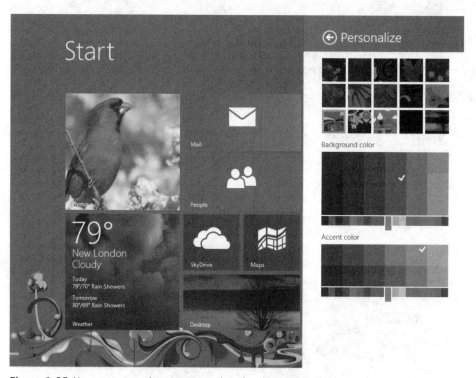

Figure 1-35 You can now select custom colors for the Start screen.

Windows 8.1 also makes your Start screen more dynamic by using motion accents. Basically, graphics move with your Start screen, providing an interesting, almost three-dimensional effect. Watch the video at the link provided at the beginning of this section to see motion accents in action.

Drastically improved searching

Perhaps my favorite improvement in Windows 8.1 is search. Now, you can simply type from the Start screen and Windows will find what you're looking for, whether it's an app, setting, document, picture, news, or webpage. As shown in Figure 1-36, Windows 8.1 displays the results using a full-screen interface that's much nicer to browse than any web search engine.

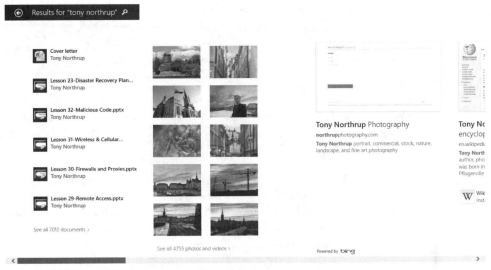

Figure 1-36 Windows 8.1 makes it easier to find anything.

More settings available with the touch interface

Windows 8 featured a handful of settings accessible from the touch interface (available from the Settings charm by selecting Change PC Settings). However, to change most settings, you still had to open Control Panel on the desktop, exactly as in Windows 7. That worked well with a keyboard and mouse, but it could be difficult to use with touch.

Windows 8.1 moves more settings from Control Panel to the touch interface. Now, all the settings most users might need to change are accessible through touch. Some settings accessed less frequently, such as configuring BitLocker or Windows Firewall, still require you to use Control Panel from the desktop.

Internet Explorer 11

In Windows 8, you could access Adobe Flash–based websites only from the desktop. The Windows 8.1 update includes Internet Explorer 11, which supports Adobe Flash, whether you're using the touch-screen interface or the desktop. Additionally, Microsoft will now distribute updates to Adobe Flash using Windows Update, which allows Adobe to more quickly fix newly discovered vulnerabilities.

Internet Explorer 11 also supports Enhanced Protected Mode (EPM) on the desktop, and EPM is enabled by default. EPM runs webpages in a sandbox, preventing them from accessing important system resources and your personal files. EPM also provides 64-bit tabs, which are less vulnerable to attacks such as buffer overflows than are 32-bit tabs.

Together, these security improvements reduce the risk of getting a malware infection from a website.

Improved security

Windows 8.1 includes several improvements to security:

- **Windows Defender network support**   Windows Defender can now monitor your network communications for suspicious activity, allowing it to detect malware that would otherwise remain hidden.

- **Biometrics**   If your PC has a fingerprint scanner (or if you've installed a USB fingerprint scanner), you can now use it to log on and to authenticate in other areas of Windows 8.1, such as User Account Control prompts. Naturally, you can still revert to a traditional password. However, fingerprint scanning can be a convenient way to log on, especially when using a touch-screen device.

- **Encryption**   All editions of Windows 8.1 support device encryption. In Windows 8, only the RT, Pro, and Enterprise editions supported BitLocker Drive Encryption. Those editions of Windows 8.1 still provide more full-featured encryption management tools than the standard edition of Windows 8.1, but standard users can now encrypt drives for better security.

- **Assigned access**   You can limit specific accounts to running only a single app. When the user logs on, that app will automatically open, and the user won't be able to switch to other apps. Assigned access is useful for kiosk environments, where a PC serves a very specific, single function.

- **Remote data removal**   With increased mobility comes the increased risk of physical loss of your PCs. Windows 8.1 provides remote data removal, which allows businesses to configure types of data to always be encrypted. If the PC is lost, the business can remotely wipe the data (provided the PC connects to the Internet).

3-D printer support

Windows 8.1 supports printing directly to 3-D printers, so you can print 3-D objects using plastic. You can do this with earlier versions of Windows, but doing so required additional software. For more information about 3-D printing in Windows, including apps to help you get started, visit *http://channel9.msdn.com/Events/Build/2013/3-9027*.

Tethering

Windows 8.1 supports tethering. With tethering, you can use Wi-Fi to share an Internet connection. For example, if your Windows 8.1 PC has a mobile broadband connection, you can enable tethering and then connect other wireless devices to a mobile Wi-Fi hotspot. Any device that connects to the hotspot will be able to use the mobile broadband connection to access the Internet. Tethering is particularly useful when you are traveling because you can share a single Internet connection between all your wireless devices.

In Windows 8, you had to follow a complex series of steps to enable tethering or use a third-party app.

New business features

This book focuses on using Windows 8.1 in the home environment. However, I do want to mention the features that Windows 8.1 adds that are primarily intended for business environments:

- **NFC tap-to-print** When administrators allow it and your printers and Windows 8.1 devices support it, you can now connect to a printer using near field communications (NFC). Just tap your device against a printer, and you'll be able to print your document.

- **Better Bring Your Own Device (BYOD) support** Administrators can configure business networks to allow users to connect their home devices, including Windows 8.1 RT tablets, to the corporate network while minimizing security risks. For more information, visit *http://www.microsoft.com/en-us/windows/windowsintune/pc-management.aspx*.

- **Work folders** If your system administrator allows it, you can now synchronize your work files with your different devices, even if you bought them yourself.

What's missing

Windows 8.1 is missing a couple of features that were part of Windows 7:

- **DVD playback** Windows 7 had DVD playback capabilities built in. You could insert a DVD movie and play it without any additional software. This is not a feature in Windows 8.1. Because of licensing fees, including DVD playback capabilities increases the cost of every computer that includes Windows. However, many new netbooks, ultrabooks, and tablets do not even include DVD hardware, so including the feature would increase costs without offering the user any benefit.

- **Media Center**   With Media Center, you can use a remote control to play music, videos, and DVDs, as well as to record and play TV. Media Center has been a popular way to create a Home Theater PC (HTPC). Some editions of earlier versions of Windows included Media Center, but Media Center is available only as an add-on for Windows 8.1 (for an additional charge). As with DVD playback, supporting the ability to record broadcast TV added costs to computers for features that many people would never use. To purchase Media Center, use the Add Features To Windows 8.1 tool in Control Panel, as shown in Figure 1-37.

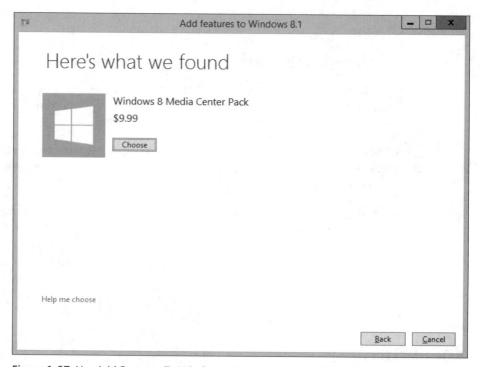

Figure 1-37 Use Add Features To Windows 8.1 to purchase and install Media Center.

For more information about watching videos, refer to Chapter 14, "Music and videos." For more information about Media Center, refer to Chapter 17, "Creating a Home Theater PC."

While Windows 8.1 does not natively support playing back DVDs, computer manufacturers are likely to include their own software for DVD playback on computers with the necessary hardware, so the user experience is not likely to change.

Inside OUT

Free Media Center alternative

I've used HTPCs for all my TV and movies since about the year 2000. In that time, I've tried many different applications. Media Center remains my favorite, but there's also a free alternative: XMBC, available at *http://xbmc.org/*. XMBC doesn't have Media Center's refinement, but for power users, it's a great choice because it has dozens of different skins and anyone can create new features for it. It has some features built in that Media Center lacks, such as automatically downloading cover art and summaries for movies and TV shows.

Using Windows 8.1 apps

Common features. 52

Using apps. 54

How Windows 8.1 apps work. 62

Changing app file associations. 64

Built-in apps 67

Windows 8.1 supports a new type of app designed for modern, mobile, and touch-enabled PCs. This new type of app provides many benefits:

- Integration with the Windows 8.1 user interface for settings, sharing, and notifications

- Background apps automatically suspend to maximize performance and battery life

- Full-screen user interface maximizes desktop space

- Support for ARM computers running Windows RT 8.1

- Persistence through a PC refresh

Using and managing these apps requires very different skills. The Windows Store completely changes the way you find, download, and install apps. Familiar tasks, such as changing app options, are still available, but they're out of sight by default. Right-clicking won't work the way you expect it to, but you'll quickly become familiar with the touch-friendly way of interacting with apps.

To provide compatibility with existing apps, Windows 8.1 and Windows 8.1 Pro can run the same desktop apps supported by Windows 7 and earlier versions of Windows, and those apps will continue to work exactly as you expect them to. Windows RT (the version of Windows 8.1 for computers with ARM processors) can run apps designed for Windows 8.1, but can't run desktop apps.

This chapter provides an overview of Windows 8.1 apps and the specific apps that are included with Windows 8.1. None of the features described in this chapter apply to desktop apps, including those apps designed for Windows 7 and earlier versions of Windows. This chapter refers only to touch-friendly apps designed for Windows 8.1. For detailed information, refer to Chapter 6, "Adding, removing, and managing apps."

Common features

Apps created for Windows 7 and earlier versions of Windows require the app developer to determine the best way to implement common tasks such as configuring app settings, finding content with the app, and printing. Not only did this flexibility increase the amount of work developers needed to do, but it meant that developers chose to implement the same features in very different ways.

For example, many desktop apps allow the user to configure settings using the Options item on the Edit menu. However, some desktop apps store the Options item under the File or Tools menu. Internet Explorer 9 doesn't display a menu bar by default, so users need to click a toolbar button to set options.

Inconsistency between apps is difficult for users. With Windows 8.1 apps, users access common features using charms. To see your charms, swipe in from the right using touch or press Windows+C on the keyboard. For more information about charms, refer to Chapter 1, "What's new in Windows 8.1."

▶ **Using charms**   Watch the video at *http://aka.ms/WinIO/charms*.

Settings

Windows 8.1 provides a common user interface for configuring app-specific settings and common system settings, as shown in Figure 2-1. To access settings and hidden menu items for the current app, press Windows+I.

If you log on to multiple computers with the same Microsoft account, app settings will roam with you to whichever computer you log on to.

By clicking the Settings charm (shortcut: Windows+I) and clicking Permissions, you can configure the resources an app can access, including your webcam, microphone, and the lock screen.

Search

With Windows 8.1, your searches can find data within Windows 8.1 apps as well as files and folders on your computer. For example, a search could find a contact from the People app, stock data from the Finance app, or messages from the Mail app.

As a result, most apps won't have their own search command. Instead, use the Search charm to search within any app. To quickly start a search using a keyboard, press Windows+F. For example, to find a new app in the Store by name, touch the Search charm, touch Store, and then type the name of the app. Similarly, to find music, touch the Search charm, touch Music, and then type the name of the artist.

Configure whether an app appears on the search bar by using the Search page of PC Settings.

Figure 2-1 Access settings for the Start screen or any Windows 8.1 app by pressing Windows+I.

Share

You can share content from many Windows 8.1 apps by clicking the Share charm (shortcut: Ctrl+H). For example, from Internet Explorer, you can use sharing to easily email a link to a webpage (using the Mail app) or share it on Facebook or Twitter (using the People app). Any app can support sharing from any other app, so you can share with apps that are not included with Windows, too.

Configure whether an app can share from the Share page of PC Settings.

Printing

Windows 8.1 apps share a common convention for printing: the Devices charm. To print a document from within an app, tap the Devices charm and then follow the prompts that appear.

Resuming

Microsoft has guidelines for Windows 8.1 app developers that will further improve consistency and usability. Most Windows 8.1 apps resume where you left off, as long as that content is still relevant. For example, Internet Explorer always returns you to the tabs you last had open, reading apps will open the book you were last reading to your current page, and games should return to your current spot without requiring you to load a saved game. Windows 8.1 apps can automatically roam settings and state, too, so you can have the same experience even if you switch between computers.

Using apps

The sections that follow provide an overview of how users find, download, and use apps.

Store

Apps designed for Windows 8.1 can be installed only by downloading them using the Store app. The Store provides a single interface for finding, buying (if an app is not free), downloading, and installing an app.

> ## Inside OUT
>
> ### The Store process and communications
>
> Like all Windows 8.1 apps written using JavaScript, the Store app runs using a process named WWAHost.exe. When you browse the Store, the app uses HTTP and HTTPS to communicate with several Microsoft web services: go.microsoft.com, services.apps.microsoft.com, wscont.apps.microsoft.com, wscont1.apps.microsoft.com, lic.apps.microsoft.com, beta.urs.microsoft.com, c.microsoft.com, fe.ws.microsoft.com, aq.v4.emdl.ws.microsoft.com, aq.v4.a.dl.ws.microsoft.com, and mscrl.microsoft.com (to verify certificates). At the time of this writing, the web service for browsing the Store is located at *http://c.microsoft.com/trans_pixel.aspx*, but you cannot access it directly with a browser.

In previous versions of Windows, finding and installing a new app typically followed this process:

1. Search the web for an app.

2. If an app seems to meet your needs, determine whether you need to pay for it. If you do, progress through the website's checkout process and provide your credit card information.

3. Find the link to download the software.

4. Follow the setup wizard to install the software.

5. If necessary, enter a product key, and record your software.

Because each software development company has its own website format, the process for buying, downloading, and installing each app was different. If the app had a free trial, users would have to return to the website later to purchase and register the app. Additionally, there was no reliable way to find user reviews.

The Store changes this for Windows 8.1 apps. Now the process is much simpler:

1. Open the Store from the Start screen to browse apps, or click the Search charm and select Store to search apps.

2. Select an app. The Store displays user reviews, the cost (if an app is not free), and the permissions the app needs for your computer, as shown in Figure 2-2. Click Buy or Try. If you buy the app, the Store confirms the purchase, asks you to retype your Microsoft account password, and then collects your payment information. You can pay with a credit card or PayPal, and Microsoft can save your credit card information so you don't have to retype it each time.

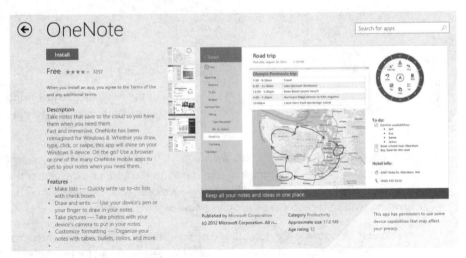

Figure 2-2 Finding and installing Windows 8.1 apps is much simpler.

3. Continue using Windows. Windows 8.1 notifies you when it has installed the app.

Only Windows 8.1 Pro computers that have been joined to an Active Directory domain can install apps without using the Store. This process is commonly known as *sideloading*, and the custom apps businesses add are called *line-of-business* (LOB) apps. Essentially, only business users can bypass the Store to install Windows 8.1 apps. While this restriction might not be popular among power users, you can still freely install desktop apps.

▶ **Using apps designed for Windows 8.1** Watch the video at *http://aka.ms/WinIO/apps.*

Inside OUT

Disabling the Store

The Store only has apps that Microsoft has approved, so downloading should be much safer than downloading random apps from the Internet. Still, you might not want your kids installing apps without checking with you first. You can disable the Store using Group Policy by following these steps:

1. Run **gpedit.msc** to open the Local Group Policy Editor.

2. Select Computer Configuration\Administrative Templates\Windows Components\Store (to apply the settings for all users) or User Configuration\ Administrative Templates\Windows Components\Store (to apply the settings for the current user).

3. Double-click Turn Off The Store Application. Select Enabled, and then click OK.

4. Restart the computer.

Updates

Developers release app updates regularly. Most of the time, they're just fixing a bug or two. Sometimes, they add new features or improve the user interface. Updates are usually a good thing.

On rare occasions, you might find an update that you don't want. For example, the developer of a free app might add aggressive advertising to the app, or a developer might remove an important feature. It's even possible that a developer will introduce a new bug that breaks an existing feature, a problem developers know as a *regression*.

By default, Windows 8.1 automatically downloads app updates and then prompts you to install them, as shown in Figure 2-3. This is the best situation for most people. You can't con-figure apps to update automatically. Every update must be initiated by the user, but since Windows 8.1 has already downloaded the files, the update doesn't take long.

You can manually check for updates by opening the Store, selecting the Settings charm, select-ing App Updates, and then selecting Check For Updates. Because updates are automatic, you shouldn't need to worry about them, but it's good to know how to check just in case you hear about an important update that Windows hasn't found yet.

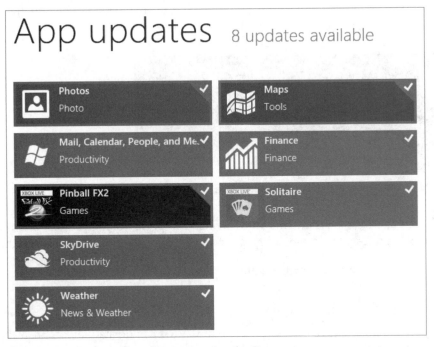

Figure 2-3 Automatically update apps using the Store.

Inside OUT
Disabling updates

I'm from Texas, where there's a popular saying: If it ain't broke, don't fix it. If you cherish stability and don't want to risk having someone else using your computer update apps, you can disable app updates by following these steps:

1. Run **gpedit.msc** to open the Local Group Policy Editor.

2. Select Computer Configuration\Administrative Templates\Windows Components\Store.

3. Double-click Turn Off Automatic Download Of Updates. Select Enabled, and then click OK.

4. Restart the computer.

App commands

Windows 8.1 apps don't have menus. Instead, they have app commands that are displayed on a toolbar that appears at the bottom of the screen, the top of the screen, or both. Figure 2-4 shows the Weather app commands at the top of the screen.

Figure 2-4 App commands replace menus in Windows 8.1 apps.

To view app commands with the touch interface, swipe up from the bottom or down from the top of the screen. To view app commands with a mouse, right-click anywhere on the app.

Some Windows 8.1 apps, such as Internet Explorer, still provide right-click context menus.

Snapping

If your computer's display has a resolution of 1024x768 or greater, you can snap apps to the short side of a screen and use them alongside another app. To snap the current app, drag the top of the screen to one side. You can also touch or hover your pointer at the upper-left corner to display previously opened apps and then drag the app you want to snap to one side of the screen.

After you have snapped an app, you can drag the divider left or right to change how the apps share screen space. Apps have a minimum width, however, and that width is usually 320 pixels. Figure 2-5 shows the Weather app snapped to the left side of the screen, multitasking with Internet Explorer.

Windows 8.1 improvements

Windows 8 requires your computer's display to have a resolution of 1366x768 or greater to run multiple apps simultaneously. It also limits you to running two apps side by side, and one of those apps must run with a width of 320 pixels. The Windows 8.1 update reduces the required resolution to 1024x768, allows you to run as many apps as can fit on your screen, and allows app windows to be resized.

Figure 2-5 Snap apps to the side of the screen to multitask.

In the desktop environment (including the Windows 8.1 desktop), the user can make app windows any size. For example, a user might place a web browser on the top half of the screen and a word-processing app on the bottom half of the screen. Windows 8.1 continues to support this flexibility for desktop apps.

While all apps designed for Windows 8.1 support snapping, some apps won't be useful when snapped, and they might simply display an icon. Even if an app does not display a user interface when snapped, snapping can still be a useful way to quickly flip between two apps.

To close a snapped app with the mouse or touch, swipe down from the top of the screen and then drag it to the bottom of the screen.

Live tiles

Apps designed for Windows 8.1 can update their tiles on the Start screen with relevant information. For example, as Figure 2-6 demonstrates, the Finance app displays current stock prices and the Weather app displays current conditions. Live tiles often give you the information you need from an app without having to open the app.

Windows 8.1 is designed to support hundreds of live tiles without substantially slowing your computer's performance or reducing battery life. Windows 8.1 receives authenticated and encrypted updates to live tiles from the Windows Push Notification Services (WNS), a web service hosted by Microsoft for free use by Windows 8.1 customers and app developers. Because WNS provides updates for all apps, Windows 8.1 can update an app's tile without starting the app itself. App developers can create custom web services to update WNS, and in turn live tiles, with up-to-the-minute text, data, and images.

Figure 2-6 Live tiles display app information without opening the app.

Apps can also update live tiles while the app is running and on a scheduled or periodic basis. For example, the Windows Calendar app uses scheduled updates to display meeting notifications based on local calendar data, without communicating on the Internet. Live tiles can cycle through up to five updates.

> ➤ For detailed information, read "Updating live tiles without draining your battery" at *http://blogs.msdn.com/b/b8/archive/2011/11/02/updating-live-tiles-without-draining-your-battery.aspx.*

Use the App History tab of Task Manager to see the bandwidth used by live tiles.

Inside OUT

Live tile data

Windows 8.1 stores the live tile arrangement for a user at C:\Users\<*username*>\ AppData\Local\Microsoft\Windows\appsFolder.itemdata-ms. You'll find a file named appsFolder.itemdata-ms.bak in that same folder; it's a backup that Windows generates automatically, and you can replace the primary file with it if you ever want to restore earlier settings.

If you want new users on your computer to have a different layout than the default, create a user account with the layout you want. Then, copy the appsFolder.itemdata-ms file from that user's profile to C:\Users\Default\ AppData\Local\Microsoft\Windows\.

Some Windows 8.1 apps allow you to use the Pin To Start option to add an extra tile to the Start screen. The new tile links you directly to content within an app, but otherwise it behaves exactly like an original tile. For example, a news app might allow users to create a tile for a specific news topic, such as technology news. The app could then update that tile with headlines and images from the latest technology news.

Lock screen

Windows 8.1 apps can display information on the lock screen, which allows users to get updates at a glance without logging on to their PC. Not all apps support displaying information on the lock screen.

You can configure up to seven apps to display information on the lock screen, with one app displaying a detailed status. Figure 2-7 shows a sample lock screen. On the right side of the screen, above the date, the Calendar app displays the details of the next meeting. Below the date, the icons show that the People app has four notifications, and the Mail app has two new messages.

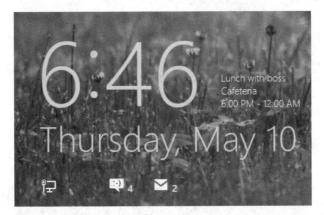

Figure 2-7 Apps can display notifications on the lock screen.

To configure which apps can update the lock screen, use the Personalize page in PC Settings.

How Windows 8.1 apps work

Windows 8.1 apps have several unique features that you won't directly interact with. Desktop apps don't have these features; only apps specifically designed for the Windows 8.1 touch interface do. For the curious, the sections that follow describe those features.

Isolation

To improve system integrity and user privacy, Windows 8.1 apps run in a sandboxed environment that isolates the app's data and minimizes the privileges the app has to the operating system and computer. Isolation improves security, reduces the risk of malware, and increases system stability.

Suspending Windows 8.1 apps

Applications use resources even when you are not actively using them. In earlier versions of Windows, users needed to manage the apps they had open and remember to close apps they were no longer using. If a user left too many apps open, the computer would run low on memory or processor resources, and the computer's performance would slow down. The computer would run out of battery power sooner, too.

Windows 8.1 automatically suspends Windows 8.1 apps that are not in use when it can make better use of the app's memory. When Windows 8.1 suspends an app, Windows 8.1 writes the app's memory to the hard disk without interfering with other disk input/output (I/O). If you are familiar with Windows hibernation, the process is similar, but for a single app.

Inside OUT

Identifying suspended apps

To view suspended apps, press **Windows+X** on a keyboard or **Windows+Power** on a slate, click Task Manager, click More Details (if necessary), and then select the Processes tab. Suspended apps have a status of Suspended.

Though Windows 8.1 makes a copy of the app's memory on the hard disk, it leaves the contents of the app's memory intact. If the user accesses the app before another app needs the memory space, Windows 8.1 resumes the app immediately without needing to read the memory contents from disk.

If the user accesses a suspended app and the app's memory contents have been overwritten, Windows 8.1 immediately reads the app's memory from the hard disk and resumes the app.

The faster the computer's disk is, and the smaller the app's memory set is, the more responsive suspended apps will be. Specifically, solid-state disks (SSDs) will provide the best performance.

Apps consume no resources while in a suspended state, improving battery life and the performance of foreground apps. On computers with large amounts of memory, Windows 8.1 might never need to suspend apps. Operating system functions, such as copying files, continue in the background without being suspended. Windows 8.1 cannot suspend desktop apps.

Inside OUT

App performance requirements

Microsoft really wants your apps to open and suspend quickly. Microsoft requires apps to launch in five seconds or less and suspend in two seconds or less on a low-power computer. Typical computers will be even faster.

Background tasks

Desktop apps continue to run even when they are not in the foreground. Though the user might not interact with them, desktop apps often perform background tasks such as retrieving data from the Internet. Sometimes, these background tasks are unnecessary and simply waste computing resources. At other times, however, they are important. For example, an instant messaging app needs to receive new messages, and a music app needs to play music.

Windows 8.1 apps are designed to be suspended when they are not in the foreground, minimizing the resources they use. However, Windows 8.1 apps can still perform background tasks triggered by a variety of different scenarios, including:

- A message is received from the Internet.
- A notification is received from the Windows Push Notification Services (WNS).
- The Internet becomes available or unavailable.
- The app is updated.
- The user leaves or returns.
- A specific time of day occurs.
- A regular interval occurs.

Applications can restrict background tasks so that they run only when the computer is plugged in or a specific amount of network bandwidth is available. Windows 8.1 restricts the processing and network resources background tasks can use so that they will not consume too many resources. Apps on the lock screen receive the following processor and network time:

- Two seconds of processor time every 15 minutes (a maximum of about 0.2% of the processor time)

- Approximately 187 kilobytes (KB) of data for each megabit of network throughput every 15 minutes (about 0.2% of the available bandwidth), based on the amount of power required by the network adapter

Apps not on the lock screen receive even fewer resources:

- One second of processor time every 2 hours (a maximum of about 0.01% of the processor time)

- Approximately 187 KB of data for each megabit of network throughput every 15 minutes (about 0.03% of the available bandwidth), based on the amount of power required by the network adapter

The network restrictions are removed when the PC is connected to a power outlet.

➤ **For more information, read "Introduction to Background Tasks" at** *http://www.microsoft.com/en-us/download/details.aspx?id=27411.*

Changing app file associations

The primary way for browsing files with a touch interface is the SkyDrive app. Most of the time, you can simply select files and let Windows choose how to open them. If you're not happy with the app Windows selects by default, you can change it. When you change a default app association, you change which app Windows uses to open all files with the same file name extension. For example, you could configure Windows to open all .jpg files with the Windows Photo Viewer desktop app instead of the Photos app.

From within SkyDrive, select a file instead of opening it. You can select a file by flicking it with your finger or right-clicking it with your mouse. Then, select Open With from the commands at the bottom of the screen. SkyDrive displays the dialog box shown in Figure 2-8, prompting you to select the app to open the file with.

Select More Options to view the full list of apps, including an option to download a new app from the Store. If you leave Use This App For All Files selected, Windows will use the selected app by default (even if you open a file from the desktop).

Figure 2-8 You can change default file associations within SkyDrive.

You can change the default app from the desktop, too. From File Explorer, right-click a file, click Open With, and, if the submenu is available, select Choose Default Program, as shown in Figure 2-9. If you simply select Open With and then the app you want to open the file with, you won't change the default app used when you open the same file type in the future.

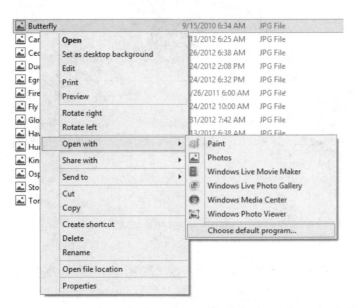

Figure 2-9 Use File Explorer to change the default app from the desktop.

If you want to change the file association for multiple file types, here's a quicker method:

1. From the Start screen search for **associations** and then select Change The File Type Associated With A File Extension.

2. Select a file association that you want to change, as shown in Figure 2-10. Then, select Change Program.

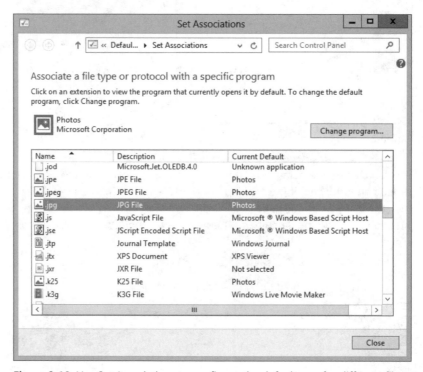

Figure 2-10 Use Set Associations to configure the default app for different file extensions.

If you have a new app and you want it to handle every file type it is capable of opening, follow these steps:

1. From the Start screen search for **default programs** and then select Set Your Default Programs.

2. As shown in Figure 2-11, select the app you want to set as the default, and then select Set This Program As Default.

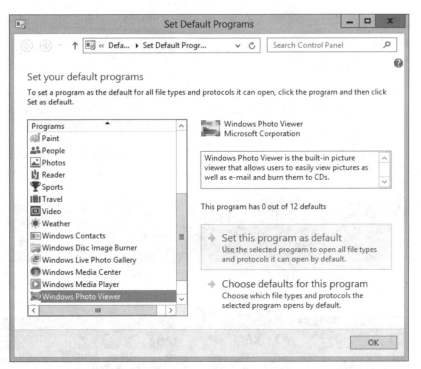

Figure 2-11 Use Set Default Programs to configure an app as the default.

Built-in apps

The apps built into Windows 8.1 work together. For example, starting the Mail app allows you to browse through the People app to select message recipients.

The sections that follow provide a high-level overview of Internet Explorer 11 and the People, Calendar, and Mail apps, among others.

Internet Explorer 11

Windows 8.1 includes two versions of Internet Explorer: a touch version and a desktop version. The desktop version of Internet Explorer 11 closely resembles Internet Explorer 9 running in Windows 7. When you launch Internet Explorer from the Start screen, however, you open the touch version of Internet Explorer, which provides a very different experience by default:

- The display is touch-friendly and full-screen.

- The user interface uses Windows 8.1–style buttons and icons.

- The address bar (which is also used for searching) is at the bottom of the screen.

- The address bar appears only before the user opens the first webpage and while pages are loading.

- Click anywhere on a webpage to hide the toolbar buttons and address bar. Right-click or swipe up from the bottom to display toolbar buttons, the address bar, and tabs at the bottom of the screen, as shown in Figure 2-12.

- The app commands include the Pin To Start button. Click this command to add the current webpage to your Start screen so that you can access it with one touch.

Figure 2-12 Starting Internet Explorer 11 from the Start screen provides a full-screen interface and touch-friendly controls.

NOTE

To search a webpage when you start Internet Explorer from the Start screen, tap the Wrench app command and then tap Find On Page. From a keyboard, press Ctrl+F.

When you launch Internet Explorer 11 from the Start screen, the app is very touch-friendly. To go back to a previous page, swipe the page from left to right. To switch between tabs, swipe down from the top of the screen, and then touch the tab you want to use. For more information about using touch, refer to Chapter 1.

Windows 8 includes Internet Explorer 10, and Windows 8.1 includes Internet Explorer 11. For users upgrading from Internet Explorer 9, Internet Explorer 10 and 11 offer several important improvements:

- Spelling checker and autocorrect to provide word-processing features to webpages.

- HTML5 support for richer websites without using plug-ins.

- CSS3 features to support more robust and efficient formatting for websites, including gradients, animations, 3-D transformations, multicolumn layouts, and grid layouts.

- Panning and zooming using touch interfaces.

- Hardware-accelerated graphics to improve the performance of interactive websites.

These capabilities won't change the way you use a website unless the website specifically takes advantage of them. Over time, however, more websites will create content that leverages the power of these features.

Internet Explorer 11 has several improvements over Internet Explorer 10:

- **Multiwindow browsing** Just as you can snap multiple apps to run side by side, you can run multiple copies of the touch version of Internet Explorer side by side, as shown in Figure 2-13. Simply right-click any link and then select Open In New Window.

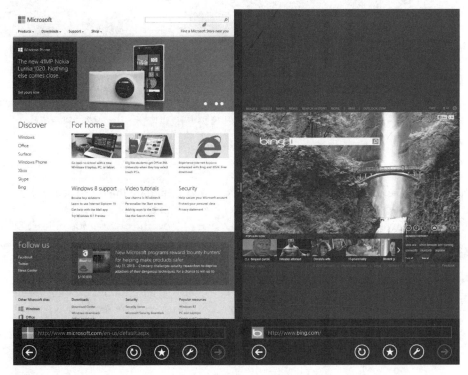

Figure 2-13 Internet Explorer 11 supports side-by-side browsing.

- **Favorites return**   The touch version of Internet Explorer 11 includes Favorites (often called bookmarks). Click the star icon beside the address bar to open your list of favorites. You can also pin a webpage to the Start screen (the approach emphasized in Internet Explorer 10) by opening the Favorites bar and clicking the pin icon, as shown in Figure 2-14.

Figure 2-14 Internet Explorer 11 supports both Favorites and pinning pages to the Start screen.

- **Unlimited tabs**   Internet Explorer 10 limited you to 10 tabs; Internet Explorer 11 removes that limitation, allowing you to open all the tabs you want.

- **Tab, history, and favorite synching**   Internet Explorer automatically synchronizes your browsing between any PC that you access with the same Microsoft account.

Behind the scenes, Internet Explorer 10 and 11 update the user agent string, which Internet Explorer uses to identify the browser's version to the web server. Some web servers provide different versions of a website depending on how the browser identifies itself. While this will not be a problem for most users, you can solve any compatibility issues by enabling compatibility mode in Internet Explorer 11. Compatibility mode configures Internet Explorer to identify itself as Internet Explorer 7 and to render webpages using the techniques implemented in Internet Explorer 7. If you are a web developer, read "Internet Explorer 11 Preview Guide for Developers" at *http://msdn.microsoft.com/en-us/library/ie/bg182636.aspx*.

File Explorer

Since the earliest versions of Windows, Windows Explorer has been the primary tool for browsing and searching files. Windows 8.1 provides the familiar File Explorer (called Windows Explorer in Windows 7) functionality with a more intuitive interface, as the sections that follow describe.

Unlike the other apps described in this section, File Explorer is a desktop app. Desktop apps are designed to be primarily controlled with a mouse and keyboard.

> ➤ **For detailed information about managing files, read Chapter 9, "Organizing and protecting files."**

Ribbon

File Explorer uses a ribbon, as shown in Figure 2-15, rather than more traditional menus. To maximize screen space, the ribbon automatically hides when it is not being used. However, you can click the arrow in the upper-right corner to keep the ribbon visible.

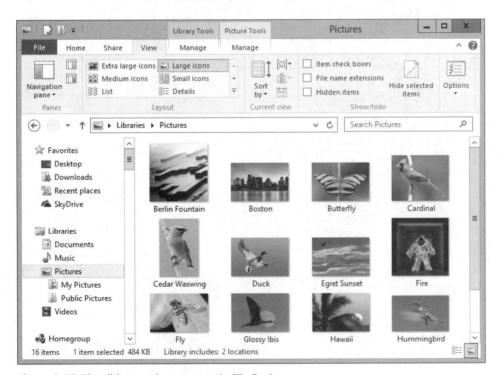

Figure 2-15 The ribbon replaces menus in File Explorer.

CHAPTER 2

File Explorer displays specialized tabs on the ribbon for the content in the selected folder. For example, if you select a folder with pictures, File Explorer provides the Picture Tools tab that you can use to rotate pictures and start a slide show. Similarly, File Explorer provides specialized tabs for videos, music, compressed files, disk image files (.iso and .vhd), searches, and more.

If you're not a fan of the ribbon, click the arrow near the upper-right corner to hide it. The next time you open File Explorer, the ribbon is hidden automatically.

Copying files

File Explorer also improves how files are copied. If users copy multiple files, File Explorer displays all copy jobs in a single window as shown in Figure 2-16, rather than displaying a separate window for each copy job. You can pause copying to improve the performance of other copying tasks, and you can click folder names to open the folder from the copy window.

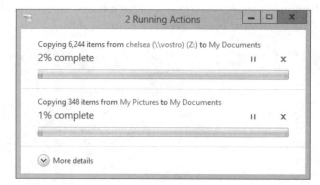

Figure 2-16 File Explorer displays all copy jobs in a single window.

Clicking More Details displays the throughput, progress, and an estimate of the time remaining for each copy job, as shown in Figure 2-17.

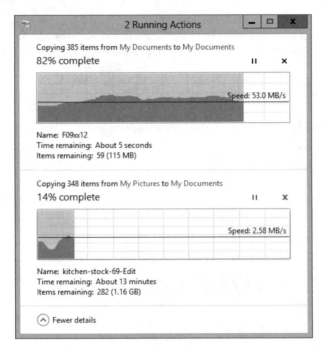

Figure 2-17 Copy details now display the progress and performance.

Conflict resolution

If you attempt to move or copy files to a folder that contains files with the same name, File Explorer detects the conflict and allows you to replace the files, skip the files, or choose which files to keep, as shown in Figure 2-18.

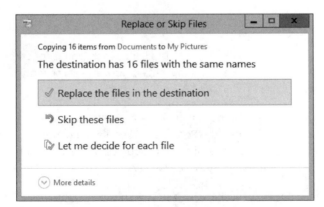

Figure 2-18 File Explorer prompts you to decide how to handle conflicts.

If you decide to choose which files to keep, File Explorer in Windows 8.1 displays the window shown in Figure 2-19. Select the files you want to keep. Selecting the check box at the top of each list will select all files from that folder. Double-click a file to open it. Then, click Continue.

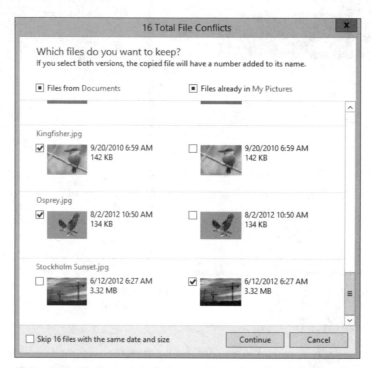

Figure 2-19 File Explorer includes a new user interface for selecting which files should be kept or overwritten.

People

The People app is much more than an address book. The People app brings together everyone in your life from many different sources: personal email, work email, Facebook, Twitter, LinkedIn, Google, and more.

The People app is the best way to keep in touch with anyone you know. Rather than visiting Facebook to check on a friend, simply open the People app. People will gather the person's status, photos, and videos from Facebook as well as other sources, and allow you to browse what they've shared using a touch-friendly interface. You can even Like and Comment.

Right-click or swipe down from the top of the screen, and then click What's New at the top of the page to browse friends with recent updates from all your different social networks, including status updates and new pictures. Tap any update to Like it, Favorite it, add a comment, or re-tweet it. How you can respond to an update depends on the social network the update was posted to.

You are part of the People app, too. Clicking Me at the top of the screen shows you your own status updates and photos, as well as updates on the people closest to you.

Calendar

The Calendar app synchronizes with your calendar service and displays your plans in daily, weekly (as shown in Figure 2-20), or monthly layouts. Editing an event is as easy as tapping it. With an event open, swipe up from the bottom or right-click the details pane to delete it.

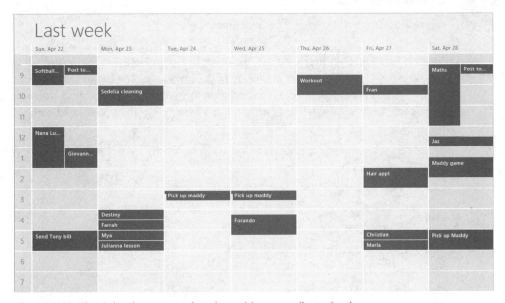

Figure 2-20 The Calendar app synchronizes with your online calendar.

The Calendar app's live tile on the Start screen displays the current date and upcoming events. The Calendar app will also remind you of upcoming events that you have set an alarm for, even when the Calendar app isn't running.

Mail

The Mail app connects to each of your different email accounts and uses the People app when you need to browse contacts. As shown in Figure 2-21, it provides a touch-friendly way to read email messages. It also supports using many different accounts.

Figure 2-21 Use Mail for each of your different accounts.

Sending email is straightforward too, as shown in Figure 2-22. Tap the To field to select recipients, and then type the subject and body of your message. The bar at the bottom of the screen provides convenient access to common formatting and for adding attachments and emoticons. To send or delete the message, tap the icons in the upper-right corner.

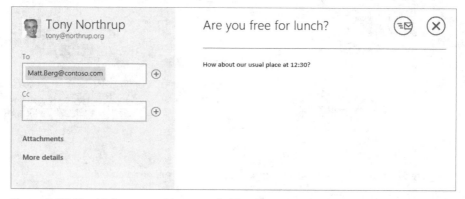

Figure 2-22 The Mail app provides a touch-friendly way to send email.

The mail server you connect to can communicate security requirements to your computer. For example, the mail server might require that you use a complex password and that the computer lock itself after a period of inactivity. Windows 8.1 will prompt you if this is the case, and if you choose to synchronize with the server, Windows 8.1 can automatically configure itself to meet your mail server's security requirements.

Games

Windows 8.1 includes the Games app. With Games, you can:

- Find, buy, download, and play games, as shown in Figure 2-23.

- Manage your Xbox LIVE account, including viewing achievements from playing Xbox.

- Find friends who are online.

- Customize your avatar.

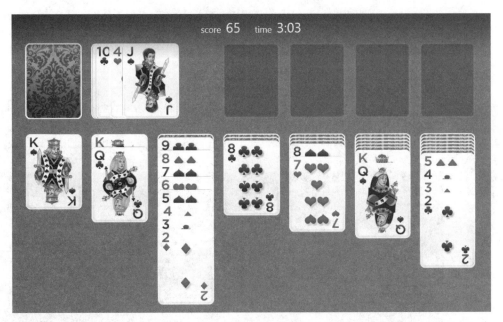

Figure 2-23 Games provides single player and online gaming directly from the Start screen, and Solitaire is still provided for free.

Music

Windows 8.1 provides the Music app to allow you to play music that's in your collection and to find new music. The intuitive interface allows you find musicians, albums, and songs and to create playlists. Your music will continue to play even if you switch away from the Music app.

If you are looking for new music, you can find music from just about any artist, and preview 30 seconds from different songs. If you like a song, you can buy it with just a few clicks.

The Music app includes songs from your Music library. For instructions for how to add a folder to your library, refer to Chapter 9. For more information about the Music app, refer to Chapter 14, "Music and videos."

Video

The Video app gives you access to your entire video collection, and lets you find and buy movies and TV shows with HD sharpness and high-quality sound. When shopping for movies and TV shows, you can watch previews. Unlike with the Music app, if you switch to another app, Video automatically pauses.

The Video app includes files from your Videos library. For instructions describing how to add a folder to your library, refer to Chapter 9. For more information about the Video app, refer to Chapter 14.

Photos

The Photos app, as shown in Figure 2-24, provides an interface for browsing and editing pictures on your local computer. Note that in the Windows 8.1 update, Microsoft removed the feature included in Windows 8 that displayed pictures from Facebook, Flickr, and SkyDrive.

Figure 2-24 The Photos app displays pictures from your local Pictures library.

Click a picture to view it full-screen, and slide up from the bottom to set the picture as the image on the app tile or as the lock screen image or to edit it. The Photos app in Windows 8 did not include editing capabilities, but these were added as part of the Windows 8.1 update. Figure 2-25 shows a picture being edited in the Windows 8.1 Photos app.

Figure 2-25 The Windows 8.1 update allows you to edit photos using touch.

Some of the ways you can edit your photos include:

- Fixing color problems, such as those caused by artificial lights.

- Fixing brightness and exposure problems.

- Applying special effects filters.

- Converting your pictures to black and white.

- Increasing the saturation to get brighter colors.

- Blurring the background.

When you finish editing your photo, the app gives you the option to update the original file or save a copy. I recommend saving a copy, because edits that seem great to you now might seem silly in a few years.

The Photos app does not let you browse or edit raw files from higher-end cameras. Raw files capture all the data from your camera's sensor, potentially providing better image quality and more powerful editing capabilities. To edit raw files, I suggest the free Picasa app available at *http://picasa.google.com*, or Adobe Lightroom, available at *http://adobelightroom.com*.

You can also select multiple pictures as you browse them, and then quickly send the pictures in an email by using the Share charm.

CHAPTER 2

The Photos app includes files from your Pictures library. To add a folder to your library, see the instructions in Chapter 9. For more information about managing your photos, refer to Chapter 15, "Photos."

Weather

People often look up the current weather, and with the Weather app (shown in Figure 2-26), the forecast is a tap away. On your Start screen, the Weather app's live view tile displays the current weather at your selected location. Open the Weather app to view the upcoming forecast hourly for the current day or daily for the entire week. Swipe from the top or bottom to choose your location, and scroll sideways to view more detail, including weather maps and historical data.

Figure 2-26 The Weather app displays the current and forecasted conditions.

Finance

The Finance app gives you quick insight into how the stock markets and your personal holdings are performing. The live tile on the Start screen shows you current stock prices with a 30-minute delay. Open the app to choose the stocks you own, view the latest financial news (as shown in Figure 2-27), check values for currencies, commodities, and bonds, and view interest rates. Add stocks to your watch list and then tap the stock to view a chart of the current prices.

Figure 2-27 The Finance app gives you recent stock prices and financial news.

Reader

Use the Reader app to view comment document formats, including PDF and XPS files. By default, the Reader app browses SkyDrive. Click the arrow to choose any folder on your computer. To access files on remote computers, use the File Explorer desktop app to map a shared folder.

Turn pages by tapping the arrows on either side of the screen or by using your keyboard's arrow keys. Swipe up from the bottom or right-click to bring up the app commands, which allow you to search within the document and view the document in one page, two page, or continuous formats. When you view a document in Two Pages mode, if the left and right pages seem to be on the wrong sides, select the Cover Page option.

Tap More to rotate the document, view the document's metadata, or navigate using the document's bookmarks (which function like a table of contents). Zoom in and out by pinching and pulling with the touch interface, or by holding down Ctrl and using your mouse's scroll wheel. Zoom out far enough, and you can view thumbnails of the document's pages and quickly find a specific page.

While reading, you can select text to highlight it, add notes to it, or copy it to the Clipboard.

Maps

The Maps app provides a touch-friendly tool for viewing street maps, satellite maps, traffic, directions, and satellite maps, as shown in Figure 2-28.

The Directions feature will create turn-by-turn steps that you can follow to drive between two locations. Use the Devices charm to print from Maps.

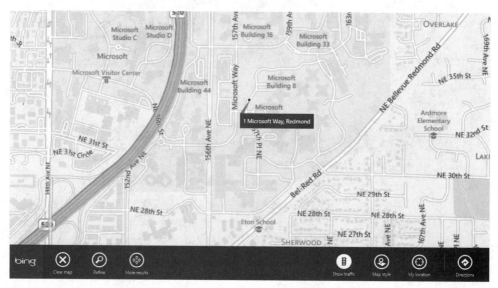

Figure 2-28 Maps provides directions.

Camera

The Camera app turns your PC into a camera, much like a camera built into a mobile phone. You can use the Camera app with any webcam; however, most users will use it with cameras built into slate PCs.

Using the camera is straightforward. Tap anywhere on the screen to take a picture or start a video recording. In video mode, tap the screen a second time to stop recording. If your PC has two cameras, the Camera app will display the Change Camera button to switch between the forward and rear-facing cameras.

Tap the Camera Options command to change the resolution of the recorded image or to select a different microphone for video recording. Click the More link on the options page to adjust brightness, contrast, flicker, and the behavior of the autofocus and autoexposure systems.

News

The News app provides a rich way to browse the news. The user interface is much more touch-friendly than any website. In fact, the News app feels more like flipping through a magazine than using a website.

You can customize the News app to show news you're especially interested in. The easiest way to do this is to add or remove sections from the home news feed, Bing News. With Bing News selected (which is the default), swipe up from the bottom or right-click to view the app commands, and then select Customize. As shown in Figure 2-29, remove any sections you don't want, and click the Plus symbol to add sections that you do want. You can also reorder sections.

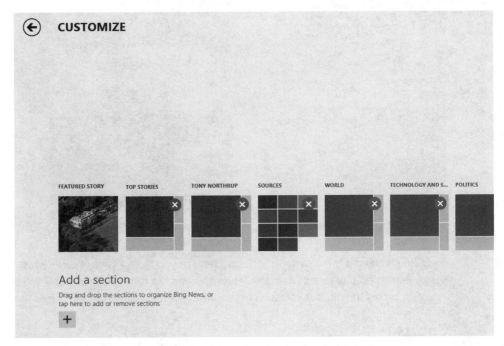

Figure 2-29 The News app can find articles related to topics you choose.

Travel

The Travel app, shown in Figure 2-30, is like a touch-friendly travel magazine. Browse photos of gorgeous places and read travel-related articles, updated regularly.

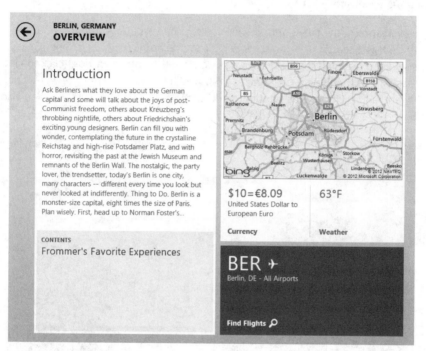

Figure 2-30 Use the Travel app to scope out a city.

If you're planning a trip to a specific destination, or you have a case of wanderlust but haven't yet picked a destination, open up the Travel app and flip through it. Not only will you find amazing places to visit, but you can choose attractions, hotels, restaurants, and more.

Sports

The Sports app is a great way to keep up with the latest scores, team schedules, and sports-related headlines. You can add your favorite teams to the Sports app, and the latest news about the team, their entire schedule, all recent scores, and their roster and stats are just a couple of taps away.

Food And Drink

The Food And Drink app, released with the Windows 8.1 update, makes your PC particularly useful in the kitchen by letting you organize recipes, maintain a shopping list, and (as shown in Figure 2-31), plan your meals.

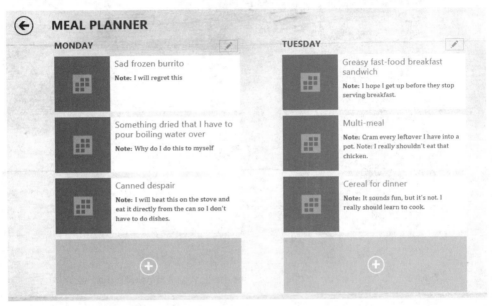

Figure 2-31 Use the Food And Drink app to organize your recipes and plan your meals.

Scroll right to use my favorite feature of the app: browsing thousands of recipes. When you find a recipe, you can add it to your meal planner and even add the ingredients to your shopping list.

Health And Fitness

This app (new in the Windows 8.1 update) can track your diet, nutrition, calories, weight, cholesterol, blood pressure, vaccinations, and exercise. You can even use it to find potential diagnoses for medical conditions by entering your symptoms, as shown in Figure 2-32.

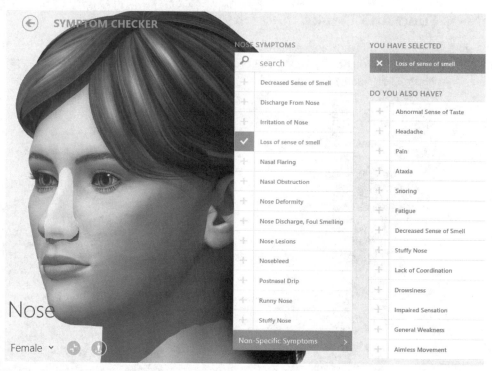

Figure 2-32 You can try to diagnose your medical problems with the Health And Fitness app.

Help+Tips

Use this app to learn more about Windows 8.1 and to get help with specific apps. I suggest visiting each of the sections on the Help+Tips app home page, shown in Figure 2-33, and watching the animations. Browsing the entire app takes only a few minutes, but having a good understanding of how to use Windows 8.1 can save you hours over the lifetime of your computer.

Many of the sections offer separate tips for using the touch interface or a mouse. Be sure to select your preference using the Show Content For option on the bottom of the page.

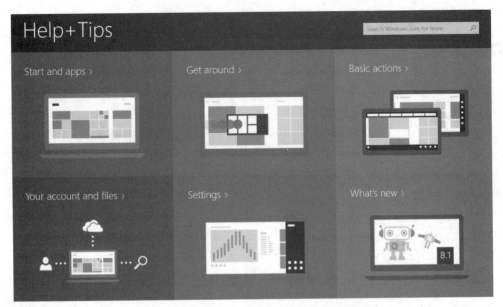

Figure 2-33 The Help+Tips app is a great way to learn to use Windows 8.1.

Reading List

If you're browsing the web and want to save an article to read later, add it to the Reading List. From Internet Explorer, find a page you want to save, select the Share charm, and then select Reading List.

Later, just open the Reading List app, and you can browse the items you've saved. You can view them even if you're no longer connected to the Internet, making Reading List ideal for offline reading while you're in a train or airplane.

Scan

Use the Scan app to scan documents. Before using the Scan app, be sure to connect your scanner by opening PC Settings, selecting PC & Devices, and then selecting Devices.

Sound Recorder

The Sound Recorder app is appropriately named; it's the perfect tool for making quick spoken notes to yourself or recording meetings and classes. The first time you launch it, you see only a big record button that you click to start recording. Once you have a recording, you can play it back, delete it, rename it, or trim it.

Buying and installing Windows 8.1

Buying Windows 8.1 89

Installing Windows 8.1 91

Dual-booting Windows 8.1. 100

f you plan to upgrade an existing version of Windows, read "Buying Windows 8.1" in this chapter, and then skip to Chapter 4, "Upgrading and migrating to Windows 8.1."

You might want to try out Windows 8.1 before installing it. If you want to get a quick idea about what it's like to use Windows 8.1, use VirtualBox to run Windows 8.1 within a virtual machine, as described in Chapter 20, "Using Hyper-V." Be careful not to use your product key to activate your virtual machine, however. If you want to see how Windows 8.1 performs with your hardware, but you don't want to change your existing operating system, you can dual-boot your PC by following the steps in "Dual-booting Windows 8.1" near the end of this chapter.

Buying Windows 8.1

Windows 8.1 is available in four different editions:

- **Windows 8.1**   The basic edition of Windows 8.1. If you're upgrading from Windows 7 Home Basic or Windows 7 Home Premium, this is the right choice.

- **Windows 8.1 Pro**   The complete edition of Windows 8.1. If you're upgrading from Windows 7 Professional or Windows 7 Ultimate, this is the right choice.

- **Windows 8.1 RT**   The only edition of Windows 8.1 for ARM-based PCs, such as the Microsoft Surface.

- **Windows 8.1 Enterprise**   The business edition of Windows 8.1, which isn't recommended for home users or even most small business users.

The decision about which version to buy is easier than it seems. If you have an ARM-based PC, such as a Microsoft Surface, it will come preinstalled with Windows 8.1 RT. There's nothing more for you to do.

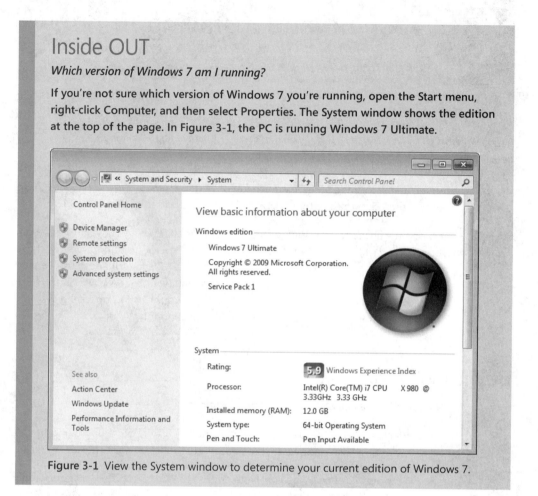

Inside OUT

Which version of Windows 7 am I running?

If you're not sure which version of Windows 7 you're running, open the Start menu, right-click Computer, and then select Properties. The System window shows the edition at the top of the page. In Figure 3-1, the PC is running Windows 7 Ultimate.

Figure 3-1 View the System window to determine your current edition of Windows 7.

Windows 8.1 Enterprise is only for business use. If you're not using your PC at a business that has an Active Directory infrastructure, you don't need it.

So, that leaves two choices for the average consumer with a typical home PC: Windows 8.1 or Windows 8.1 Pro. Windows 8.1 Pro is a bit more expensive, but it includes many more features. If you decide to start with Windows 8.1, you can easily upgrade to Windows 8.1 Pro later, so don't stress too much about the choice.

Windows 8.1 Pro offers these features that are not available in Windows 8.1:

- **Remote Desktop host**   Lets you accept Remote Desktop connections, which allow you to control a PC remotely from another PC. I love using Remote Desktop to connect from a laptop or tablet to my desktop PC when I'm at home or traveling and need to access something on my desktop.

- **Encrypting File System (EFS)**   Encrypt your files with Encrypting File System, which helps to protect individual files from other users on your PC or from someone with physical access to your PC. For more information about EFS, refer to Chapter 9, "Organizing and protecting files."

- **BitLocker**   Encrypt entire drives with BitLocker, which can help to protect you from some malware and helps to protect your confidential files if someone steals your PC or hard drive. For more information about BitLocker, refer to Chapter 9.

- **Hyper-V**   Allows you to run virtual machines, which act like another PC within a window on your PC. Virtual machines are useful for testing apps and running other operating systems. For more information about virtual machines, refer to Chapter 20.

- **Windows Media Center**   Enables your PC to act as a Home Theater PC (HTPC) and supports DVD playback. Windows Media Center requires a separate download, which might (or might not) be free, depending on when you bought Windows 8.1 and whether you are upgrading from a previous version of Windows that had Media Center installed. For more information, refer to Chapter 17, "Creating a Home Theater PC."

- **Virtual hard disk (VHD) booting**   Allows you to boot directly from a VHD file. A VHD file is like a separate hard drive stored within a file on your hard drive. You might boot from a VHD file if you want to run a separate copy of Windows with different settings and Hyper-V isn't powerful enough to meet your needs (for example, if you want to be able to play games or connect hardware accessories that Hyper-V doesn't support.)

- **Active Directory domain join**   Allows you to join an Active Directory domain. Businesses use Active Directory domains to manage large numbers of computers. If you don't plan to have your PC join a domain, or you don't know what this is, then it doesn't matter to you.

For information about purchasing Windows 8.1, visit *http://windows.microsoft.com/*.

Installing Windows 8.1

This section describes how to install Windows 8.1 if you're installing Windows 8.1 on a new PC without an operating system, or you want to perform a clean install of Windows 8.1 to remove any apps, settings, and files.

If you want to upgrade an existing installation of Windows to Windows 8.1, refer to Chapter 4. If your PC is misbehaving and you just want to reinstall Windows to clean out whatever unwanted software might be causing problems, you should start by refreshing or resetting your PC, as described in Chapter 27, "Troubleshooting startup problems, crashes, and corruption."

CHAPTER 3

▶ **Installing Windows 8.1** Watch the video at *http://aka.ms/WinIO/install*.

Making a bootable flash drive

Many new tablets and ultrabooks don't have a DVD drive. You can purchase USB DVD drives that you can then use to install Windows from a DVD, but there's an easier way: create a bootable flash drive from an ISO file. Unfortunately, this isn't as simple as copying the files from the DVD to the flash drive, because that wouldn't result in a bootable DVD.

If you don't have an ISO file of Windows 8.1, you can create one from the Windows 8.1 DVD (presuming you have access to a PC with a DVD drive). Download and install ISODisk from *http://www.isodisk.com/*. Insert your Windows 8.1 DVD, run ISODisk, select the Create ISO Image From CD-ROM tab, and click the Save button to select the file to create. Figure 3-2 shows ISODisk in action.

Figure 3-2 Use ISODisk to create an ISO file from a bootable DVD.

After saving the ISO file, use the UNetbootin tool (available at *http://sourceforge.net/projects/unetbootin/*) to create a bootable USB flash drive. Select the Diskimage option, specify your Windows 8.1 ISO file, select the USB flash drive that you want to be bootable, and click OK. Figure 3-3 shows UNetbootin in action.

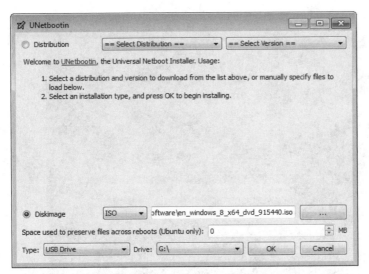

Figure 3-3 Use UNetbootin to create a bootable flash drive from an ISO file.

Starting the installation

If Windows prompts you to press a key to start from the CD or DVD, that means that the Windows setup program found an existing operating system on your PC. This is normal if you're installing Windows over an existing version of Windows, and you should press a key to start setup. Otherwise, your existing operating system will load as if the Windows 8.1 DVD were not connected.

TROUBLESHOOTING

Why isn't my PC booting from the DVD or flash drive?

If your PC doesn't boot from your DVD or flash drive, it's probably because the BIOS isn't configured to start from that media. Enter your PC's BIOS settings and change the configuration options. Unfortunately, every PC's BIOS is a little different, so I can't give specific instructions. Refer to your PC or motherboard's manual for more information.

On the first page of Windows Setup, as shown in Figure 3-4, select your language, time and currency format, and input preferences, and then click Next. On the next page, click Install Now.

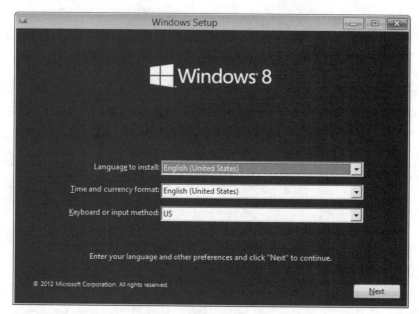

Figure 3-4 Windows Setup prompts you to select your preferences before setup begins.

Windows prompts you for your product key as shown in Figure 3-5. There's no way to bypass this; you need to enter a valid product key to continue. Windows Setup hasn't made any changes to your PC at this point, so if you don't have a product key, you can just restart your PC and any existing operating system will still work. By the way, the product key shown in Figure 3-5 is the result of me mashing the keys. It doesn't work.

Windows doesn't need to immediately activate your product key. Therefore, if you enter a product key for a different PC, setup will continue, but once Windows is running and connected to the Internet, Windows will detect that your product key is already in use and prompt you to enter a new product key or purchase a valid product key for Windows 8.1.

Prepare yourself to smirk: on the next page, you should carefully review the license terms before accepting them. It wouldn't hurt to also search the Internet for "Windows 8.1 license agreement" and find a good summary or two. Who am I kidding, most people won't even read this entire paragraph.

On the Which Type Of Installation Do You Want page, as shown in Figure 3-6, click Custom. I have no idea why it's called Custom or Advanced, or why this page even exists. If you were to click Upgrade, Windows Setup would tell you that you have to start an upgrade from a running version of Windows and then force you to restart the entire setup process. So, click Custom, but don't worry, there's nothing custom or advanced about this process.

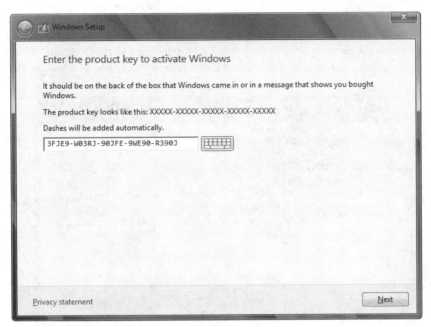

Figure 3-5 You must enter a product key to continue setup.

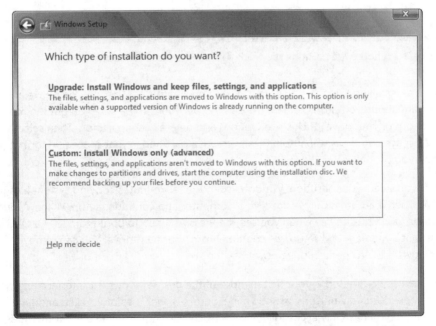

Figure 3-6 Click Custom to continue your very non-custom setup process.

The Where Do You Want To Install Windows page shows all available partitions. Most of the time, you can just click Next and go on with setup. If you're installing Windows 8.1 onto a hard drive that has never been used before, you might see only a single partition. Otherwise, you might see a small reserved partition and a larger primary partition, as shown in Figure 3-7.

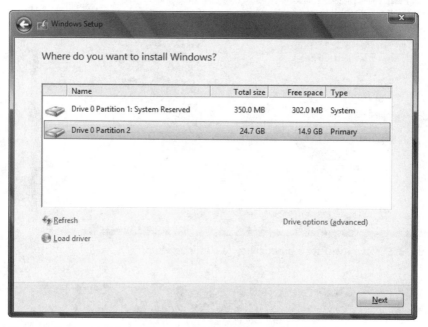

Figure 3-7 Choose the partition on which you want to install Windows.

If you're installing Windows on a new PC or a new hard drive, or you don't have any files that you care about, you should delete the existing partitions to be sure you get the most usable space out of your drive. Click Drive Options and delete every partition. Then select the unallocated space. Windows will automatically create a partition in that space and format your drive when you click Next.

After you select your partition, Windows spends a few minutes copying system files to your drive. Then it automatically restarts your computer and continues setup. When Windows restarts, don't press a key when you see the Press Any Key To Boot From CD Or DVD prompt. Just wait a moment and setup will continue from your hard drive. You can remove the Windows 8.1 DVD or flash drive now.

The next stage of setup is your first glimpse of the new Windows 8.1 interface: big type and large, touch-friendly buttons, as shown in Figure 3-8. Pick a color you like and type a name for your PC. If you have any accessibility needs (such as using alternative input methods, requiring text-to-speech, magnifying the screen, or using high contrast), click the icon in the lower-left corner.

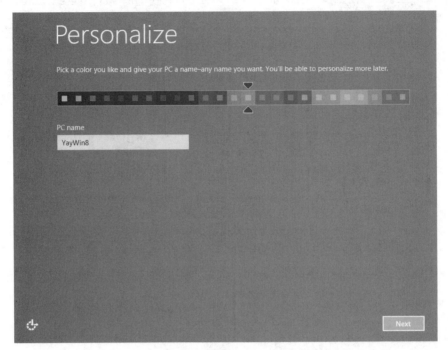

Figure 3-8 Name your PC and select your favorite color.

The PC name is important because you'll see it when you browse shared files or connect to the PC across the network. Make it a name everyone in your family can remember. I tend to name my PC after the model number, such as "XPS13," but my eight-year-old daughter has an easier time remembering them as "Tablet," "SmallLaptop," or "BigLaptop." You can't use spaces or any special characters in the PC name. As discussed in Chapter 5, "Personalizing Windows 8.1," users can select their own color, so don't worry if not everyone in your family likes the color you choose. You can change the PC name later, too.

Configuring express settings

On the Settings page of Windows Setup, I usually just click Use Express Settings. Express settings make the following default choices for your PC, any of which you can change after Windows is installed:

- Send anonymous usage information to Microsoft, including some URLs that apps use, information about potentially malicious apps, and some location data with location-aware apps. Express settings also configure your computer to participate in the

Customer Experience Improvement Program (CEIP) and Help Experience Improvement Program (HEIP), which sends Microsoft information about how you use Windows. If you're really sensitive about your privacy, you might not want these settings enabled.

- Automatically install important and recommended updates, including updated drivers. For more information about updates, refer to Chapter 25, "Maintaining your PC."

- Check online for solutions to problems using Windows Error Reporting, which sends crash reports to Microsoft and helps Microsoft identify the bugs that are impacting the most customers.

- Turn on Do Not Track in Internet Explorer, which configures Internet Explorer to send requests to websites that they not track you, but whether the websites do anything to respect that request is up to each website. It doesn't hurt, though.

- Turn on SmartScreen, which checks URLs you visit and warns you if they're known to be phishing sites or malware sites or present some other threat. SmartScreen requires Windows to send anonymous browsing information to Microsoft. For more information about SmartScreen, refer to Chapter 19, "Windows, application, and network security."

- Use Internet Explorer Compatibility lists to help identify optimal settings for Internet Explorer to use on different websites.

Of course, you don't have to use Internet Explorer. If you install a different browser and use it, the settings related to Internet Explorer won't impact you.

Selecting custom settings

If you select Customize instead of Express Settings, Windows 8.1 will walk you through several different prompts. You can change any of the settings later.

- **Sharing**   If you're connected to a home or work network, and you trust the other people and devices connected to the network, select Yes, Turn On Sharing And Connect To Devices. If not, select No, Don't Turn On Sharing Or Connect To Devices. For information about changing this setting after setup is complete, refer to Chapter 24, "Sharing and managing files and printers."

- **Help Protect And Update Your PC**   The default settings are almost always the right choice. For more information about updates, refer to Chapter 25. For information about SmartScreen, refer to Chapter 19.

- **Send Microsoft Info To Help Make Windows And Apps Better**   By default, Windows will not send any usage information to Microsoft, and those settings (see Figure 3-9) will work well for you. Turning these options on doesn't impact your daily usage of Windows in any way, but it does cast an anonymous vote with Microsoft about how you use your computer, which can help guide Microsoft's development efforts in a direction that might better suit your needs.

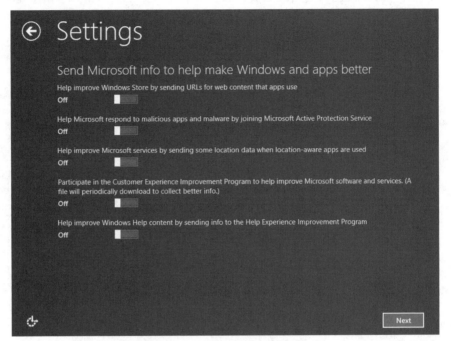

Figure 3-9 Sending usage information to Microsoft is like casting an anonymous vote for the company to optimize future updates for how you use your PC.

- **Check Online For Solutions To Problems**   Enabling these settings can improve your experience with Windows. If you turn on Windows Error Reporting, Windows will send information about any crashes you experience to Microsoft. This lets Microsoft know that you're having a problem with something, and while Microsoft doesn't respond to every problem, it does prioritize troubleshooting efforts based on the number of people having a problem. Therefore, by turning on Windows Error Reporting, you're casting a vote that any problems you have are important. Windows Error Reporting can also find existing solutions to a problem you have, so you might be able to get an update that solves your problem. The information sent in is quite anonymous, but if you're really concerned about your privacy, you should turn this setting off. Using Internet Explorer compatibility lists just refers to a list Microsoft has created of websites that work bet-ter with older versions of Internet Explorer. If a website is on that list and you have this option enabled, Internet Explorer can automatically render the website as you would see it in an older version of Internet Explorer, improving your experience. Most popular web-sites don't need this, however.

- **Share Info With Apps**   Windows 8.1 apps that you install can communicate with Windows to find some information about you, including your name, your picture, and your location. If you only install apps that you trust, enabling these settings shouldn't be a problem. If you're worried that an app might share your name, picture, or location, turn these settings off.

Signing in to your PC

Whether you choose express settings or custom settings, Windows Setup will prompt you to create a user account for your PC. Most of the time, you should sign in with your email address. This creates a Microsoft account (if you didn't already have one) and synchronizes your settings with Microsoft's servers on the Internet.

Much of what's great about Windows 8.1 is built around using your Microsoft account. How-ever, if you don't want Microsoft to manage your account information and credentials, click Sign In Without A Microsoft Account to create a local account, the same as you used in earlier versions of Windows. For detailed information about account types, refer to Chapter 18, "Man-aging users and Family Safety."

After you configure your user account, Windows starts for the first time, and setup is com-plete. Refer to Chapter 5 for information about how you can further customize Windows.

Dual-booting Windows 8.1

Dual-booting allows you to run multiple operating systems (one at a time) on your PC. When you start your PC, you can choose which operating system you want to start.

Ten years ago, dual-booting was incredibly common. Just about every geek out there had set up a system to boot between two or more operating systems. Today, virtual machines provide most of the same capabilities as dual-booting, and with much less hassle. For information about using a virtual machine to run different operating systems, refer to Chapter 20.

There are still many valid reasons to dual-boot your PC. When you dual-boot your PC, the operating systems communicate directly with your PC's hardware, providing many benefits:

- Operating systems run faster than they would in a virtual machine.

- Operating systems take full advantage of tablet features, such as touch screen, acceler-ometers, and gyroscopes.

- Operating systems can communicate with all your hardware accessories.

Therefore, if you want to be able to choose from different operating systems when starting your PC, and the drawbacks of using a virtual machine are too great, you should configure your PC for dual-booting.

Windows 8.1 supports two different techniques for dual-booting:

- Installing Windows 8.1 to a separate partition

- Booting Windows 8.1 from a virtual hard drive (VHD) file

Both approaches can be a little complicated to configure. Typically, installing Windows 8.1 to a separate partition is easier, but booting from a VHD file can make more efficient use of free space. The sections that follow describe both techniques, as well as how to configure startup options.

Installing Windows 8.1 on a separate partition

Every installation of Windows 8.1 requires a separate partition. A partition is a section of your hard disk. Usually, each partition has its own drive letter, such as C, D, or E.

Most PCs have only a single hard drive, and Windows automatically configures that hard drive with a single partition. That's perfect if you have only one operating system installed, but you'll need to create a separate partition for each installation of Windows.

If your drive has plenty of free space, you can probably split the existing drive into multiple partitions. If your drive doesn't have at least 30 gigabytes (GB) of free space, you should free up some disk space (refer to Chapter 9) or install another disk (refer to Chapter 12, "Managing storage").

To split an existing drive into multiple partitions, first free up all the disk space you can. Within Windows 7 or Windows 8.1, open the Computer Management console by running **compmgmt.msc** from the Start screen or, from Windows 8.1 only, by using the WinX menu. Select Storage, Disk Management.

In the Disk Management console, right-click your C drive and then click Shrink Volume. The Shrink dialog box appears, as shown in Figure 3-10. The default value shows the maximum amount of space you can shrink your C drive, which is also going to be the maximum size of your new partition. If it doesn't read at least 20,000, you won't be able to shrink the volume enough to create a new partition large enough to install Windows 8.1.

Once you click Shrink, Disk Management reduces the size of your existing Windows partition and leaves the remaining space unallocated. Now, you can install Windows 8.1 to the unallocated space as described in "Installing Windows 8.1" earlier in this chapter. On the Where Do You Want To Install Windows page, select the drive that matches the size you specified for the new partition and shows Unallocated Space.

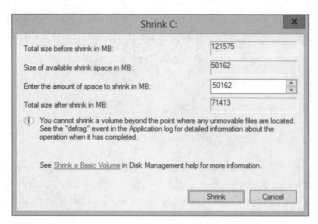

Figure 3-10 Shrink an existing volume to make room for a new Windows 8.1 partition.

TROUBLESHOOTING

Why can't I shrink my drive more?

The amount you can shrink your drive is often much less than the available free space. That's because Windows needs the free space to be contiguous; that is, to maintain one big undivided block. Often, free space on a disk is broken up by random blocks of data. The longer you've been using your PC, the more likely it is that your free space is segmented.

In theory, Windows could simply rearrange your data for you so you can free up more disk space. Windows 8.1 won't do this for you, but you can use a free tool called GParted, available at *http://www.hirensbootcd.org/*. Though I've never had a problem with the tool, you should back up your PC before using it, because Microsoft does not support it, and if something goes wrong, you could lose your data. After unzipping the ISO file, insert a blank CD into your computer, right-click the ISO file in File Explorer on the desktop, and then click Burn Disk Image. If you can't boot from a CD, use the Unetbootin tool (available at *http://sourceforge.net/projects/unetbootin/*) to create a bootable USB flash drive.

When you start from Hiren's BootCD, select Linux Based Rescue Environment and start with the default settings. Then, launch Partition Manager from the desktop to open the GParted tool. Right-click your system drive (check the size of the drive to identify it) and click Resize/Move, as shown in Figure 3-11.

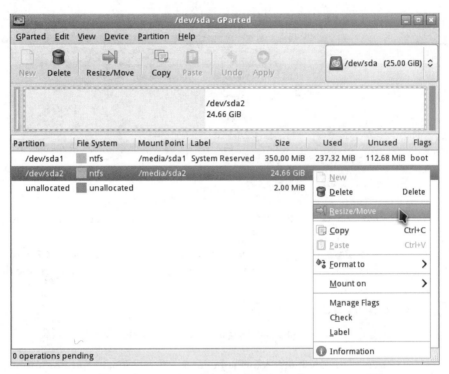

Figure 3-11 Use GParted to squeeze the most free space from your partition.

The Resize/Move dialog box in GParted works very differently from the Shrink dialog box in Windows. The default settings don't do anything useful, and you might even have to resort to doing math.

To calculate the maximum size of your new partition, first subtract the Minimum Size from the Maximum Size, as shown in Figure 3-12. If you choose that size, you won't leave any free space for your existing installation of Windows. So, subtract at least a few gigabytes of space, and then enter the size of the new partition you want in the Free Space Following box.

Figure 3-12 Use the Resize/Move dialog box to shrink your existing partition.

Click Resize/Move, and then click Apply on the toolbar. Because GParted actually rearranges your data on the disk, resizing your partition can take some time.

Booting from a VHD

These steps apply equally well to Windows 7 or Windows 8.1:

1. Open the Computer Management console by running **compmgmt.msc** from the Start screen or from the WinX menu.

2. Select Storage, Disk Management.

3. Wait until you see the list of drives, and then right-click Disk Management and select Create VHD.

4. As shown in Figure 3-13, select a location for your VHD file.

    To make the next steps easy for you, I suggest placing the file in the root of a drive. Set the size to at least 20 GB. This is going to be a very large file, so be sure you have plenty of disk space. If you want to minimize wasted disk space, select Dynamically Expanding. If you want better performance, select Fixed Drive.

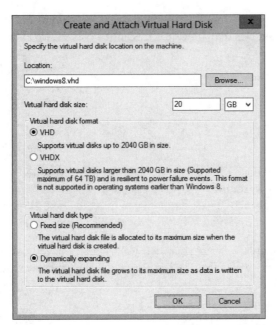

Figure 3-13 Use the Computer Management console to create a VHD.

5. When you click OK, the Disk Management console creates the file you specified and adds it as if it were a physically separate drive. On the new drive, right-click Not Initialized and then click Initialize Disk. You can accept the default setting of Master Boot Record (MBR).

6. Now, insert your Windows 8.1 setup DVD or connect your bootable flash drive and restart your computer. If prompted, press a key at the Press Any Key To Boot From CD Or DVD prompt.

    Windows Setup isn't going to be able to find the VHD file you just created, so you need to mount it as a drive. Fortunately, you can open a command prompt and run a command to mount the VHD as a drive.

7. Once Windows Setup prompts you to select the language, press Shift+F10 to open a command prompt.

    The first thing you need to do from the command prompt is determine the drive letter of the drive you stored the VHD file on, because the drive letters aren't necessarily the same as when you're running Windows.

CHAPTER 3

8. From the command prompt, run the command **wmic logicaldisk get name**. This command lists all the drives that are visible to Windows, as shown in this example output:

```
wmic logicaldisk get name
Name
C:
D:
E:
X:
```

9. Normally, your system drive is your C drive. However, the drive lettering can change when you start Windows setup. To find your system drive, run the command **dir <*drive_letter*>:** for each drive letter until you find the one that contains the Windows folder. For example, you might run **dir C:**, **dir D:**, and **dir E:**.

10. Now that you know the drive letter your VHD file is stored on, you can run the DiskPart command to mount the VHD file as a drive. Run the following commands:

```
diskpart
select vdisk file=<drive_letter>:<vhd_file>
attach vdisk
exit
```

The commands and output will resemble the following, with user input shown in bold:

```
X:\Sources>diskpart

Microsoft DiskPart version 6.2.9200

Copyright © 1999-2012 Microsoft Corporation.
On computer: MINWINPC

DISKPART> select vdisk file=C:\Windows8.vhd

Diskpart successfully selected the virtual disk file.

DISKPART> attach vdisk

  100 percent completed

DiskPart successfully attached the virtual disk file.

DISKPART> exit

Leaving DiskPart...
```

11. Now, close the command prompt and continue your Windows 8.1 installation. On the Which Type Of Installation Do You Want page, select Custom.

CHAPTER 3

12. On the Where Do You Want To Install Windows page, select the drive that matches the size you specified and shows Unallocated Space. As shown in Figure 3-14, you'll see the warning message Windows Can't Be Installed On This Drive. Ignore that and click Next, you reckless daredevil, you.

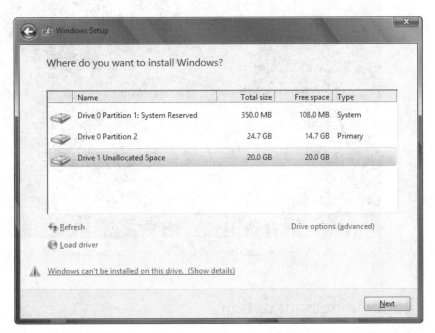

Figure 3-14 Ignore the warning that Windows can't be installed on the drive.

13. Setup will continue normally. Once it's done, Windows will greet you with the Choose An Operating System page, as shown in Figure 3-15. The first choice is your new Windows 8.1 installation, and you'll have to select it to continue setup. For information about how to configure the names of the options, the default choices, and how long the menu waits, refer to the next section, "Configuring boot options."

CHAPTER 3

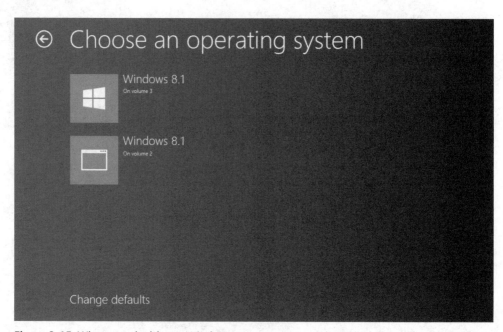

Figure 3-15 When you dual-boot, Windows prompts you to select which operating system to start.

Configuring boot options

Once you configure dual-booting, Windows 8.1 shows you a startup menu each time your PC boots. However, it displays the menu for only three seconds by default. That's plenty of time if you're staring at the screen and you have the reflexes of a PC gamer. If you have an attention span like mine, though, you're probably already distracted by reddit.com on your smartphone.

To change the timer and other startup options, restart your PC (assuming it's already con-figured to dual-boot) and be patient for once. Stare at the screen. When the menu appears, quickly click Change Defaults Or Choose Other Options at the bottom of the screen. You'll see the options page, as shown in Figure 3-16. If you don't have your PC configured for dual-boot, you can view the startup options on the General page of PC Settings. Under Advanced Startup, select Restart Now.

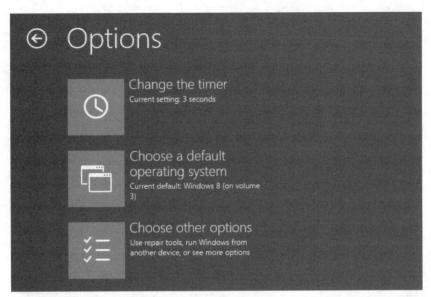

Figure 3-16 Use the Options page to configure how long Windows waits for you to select an operating system.

The options are self-explanatory. For example, the Options page allows you to choose startup timers of 3 seconds, 30 seconds, and 5 minutes.

If you want to set it for one minute, or to wait indefinitely, you'll need to use more powerful tools. Windows includes the command-line tool BCDEdit for this purpose, and I could tell you how to use it, but there's an easier way: EasyBCD.

To use EasyBCD, visit *http://neosmart.net/EasyBCD/*. There's a version of the tool that's free for home use. Once it's installed, click Edit Boot Menu. Then, you can reorganize and rename the different boot menu items. The Timeout Options at the bottom of the screen allow you to control how long the menu waits. Figure 3-17 shows EasyBCD configuring a PC with separate Windows 8.1 installations for home and work. The timer is set to wait indefinitely for the user.

CHAPTER 3

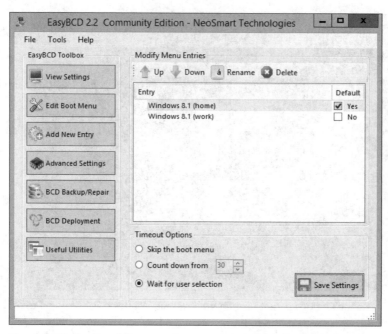

Figure 3-17 Use EasyBCD to configure startup options if you need to customize them beyond what Windows 8.1 allows.

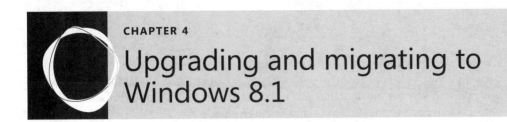

CHAPTER 4

Upgrading and migrating to Windows 8.1

Preparing for an upgrade 111

Upgrading from Windows XP or Windows Vista to Windows 8.1 112

Performing the upgrade to Windows 8.1 113

Migrating from an old PC to a new PC 116

Post-upgrade tasks 120

Uninstalling Windows 8.1 122

You can upgrade a PC running Windows XP, Windows Vista, or Windows 7 to Windows 8.1. That's pretty amazing, especially considering Windows XP was released more than 11 years before Windows 8.1. Additionally, if you buy a new PC, you can easily transfer your files and settings from your old PC to your new PC.

This chapter prepares you for the upgrading process and teaches you all the tricks you need to know to make sure an upgrade goes smoothly. For information about buying Windows 8.1, refer to Chapter 3, "Buying and installing Windows 8.1." If you're looking for information about upgrading from the original release of Windows 8 to Windows 8.1, you really don't need any. Simply run Windows Update and follow the prompts that appear.

Preparing for an upgrade

To prevent yourself from losing data and to ensure that an upgrade goes smoothly, you should take care of a few things before performing your upgrade:

- **Back up your PC** This is really important. If you are running Windows Vista, perform a Complete PC backup. If you are running Windows 7, perform a system image backup. Windows XP didn't include good software for backing up your entire PC, including apps and settings, so find third-party software. Be sure you have a bootable CD or flash drive that will allow you to restore your PC from the backup.

- **Upgrade your BIOS and other firmware** Motherboard and PC manufacturers occasionally release BIOS upgrades for PCs to update the lowest-level software that runs on the PC. Often, they release updates specifically to improve compatibility with new versions of Windows. Search for your PC model or make of motherboard to find a BIOS upgrade, and install the latest version of your PC's BIOS.

- **Uninstall unwanted apps**   From Control Panel, access the Add Or Remove Programs tool in Windows XP or the Uninstall Or Change A Program tool in Windows Vista and Windows 7. Remove any app that you aren't using. This frees up disk space, improves the performance of your PC, and simplifies the upgrade.

- **Deactivate or deauthorize apps**   Some apps, including Apple iTunes and Adobe Photoshop, can be authorized on only a limited number of PCs. Your upgraded PC might count as another PC. To avoid this, deactivate or deauthorize such apps prior to your upgrade.

- **Free up disk space**   Windows 8.1 requires at least 16 gigabytes (GB) of free disk space, but more is better. Right-click your drive in Windows Explorer, and click Properties. On the General tab, click Disk Cleanup, and free up as much space as possible. Also delete any unwanted files.

- **Verify that you have enough memory (RAM)**   Your PC needs to have 1 GB of RAM for the 32-bit version of Windows 8.1 or 2 GB of RAM for the 64-bit version of Windows 8.1. To determine how much memory you have installed, right-click My Computer and then click Properties.

- **Verify that your PC supports Data Execution Prevention (DEP)**   Your CPU and motherboard must support DEP (a feature of newer CPUs and motherboards) and have it enabled. Check your BIOS settings and verify that DEP is enabled. If it's not an option, you might be able to find a BIOS upgrade for your PC that adds support, but probably not.

- **Make sure you know your Wi-Fi password**   Windows 8.1 won't transfer your Wi-Fi password, and you don't want to be left without Internet access after upgrading.

Upgrading from Windows XP or Windows Vista to Windows 8.1

You can upgrade PCs running Windows XP and Windows Vista to Windows 8.1. In fact, many users report that their system actually feels quicker after installing Windows 8.1. It'll certainly be more powerful and secure.

If you're running Windows XP, you must have Windows XP Service Pack 3 installed. You can download Service Pack 3 by using Microsoft Update or directly from *http://www.microsoft.com/en-us/download/details.aspx?id=24*.

If you're running Windows Vista and you want to keep your apps and settings, you must have Windows Vista Service Pack 1 or Service Pack 2 installed. If you already have Service Pack 1 installed, don't bother to install Service Pack 2 before upgrading. If you have never installed a service pack, you can still perform an in-place upgrade, but you will only be able to transfer your personal files. To install Service Pack 2, visit *http://windows.microsoft.com/en-us/windows/ service-packs-download#sptabs=win8*.

If you are running the 32-bit version of Windows XP or Windows Vista, you can only upgrade to the 32-bit version of Windows 8.1. Unless you plan to use more than about 3.5 GB of RAM, the 32-bit version of Windows 8.1 should work just fine for you. To determine whether you're running 32-bit or 64-bit Windows XP or Windows Vista, right-click My Computer and then click Properties.

Inside OUT

What if you really want to upgrade from 32-bit Windows XP or Windows Vista to 64-bit Windows 8.1?

If you really want the 64-bit version of Windows 8.1, follow the instructions in "Migrating from an old PC to a new PC" later in this chapter, and transfer your files and settings to an external hard drive. Then, install 64-bit Windows 8.1 on your PC as described in Chapter 3 and use Windows Easy Transfer to copy your files and settings to Windows 8.1 from your external hard drive.

Performing the upgrade to Windows 8.1

To perform the upgrade, launch Windows 8.1 Setup while your existing version of Windows is running. You can't upgrade by booting your PC from Windows 8.1 Setup.

The upgrade process is straightforward, and I won't walk you through every page of the wizard. I'll cover the few tricky parts, however.

Unlike earlier versions of Windows, in Windows 8.1 you can't easily bypass entering the product key, as shown in Figure 4-1. Windows Setup hasn't made any changes to your PC at this point, so if you don't have a product key, just close Setup and restart it when you have a product key. If you enter a product key that has already been used, Windows Setup will continue, but you'll be required to purchase a new product key once Windows 8.1 is running.

▶ **Upgrading to Windows 8.1** Watch the video at *http://aka.ms/WinIO/upgrade*.

CHAPTER 4

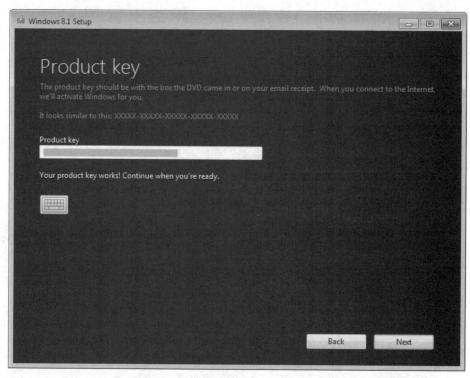

Figure 4-1 You can't easily bypass entering the Windows 8.1 product key.

The Choose What To Keep page presents a very important choice:

- **Keep Windows Settings, Personal Files, And Apps**   Choose this option (available in Windows 7 and Windows Vista with Service Pack 1 or later only) to migrate everything to Windows 8.1. This is the right choice for most people.

- **Keep Personal Files Only**   This option forgets your Windows settings (such as your desktop background) and your apps. This is the right choice if you are upgrading from Windows XP. If you're using Windows 7, choose this option only if you haven't customized Windows and the only app you use is a web browser.

- **Nothing**   This performs a clean install of Windows 8.1, deleting all your files, apps, and settings. Only do this if you want to start completely clean and you have anything important backed up to an external hard drive.

If you choose Keep Personal Files Only or Nothing, Windows Setup will move the data it couldn't migrate, including the data in your Program Files and Documents And Settings folders, into C:\Windows.old, so you can access it after setup is complete. You will need to reinstall every app that you need.

If you choose to keep your apps, Setup will analyze your apps to determine if there's anything that definitely won't work in Windows 8.1. As shown in Figure 4-2, it prompts you to uninstall those apps to continue setup. In Figure 4-2, the compatibility report for my ultrabook shows two hardware related apps. While both those apps provide important functionality in Windows 7, Windows 8.1 has hardware support for those components built in, so I can uninstall the apps and still be able to use my trackpad and wireless.

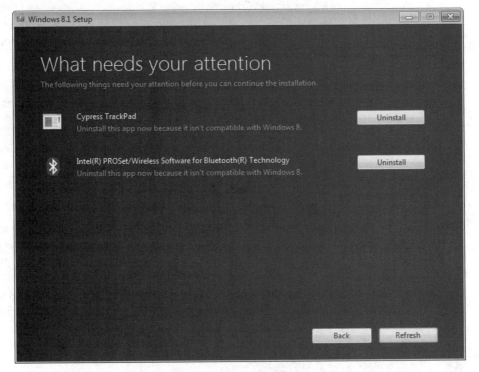

Figure 4-2 Uninstall any apps that won't work with Windows 8.1.

You might have to restart your computer and then start setup again after uninstalling the apps. However, if an app's uninstaller warns you that you need to restart your PC for the changes to take effect, you can probably ignore the warning and continue with setup.

CHAPTER 4

If there are any apps you absolutely need that Windows 8.1 does not support, you have a few options:

- Upgrade to Windows 8.1 and run the app with compatibility settings, as described in the section "App compatibility settings" in Chapter 6, "Adding, removing, and managing apps." This won't work for some apps, however.

- Upgrade to Windows 8.1 and run an earlier version of Windows within a virtual machine. Then, install the app in the virtual machine. This will work for many apps, but it might not work for games or apps that require a specific hardware accessory. For more information, refer to Chapter 20, "Using Hyper-V."

- Install Windows 8.1 separately from your current Windows installation, and then dual-boot your PC. This will allow you to start either your existing Windows installation or Windows 8.1. However, Windows Setup will not automatically migrate your apps and settings. For more information, refer to Chapter 3.

Once you begin the installation, Windows will take about 20 minutes before it prompts you to personalize Windows. The process closely resembles that used to perform a clean installation of Windows 8.1, as described in Chapter 3.

All your hardware, including Bluetooth accessories, should work properly during Windows 8.1 setup. If you need to run a command to configure hardware, press Shift+F10 to open an administrative command prompt.

The Sign In To Your PC page will prompt you to enter your email address. We're so accustomed to entering our email address in forms that it would be easy to overlook the significance of this step. If you enter your email address, your existing local account will be associated with a Microsoft account, and Windows 8.1 will use your Microsoft account for future logins and to synchronize your files. I'm a huge fan of using a Microsoft account, but if you prefer to keep your login local, choose Skip on the Sign In To Your PC page. For detailed information about account types, refer to Chapter 18, "Managing users and Family Safety."

Migrating from an old PC to a new PC

If you buy a new PC with Windows 8.1 and you want to replace an existing PC, you can use Windows Easy Transfer to copy the files and settings from your old PC to your new Windows 8.1 PC. You'll feel instantly at home at your new PC, though you will need to reinstall any apps.

As shown in Figure 4-3, Windows Easy Transfer provides three ways to copy your files and settings. The network option is going to be easiest for most people, and that's the method that I'll describe. If you have a large number of files, it might be worth your while to connect both PCs to a wired network to reduce the time the transfer takes.

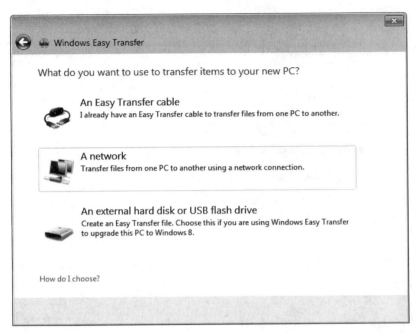

Figure 4-3 Windows Easy Transfer provides three ways to move your files to a new PC.

If your old PC is running Windows XP, make sure you have Service Pack 3 installed. You can download the service pack by using Microsoft Update or directly from *http://www.microsoft.com/ en-us/download/details.aspx?id=24*.

Here's an overview of the Windows Easy Transfer process:

1. On your new PC running Windows 8.1, open the Start screen, type **transfer**, and then select Windows Easy Transfer. Follow the prompts that appear. On the Do You Need To Install Windows Easy Transfer On Your Old PC page, select I Already Installed It On My Old PC. Don't worry if you haven't actually done that, because you'll install it in the next step.

2. On your old PC, download and install Windows Easy Transfer from *http:// windows.microsoft.com/en-us/windows7/products/features/windows-easy-transfer*. Windows Easy Transfer hasn't changed since Windows 7, so the Windows 7 version of Easy Transfer will work.

3. When you reach the Go To Your New Computer And Enter Your Windows Easy Transfer Key page (as shown in Figure 4-4) on a computer running Windows XP, make note of the key and type it into your new PC.

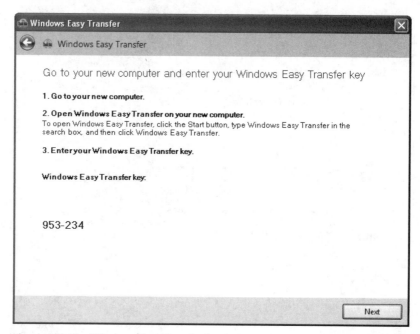

Figure 4-4 The Windows Easy Transfer key helps your PCs communicate across the network.

4. Windows Easy Transfer will verify compatibility. If it finds any problems, such as a missing service pack, it will warn you.

5. After it verifies compatibility, Windows Easy Transfer prompts you to choose what to transfer. Click the Customize link to choose exactly which files and settings should be transferred, as shown in Figure 4-5. To reduce clutter and speed the migration process, you should transfer only files and settings that you need. Click Advanced Options to configure how user accounts on your old PC are mapped to user accounts on your new PC, and how drives on your old PC are mapped to your new PC. If you have only one drive and one user on each PC, you don't need to bother changing the defaults.

6. Windows Easy Transfer now copies over your files and settings. On the last page, be sure to click See A List Of Apps You Might Want To Install On Your New PC to view the App Report, as shown in Figure 4-6. Before you install the same desktop app on your Windows 8.1 PC, you should check the Windows Store to see if there's a newer version of the same app, or an app with similar functionality, that was designed specifically for Windows 8.1.

Restart your PC, and Windows 8.1 is ready to use.

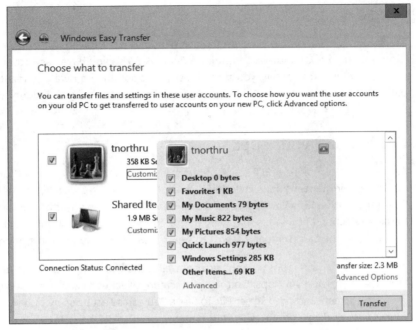

Figure 4-5 Windows Easy Transfer allows you to customize what it transfers.

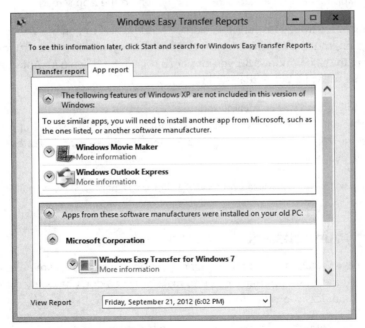

Figure 4-6 View the App Report tab to see what apps you might need to install.

CHAPTER 4

Post-upgrade tasks

Feel free to play around as soon as you get Windows 8.1 installed. At some point, though, you should spend a few minutes configuring Windows 8.1 so you have easy access to the apps you use most often. Additionally, you should test your apps and hardware to identify any incompatibilities that weren't found during setup and remove the massive amount of unnecessary files that setup leaves behind.

Configuring your apps

After setup is complete, you'll see the Start screen for the first time. The left side of the Start screen has the standard apps included with every Windows 8.1 installation, as described in Chapter 2, "Using Windows 8.1 apps." Scroll right (or scroll down with your mouse scroll wheel) to see a selection of the apps that were migrated to Windows 8.1. Windows 8.1 doesn't add all your apps to the Start screen; it seems to select those apps you use most often.

If any of your favorite apps are missing, right-click the Start screen or swipe up from the bottom, and then select All Apps. On the Apps screen, select each app that you want to appear on your Start screen, and then select Pin To Start. You can select apps by right-clicking them with your mouse or flicking them with your finger.

Of course, you don't need to add every app to the Start screen. You can always access apps by typing the app name on the Start screen or by opening the App screen.

All apps migrated from your earlier version of Windows will run on the Windows 8.1 desktop, which isn't optimized for mobile devices or touch. It's a good idea to search for your apps in the Store to see if Windows 8.1 versions are available for download. Apps designed for Windows 8.1 will work better than desktop apps.

The Store will probably have several updates to apps that are preinstalled with Windows 8.1, so start Store and click Updates in the upper-right corner to install those updates. You should also select the Windows Update page from PC Settings to see if any updates to Windows components are available.

Now, you're ready to customize Windows 8.1. Refer to Chapter 5, "Personalizing Windows 8.1," for information.

Testing your apps and hardware

After you have Windows 8.1 up and running, you should spend a few minutes going through the tasks that are most important to you to make sure you don't have any compatibility problems. Here's a quick list of steps to take:

- Run every app that you might want to use in the future.

- Use every piece of hardware that you care about.

- Make sure components such as Bluetooth and wireless networking work properly.

- Verify that you can print.

- Test features that you might use only when traveling.

I suggest these steps not because my experience leads me to believe you'll have problems. On the contrary, I haven't had any compatibility problems with Windows 8.1. However, in the unlikely event you do have a compatibility problem, I don't want you to be stranded without being able to use your PC.

Freeing up disk space

Naturally, Windows 8.1 has different system files from earlier versions of Windows. Windows 8.1 doesn't delete any of your existing system files or apps. Instead it saves them in the C:\Windows.old folder, which will probably be about 16 GB if you're upgrading from Windows 7.

TROUBLESHOOTING

Where did my app data go?

If during the upgrade you chose the Keep Personal Files Only option on the Choose What To Keep page, Windows Setup will move your Program Files folder (which contains all your desktop app files, possibly including app settings and data) into the Windows.old folder. If you reinstall an app and discover that it can't find its data, you might be able to rescue the data by finding the files in C:\Windows.old\Program Files\.

If you chose the Nothing option on the Choose What To Keep page, Windows will also move your user profile folder (such as the Documents And Settings folder) into Windows.old. Therefore, it's not too late to recover your files.

Wait a week or two, and once you're sure you don't need any of your system files, delete that folder to free up some disk space. You can remove it by using the Disk Cleanup tool (described in Chapter 9, "Organizing and protecting files") and choosing Clean Up System Files. Then, in the Disk Cleanup dialog box, select Previous Windows Installations, as shown in Figure 4-7. You can also select Temporary Windows Installation Files (about 5 GB) and Windows Upgrade Log files (about 170 MB).

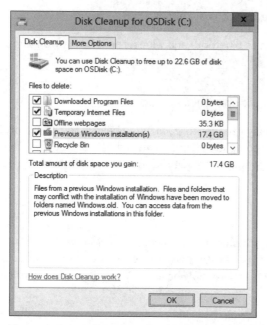

Figure 4-7 Remove your previous Windows installation to save space.

Uninstalling Windows 8.1

I haven't had any compatibility problems with Windows 8.1, but if Windows 8.1 doesn't support an important piece of hardware or software and the vendor won't provide you with an update, the easiest way to get back to your Windows 7 installation is to restore the system image backup I suggested you make at the beginning of the chapter. If you don't have a recent backup, you should copy your files to an external drive and reinstall Windows 7 by deleting all existing partitions during the setup process. Then, restore your files from your external drive.

If you just don't like the Windows 8.1 user interface, I suggest giving it a couple of weeks. You'll probably learn to love it, as I have. If you still don't like it, read Chapter 5 for information about customizing Windows 8.1 to be a bit more like earlier versions of Windows.

Personalizing Windows 8.1

The Start screen 123

Tiles. 128

Notifications 129

Lock screen 130

Desktop 132

Searching 135

Power settings. 136

Multiple monitors 139

Language settings 142

WinX menu 143

Ever since you were a small child, you've had your own unique preferences: your favorite color, your favorite food, and your favorite animal. Preferences like these don't go away when you become an adult. In fact, they only become more complex.

You have a unique personality, with a set of preferences that you share with nobody else on the planet. Your friends, home, and music reflect those preferences, and so should your PC.

Yet the power to personalize a PC comes with a heavy cost. Simply allowing users to choose from round corners or square corners requires developers to test their app (and every update to that app) with both styles. Allowing users to choose translucent borders (such as the Aero theme in Windows 7) creates a user interface that can't be supported on mobile devices with lower processing capabilities.

This chapter provides an overview of how you can personalize Windows 8.1 by using built-in settings or third-party tools, but it does not describe personalizing the desktop.

The Start screen

The Start screen is the first screen you see when you log in to Windows. It's more than just a way to launch your apps: it's an entire dashboard, showing live updates from your social networks, weather, news, and more. If you arrange the Start screen properly, you can have all the most important apps and updates available at a glance, without scrolling, and that can save you enormous amounts of time.

The next sections show you how to customize your Start screen and give you advice about the best ways to do it.

▶ **Customizing the Start screen** Watch the video at *http://aka.ms/WinIO/startscreen*.

Arranging tiles

By default, Windows 8.1 adds the standard apps to the left side of your Start screen and displays those same apps every time Windows starts. That left side of the Start screen is the most valuable real estate on your PC though, and it's best filled with the tiles containing the most useful updates and the apps you launch most often.

Arranging tiles is intuitive: drag them on the Start screen. To change the size of a tile, select it by flicking or by right-clicking it, and then click Resize.

Inside OUT

Default icons for app tiles

The app tile icons are not meant to be edited, but if you are curious about where these files are located, browse the %ProgramFiles%\WindowsApps\ folder. You might need to take ownership of it before you browse it. Most tile files use the PNG image format and have a .png file name extension.

Grouping apps

Although it might not be obvious, apps on the Start screen are divided into groups, as shown in Figure 5-1, and each group has a name. To move an app between groups, simply drag the app to the new group. To rename a group, select any app in the group by right-clicking or flicking it, and then type the new group name.

Figure 5-1 Zoom back on the Start screen to change app groups.

You can zoom out by pinching with your fingers or by pressing Ctrl+Minus Sign on the keyboard. With the Start screen zoomed out, you can rearrange entire groups by dragging them left or right.

I arrange the tiles so that all the apps I use regularly are at the left and appear by default on the Start screen. Apps I use less frequently are grouped logically according to the type of app.

One of my apps is missing from the Start screen

If an app is installed but doesn't have a tile on the Start screen, follow these steps to add it:

1. On the Start screen, click the arrow in the lower-left corner. This displays all apps installed on your computer, even if they are not pinned to the Start screen.

2. Select an app by flicking it with your finger or right-clicking it with the mouse.

3. Click the Pin To Start command at the bottom of the screen.

You can also quickly launch any app by typing its name from the Start screen. With touch, use the Search charm from the Start screen to find an app.

Changing the Start screen background

While you don't have as many options as you do on the desktop, you can still configure the color of the Start screen and choose from a few graphical themes. From the Start Screen, select the Settings charm, and then select Personalize. In the right pane, select the graphic you want, as shown in Figure 5-2, or select your desktop wallpaper (always the last item). Then, pick your color and the background style you want. That's really it!

Figure 5-2 There are only a few ways to customize the Start screen.

Showing administrative tools on the Start screen

In the early versions of Windows, Microsoft expected everyone to have some basic systems administration skills, but each version has gotten progressively more automated. If everything goes as planned with Windows 8.1, most users will never need to launch an administrative tool.

That's a step in the right direction, but power users still need every tool available to them. Especially if you're familiar with earlier versions of Windows, you want to have the same tools at your fingertips. While the Windows 8.1 Start screen doesn't show administrative tools by default, you can turn them on with a few clicks: from the Start screen, open the Settings charm, click Settings, click Tiles, and then click Show Administrative Tools.

Windows 8.1 displays the administrative tools only on the All Apps page (accessed by clicking the down arrow from the main Start screen), as shown in Figure 5-3. To add individual tools to your main Start screen, right-click or flick the tool and then select Pin To Start.

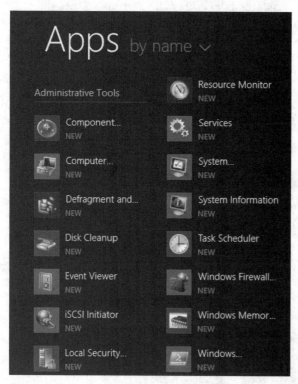

Figure 5-3 You can add the administrative tools to your Start screen.

Adding restart and shutdown to the Start screen

Most users will not need to manually shut down or restart their computer; they'll simply close the lid or press the power button. Those who do can open the Settings charm and then click Power. For me, that's quick enough.

If you'd rather bypass the Settings charm, you can add links to shut down or restart your computer to your Start screen by following these steps:

1. Open the desktop by clicking the Desktop icon from the Start screen or by pressing Windows+D.

2. Right-click, choose New, and then click Shortcut. In the Type The Location Of The Item box, type one of the following:

    - To restart Windows without restarting open applications, type **shutdown /r /t 0**.

    - To restart Windows and any open applications, type **shutdown /g /t 0** (as shown in Figure 5-4).

    - To shut down Windows, type **shutdown /s /t 0**.

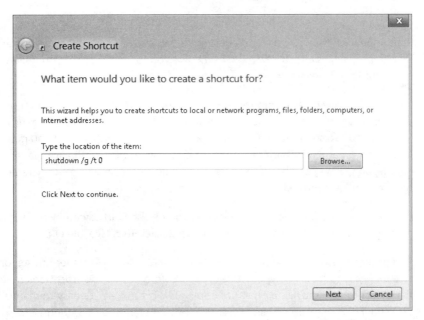

Figure 5-4 Create a special shortcut to restart your computer from the Start screen.

CHAPTER 5

3. Click Next. On the What Would You Like To Name The Shortcut page, type a name for the shortcut, and then click Finish.

4. Right-click the newly created shortcut, and then click Properties.

5. On the Shortcut tab, click Change Icon.

6. In the Change Icon dialog box, select an appropriate icon, such as the power icon. Click OK twice.

7. Right-click the shortcut, and then click Cut.

8. Open File Explorer. Type the following path into the address bar, and then press Enter: **%UserProfile%\AppData\Local\Microsoft\Windows\Application Shortcuts**

9. Paste the shortcut into the folder by pressing Ctrl+V or by right-clicking and selecting Paste.

Now, open the Start screen. Your new app tile will be at the far right side. Drag it anywhere you want it.

Tiles

Tiles appear on the Start screen, replacing app icons. You can click a tile to start an app, but if an app uses tiles effectively, the tile will give you the information you need to completely avoid starting the app.

Tiles can display content from the app and display updates without requiring you to open the app. Fortunately, tiles are designed to use very little battery power and bandwidth. Nonetheless, they do use some trace amount of power and bandwidth, and if you don't use the live tile feature for an app, you might as well turn it off. I've turned off the live tile feature for the Mail, People, and News apps because I find the updates too distracting—they tempt me to check my email or Facebook when I'm supposed to be working.

To disable a live update for a tile, select an app on the Start screen by flicking it or right-clicking it. Swipe up from the bottom, and then click Turn Live Tile Off.

It's entirely possible for live tile data to show something you'd rather not see on your Start screen. Realistically, it's only a matter of time before one of your Facebook friends posts something absurd that shows up on your People tile. Fortunately, it's easy to manually clear the live tile data. From the Start screen, select the Settings charm, click Settings, click Tiles, and then click Clear.

Windows 8.1 will clear all data from your live tiles, so you will see the default tiles. At some point, though, it will refresh the tile data, and your friend might make another appearance unless you disable live tile updates for that app.

To automatically clear live tile data when you log off from Windows 8.1 Pro or Windows 8.1 Enterprise, follow these steps:

1.   Run **gpedit.msc** to open the Local Group Policy Editor. You can run an app by typing the name at the Start screen. For example, simply open the Start screen, type **gpedit.msc**, and then press Enter.

2.   Select User Configuration\Administrative Templates\Start Menu And Taskbar.

3.   Double-click Clear History Of Tile Notifications On Exit. Click Enabled, and then click OK.

4.   Restart the computer.

Notifications

Apps can display notifications that appear as a message on top of other apps for 10 seconds. These messages appear any time the app has something it wants to tell you immediately. For example, an instant messaging app would show a notification each time you receive a new message, and Windows shows a notification each time you insert a memory card with pictures on it.

Unfortunately, it's also possible for apps to show annoying notifications. For example, you probably don't care if a role-playing game you installed six months ago is now offering 50 percent off bronze armor, or if a social networking app thinks you've gone too long without updating your status.

In those situations, you can turn off notifications for the offending app. Select the Settings charm, and then click Change PC Settings. In the left pane, click Search & Apps, and then click Notifications. In the right pane, turn off notifications for individual apps as shown in Figure 5-5. You can also use this page to set quiet hours during which Windows hides notifications. This is a good way to stop your PC from waking you up while you're sleeping.

CHAPTER 5

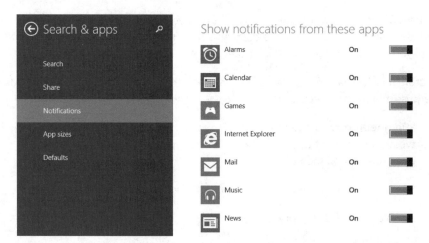

Figure 5-5 Use PC Settings to turn off an app's notifications.

You should temporarily turn off notifications before giving a presentation or sharing your computer with a coworker (unless, of course, you want them to see the unexpected love note from your spouse/partner). To temporarily disable all notifications, select the Settings charm, and then click Notifications in the lower-left corner of the settings bar. You can then choose to hide notifications for one hour, three hours, or eight hours.

When the Notifications icon shows a clock over it, notifications are disabled. Click the icon to reenable notifications.

▶ **Personalizing Windows 8.1** Watch the video at *http://aka.ms/WinIO/personalize.*

Lock screen

The lock screen is the first thing you see when you start Windows. The lock screen shows a picture along with app notifications, both of which can be customized by changing the lock screen picture or personalizing lock screen notifications.

Ideally, you should set up the lock screen to tell you that you don't need to log in to your computer. For example, if you regularly log in just to see if you have any new email messages, you should display email notifications on the lock screen. Then, you can tell at a glance, without logging in, whether you have any new messages. I have it set up to display the details about the next appointment on my calendar and the number of new messages waiting for me.

To set the lock screen picture, select the Settings charm and then click Change PC Settings. Select PC & Devices, click Lock Screen, and then click Browse to select a picture. To control which apps display notifications on the lock screen, under Lock Screen Apps, click a plus symbol to add an app, as shown in Figure 5-6. To remove a notification, click the icon and then click Don't Show Quick Status Here.

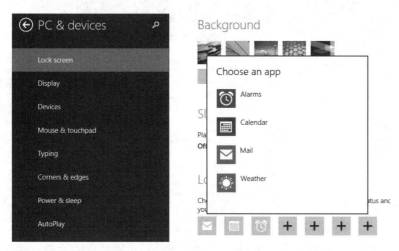

Figure 5-6 Use PC Settings to show app notifications on the lock screen.

Whereas a standard notification simply shows a number (which might indicate the number of new messages), a detailed notification shows text (which might show a preview of the most recent message). Only one app can show detailed notifications, so choose the one that will save you from having to log in to your computer most often, and be sure you're comfortable with other people seeing those notifications, because anyone can see the lock screen without logging in.

To choose which app shows a detailed notification, click the icon below Choose An App To Display Detailed Status, and then click the app.

You can also completely disable the lock screen. Even though the lock screen is useful for giving you information without logging in and for preventing accidental input on touch-screen computers, it's rather unnecessary on desktop computers, because you can usually get more detailed information from the live tiles on the Start screen.

If you'd rather skip the lock screen and jump directly to the login screen, run **gpedit.msc** (only available on Windows 8.1 Pro and Windows 8.1 Enterprise) to open the Local Group Policy Editor. Select Computer Configuration\Administrative Templates\Control Panel\Personalization, as shown in Figure 5-7. Double-click Do Not Display The Lock Screen. Select Enabled, and then click OK. The next time you restart the computer, Windows will display the login screen when it starts, bypassing the lock screen.

CHAPTER 5

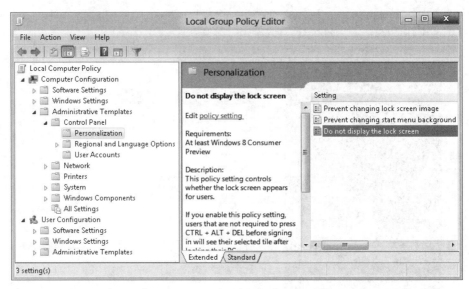

Figure 5-7 Some advanced settings must be changed using the Local Group Policy Editor.

Desktop

Over time, more applications will be designed for Windows 8.1, and users will rarely need to access the desktop. Windows 8.1 is designed with that long-term goal in mind. While Windows 8.1 is new, however, many of us will still spend a great deal of time running desktop apps created for Windows 7. If that sounds like you, you might also find it frustrating that Windows 8.1 deemphasizes the desktop. Fortunately, there are several steps you can take to make the Windows 8.1 desktop more usable while waiting for your apps to catch up with your new operating system.

Adding the Windows 7 Start menu

If you missed it in Chapter 1, "What's new in Windows 8.1," you can download and install a desktop app that provides a Start menu very similar to the one built into Windows 7. My favorites are ViStart, available at *http://lee-soft.com/vistart/*, and Start 8, available at *http://www.stardock.com/products/start8/*. Also check out Classic Shell at *http:// classicshell.sourceforge.net/*.

How to launch apps

You can launch any app simply by typing its name from the Start screen. However, if you're a desktop user and you'd rather not use the Start screen to launch apps, you can create a special folder containing shortcuts to your Windows 8.1 apps. The easiest way to launch desktop apps is still by pinning the apps to the desktop taskbar.

To launch Windows 8.1 apps directly from the desktop, create a shortcut that links to the special folder location containing the apps. Follow these steps:

1. Open the desktop by clicking Desktop from the Start screen or by pressing Windows+D.

2. Right-click the desktop, select New, and then click Shortcut.

    The Create Shortcut wizard appears.

3. On the What Item Would You Like To Create A Shortcut For page, type **%windir%\ explorer.exe shell:::{4234d49b-0245-4df3-b780-3893943456e1}**, and then click Next.

4. On the What Would You Like To Name The Shortcut page, type **Apps**, and then click Finish.

5. To make the folder easier to access, right-click it and then click Pin To Taskbar.

To launch an app from the desktop, open the folder you created and double-click the app. You might not be able to see the icons for Windows 8.1 apps because most of them are white, and File Explorer shows a white background by default. To see the icons, select them with your mouse or press Ctrl+A, as shown in Figure 5-8.

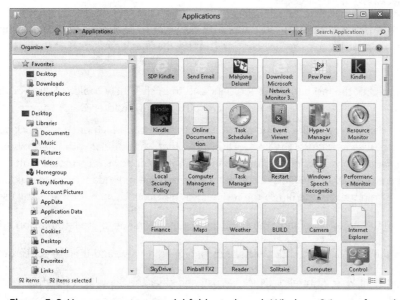

Figure 5-8 You can create a special folder to launch Windows 8.1 apps from the desktop.

CHAPTER 5

How to pin apps

If you have a desktop app that doesn't use a conventional installer (for example, an .exe file that you run directly), you can still add it to the Start screen. From the desktop, right-click the .exe file and click Pin To Start. Press the Windows key to open the Start screen; the new tile for the app will be the last item.

How to add the Recycle Bin to the taskbar

The Recycle Bin is always located on your desktop, and you can drag files and folders to it to delete them. To make it even easier, you can add the Recycle Bin to your taskbar, as shown in Figure 5-9.

Figure 5-9 Add the Recycle Bin to your taskbar for easy access.

To add the Recycle Bin to your taskbar, follow these steps:

1.   Open the desktop by clicking the Desktop icon from the Start screen or by pressing Windows+D.

2.   Start File Explorer by clicking it on the taskbar. On the View tab, select the Hidden Items check box. Close File Explorer.

3.   If the taskbar is locked, unlock the taskbar by right-clicking it and then selecting Lock The Taskbar. If Lock The Taskbar does not have a check mark next to it, the taskbar is already unlocked.

4.   Right-click the taskbar, select Toolbars, and then click New Toolbar. Select C:\Users\ <*username*>\AppData\Roaming\Microsoft\Internet Explorer\Quick Launch.

     This displays the Quick Launch toolbar on the taskbar, which provides quick access to shortcuts and folders. The Quick Launch toolbar was popular with Windows Vista and earlier versions of Windows, but Windows 7 and Windows 8.1 support pinning shortcuts to the taskbar, so the Quick Launch toolbar became redundant. However, you cannot easily pin the Recycle Bin to the taskbar, so the Quick Launch toolbar is still useful.

5.   Grab the dotted line and drag the Quick Launch toolbar to the left, making it larger.

6.   On the taskbar, right-click Quick Launch, highlight View, and then select Large Icons.

7.   On the taskbar, right-click Quick Launch and clear the Show Text option.

8. On the taskbar, right-click Quick Launch and clear the Show Title option.

9. Drag the Recycle Bin from the desktop to the Quick Launch toolbar.

10. Once again, grab the dotted line to resize the Quick Launch toolbar. This time, drag it all the way to the right, making it as small as possible.

11. Right-click the taskbar, and select Lock The Taskbar.

Now, you can drag items to the Recycle Bin on your taskbar to delete them, and empty the Recycle Bin by clicking it on the taskbar.

Searching

Windows 8.1 provides an entirely new system for searching content on your computer and the Internet. Whereas Windows 7 simply searched files on your computer, Windows 8.1 allows applications to include their own search results. Windows 8.1 also stores your search results so that it can automatically suggest similar searches in the future.

To configure which applications can be searched and to clear your search history, select the Settings charm and click Change PC Settings. In the left pane, select Search & Apps, and then select Search.

Now, you can perform several different actions:

- **Clear your search history**   Click the Clear button in the right pane.

- **Stop Bing from searching the web**   Change the settings under Use Bing To Search Online to prevent all automatic Bing searches or to prevent them just when you're using a metered connection (to reduce your data usage).

- **Stop Bing personalization**   Under Your Search Experience, select Don't Get Personalized Results From Bing. This option stops Bing from tracking your specific interests, so the results you get will be more generic.

- **Allow Bing to use your location**   Under Your Search Experience, select Get Personalized Search Results From Bing That Use My Location. This option sends your location along with Bing queries, potentially allowing Bing to provide catered results. For example, searching for "pizza restaurant" might return local results rather than more generic results.

- **Filter (or stop filtering) adult content**   Under SafeSearch, choose Strict, Moderate, or Off to control which types of results searches will return.

CHAPTER 5

Power settings

All computers, but especially mobile computers, must balance performance and power usage. Windows 8.1 default settings are effective for most users, and if you buy a new computer with Windows 8.1 installed, the computer manufacturer has probably tuned the settings specifically for your computer.

The Windows 8.1 update includes Power & Sleep options, which you can access by opening the Settings charm, selecting PC & Devices, and then selecting Power & Sleep. These options allow you to control whether Windows 8.1 automatically adjusts the screen brightness and to specify how long it waits to turn off the screen or to enter Sleep mode.

There are times when you might want to fine-tune power settings. For example, if you are on an eight-hour flight and you need your battery to last for as long as possible, you might be willing to tolerate slower performance. On the other hand, if you need to finish a report in the next 30 minutes, you want every bit of performance your computer has to offer.

Inside OUT
Power-saving changes since Windows 7

Though you can now adjust the screen brightness using the Settings charm, most of the power settings have not changed since Windows 7. Windows 8.1 should give you better battery life, however, because apps designed for Windows 8.1 are also designed to be highly efficient.

Windows 8.1 includes three power plans. Each one adjusts performance differently depending on whether the computer is plugged in or running on battery power. The three plans are:

- **Balanced**   The default plan, which is sufficient for most users. Performance is maximized when the computer is connected to power, but the balance shifts toward efficiency when the computer is running on battery.

- **Power Saver**   This plan reduces power usage even when the computer is plugged in. You might see less performance from your wireless network, but your batteries will last longer.

- **High Performance**   This plan maximizes performance even when the computer is running on battery power. You won't notice a difference when the computer is plugged in, but performance will improve when you are using batteries. Switch to this plan when you have more than enough battery power and you want your computer and wireless network to be as fast as possible.

I usually leave my computer on Balanced mode and adjust the advanced settings for my typical usage. When I need my batteries to last as long as possible (for example, on a long flight), I switch to Power Saver mode. When I have more than enough battery power, I switch to High Performance mode.

To change your power plan or adjust a power plan's settings, search for **power options** and then select Power Options. Select a power plan, as shown in Figure 5-10. (If you don't see High Performance, click Show Additional Plans.)

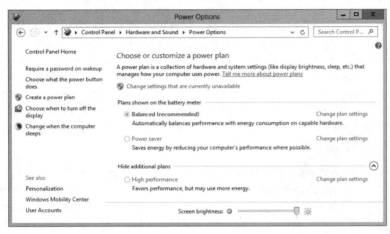

Figure 5-10 Change your power plan to get more battery life or faster performance.

The first setting you might want to change is Require A Password On Wakeup. If you are not worried about other people using your computer or accessing your files, change this setting to No.

You might also need to customize power settings for specific scenarios. If you are uploading a large file, you don't want your laptop to automatically go into Sleep mode when you close the lid. If you have a really weak Wi-Fi signal, you might want to boost the power of your wireless network radio without changing the power settings for other aspects of your computer. To customize a power plan's settings, click Change Plan Settings, and then click Change Advanced Power Settings. Some of the more useful settings include:

- **Wireless Adapter Settings**   Choose how much power your wireless network adapter uses. If your wireless signal is too weak when on battery power, if you know there's a wireless network available but your computer can't see it, or you just need as much bandwidth as possible, change it to Low Power Saving or Maximum Performance.

- **Processor Power Management, System Cooling Policy**   The more work your PC's processor is doing, the hotter it gets. When the processor gets hot, Windows can cool the processor in one of two ways: active cooling or passive cooling. Active cooling runs a fan, whereas passive cooling slows down the processor. By default, Windows uses active processing when the PC is plugged in and passive cooling when the PC is on battery power. If you're like me and you find it annoying that your PC slows down when it gets busy, change the On Battery setting to Active.

- **Power Buttons And Lid**   Choose what happens when you press the power button or close a laptop's lid. For example, if you are transferring a file or encoding a video, you might want to close the lid on your laptop without putting the laptop into Sleep mode.

- **Display, Enable Adaptive Brightness**   Adaptive brightness uses a light sensor on a mobile computer to adjust the screen brightness based on the amount of light in the room. The brighter the room, the brighter the screen. In dim rooms, adaptive brightness decreases the screen brightness to reduce power. Disable adaptive brightness if you prefer to manually control the brightness. To manually change the screen brightness, select the Settings charm, click the Brightness icon, and then adjust the brightness. Many computers also have dedicated hardware buttons for changing the screen brightness. Dimmer settings extend battery life.

- **Multimedia Settings, When Sharing Media**   If you use a mobile computer to share music or videos across your network, you definitely do not want it to turn off automatically. It won't turn off when plugged in, but, by default, it will turn off when on battery power.

- **Multimedia Settings, When Playing Video**   If you use your computer to watch videos on battery power (for example, on an airplane), adjust this setting to balance video quality with power consumption. I would rather have my battery last through a long flight and tolerate lower video quality, so I set Multimedia Settings, When Playing Video, On Battery, to Optimize Power Savings.

- **Battery**   Windows will warn you and then automatically hibernate your computer as your battery runs down. This works well when the battery is new, but when the battery is older, you might need more warning. If your computer warns you only seconds before the battery runs out, or it doesn't have time to hibernate, increase the percentage for Critical Battery Level.

Inside OUT
Adjusting power settings from the command line

Use the PowerCfg command-line tool to change power settings from a command prompt or command script (commonly known as a batch file). For example, you could create several command scripts that adjust settings for the current power plan to your specific needs for different scenarios, such as airplane travel, presentations, and sharing media. For more information about PowerCfg, open a command prompt and run **PowerCfg /?**. For information about writing command scripts, read "How to Write a Batch File" at *http://www.wikihow.com/Write-a-Batch-File*.

Multiple monitors

Using multiple monitors is a great way to improve the productivity of anyone working in a traditional computing environment with a desk, keyboard, and mouse. When you have more than one screen, you can keep more windows open simultaneously. Instead of returning to the Start screen to switch apps, you can simply move your mouse over to the other monitor.

Some apps can take advantage of multiple monitors, also. For example, Adobe Lightroom provides tools for cataloging and editing pictures. If you have more than one monitor, you can display thumbnails of all your pictures on one monitor while viewing the selected image full-screen on your second monitor, making it much faster to browse pictures.

If you use Windows 8.1 with more than one monitor, the Start screen and apps designed for Windows 8.1 will use the primary monitor, while the desktop will use all additional monitors. You can also use the primary monitor for desktop apps.

The sections that follow describe how you can customize the way Windows 8.1 uses your monitors.

Configuring multiple monitors

Windows 8.1 will automatically configure the resolution for each monitor, and you will be able to move your mouse between monitors. However, Windows 8.1 might incorrectly guess the arrangement of your monitors. Follow these steps to correctly arrange your monitors:

1. Open the Settings charm, click Change PC Settings, select PC & Devices, and then select Display.

2. On the Customize Your Display page, click Identify to display a number on each monitor. Drag the monitors shown on the page so that they match the physical arrangement on your desk.

3. Select the monitor that you want to use for the Start screen and Windows 8.1 apps. If the Customize Your Display page shows Make This My Main Display, select the check box, as shown in Figure 5-11.

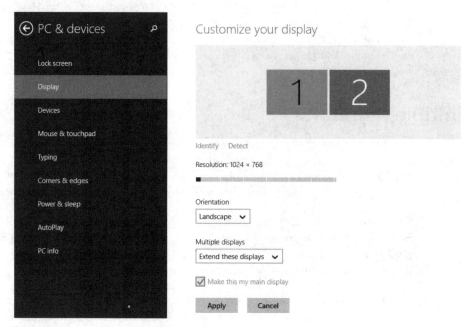

Figure 5-11 Use the Screen Resolution settings page to configure multiple monitors.

4. By default, Windows 8.1 extends your display across all desktops, which is the best way to use multiple monitors in most scenarios. If you want to show the same desktop on multiple displays (for example, if one display is a projector for a presentation), click the Multiple Displays list and then select Duplicate These Displays.

5. Click Apply.

Setting up your taskbar

Windows 7 was only capable of displaying the taskbar on your main display. Windows 8.1 makes an important improvement: it can display the taskbar on every monitor that displays the desktop. That feature is disabled by default, however. Follow these steps to enable it:

1. Right-click the taskbar, and then click Properties.

2. In the Multiple Displays group, select the Show Taskbar On All Displays check box, as shown in Figure 5-12.

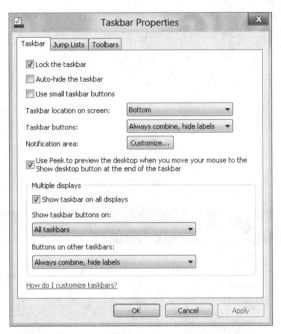

Figure 5-12 You can configure Windows 8.1 to display the taskbar on every monitor.

3. Open the Show Taskbar Buttons On list, and then select Taskbar Where Windows Is Open. I find the other settings confusing.

4. Click OK.

Inside OUT

Using peek preview

Just like in Windows 7, you can hover your pointer in the lower-right corner for a few seconds to make all desktop windows transparent so you can see the desktop.

CHAPTER 5

Language settings

You'll definitely want to configure Windows 8.1 to use the language you're most comfortable with. If you have people in your household who speak different languages, or are trying to learn other languages, you can add multiple languages to Windows 8.1, regardless of where you bought your computer.

To add a language, follow these steps:

1. Open the Settings charm, click Change PC Settings, select Time & Language, and then select Region & Language.

2. Click Add A Language.

3. Select the language. If prompted, also select the dialect, as shown in Figure 5-13.

Figure 5-13 Use PC Settings to add a language.

As shown in Figure 5-14, you can switch between installed languages at any time. Click the Settings charm, click the language in the lower-right corner, and then select the new language.

Figure 5-14 Switch between languages with two clicks.

WinX menu

Pressing Windows+X on the keyboard or right-clicking the lower-left corner opens a list of commonly used power user tools, such as a command prompt with administrator privileges, as shown in Figure 5-15. This menu is commonly known as the WinX menu.

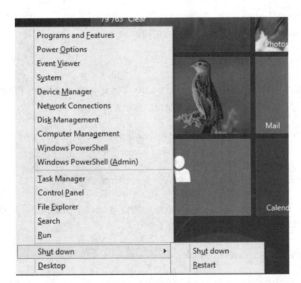

Figure 5-15 The WinX menu displays helpful power user commands.

As you might guess, most users won't ever stumble across the WinX menu. That's okay, because most users won't need these tools frequently enough to want a special menu. After all, all these tools can be started in other ways, such as by using the Start screen. However, the

WinX menu can save power users a great deal of time, especially if you take a few minutes to add your own custom items to it.

Inside OUT

Running an app as an administrator

Some apps require administrator privileges to make changes to your computer. To run an app as an administrator, follow these steps:

1. Select an app by flicking it with your finger or right-clicking it with the mouse.

2. In the app commands, click Run As Administrator. The prompt will not be available for apps that cannot use administrator privileges.

Adding items to the WinX menu

The simplest way to update the WinX menu is to use the Win+X Menu Editor tool, available for download from *http://winaero.com/*. You can manually add your own items to the WinX menu by following these steps:

1. In File Explorer, type **%LocalAppData%\Microsoft\Windows\WinX** in the address bar, and then press Enter. This opens the hidden folder.

2. On the Home tab, click the New Folder button. Create a folder named Group4.

3. Copy a shortcut from the %ProgramData%\Microsoft\Windows\Start Menu\Programs folder to the %LocalAppData%\Microsoft\Windows\WinX\Group4 folder.

4. Download the HashLink tool from *http://www.withinwindows.com/2012/04/04/windows-8-secrets-the-winx-menu-and-its-hashing-algorithm/*.

5. Extract the hashlnk.exe file and save it to your Windows folder.

6. Open an administrative command prompt. Switch to the %LocalAppData%\Microsoft\Windows\WinX\Group4 folder.

7. Run the command **hashlink *<shortcut>*.lnk**.

8. Restart your computer. Technically, you only need to restart Explorer, but it is probably easier just to restart Windows.

Your custom shortcuts will appear at the top of the WinX menu.

Inside OUT

How the WinX menu works

Windows 8.1 stores the WinX menu entries in the %LocalAppData%\Microsoft\ Windows\WinX folder. Entries are divided into group folders, with Group1 appearing at the bottom of the menu. Each group folder contains .lnk shortcuts that start with a number and a hyphen. The number defines the sequence the commands are displayed in, with lower numbers being displayed at the bottom of the group.

I can't explain why, but Windows 8.1 only adds links that contain a valid hash of the shortcut's path and arguments along with a salt. A hash is a piece of cryptographic data that software can use to verify that a file has not been changed. A salt is a static string used in cryptography to make it more difficult for an attacker to crack encryption.

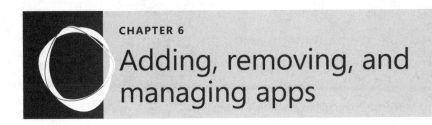

CHAPTER 6

Adding, removing, and managing apps

Installing Windows 8.1 apps 147

Uninstalling Windows 8.1 apps 148

Setting default programs 149

Configuring AutoPlay 151

Managing startup apps 152

Recording app problems 157

Understanding app permissions 158

The .NET Framework 159

The parts of a Windows 8.1 app 160

App compatibility settings 165

Managing Windows 8.1 app packages 168

Monitoring app events 170

You shouldn't ever need to peek under the hood to see how Windows 8.1 apps work. Microsoft has standardized installation, file locations, configuration settings, and permissions. Microsoft reviews apps in the Store to help verify that they are safe and reliable, and Windows 8.1 runs them with minimal permissions to limit the damage they could do even if there was a bug or the app developer managed to sneak malicious code through the review process.

Apps designed for Windows 8.1 should just work.

If you're curious about how Windows 8.1 apps work, or if at any time they don't just work and you need to troubleshoot them, this chapter provides an inside look at installing, configuring, and running Windows 8.1 apps. It also covers how to prevent apps from being automatically installed for new users and how to examine the app event logs. For desktop apps, this chapter shows you how to configure desktop apps to start automatically, choose which apps open when you double-click a file, and troubleshoot desktop apps that don't work properly.

For information about monitoring app resource usage and stopping problem apps, refer to Chapter 26, "Monitoring, measuring, and tuning performance."

Installing Windows 8.1 apps

Unless you are a developer or a business user connected to an Active Directory infrastructure, the only way to install Windows 8.1 apps is through the Store. You can still freely download and install desktop apps, however.

▶ **Installing, updating, and removing Windows 8.1 apps** Watch the video at *http://aka.ms/ WinIO/installupdateremove*.

While the restriction on Windows 8.1 apps might seem harsh, most users will quickly learn to appreciate it. Apps from the Store:

- Are tested by Microsoft to be reliable and free of malware.

- Are publically reviewed by other users.

- Show the permissions they need to run on your PC.

- Install without prompting.

- Uninstall cleanly.

Installing an app from the Store is simple: click Install on the app page and wait a few moments. Windows 8.1 will notify you (via a pop-up notification that appears in the upper-right corner) when installation is complete. The app's tile will appear on the Start screen before the app has completed installation. You can view the installation progress for an app by clicking the tile, as shown in Figure 6-1.

← Installing apps

Home

Hydro Thunder Hurricane
Downloading

Figure 6-1 Click an app tile to view installation progress.

Windows 8.1 also maintains the app for you. If a file becomes corrupted, Windows 8.1 will detect this and then prompt you to reinstall the app from the Store.

Uninstalling Windows 8.1 apps

To uninstall a Windows 8.1 app, follow these steps:

1. Open the Start screen.

2. Select the app by flicking it or right-clicking it.

3. Select Uninstall.

Apps designed for Windows 8.1 are installed separately for every user. Therefore, you can uninstall an app on your account without impacting other users of the same computer. If another user has installed an app and you no longer want the app on your computer, you need to log on with the other user's account and uninstall the app as well.

People, Messaging, Calendar, and Mail are all part of a single app. If you uninstall one, you uninstall them all. Some apps, such as Internet Explorer, Remote Desktop, Windows Defender, and the Store can't be uninstalled. However, you can unpin the tile from the Start screen.

To prevent users from uninstalling apps on Windows 8.1 Pro or Windows 8.1 Enterprise, follow these steps:

1. From the Start screen, type **gpedit.msc**, and then press Enter to open the Local Group Policy Editor.

2. Select User Configuration\Administrative Templates\Start Menu And Taskbar.

3. Double-click Prevent Users From Uninstalling Applications From Start. Select Enabled, and then click OK.

4. Restart the computer.

Setting default programs

When you open a file in File Explorer, Windows 8.1 starts that file type's default program to open the file for you. For example, when you open a picture file ending in .jpg, Windows 8.1 determines that the .jpg file extension is associated with the Photos app. Windows 8.1 opens the Photos app, and the Photos app shows you the picture.

Switching away from the desktop can be a jarring experience, however. If you would rather use a different app, such as a desktop app, to open files of a specific type, follow these steps:

1. Click the Search charm.

2. Click Settings.

3. Type **default**.

4. In the search results, select Set Your Default Programs.

5. In the Set Default Programs dialog box, select the program you want to use to open your files, as shown in Figure 6-2.

CHAPTER 6

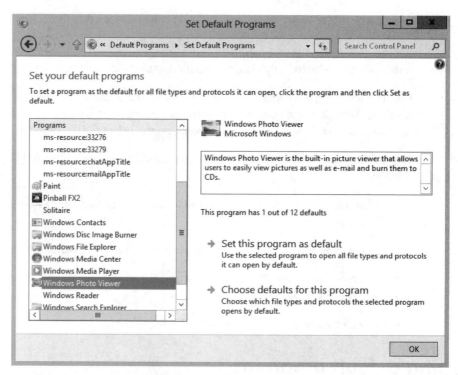

Figure 6-2 Use the Set Default Programs tool to configure how files open from File Explorer.

6. Click Set This Program As Default to associate it with all file types that it can open.

7. Click OK.

Inside OUT

Selecting specific file types

If you only want to use an app to open some file types, but not all types that it can handle, click Choose Defaults For This Program, select the file types, and then click Save.

You can always open a file with a nondefault app by right-clicking it in File Explorer and then clicking Open With. Figure 6-3 shows how File Explorer handles pictures. It displays a different interface with similar functionality for other file types. Select Choose Default Program or Use This App For All Files to quickly change the default app for that file type.

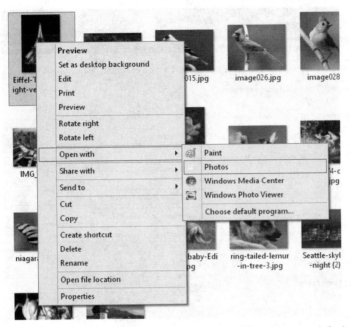

Figure 6-3 Use the Open With menu to open a file with a nondefault app.

Configuring AutoPlay

Windows can automatically run an app when you connect media such as a camera's memory card or a USB flash drive. To configure the app that Windows uses when you connect media with different file types, follow these steps:

1. At the Start screen, type **AutoPlay**.

2. In the search results, click AutoPlay.

   The AutoPlay Control Panel tool appears.

3. If you want to turn off AutoPlay completely, clear the Use AutoPlay For All Media And Devices check box, and then click Save. Windows will no longer prompt you when you connect media.

4. Otherwise, choose what you want Windows 8.1 to do when you connect different types of media, as shown in Figure 6-4. If you don't want AutoPlay to appear for some file types, select Take No Action. Then click Save.

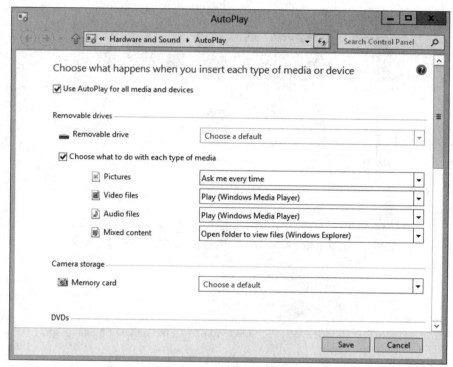

Figure 6-4 Use Control Panel to configure AutoPlay.

If you turn off AutoPlay, you can hold down the Shift key when connecting media to cause Windows to open AutoPlay just that one time.

There's also a touch-friendly interface for configuring AutoPlay, but it's not as powerful. To configure AutoPlay for touch, open the Settings charm, select Change PC Settings, select PC & Devices, and then select AutoPlay.

Managing startup apps

Startup apps open automatically when you log on to Windows. In earlier versions of Windows, startup apps were very important. If a user wanted to receive instant messages, their instant messaging app needed to start automatically. Apps often created agents that ran at startup to check for new updates.

However, each startup app made Windows take even longer to start, and slightly decreased the overall performance of Windows. The performance impact can be so severe that Windows 8.1 Action Center will warn you if you have three or more apps configured to start automatically.

Windows 8.1 eliminates most of the reasons you might start apps automatically and handles background tasks for apps. Live tiles and notifications eliminate the need to have messaging apps running continuously. The Store's centralized app updates replace separate update agents that desktop apps use.

With Windows 8.1, few apps should need to run at startup. Those that do should use a Windows service, which doesn't require any user configuration.

Windows still supports many different ways for apps to start automatically. Some of them are:

- **Scheduled tasks**   The Task Scheduler can launch apps at startup, as well as run apps at any time of the day or week. Scheduled tasks are the simplest way for users to configure startup apps.

- **Services**   Processes that run in the background without directly interacting with the user. In Windows 8.1, services are the preferred way for apps to start automatically.

- **Group Policy**   Several different Group Policy settings can start apps at startup or logon. To view or edit these policies, run Gpedit.msc.

  - Computer Configuration\Administrative Templates\System\Logon\Run These Programs At User Logon

  - User Configuration\Administrative Templates\System\Logon\Run These Programs At User Logon

  - Computer Configuration\Windows Settings\Scripts\Startup

  - User Configuration\Windows Settings\Scripts\Logon

- **Registry**   The registry is a massive collection of settings that earlier versions of Windows relied on heavily. While Windows 8.1 relies primarily on Group Policy settings and profile data instead of the registry, apps can still use the registry to automatically start. To view or edit these settings, run Regedit. In the following list, HKLM stands for HKEY_LOCAL_MACHINE (a registry hive that defines settings for all users) and HKCU stands for HKEY_CURRENT_USER (a registry hive that defines settings for only the current user). The relevant keys are:

  - HKLM\Software\Microsoft\Windows\CurrentVersion\Run

  - HKLM\Software\Microsoft\Windows\CurrentVersion\RunOnce

  - HKLM\Software\Microsoft\Windows\CurrentVersion\RunOnceEx (doesn't exist by default, but can be added)

  - HKCU\Software\Microsoft\Windows\CurrentVersion\Run

  - HKCU\Software\Microsoft\Windows\CurrentVersion\RunOnce

CHAPTER 6

- HKCU\Software\Microsoft\Windows\CurrentVersion\RunOnceEx (doesn't exist by default, but can be added)
- HKLM\Software\Microsoft\Windows NT\CurrentVersion\Winlogon\Userinit
- HKLM\Software\Microsoft\Windows NT\CurrentVersion\Winlogon\Shell
- HKLM\System\CurrentControlSet\Control\Session Manager

- **Shell service objects**   Windows can load tools at startup to add features to the desktop.

The sections that follow describe how to examine, remove, and add startup apps.

How to examine startup apps

To examine apps that start automatically, follow these steps:

1. Open Task Manager from the Start screen by typing **Task** and then clicking Task Manager. You can also press Ctrl+Shift+Esc or use the WinX menu.

2. Select the Startup tab.

   Task Manager displays every app configured to start automatically, regardless of how it is configured. Notice the Startup Impact column, which summarizes how much that app might be slowing down your computer's startup.

3. Right-click the column heading to select additional columns. These columns display interesting information about each startup app and the resources each uses during the Windows startup process:

   - **Start Type**   The mechanism by which the app is configured to start automatically.
   - **Disk I/O At Startup**   The amount of data the app transferred to and from the disk.
   - **CPU At Startup**   The processing time the app used.
   - **Command Line**   The full command line, including any parameters.

The System Information tool provides more useful information about startup apps. Follow these steps to view that information:

1. From the Start screen, type **System Information**. Click System Information when it appears in the search results.

   The System Information tool appears.

2. In the left pane, select System Summary\Software Environment\Startup Programs.

3. In the right pane, view the information about each startup app.

Besides the information displayed in Task Manager, System Information shows the user account running the app and the specific location of the startup command. The Program column provides different information than Task Manager, too.

How to remove startup apps

To remove a startup app, follow these steps:

1. Open Task Manager from the Start screen by typing **Task** and then clicking Task Manager. You can also press Ctrl+Shift+Esc or use the WinX menu.

2. Select the Startup tab.

3. Right-click the app you no longer want to start automatically, and then click Disable.

If you later change your mind and you want the app to start automatically, repeat the process, right-click the app, and then click Enable.

Inside OUT

What happened to MSConfig?

Previous versions of Windows used the System Configuration tool, MSConfig, to configure Startup apps. Windows 8.1 moves that important functionality into the more commonly used Task Manager.

How to add startup apps

Unfortunately, you can't automatically start apps designed for Windows 8.1. Fortunately, this isn't as important as it used to be, because Windows 8.1 provides background processing and updates for Windows 8.1 apps. You still might want to start a desktop app automatically, however. Follow these steps to start a desktop app automatically when you log on:

1. From the Start screen, type **Task**. In the search results, click Task Scheduler.
    Windows opens Task Scheduler.

2. On the Action menu, select Create Basic Task.
    Task Scheduler opens the Create Basic Task Wizard.

3. On the Create A Basic Task page, type a name for the task, and then click Next.

4. On the Task Trigger page, select When I Log On, and then click Next.

5. On the Action page, select Start A Program, and then click Next.

6. On the Start A Program page, click the Browse button.

   The Open dialog box appears.

7. In the address bar, type **C:\ProgramData\Microsoft\Windows\Start Menu\ Programs**. The folder is hidden, so it might not appear when you browse. Press Enter, and then browse the subfolders to find your app. Select your app, and then click Open.

8. Click Next.

9. On the Summary page, as shown in Figure 6-5, click Finish.

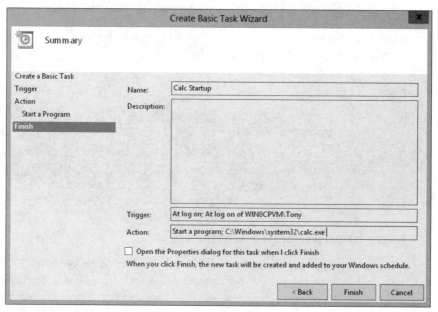

Figure 6-5 Use Task Scheduler to start a desktop app automatically.

The next time you log on to your computer, the app will start automatically after a brief delay. It might be hidden behind the Start screen, however. Switch to the desktop to see it. For information on how to display the desktop automatically when you log on, refer to Chapter 5, "Personalizing Windows 8.1."

Recording app problems

If an app isn't working properly, you can use Steps Recorder to record the problem. Then, you can send the recording to the app support staff so they can better see the problem.

To use Steps Recorder, follow these steps:

1. On the Start screen, type **Steps**, and then select Steps Recorder.

   Windows 8.1 displays the desktop and opens the Steps Recorder app.

2. Click Start Record.

3. Switch back to the Start screen, open the app causing the problem, and repeat the steps that demonstrate the problem.

4. Switch back to the desktop (for example, by clicking Desktop on the Start screen or by pressing Windows+D). In the Steps Recorder app, click Stop Recording.

   Steps Recorder displays your recording, as shown in Figure 6-6.

Figure 6-6 Use Steps Recorder to record actions on your PC.

5. Click Save or Email, and send the recording to the support staff.

Steps Recorder is also a useful way to create step-by-step instructions for friends who need help.

Understanding app permissions

By default, apps designed for Windows 8.1 have permission to do very little on your computer. While apps can read and write files for their own use, they can't read your documents or even communicate on the Internet without requesting additional permissions. App developers must request every permission that their app needs.

When you browse apps, the Store shows you exactly which permissions an app uses. Figure 6-7 shows the required permissions for a weather app, which needs to determine your location and then communicate with an online service to determine the weather.

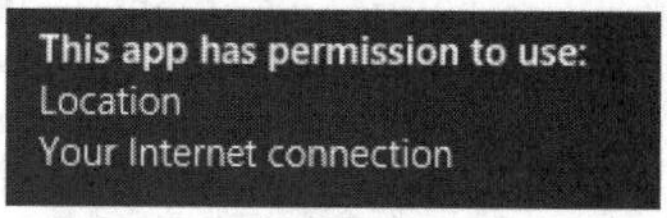

This app has permission to use:
Location
Your Internet connection

Figure 6-7 The Store displays the permissions an app needs.

Permissions allow apps to gain access to everything they need while making the user aware of an app's requirements. In the past (and in the present, in the case of desktop apps), apps often took actions that the user might not want them to take, such as accessing private files and transmitting them across the Internet. A Windows 8.1 app could still do this, technically. However, the app would require Your Documents Library and Your Internet Connection permissions, which would make the user aware of the potential security concern. Additionally, the app would probably be rejected as part of the Microsoft app approval process. Restrictive permissions also reduce the risk that another app will exploit a vulnerability to take advantage of excessive permissions.

Different permissions apps can require are:

- Your documents library

- Your pictures library

- Your videos library

- Your music library

- Use of your webcam

- Your location

- Your Internet connection

- Your Internet connection, including incoming connections from the Internet

- A home or work network

- Your Windows credentials

- Software and hardware certificates or a smart card

- Removable storage

You can view the permissions for an app you have already installed by following these steps:

1. Start the app.

2. Click the Settings charm.

3. Click Permissions.

Desktop apps that you might install from the Internet or sources other than the Store don't have these same restrictions.

The .NET Framework

The Microsoft .NET Framework is a component of Windows that is required to run .NET apps. A large number of the apps written for Windows Vista and Windows 7 were .NET apps, and many Windows 8.1 apps use the .NET Framework.

The .NET Framework has gone through a series of versions, starting with .NET 1.0, released in 2002. Windows XP included .NET 1.0, Windows Vista included .NET 3.0, Windows 7 included .NET 3.5, and now Windows 8.1 includes .NET 4.5.

Typically, apps created for earlier versions of the .NET Framework will run in later versions. For example, most apps created for .NET 3.5 will run on Windows 8.1 and .NET 4.5. However, you can install the .NET Framework 3.5 (which also supports earlier versions) from the Turn Windows Features On Or Off link in Control Panel, as shown in Figure 6-8. You will rarely need to do this because most apps will automatically install any prerequisites.

Figure 6-8 Use Control Panel to install earlier versions of the .NET Framework.

The parts of a Windows 8.1 app

Desktop apps, including apps designed for earlier versions of Windows, typically consist of .exe files, .dll files, and other supporting resources. Desktop apps are usually installed in the %ProgramFiles% folder, which is C:\Program Files\ by default. Desktop apps can be installed for all users or just for a single user.

Apps designed for Windows 8.1 work very differently. First, all apps are installed for only a single user, so other users on the same computer need to install the app for themselves. The files Windows 8.1 apps use are different, too.

Types of Windows 8.1 apps

Windows 8.1 can run three different types of apps:

- **Desktop** Traditional apps that can also run in earlier versions of Windows.

- **XAML** Apps written in C#, Visual Basic.NET, C++, or other .NET Framework languages.

- **HTML5** Apps are created using the same technologies used for websites: HTML5, JavaScript, and CSS3. Essentially, these apps are dynamic webpages that run on your local computer, but they are more powerful because they can use the Windows Library for JavaScript, which provides controlled access to local computer resources beyond what a website could access.

XAML and HTML5 apps provide the full-screen, touch-friendly experience of apps designed for Windows 8.1. The user can't tell whether an app was created with XAML or HTML5; the different development environments simply appeal to developers with different programming backgrounds. However, being familiar with the different types of apps is important if you want to understand the structure of apps and the files contained within.

The sections that follow focus on XAML and HTML5 apps. Desktop apps haven't changed significantly since Windows 7.

XAML app file types

Windows 8.1 uses the .NET Framework and the Windows Runtime to run XAML apps. File types in a XAML app include:

- **.exe**   The app executable. This is the file that Windows 8.1 runs when you start the app. Windows 8.1 won't allow you to start XAML apps directly from File Explorer. Instead, use the Start screen.

- **.xaml**   An XML-based description of the app's user interface. Apps can have separate .xaml files for every page the app displays.

- **.xml**   A text-based file that might include metadata or settings. The AppManifest.xml file is described later in this section.

- **.p7x**   The app's digital signature, which allows Windows 8.1 to verify the app's integrity.

- **.winmd**   A description of the different methods that the app uses.

- **.pri**   A binary file that contains app resource information.

- **.dll**   A binary file, known as a library, that includes code that the app can run.

Additionally, most apps have images (such as .png files) that they display as part of the user interface.

HTML5 app file types

Windows 8.1 uses web technologies to run HTML5 apps. File types in an HTML5 app include:

- **.html**   An HTML file that describes the app's user interface. Apps can have separate .html files for every page the app displays.

- **.xml**   A text-based file that might include metadata or settings. The AppManifest.xml file is described later in this section.

- **.js**   JavaScript code that contains an app's logic, including how it responds to your touches and clicks.

- **.css**   A cascading style sheet (CSS) file that can describe aspects of the user interface such as color and shape. CSS files often include some logic, such as how text might expand or change when you click it or hover over it.

- **.resjson**   A text file that contains app resource information, such as the text for the user interface in a variety of languages.

- **.p7x**   The app's digital signature, which allows Windows 8.1 to verify the app's integrity.

- **.winmd**   A description of the different methods that the app uses.

- **.dll**   A binary file, known as a library, that includes code that the app can run.

You are free to explore many aspects of both XAML and HTML5 apps. However, some developers will obfuscate their code, scrambling it so that it is more difficult to understand. If you change an app, Windows 8.1 might not run it.

Configuration settings

In the past, desktop apps frequently stored user settings in .ini or .xml files. Apps designed for Windows 8.1 typically store data in the local application data store. The local application data store is isolated by both the app and the user, so one app can't access another app's data, and an app can't access data created by another user of the same app. This improves security, but because the data is stored in a binary format (and typically encrypted), you can't easily access or edit it directly.

Basically, you need to use the Settings charm to change settings within an app. You can't easily edit app configuration settings when an app isn't running.

File locations

Windows 8.1 apps often have different components in different folders, as described in Table 6-1.

Table 6-1 Windows 8.1 app file locations

Data	Location
Executable files	%UserProfile%\AppData\Local\<*Developer*>\<*App*>
App packages	%UserProfile%\AppData\Local\Packages\
Shortcuts	%UserProfile%\AppData\Local\Microsoft\Windows\Application Shortcuts\
Manifest	%ProgramFiles%\WindowsApps\<*App*>\AppXManifest.xml
Shared components/assemblies	%WinDir%\WinSxS\x86_*

Inside OUT

Environment variables and restricted permissions

%UserProfile% is an environment variable that represents the current user's profile folder, which is by default located at C:\Users\<*First_Name*>\. By default, %ProgramFiles% is C:\Program Files\, and %WinDir% is C:\Windows\. You can type environment variables such as %UserProfile% directly into Windows, and Windows will use them correctly. For a complete list of environment variables, open a command prompt and type the command **Set**.

By default, your user account won't have access to open some folders, including %ProgramFiles%\WindowsApps\. This isn't to protect Windows from you, it's to protect Windows from potentially malicious apps. Even if you are an administrator, you need to take ownership of the folder before you can access it. Using an account that is a member of the local Administrators group, follow these steps to access the folder:

1. Attempt to open the folder in File Explorer.

2. Windows 8.1 will prompt you to grant yourself permission to the folder. Click Continue.

3. If prompted, type an administrator password or respond to the User Account Control (UAC) prompt.

4. When Windows tells you that you have been denied permission to the folder, click the Security Tab link.

5. In the WindowsApps Properties dialog box, click Advanced.

6. Beside the Owner label at the top of the dialog box, click Change. Respond to the UAC prompt that appears.

7. In the Select User Or Group dialog box, click Advanced.

8. Click Find Now. In the Search Results list, click your user name, and then click OK.

9. Click OK three more times, and then click Close to close all dialog boxes.

10. Now that you are the owner of the folder, attempt to open the folder in File Explorer again.

11. Once again, Windows 8.1 prompts you to grant yourself permission to the folder. This time it will work because you're the folder's owner, so click Continue.

Some folders, such as %ProgramFiles%\WindowsApps\ and %UserProfile%\AppData\, are hidden. You can access them by typing the folder name directly into the File Explorer address bar. Alternatively, you can display hidden folders by selecting the View tab in File Explorer and then selecting Hidden Items in the Show/Hide group.

CHAPTER 6

App manifests

Apps have manifests, which are XML files that list the app's name, publisher, logo, and description and describe an app's prerequisites, dependencies, and requirements. The manifest file is typically named AppXManifest.xml, and it is stored in the app's folder under %ProgramFiles%\ WindowsApps\.

There's probably no legitimate reason for users to access the manifests, though the information within the file might be insightful for troubleshooting. Manifests are really interesting if you're curious about how an app works, however. The easiest way to view a manifest is to double-click it in File Explorer, which by default opens it with Internet Explorer. The Properties section lists basic information about the app:

```
<Properties>
    <Framework>false</Framework>
    <DisplayName>ms-resource:///photo/residAppNAme</DisplayName>
    <PublisherDisplayName>Microsoft Corporation</PublisherDisplayName>
    <Description>ms-resource:///photo/residAppDescription</Description>
    <Logo>ModernPhoto\Images \storelogo.png</Logo>
</Properties>
```

The Prerequisites section lists the version of Windows the app was developed for. Windows 8.1 is technically considered Windows version 6.2; Windows 7 was 6.1, and Windows Vista was 6.0:

```
<Prerequisites>
    <OSMinVersion>6.2.1</OSMinVersion>
    <OSMaxVersionTested>6.2.1</OSMaxVersionTested>
</Prerequisites>
```

The Capabilities section lists low-level features that the app implements. In the case of the Photos app, the capabilities show that it acts as a picture library, that it creates both outgoing and incoming network connections, and more:

```
<Capabilities>
    <Capability Name="picturesLibrary" />
    <Capability Name="internetClientServer" />
    <Capability Name="privateNetworkClientServer" />
    <Capability Name="removableStorage"/>
</Capabilities>
```

The Extensions section describes ways that the app can interact with Windows and other apps. In the case of the Photos app, it supports searching, AutoPlay (which launches the app if the user connects removable storage with pictures or video), and file extension mappings (which automatically open the app when the user selects a file with a matching extension.)

```
<Extension StartPage="ModernPhoto\PhotosApplication\PhotosApplication.htm"
Category="windows.search"/>
<Extension Category="windows.autoPlayContent">
    <AutoPlayContent>
        <LaunchAction ContentEvent="CameraMemoryOnArrival" ActionDisplayName=
          "ms-resource:///photo/residAutoplayDisplayText" Verb="storageDevice"/>
        <LaunchAction ContentEvent="ShowPicturesOnArrival" ActionDisplayName=
          "ms-resource:///photo/residAutoplayDisplayText" Verb=
          "storageDeviceWithPhotos"/>
    </AutoPlayContent>
</Extension>

<Extension StartPage="ModernPhoto\PhotosApplication\PhotosApplication.htm"
Category="windows.fileTypeAssociation">
    <FileTypeAssociation Name="imagetypes">
        <Logo>ModernPhoto\Images\Icon.png</Logo>
        <SupportedFileTypes>
            <FileType>.jpg</FileType>
            <FileType>.jpeg</FileType>
            <FileType>.png</FileType>
            <FileType>.bmp</FileType>
            <FileType>.gif</FileType>
        </SupportedFileTypes>
    </FileTypeAssociation>
</Extension>
```

The manifest often has a great deal more information in it, including a list of libraries that the app uses. While you can edit a manifest file using a text editor such as Notepad, the results will be unpredictable; the app might not work at all.

App compatibility settings

Windows 8.1 is designed to work with apps created for earlier versions of Windows, and most people will never have an app compatibility problem. However, some apps created for Windows XP and earlier versions of Windows have compatibility problems for one of these reasons:

- They require administrative privileges, which Windows XP and earlier versions of Windows gave to all apps by default.

- They attempt to read files they don't have permission to access but might have had permission to access by default in earlier versions of Windows.

- They attempt to save files to locations they don't have access to.

- They make changes to the system.

- They attempt to install unsupported drivers (typically, drivers created for Windows XP).

If an app doesn't work the way you expect it to, use the Program Compatibility Troubleshooter. By adjusting the compatibility settings, Windows 8.1 can work around most of the common compatibility problems, though it can't fix apps that require unsupported drivers. The troubleshooter works pretty well, and it walks you through the process itself, but here are steps you can follow:

1. Open File Explorer on the desktop.

2. In the address bar, type **%ProgramData%\Microsoft\Windows\Start Menu\ Programs**. Press Enter.

3. Browse to find the shortcut to the app you want to troubleshoot. Select the shortcut.

4. At the top of the File Explorer window, select the Manage tab under Application Tools as shown in Figure 6-9. Then, click the Troubleshoot Compatibility button. You can also right-click the app and then click Troubleshoot Compatibility.

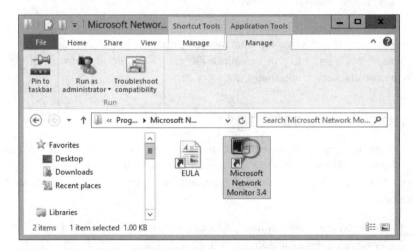

Figure 6-9 Use File Explorer to troubleshoot desktop app compatibility problems.

5. The Program Compatibility Troubleshooter appears, as shown in Figure 6-10. Select the options that describe the problem you're having, and then click Next.

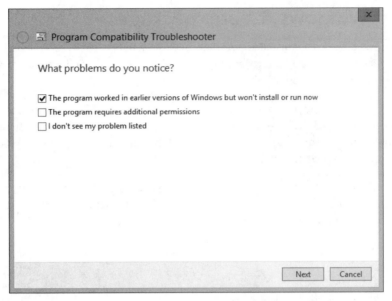

Figure 6-10 Use the Program Compatibility Troubleshooter to automatically identify compatibility problems.

The Program Compatibility Troubleshooter might prompt you for additional information. If the app still doesn't work correctly, you have another option: run the app in a virtual machine (VM). Windows 8.1 Professional includes Hyper-V, which can run Windows XP in a window on your desktop. You can then run almost any Windows XP app within that virtual machine. For more information, read Chapter 20, "Using Hyper-V."

If you don't have Windows 8.1 Professional, you can use VirtualBox to create a virtual machine for Windows XP. Download VirtualBox at *https://www.virtualbox.org/*.

Inside OUT
Use caution when running the Program Compatibility Troubleshooter

Only run the Program Compatibility Troubleshooter for apps that you trust. Often, it will grant additional permissions to the app. If the app is malware, those additional permissions would allow it to violate your privacy or compromise your system integrity.

CHAPTER 6

Managing Windows 8.1 app packages

Windows 8.1 apps are installed automatically using an app package. As a user, you never have to understand how app packages work. The Windows Store will download and install the packages for you automatically.

One of the many ways apps designed for Windows 8.1 are different from desktop apps is that Windows 8.1 apps are always installed on a per-user basis. Therefore, if you install an app, and then your sister logs on to your computer with her own account, she won't have access to that app unless she installs it herself.

Because you can't install Windows 8.1 apps for all users of a computer, Windows 8.1 needs to install default apps for each new user on a computer. By default, Windows 8.1 installs the following list of new apps for each new user on the computer:

- Finance
- Maps
- Weather
- Camera
- SkyDrive
- Messaging
- Photos
- Games
- Music
- Video

A copy of the app package for each of these apps is stored in the default installation of Windows 8.1. You can use the Dism tool to examine these app packages and remove any app packages you don't want automatically installed.

Other apps, such as the Store, aren't installed as an app package and thus can't be removed using these techniques. For information about how to disable the Store, refer to Chapter 2, "Using Windows 8.1 apps."

Inside OUT

Managing Windows 8.1 image files with Dism

Dism is primarily designed to manage Windows 8.1 images. An image is a copy of a Windows installation that is stored in a file. IT professionals at large companies use images to rapidly deploy dozens, hundreds, or thousands of new Windows 8.1 computers using standardized settings and apps.

How to run Dism

To run Dism, open a command prompt with administrator privileges and then type **dism**. The easiest way to do this is by using the WinX menu: Press Windows+X (or right-click the lower-left corner) and then click Command Prompt (Admin).

How to list Windows 8.1 app packages

To list Windows 8.1 app packages that will be automatically installed for each new user you create on your computer, run the following command at an administrator command prompt:

```
Dism /Online /Get-ProvisionedAppxPackages
```

Dism lists every Windows 8.1 app package installed on your computer. These are only the apps that Windows installs automatically for new users; they do not include apps you might have installed after Windows created your account.

How to remove Windows 8.1 app packages

To remove a Windows 8.1 app package so that Windows 8.1 won't automatically install the app for new users, first identify the package name using the **Dism /Online /Get-ProvisionedAppxPackages** command. You can copy the package name to the Clipboard by following these steps:

1. Click the command box in the upper-left corner of the command prompt, click Edit, and then click Mark.

2. Use your mouse to select the text to copy. In this case, select the package name.

3. Press Enter.

CHAPTER 6

Now you can use the package name to uninstall the app. Run the following command at an administrator command prompt:

```
Dism /Online /Remove-ProvisionedAppxPackage /PackageName:<package_name>
```

For example, to remove the Sports app, you would run the following command:

```
Dism /Online /Remove-ProvisionedAppxPackage
/PackageName:Microsoft.BingSports_1.2.0.135_x64_8wekyb3d8bbwe
```

To paste the package name from the Clipboard to the command prompt, click the command box in the upper-left corner of the command prompt, click Edit, and then click Paste.

If Dism successfully removes the app, it will display a message resembling the following:

```
Deployment Image Servicing and Management tool

Version: 6.2.9200.16384

Image Version: 6.2.9200.16384

The operation completed successfully.
```

If you get an error message, view the Dism log file at %WinDir%\Logs\DISM\Dism.log. A convenient way to view the log file while at the command prompt is to run the following command:

```
Notepad %WinDir%\Logs\DISM\Dism.log
```

Monitoring app events

Windows 8.1 adds events to the event log every time it installs an app, uninstalls an app, or applies compatibility fixes for an app. You can open the Event Viewer by pressing Windows+X (or right-clicking the lower-left corner) and then clicking Event Viewer.

Within Event Viewer, the most useful logs for examining app installs are:

- **Windows Logs\Application**   Logs actions by Windows Installer, also known as MSI, when desktop apps are installed or uninstalled. This log also includes events created by apps that don't have their own log.

- **Applications And Services Logs\Microsoft\Windows\AppHost\Admin**   Lists errors that Windows 8.1 experienced while running apps designed for Windows 8.1, such as missing resources. If an app isn't working properly, the events in this log might give you a hint as to what is missing.

- **Applications And Services Logs\Microsoft\Windows\Application-Experience\ Program-Telemetry**   Lists desktop apps that Windows 8.1 applied compatibility fixes to. Windows 8.1 applies compatibility fixes when it detects an app was designed for an earlier version of Windows and won't work properly with Windows 8.1.

- **Applications And Services Logs\Microsoft\Windows\AppXDeployment-Server\ Microsoft-Windows-AppXDeploymentServer/Operational**   Lists app packages that are installed and uninstalled.

- **Applications And Services Logs\Microsoft\Windows\AppXPackagingOM\ Microsoft-Windows-AppxPackaging/Operational**   Logs changes to app packages.

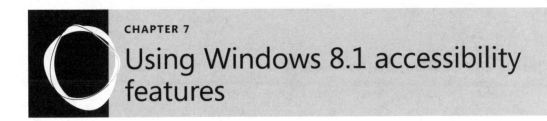

CHAPTER 7

Using Windows 8.1 accessibility features

Choosing accessible hardware 174

Configuring accessibility options. 174

Visual accessibility 175

User input accessibility 187

Dyslexia and reading accessibility 192

The Windows 8.1 defaults are designed to work well for people with common levels of vision, hearing, and motor skills. Many people have different levels of abilities, however. The Windows 8.1 accessibility features are designed to make Windows 8.1 and the applications it runs as usable as possible for people with varying capabilities.

For example, many people can't easily read text on a computer screen. Using the accessibility features in Windows 8.1, users can increase the size of all text, magnify portions of the screen to view individual words and letters close-up, choose high-contrast settings to make the text clearer, or use the Narrator tool to audibly read the text.

Accessibility isn't only for people with varying physical capabilities. For example, dyslexic users might find that the Narrator tool makes it easier to read text and voice recognition makes it easier to write messages. These features sound simple enough, but don't underestimate their power; they can change lives.

In this chapter, I'll start by giving you some examples of specialized hardware used in accessibility scenarios. Then, I'll walk you through the accessibility features that Windows 8.1 provides. I'll also mention several great third-party apps that extend Windows accessibility even further.

Inside OUT

App accessibility

Microsoft gives app developers great tools to make accessible apps and encourages them to follow accessibility guidelines. Ultimately, though, apps you buy from the Store might or might not be accessible. If you find apps that you can't use, I encourage you to contact the app vendor to discuss the issues with them; many vendors care deeply about making their apps accessible. You might also find a different app in the Store that provides similar features with greater accessibility.

Choosing accessible hardware

For some users, adjusting the accessibility settings will be enough for them to happily use their computers. Many users, however, require specialized hardware. For example, a user with a C4 (cervical vertebra 4) injury doesn't have movement below the collarbone. However, since they can control their neck and head, they can use a head mouse, which controls the pointer by tracking head movement. A head mouse connects to a computer exactly like a traditional mouse; Windows 8.1 simply supports the hardware driver.

Even though these users can control the mouse, they might not have the precision they need to perform some actions, such as swiping or dragging. Switching between applications is a common challenge for users with accessibility issues. Therefore, it's a good idea to get the largest monitor possible; this allows them to keep multiple desktop applications on the screen simultaneously. Additionally, it leaves more room for the on-screen keyboard, an important tool for users who can't use a traditional keyboard.

If the user can speak, they can use voice recognition software for text input. While the on-screen keyboard is good for tapping out a few letters, it would be pretty time-consuming to write a book using it. Windows 8.1 includes basic voice recognition capabilities, and a product such as Dragon by Nuance, available at *http://www.nuance.com/dragon/*, provides more advanced options. To get the most out of voice recognition software, connect a headset that has been designed specifically for voice recognition to the computer.

Windows 8.1 tablets are excellent choices for many vision impaired users because users can easily control the distance and angle of a tablet's screen. The updated Magnifier and Narrator tools work great with touch, too. Stationary screens with touch support can be very useful to users with a mouse stick, which is a pointing device held in the mouth that allows a user to press keys on the keyboard or touch a screen.

There are as many different accessibility tools as there are capabilities, and many people create specialized tools exactly for a specific person. I won't try to describe every type of specialized hardware, but it's important to understand that some of these accessibility features aren't really designed to be used with a keyboard and mouse, even though they work with keyboard and mouse input.

Configuring accessibility options

The quickest way to improve accessibility is to run the Ease Of Access wizard, as shown in Figure 7-1. To launch the wizard, search Settings for **ease**, and then click Let Windows Suggest Ease Of Access Settings.

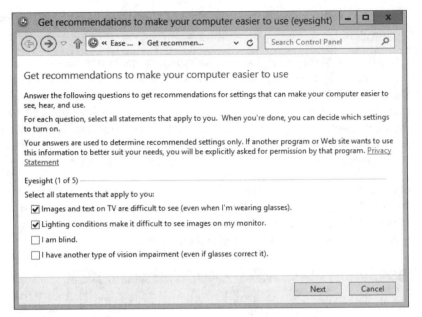

Figure 7-1 Use the Ease Of Access wizard to improve accessibility.

The wizard is a good starting point, but you will need to customize the settings further to optimize Windows to your individual needs. Notably, selecting the reasoning options on the last page does not seem to change any settings. However, following the guidelines near the end of this chapter can help.

Visual accessibility

Not everyone sees the same way. For many users, text on computer screens is too small to read comfortably, but they can read it if it's zoomed in larger. Some users can read the text, but only when the text is white on a black background, or vice versa. Other users cannot see at all and must rely on their hearing to get feedback from a computer.

The sections that follow cover visual accessibility tools in more detail.

Making everything bigger

If a user can see but finds the text on the screen too small, turn on Make Everything On Your Screen Bigger from the Ease Of Access page of the PC Settings screen. This option does what it says, but it works best on high-resolution screens. If your screen is near the minimum resolution for Windows 8.1, some text might get pushed off the screen, reducing readability. If the bigger display isn't easily readable, you have other options: using Magnifier or scaling screen content within apps.

Despite its name, the Make Everything On Your Screen Bigger option does not change the desktop appearance. To adjust the size of the desktop, search Settings for **text size** and then select Make Everything On Your Screen Bigger. If the option with the same name is enabled, select it. Windows 8.1 scales the Start screen and apps designed for Windows 8.1 to your high-resolution screen, making tiles, images, and text larger. It does not, however, change the appearance of the desktop. If the Make Everything On Your Screen Bigger option is not enabled, your screen resolution is not high enough to use that option.

To increase the size of the desktop, search Settings for **text size** again, and this time select Make Text And Other Items Larger Or Smaller. Select the text size, as shown in Figure 7-2, or click Custom Sizing Options to select a different size. The sizes available to you vary depending on your screen's resolution. Click Apply, and then sign out and sign back on.

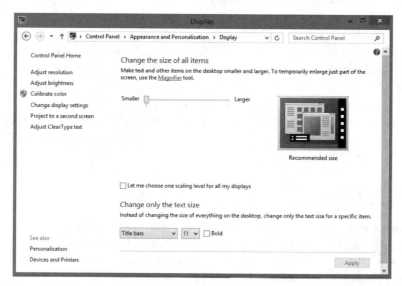

Figure 7-2 Use Control Panel to adjust the size of text on the desktop.

In many apps, a better option is to zoom in within the app. For example, when you zoom in with Internet Explorer (by pressing Ctrl+Plus Sign) or by using the Internet Options selection from the Settings charm), Internet Explorer smoothly scales text and images, making them larger on-screen. Other apps, including e-book reader apps and Microsoft Office, provide similar capabilities.

Increasing contrast

If a user finds it easier to read black-and-white text rather than text on colored backgrounds, you can enable high contrast mode from the login screen or the Ease Of Access section in PC Settings, as shown in Figure 7-3.

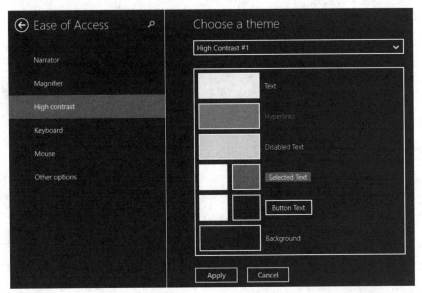

Figure 7-3 High contrast mode can make Windows easier to see for many users.

Magnifying the screen

Magnifier is a tool that zooms in to your computer's display, showing a small part of the screen much larger. This is perfect for users who find it difficult to see small details on the screen or who cannot increase the size of text to be large enough to be readable.

You can adjust Magnifier options from PC Settings, Ease Of Access. Invert Colors changes the screen colors, which makes it more obvious that Magnifier is enabled and can make some text easier to read. Screen colors go back to normal when you close Magnifier. The default settings typically work well for the remaining options—Follow The Keyboard Focus and Follow The Mouse Cursor. You might also want Magnifier to start automatically when you log in, which you can do by enabling the Start Magnifier Automatically option.

▶ **Using Magnifier** Watch the video at *http://aka.ms/WinIO/magnifier*.

Inside OUT

Larger but not always clearer with Magnifier

Whereas a real-world magnifying glass allows you to see greater detail, Magnifier doesn't increase detail; it just shows everything larger. So, as you zoom in with Magnifier, you're going to experience a great deal of pixilation. Basically, everything gets either blocky or blurry, as Figure 7-4 shows.

Figure 7-4 Magnifier increases size but not detail.

Worst of all, the 1000% text, which appears as black on white when the view is not zoomed in, becomes a mosaic of colors. These colors are there when you are not zoomed in with Magnifier, but most people don't see them. They're a font-smoothing technology within Windows, known as ClearType, that uses intermediate colors to smooth the appearance of text and reduce the visibility of individual pixels on computer screens.

While ClearType makes text easier to read at normal zoom levels, it has the opposite effect when using Magnifier. If you search for Performance Options in your computer's settings, you'll find the Adjust The Appearance And Performance Of Windows dialog box. Open it and clear the Smooth Edges Of Screen Fonts option. Now, some magnified text appears more readable, as shown in Figure 7-5.

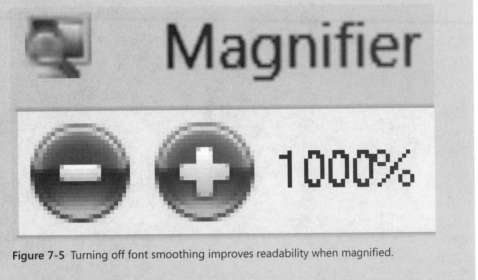

Figure 7-5 Turning off font smoothing improves readability when magnified.

You definitely should turn font smoothing off if you plan to use Magnifier regularly, but be warned: most apps will still use font smoothing. I can't explain why this is, but even some of the text in the Ease Of Access Center continues to use font smoothing after the setting has been disabled.

Using Magnifier with touch

Touch devices, and specifically tablet computers, are great for many users with varying visual capabilities. Because you can hold tablet computers in your hand, you can bring them closer to or move them farther from your eyes. You can also easily tilt the screen to reduce reflections and glare, or move the computer into a part of the room with less light.

The Windows 8.1 touch interface provides an entirely new way to use Magnifier. After you turn on Magnifier, you can zoom in and out by touching + and – at each corner, as shown in Figure 7-6. When zoomed in, pan around the screen using the scroll bars along each edge. When a scroll bar disappears, you know you've reached the edge of the screen. If you move to the right edge of the screen until the scroll bar disappears, you can swipe in to access the charms.

To quickly zoom in and out with touch, pinch and pull your fingers together along any of the scroll bars at the edge of the screen.

Figure 7-6 Magnifier is optimized for use with a touch screen.

If you get lost, tap on opposite borders of the screen. In other words, tap both the left and right borders at the same time, or tap the top and bottom borders at the same time. This shows the full-screen view, with the portion of the screen you're looking at highlighted, as shown in Figure 7-7. You can drag the highlighted rectangle around to view a different portion of the screen.

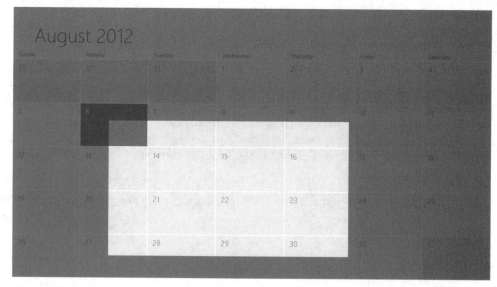

Figure 7-7 Tap both borders to briefly zoom out.

Using Magnifier with a mouse

The simplest way to launch Magnifier is at login, by clicking the icon in the lower-left corner of the login screen. After logging on, open Magnifier and configure it to start automatically using the Ease Of Access Center.

By default, Magnifier zooms in 200 percent. Simply move the mouse to the edge of the screen to pan the screen around. To zoom in or out, click the magnifying glass icon and then click the buttons on the Magnifier window.

To quickly see the entire screen (a great way to get your bearings), click the magnifying glass icon and then click Preview Full Screen on the Views menu. You can pan around the screen with the mouse and click to zoom back in.

Magnifier also supports lens mode, which shows a small portion of the screen magnified, as shown in Figure 7-8. To switch between modes with a mouse, just select Lens or Full Screen from the Views menu in Magnifier.

Figure 7-8 Magnifier is shown here in lens mode.

Using Magnifier with a keyboard

Magnifier is definitely easiest to use with either touch or a mouse. However, if you are limited to a keyboard, you can launch Magnifier by pressing Windows+Plus Sign. Press Windows+Plus Sign again to zoom in further, or press Windows+Minus Sign to zoom out. Use Ease Of Access to start it automatically when you log in to Windows.

Press Windows+Esc to cancel Magnifier. When the view is magnified, pan around the screen by holding down both Ctrl and Alt and pressing the arrow keys.

To quickly see the entire screen, press Ctrl+Alt+Spacebar on the keyboard. You can then use the keyboard to pan around the screen.

To open lens mode with a keyboard, press Ctrl+Alt+L. To switch back to full-screen mode (the default), press Ctrl+Alt+F.

If you are using the keyboard with Magnifier, there are a couple of options you'll want to turn on: Follow The Keyboard Focus and Follow The Mouse Cursor. Selecting these options causes the screen to follow the user's action as the user tabs between elements. If you were using Magnifier with a mouse, this would quickly become disorienting, however. You can access these options from the PC Settings, Ease Of Access, Magnifier page, as shown in Figure 7-9.

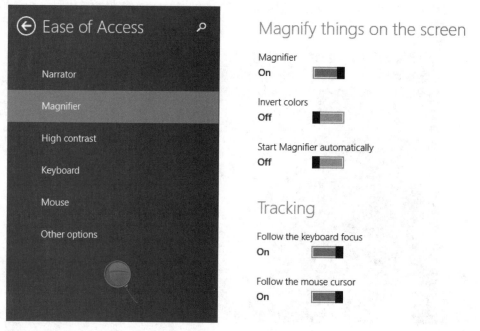

Figure 7-9 Set Magnifier options for use with a keyboard.

Third-party screen magnification software

Magnifier is free and well integrated into Windows. Some users might need more powerful features, such as control over screen tinting, help following the mouse pointer, and extended support for multiple monitors. MAGic Screen Magnification provides those features (for a fee). You can purchase MAGic at *http://www.freedomscientific.com/products/low-vision/MAGic-screen-magnification-software.asp*.

Narrator

Narrator reads text on the screen and can provide audible descriptions of different user interface elements. Earlier versions of Windows had the Narrator tool, but it has been much improved in Windows 8.1: it's faster, it supports more languages and voices, it can read more user interface elements, and it has been optimized for touch screens. You can start Narrator from the login screen or the Ease Of Access Center.

On a touch computer, press Windows+Volume Up to start Narrator. Then, you can explore the screen by touching it. Narrator will read a description of the element under your finger. Touch the screen with a second finger to activate the element.

Narrator is useful in Internet Explorer, too. To read an entire webpage, press Windows+Alt+\. Pressing Ctrl stops the reading and allows you to click links. Press Windows+Alt+Enter to select a hyperlink, and Windows+Alt+Spacebar to follow the link.

Narrator settings

Figure 7-10 shows the Narrator Settings page (accessed from PC Settings, Ease Of Access, Narrator), which you can use to customize different aspects of Narrator's behavior, as well as accessibility settings that aren't necessarily directly related to Narrator, such as how long notifications stay on the screen. Many of these settings are very important to customize; because users have very different accessibility needs, the default settings will not be perfectly suited to every user.

You should adjust the voice speed and pitch settings so that you can comfortably understand your favorite of the three voices. Faster speeds can greatly improve your efficiency when using your PC. If you are an accurate typist, you should clear the Characters You Type and Words You Type options.

▶ **Using Narrator** Watch the video at *http://aka.ms/WinIO/narrator*.

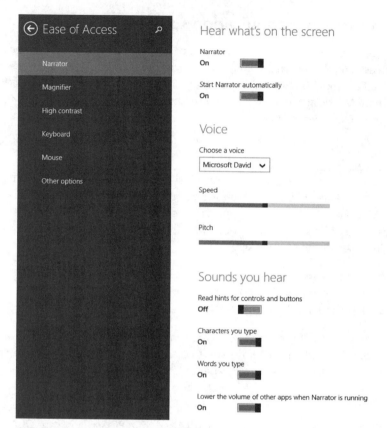

Figure 7-10 Narrator reads screen text aloud through your PC's speakers.

Narrator keyboard shortcuts

Because many Narrator users also have difficulty with pointing devices such as a mouse, Narrator is designed to be controlled using keyboard shortcuts. You can configure these short-cuts using the Commands settings in the Narrator Settings desktop tool, as shown in Figure 7-11. You can open the tool by typing **narrator** at the Start screen and selecting the icon with the computer and the voice bubble.

However, for best results, try to learn to use the default keyboard shortcuts. If you rely on cus-tomized shortcuts, you might find that your own PC is easier to use, but you'll be lost if you ever need to use another PC.

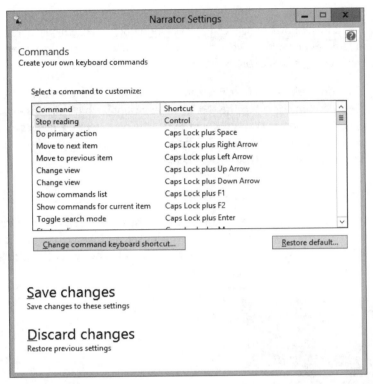

Figure 7-11 Use the Commands settings in Narrator to configure keyboard shortcuts.

Third-party text-to-speech software

Narrator is useful, but app-specific text-to-speech software can be more useful because it can handle the app's content more intelligently. Browsers are an important example: all popular browsers have several different plug-ins that support text-to-speech; simply visit the browser's plug-in library and search for the phrase "text-to-speech."

Only the desktop version of Internet Explorer supports plug-ins. Therefore, if you require text-to-speech with Internet Explorer, you need to use Narrator or switch to the desktop version and use a third-party plug-in.

Third-party screen readers that work with any app within Windows include:

- **NVDA (NonVisual Desktop Access) screen reader**   Available at *http://www.nvaccess.org/*, NVDA supports 30 languages and a variety of different voices.

- **Thunder**   Free screen-reading software available at *http://www.screenreader.net*. Thunder supports a handful of languages.

- **JAWS**   It's not free, but it's quite powerful and supports Braille output in addition to speech. It also supports optical character recognition (OCR), which can read text that is rendered as an image (a very common problem with webpages). Available at *http://www.freedomscientific.com/products/fs/jaws-product-page.asp.*

If you're using someone else's computer, you can use WebAnywhere to audibly read the contents of a webpage from any browser. The URL is rather complex, so it's easier simply to search for it. Choose the beta version of WebAnywhere to get the best results. Once it's loaded, WebAnywhere provides its own address bar at the top of the page. This address bar doesn't support searching, so you need to type a URL, such as *http://bing.com.*

Making the pointer easier to find

If you have difficulty finding the mouse pointer, you can increase the pointer size from PC Settings, Ease Of Access, Mouse. Search Settings for **pointer**, and then click Make It Easier To See The Mouse Pointer. As shown in Figure 7-12, Windows 8.1 provides options for large and extra-large pointers in several different sizes and styles.

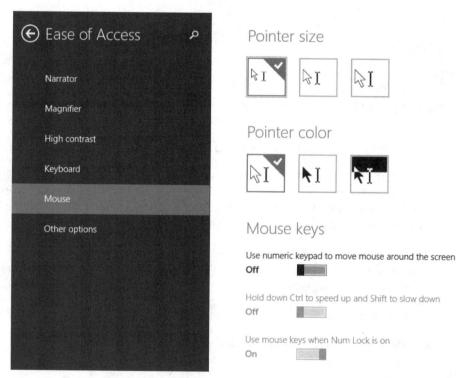

Figure 7-12 Choose a larger mouse pointer to make the pointer easier to find.

Other useful mouse settings are available. Turning on Use Numeric Keypad To Move Mouse Around The Screen helps users who are more comfortable with buttons than a mouse. You can fine-tune mouse behavior by using the Ctrl and Shift keys to control the speed of the mouse and by enabling the mouse keys to work whether or not Num Lock is on. By default, when Mouse Keys is enabled, it works only when the Num Lock button is off.

User input accessibility

Windows 8.1 and Windows 8.1 apps are designed to be used with either touch or a mouse and keyboard. If those options aren't ideal for you, you can accomplish most tasks using just a keyboard or just a mouse. Additionally, speech recognition is useful for dictation and many common Windows tasks.

If you have difficulty typing a password to sign on to Windows, you might find it easier to use a picture password or a PIN. For information about changing your sign-in settings, refer to Chapter 18, "Managing users and Family Safety."

Using Windows 8.1 with only a keyboard

The login screen's password field is selected by default. Therefore, users with access to a keyboard but without a mouse can simply type their password and press Enter.

Users who cannot press two keys simultaneously, but who need to type capital letters or symbols in their password, should use Sticky Keys. To activate Sticky Keys, press the Shift key five times and then press the Spacebar to select Yes when prompted to confirm, as shown in Figure 7-13.

Inside OUT

Accessible complex passwords

To save yourself the trouble of enabling Sticky Keys just to type your password, create a complex password without using the Shift key. Mix lowercase letters, numbers, and symbols that don't require the Shift key, such as square brackets, slashes, and the apostrophe. If an attacker was aware that the password does not use the Shift key, it would make the password much easier to guess. Therefore, make the password a few characters longer than you normally would.

Press Tab to access other elements of the login screen, just as you would with most aspects of Windows. By tabbing multiple times, you can access the power button in the lower-right corner to shut down or restart your computer or the Ease Of Access button in the lower-left corner to turn on Narrator, Magnifier, the on-screen keyboard, high contrast, Sticky Keys, or FilterKeys.

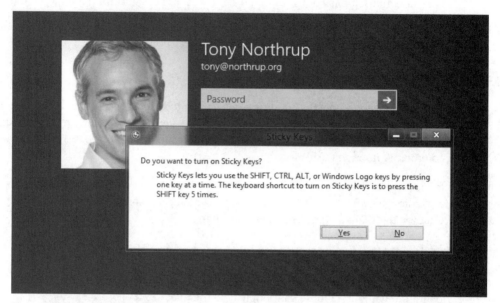

Figure 7-13 Enable Sticky Keys by pressing Shift five times.

Table 7-1 lists keyboard shortcuts that are particularly useful to users without a mouse. Note that this isn't the complete list of keyboard shortcuts; these are the most important keyboard shortcuts that can be performed by pressing a single key.

Table 7-1 Accessibility shortcuts

Shortcut	Action
Tab	Switch between elements.
Enter	Send the current form data or click OK.
Esc	Reject the current form data or click Cancel.
Backspace	Return to the previous page.
Home	Jump to the beginning of the current line of text.
End	Jump to the end of the current line of text.
Page Down	Scroll down one page
Page Up	Scroll up one page

Some users, especially those who don't have steady hands, find it easier to type when they have FilterKeys enabled. FilterKeys is a feature that slows down keyboard input. Basically, you have to hold down a key for a full second before it registers. Enabling FilterKeys reduces the precision required when typing, because if someone briefly bumps the wrong key, Windows ignores the keystroke. To turn on FilterKeys, hold the right Shift key for eight seconds.

Using Windows 8.1 with only a mouse

To log in without a keyboard, click the Ease Of Access icon in the lower-left corner and then click On-Screen Keyboard. The on-screen keyboard, as shown in Figure 7-14, works exactly like a regular keyboard except that the Shift, Fn, Ctrl, and Alt keys are sticky. So, to type a capital A, you would click Shift and then click A.

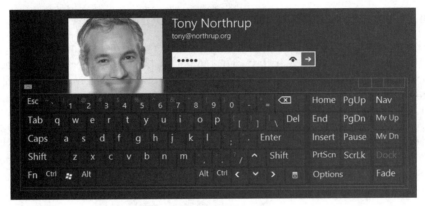

Figure 7-14 Use the on-screen keyboard to type with a mouse.

Inside OUT
Security uses for the on-screen keyboard

If you use an external keyboard, attackers can gather your password and anything else you type by connecting a keylogger between your keyboard and your computer. Using the on-screen keyboard is a great way to reduce the risk of a hardware keylogger getting your password (though it can make it easier for someone to read your password over your shoulder).

Windows 8.1 hides your password when you type it to make it harder for someone to read it over your shoulder. Typos are easy, though, especially when using the on-screen keyboard. You can double-check what you've typed by clicking and holding the eye icon next to the password.

Inside OUT

Have Narrator read your keystrokes

To be reassured of what you're typing, use Narrator to read your keystrokes as you type them. Just open the Narrator settings, enable Narrator, and turn off every option except Characters You Type. It won't take effect until after you log on, however, so you don't have to worry about having your password read aloud.

Using Windows 8.1 with speech recognition

You can control many aspects of Windows 8.1 and Internet Explorer with your voice. Previous versions of Windows have had speech recognition, but it has never been this useful. With Windows 8.1, you really can navigate Windows and perform most common tasks with your voice, without touching a keyboard or mouse.

First, you'll want a good quality headset microphone recommended for use with voice recognition. A headset microphone stays close to your mouth, which helps to reduce the impact of outside noises. It also maintains a more consistent volume level as you move your body and head. Speech recognition works with other types of mics, but it won't be reliable enough for anything more than occasional use.

To set up speech recognition, type **speech** at the Start screen, and then click Windows Speech Recognition. The wizard, as shown in Figure 7-15, helps you configure your mic and train speech recognition to understand your voice.

Once you've set up speech recognition, you can perform basic tasks such as opening the Start screen (say "Start screen"), opening apps (say "Start *<name of the app>*"), scrolling (say "Scroll up" and "Scroll down"), clicking links in Internet Explorer (say "Click *<name of link>*"), or selecting items in dialog boxes (say the name of the item). There are dozens of commands.

You can also use speech recognition to dictate documents and messages. Once in an app, simply speak, and Windows will do its best to interpret what you say. It doesn't have grammar skills, so you need to say every piece of punctuation. For example, you might say, "Hello comma world period," to write "Hello, world."

Figure 7-15 Speech recognition allows you to control your computer with your voice.

Inside OUT

The imperfection of speech recognition

Relying on speech recognition has some downsides:

- The login screen does not support voice recognition for selecting your user name or typing your password, so you might want to set up Windows 8.1 to log you on automatically. From the Start screen, type **netplwiz** and press Enter. Then, clear the Users Must Enter A User Name And Password To Use This Computer check box, and follow the prompts that appear.

- Some apps won't work well or at all, especially third-party apps. Many developers simply don't test their apps with speech recognition.

- Speech recognition isn't perfect, especially during dictation. You need to carefully review everything you write.

Speech recognition in Windows 8.1 is not perfect, but no speech recognition software is (yet). If it's not good enough for you, try Dragon by Nuance. It's not free, but it's more accurate and powerful.

Using Windows 8.1 with touch

Windows 8.1 has a setting that can improve the usability of the touch keyboard by activating keys only once you remove your finger from the keyboard. This allows you to hold your finger against the screen, slide to the right key, and then lift your finger to type the key.

This setting is hidden in a rather unexpected place: Narrator. On the Narrator settings page, turn Narrator on, and then select the Activate Keys On Touch Keyboard When I Lift My Finger Off The Keyboard option, as shown in Figure 7-16. Be sure to configure Narrator to start auto-matically (as described in the section "Narrator" earlier in this chapter), even if you must dis-able Narrator's other functionality.

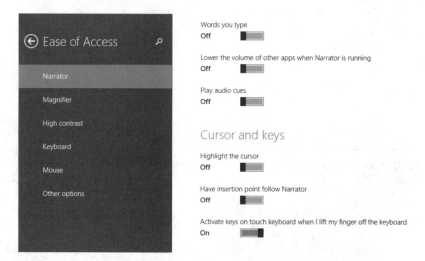

Figure 7-16 Use Narrator to make the touch keyboard more accessible.

Dyslexia and reading accessibility

Though it has improved over time, using a computer and the Internet still relies heavily on a user's ability to read and write. This makes using a computer more difficult for many users, especially users with dyslexia and similar conditions.

Narrator translates written text to spoken word. While Narrator is capable of reading just about every aspect of the Windows user interface, many dyslexic users feel comfortable navi-gating Windows without it. Windows 8.1, in particular, uses icons heavily, reducing the need to rely on the written word for navigation. Where Narrator comes in handy for dyslexic users is with large blocks of text—webpages and e-books, for example.

Speech recognition can make entering large amounts of text easier for dyslexic users. While most won't want it for entering a few keystrokes (for example, typing their password or using keyboard shortcuts), speech recognition can greatly reduce the time it takes to write papers, emails, and instant messages. It might also improve spelling accuracy.

Speech recognition software is never perfect, however, so you should still reread important messages, even if you use Narrator to do it.

Another way to improve readability for some users is to select specific fonts. For example, a recent study showed that readers with dyslexia made fewer errors when using the Dyslexie type, a type designed specifically for their style of learning. Dyslexie (available at *http://www.studiostudio.nl/home/en/*) and a similar font named Lexia Readable (available at *http://www.k-type.com/?p=520*) are currently free for personal use and can be installed in Windows 8.1.

Figure 7-17 contrasts the Segoe font (top) built into Windows 8.1 with Dyslexie (bottom). As you can see, the lowercase q (easily confused with a p, b, or d) is written using an uppercase style. Lowercase b and d are visually weighted at the bottom, preventing them from appearing the same when rotated.

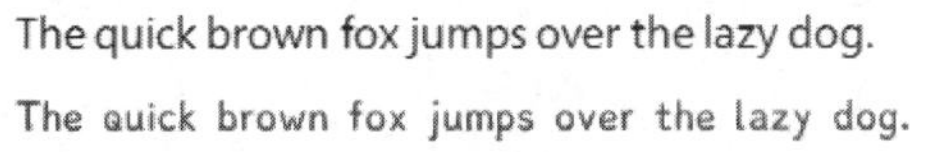

The quick brown fox jumps over the lazy dog.

The quick brown fox jumps over the lazy dog.

Figure 7-17 Characters like Q can be easier to read in the Dyslexie font.

To install fonts that aren't built in, download them, right-click the font file (with a .otf or .ttf file extension), and then click Install. If you don't have the option to install a font, many users consider Trebuchet MS, Georgia, and Comic Sans to be the best built-in fonts for readers with dyslexia.

You can't change the font for all of Windows, but you can select fonts in some applications, including many document and e-book readers. In the desktop version of Internet Explorer, you can choose a default font, but Windows uses it only when the website you are viewing doesn't specify a font, which is uncommon. So, you also need to configure Internet Explorer to ignore website fonts. Therefore, you need to make two configuration changes from the General tab of the Internet Options dialog box in the desktop version of Internet Explorer:

- Click Accessibility, and then select Ignore Font Styles Specified On Webpages.

- Click Fonts, and then select your preferred font.

With these few tweaks, PCs can be much more usable to people with dyslexia or other reading conditions.

Obtaining help and support

Obtaining professional support. 195

Help and support. 196

Determining who to contact for support. 197

Searching the Internet. 198

Asking for help. 199

Connecting with Remote Assistance. 202

Recording problems. 206

Nobody is such a computer expert that they have the answer to every problem memorized. Typically, experts learn the basics of computers and then rely on Internet searches and technical resources to find the information they need.

The goal of this chapter is to teach you the basics of finding help for any problem that might arise within Windows by using different forms of support: professional support, online help, information on the Internet, and online forums. This chapter also shows you how to connect to remote computers using Remote Assistance and how to record a problem so you can show someone else exactly what's happening.

This book also provides some troubleshooting assistance in Chapter 23, "Troubleshooting your network," and in Part 6, "Maintaining, tuning, and troubleshooting." However, there's also an entire Inside Out book dedicated to the topic: *Troubleshooting Windows 8 Inside Out* (Microsoft Press, 2012).

Obtaining professional support

For the first time, Windows 8.1 comes with 90 days of free premier phone support. If you run into a problem with your new computer, you can get free help at *http://answerdesk.com* or you can call the Microsoft Answer Desk at 800-MICROSOFT (800-632-7676).

After your first 90 days, you might still have free support available from your computer manufacturer. Therefore, if you have a Dell computer, you should contact Dell support. If you have an HP computer, you should contact HP support.

Support never lasts indefinitely. Therefore, when you contact your hardware manufacturer, it's possible that your warranty will have expired. Typically, the manufacturer will still help you, but they'll charge a fee. When you purchase your computer, the manufacturer often offers an extended support contract (for a fee). If you regularly need help, that fee might be worthwhile.

If you are not eligible for free support, you can hire computer support from a wide variety of companies. Microsoft Answer Desk, available at *http://www.answerdesk.com*, is an option. You can also schedule an appointment for in-person help at a Microsoft Store (if there is one in your area). Visit *http://content.microsoftstore.com/Home.aspx* to schedule an appointment.

An Internet search for "computer support" returns dozens of different businesses willing to help you with your computer problems for a fee. Often, however, you can find the answers to your problems for free using the Internet. The sections that follow describe these free support options.

Help and support

Windows 8.1 and Windows 8.1 apps are designed to be easy enough to use that you don't need help. Online Help is still available, though. You might be accustomed to pressing F1 to get help. That won't work from the Windows 8.1 Start screen or from most apps designed for Windows 8.1. This makes sense, because Windows 8.1 is designed to be used without a keyboard. However, pressing F1 for help will still work in many desktop apps.

Instead, to get help at the Start screen or within an app, open the Settings charm and then click Help. Not all apps offer help, however. As shown in Figure 8-1, the Help system slides in from the right while your app remains open. Simply click the topic you're interested in, or click your app to return to it. Many of the topics link to webpages on the Internet, so you might need Internet access to read them.

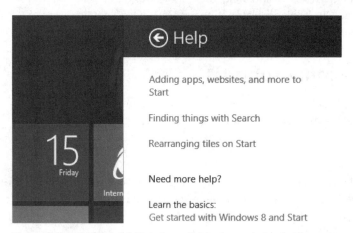

Figure 8-1 Windows 8.1 Help is available through the Settings charm.

Opening Help from the Start screen also provides a link for learning the basics of Windows 8.1.

Help isn't as important as it used to be. In the past, users needed to study the Help system to learn how to use an app. Today, apps are designed to be intuitive. When users want to learn general information about a product, they tend to purchase a book (such as this one). When users need help performing a specific task, most of them prefer to search the Internet. For more complex tasks, you might even search YouTube—there's a large community of people, including the author of this book, who publish how-to videos.

Determining who to contact for support

Accessories you buy for your computer might be made by a different company than the one that manufactured your computer. Apps are made by yet another company. So, who should you contact for support about any particular problem?

First, a bit of background about Windows architecture. There are four basic layers, from top to bottom:

- Apps

- Windows

- Drivers

- Hardware

As a general rule, each layer communicates only with the layer above or below it. So, apps never communicate directly with hardware. If you want to print from an app, the app sends a message to Windows, Windows sends a message to the printer driver, and the printer driver communicates with the hardware printer.

If you have a problem printing from an app, it could be a problem with the app, Windows, the driver, or the hardware. Who should you call? Your first step should be to isolate the problem to a single layer. To isolate a problem, change the scenario and see whether the problem still exists.

To isolate the printer problem, you could:

- Attempt to print from the same app to a different printer. If this works, you know the problem is specific to the printer or its driver, and you can contact the hardware manufacturer because the manufacturer is responsible for both.

- Attempt to print from a different app to the same printer. If this works, you know Windows, the printer, and the driver are working, and you can contact the app developer.

CHAPTER 8

- Attempt to print from the same app to the same printer but from a different computer. If this works, the problem is specific to the computer, which could mean a hardware problem, a software configuration error, or a problem with software versions.

Some problems are more difficult to isolate. If you can't isolate a problem, start by searching the Internet for help. Then, post a message in a support forum. Finally, contact technical support.

Inside OUT

What are drivers?

Drivers are pieces of software that handle communications between Windows and your computer hardware. Think of it like world languages: Windows speaks only one language, but each piece of hardware speaks its own unique language. The driver is the translator, allowing Windows to speak to any piece of hardware without having to learn thousands of different languages.

Hardware manufacturers create most drivers because they're the ones who best understand the language their devices speak. However, Microsoft tests and approves many drivers to reduce the risk that they'll cause your computer to crash. When Microsoft approves a driver, they distribute it through Windows Update, so you can install the driver automatically when you first connect hardware to your computer. Windows Update also allows you to automatically receive new versions of drivers.

Technically, it would be possible for Windows to learn every different language. However, that would require hardware manufacturers to contribute code directly to Windows, which would reduce reliability and make the development process very difficult. It would also make distributing updates more difficult.

NOTE

If you're not sure who the app developer is, open the app, access the Settings charm, and then click About. This usually provides the name of the developer.

Searching the Internet

For better or worse, you're probably not the first person to have any specific problem. Odds are very good that someone else had the problem and posted a message about it. There's even a good chance that they found the solution to their problem, and that solution will work for you, too.

Here's a good process for finding webpages related to your problem. If at any time you find no useful results, it's probably time to post your own question.

- Search the Internet for your exact problem, enclosing the phrase in quotation marks. For example, if the Computer Management console crashes with an error message, you might search for **"Microsoft Management Console has stopped working."**

- If the results are related to different problems, make your search more specific. For example, you might search for **"Computer Management" "Microsoft Management Console has stopped working."**

- If you still have too many results, try narrowing the scope of your search to people discussing the problem on Internet forums. Google allows you to do this by selecting Discussions from the left side of the search results.

If the problem is related to Windows (as opposed to an app), use these same techniques to search Microsoft Support, available at *http://support.microsoft.com*. Microsoft Support includes Microsoft's massive public knowledge base of technical information and answers from Microsoft communities. When Microsoft discovers a bug or other technical issue, they often create a TechNet article that describes the issue and suggests a workaround.

Asking for help

The Internet community has a bad reputation for responding to sincerity with sarcasm and hostility, and that reputation isn't completely undeserved. However, there's a massive population of generous and knowledgeable people willing to do their best to help complete strangers with problems.

Before you ask for help, make sure you have done your best to find an answer to your problem:

- Restart your computer and any hardware devices related to the problem.

- Install all important updates from Windows Update.

- Install any updates available from the app developer or hardware vendor.

- Examine online Help, if it's available.

- Search the web for your error message.

- Check the app developer or hardware vendor's website for troubleshooting instructions.

Now you're ready to find a help forum. You want to find the forum most closely related to the problem you're experiencing. If you can't print from any app on your computer,

you should browse the printer manufacturer's website for a support forum. If you're having a problem with an app, find the app developer's website and visit their forum. If you're
having a problem with Windows, visit the Windows Community (see Figure 8-2) at *http://
windows.microsoft.com/en-us/windows/help/community*. Microsoft Most Valuable Professionals
(MVPs) and even Microsoft full-time employees often help answer questions.

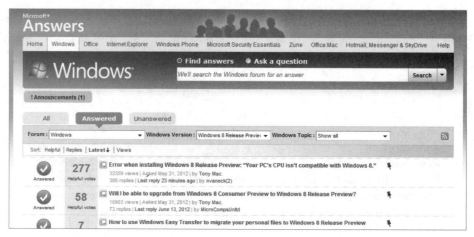

Figure 8-2 The Windows Community is a great place to find free volunteer help.

You're almost ready to post. Before you do, make one last search for your problem using the
forum's search engine. Internet search engines don't always return the latest messages, so you
might find a recent message related to your problem.

Some websites have forums for different types of issues. For example, the Windows Community has separate forums for Windows 8.1, Windows 7, and Windows XP. Find the forum that
best suits your question, and create a new message.

You want to provide people all the information they might need to diagnose your problem
and provide a recommendation. At a minimum, provide:

- A detailed description of the problem. Specify the exact steps you follow to reproduce
  the problem. For example, you might say, "When I try to print from any app, I get the
  error message, 'Could not connect to printer.'"

- An overview of the troubleshooting you've already done and what the results were. For
  example, you might say, "I installed the latest drivers from the hardware manufacturer.
  I rebooted my computer and my printer and tried connecting the printer to a different Windows 8.1 computer, but the problem continues. When I connect the printer to a
  Windows 7 computer, it works properly."

- The version of Windows that you're using, including the service pack, if any. Mention that you've installed every important update from Windows Update. For example, you might say, "I'm running Windows 8.1 with all available updates."

- If it's an app problem, the full name of the app, and the version if you can find it. For example, you might say, "I'm running the Photos app version 1.2."

- If it's a hardware problem, the make and model of the device and how it is connected to your computer. For example, you might say, "My printer is the Brother MFC-J825DW, and I connect to it with a USB cable."

- If it's a performance problem, provide your computer's specifications. For example, you might say, "I'm using a Dell XPS 13."

With your message crafted, you need to wait anywhere from several hours to several days for a reply. You might not get a reply at all; if you have a problem nobody has experienced before, no one on the forum will know how to solve it.

▶ **Finding help online** Watch the video at *http://aka.ms/WinIO/help*.

Here are a few etiquette tips to follow:

- Post one message. If you don't get any replies in two days, you can post in a different forum.

- Be responsive. If someone writes back with questions, do your best to answer them promptly.

- Follow up. If you solve your problem, write a reply describing exactly how you solved it. Others with the same issue will benefit from your experience.

- Be polite. The people helping you are volunteers and are not paid for their work. They deserve a BIG thank you!

- Relax. The problem feels urgent to you, and other people want to help, but they are volunteers, and your problem isn't an emergency to them. Don't say things like, "URGENT: NEED HELP!!!" If you really need a response within minutes, contact professional technical support.

- Return the favor. Browse the forum and see whether other people are having problems you can solve. If you have skills that aren't related to computers, there are forums where people need your skills. Help them out, and you help to keep the best part of the Internet alive.

CHAPTER 8

Connecting with Remote Assistance

With Remote Assistance, someone can connect to your computer across the local network or the Internet and share your desktop with you. This way, you can easily show them what's happening and they can try to fix it. Of course, since you're reading this book, it's more likely that you'll be the one providing the assistance.

> ## Inside OUT
> ### *The technology behind Remote Assistance*
>
> Remote Assistance, and the very closely related Remote Desktop, offer really amazing performance. Over all but the slowest of Internet connections, you'll feel like you're sitting right at the other computer.
>
> Remote Assistance and Remote Desktop are based on the Remote Desktop Protocol (RDP). It doesn't work by streaming the computer's display across the Internet; if it did, the performance and quality would be more like watching a video across the Internet. You'd need a great deal of bandwidth for reasonable performance, and it wouldn't work at all across slower links.
>
> Instead, RDP connects deeply into Windows, transmitting low-level messages about the desktop environment rather than individual pixels. Therefore, when you open the Calendar app across a remote connection, RDP sends a message saying, "Draw a gray background. On that background, write June 2012 in the upper-left corner. Draw a series of boxes with numbers in their lower-right corners." This is much more efficient than individually describing the color of the roughly one million pixels that appear on the screen.
>
> This method is in stark contrast to the best free tool I've used: Virtual Network Computing (VNC). VNC seems to transmit your screen pixel by pixel without knowledge of the underlying apps. As a result, it's much slower.
>
> With this understanding of how RDP works, you can understand the scenarios when it doesn't work very well: viewing pictures and videos. While both types of content can be compressed before transmitting, it's not nearly as efficient as transmitting low-level application messages. Therefore, don't plan on using RDP for watching videos or editing pictures—unless you're on a very fast network, it'll probably be too slow.

Enabling Remote Assistance

Remote Assistance is enabled by default. If you're security conscious, this might sound scary, as if anyone could connect to your computer. It's not that easy; before anyone connects to your computer, they need an invitation, and the invitations are cryptographically protected. Of course, if you don't plan to use Remote Assistance, you should disable it, because reducing the attack surface is always a useful way to improve security.

To enable or disable incoming Remote Assistance invitations, use the Remote tab of the System Properties dialog box, as shown in Figure 8-3. You can open this dialog box by searching Settings for **Assistance**, and then clicking Allow Remote Assistance Invitations To Be Sent From This Computer.

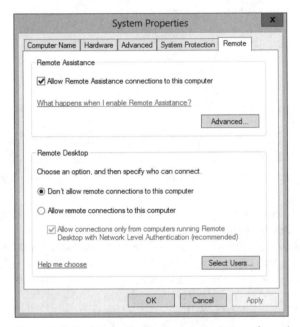

Figure 8-3 Enable or disable Remote Assistance from the System Properties dialog box.

If you want other people to be able to view your computer but not control it, click Advanced, and then clear the Allow This Computer To Be Controlled Remotely option. You don't need to enable or disable Remote Assistance for outgoing connections, which you would use to help someone else; you can always accept a Remote Assistance invitation.

Creating a Remote Assistance invitation

To create a Remote Assistance invitation (which you can use to help someone or get help), search Settings for **Assistance**, and then click Invite Someone To Connect To Your PC And Help You, Or Offer To Help Someone Else. This opens the Windows Remote Assistance wizard, shown in Figure 8-4.

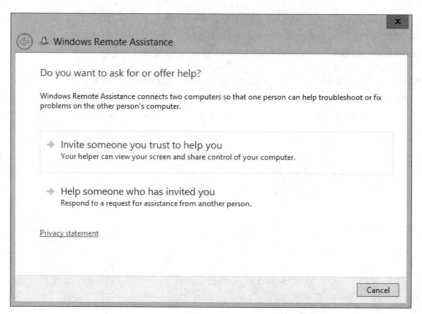

Figure 8-4 Use the Windows Remote Assistance wizard to invite someone to connect to your PC.

The wizard is self-explanatory, with one exception: Easy Connect. Easy Connect allows you to find and connect to a computer anywhere on the Internet by typing the password Remote Assistance provides you (as shown in Figure 8-5) into the Remote Assistance window. Easy Connect requires both computers to be running either Windows 7 or Windows 8.1. Try Easy Connect; if it doesn't work, send the invitation another way.

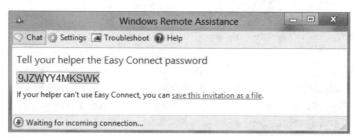

Figure 8-5 Easy Connect lets you connect to almost any computer by typing a password into the app.

If you send the invitation as a file or an email attachment instead of using Easy Connect, the recipient simply needs to double-click the .msrcIncident file from a computer running Windows XP, Windows Vista, Windows 7, Windows 8, or Windows 8.1. Then, the recipient needs to type the password shown in the Remote Assistance window. You need to confirm that they are allowed to connect to your computer.

No matter which method you use to connect, you need to leave the Windows Remote Assistance window open. Closing it prevents the expert from connecting to your computer. That's also a bit comforting, because protecting your computer is as easy as closing the window. By default, invitations expire after six hours.

Using Remote Assistance

Within the Remote Assistance session, the expert will be able to view your computer and see anything you do on it. If your computer has a high screen resolution (most common on large monitors) or multiple displays, the expert will see the entire screen scaled down to the size of their Remote Assistance window. This is in contrast to Remote Desktop, which automatically changes the screen resolution.

To allow the expert to control the computer, the expert must click the Request Control button, and then you must confirm that they can have control. Until you confirm that the expert can control your computer, the expert can only view your screen. If you want to hide your screen temporarily, click the Pause button.

By clicking the Settings button on your computer, you can configure the bandwidth usage, as shown in Figure 8-6. The default setting of Low is ideal for helping someone, but you can increase the bandwidth to show the background and visual effects.

Figure 8-6 Configure Windows Remote Assistance Settings to optimize performance.

Inside OUT

Is Easy Connect not so easy for you?

Most of the time, Easy Connect does exactly what its name indicates. If you run into a problem, it's probably because of a network configuration issue. You probably need to change your router configuration to support Universal Plug and Play (UPNP) and the Peer Name Resolution Protocol (PNRP). If you have an older router, you might need to upgrade it.

It's probably easier just to send the invitation as a file or an email message; however, if you want to troubleshoot the network configuration issue, use the Microsoft Internet Connectivity Evaluation Tool at *http://www.microsoft.com/windows/using/tools/igd/default.mspx*. You must use Internet Explorer.

Recording problems

You can use Steps Recorder to record a problem that's occurring. Then, you can send the recording to an expert so that they can better see the problem.

To use Steps Recorder, follow these steps:

1. From the Start screen, search for **Problem Steps**.

2. In the left pane, click Record Steps To Reproduce A Problem.

    Windows 8.1 displays the desktop and opens the Steps Recorder app.

3. Click Start Record.

4. Switch back to the Start screen, open the app causing the problem, and repeat the steps that demonstrate the problem.

5. Switch back to the desktop (for example, by clicking Desktop on the Start screen or by pressing Windows+D). In the Steps Recorder app, click Stop Recording.

    Steps Recorder displays your recording, as shown in Figure 8-7.

Figure 8-7 Use Steps Recorder to record actions on your PC.

6. Click Save or Email, and send the recording to the support staff.

Steps Recorder is also a useful way to create step-by-step instructions for friends who need help.

PART 2

File management

CHAPTER 9
Organizing and protecting files 211

CHAPTER 10
Backing up and restoring files 233

CHAPTER 11
Managing Windows search 249

CHAPTER 12
Managing storage 261

CHAPTER 13
Using SkyDrive 289

Organizing and protecting files

The Windows 8.1 way of organizing files 212

File system concepts 212

Working with libraries 215

Zipping folders 218

Protecting files 219

Advanced searching 225

Freeing up disk space 228

File organization tips 230

Windows 8 takes an app-first approach to managing files. If you want to view your photos, open the Photos app. To find your music, open the Music app.

This approach is very different from how you managed files in Windows 7. In Windows 7, most users ran Windows Explorer to access files of any type. For example, to view your photos in Windows 7, you use Windows Explorer to browse to the Pictures library. Then, to view a specific picture, you double-click it, and Windows opens the file in Windows Photo Viewer. The same process applies to finding your music: open the Music folder in Windows Explorer, and then double-click a song to open it in Windows Media Player.

Because in Windows 7 you use Windows Explorer to manage files of every type, it can become rather complicated. You can use Windows Explorer to add tags to your photos or associate a song with a different artist, but it isn't necessarily the easiest or most efficient way to do it. Photos deserve their own app with a specialized user interface, and so do music, videos, and every other type of file you use.

This chapter describes the most useful concepts of file management for Windows 8.1. I'll show you how to manage, compress, and protect your files, folders, and libraries in the File Explorer desktop app (previously known as Windows Explorer, which many users accessed by clicking Computer or Documents). I'll also show you how to find lost files and how to free up space on a full disk. I won't, however, show you every aspect of using File Explorer. If you were a Windows 7 user, you already know how, and if you're new to Windows 8.1, you'll never need to learn.

The Windows 8.1 way of organizing files

The Windows 8.1 app-first approach to file management makes sense. When you use many apps designed for Windows 8.1, you don't even need to know which file system folders the data is stored in, and you certainly don't need to understand how to view file metadata, group files, or change the thumbnail size. The individual apps know best how to organize files of that type, and they hide the underlying file system structure from the user.

You can still take a file-first approach in the Windows 8.1 interface: open the Search charm and search for files. For most users, searching is a quicker and more accurate way of finding files than browsing the relatively complex file system.

Of course, for those of us comfortable with the file system, File Explorer is still available on the desktop. In fact, as described in Chapter 2, "Using Windows 8.1 apps," the user interface has been significantly improved. To open File Explorer, simply launch the Desktop from the Start screen, and then click the pinned File Explorer window on the taskbar. (It looks like a yellow folder.)

File system concepts

When you use Windows 8.1 apps and everything works like it is supposed to, you really don't need to understand how a file system works. For those of us who still use desktop apps or who want to understand the inner workings of an operating system, this section provides an overview of basic file system concepts.

Windows 8.1 uses a file system called NTFS. NTFS stands for New Technology File System, which was a completely appropriate name when the file system was originally released in 1993. NTFS is old enough to vote now, but Microsoft has regularly added new features to keep it up to date.

> ➤ **Windows 8.1 should automatically fix most file system corruptions. For more detailed information, refer to Chapter 12, "Managing storage."**

NTFS uses a hierarchy of folders inside other folders, including C:\Users\<*username*>\My Documents, which is your documents folder, and C:\Windows\, which (by default) stores your Windows system files. Each folder can contain files and other folders. Figure 9-1 shows a portion of the file system tree of the C drive in File Explorer.

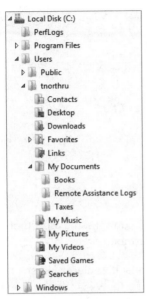

Figure 9-1 Your file system stores folders within folders.

File names

File names can be long (up to 255 characters) and contain some special characters, such as spaces and parentheses. File names can't contain other characters, including slashes, backslashes, and asterisks (*). You can type file names in uppercase and lowercase, such as MyFile.txt, and Windows remembers the case you used. However, file names aren't case sensitive, so if you later attempt to open myfile.txt without using the uppercase letters, it still works.

File names almost always end with an extension that indicates the file type and which app the file should be opened with. For example, many image files have a .jpg extension (for example, MyPicture.jpg), and Windows knows to open .jpg files with the Photos app. Text files often have a .txt extension (such as MyTextFile.txt), and Windows opens .txt files in Notepad by default. Chapter 2 describes how to change which app opens a specific file type by default.

File Explorer hides file name extensions by default, but it's very useful to see them. To show file name extensions, select the View tab in File Explorer, and then select File Name Extensions, as shown in Figure 9-2.

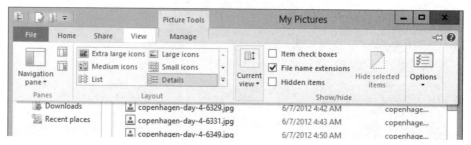

Figure 9-2 You can choose to show file name extensions.

Attributes

Besides names, files and folders have attributes. Attributes control some aspects of how Windows interacts with a file. The most commonly used attributes are:

- **Hidden**   Prevents a file from being displayed by default. Hiding a file isn't at all secure; you can show hidden files in File Explorer by selecting the View tab and then selecting the Hidden Items check box. I describe how to protect files later in this chapter.

- **Read-only**   Indicates that a file shouldn't be changed or deleted. This attribute also shouldn't be trusted; any app or user can overwrite read-only files. Most apps provide an extra warning if a file is read-only. Some apps don't allow you to overwrite a read-only file. You need to go to File Explorer to remove the read-only attribute.

- **Compressed**   Compresses a file so that it consumes less disk space. When you compress a folder, you can compress all files within that folder. Accessing compressed files can be a little slower than accessing noncompressed files, but if there's any performance impact, you probably won't notice it. Compression is always lossless, which means that your file contents aren't changed in any way; the original data is still stored in its entirety, it's just stored a little more efficiently. It won't do you any good to compress image, music, or video files, but text files and documents become much smaller when they're compressed.

- **Encrypted**   Encrypts a file so that only authorized users can access it, even if they bypass Windows by connecting the hard disk to another computer. Encrypting files is discussed in more detail later in this chapter.

To modify a file's attributes, right-click the file in File Explorer and then click Properties. The General tab gives you check boxes for Read-Only and Hidden, as shown in Figure 9-3. To modify the compressed or encrypted attributes, click the Advanced button.

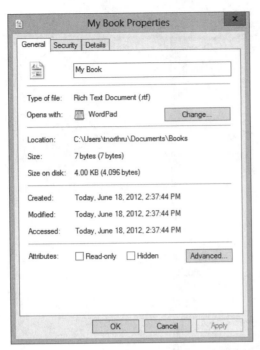

Figure 9-3 Modify a file's attributes in its Properties dialog box.

Working with libraries

Libraries are collections of folders that make it easy to find files in different places. You use libraries all the time, even though you might not be aware of them.

For example, Documents, Pictures, Music, and Videos are all libraries, even though they behave very similarly to folders. Each library, by default, contains two separate folders: a private and a public folder.

Figure 9-4 shows the properties for the Documents library (which you can view by right-clicking Documents in File Explorer and then clicking Properties). As you can see, my Documents library contains two different folders: C:\Users\tnorthru\Documents (my private documents folder) and C:\Users\Public\Documents (the public documents folder that all users on my computer can access).

As you can see by the check mark in Figure 9-4, your personal Documents folder is set as the default save location. Therefore, any newer Windows apps will automatically save your documents in this folder. Different file types, such as music, pictures, and videos, will be saved in the appropriate library's save location. You can select a different folder as your default location by selecting the folder and then clicking Set Save Location.

Figure 9-4 Libraries can contain multiple folders stored anywhere.

Here's why libraries are useful: you can access and search multiple folders as if they were a single folder. For example, if you run out of room on your C drive, you could buy a USB drive and connect it to your computer, create a new Documents folder on it, and then add that folder to your library. If you want new files to be saved to your external drive by default, select the new folder and then click Set Save Location.

Inside OUT

Where is the library data stored?

Windows stores library data in the C:\Users\<*username*>\AppData\Roaming\Microsoft\ Windows\Libraries folder by default. The library data files are just XML files with an .ms-library file extension. An XML file is a text file designed for computers to read. If you're curious, browse to that folder, right-click a library, and then click Open With. Click Try An App On This PC, and then click Notepad. In theory you could edit a library data file, but it's much easier to use the graphical interface.

Similarly, if you decide to move all your documents to a different drive, just move your Documents folder to the new drive, add the new folder to the library (and set it as your default save location), and then remove the old folder from the library.

Inside OUT

Creating custom libraries

I don't recommend creating custom libraries; Windows won't know about them or use them by default. It's better just to add folders to the existing libraries.

However, if you find a need to create a custom library, right-click Libraries in File Explorer, point to New, and then click Library. Then, right-click and select Properties to configure the library. As shown in Figure 9-5, you can add folders to the new library, specify the document type, and change the library icon.

Figure 9-5 Create a custom library for special file types (if you must).

You don't really need to use libraries. You could simply select a different folder to save your files in. However, using libraries saves you a few clicks each time you open and save files, which can add up to thousands of clicks over time. Libraries are also backed up by default, assuming you configure backups as described in Chapter 10, "Backing up and restoring files." Adding folders to your Pictures, Music, and Videos libraries allows the associated apps to automatically find your files, too, and the Search charm searches your libraries by default.

Zipping folders

You can compress files and folders using attributes, but the compression isn't very efficient. However, you can dramatically reduce the size of many types of files by zipping them. Accessing files in a zipped archive takes a bit longer, so you only want to zip folders that you don't frequently use. Zipping doesn't reduce the size of most pictures, videos, or music, however, because those files types are (usually) already compressed.

To zip a folder, right-click it in File Explorer, click Send To, and then click Compressed (Zipped) Folder. Windows makes a new file with a .zip extension. This file contains a compressed copy of every file that was in your folder, including all subfolders. To view the contents of the compressed file, simply open it like you do a folder.

To unzip an archive and return it to its original state, right-click it, and then click Extract All.

Zipping a folder is also a good way to send several files to someone as an email attachment. Zipping a folder creates a second copy, so if you are archiving the folder, you should delete the original folder after zipping it.

Inside OUT

Password protecting a zip archive

You can use the free 7-Zip tool to create zip archives that are encrypted and password protected. This is useful if you want to send someone a file (or many files) through email but want to minimize the risk that someone else will be able to open the files. After installing 7-Zip from *http://www.7-zip.org*, right-click the file or folder you want to protect and click Add To Archive. Then, type your password twice. If you use the ZIP format, consider changing the encryption from the default of ZipCrypto to AES-256.

Obviously, recipients need to know the password to open the .zip file. Don't just tell them the password in the same email message you send the attachment in, because then anyone who has access to the email can decrypt your zip archive. Don't send the password in a separate email either, because that also makes the password vulnerable. Instead, send the password "out-of-band" using a different communication mechanism. In other words, call or text the password to recipients. For even better protection, text them half the password and call them with the other half.

Protecting files

Windows 8.1 offers two ways to protect your files and folders: permissions and encryption.

Using permissions

Every file and folder has its own set of permissions. These permissions define which users can open, edit, and delete files. The default settings work for most users, so you might never have to see or change permissions.

However, if you're curious, right-click a file or folder in File Explorer, click Properties, and then select the Security tab. As Figure 9-6 shows, permissions consist of a list of different users and groups and the rights they have to that file or folder. This list is known as an access control list (ACL).

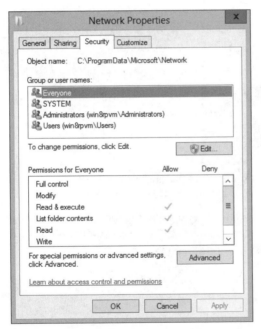

Figure 9-6 The Security tab shows the permissions of a file or folder.

Figure 9-6 shows typical permissions for a system folder: the Everyone group (which, logically, applies to everyone on the computer, including guests) can read files and run apps. The SYSTEM account and the Administrators group (both of which are also logically named) can also update files. These permissions allow a user with administrator privileges (such as the first account you created on your computer) to update system files but prevent standard users from updating files, reducing the risk of malware infecting your computer.

CHAPTER 9

Figure 9-7 shows typical permissions for a user folder. A user can access his or her own files, as can the SYSTEM account and members of the Administrators group. No other users are allowed to access the files, however. Because the Everyone and Users groups are not listed, members of those groups can't view or edit files in this folder.

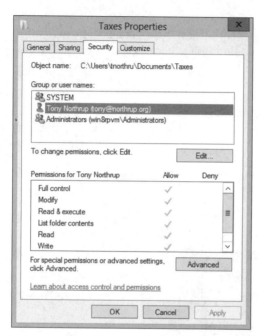

Figure 9-7 This Security tab shows the author has Full Control permissions for his Taxes folder.

If you want to share a folder or files with another user on the same computer, simply drag them to a public folder. Public folders are located within C:\Users\Public. Other users on the same computer will be able to access files in the same folder.

Inside OUT

Booting from a live CD

A live CD is a CD or flash drive containing an operating system that doesn't need to be installed on a computer. Simply insert the CD or connect the flash drive, start your computer, and the operating system on the live CD will start, allowing you to perform basic tasks such as browsing the web, opening files, and recovering corrupted files.

You should always keep a live CD ready because they're extremely useful for recovering a failed Windows installation and saving corrupted files. There are dozens of different live CDs available, but my favorite is Puppy Linux, available from *PuppyLinux.org*.

Live CDs are usually distributed as ISO files. It's surprisingly hard just to find the ISO file to download on the Puppy Linux website, so you might have better luck searching the Internet for the phrase "Puppy Linux ISO." After downloading the ISO file, insert a blank CD into your computer, right-click the ISO file in File Explorer on the desktop, and then click Burn Disk Image. To create a bootable USB flash drive, download the free UNetbootin tool from *http://sourceforge.net/projects/unetbootin/*, and use it to copy the ISO file to a flash drive.

After burning the CD, restart your computer to load the live CD. If the computer doesn't automatically start from the CD, change the startup sequence in your computer's BIOS settings to start from a CD first.

Once Puppy Linux loads, you can browse your files by clicking the hard disk icons in the lower-left corner, as shown in Figure 9-8. This is useful when Windows won't start, but it also has a more nefarious purpose: bypassing permissions. The permissions discussed in this section apply only when Windows 8.1 is running. If you load a different operating system, that operating system will completely ignore those permissions.

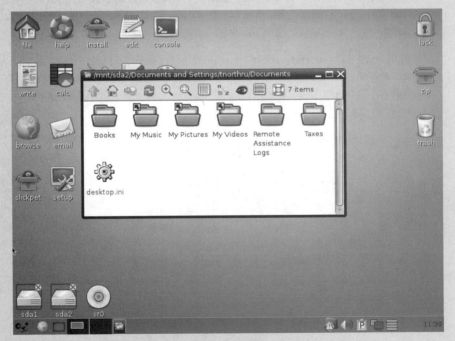

Figure 9-8 Using the Puppy Linux live CD enables you to access your files.

For security that can't be ignored, use encryption, as described in the next section.

CHAPTER 9

Permissions are useful for protecting your privacy because other users who log on to your computer by using their own account won't be able to accidentally access your files. However, you shouldn't rely on permissions for security purposes. Permissions can be bypassed simply by starting a computer from an operating system other than Windows.

▶ **Protecting your files** Watch the video at *http://aka.ms/WinIO/protect*.

Using encryption

Encryption changes how Windows stores your files but not how you access them. Encryption is a process that replaces your files with seemingly random data. With the right security key, however, you can decrypt the files and access their contents.

Encryption complements permissions perfectly. Whereas permissions can be bypassed by starting your PC from a different operating system, encrypted files are completely unreadable to other operating systems.

Windows 8.1 provides file encryption using a feature called Encrypting File System (EFS). EFS encrypts each user's files with a unique key. When you log on, all your files are automatically decrypted when you access them, so there are no additional steps for you to take. Other users can decrypt your files only if you specifically share the files with them.

To encrypt a file or folder, right-click it in File Explorer and then click Properties. On the General tab of the Properties dialog box, click the Advanced button. As shown in Figure 9-9, select Encrypt Contents To Secure Data. Click OK twice, and you'll be given the option to encrypt subfolders and files.

Figure 9-9 Encrypt files to protect them from offline access.

The first time you encrypt something, Windows prompts you to back up your recovery key, as shown in Figure 9-10. While you will probably never need to directly access your key, backing up your key is really important, because if your key gets corrupted for some reason, you won't be able to access your encrypted files.

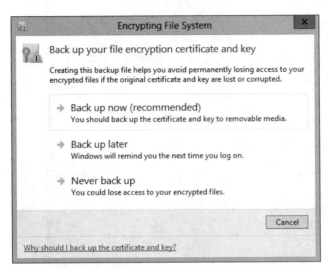

Figure 9-10 Back up your key or risk losing access to your encrypted files.

Windows stores your key in a certificate, so to back up your key, Windows uses the Certificate Export Wizard. The wizard is used for other types of certificates as well, so it has many options you won't use. Simply accept the default settings on the Export File Format page and provide a password on the Security page.

If you miss the notification to back up your key, you can back up your key at any time by using the Encrypting File System tool. Search Settings for **encrypt**, and then select Manage File Encryption Certificates. On the Select Or Create A File Encryption Certificate page, accept the default settings. On the Back Up The Certificate And Key Page (shown in Figure 9-11), provide a password and select a backup location. Don't select any files on the Update Your Previously Encrypted Files page.

You should back up your encryption key somewhere other than your computer: use SkyDrive, a USB flash drive, a writable CD or DVD, or a different computer.

CHAPTER 9

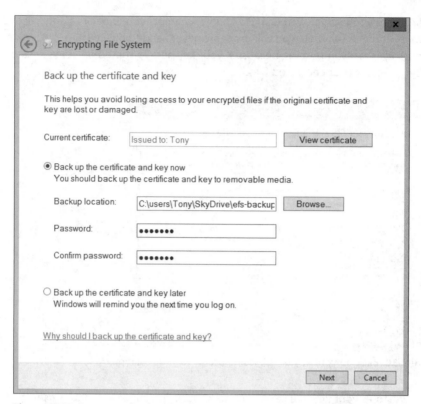

Figure 9-11 Store your backup key somewhere other than your PC.

If you ever need to recover your EFS-protected files (for example, if you connect your drive to a different computer), follow these steps:

1. At the Start screen, type **certmgr.msc**. Select Certmgr.

2. Select the Personal folder.

3. On the Action menu, click All Tasks, and then click Import.

   The Certificate Import wizard appears.

4. Click Next.

5. On the File To Import page, click Browse. In the lower-right corner, click the file types drop-down list and select Personal Information Exchange. Now, select your EFS certificate backup. Click Open, and then click Next.

6. On the Private Key Protection page, type the password and select the Mark This Key As Exportable check box. Do not enable strong private key protection. Click Next.

7. On the Certificate Store page, click Next.

8. Click Finish.

Now, you should be able to open the EFS encrypted files.

Advanced searching

The easiest way to search files is to use the Search charm. However, File Explorer offers more advanced file search capabilities.

First, open File Explorer and select a folder that you want to search. Searching automatically searches all subfolders. If you're not sure which folder your file might be in, simply select Libraries in the left pane to search all folders where users typically store files.

With the folder selected, simply type a search term in the search box in the upper-right corner. By default, File Explorer returns results that have a matching file name, matching metadata (such as tags on picture files), or matching file contents (such as a word within a text file). Figure 9-12 shows how to search all user libraries for files matching the term *Ireland*.

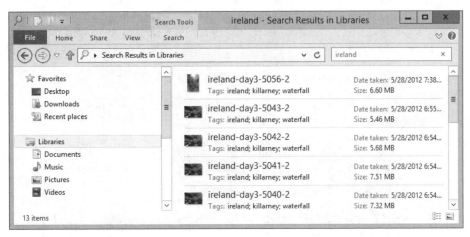

Figure 9-12 Select Libraries and use the search box to search all your libraries for any text you specify.

Searching with File Explorer works very similarly to the Search charm. However, File Explorer uses a very different technique for finding files.

You can also use either File Explorer or the Search charm to find files by file name. If you don't know the exact name of a file, use the asterisk (*) wildcard. An asterisk replaces any number of characters in the file name. For example, searching for **Book*** returns all files with a name that starts with Book, including Book1.rtf, BookingTickets.docx, and BookPages.jpg. Searching by using the term ***.jpg** returns all files with a .jpg extension, including File1.jpg, Picture.jpg,

and MyCat.jpg, as shown in Figure 9-13. You can use multiple wildcards in a single search, so
*ope*ge*.jpg would return .jpg files with Copenhagen in their name (and perhaps other files).
Basically, if you know part of the file name, replace any part you don't know with an asterisk
and then search.

Figure 9-13 Use wildcards to find files by file name.

If you don't know the name of a file, but you know you worked on it recently, you can use File
Explorer to sort by when files were last updated (you can't do this using the Search charm).
Follow these steps:

1. Open the desktop, and then open File Explorer.

2. Select a folder to search. If you don't know which folder the file might be in, select
    Computer to search everything.

3. In the search box (in the upper-right corner), type your search term, such as part of the
    file name. If you don't know anything about the file, type an asterisk (*).

    File Explorer displays every file and folder on your computer.

4. On the View tab, select Details. This sorts the files in a list form.

5. Click the Date Modified column heading to sort the files from newest to oldest. If the
    arrow at the top of the column points up, the list is sorted from oldest to newest. Click
    the column heading again so that the arrow points down.

6. If you think your file might be hidden (for example, if you're attempting to find a
    temporary file or an automatic backup copy of a file saved by a Microsoft Office app),
    select the View tab and then select the Hidden Items check box.

You can use the same technique to find recently created files. Right-click any column heading
in Details view and then select the Date Created column. Then, click that column to sort by it.

Date Created is the time the file was first written, whereas Date Modified is the time the file was most recently updated.

By right-clicking a column and then clicking More, you can choose from a wide variety of useful details about files, including photo metadata (such as the shutter speed or aperture setting), music metadata (such as the artist and album), and Date Accessed (the last time a file was used).

If you know when you last updated the file, you can search by Date Modified. First, open a folder or perform a search. Select the Search tab, click Date Modified, and select a date range, such as Today, Yesterday, This Week, or Last Year, as shown in Figure 9-14.

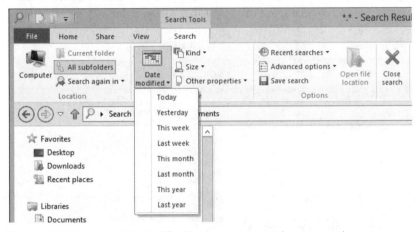

Figure 9-14 Use the Date Modified button to narrow down a search.

To specify a custom date range, switch to Details view and then click the drop-down list on the Date Modified or Date Created column, as shown in Figure 9-15. Drag your pointer across the dates you want to search for.

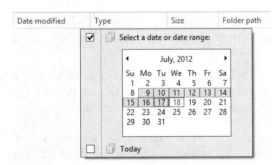

Figure 9-15 Use the drop-down list to the right of the column headings to narrow a search to custom dates.

Freeing up disk space

You never have enough disk space. No matter how large your hard disk, at some point you'll fill it up.

Here are some ways to free up disk space. Before you do anything, though, make a complete backup of your computer as described in Chapter 10. That way, if you accidentally delete something important, you can restore your backup.

- **Run Disk Cleanup**   Search settings for **disk** and choose Free Up Disk Space By Deleting Unnecessary Files. As shown in Figure 9-16, you need to select the types of files to delete (you can typically select all the check boxes) and then click OK. Click Clean Up System Files to free additional space used by Windows Defender and Windows Error Reporting.

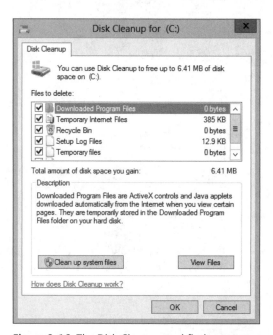

Figure 9-16 The Disk Cleanup tool finds space you can reclaim.

- **Uninstall apps**   Remove apps you no longer need. To remove Windows 8.1 apps, select them from the Start screen and then select Uninstall. To remove desktop apps, use the Search charm to search for **uninstall**, and then click Uninstall A Program.

- **Compress your drive**   In File Explorer, right-click your C drive and then click Properties. Select the Compress This Drive To Save Disk Space check box. You'll probably receive at least one error because a file is in use. Click Ignore All to continue.

- **Reduce your Internet Explorer cache size**   Web browsers spend a great deal of time downloading the same data. For example, the first time you visit your favorite social networking site, Internet Explorer downloads a copy of the site's logo. Although Internet Explorer could download the logo every time you visit the site, Internet Explorer keeps a copy of the logo (and most images on a webpage) cached locally. When you visit the site in the future, Internet Explorer shows you the cached version of the logo instead of downloading the logo again. All these cached files take up disk space. To reduce the disk space Internet Explorer uses (and free it up for other apps), open Internet Explorer from the desktop. Then, click the Tools button (Alt+X) and select Internet Options. On the General tab, click Settings, and then choose how much space you want to dedicate to the cache. 100 megabytes (MB) is usually plenty.

- **Analyze your disk space**   If you have no idea why you're out of disk space, use a disk space analyzer tool, such as the free Scanner tool shown in Figure 9-17, available at *http://www.steffengerlach.de/freeware*. Because Scanner is a desktop app from the Internet, Windows 8.1 will warn you about running it; click More Info and then click Run Anyway. Inner sections of the chart show folders, while outer sections show subfolders. Hover your pointer over a folder to show the name and size in the upper-left corner, click a folder to zoom in, or right-click a folder and then click Open to view the folder in File Explorer.

This is a good way to find large files that you forgot about and no longer need, but don't delete files that you aren't sure about.

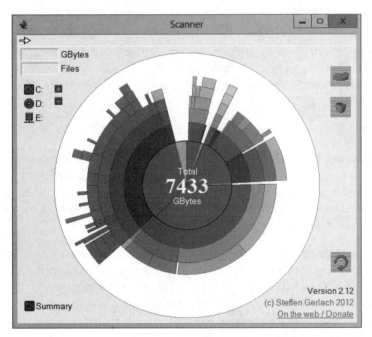

Figure 9-17 Use a disk space analyzer tool to find large files and folders.

CHAPTER 9

Inside OUT

Files you can and can't delete

When you analyze your disk space usage, you're going to find some files that you definitely shouldn't touch because they're used by the system. Some of the largest are:

- C:\Pagefile.sys
- C:\Windows (and everything inside of it)
- C:\Program Files

You might, however, find files you can delete in these folders:

- C:\users\
- C:\temp\

If you aren't sure what a file does, don't delete it. Sometimes apps store important data in cryptic and unlikely locations. If you're willing to take the risk, be sure you have a full backup of your computer, and move the file to the Recycle Bin rather than permanently deleting it. You can easily recover files from the Recycle Bin by opening it from the desktop.

File organization tips

Windows gives you complete flexibility to create any folder structure you want. If you're a naturally organized person, this is really useful. If you're more like me and your files are chaotic and lost, this can lead to many moments of frustration and even terror when you can't find important files.

Here's some advice on keeping your files organized:

- **Save your files**   This sounds obvious, but I've known people who never save their files. For example, if you close Microsoft Word without saving your files, it will automatically reopen them for you. Word is storing your files in a temporary location, though, and if you ever need to find those files, it's going to be difficult. Every time you create a new file, save it somewhere you can find it later.

- **Create folders for every project**   For example, if you're creating a presentation for work, create a folder called Contoso Presentation. Then, save all the files related to that presentation in that folder. Some people create different folders for each different file type, such as Word Documents, Excel Spreadsheets, and PowerPoint Presentations. It's easy to sort files by file type, so this organization doesn't help you at all.

- **Create a logical folder hierarchy**   For example, if you previously created a folder called Contoso Presentation and your boss has asked you to create a contract and an invoice for Contoso, create a top-level folder named Contoso. Within the Contoso folder, create subfolders named Presentation, Contract, and Invoice. It takes a few seconds the first time, but you'll save yourself time in the long run.

- **Be consistent**   If you have many different projects, use the same naming strategy for all of them. For example, if you create a new folder for your taxes every year, name them Taxes 2012, Taxes 2013, and Taxes 2014. Don't name them Taxes 2012, 2013 Taxes, and I HATE TAXES 2014. You'll have a hard time finding them later.

- **Use favorites**   File Explorer shows a list of favorite folders in the upper-left corner. By default, your Desktop, Downloads, and Recent Places folders are your only favorites. If you often open a folder from File Explorer, just drag it to the favorites list. Later, you can open that same folder by clicking the Favorites link.

CHAPTER 9

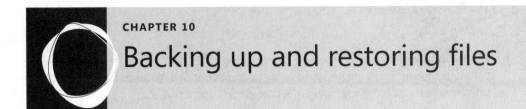

Backing up and restoring files

Backup concepts. 233

Connecting a backup disk. 235

Backing up and recovering files. 239

Backing up and recovering apps and settings. 243

Using cloud services 244

Online backup services 246

Backup concepts. 233

At some point, you're going to lose files that are really important to you. It happens to everyone, no matter what type of computer you buy. It could happen today, or 10 years from now, but it will eventually happen. Storage never lasts forever.

Therefore, if you store files on your PC that you don't want to lose, you need to keep a second copy of them somewhere safe. If you're not ready to lose your family photos and videos, your accounting records, or that book you're writing, you need to immediately create a backup plan and begin following it.

There's no single backup solution that meets everyone's needs, however. To teach you what you need to know to keep your files safe under any circumstances, this chapter describes the basic concepts of disaster recovery, lists the different types of backup technologies, and shows you how to implement specific solutions, including using the File History feature of Windows 8.1.

Backup concepts

First, let's discuss the most common data loss scenarios. In rough order of frequency, they are:

- **Accidentally deleting a file**   By default, deleted files are stored in the Recycle Bin, giving you a chance to recover them. However, accidentally deleting files is still the most common way users lose files.

- **Accidentally messing up a file**   One time, my cat stepped on my keyboard while I was writing a chapter. He somehow selected the entire chapter (Ctrl+A), typed over the text, and then closed the document (Ctrl+W), saving it as he did. I had to restore the file from my most recent backup, causing me to lose a full day's work. I was lucky because I immediately knew the file was damaged. If you don't notice for a few days or weeks, the uncorrupted version might no longer be available.

- **File corruption**   Cats aren't the only source of file corruption. Failing hardware, fluctuating power, and odd magnetic fields can corrupt your files, requiring you to restore them from a backup created before the corruption occurred.

- **Failed disk**   Hard disks can fail either partially or entirely. If a hard disk partially fails, you can recover some of your data by using special data recovery tools (some of which I describe in the last section of this chapter). If a hard disk fails completely, your data is typically gone. You might be able to send the disk to a data recovery service specializing in PC forensics, but they can charge thousands of dollars.

- **Theft or loss**   Any PC can be stolen. For example, someone might break into your house to steal your desktop, or you might leave a PC behind while going through security at the airport. Backups only help in this scenario if the backup isn't stored on your PC.

- **Natural disaster**   Fires, earthquakes, flooding, hurricanes, and many other events can cause catastrophic damage. Your PC might be lost, but your data doesn't need to be if you back it up properly.

Inside OUT
Improving system stability

One of the best things you can do to improve system stability is to use an online uninterruptable power supply (UPS). UPSs are designed to provide backup power to your PC in the event of a power failure. If you use one of the more expensive online varieties, you'll also benefit from power conditioning. This improved stability can reduce the occurrence of failed hardware (including hard disks) and corrupted files.

At a high level, you can use several different backup techniques:

- **Same disk backup**   Backing up files to the same disk seems like an awful idea, but it does protect you against the most common data loss scenarios: accidentally deleted files and messed up files. Windows provides same disk backup automatically using two different technologies: the Recycle Bin and System Restore. Therefore, even if you have never configured a backup, you might be able to restore a file from the same disk.

- **Different disk backup**   Backing up files to another disk connected to your PC protects against the failure of your primary disk. It also requires you to buy and connect a separate disk and configure backups.

- **Off-site backup**   Storing backups in a location other than your PC protects you in the event of theft or natural disaster. This can be done easily using online backups (described later in this chapter), although you need to pay for the service. You can also back up to an external disk and take the disk to a different location, but backup techniques that require you to do something on a regular basis tend not to work well over a long period of time.

- **Redundant array of independent disks (RAID)**   RAID protects data by keeping multiple copies of files on separate disks. RAID works automatically and continuously, and if a disk fails, it can allow you to keep using your PC. However, it's not sufficient as a backup solution because it doesn't protect you from accidentally deleting files, messed up files, corrupted files, theft, or natural disaster. Windows 8.1 supports software RAID 1, commonly known as mirroring. However, most people use hardware RAID.

Table 10-1 shows which backup techniques protect against each common data loss scenario.

Table 10-1 Data loss scenarios and backup techniques

Data loss scenario	Same disk backup	Different disk backup	Off-site backup	RAID
Deleted file	X	X	X	
Messed-up file	X	X	X	
Corrupted file	X	X	X	
Failed disk		X	X	X
Theft			X	
Natural disaster			X	

TROUBLESHOOTING

How do I recover app-specific backups?

Many apps, including Microsoft Word, Apple iTunes, and Adobe Lightroom, automatically create backup copies of important files. While the apps automatically generate backup files, they don't always automatically restore them. If you find that an app can't open its catalog or a specific file, search the Internet for your error message. You just might find a response that shows you where the backup file is hidden.

Connecting a backup disk

Any hard disk can work as a local backup disk, including external and internal disks. However, external disks are the most common because they are easy to connect and configure. If you connect an external disk, configuring backup is as easy as selecting Configure This Drive For Backup when the notification appears, as shown in Figure 10-1.

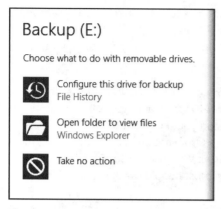

Figure 10-1 Windows 8.1 prompts you to use an external drive for backup.

Inside OUT

Connecting an internal disk

If you have a desktop PC with some additional space and an extra connection for a disk, you can add a disk inside your computer. Internal disks tend to be less expensive, faster, and more efficient than external disks. Internal disks also reduce the amount of clutter on your desk.

Before you buy an internal disk for backups, open your case and verify that you have an extra SATA (Serial AT Attachment) connection and a power connection for your new disk. Some desktop PCs come with an extra SATA cable and a power connector, so all you need to do is physically install the disk in your desktop, secure it to the case with screws, and connect the cables.

If your PC does not have an extra SATA cable, it still might have an available SATA slot on the motherboard. Examine your motherboard and find the existing SATA cable connected to your disk and trace it back to the motherboard. Typically, motherboards have several SATA slots grouped together, as shown in Figure 10-2. An extra SATA cable costs only a few dollars.

If your PC does not have an extra power cable, you can purchase a SATA power Y splitter, as shown in Figure 10-3, for about $5. Y splitters have one male connection and two female connections. Unplug the power from one of your existing disks, connect the male end of the Y splitter to the existing power cable, and then connect the two female connections to your existing disk and your new disk.

CHAPTER 10

Figure 10-2 This motherboard has one occupied and three available SATA slots.

Figure 10-3 Use a SATA power Y splitter if you need an extra power cable.

If Windows does not start correctly, you might have to access your PC's BIOS and change the boot settings to start from your Windows disk. Once you start Windows, launch the Computer Management console and select Storage\Disk Management. Windows should automatically prompt you to initialize the disk, as shown in Figure 10-4.

CHAPTER 10

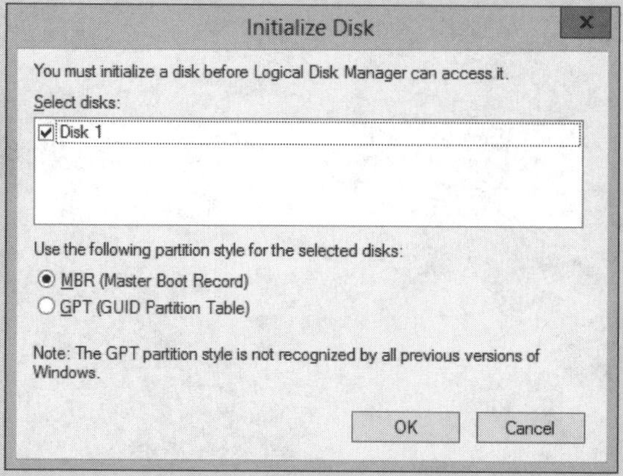

Initialize Disk

You must initialize a disk before Logical Disk Manager can access it.

Select disks:

☑ Disk 1

Use the following partition style for the selected disks:

◉ MBR (Master Boot Record)
○ GPT (GUID Partition Table)

Note: The GPT partition style is not recognized by all previous versions of Windows.

[OK]   [Cancel]

Figure 10-4 New disks must be initialized before you can use them.

Once the disk is initialized, you then have to partition and format the disk. Right-click Unallocated Disk 1 in Disk Management and then click New Simple Volume. The Master Boot Record (MBR) partition style is a good choice for drives 2 TB and smaller, but choose GUID Partition Table (GPT) for larger drives. For detailed information, read "Windows and GPT FAQ" at *http://msdn.microsoft.com/en-us/library/windows/hardware/gg463525.aspx*.

Be sure to assign a meaningful volume name, such as Backup, because this will make it easier for you to distinguish the backup volume from your system disk. Now you can access the disk from File Explorer and File History. For more information, refer to Chapter 12, "Managing storage."

When buying a disk for backups, buy the largest capacity disk you can afford. Naturally, it needs to be at least as large as the files you want to back up. However, it's good practice to have a backup disk that's bigger than your system disk. Having extra space allows Windows to keep multiple versions of your files, allowing you to restore an older version of a file in the event it is corrupted.

While disk performance is extremely important for your system disk, performance isn't an important factor for backup disks. Slower disks tend to be less expensive to purchase, and because they typically use less power, they are less expensive to own. Slower disks also tend to be more reliable.

If you create important files when you travel (for example, if you move pictures from your camera to your PC), you should plan to bring an external backup disk with you. For travel, look for a backup disk that is small, lightweight, and does not require an extra power supply. If your backup disk does require an external power supply, you might also need to bring a power strip because many hotel rooms don't have enough power outlets. If you're travelling internationally, you might also need a power adapter.

Backing up and recovering files

Windows 8.1 includes the File History feature, which allows you to back up and restore files to an internal disk, an external disk, or to another PC across your home network. File History is the right choice for local file backups for PCs at a desk where you can easily connect an extra disk. File History is also the right choice for backing up files from a mobile PC across your local network to a desktop PC with backup space.

File History is not a complete backup solution, however, because it does not perform off-site backups and does not back up desktop apps and settings. Later sections in this chapter discuss backup solutions for those needs.

The sections that follow tell you more about how and why to use File History.

TROUBLESHOOTING

My backups aren't working

If your backups aren't working, you might be able to get some useful information from the backup logs about why the failure is happening. To view the backup logs, launch the Computer Management console from the WinX menu by pressing Windows+X or right-clicking the lower-left corner. Then, browse to System Tools\Event Viewer\ Applications and Services Logs\Microsoft\Windows\FileHistory-Engine\File History Backup Log.

▶ **Backing up and restoring files** Watch the video at *http://aka.ms/WinIO/backuprestore*.

Backing up files

To use File History, navigate to PC Settings, Update & Recovery, File History. Figure 10-5 shows the File History settings page.

CHAPTER 10

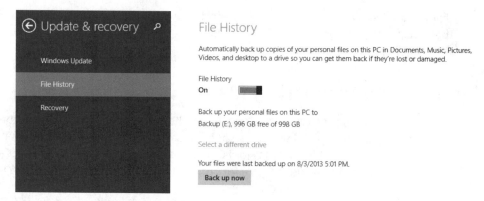

Figure 10-5 Use File History to create a local backup of your files.

In most cases, all you need to do is turn on File History, and follow the prompts that appear. If File History doesn't select the right disk for backups, or if you want to back up to a shared folder on the network (a great idea if you have multiple PCs), click Select A Different Drive.

The default settings are good for most people. If you don't want to back up specific folders (for example, music files that you could easily download again), search from the Start screen for **file history** and select the Control Panel tool. Then, click Exclude Folders and select those folders.

Click Advanced Settings in the File History Control Panel tool to fine-tune your backup configuration, as shown in Figure 10-6. Set Save Copies Of Files to the maximum amount of work you're willing to lose. By default, this is set to one hour, and that means that you might lose a full hour of saved work. If that's not okay with you, change the setting to a shorter time period, but this might have some small impact on your PC's performance. Additionally, saving files more frequently will increase the size of your backups because File History will keep every separate version of your file by default.

Change the Keep Saved Versions list setting to reduce the number of copies of a single file that File History retains. Keeping multiple versions of a single file allows you to go back in time and restore an earlier version of a file, which is really important for those of us who make mistakes and then save them. While keeping saved versions forever sounds nice, the Until Space Is Needed option is generally more useful because it allows backups to keep working even after you fill up your backup disk. Click Clean Up Versions to manually delete old versions of files.

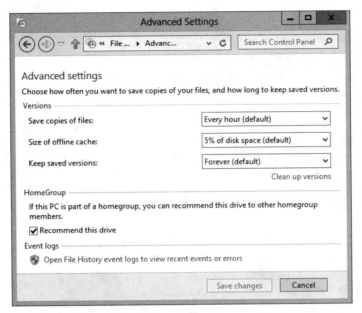

Figure 10-6 The advanced settings let you control backup frequency and the number of saved versions.

If you have created a homegroup on your network, select the Recommend This Drive option to allow other PCs to back up to the same drive. This is a great idea because it allows you to easily back up every PC on your network to a single disk, saving you the trouble of connecting backup disks to each PC. Enabling this feature is especially important for tablet PCs because they tend to be left in different rooms and are rarely connected to an external disk. For more information about homegroups, refer to Chapter 21, "Setting up a home or small office network."

Restoring files

You can restore files any time you lose a file or need to return to an earlier version. If you need to restore files to a different PC, connect your backup disk to that PC, and then select the disk in File History.

To restore files, from the Start screen, search for **restore files**, and then select Restore Your Files With File History. Figure 10-7 shows the window that appears.

CHAPTER 10

Figure 10-7 Restore files that are lost or damaged.

From this window, simply browse to the file you want to restore, select it, and then click the big button at the bottom of the window to restore the file to its original location. If you're recovering an older version of an existing file and don't want to overwrite the newer file, rename the newer file first. This is useful if, for example, you're writing a book and need to recover a paragraph that you deleted a week earlier without losing the work you've added since. (I might be speaking from personal experience.) You can also right-click a file and then click Restore To and select a different location.

Windows 7 allowed you to restore files directly from Windows Explorer by right-clicking the file and then clicking Restore Previous Versions. In case you're looking for that feature, Windows 8.1 doesn't have it.

Inside OUT

Testing your backups

Put a reminder in your calendar to test a file restore the first day of every month. I've seen diligent users start the process of creating backups, only to discover when they go to restore a file that the backups weren't working properly. Backup problems do happen, and if you don't test them, you won't discover the problem until it's too late.

Backing up and recovering apps and settings

Files are your most important assets, but they're not everything that's unique about your PC. You also have personalized settings and apps installed, and backing up your files alone won't let you recover apps and settings.

If you're doing everything the Windows 8.1 way, File History is sufficient for local backups (but you still need an off-site backup). When I say "the Windows 8.1 way," I mean:

- **Using only Windows 8.1 apps**   You don't need to worry about backing up Windows 8.1 apps. If their files get corrupted, you can just download them again from the Store.

- **Signing in with a Microsoft account**   If you sign in with a Microsoft account, as opposed to a local account, Microsoft automatically backs up your settings.

If your PC bursts into flames and you're doing everything the Windows 8.1 way, you simply buy a new PC, sign in with your Microsoft account, and then restore your files with File History. If your hard disk melts, you just replace the disk, reinstall Windows, sign in with your Microsoft account, and then restore your files.

Many Windows 8.1 users will have desktop apps, however, and File History doesn't back up desktop apps or their settings. In the event of a disk failure, you could simply reinstall your apps and reconfigure them. That can be more difficult than it sounds, however, because settings are often complex (for example, configuring Photoshop plug-ins), and you'd better have records of the product keys you need for every desktop app, or you're going to need to purchase another copy or contact the software developer (which might not be an option).

Windows 7 and Windows 8 included system image backups, which created an exact copy of your entire disk. This capability allowed you to quickly restore your PC, including all apps, but Windows 8.1 has removed it. If you want to be able to restore your desktop apps without reinstalling and reconfiguring them, you can use free third-party backup software, such as Macrium Reflect Free, available at *http://www.macrium.com/reflectfree.aspx*.

TROUBLESHOOTING

How do I fix Windows when it won't start?

If Windows won't start, your disk might have failed. There might be many other causes for the same problem, too. A portion of your motherboard might have failed, a cable might have come loose, your BIOS settings might have changed, or an important section of the disk might be corrupted while the rest of the data remains intact. Actually, many different things might have happened. For detailed troubleshooting information, refer to the book, *Troubleshoot and Optimize Windows 8 Inside Out* (Microsoft Press, 2012).

CHAPTER 10

Inside OUT

Configure Windows to always show startup options

If you're an old-school Windows user, you like to be able to start in Safe Mode or to enable debugging options at startup, and you're using a keyboard, run this command at an administrator command prompt (which you can launch from the WinX menu, as described in Chapter 5, "Personalizing Windows 8.1").

```
Bcdedit /set {bootmgr} displaybootmenu yes
```

Once you run that command, Windows displays a start menu for 30 seconds before starting. Press Enter to start Windows sooner, or press F8 to display the Startup Settings page, as shown in Figure 10-8. To start the recovery environment, press F10 from that page, and then press F1.

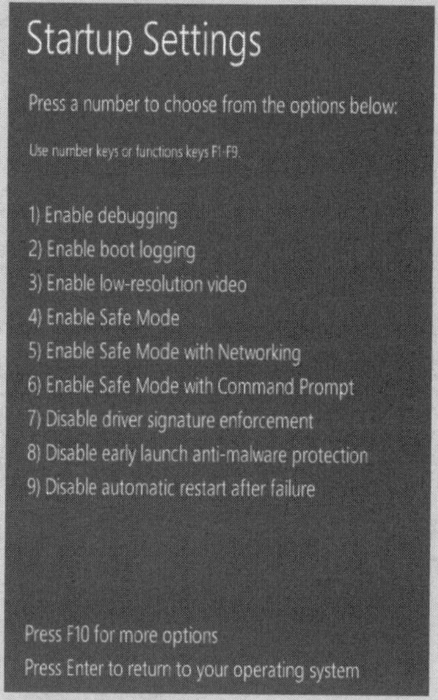

Startup Settings

Press a number to choose from the options below:

Use number keys or functions keys F1-F9.

1) Enable debugging
2) Enable boot logging
3) Enable low-resolution video
4) Enable Safe Mode
5) Enable Safe Mode with Networking
6) Enable Safe Mode with Command Prompt
7) Disable driver signature enforcement
8) Disable early launch anti-malware protection
9) Disable automatic restart after failure

Press F10 for more options
Press Enter to return to your operating system

Figure 10-8 Configure Windows to show startup options to launch the Startup Settings page.

Using cloud services

Cloud services can store files, settings, and even apps on servers on the Internet. Exactly what's stored on the Internet depends on the cloud service. Cloud services are great for data recovery because they're professionally managed by experts who know how to make storage reliable.

Services vary, but typically they're very reliable and provide automatic off-site backups without you having to configure anything.

Basically, with cloud services, your files are stored somewhere on the Internet and a professional makes sure they're always available. So, you don't even need to think about backing up your files.

The most common form of cloud services are online email and messaging services. For example, Hotmail, Gmail, and Facebook all automatically store your email and keep it backed up. If you use one of these services instead of downloading your mail to your PC, you (usually) don't need to worry about backing it up. As an added benefit, you can also access it from many different PCs. Unless you need to store a massive amount of email, most users can use these services completely free.

There are a large number of services that store files in the cloud, including Microsoft SkyDrive, Dropbox, Apple iCloud, and Google Drive. These services all provide a small amount of storage for free. For example, SkyDrive currently allows users to store 7 gigabytes (GB) of files for free.

Some apps are available as cloud services, too. Microsoft Office 365 and Google Docs are two common cloud services that automatically store your documents online and allow you to run word-processing, spreadsheet, presentation, and other services from a web browser, even if you don't have the apps installed on a PC. Google Docs is free for most personal users, and the Office 365 small business plan is currently $6 per month.

Cloud services have a couple of drawbacks, though. Free services allow you to store only a few GB of data. If you just have a few documents and pictures, that's fine, but if you have more, cloud services can be expensive. I personally have about 3 terabytes (TB) of documents, photos, and videos that I've created over the years and wouldn't want to ever lose. Right now, Microsoft SkyDrive has the best price for large amounts of online storage: 100 GB for $50/year. For me, with my 3 TB of files, however, that adds up to $1,500/year. A 3-TB hard disk costs only about $140 dollars, so it's far more cost-effective for me to store my files locally.

If you store your data only on a cloud service, you're still accepting some risk of data loss. Cloud services always provide some form of backup, but how much do you trust your cloud service? Historically, data loss has been rare, but even professionals make mistakes. If your data is really important, you should still store a copy of your most important files on your local PC or in a different cloud service.

Finally, cloud services require you to use your Internet connection. Therefore, accessing files is slower than if they were stored on your local PC. For small files, this won't matter much, but it can become a problem if you need to back up a large number of pictures or many video files. Depending on the size of your files and your upstream bandwidth (the speed at which you can upload files to the Internet), you might need months to complete a full backup. Also, if your Internet connection is offline, you won't be able to access any files that are stored only in the cloud.

CHAPTER 10

Online backup services

Online backup services are slightly different from cloud services. With an online backup service, you store your files on your PC's disk, just like you always have. The online backup service makes a copy and stores it online, and you typically access that copy only if you lose your original file. With a cloud service, the primary copy of your file is stored by the cloud service, and you don't need to store local copies. For backing up large numbers of files, online backup services tend to be less expensive than cloud services.

If you have less than about 50 GB of data, an online backup service might be a perfect backup solution, completely replacing the need for File History. Online backup services use custom software to copy your personal files from your PC to servers on the Internet. If you ever lose a file or your hard disk fails, you can recover your files by downloading them from the Internet.

Online backup services have several advantages:

- They provide automatic off-site backups, protecting your files from theft or natural disaster without requiring you to remember to move a hard disk to a different location.

- You can access your files from different locations, allowing you to download files from your home PC when you travel, even if your home PC is turned off.

- You don't have to buy or connect any extra hardware.

- They work from anywhere with an Internet connection, which is especially important for mobile PCs.

They also have a few disadvantages:

- They use your Internet connection, so you cannot back up or restore files while you're offline.

- Backing up and restoring more than 100 GB of data can be expensive and, depending on the speed of your Internet connection, time-consuming.

I've used both Carbonite and MozyHome, but an Internet search for "online backup services" will return many different services.

What if disaster strikes and you don't have a backup?

It's happened to all of us: our disk fails and we discover we don't have a backup, either because we never set it up or because our backup didn't work. It seems dire: Windows won't start, and even loading the Windows recovery tools from a CD or flash drive won't fix the problem. All hope is not yet lost, though.

You can use another PC to download live CDs containing free Linux and open-source file recovery tools. Then, you can copy the files to a CD or flash drive, boot your PC from that media, and use the tools to attempt to repair your disk or recover your files. These tools can't fix every problem, but in my personal experience, I've always been able to recover most of the files from a failed disk.

Compared to Windows 8.1, these tools have rather unfriendly user interfaces. However, if you're willing to spend some time reading the documentation on their websites, you just might be able to recover your precious files. Some of the more popular live CDs for data recovery include:

- Ubuntu Rescue Remix (*http://ubuntu-rescue-remix.org/*)

- Ultimate Boot CD (*http://www.ultimatebootcd.com/*)

- SystemRescueCD (*http://www.sysresccd.org/SystemRescueCd_Homepage*)

- Trinity Rescue Kit (*http://trinityhome.org/Home/index.php?content=TRINITY_RESCUE_ KIT___CPR_FOR_YOUR_COMPUTER&front_id=12&lang=en&locale=en*)

Booting from the live CD won't automatically fix your disk or find your files. Once you get the live CD booted, you need to use specific tools to fix your disk or recover your files. Two of the more useful tools include:

- **TestDisk**   A data recovery tool that attempts to recover lost partitions and allows you to start from disks that should be bootable but have become corrupted.

- **PhotoRec**   A tool that scans a hard disk and attempts to recover common file types, including images, audio files, Office documents, and more.

If you can't tell, I've learned the hard way how to recover data from a failed drive. It's not fun, because the entire time I've felt rather panicked that I was going to lose my files. Please, heed my warning: always have a current and off-site backup of all your important data so you never have to experience that heart-stopping moment when your files seem to disappear.

CHAPTER 10

Managing Windows search

App search concepts 249   Managing file indexing 251

Managing search suggestions 250

Windows 8.1 includes several different types of search:

- **Searching everywhere**   Type at the Start screen to display a list of apps with names that match what you type, as well as settings, files, and results from the web. Typing at the Start screen is the easiest way to find anything. On touch devices, open the Start screen and then open the Search charm**.**

- **Searching within apps**   Open the Search charm when an app is open to search within that app. For example, searching within the Music app finds matching songs. This chapter shows you how to control which apps appear in the search list and which appear at the top of the list.

- **Searching settings**   Open the Search charm and select Settings to search all settings, including Control Panel. There's nothing to configure, so it isn't discussed further.

- **Searching files and folders**   Like Windows 7, Windows 8.1 indexes files and folders and allows you to search their properties and contents. This chapter shows you how to move the index, prevent indexing for specific files and folders, or stop indexing entirely.

This chapter covers the underlying concepts of Windows 8.1 search and how to manage it. For information about finding files, refer to Chapter 9, "Organizing and protecting files." For information about finding information within apps, refer to Chapter 2, "Using Windows 8.1 apps."

App search concepts

Windows 7 allowed you to search files, and that functionality has changed very little with Windows 8.1. Windows 7 search allows you to find many different file types, but apps have to provide tools, known as protocol, filter, and property handlers, that tell Windows 7 how to extract searchable text from the file. This works well for many apps, such as Microsoft Word, where the data you are searching is contained in the file either as metadata or as content.

You can still search files in Windows 8.1 using the same technology built into Windows 7—just open the Search charm, select Files, and type your search. Searching from File Explorer works exactly as it did with Windows 7, too.

Inside OUT

Extending Windows 7 search

Technically, Windows 7 search could be extended to index data sources other than files. Not many developers took advantage of the capability, however, and not many users attempted to search for anything but files.

Windows 8.1 also adds the ability to search within apps by using a common interface, allowing searches to be more intelligent and content-aware. The following two sections discuss how to manage this new capability. The section "Managing file indexing" describes how to manage Windows 7–style file indexing.

▶ **Searching with Windows 8.1** Watch the video at *http://aka.ms/WinIO/search*.

Managing search suggestions

Windows 8.1 automatically records your searches and suggests previous searches when you start typing something similar. This can really help speed up data entry, which is particularly important on computers without a keyboard because typing can be more time-consuming.

It's helpful until your neighbor borrows your computer, attempts a search, and sees your search for some weird medical symptom you'd rather keep private. To remove the history of your searches, open PC Settings, Search & Apps, Search, and then, under Clear Search History, click Clear.

Inside OUT

File search suggestions

You can't turn off file search suggestions, which lists files and folders with names that contain letters you're searching for. Basically, if you type *My*, Search will suggest My Pictures and My Documents. Again, that's genuinely helpful until it suggests a Word document with the file name "Why I Hate My Neighbor, Bob.docx."

If you have files or folders that you don't want suggested, disable indexing for those files or folders by following the steps described in "Managing searchable files and folders" later in this chapter.

CHAPTER 11

Managing file indexing

File indexing is the behind-the-scenes process of cataloging every bit of text in a file's contents and properties. Every time you save or update a file, Windows indexes the file to make future searches faster. This feature really hasn't changed much since Windows 7, which is good news—file indexing is mature, and if you want to customize it or you happen to have a problem with it, you can rely on documentation created for Windows 7.

My search is not working correctly

Most search problems can be fixed by deleting the index and allowing Windows to regenerate it. To delete the index, search Settings for Indexing Options. Click the Advanced button to open the Advanced Options dialog box, and then click the Rebuild button. You should also use the Computer Management console and double-check that the Windows Search service is started and set to Automatic (Delayed Start).

This section describes the basics of managing searchable files and shows you how to disable indexing.

Managing searchable files and folders

Windows automatically indexes your personal files that have a format it can understand. For example, it will index the attributes of any pictures and the content within all Microsoft Word documents. When you search files, Windows will return a list of matching files.

If you want to add folders to the search index, add them to one of your libraries: Documents, Pictures, Videos, or Music, as described in Chapter 9. Search automatically indexes folders in your libraries.

What if you have files you don't want to pop up in search results? For example, if you keep your diary or confidential work documents on your computer, you probably don't want them appearing when your daughter is looking for her homework assignment. Unfortunately, disabling indexing for specific files and folders isn't nearly as easy as disabling search for an app.

Inside OUT

Search index storage

Like Windows 7, Windows 8.1 stores the search index at C:\ProgramData\Microsoft\ Search\Data\. The files in there aren't anything you can edit yourself, however. You can move the folder by using the Advanced Options dialog box, which you can access by clicking Advanced in the Indexing Options dialog box.

To disable content indexing for a file or folder, follow these steps:

1. Search Settings for Indexing Options.

   The Indexing Options dialog box appears, as shown in Figure 11-1.

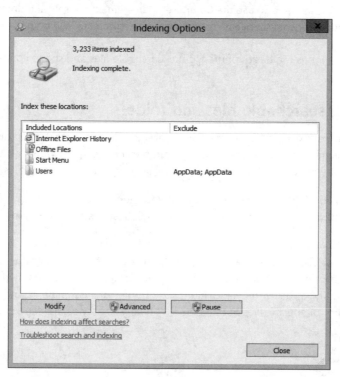

Figure 11-1 Use Indexing Options to configure which folders should be searched.

2. Click Modify.

The Indexed Locations dialog box appears as shown in Figure 11-2.

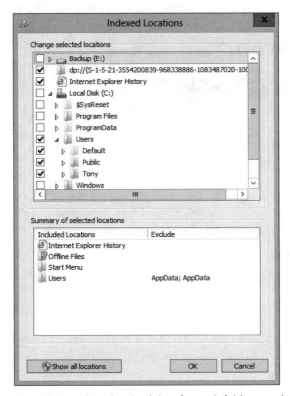

Figure 11-2 Clear the check box for each folder you do not want indexed.

3. If you want to change settings for other users, click Show All Locations.

4. Expand drives and folders to find the folders you want to index. Clear the check box for folders you do not want indexed.

5. Click OK.

You can also allow the file name and properties to be indexed, but not index the contents of files. Do this if you regularly search for file names but never for the contents of a file:

1. Open the desktop and then open File Explorer.

2. Browse to the file or folder you don't want indexed. Right-click it and click Properties.

3. On the General tab, click Advanced.

4. In the Advanced Attributes dialog box (as shown in Figure 11-3), clear the check box for Allow Files In This Folder To Have Contents Indexed In Addition To File Properties.

Figure 11-3 Use the Advanced Attributes dialog box to disable search for a file or folder.

5. Click OK twice.

6. If you're changing the properties for a folder, in the Confirm Attribute Changes dialog box, choose whether to change the properties for the contents of the folder or just the folder itself. If you change the folder properties but not its contents, only new files you add to the folder will be indexed.

Managing the search index

You can adjust a few settings to control which files Windows indexes and where it stores the index. To open the Advanced Options dialog box (shown in Figure 11-4), open the Indexing Options dialog box and then click Advanced.

The most useful option here is Index Encrypted Files, which does exactly what it says. Selecting the Index Encrypted Files option allows encrypted files to appear in your search results. That sounds useful, but it also compromises the security provided by the encryption. Any time a file is indexed, Windows makes a copy of the words within the file, which could make it easier for a very clever attacker to extract some portion of the data contained within it. It also means your encrypted files might pop up as search results. Basically, selecting the option might expose your encrypted files to people logged on to your computer. If you're using encryption just to protect files in the event your computer is stolen, then it's probably safe to select the option. If you're using encryption to prevent other legitimate users of your computer from seeing your files, then you shouldn't select the option.

Figure 11-4 Use the Advanced Options dialog box to delete or move the search index.

The Treat Similar Words With Diacritics As Different Words isn't going to be useful for most users. Basically, it would treat the words *fiancé* and *fiance* differently (note the missing accent over the final *e*). If you're regularly searching for the word *resume* and you're tired of getting results that also include the word *résumé*, go ahead and select this option, but be sure you include diacritics when you search for them.

You can also use this dialog box to move your index to a different location. The default location is typically fine. However, if you have multiple disks, you might want to move the index to a disk with more room. It's not unusual for an index to grow to more than 1 gigabyte (GB), so if your system disk is low on space and you have another disk (a common scenario on a desktop computer with a high-performance solid-state drive (SSD) system disk), move the index to a different disk. Search performance might change, but you probably won't notice the difference.

CHAPTER 11

Indexing other file types

Windows 8.1 needs a filter for each file type that it indexes. Windows 8.1 includes several different filters that allow it to index text, HTML, XML, Microsoft Office documents, RTF files, PDF files, JavaScript files, media file properties, and a handful of other formats.

If you install an app that uses a different document format, that app might install its own filter, allowing you to search for and find documents based on their contents. Or, the app might not install its own filter, in which case, you'll only be able to search for file names and document properties.

If you use files with an unusual file extension but a common format, such as a text file with a .words extension, you can configure search to look for that extension. Open the Indexing Options dialog box, click the Advanced button, and then select the File Types tab in the Advanced Options dialog box (as shown in Figure 11-5). Type your new file extension in the box at the bottom and then click Add. Then, select either Index Properties Only (for everything except plain text files) or Index Properties And File Contents (for text files).

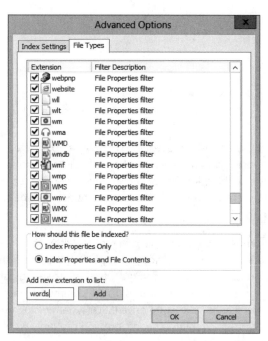

Figure 11-5 Add file extensions to index custom file types.

Inside OUT

Monitoring index performance

Use Task Manager to monitor the resources that the indexer is using. Start Task Manager from the WinX menu. If necessary, click More Details. On the Processes tab, look within the Background Processes group for Microsoft Windows Search Indexer, as shown in Figure 11-6. The CPU utilization should increase only when Windows is indexing new files or when you rebuild the index, and even then, indexing shouldn't interfere with you using the computer. The memory utilization is typically between 15 and 40 MB, or about 1–2 percent of the memory on a computer with 2 GB of RAM.

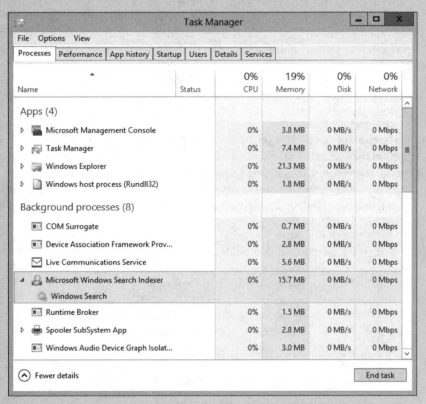

Figure 11-6 Use Task Manager to assess the performance impact of Windows Search.

> If indexing files is your top priority, you have a great many files to index, and you don't want Windows Search to slow down indexing when you're using the computer, run the Local Group Policy Editor (gpedit.msc), select Local Computer Policy\Computer Configuration\Administrative Templates\Windows Components\Search, and enable the Disable Indexer Backoff setting. Then, restart your computer. Indexing will go full-speed no matter what you do on the computer.

Disabling indexing

File indexing is a big job; it requires Windows to read the content of every user document on the disk and index every word within it. That does require quite a bit of processor time and disk input/output (I/O), but it's smart about minimizing the impact on your computer's performance. For example, it does most of its indexing while you're not using your computer.

Nonetheless, indexing does consume some computing resources, and if you like to run only required services, you can stop it temporarily, prevent Windows from indexing while you're on battery power, or disable it completely.

To temporarily stop indexing, open the WinX menu and then select Computer Management. Within the Computer Management console, select the Services And Applications\Services node. Then, right-click Windows Search and click Stop. Choose Start to restart indexing, or just wait until you restart your computer. You can also run the command **net stop wsearch** from a command prompt with administrator privileges.

To prevent indexing while you're on battery power, run the Local Group Policy Editor (gpedit.msc), select Local Computer Policy\Computer Configuration\Administrative Templates\ Windows Components\Search, and enable the Prevent Indexing When Running On Battery Power To Conserve Energy setting. Then, restart your computer.

To permanently disable indexing, open the WinX menu and then select Computer Management. Within the Computer Management console, select the Services And Applications\ Services node. Then, double-click Windows Search to open the Windows Search Properties dialog box, as shown in Figure 11-7. Click the Stop button to stop indexing just for your current session. To stop all future automatic indexing, change the Startup Type to Disabled.

Figure 11-7 Set the Startup Type to Disabled to prevent automatic indexing and potentially reduce your computer's power usage.

Once you stop the service, you can't search for files using the Search charm. Well, you can try, but you won't find any results or even get an error message. You can, however, search using File Explorer on the desktop. It will take much longer to find results, however, because Windows needs to read every file after you initiate the search.

To configure how File Explorer searches non-indexed folders (which is every folder if you disable indexing), select the View tab in File Explorer and click Options. In the Folder Options dialog box, select the Search tab as shown in Figure 11-8. The options are self-explanatory; you can choose to search ZIP files and to search both file name and contents (even though the search would be very slow).

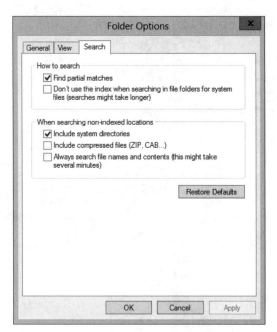

Figure 11-8 Use the Folder Options dialog box to configure desktop file search.

CHAPTER 12

Managing storage

Storage Spaces 261

BitLocker 268

Fixing errors 283

Choosing a new drive 286

Storage is the most important part of your PC. Storage is all the data you hold dear—your documents, pictures, and videos, plus the drives that they're stored on. Most PC users never need to worry about their storage because the drive their PC came with is good enough for them and they aren't worried about data security.

For the rest of us, this chapter shows how to take advantage of Storage Spaces, allowing you to easily and cheaply expand your storage however you see fit. This chapter also discusses BitLocker, which encrypts entire drives and can help to protect you from rootkits, a type of malware that might watch your every move without being detected by tools such as Windows Defender.

Storage Spaces

When I first read about Storage Spaces, my response was "Finally!" Storage Spaces takes whatever random drives you connect to it and combines them to make useful, and optionally redundant, storage.

Here's why that's great:

- You never have to think, "Did I save that on my C drive, my D drive, or my E drive?" All your drives can have a single drive letter.

- You don't have to reorganize your files when you add a new drive; just add the drive to the storage pool and expand the capacity.

- You can buy drives with the best price per terabyte, rather than buying larger capacity drives just to simplify your file management.

- You can get redundancy (allowing a drive to fail without you losing data) without spending extra on a proper RAID (redundant array of independent disks) array.

- You can connect all those old drives you have lying around from outdated PCs and use their storage without needing to manage your files on many different drives.

Storage Spaces concepts

Instead of accessing drives directly, you access Storage Space pools. Pools are a collection of one or more drives of varying sizes. As you do drives, you access pools using a drive letter such as E:\.

One of the features of a pool is resiliency. Resiliency is a form of redundancy, which sounds wasteful: it stores multiple copies of your data on different drives. That does waste space, but if you ever lose a drive, redundancy will enable Storage Spaces to regenerate the data that was on your drive. With redundancy, a lost drive doesn't mean lost data.

Storage in a pool is written to the underlying drives in blocks. By default, blocks are 4 kilobytes (KB) in size (4,096 8-bit bytes), so a 1-terabyte (TB) drive is divided into about 250 million blocks.

When you save a file to a drive without using Storage Spaces, the entire file is written to blocks on a single drive using the FAT file system or the NTFS file system format, which all modern operating systems can access. Therefore, you can take that drive and connect it to a different PC (even if it's running an earlier version of Windows) and that PC can still read the same file.

Storage Spaces completely separates the layout of your files from the physical arrangement of drives in your PC. If you configure three drives in a single pool and then save a file to that pool, blocks from the file might be saved across different drives. They might not. It's entirely up to Storage Spaces to decide how to store files, and you don't have much insight into it.

Storage Spaces also uses a new format that is not supported by earlier versions of Windows. Therefore, you can't move drives that are part of a Storage Spaces pool to a PC running an earlier version of Windows. You also can't access data in a pool if you multiboot to an earlier version of Windows on a single PC.

Inside OUT

Comparing Storage Spaces to RAID

Like Storage Spaces, RAID also divides data from individual files across multiple drives. However, there are some key differences. If you add a drive to a RAID array, the RAID array will integrate the new drive into the array by rewriting all of the existing files across every drive in the array. If you add a drive to a pool, Storage Spaces does not rewrite any of the existing files. It will use the new drive for future data, however.

Another difference is that you can use RAID to protect your system drive. You can't use your system drive as part of a Storage Spaces pool, however.

You can, however, move all the drives that make up a pool to a different PC running Windows 8.1 and access that pool. Windows will detect the drives and configure the pool automatically.

▶ **Using Storage Spaces** Watch the video at *http://aka.ms/WinIO/storage*.

Evaluating Storage Spaces

In practice, the architecture of Storage Spaces means a few things might have to change about how you work with files and drives:

- Read performance might be improved if your PC can communicate with the separate drives faster than with a single drive. For most PCs, however, you won't notice a substantial difference.

- If you use resiliency, write performance might be decreased. Parity (one form of resiliency) requires the PC to perform some mathematical calculations and then write both your data and its parity information, which can be one-third the size of the original data. If you use mirroring (another type of resiliency), your PC has twice as much data to write for every update. In theory, your PC might be able to write to multiple drives simultaneously, but in practice, most home PCs aren't designed for parallel input/output (I/O) to multiple drives, and drive I/O performance is bottlenecked at a much slower pace.

- If you configure multiple drives in a pool, you cannot access the data on the drives individually, because each drive has only part of any given file. Therefore, if you want to move a storage pool to a different PC (which must be running Windows 8.1), you must move every drive in the pool.

- If one drive fails and you have not configured redundancy, all your data is lost. Therefore, if you have a 6-TB storage pool consisting of three 2-TB drives, and one of the drives fails, you lose access to all 6 TB of data. If you had configured those three 2-TB drives as separate drive letters without using Storage Spaces, you would need to restore only the one drive instead of the data from all three.

- The risk of failure increases because the failure of any one drive causes an entire nonredundant storage pool to fail. Consider two scenarios: one 3-TB drive or three 1-TB drives in a storage pool. It might be less expensive to buy three 1-TB drives and configure them in a storage pool, but the odds of any one of those three drives failing are much higher than the odds of the single 3-TB drive failing.

- Drives that are added to a pool must be formatted, which erases all the data from the drive. Therefore, you cannot integrate an existing drive with data into a storage pool. Instead, you need to copy the data to your storage pool (assuming you have enough free space) and then reuse the original drive.

There's one other factor you should consider before you trust your data to Storage Spaces: the technology hasn't yet been proven over a long period of time. People like me, who study storage reliability, have a great respect for well-proven technologies, even if they're not the most cutting-edge. I'm not telling you to avoid Storage Spaces, but if you use it, configure resiliency and have a reliable backup. For more information, refer to Chapter 10, "Backing up and restoring files."

Inside OUT

Drive Mean Time to Failure (MTTF)

According to the study "Disk failures in the real world: What does an MTTF of 1,000,000 hours mean to you?," available at *http://www.cs.toronto.edu/~bianca/papers/fast07.pdf*, the odds of any drive failing in a given year are 2–4 percent. Drives are more likely to fail in the first year, and then again as they get older; drives that are one to seven years old are the least likely to fail.

If you assume that 3 percent of all drives fail, the odds that a single 3-TB drive will fail in a given year is 3 percent. The odds that a storage pool consisting of three drives fails is 9 percent. So, either way, the odds are in your favor in any given year, but if you have a storage pool of three drives for six years, there's about a 54 percent chance that one of the drives will fail. If you've configured resiliency, you shouldn't lose any data, but you should still have a backup of the entire storage pool ready.

Configuring Storage Spaces

To manage Storage Spaces, search Settings for **storage spaces**, and then select Storage Spaces to open the Control Panel tool, as shown in Figure 12-1.

When you click the link to create a new pool, Windows prompts you to select the drives to add to the pool. As shown in Figure 12-2, Windows automatically selects all unformatted drives. Those are drives you wouldn't be able to access anyway, and they definitely don't have any useful data on them (at least not data created by a PC running Windows). If you select a formatted drive, all the data from that drive will be lost forever, so be sure there's nothing you love on it.

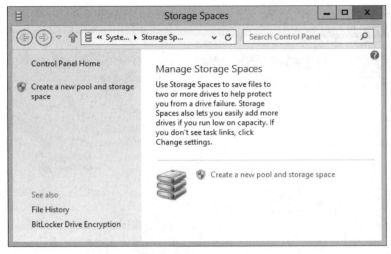

Figure 12-1 You manage Storage Spaces using the Control Panel tool.

Figure 12-2 You can create a pool from multiple drives of different sizes.

After selecting your drives and clicking Create Pool, you'll be prompted to configure your resiliency, as shown in Figure 12-3.

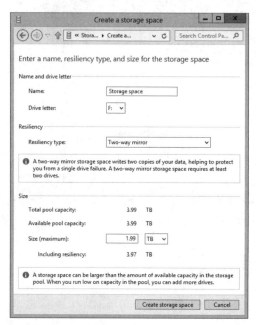

Figure 12-3 Configure resiliency to help protect yourself from the failure of a single drive.

The Size (Maximum) option is set by default to the maximum available capacity for the physical drives you have allocated. You can set it to a larger value, but I have no idea why you'd want to. For example, if you connect 4 TB of physical drives, you can set a 10-TB capacity. Naturally, Windows can't actually save 10 TB of files in that pool, but when you start to run out of physical space (for example, if you have used 3.9 TB of your physical drives), Windows will prompt you to add more physical drives to the pool.

Configuring resiliency

Storage Spaces supports four levels of resiliency, each with its own advantages:

- **Simple (no resiliency)**   Storage Spaces writes one copy of your data, so if a drive fails, you lose all the data in the pool. This requires only one drive and you can access 100 percent of your physical capacity.

- **Two-way mirror**   Storage Spaces writes two copies of your data, allowing you to lose one drive without data loss. This requires at least two drives, and you can access only 50 percent of your physical capacity.

- **Three-way mirror**   Storage Spaces writes three copies of your data, allowing you to lose two drives simultaneously without data loss. This requires at least three drives, and you can access only 33 percent of your physical capacity.

- **Parity**   Storage Spaces uses mathematical algorithms to protect your data more efficiently than by simply creating additional copies of it. Parity requires at least three drives. The portion of the physical capacity that you can access is related to the number of drives you add. To calculate the maximum capacity you can access, take the reciprocal of the number of physical drives, and then subtract that from one. Basically, divide one by the number of drives you have to calculate the capacity used by parity. If you have three drives, you can access up to 66 percent of your physical capacity. If you have four drives, you can access up to 75 percent of your physical capacity.

If you have one drive, you can't use resiliency.

Inside OUT

Resiliency doesn't replace backups

Resiliency isn't a replacement for a backup. Resiliency can protect your data from a failed drive, but it can't protect your data from theft, a fire, or you accidentally deleting a file. For more information about backups, refer to Chapter 10.

If you have two drives, you can choose to create a two-way mirror, which protects your data but limits your capacity to the size of the smaller drive. In other words, a two-way mirror uses at least 50 percent of your space for resiliency.

If you have three or more drives, you can choose from any of the options without any major drawbacks:

- If you have frequent backups and you don't mind the elevated risk of data loss by combining multiple drives, choose Simple.

- If you don't want to lose the data in your pool and you don't mind if your drive is a little slow, choose Parity.

- If you don't want to lose the data in your pool, but performance is really important to you, choose Two-Way Mirror. Mirrors offer no performance penalty when reading data, and the performance penalty for writing data is typically less than other types of resiliency.

- If you really, really don't want to lose the data in your pool and you don't mind losing two-thirds of your storage capacity, choose Three-Way Mirror.

CHAPTER 12

You can't change your resiliency choice after you click Create Storage Space. You would need to delete the Storage Space and then re-create it, which would delete all of your data. So, be really sure that you're going to be happy with your resiliency choice over the long term.

BitLocker

On PCs running Windows 8.1 Pro and Windows 8.1 Enterprise, BitLocker encrypts your entire drive, helping protect your data in the event someone steals your PC and you haven't left your PC logged on. It also prevents your PC from starting if any of the monitored system files have been tampered with. This primarily helps reduce the risk of rootkits, a clever type of malware that installs itself underneath the operating system so it cannot be easily detected.

Other editions of Windows 8.1, including Windows RT 8.1, support device encryption but do not include the BitLocker tools described in this section. Device encryption is turned on by default for new installations of Windows 8.1. If you upgraded from Windows 8, device encryption is not automatically turned on. To turn device encryption on or off, open PC Settings, PC & Devices, and then PC Info.

Inside OUT

What are rootkits?

Rootkits are the scariest type of malware. While all apps (and most malware) run within Windows, rootkits run outside Windows, communicating directly with your computer's hardware. They do many of the same things that other types of malware do, including monitoring your computer and sending your private data across the Internet. However, because rootkits run outside Windows, they can be impossible for Windows to detect and remove.

Not a lot has changed for consumers using BitLocker at home, but there are a few improvements:

- Windows 8.1 now supports offloading drive encryption and decryption to specialized hard drives that have those features. If you happen to have one of these drives, you won't suffer the same performance degradation after enabling BitLocker.

- Windows 8.1 now supports encrypting just the part of your drive with data on it, a feature known as Used Drive Space Only encryption. This means that BitLocker doesn't encrypt all the free space on your drive, which reduces the time the initial encryption requires. This makes first enabling BitLocker quicker (though the interruption is pretty minimal, anyway), and it's the right choice for a brand new PC or hard drive.

Inside OUT
Select Used Disk Space Only encryption for new disks

When you permanently delete a file, that file is still entirely intact on your drive. However, the file seems to be gone because its entry in the file system has been removed. Windows will mark the space the file occupies as available for other apps to use when they save files; however, until another app overwrites that exact location, the file will remain intact.

If you've been using your hard drive, deleted files might still be accessible on your drive. If you use the BitLocker Used Disk Space Only encryption option, BitLocker will not encrypt those previously used parts of the drive, because BitLocker considers them completely unused. Therefore, even with BitLocker enabled, a skilled attacker could access some of your permanently deleted files.

The lesson here is to use Full Volume encryption instead of Used Disk Space Only encryption if you've been using a drive long enough to have deleted files. Full Volume encryption isn't that much more time-consuming to enable, because it encrypts in the background.

Evaluating BitLocker

BitLocker isn't right for everyone, and it might not even be right for most people, because it has a few major drawbacks:

- It slows down your drive performance. Every bit of data read from the drive must be decrypted by your CPU. Likewise, data written to the drive must be encrypted. How much you notice this performance depends on your drive and CPU speed.

- You might lose your data. BitLocker is well proven at this point, but a corrupted key or damaged Trusted Platform Module (TPM) chip will result in your PC being unbootable and your data being inaccessible. To offset this risk, make frequent backups, as described in Chapter 10. You should keep your backups secure, too, because if someone steals your backup, they'd have access to all your files, anyway.

- It makes data recovery much more difficult. If you ever have drive corruption issues, the odds of you recovering files from a BitLocker-encrypted drive are almost zero. After all, BitLocker is specifically designed to prevent that type of data recovery. For more information about data recovery, refer to Chapter 10.

Inside OUT
Understanding TPM chips

The TPM chip securely stores the keys required to decrypt your data, and it gives those keys up only to trusted software. This means that if malware (such as a rootkit) corrupts your system files, the TPM chip won't give up the decryption key. This is a good thing if you're really concerned about the privacy of your data, because if the corrupted version of Windows is able to start, the malware could read your secret files and send them off to anyone on the Internet.

TPM chips are designed to make it really, really difficult for an unauthorized attacker to extract the secret data contained within the chip. Theoretically, it's possible to extract the bits and bytes that make a secret key from any sort of storage device. To minimize this risk, TPM chips are physically secure. TPM chips are designed so that if an attacker attempts to open a chip's casing, the chip will break apart in such a way that the secret keys would be permanently lost.

You can't just buy a TPM upgrade for your PC; the chip must be built into the motherboard when it's new. So, if you want to use BitLocker with a TPM chip, make a point of choosing a PC with TPM built in the next time you upgrade. Because TPM chips are primarily used by businesses, many PCs designed for consumers don't have one (it helps the PC manufacturer keep costs down).

BitLocker is right for some people, though: those who have secrets on their PC that they really want to keep secret. If you're willing to accept a bit slower performance and give up some data recovery options to reduce the risk of someone seeing your secret files, turn on BitLocker.

▶ **Using BitLocker** Watch the video at *http://aka.ms/WinIO/bitlocker*.

Drive types that can be encrypted

You can use BitLocker to encrypt three different types of drives:

- **System drive**   BitLocker's primary purpose is protecting your system drive (your C drive, which has Windows installed on it). When you enable BitLocker for your system drive, the entire system drive is encrypted, including Windows files. If your PC has a TPM chip, this helps protect you from malware that modifies the system, including rootkits. You can use BitLocker on the system drive to require a PIN, password, or USB flash drive for Windows to start.

- **Data drive**   You can also encrypt data drives with BitLocker. Protecting a data drive benefits you only if someone attempts to access the data offline by starting your PC from a different operating system or by stealing your drive and connecting it to a different PC. As an alternative, consider using Encrypting File System (EFS), as described in Chapter 9, "Organizing and protecting files."

- **Removable drive**   If you use BitLocker to protect a removable drive, whoever you give the drive to will be prompted for a password or a smart card when they connect the drive to a PC. This helps protect your data if someone steals your flash drive.

Choosing the startup mode

Of course, encrypting a drive isn't useful if BitLocker simply decrypts the drive for everyone. When you configure BitLocker to protect your system drive, you're given two or three of these choices:

- **Enter A PIN**   You must enter a numeric PIN each time your PC starts. This option is available only when your PC has a TPM.

- **Enter A Password**   You must enter a password (which can contain letters, numbers, and special characters) each time your PC starts. This option is available only when using BitLocker without a TPM.

- **Insert A USB Flash Drive**   Connect a USB flash drive to your PC the way you would use a key to start your car. If you lose your flash drive, you won't be able to start your PC.

- **Let BitLocker Automatically Unlock My Drive**   BitLocker doesn't prompt you for a PIN, a password, or a USB flash drive. Instead, it only verifies the system's integrity and then automatically starts up. This option doesn't offer any protection from someone who steals your entire PC, but it does protect your data in the event someone steals just the drive from inside your PC (a scenario that is more common in business environments). It also helps protect you from rootkits and other malware that might modify your system files.

If you have a TPM chip, your PC's BIOS will prompt you to enter a PIN. Therefore, the prompt happens before any part of Windows has loaded. If you don't have a TPM chip and you decide to use a password, the Windows boot loader starts, prompts you to select an operating system (if you have multiple operating systems installed), and then BitLocker starts and prompts you to enter your password, as shown in Figure 12-4.

CHAPTER 12

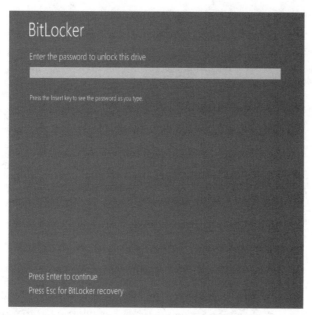

Figure 12-4 BitLocker prompts you for a password.

When you configure BitLocker and your computer has a TPM chip, you'll see the BitLocker wizard page for choosing how to unlock your drive, as shown in Figure 12-5.

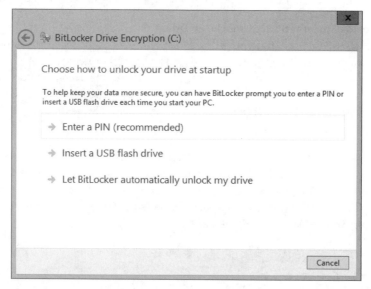

Figure 12-5 You have three choices for starting your PC with BitLocker and a TPM.

However, if your computer does not have a TPM chip, you'll instead see the BitLocker wizard page shown in Figure 12-6. As you can see, you have the option to enter a password instead of a PIN, and there's no option to let BitLocker automatically unlock your drive.

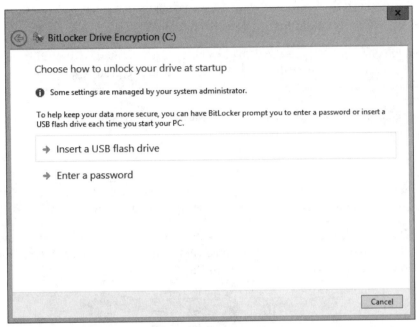

Figure 12-6 You have two choices for starting a PC that doesn't have a TPM.

You can always change the startup options after you enable BitLocker.

Inside OUT

Locking your computer

BitLocker only protects your computer during startup. After Windows starts, it automatically decrypts everything, nullifying any protection.

Obviously, if someone steals your computer while you're logged on, the thief is going to get the same transparent access to your data that you enjoy. Therefore, it's very important that you not leave your computer logged on when someone might steal it.

For best results, configure your computer to lock when not in use. That way, if you walk away from your computer or stash it in a bag, someone would need to know your password to log on to it. If they attempt to restart your computer to access your files offline, BitLocker's encryption will protect your data.

CHAPTER 12

Using BitLocker without a TPM

BitLocker is designed to be used primarily with a TPM chip. If you use it without a TPM chip, your PC won't be able to start up automatically like a BitLocker-protected PC with a TPM chip is able to. Instead, you'll need to authenticate yourself by typing a password or by connecting a USB key with a secret certification before Windows 8.1 starts.

If you don't have a TPM, you also won't be able to take advantage of the TPM's system-integrity checks. That means that BitLocker won't be able to protect you from rootkits. You'll still enjoy the benefits of an encrypted drive, however.

If your PC doesn't have a TPM chip and you want to use BitLocker, you need to change a Group Policy setting:

1. Run **gpedit.msc**.

2. Browse to Local Computer Policy\Computer Configuration\Administrative Templates\ Windows Components\BitLocker Drive Encryption\Operating System Drives.

3. Double-click Require Additional Authentication At Startup, select Enabled, and select Allow BitLocker Without A Compatible TPM (Requires A Password Or A Startup Key On A USB Flash Drive), as shown in Figure 12-7.

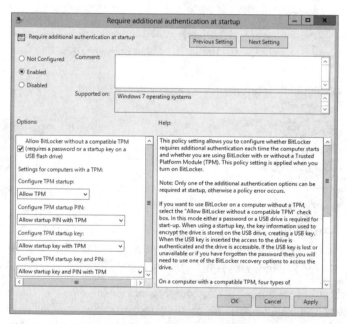

Figure 12-7 If your PC doesn't have a TPM chip and you still want to use BitLocker, you need to enable it from this Group Policy setting.

4. Click OK.

Now, you can enable BitLocker using Control Panel.

Suspending and removing BitLocker

After you enable BitLocker, the Control Panel tool gives you options to suspend BitLocker or turn it off, as shown in Figure 12-8.

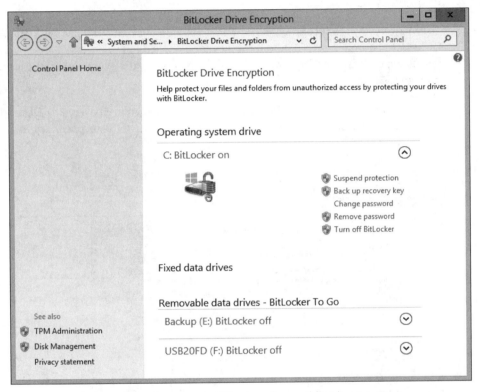

Figure 12-8 You can suspend or remove BitLocker after enabling it.

You'll want to use these options in different circumstances:

- **Turn off**   Turning off BitLocker decrypts your drive. Of course, you lose the benefits of BitLocker, but you also lose the drawbacks. You'll be able to access data directly from other operating systems, and you won't suffer any performance penalty for encryption and decryption. If you turn BitLocker back on, it will need to re-encrypt all of your files.

- **Suspend**   Suspending BitLocker keeps your drive encrypted but stores the decryption key in plain text. Suspending BitLocker allows you to start Windows without a password,

PIN, flash drive, or recovery key. If you're using a TPM, Windows will start even if system files have been modified. Suspend BitLocker when you don't need to access the files from other operating systems and you plan to reenable it in the near future.

BitLocker recovery

The consequences for losing your decryption key are pretty severe: you permanently lose access to every file on your PC. You really don't want that to happen, so BitLocker provides a recovery key.

The recovery key is a second type of key that you don't use on a regular basis. The recovery key is never stored in the TPM, so it can never be applied automatically. Instead, you need to save it some place safe where you will be able to find it in the event you can't start BitLocker normally.

Figure 12-9 shows the options BitLocker provides to save your recovery key. Depending on your PC's configuration, you might also be prompted to save the recovery key to a USB flash drive.

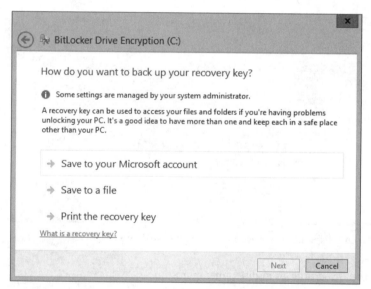

Figure 12-9 There are several ways to store your BitLocker recovery key.

No matter where you back up your key, keep in mind that your data is only as safe as your key backup. If you save the key to a file, save that file to a disc and lock the disc up. If you print the recovery key, lock the page you printed it on in a safe. If you save it to your Microsoft account, make sure you have a strong password that you don't use on any other sites and that you haven't told anyone else. For the best level of protection, save your recovery key in multiple locations.

The option to save your recovery key to your Microsoft account is new with Windows 8.1. Choose this option if you're at all concerned that you might lose your recovery key or if you travel with a mobile PC and don't bring your recovery key everywhere with you. It's great for people like me who constantly misplace small things like flash drives.

If you choose to print the key or save it to a file or a USB flash drive, the file will resemble the following:

```
BitLocker Drive Encryption recovery key

To verify that this is the correct recovery key, compare the start of the following
identifier with the identifier value displayed on your PC.

Identifier:
....4641E004-E05D-4890-8018-1D307E793C16

If the above identifier matches the one displayed by your PC, then use the following key
to unlock your drive.

Recovery Key:
....243276-554829-375265-700414-356246-257708-607915-497486

If the above identifier doesn't match the one displayed by your PC, then this isn't the
right key to unlock your drive.
Try another recovery key, or contact your administrator or IT Help Desk for assistance.
```

Notice that the file contains two separate, really long series of numbers, letters, and dashes:

- **Identifier**   A series of 32 hexadecimal characters (which consist of the numbers 0–9 and A–E). If you need to recover BitLocker, BitLocker will display this identifier. This isn't especially useful if you have only one PC, but if you have several PCs, this will make it much easier to find the recovery key that matches a particular PC.

- **Recovery Key**   A series of 48 numbers, broken into eight groups of six; memorize this sequence so that you can start your PC if you ever have a problem with BitLocker. Just kidding, of course. It's hard enough just remembering where you saved the recovery key.

As shown in Figure 12-10, BitLocker prompts you with the recovery key ID when you attempt to recover your PC. If you type the recovery key correctly, Windows will start normally.

If you saved your recovery key to your Microsoft account, press Esc from the page shown in Figure 12-10. Windows 8.1 will prompt you to enter the recovery key again, but this time it will provide you a URL you can type into a different PC. Visit that URL (which redirects you to *https://skydrive.live.com/P.mvc#!/recoverykey*), log in with your Microsoft account (you might need to verify the new PC), and you'll be able to retrieve your recovery key, as shown in Figure 12-11.

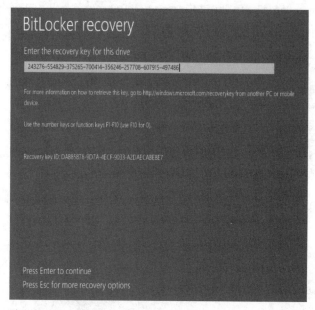

Figure 12-10 Type the BitLocker recovery key if you cannot start BitLocker normally.

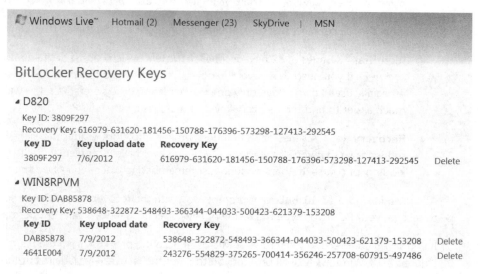

Figure 12-11 You can retrieve your recovery key online using your Microsoft account.

When you save the recovery key to a file, the file name includes the identifier. Don't confuse this with the recovery key. If you lose your recovery key while your PC is still running, you can save a new copy of it by clicking Back Up Recovery Key from the BitLocker tool in Control Panel.

As you might imagine, typing a series of 48 numbers is an error-prone experience. Fortunately, BitLocker warns you if you make a mistake within each of the six-digit groups. Also, you need to use the recovery key only in the event of a BitLocker failure, which might never happen.

Enabling BitLocker

BitLocker's initial encryption will fail if your drive has any errors. Therefore, your first step should be to preventatively find and fix any errors. Windows 8.1 is supposed to do this automatically, and it does a good job of it. However, in my experience, quite a few attempts at enabling BitLocker fail in a frustrating way because of drive errors, so it's better to fix them ahead of time. For more information, read "Fixing errors" later in this chapter.

To enable BitLocker, search Settings for **bitlocker** and select BitLocker Drive Encryption. Then, click Turn On BitLocker, as shown in Figure 12-12.

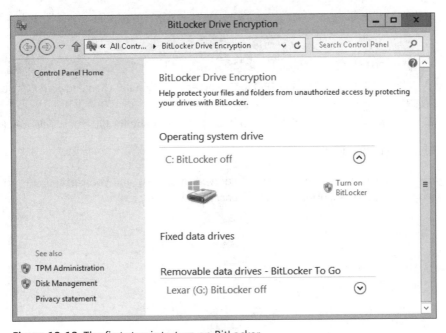

Figure 12-12 The first step is to turn on BitLocker.

CHAPTER 12

Enabling BitLocker is a three-step process:

1. Turn on the TPM security hardware.

    It's possible that your TPM security hardware is already enabled. If not, Windows will prompt you to configure your TPM hardware and restart your PC. Depending on your PC, it's possible that your BIOS will prompt you to allow the change, as shown in Figure 12-13. It's also possible that you will need to enter your BIOS configuration and modify the TPM settings yourself.

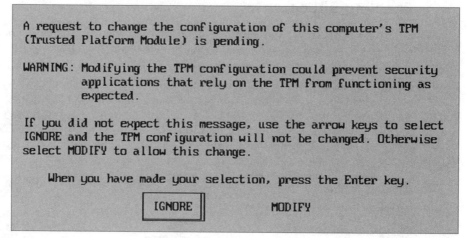

A request to change the configuration of this computer's TPM (Trusted Platform Module) is pending.

WARNING: Modifying the TPM configuration could prevent security applications that rely on the TPM from functioning as expected.

If you did not expect this message, use the arrow keys to select IGNORE and the TPM configuration will not be changed. Otherwise select MODIFY to allow this change.

When you have made your selection, press the Enter key.

IGNORE   MODIFY

Figure 12-13 Enabling the TPM for BitLocker often requires changing your PC's BIOS settings.

2. Perform a system check to ensure that the PC is ready for BitLocker. This step is optional.

3. Encrypt the drive.

You can keep using your PC during the encryption process, and you can even restart if you need to. BitLocker will notify you when encryption is complete.

Windows says I don't have a TPM

If you see the message in Figure 12-14, there are two possible causes: either your PC doesn't have a TPM chip, or it has a TPM chip and it is disabled in the BIOS. Check your PC's manual to determine how to adjust the BIOS settings, and look for an option to turn on the TPM chip. On most PCs, the TPM is disabled by default (for no reason I've been able to understand).

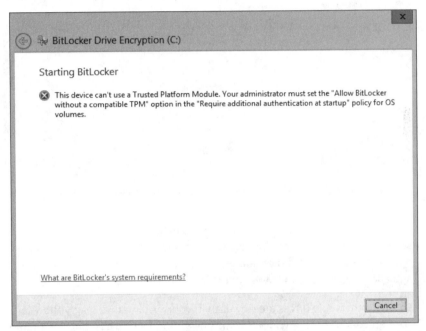

Figure 12-14 If you see this error message, there might be a couple of ways to fix it.

If you don't have a TPM chip, you can still use BitLocker. Refer to the section, "Using BitLocker without a TPM," earlier in this chapter.

Using BitLocker with removable drives

You can also use BitLocker to encrypt removable drives. Simply connect your removable drive, right-click it in File Explorer, and then click Turn On BitLocker. BitLocker initializes the drive and then prompts you to protect it with a password, a smart card, or both (see Figure 12-15).

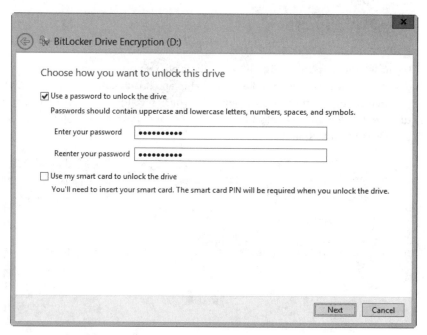

Figure 12-15 You can also protect data on removable drives with BitLocker.

As with protecting fixed drives, you'll have a recovery key that you can save to your Microsoft account, save to a file, or print. Recovery keys for removable drives aren't usually as important, however, because the files on the drive are typically copies of files you have stored elsewhere, and a lost password won't stop your PC from booting.

Because removable drives are slower than your system drive, encryption can take much longer. You can continue using your PC while encryption takes place, but don't remove the drive until encryption is finished, or you might damage your files.

When you connect a BitLocker-protected drive, Windows 8.1 notifies you. Click the notification and type a password to quickly unlock the drive, or click More Options to recover it. Clicking More Options also gives you the option to automatically unlock the drive in the future, as shown in Figure 12-16.

You can use BitLocker-protected removable drives with Windows 7, too. If you want to use them on PCs running Windows XP or Windows Vista, you need to run the executable file stored on the drive to access the drive. For Windows XP and Windows Vista users, the drive is read-only, so you can copy the files to your PC and edit them there, but you can't edit the files directly on the removable drive.

Figure 12-16 Configure removable drives to automatically unlock to save some time.

Fixing errors

Drives aren't perfect. They're physical devices subject to fluctuating power, unexpected shut-downs, and (especially for mobile PCs) sudden impacts. Sometimes they get errors.

Total failures happen occasionally, and your only recourse is to recover from a backup (as described in Chapter 10). More frequently, small errors appear that might only change a byte or two on the drive. These happen so frequently that Windows 8.1 actually looks for them and attempts to fix them automatically, a process known as *online self-healing*. As part of that process, Windows 8.1 performs an online verification to make sure the error is the drive's fault, and not an error occurring in some other part of the PC (such as a memory error).

Some types of drive errors must be fixed while Windows is offline. For example, if a drive error has corrupted a system file, Windows 8.1 can replace the corrupted file with a genuine version of the file—but only while Windows is offline. If Windows 8.1 automatically detects a drive error that it cannot fix while online, it will prompt you using a notification in the Action Center. You can then restart your PC to allow Windows to fix the problem, or simply wait until the next time you normally restart your PC.

To manually find and fix errors, switch to the desktop and open File Explorer. Within Computer, right-click your drive and then click Properties. On the Tools tab, click the Check button. If you're prompted, click Scan Drive. Windows scans your drive, as shown in Figure 12-17.

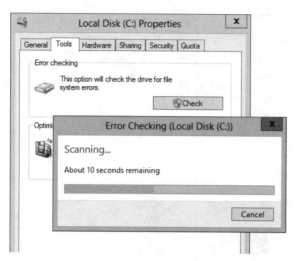

Figure 12-17 Windows 8.1 can scan your system drive without restarting.

Windows 8.1 is the first version of Windows to allow you to scan for and fix some problems with your system drive while Windows is running. Previous versions of Windows required you to restart your PC to scan for errors, which often prevented you from using your PC for several minutes or even hours. Sometimes, Windows would automatically start the scan when you were restarting your PC, preventing you from using your PC without much warning (it did give you 8 seconds to abort the scan, but if you happened to be getting some coffee while the computer rebooted, your coffee break might extend into a lunch break).

Windows 8.1 will still need to fix some types of problems while offline, a process known as a spot fix. However, the scan was the time-consuming part, so if it does identify a serious problem during the online scan, it should be able to fix it during your next reboot within just a few seconds.

If you're in the habit of manually scanning your drive for errors, or if you run ChkDsk regularly, you can stop once you upgrade to Windows 8.1. Like defragmentation (a process that was manual in earlier versions of Windows but is now automated), scanning for drive errors is best handled by Windows.

You still have the option of manually performing an offline scan, though you need to do this only when the file system is so corrupted that Windows cannot mount it. Use the WinX menu to open an administrative command prompt and then run this command (replacing C: with the drive you want to scan):

```
chkdsk C: /f /r
```

Inside OUT

Viewing ChkDsk output

Whereas earlier versions of Windows displayed the results from ChkDsk on the screen, Windows 8.1 shows a more attractive (if less informative) screen. To view the ChkDsk results, open the Computer Management console from the WinX menu. Browse to Event Viewer\Windows Logs\Application, and then click Find on the Action menu. Search for the phrase **chkdsk**, and open the most recent event. Figure 12-18 shows an example of the ChkDsk output containing several errors that have been fixed.

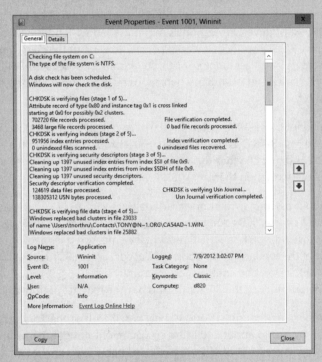

Figure 12-18 Windows stores the ChkDsk results in the Application event log.

Choosing a new drive

Drives are one of the best upgrades you can make to improve the performance of an older PC (especially if you upgrade the system drive). If you happen to be running out of space, choose a fast drive to get some extra performance along with your capacity.

You can choose from two types of drives: magnetic drives and solid-state drives (SSDs). Magnetic drives have been common in PCs since the 1980s, and they're still the best choice if you're on a budget or you need lots of drive space.

Magnetic drive performance is typically illustrated using rotations per minute (RPMs): 5,400-RPM drives are the slowest common drives, 7,200-RPM drives are quite a bit faster, and there are also 10,000-RPM drives. Professionals might use higher-RPM drives, but they're not common in consumer PCs. Drives with lower RPMs are slower, but they also tend to be less expensive, use less power, and last longer. For those reasons, choose low-RPM drives any time performance doesn't matter: for example, when choosing a backup drive or a drive for a home theater PC (HTPC).

Generally, larger magnetic drives are faster than smaller drives. So, if you upgrade from a 500-MB, 7,200-RPM drive to a 3-TB, 7,200-RPM drive, you'll probably discover that it's much faster, even though the RPMs didn't change. This makes sense, because a 3-TB drive accesses six times more data in every rotation than a 7,200-RPM drive.

If you really care about performance or power usage (for example, if you're using a mobile PC), SSDs are the best choice. SSDs don't spin like a magnetic drive, so their performance isn't measured in RPMs. Instead, you'll see their performance measured in megabytes per second (MB/s or MBps). As of the writing of this book, typical consumer SSDs read data at 500 MB/s and write it at 250 MB/s. Don't be confused by measurements of 6 Gb/sec or 3 Gb/sec; those are the maximum throughput of the SATA bus, and not the realistic performance of the drive.

The bus speed is important, though. If your PC only has SATA II connectors, read and write performance will be limited to about 240 MB/s, so you might not get the full performance out of an SSD unless you use SATA III. If you have a desktop PC, you might be able to add a SATA III card, but there's still no guarantee that you'll get the full performance from your SSD, because performance might be limited by the motherboard's bus. If you connect an external drive using USB 2.0, you're going to be limited to a maximum of 60 MB/s (though you'll usually get even less).

MB/s measures the sequential read of a drive, which is how fast the drive could read a single file. There's another important performance metric: access time (also known as seek time). Access time is the time required to start reading a new piece of data, and it's typically measured in milliseconds (ms). Magnetic drives typically have access times of 4–8 ms, while SSDs often have access times of less than 1 ms. Naturally, faster is better.

If you want to measure the performance of your drive, use the free version of HD Tune, available at *http://www.hdtune.com/*. Run it on your drive before and after you upgrade so you can measure the performance difference. Figure 12-19 shows a screen shot of HD Tune running on an SSD drive that is limited by a SATA II connector.

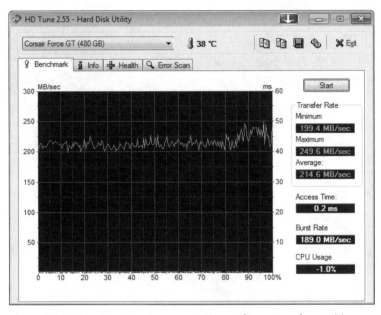

Figure 12-19 Use HD Tune to measure the performance of your drives.

SkyDrive overview 289

Using the SkyDrive app for Windows 8.1 290

Accessing SkyDrive from mobile devices 292

Accessing SkyDrive from a browser. 294

Using SkyDrive on the desktop 295

Editing documents simultaneously with
other users. 302

Microsoft SkyDrive is a cloud-based storage service, and I'm using it right now to write this chapter. Where are chapter files that I've put so many hours of work into? I don't know, but I do know I moved between my desktop, my ultrabook, my tablet, and my phone without ever copying a file between them. When it was time to send the file to my editor, I tapped the Share charm and it was sent in seconds, without the usual bulky file attachments.

SkyDrive is more than just magical file synchronization. SkyDrive provides continuous, off-site backups for your files and data anytime you have Internet access. While making your own backups is still a good idea, you'll probably never need them. SkyDrive also creates a version history, allowing you to go back in time to an earlier version of a document. If you accidentally delete a chapter from your novel and save the file, SkyDrive can rescue the lost chapter.

How integrated is SkyDrive into Windows 8.1? Well, there's no touch-friendly app for accessing files on your hard drive, but there is a touch-friendly app for accessing SkyDrive. And, for the way people use mobile PCs, SkyDrive is a much better choice than your local drive. In fact, SkyDrive is a better choice than your local drive for just about anything.

In summary: store all your files in SkyDrive, and stop using your C drive.

SkyDrive overview

SkyDrive is a cloud storage service, similar in many ways to Dropbox, Google Drive, and Apple iCloud. SkyDrive stores your files on servers connected to the Internet, allowing you to view and edit your files from anywhere with an Internet connection, on just about any device that can connect to the Internet. You can use the optional SkyDrive desktop app to synchronize your SkyDrive files with your PC's hard drive, allowing you to work with files when you're offline.

Figure 13-1 illustrates this relationship.

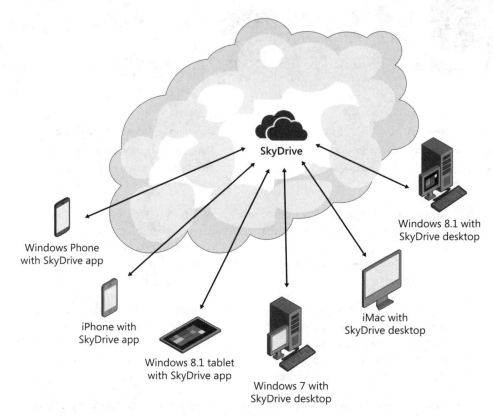

Figure 13-1 SkyDrive apps for Windows Phone, iOS, and Windows 8.1 provide direct access to SkyDrive files, and the SkyDrive desktop app synchronizes files with the local PC.

Once you use SkyDrive for a month, you'll be amazed that you ever lived without it. You never have to manually copy files between your desktop and laptop. Every file on your PC is accessible from your phone. And if you use SkyDrive for everything, you might never need to worry about backing up your files.

▶ **Using the SkyDrive app**   Watch the video at *http://aka.ms/WinIO/skydriveapp*.

Using the SkyDrive app for Windows 8.1

The SkyDrive app's controls are similar to the other Windows 8.1 apps, including Photos, Video, and Music. Swipe left and right to browse, and click the arrow in the upper-left corner to go back one page.

Swipe up from the bottom or right-click anywhere to use the commands:

- **Add Items**   Upload files from your local PC.

- **Details/Thumbnails**   Change how you view the files and folders.

- **Make Offline**   With a file selected, this command copies the file to your local PC.

- **Delete, Rename, Copy, and Cut**   Manage selected files and folders.

Figure 13-2 shows the SkyDrive app with several files selected and the commands visible.

Figure 13-2 The SkyDrive app provides access to your files and limited management functions.

The SkyDrive app provides a convenient way to browse your files, but browsing your files is a very Windows 7 kind of way to think. A more Windows 8.1 approach is to start with your app. For example, if you want to browse your pictures, launch the Photos app. From within Photos, you can access your SkyDrive folder. Many apps provide direct access to SkyDrive, so you won't have to use the SkyDrive app regularly.

Inside OUT

Using the Photos app instead of the SkyDrive app

Another good reason to browse pictures using the Photos app instead of the SkyDrive app is that the Photos app is more specialized. SkyDrive does a decent job of allowing you to flip through pictures stored on SkyDrive, but the Photos app provides slide shows and printing as well.

When you use SkyDrive from Windows 8.1, your files stay in the cloud. You can manually copy individual files to your local PC, but Windows 8.1 never synchronizes files to or from SkyDrive. This eliminates versioning conflicts that occur with synchronization, and it overcomes the limited storage of many mobile PCs. If you want file synchronization (and your PC has the local storage for it), install the SkyDrive desktop app, described later in this chapter.

Inside OUT

Where exactly are my files?

Your files are in the "cloud," which is a deliberately vague term. They're stored on some sort of hard drive, and some sort of server listens for requests on the Internet and sends the bits and bytes that a file consists of when you request it.

At the moment, I'm accessing my SkyDrive files through a server with the IP address 207.46.0.174, which I determined by capturing network communications using Microsoft Network Monitor. By checking *http://whois.arin.net*, I can tell that the IP address is registered to Microsoft. By performing a geolocation lookup, I know that the server is somewhere in New York City, the closest Internet hub to where I live. If you live somewhere else, I bet you'll connect to a server closer to you.

If you open a Microsoft Office document from SkyDrive, SkyDrive opens it using Internet Explorer and the free web viewer. You can use the Office web app to edit files, too, and if you have Office installed on your PC, you can edit the files directly in the Office apps.

You can share your files directly from SkyDrive without copying them to your local PC; simply open the file or folder in SkyDrive and select the Share charm. SkyDrive will share a link to the online files. Not only is this more efficient than copying files and creating an email attachment, but it allows the recipient to receive changes you make after you share the files.

Accessing SkyDrive from mobile devices

You can install the SkyDrive app on your Windows Phone, iPhone, iPad, or Android. Additionally, third-party developers have created apps for other platforms. Microsoft lists some recommended apps at *http://windows.microsoft.com/en-us/skydrive/download#apps*. If there isn't a SkyDrive app for your mobile device, just use your browser to visit the *http://www.skydrive.com* website.

The mobile apps work great. Figure 13-3 shows the app running on an iPhone. The app can natively display most common file types, including text files, images, and Office documents.

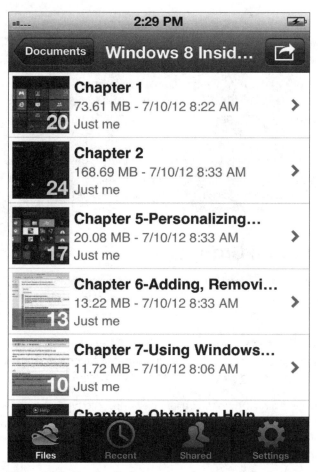

Figure 13-3 Use the SkyDrive app on an iPhone to view your files.

The SkyDrive app can't edit files directly, but it can move files, rename them, and open files in other apps that you might have installed. To edit a file, open it, select the Forward link in the lower-right corner, and then select Open In Another App. You can use the same technique to rename files.

Be aware of fees your carrier might charge you for accessing data, especially when opening large files. Particularly when travelling to other countries/regions (when roaming charges can be very high), you might save yourself money by waiting until you have access to Wi-Fi to open large files from SkyDrive. Or, plan ahead and copy the files to your mobile device before leaving home.

Inside OUT

Microsoft OneNote and SkyDrive

My favorite smartphone app is the OneNote app, which lets me update my personal notes (which I store in the Microsoft OneNote desktop app) from my mobile device. It uses SkyDrive to synchronize changes with my PC. The mobile app is free and it works, so what else could you want?

To share your OneNote notebook, select the File tab and then select Share. This stores the OneNote file in your Documents folder on SkyDrive. You can open the file in your browser or use the OneNote app on other PCs or your mobile devices.

Accessing SkyDrive from a browser

SkyDrive has specialized apps for many different devices, and those apps will always give you the best experience. If you're on a PC, Mac, or mobile device that doesn't have the SkyDrive app installed, you can access SkyDrive from almost any browser.

In other words, if you're an iPhone user, you should install the SkyDrive app on your iPhone and use that. If you want to quickly show a friend a file using the friend's tablet, there's no need to install an app; just open the browser, visit *https://skydrive.com,* and log in.

When you log in to SkyDrive from a browser, you can view most file types directly within your browser. If you're on a PC or Mac, SkyDrive will even let you edit Office documents without having Office installed, as shown in Figure 13-4. The web apps aren't as full-featured as the desktop Office apps that you buy, but they're useful, free, and work with many web clients.

▶ **Using the SkyDrive website** Watch the video at *http://aka.ms/WinIO/skydriveweb*.

You can't edit Office documents directly from SkyDrive mobile apps. However, you can view your Office documents and open them in a different app for editing.

The SkyDrive website has several features that you can access by right-clicking files:

- **Share** Send your files in email or post them to Facebook, Twitter, LinkedIn, Flickr, and other services you might add. Your friends won't even need to log in to access them, though you can require them to log in if you want to. You can even allow recipients to edit your documents.

- **Embed** Generates HTML code that you can add to a webpage using an iframe. This is perfect for web designers and bloggers who want to share a file. Embedding is better than simply copying the content into your webpage because any updates you make to the file are immediately reflected on your webpage, no matter which PC or mobile device you use to edit the file. Here's a sample of the HTML code:

```
<iframe src="https://skydrive.live.com/embed?cid=D465B387E587EF71&resid=
D465B387E587EF71%215415&authkey=ALYzTme1wUa3iUE" width="98" height="120"
frameborder="0" scrolling="no"></iframe>
```

- **Version history**   Retrieve earlier versions of a file that you have saved over. This lets you recover parts of a document that you might have changed or deleted.

- **Download**   Copy the file to your local PC. Any changes you make to the copy won't be reflected in SkyDrive, however.

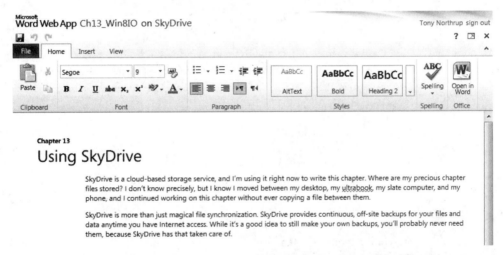

Figure 13-4 View and edit Office documents on SkyDrive from most desktop browsers.

While it's easier to use the SkyDrive desktop app (described in the next section) to add files to SkyDrive, you can also drag files from File Explorer to SkyDrive in your browser. SkyDrive uploads the files and allows you to monitor the progress. The upload tool even gives you an option to automatically resize your pictures to speed up viewing time later.

Using SkyDrive on the desktop

SkyDrive integrates itself into File Explorer by adding the SkyDrive item between your Favorites and your PC. You can work with files and folders on SkyDrive exactly as you would locally stored files and folders, except that files will take a few moments to download when you open them.

To keep a local copy of a file or folder automatically synchronized, right-click it and then click Make Available Offline. To disable local caching, right-click a file or folder and then select Make Available Online-Only. To synchronize all your files, open the SkyDrive app, select the Settings charm, select Options, and then select Access All Files Offline.

You can control whether SkyDrive synchronizes over metered connections by opening PC Settings, SkyDrive, and then Metered Connections. To change the quality of pictures that are synchronized and whether videos are automatically synchronized, select PC Settings, SkyDrive, and then Camera Roll.

Inside OUT

Only use the SkyDrive desktop app on one PC

If you have PCs running Windows Vista, Windows 7, or Windows 8, you can install the SkyDrive desktop app to keep files synchronized on those PCs. The SkyDrive desktop app is available for free from *http://windows.microsoft.com/en-US/skydrive/ download-skydrive.*

My first instinct was to install the SkyDrive desktop app on every PC on my home network to keep files synchronized. However, when I switched from my desktop to my tablet or my ultrabook, the files I was working on were often not synchronized. Naturally, my mobile PCs turn themselves off to save power, so synchronization didn't even begin until I started to use them, and SkyDrive needed to synchronize so many files that it would have taken hours.

I ran into another problem when I uploaded 25 gigabytes (GB) of files to SkyDrive. My desktop has more storage space than my tablet and ultrabook, and when my mobile PCs tried to synchronize 25 GB, they filled up their drives and stopped synchronization (and also stopped saving any new files).

A better approach is to share your SkyDrive folder from the PC that tends to stay on and connected to your home network the most. Then, connect to that shared folder across the network. Homegroups are an excellent way to do this. For more information, refer to Chapter 21, "Setting up a home or small office network."

SkyDrive performance

SkyDrive is designed to have very little impact on your PC's performance. It requires very little memory, and it uses very little processor time even when it's synchronizing files. Basically, SkyDrive won't slow down your PC.

Figure 13-5 shows the Performance Monitor analysis of SkyDrive's processor utilization during a very large synchronization. As you can see, the average processor utilization is less than 3 percent, and the peak processor utilization during a 1-second period is only 15.4 percent

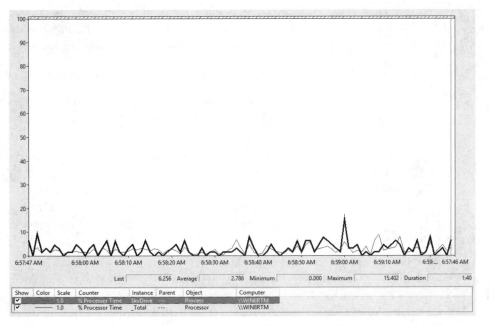

Figure 13-5 The SkyDrive desktop app uses very little processing time.

How SkyDrive desktop synchronization works

SkyDrive's desktop synchronization technique will be familiar to readers who happen to have a background in the exciting field of distributed enterprise databases; it's called lazy synchronization. Lazy synchronization has some important advantages:

- It doesn't slow down accessing files. You're actually saving to your local PC, so there's no performance hit when viewing and editing files. SkyDrive works behind the scenes to synchronize your changes.

- You can view and edit files while you're offline. If you grab your laptop and go, you'll continue working from the local file, and SkyDrive will automatically synchronize it with the copy on the Internet the next time you have Internet access.

Lazy synchronization also has some disadvantages that you should understand:

- Saved changes aren't immediately available to other PCs. Depending on your Internet connection speed and the size of the file, it might take just a few seconds, or it might take several minutes.

- If you save a file and then immediately shut down your PC, your file won't be synchronized until you connect to the Internet and allow SkyDrive the time it needs to synch. In other words, when the flight attendant warns you that you must immediately power down your PC before the flight can leave, your recent changes won't be available on SkyDrive until that PC can spend a few minutes connected to the Internet.

- Versioning issues can occur. Imagine that you maintain a Microsoft Excel spreadsheet with your home expenses. You lose power and Internet access at home, so you call an electrician and use your laptop to update the spreadsheet while offline. Your wife, meanwhile, buys a flashlight at the hardware store and updates the spreadsheet from her phone. Now you have two different versions of the document that you will need to merge manually.

The list of disadvantages seems much longer than the list of advantages. However, lazy synchronization is definitely the right choice for working with large files or when you regularly work offline.

The time it takes SkyDrive to synchronize your files depends primarily on your Internet bandwidth. In my experience, SkyDrive will use about 80-90 percent of your upstream or downstream bandwidth during synchronization. Synchronizing files from SkyDrive to your local PC uses your downstream bandwidth. Synchronizing files from your local PC to SkyDrive utilizes your upstream bandwidth, which is usually a fraction of your downstream bandwidth. Therefore, the first time you copy files to SkyDrive, synchronization might take a long time, but copying files from SkyDrive to other PCs should happen much more quickly.

Handling versioning conflicts

As discussed earlier, SkyDrive's lazy synchronization can lead to versioning conflicts in which a single file is updated in two different locations. Resolving these conflicts really requires human levels of intelligence; SkyDrive can't determine how to merge two different files possibly updated by different people. So, it's up to you to resolve the conflict, but SkyDrive makes it as simple as possible.

If SkyDrive detects a versioning conflict, it uses the most recently updated version of the file. Imagine you are editing a text file on both your desktop and your laptop:

1. On your desktop (with the clever PC name "mydesktop"), you save diary.txt to your SkyDrive folder with one line, "Dear diary," and SkyDrive synchronizes the update with the cloud.

2. Later, still on your desktop, you add a second line to the diary.txt file, "I feel like I'm never in one place long enough to complete a thought." You immediately shut down your desktop, before SkyDrive can synchronize the changes.

3. That evening on your laptop, you open diary.txt from your SkyDrive folder and discover that it reads only, "Dear diary," The second line isn't there because the change wasn't synchronized. So, you edit diary.txt and add the line, "I might be losing my mind. I swear I already started this entry." SkyDrive synchronizes the changes.

4. The next day, you start your desktop and let it run long enough for SkyDrive to synchronize the changes. You go to open your diary.txt file and discover there are two files in the folder: diary.txt and diary-mydesktop.txt.

In this scenario, diary.txt would read:

```
Dear diary,
I might be losing my mind. I swear I already started this entry.
```

And diary-mydesktop.txt would read:

```
Dear diary,
I feel like I'm never in one place long enough to complete a thought.
```

As you can see, SkyDrive didn't throw out any useful data. When the desktop PC synched with SkyDrive, SkyDrive discovered there was a newer version of the same file in the cloud. So, it left the newer version named diary.txt and renamed the older version on the desktop to *<filename>-<PCname>.<extension>*.

Now it's up to you to merge the changes. The best way to do that depends on the file type and app. For most files, you'll simply need to examine the two files and copy any changes from the renamed file into the master file.

Some apps, however, support merging changes. Most notably, Microsoft Office apps can examine two versions of a file and intelligently merge changes. For example, in Microsoft Word 2010, on the Review tab, click Compare and then click Combine to merge two versions of a single document.

Inside OUT

Backing up SkyDrive files

Consider excluding files synchronized to SkyDrive from your backups, since they're already backed up by SkyDrive. For more information about configuring backups, refer to Chapter 10, "Backing up and restoring files."

Accessing PCs through SkyDrive

In theory, you'll just store all your files on SkyDrive, and SkyDrive will automatically synchronize the files you choose for offline use. In practice, many people will move some of their files over to SkyDrive while leaving many more stored on their local PC. Then, they'll get used to having their files accessible from anywhere and realize when they're away from home that they didn't move over an important file.

Not to worry. SkyDrive can give you access to files stored only on your PCs as long as you enable the option, your PC has access to the Internet, your PC is turned on, and you are logged on. Figure 13-6 shows the website's interface for accessing files on remote PCs that are not stored in the cloud.

If you think you might want to use this feature, adjust the power settings on the PC that you plan to access so that it does not automatically go into Sleep mode. On laptop PCs, this might also require you to change what happens when you close the lid.

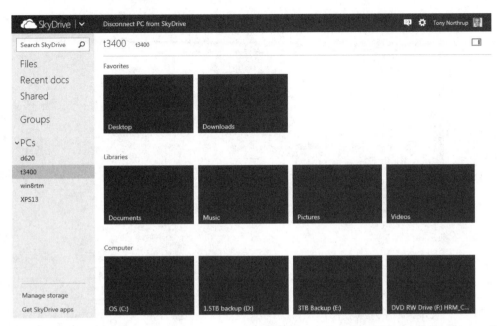

Figure 13-6 With your permission, you can access files stored on online PCs even if the files aren't in the cloud.

Inside OUT

Your security is only as good as your passwords

If you store all your files on your home PC, someone only needs to break into your house to get those files (well, unless you go out of your way to share them). Once you put your files on SkyDrive, if someone can guess your password, they can access your files. Note that they might have to confirm that their PC is a trusted PC, which also requires email confirmation, so don't use the same password for SkyDrive and your email.

Enable the option by right-clicking the SkyDrive icon in the system tray and then clicking Settings. Then, select the Make Files On This PC Available To Me On My Other Devices check box as shown in Figure 13-7.

Figure 13-7 Edit the SkyDrive desktop options to access files on your local PC across the Internet.

Editing documents simultaneously with other users

If you often have multiple people working on a single document, look into Office 365 (*http:// www.microsoft.com/office365*). Office 365 supports online collaboration using the Office web apps, so two people can edit a document simultaneously in their browser. You have to pay for the service, but if you frequently collaborate online, it's worth it.

SkyDrive does allow two or more people to edit the same documents online with the free Word Web App. However, it doesn't allow for simultaneous changes. Instead, you must refresh the document to see other users' changes. If two users update the same version of a document in different locations, the second user will receive the message shown in Figure 13-8.

Figure 13-8 SkyDrive allows multiple users to edit a single document, but you should avoid it because only one user's changes are saved.

Though it might not happen instantly, eventually SkyDrive will notify you that another user is editing the document with a message such as "Tony Northrup is editing this document." If the other user saves changes before you, you'll also receive the message, "This document has been updated by another author. Click Save to refresh this document." To see other users who are editing the same document, select the View tab and then click the Other Authors button, as shown in Figure 13-9.

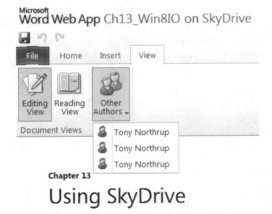

Figure 13-9 SkyDrive shows you other authors editing a document (even if it's you in another location because you forgot to close the window).

If you want multiple users to be able to edit the same document simultaneously, you'll need to purchase either Office 2010 or Office 365. Office 2010 is the traditional desktop apps, whereas Office 365 is Microsoft's cloud-based application service. Whichever you use, you'll be able to see other users' changes appear on your screen each time you save your file.

Figure 13-10 demonstrates the Word 2010 update notification: a bracket with a refresh symbol appears when an update is available on the server. Changes don't appear until you save your file. Once you save your file, changes made by other users appear highlighted in green. You can view a list of other users editing the same file by clicking the authors icon in the lower-left corner of the status bar.

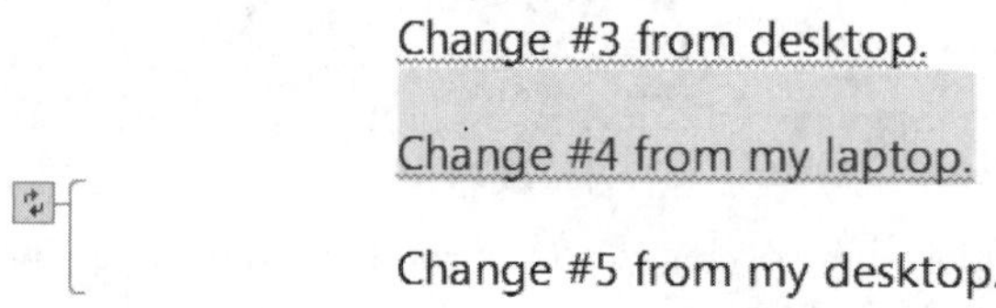

Change #3 from desktop.

Change #4 from my laptop.

Change #5 from my desktop.

Figure 13-10 The desktop version of Word 2010 notifies you when other users have edited a file and automatically merges those changes.

The Office 2010 desktop collaboration features work only when you open files from your web browser, which must be Internet Explorer. If you open a document from File Explorer (for example, by browsing to the C:\Users\<*username*>\SkyDrive\ folder), the online collaboration features don't work. Instead, SkyDrive will rename your file for you when it detects conflicts, as described in "Handling versioning conflicts" earlier in this chapter.

Office also allows you to go back in time to earlier versions of a file, just in case a coworker or a friend destroys an important part of your document. From Word 2010, select the File tab, select Info, and then use the Versions list to view earlier versions of a file.

PART 3

Music, videos, TV, and movies

CHAPTER 14
Music and videos 307

CHAPTER 15
Photos 325

CHAPTER 16
Sharing and streaming digital media 343

CHAPTER 17
Creating a Home Theater PC 359

CHAPTER 14

Music and videos

Using the Music app 307

Ripping CDs. 313

Editing metadata 315

Watching videos 316

Purchasing TV and movies 317

Editing videos 319

Imagine a technology that could multicast live music and video wirelessly around the world with an unlimited audience, all without any buffering. Now, imagine that whatever tech company built out that global infrastructure also built incredibly inexpensive clients into almost every car and house, allowing people around the globe to consume that audio and video anywhere they travelled.

A new tech startup? Hardly. Radio has been popular for about 90 years, while TV has been around for about 60. They're amazing technologies that have forever changed human culture, and I'm tired of them both.

There's a better way. The power of PCs, the bandwidth of the modern Internet, and the flexibility of home networks have come together to create new ways to enjoy music, movies, and shows. Read this chapter and set up Windows 8.1 properly, and you may never again have to rush home to catch your favorite show, listen to that annoying DJ, or be forced to watch an advertisement while waiting for your entertainment to resume. Even your digital video recorder (DVR) will seem antiquated.

This chapter provides an overview of how to listen to music and watch TV shows and movies on your PC. You should also read Chapter 16, "Sharing and streaming digital media," which shows you how to get your media everywhere you want it, including to TVs and stereos throughout your home.

Using the Music app

As described in Chapter 2, "Using Windows 8.1 apps," Windows 8.1 has a touch-friendly Music app built in. Select Collection to see the music in your local music library, select Radio to listen to streaming music, or select Explore to browse (and purchase) specific songs and CDs. It's quite easy to use, and it (mostly) replaces both Windows Media Player and Windows Media Center.

If you're very particular about your music, and you only like to listen to specific albums and songs, rip the songs you have on CD to your computer's Music folder (described later in this chapter), share the folder using a homegroup, and enjoy the music throughout your house.

The success of music on the radio has been dependent on a specific trait that many people, including myself, have: we enjoy discovering new music and would rather have music selected for us automatically. The Music app can provide that, too, using the Xbox Music service.

Inside OUT

Getting your music and videos into the apps

Windows doesn't scan your entire system to find music or videos. Instead, it looks in your Music and Videos libraries. Therefore, when you download new music and video files, it makes sense to store them in your existing Music and Videos libraries.

If you already have music and video files on your computer and you don't want to move them, add the existing folder to your Music or Videos library. This is particularly useful if you use homegroups, as described in Chapter 21, "Setting up a home or small office network." After joining a homegroup, add the Music and Videos folders for any computers in your homegroup that have shared media to the libraries on other computers. Then, you'll be able to access files on any computer connected to your home network. For detailed instructions, refer to Chapter 9, "Organizing and protecting files," and Chapter 16.

Listening to music

There are several different ways you can browse and play music:

- **One song at a time**   For those times when there's one specific song that fits your mood perfectly or, if you're like me, a song has annoyed you so much that you have to hear it again just to make fun of it. To repeat a song until you're sick of it, click the ellipses (...) in the lower-right corner and turn on Repeat.

- **One album at a time**   While pop music has largely become focused on singles, some artists still create structured albums that are best listened to in their entirety. From the Collection screen, select an album by flicking it or right-clicking it, and then select Play Selected. Selecting an album displays the songs and album artwork (if the song is available on Xbox Music), as shown in Figure 14-1. To play the songs in random order, click the ellipses (...) in the lower-right corner and then turn on Shuffle.

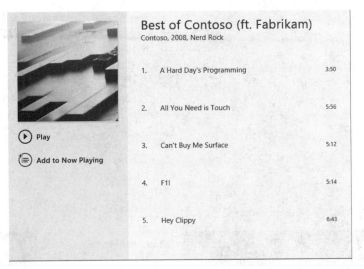

Best of Contoso (ft. Fabrikam)
Contoso, 2008, Nerd Rock

1.	A Hard Day's Programming	3:50
2.	All You Need is Touch	5:56
3.	Can't Buy Me Surface	5:12
4.	F1!	5:14
5.	Hey Clippy	6:43

▶ Play

☰ Add to Now Playing

Figure 14-1 Use the Music app to play entire albums.

- **Playlists**   A playlist is a set of songs from your music library that are played in a particular order. Playlists are the modern equivalent of the mix tapes some of us made in the 80s: a set of songs for a particular mood. For example, you might create a playlist for working out, eating dinner, or falling asleep. On the Collection screen, click New Playlist.

When playing music from your music collection, you can click the Play button to play the song immediately, or click the Plus button to add the song to the Now Playing list, as shown in Figure 14-2. The Play button should be labeled Interrupt My Music To Play Right Now, but that might be a bit wordy. Usually, Add To Now Playing is the better choice. If you keep adding songs to Now Playing, they'll play in order. If you just select Play, Windows will stop the song that's playing to play the currently selected song, and it won't resume your playlist when it's done.

Naturally, your music will keep playing in the background if you switch to another app. To quickly see the current song, pause the music, or switch to another song, press the physical volume up or down button on your computer and use the controls that appear in the upper-left corner. You can also dock the Music app along the left or right side, as discussed in Chapter 2.

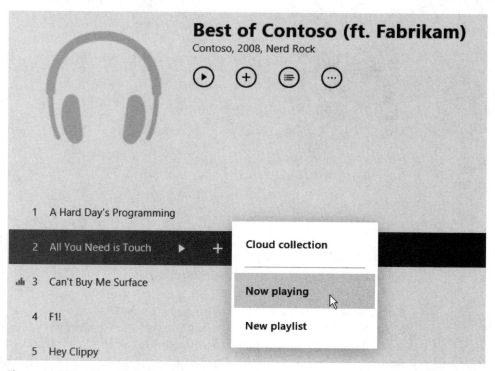

Figure 14-2 Use Now Playing if you don't want to interrupt your music.

If you like to organize your music by genre, select Collection, click the list at the far right at the top of the screen (it displays By Artist by default), and then select By Genre, as shown in Figure 14-3.

Figure 14-3 Change the sort order to view songs by genre.

Creating and managing playlists

Playlists group songs together in any order you choose—just like those custom mix tapes we used to make in the 1980s. Add songs from either the Collection or Explore page in the Music app by selecting the Plus (+) sign beside the song. Figure 14-4 shows a song being added to a custom playlist. To add multiple songs, select them all and then select Add To from the app commands at the bottom of the screen.

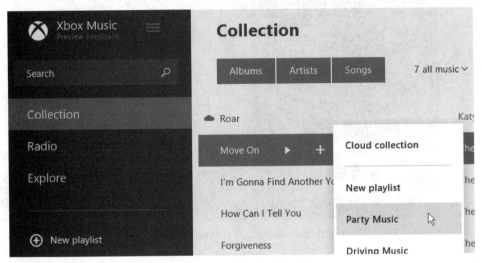

Figure 14-4 Use playlists to create sets of music for different moods.

To reorder songs or remove them from a playlist, open the playlist and select a song. As shown in Figure 14-5, use the Move Up and the More or Move Down buttons to change the order of songs in a playlist.

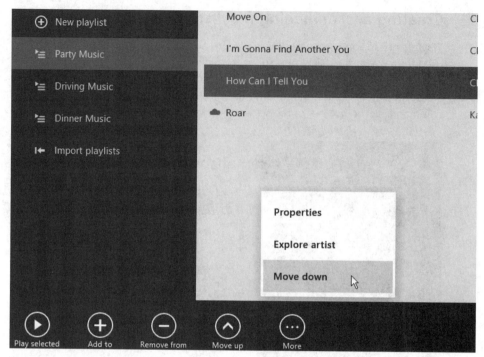

Figure 14-5 Select songs in a playlist to reorder or remove them.

Using Xbox Music

The Explore page in the Xbox Music app gives you access to the Xbox Music service. Without a subscription, you can play a 30-second clip of any song. If you want to be able to play whatever songs you want, sign up for the Xbox Music service. There's a monthly fee, but if you love music, it's probably less expensive than buying individual albums and songs. If you have a Zune account, Xbox Music automatically replaces it.

After selecting a song, you can play it or add it to a playlist. You can't keep the music forever (as you can a CD that you buy), but it's a convenient way to listen to whatever you want, whether on your PC, your Xbox, or your Windows Phone. Not having to pay for every song makes it much easier to explore new music and find new artists.

Note that songs you download through Xbox Music are downloaded in Windows Media Audio (WMA) format. The audio quality is great, but the WMA format isn't the most widely accepted. For example, you can play WMA files on your Windows Phone and on other Windows computers after you log in to Xbox Music, but you can't play WMA files directly in iTunes or on an iPhone or iPad because those devices don't support the Xbox Music copy protection format. Copy protection also prevents you from burning the songs to an audio CD.

Inside OUT

How Xbox Music copy protection works

Because the WMA music files you download from Xbox Music are copy-protected, you can't easily convert them into a more widely accepted format, such as MP3. This is by design; the Xbox Music service allows you to download all the music you want, but you are only allowed to listen to it while you have an active subscription.

If you cancel your subscription, you can't listen to the songs you've downloaded. The way Xbox Music enforces that is by distributing rights-protected and encrypted WMA music files. Only approved software that properly enforces those rights (including the Windows 8.1 Music app, Windows Media Player, and Windows Phone) are allowed to decrypt the files and play the WMA rights-protected music. Mobile devices (which don't always have an Internet connection) need to connect every 30 days to verify that you still have rights to play the music.

If that arrangement doesn't fit how you listen to music, just buy songs or albums from the XBox Music service. The Music app will automatically download them in the universally compatible MP3 format. It'll cost more, but you'll be able to listen to them with any device.

To manage your Xbox Music account, including your payment options and Zune Pass devices, open the Music app, open the Settings charm, and then select Account.

Ripping CDs

Ripping a CD is the process of converting a CD into files that you can play on your PC or media player. The term "rip" sounds rather violent, but it doesn't damage your CD at all. To rip an audio CD, insert a blank CD into your computer and open it with the Windows Media Player desktop app. If you have Windows Media Center installed, you can rip an audio CD by inserting a blank CD into your PC and opening it with the Windows Media Player desktop app. In Windows Media Player, right-click the CD and then click Rip CD To Library, as shown in Figure 14-6.

By default, Windows Media Player rips the music to WMA format. If you'd rather use the more widely compatible MP3 format, press the Alt key on your keyboard to open the menu, select Tools, and then select Options. On the Rip Music tab, open the Format list and then select MP3. If you're burning many CDs, save yourself a few clicks and select Rip CD Automatically, as shown in Figure 14-7.

▶ **Ripping CDs** Watch the video at *http://aka.ms/WinIO/ripping*.

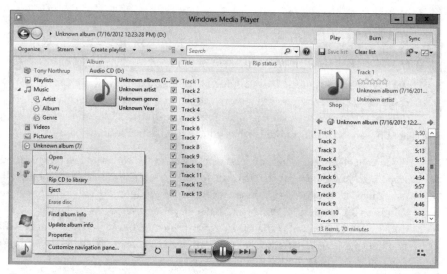

Figure 14-6 Use the Windows Media Player desktop app to rip a CD to your music library.

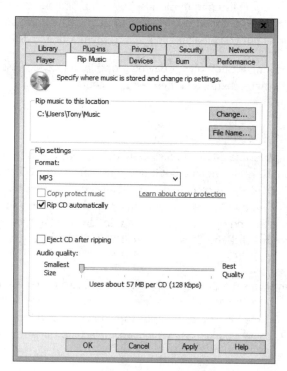

Figure 14-7 Configure Windows Media Player to automatically rip CDs to MP3s.

Windows Media Player isn't particularly good at detecting the album or song names. Other ripping software, including Apple iTunes, can do a better job.

Editing metadata

Metadata is a song's properties. Metadata is typically text information used to find and organize files. For songs, the metadata includes the album, title, and artist.

If you rip songs from CDs or create your own music, you might have to manually set the metadata. To do that, follow these steps:

1. Start the desktop, and then launch File Explorer.

2. Browse to the folder containing the files you want to edit the metadata for.

3. Right-click the file, and then click Properties.

4. Select the Details tab.

5. As shown in Figure 14-8, click any field to edit it. Then click OK to save the change.

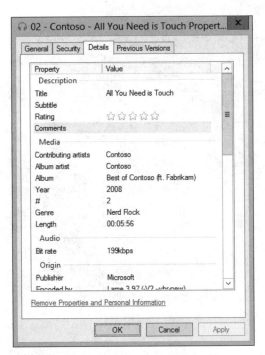

Figure 14-8 Use File Explorer to edit a file's metadata.

The Music app will immediately detect the change and update its catalog. You can't edit files that are currently playing, however. You can use the same technique to edit metadata for photos, but you can't edit the metadata for other file types, such as videos.

This could be a very slow process if you have a large number of files to update. MP3Tag (available at *http://www.mp3tag.de/en/download.html*) makes it much quicker to update large numbers of files, and you can even use it to add custom album art. If you want to add your own album art, create a 300x300 pixel JPG file. The Music app won't show your custom artwork (it only displays album covers from Xbox Music), but your smartphone or media player might.

Watching videos

You can use the Video app to watch videos that you download using the app or other sources. To watch videos that you have downloaded and saved in your Videos library, scroll left and select My Videos.

As shown in Figure 14-9, the Video app organizes your videos into broad categories: Personal Videos, My TV, Home, New Movies, Featured Movies, New TV Shows, and Featured TV Shows. Movies contains only movies that you download using the Video app. Similarly, My TV contains only TV shows downloaded using Video. All local files are shown under Personal Videos.

Figure 14-9 Videos are organized in categories on your local computer.

Selecting a video plays it using a touch-friendly interface as shown in Figure 14-10. Drag the green circle to jump to any portion of the video. If you're streaming a video, jumping too far forward can cause a delay of a few seconds while that portion of the video is downloaded. Be patient; it'll catch up. The big circle in the middle pauses and plays the video, and the arrow in the upper left returns you to the Video screen.

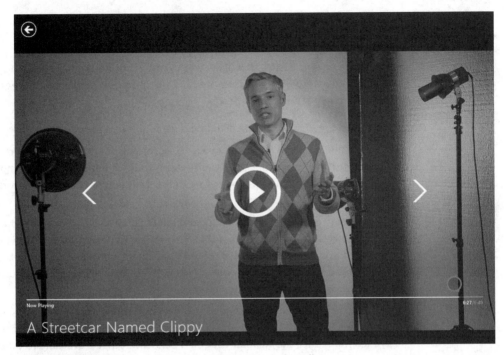

Now Playing

A Streetcar Named Clippy

Figure 14-10 The Windows 8.1 video player is touch-friendly.

Swipe up or right-click to view a few additional controls: Repeat (which plays the video file again when it ends), Previous, Play, Next, and, if you downloaded the video using the app, Play On Xbox.

Purchasing TV and movies

You can use the Video app to purchase or rent TV shows and movies. Different shows and movies can have different usage terms. It's common for a rented movie to be available for 24 hours after you start to watch it, up to 14 days after you rent it. For TV shows, you are often allowed to watch the show indefinitely. If you purchase an entire season, you might be eligible to download future episodes as they become available (not unlike the way new episodes of a show are available on a DVR after they air using conventional TV).

You can purchase entire seasons of a TV show. If you've never watched a show this way, the experience is so vastly superior to waiting a week or more for the next episode to air that you'll never want to go back to conventional TV. In fact, if you don't need live TV (such as news and sports), you might even be able to save money by cancelling your cable or satellite

TV subscription and purchasing individual shows online. As an added bonus, purchased shows have no advertising, so they take less time to watch.

TROUBLESHOOTING

I have trouble watching videos. Is my Internet connection fast enough?

There are quite a few websites that allow you to test your Internet bandwidth. My favorite is *http://www.bandwidthplace.com/*. For the purposes of watching videos, you only need to test your download speed.

Your download speed could be impacted by several different factors:

- The maximum speed allowed by your ISP according to the service that you have purchased. This is the ideal; if you test your bandwidth at 90 percent or more of this speed, then your network is operating perfectly. If you need more bandwidth, talk to your ISP, or find a different ISP.

- The current bandwidth available to your ISP. Most ISPs sell far more bandwidth than they can actually deliver to all of their customers. Therefore, during busy periods (like in the evening), you probably won't be able to reach the maximum bandwidth your ISP advertises for the service you purchased. You can call your ISP to complain, but they probably won't do anything about it.

- The current bandwidth available to your Internet connection. If you have multiple computers sharing your network, another computer might be downloading files, which will reduce the share of your ISP's bandwidth that is available to other computers on your network. If you don't have enough bandwidth to watch a video, stop file transfers and streaming media on your other PCs.

- The current bandwidth available on your local area network (LAN). If you have wired Ethernet, your LAN is almost certainly much faster than your Internet connection. Therefore, it's unlikely that your LAN is your performance bottleneck. If you're connected to a wireless LAN, there's a good chance that the wireless LAN is slower than your Internet connection. Wireless LANs never achieve their advertised speed; for example, 802.11n wireless networks often advertise speeds of 300 Mbps. As I write this, my state-of-the-art 802.11n network is capable of only about 5 Mbps, but I'm outside and rather far away from the wireless access point, my neighbors have an interfering wireless network, and the screens in my windows scramble the signal. All these factors can impact wireless network performance.

In summary, understanding your bandwidth is difficult because neither your ISP nor your LAN gives you the bandwidth they advertise, and bandwidth varies depending on many different factors. If you plan to stream hi-def video, get the highest level of Internet service from your ISP. On your LAN, use wired Ethernet when possible, followed by powerline networking, and resort to wireless networking only when no other option is available.

You don't pay for TV and movies directly using your credit card. Instead, all prices are in Microsoft Points, and you must purchase a number of Microsoft Points in advance to purchase TV shows and videos. If you want to test a show before buying it, open the TV Marketplace and select Free TV.

After you purchase a movie or TV show, the Video app will give you two options: Play and Download. Play streams the movie or show to your computer, allowing you to watch it instantly. However, if your network connection isn't fast enough, you'll experience buffering delays, wherein the video playback stops while your computer retrieves more of the video from the Internet.

If you select Download, the entire video is copied to your computer. You'll still be able to watch video immediately, and you'll be able to watch it later offline (for example, while on an airplane). The longer you wait to start playing the video, the less likely you are to experience buffering delays. You will need enough drive space to store the entire video, and downloading a large number of TV shows and movies can quickly fill up a mobile PC's drive.

When the video starts playing, you'll probably want to select the full screen icon in the lower-right corner of the video. If you love multitasking, dock the Video app to one side of the screen so that you can watch TV in a smaller window while you use another app.

Editing videos

Editing your videos is really important. This is the Internet age, and people don't have the patience for long videos. If you record your kid's hour-long baseball game and want to show it to your friends, you really should edit it down to a minute or two. If you want to keep your audience's attention, edit out everything but the most important seconds of the most important moments.

Videos are also an excellent way to share your photos. By inserting your pictures into a video, you can create a slide show with your own voice over and easily share the video on sites such as Facebook and YouTube.

Installing Movie Maker

Windows 8.1 doesn't include software to edit videos, but Windows Live Essentials (a free download from *http://windows.microsoft.com/en-US/windows-live/essentials-home*) includes Movie Maker, a desktop app you can use to edit your videos.

When installing Live Essentials, on the What Do You Want To Install page, be sure to select Choose The Programs You Want To Install. Otherwise, you might install several apps you don't need. On the Select Programs To Install page, as shown in Figure 14-11, you can clear all the check boxes except the one for Photo Gallery And Movie Maker.

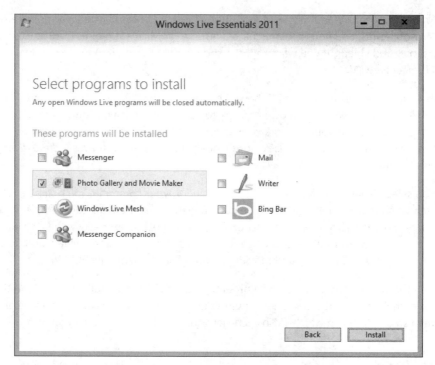

Figure 14-11 You need to install only Photo Gallery and Movie Maker to edit your videos.

By default, Movie Maker can handle only a few different types of files because Windows includes only a few codecs. *Codecs* allow Windows to understand different video formats. To allow Movie Maker to handle a wider variety of files (and thus increase the odds that it will support the files created by your camera), search for and install the K-Lite Codec Pack. Don't accept the default settings for the installation; you don't need to install Media Player Classic, which might be included with your download, and you should definitely turn off the options for installing different toolbars and changing your browser settings.

▶ **Editing a video with touch** Watch the video at *http://aka.ms/WinIO/editing*.

Editing a video

Once Movie Maker is installed, launch it from the Start screen. Your first step is to import a photo or video. Click Add Videos And Photos on the Home tab, or simply drag the files from File Explorer into the Movie Maker window.

If you add more than one file to your project, drag clips into the order you want to view them. At this point, the video is probably far longer than you would want to share. Click Play, and watch your video. When the action starts, pause the video. On the Edit tab, click Split to break your video into two clips, as shown in Figure 14-12. Then, delete the first clip.

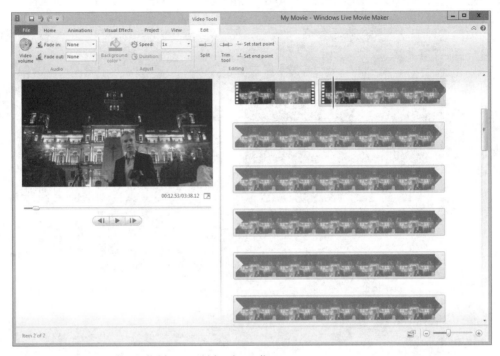

Figure 14-12 Use Split to divide your video into clips.

Now, your video is off to a strong start, but there's probably much more in the middle of the video that you want to remove. Click Play again. As soon as the action stops, and you get to a part of the video you don't want to share, click the Split button again. Continue watching, and click Split once more when you reach a portion of the video you want to share, and delete the boring clip you just created.

Repeat the process of splitting clips and deleting the boring parts until you have a fast-paced video suited to the hummingbird-like attention span of Facebook users.

You don't really need to do anything else. With video, less is more, and music, video effects, and transitions are completely unnecessary. However, if you want to play with them, check out the other tabs on the ribbon:

- Home

- Animations

- Visual Effects

One exception to the less-is-more philosophy is still photos. Apply an animation to your photos to slowly zoom them in and out, a technique known as the Ken Burns effect. As shown in Figure 14-13, expand the Pan And Zoom tools to view the full gallery of effects.

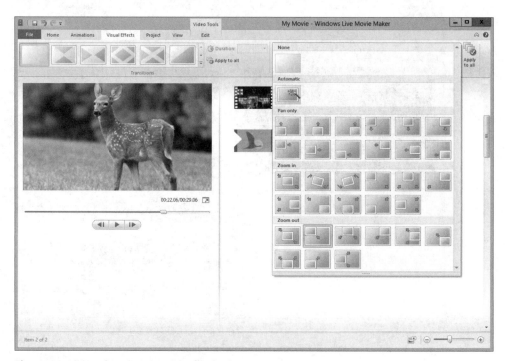

Figure 14-13 Apply animations to still photos to make them more interesting.

Publishing a video

When you're done editing your video, use the Home tab to publish and share it in a variety of formats. Movie Maker includes tools to share your video on SkyDrive, Facebook, YouTube, and Flickr. As shown in Figure 14-14, you can also click the Save Movie list to save a video file to your local computer, which you can then copy anywhere.

Figure 14-14 Movie Maker can save your edited movie in a variety of formats.

Other video editing apps

Movie Maker is powerful enough for most home users and it's free, so it's hard to beat. If you decide you need something more powerful (for example, if you record with multiple cameras and you want to more easily switch between tracks), it might be time to purchase a video-editing app.

My favorite home video-editing app is Adobe Premiere Elements, available at *http://www.adobe.com/products/premiere-elements.html*. It provides most of the power of professional video-editing software with a greatly simplified user interface.

For professional power, upgrade to Adobe Premiere Pro, available at *http://www.adobe.com/products/premiere.html*. Premiere Pro is the same tool many commercial TV series and movies are edited with. The power is unlimited, but the tool is complex and can be difficult to learn.

CHAPTER 15

Photos

Viewing pictures with the Photos app 325

Importing photos................................. 326

Printing photos................................... 330

Working with RAW files........................... 332

Selecting and sharing photos...................... 334

Working with photos on the desktop............... 336

Organizing photos 337

When I grew up—before the Internet—my family often had to entertain each other with conversation. I know, it was hard times. We played games where we asked each other hypothetical questions. I remember asking my mom which item she would take if our house were on fire, and she said the photo album.

Times haven't changed that much. The modern disaster scenario is, of course, the hard drive failure, and I regularly get email messages from readers asking how they can recover their digital pictures from their failed drive. To this day, nobody has ever asked me how they can recover their spreadsheets or their presentations from a failed drive. It's all about the photos.

And I understand that. I've been a serious photographer for about 15 years, and the tens of thousands of digital pictures I've taken are indeed my most cherished digital possessions. In this chapter, I'll walk you through how to view, import, print, share, and organize your photos. I won't, however, show you how to take pictures. If you'd like to learn how to be a better photographer, check out another of my books, *Tony Northrup's DSLR Book: How to Create Stunning Digital Photography* (Mason Press, 2011).

Viewing pictures with the Photos app

The Photos app is a touch-friendly way to browse your pictures, as shown in Figure 15-1. If you've managed to navigate the Start screen well enough to open the Photos app, you won't have any problem using the app itself. Select a folder to view the pictures within it, tap a picture to view it full screen, and then right-click or swipe up to access the Slide Show command.

Notice the option (available using the Settings charm) shown in Figure 15-2, which creates a miniature slide show in the Photos live tile on your Start screen. I suggest turning this option off because it can actually make finding the Photos app tile difficult when it changes regularly; the app name is difficult to read on top of light-colored photos.

CHAPTER 15

Figure 15-1 Browse your pictures with the Photos app.

Figure 15-2 Use the Settings charm to hide folders in the Photos app.

Importing photos

I have many friends with digital cameras who just leave their pictures on their camera. If they want to show them to you, they pull their camera out and show you on the tiny screen on the back of the camera.

Don't let your photos live their entire life trapped in a camera. Your pictures want to be on the big screen and be shared with your friends. Copying pictures from your camera to your computer is also a great way to free up room on your memory card and to back up your pictures.

To import your photos, connect your camera or memory card to your computer. There are three ways to do this:

- **With a USB cable**   Most cameras include a USB cable that you can use to plug your camera directly into your computer. This is a great approach if your computer doesn't have a memory card reader, especially when travelling, because you only need a USB cable. For smartphones that don't record images to a separate memory card, this is your only option.

- **With a memory card reader**   Almost all digital cameras record their images to a removable memory card. Take the memory card out and connect it to a memory card reader on your computer. Most desktop PCs and many mobile computers have memory card readers built in, as shown in Figure 15-3. If yours doesn't, you can buy very inexpensive USB memory card readers. If your computer supports USB 3.0, be sure to buy a memory card reader that also supports USB 3.0, because you will be able to copy your pictures must faster.

Figure 15-3 Desktop computers often have a built-in memory card reader.

- **Wirelessly**   Some cameras support copying your pictures wirelessly using Bluetooth or Wi-Fi. Wireless transfers aren't as fast as the wired options, but professionals often use wireless transfers in studio environments to allow them to continuously copy pictures to a computer during a photo shoot so that the models and art directors can see the photos on larger displays in real time. If your camera doesn't have wireless capabilities built in, you can use an Eye-Fi SD card (with a CF adapter, if your camera requires it) to send pictures to a computer, tablet, or smartphone over Wi-Fi. For best performance, use Eye-Fi direct mode. For more information, visit *http://www.eye.fi/*.

The first time you connect a memory card to your computer, Windows displays the notification shown in Figure 15-4. Select Import Photos And Videos. If the notification disappears before you can get to it, just remove the memory card and reconnect it, and wait for 5 or 10 seconds.

▶ **Transferring photos wirelessly to your PC**   Watch the video at *http://aka.ms/WinIO/transfer*.

Figure 15-4 Windows prompts you to choose what happens when you connect a memory card.

Windows will then display the import screen, as shown in Figure 15-5. This screen appears automatically the next time you insert a memory card, without Windows prompting you. By default, Windows stores pictures in a new folder in Pictures named for the current date.

Figure 15-5 Import pictures into a new folder.

TROUBLESHOOTING

How can I fix what Windows does with a memory card?

If you pick the wrong action for memory cards, you can change it later. Search Settings for **AutoPlay**, and then select AutoPlay. In the AutoPlay Control Panel tool, shown in Figure 15-6, click the Memory Card list and select your preferred response.

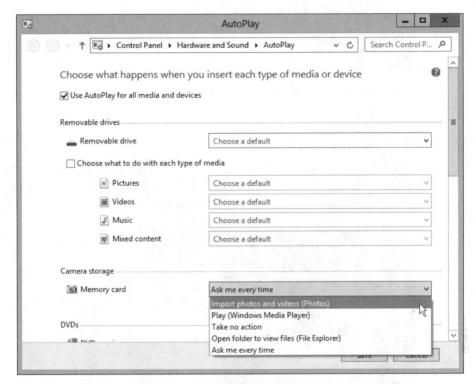

Figure 15-6 Use Control Panel to change the default action for memory cards.

You can use this same tool to change the default actions for other types of removable media and devices. Just remember that the feature is called AutoPlay, and you'll always be able to find it in Search.

Type a new name in the text box at the bottom of the import screen to describe the pictures you're importing, because the default name is rather meaningless: it's not the date the pictures were taken (which is stored in each picture's metadata anyway), but rather the date you imported them. For example, you might name the folder "Madelyn's 9th birthday party," which would allow you to find the folder years from now by searching for "Madelyn," "birthday," or "party." You can't browse to select a folder, but if you type the name of an existing folder, Windows will store your pictures in that same folder.

Once you click Import, Windows copies the pictures from your memory card to the folder you specified. This might take several minutes. When it's done, click Open Album to view your pictures.

If Windows doesn't automatically import your pictures, start the Photos app, swipe up or right-click to view the app's commands, and then select the Import button, as shown in Figure 15-7.

Figure 15-7 Use the Import button to manually import pictures.

Printing photos

As with most apps, you can print from the Photos app by opening the Devices charm and selecting your printer. As shown in Figure 15-8, the Photos app does a nice job of arranging your photos to get the most use out of your paper.

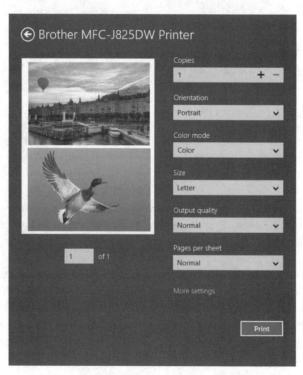

Figure 15-8 Print photos using the Devices charm.

Notice that in Figure 15-8, Photos decided to print two pictures on a single page. It did this because I chose to print two landscape photos using portrait orientation. In discussions about printing, the term landscape means that a photo is horizontal, and the term portrait means that a photo is vertical. In other words, landscapes are wider than they are tall, and portraits are taller than wide, regardless of what the subject of the photo is.

If you want to fit two landscape photos on a single page, choose portrait orientation. If you want to fit two portrait photos onto a single page, choose landscape orientation. On the other hand, choose the print orientation that matches the photo orientation if you want to print using the entire sheet of paper, as shown by Figure 15-9.

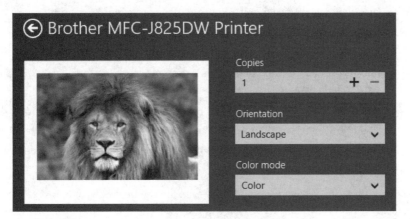

Figure 15-9 To print a photo full page, choose portrait or landscape to match the photo's orientation.

If you want to print a black-and-white photo, change the Color Mode to Monochrome. This isn't the best way to make a black-and-white print; it's better to make the adjustment in photo editing software so you can tweak the brightness and contrast, which are critical in black-and-white prints.

For better print quality, use paper designed for printing photos, and change the Output Quality to Photo. This uses more ink and takes longer to print, but your prints will look much better.

▶ **Printing photos** Watch the video at *http://aka.ms/WinIO/printphotos*.

Inside OUT

Get cheaper, better quality prints by ordering them online

As a photographer, I'm often asked which printer I use. The answer surprises many people: I don't print my own photos. I always order my prints from an online service (specifically, *mpix.com*).

I decided to order my prints online after a long battle with printing at home. I discovered that online services have many advantages over home printing:

- Using my own photo paper and ink actually costs more per photo.

- Good quality photo printers that can print larger sizes are very expensive and take up desk space.

- Photos printed at home don't have a protective coating over the ink, so they tend to fade, smudge, and stick to the glass when framed.

- You need to cut the white borders off most photos you print at home, and getting straight edges requires a large paper cutter, which takes up desk space.

- Photo printing is hard, and I often have several failed attempts at printing before I'm satisfied with one.

For those reasons, I leave printing to the experts. The only downside is that I have to wait a few days for the prints to arrive in the mail. I've tried using local one-hour print shops to get quicker results, but their print quality is no better than what I get by printing the photos at home.

Working with RAW files

Most digital cameras create a JPG file by default when you take a picture, and this file format is a great choice for the casual photographer. The files are compressed, so you can fit more pictures onto your memory card and Windows can copy them faster. JPG files are also ready to share in email or on Facebook.

However, JPG files have some serious drawbacks for photographers who really care about image quality:

- JPG uses lossy compression, which reduces image size by very slightly degrading the image quality. Most cameras use a very high-quality JPG setting by default, so the casual observer might never notice the slight loss in sharpness or the extra jaggedness JPG compression can add to a picture.

- Because your camera is creating the JPG file, you have to accept the camera's settings for color, brightness, contrast, and sharpening. If you don't know what those terms are, or you never edit your photos, then perhaps that doesn't matter. If you do edit your photos, or you might want to edit them in the future, using JPG means that your camera is making changes to your original picture that you can't undo.

- If you use special effects like converting your picture to black and white or sepia, then your pictures will have those effects applied forever—even after photographic trends change and washed-out pictures become as cool as the paint splatter backdrop used by every portrait photographer in the 1980s.

Higher-end point-and-shoot cameras and most digital single lens reflex (DSLR) cameras can be configured to save pictures as RAW files. RAW files save every bit of data that your camera's digital sensor produces. Your camera doesn't process the RAW file in any way; instead, you must use software on your computer to process the RAW file.

That's an important advantage. Your computer is much more powerful than your camera, so it might be able to do a more effective job of converting the RAW file into a JPG. Often, RAW files processed on your computer produce images with much less noise (which is the digital equivalent of grain in film), because the image processing algorithm in the computer software is more intelligent than the algorithm in your camera.

More importantly, using RAW files allows you to fix problems with your picture that you couldn't fix as well if you were using a JPG:

- You can adjust a photo's exposure after you take the picture without significant quality loss.

- If just part of a picture is overexposed (appearing completely white), you can recover the blown-out highlights in that part of the picture without impacting the overall exposure.

- White balance problems (where your picture has an orange, blue, or green tint) can be fixed.

The downside to RAW files is that RAW files are bigger than JPGs, so they fill up your memory card faster and take longer to copy to your computer. For me, the benefits of RAW files outweigh the drawbacks, so I always use them.

While JPG is a file format that can be read by anyone, RAW files are specific to an individual camera, and can only be read by software specifically designed to read that camera's RAW files. Because new cameras are constantly being released, Windows doesn't have built-in support for every RAW format. However, you can probably download a RAW codec from your camera's manufacturer. If they don't have a codec specifically for Windows 8.1, a Windows 7 codec will work.

CHAPTER 15

Here are links to different camera manufacturers' RAW codecs:

- Canon: *http://www.usa.canon.com/cusa/windows_vista/cameras/*

- Nikon: *http://www.nikonimglib.com/nefcodec/*

- Sony: *http://esupport.sony.com/perl/swu-download.pl?template= EN&mdl&upd_id=4022&SMB=YES*

- Fuji: *http://www.fujifilm.com/support/digital_cameras/software/*

- Panasonic: *http://panasonic.jp/support/global/cs/dsc/download/raw/index.html*

Manufacturers update their RAW codecs when they release new cameras. After you install the RAW codec for your camera, you'll be able to view your RAW pictures in Windows Photo Gallery and see the thumbnails in File Explorer (if you've enabled thumbnails as described in "Working with photos on the desktop" later in this chapter).

Selecting and sharing photos

Like other Windows 8.1 apps, the Photos app lets you share photos by using the Share charm. To share a single photo, view it, and then open the Share charm.

To share multiple photos, select all the photos you want to share before opening the Share charm. As a reminder, you can select objects in Windows 8.1 by right-clicking them or by flicking them with your finger. Once you select your first picture, Windows keeps the commands visible at the bottom of the screen (see Figure 15-10) to display how many photos are selected. You can change folders without clearing your selection.

Selecting Slide Show remembers your selection but displays a slide show containing all the photos from the current folder.

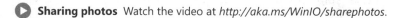 **Sharing photos** Watch the video at *http://aka.ms/WinIO/sharephotos*.

Sharing photos in email

If you share your photos in email, Mail creates a new message with the selected images as file attachments, as shown in Figure 15-11. Windows might resize your pictures to make them small enough to easily send as an attachment.

Figure 15-10 The commands stay visible once you select photos.

Figure 15-11 Send multiple pictures as attachments in email.

Working with photos on the desktop

By default, Windows opens pictures in the touch-friendly Photos app even when you open them from File Explorer on the desktop. If you'd rather use Windows Photo Viewer (the same app used by Windows 7), follow these steps:

1. Open the desktop.

2. Open File Explorer.

3. Browse to your Pictures folder (or wherever you have pictures stored).

4. Right-click a picture, click Open With, and then click Choose Default Program.

5. Select Use This App For All .Jpg Files (or whatever file extension your pictures have), as shown in Figure 15-12.

Figure 15-12 Windows Photo Viewer isn't touch-friendly, but it's much more powerful than the Photos app.

6. Select Windows Photo Viewer, as shown in Figure 15-12. If you'd rather use a different app, click More Options.

Another problem when working with the desktop is that File Explorer in Windows 8.1 doesn't show you thumbnails by default. To fix that, follow these steps:

1. Open File Explorer.

2. Click the View tab on the ribbon.

3. Click the Options button, and then click Change Folder And Search Options.

4. Select the View tab in the Folder Options dialog box. As shown in Figure 15-13, clear the first check box: Always Show Icons, Never Thumbnails. Click OK.

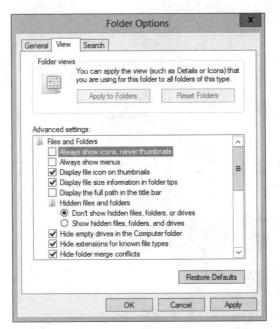

Figure 15-13 Clear this check box if you want to see thumbnails in File Explorer.

Now Windows will show thumbnails. This requires Windows to do some extra work when you view folders containing pictures, which could have a very minor impact on a mobile computer's battery life, but it isn't a problem on desktop computers.

Organizing photos

If you've owned a digital camera for more than a year or two, you've probably noticed a problem: finding that one awesome picture among the thousands you've taken. Taking large numbers of photos definitely improves your chances of getting a great one, but it also improves your chances of banging your head against the keyboard when you're trying to find the specific picture you want years later.

Fortunately, organizing your photos is easy. Windows 8.1 does include the same photo organization capabilities that were built into Windows 7: you can use the Details pane of File Explorer (which you turn on from the View tab on the ribbon) to view and edit a picture's properties. These properties include a title, subject, tags, and a rating, as shown in Figure 15-14. You can even select multiple pictures by Ctrl+clicking each of them, and then edit the properties for all of the pictures at once. After you define these properties for a picture, you can use the Search charm to find the picture based on any criteria you added.

Figure 15-14 You can view and edit picture metadata in the Details pane of File Explorer.

Here's an efficient workflow for organizing a new batch of photos:

1. Use the Photos app to import the photos to the computer.

2. Switch to the desktop and open File Explorer. On the View tab, select Details Pane (and resize the window wide enough that it displays correctly.)

3. Browse to the folder you just imported your pictures to.

4. Select a group of related photos. For example, I might select all the photos that include my daughter, Madelyn.

5. In the Details pane, add a descriptive tag such as "Madelyn," and then click Save.

6. Repeat steps 4 and 5 for every way to describe the pictures, including the name of everyone in the photo, the location, and the event.

7. Now select individual photos and rate them from 1-5 stars. I use the following system for star ratings:

- **1 star**   A blurry or poorly exposed picture, or a portrait with the person's eyes shut. Eventually, I delete all 1-star pictures to save space.

- **2 stars**   A generally bad picture that I can't bring myself to delete.

- **3 stars**   An OK picture that's not special in any way.

- **4 stars**   A picture that I want to show off. Four-star pictures have something special about them, such as a great expression or nice lighting.

- **5 stars**   A fantastic picture that I'll want to make a large print of or put in my portfolio.

By combining star ratings and tags, you can easily find your best pictures of any person or place. To find photos with a particular tag, simply search in File Explorer or the Photos app. To find just your best pictures based on the star rating, use the Details view of File Explorer and click the Rating column heading to sort the photos by rating. Use the Preview pane to view the photo you select, as shown in Figure 15-15.

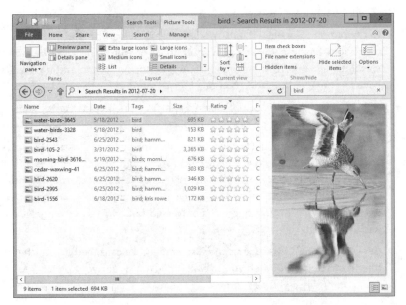

Figure 15-15 Use search, Details view, and the Preview pane to find your best-rated pictures of any subject.

File Explorer is actually pretty good for finding and organizing folders. However, Windows doesn't have powerful photo editing built in, and I believe everyone should do at least a bit of editing before printing or sharing a photo. Think of photo editing as cleaning up your house before guests visit; not only is it polite, but it makes you look better.

Inside OUT

Design a computer for photo editing

The more serious you get about photography, the more time you spend editing your photos, and the more time you spend waiting for your computer to perform different photo editing tasks. If you're buying a new computer, it makes sense to choose one that will be particularly quick when editing photos. Here are some tips:

- Get at least 8 gigabytes (GB) of RAM. Especially if you shoot RAW photos, opening pictures in applications such as Photoshop takes a lot of memory. If you don't have enough memory, Windows needs to access your hard drive, which is comparatively slow.

- Get a fast processor. Tasks such as applying a filter to your pictures require a great deal of processing. The faster your processor and the more cores you have, the less time those tasks take.

- Get two monitors. Having dual monitors really helps with applications such as Lightroom, because you can view thumbnails of your library on one monitor and view images full-screen on your second monitor. For photo editing, I'd rather have two smaller monitors than one bigger monitor.

- Get the cheapest video card you can. Expensive video cards are for gamers. Your money is better spent on other components.

- Get two disks: one small SSD and one high-capacity drive. Install Windows and your apps on the SSD drive, and use it to store your newest pictures. When you start to fill up your SSD drive (which only needs to be about 256 GB), move your pictures to your high-capacity drive (which might be 3 terabytes or more). Because your high-capacity drive is only used for long-term storage, it doesn't need to be fast.

- Get USB 3.0. USB 3.0 supports the fastest memory card readers, which reduces that frustrating time when you're waiting anxiously for your pictures to copy to your computer so you can comb over them.

25

For powerful photo organization and light photo editing, I highly recommend exploring one of these two apps:

- **Windows Live Essentials: Photo Gallery**   This app, available at *http://windows.microsoft.com/en-US/windows-live/photo-gallery-get-started*, is powerful and free. You can do the most common photo-editing tasks: crop, rotate, fix color problems, create panoramas, and even blend the best of multiple photos together.

- **Adobe Photoshop Lightroom**   This app, available at *http://www.adobe.com/products/photoshop-lightroom.html*, is not free. However, it has features that serious photographers need, such as automatically processing RAW files, powerful image editing capabilities, flexible publishing, bulk edits, virtual copies, and change control.

Even for my professional photography, those apps are sufficient for most of my photo editing. For more serious editing using powerful technologies such as layers and masks, try out the free Gimp app (available at *http://www.gimp.org/*) and, of course, Adobe Photoshop (available at *http://www.adobe.com/Photoshop*).

CHAPTER 15

Sharing and streaming digital media

Xbox Music	343	Car	348
Streaming to the Xbox	344	Other computers	350
Stereos and TVs	345	Video-streaming services	353
Smartphone	347	Creating media	354

You don't just listen to your music at your computer. Once you get spoiled by the Music app, you won't be able to stand listening to music that a DJ on the radio selected while you're in your car or at the gym. Similarly, the on-demand nature of digital video will make traditional TV seem slow-paced and annoying.

Fortunately, Windows 8.1 gives you many ways to connect the music and video on your computer to just about every stereo and TV in your life.

Xbox Music

The easiest way to get music from your computer to your stereo is by using the Xbox Music service, the Xbox Companion app, and an Xbox 360. Together, these allow you to manage your music in one place. The Play On Xbox button (which uses the free Xbox Companion app) allows you to control the music on your stereo from any computer.

It's important to understand how the Xbox Music service, the Xbox Companion app, and an Xbox 360 work together. First, you need to log in to Xbox Live on your Xbox and to the Xbox Companion app on your Windows 8.1 computer using the Microsoft Account that you used to subscribe to Xbox Music. Both Windows 8.1 and your Xbox will connect directly to Xbox Music, so it's important that you use the same credentials for both.

Next, start the Music app on Windows 8.1, and browse to the song, artist, album, or playlist you want to play. With good luck, it shows the Play On Xbox button. If it doesn't show that button, that means Xbox Music doesn't have rights to at least one of the songs you want to play. It's easy to tell which songs Xbox Music can play on your Xbox because the Music app will display album thumbnails for the song. If the Music app doesn't automatically download a thumbnail, the song isn't in the Xbox Music library, and you won't be able to play it on your Xbox.

Inside OUT
How Xbox Companion and your Xbox 360 communicate

The Play On Xbox feature of the Music app and Xbox Companion doesn't work by streaming your music files across the network. First, the Music app looks up your song to see if it's available on Xbox Music, even if you didn't download it from Xbox Music. If it is available on Xbox Music, the Music app shows you the Play On Xbox button. If not, you won't see that button.

When you click the Play On Xbox button, Music opens the Xbox Companion app. Xbox Companion then communicates with your Xbox. You might expect it to say something like, "I have a song I'd like you to play. I have a copy of it right here that you can use across our local area network." Instead, Xbox Companion says something like, "I have a song I'd like you to play. Connect to Xbox Music on the Internet to get your own copy of the song."

Connecting to the Internet to download music that you already have on your local network clearly isn't the most efficient technique. On the other hand, it can actually improve your performance if both your computer and your Xbox are connected to your wireless network. The approach also means there is a delay of several seconds after you select a song to play. It's not an issue if you start a playlist or an album because the delay occurs only before the first song.

Streaming to the Xbox

You can stream music and videos to your Xbox in two different ways:

- **Music and Video apps**   From your Xbox, browse to Music, select My Music Apps, and then select Music Player. Similarly, for videos, browse to Video, select My Video Apps, and then select Video Player.

- **Windows Media Center**   If you have the Windows Media Center add-on for Windows 8.1, you can use Xbox as a Media Center Extender and stream music and video directly from your PC. This works much better than the Music and Video apps on the Xbox; the user interface is nicer, and it's better at detecting new files and folders.

Stereos and TVs

The Digital Living Network Alliance (DLNA) has established guidelines that allow devices such as stereos and TVs to stream music, pictures, and videos from computers and other devices. Connect a DLNA-certified digital media receiver (DMR) to your network, allow media devices to stream content (configured using the Network, HomeGroup page of PC Settings, as shown in Figure 16-1), and you can play music, view pictures, and watch videos without connecting an Xbox or another computer.

▶ **Playing your music on your stereo** Watch the video at *http://aka.ms/WinIO/stereo.*

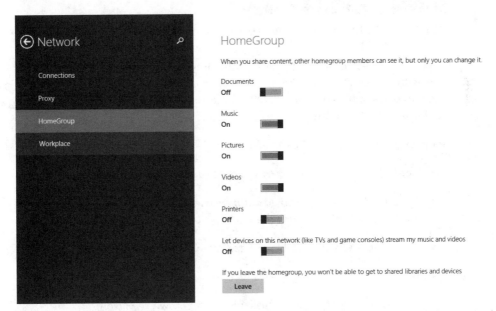

Figure 16-1 Use HomeGroup settings to allow media devices to access your music, pictures, and videos across your network.

You can even use the Devices charm to push songs directly from the Music app to your stereo, as shown in Figure 16-2. Play a song that's not copy protected (for example, a song in MP3 format rather than a song from Xbox Music), open the Devices charm, and then select your receiver. Within a second or two, the song will start playing on your receiver. The same technique can work for albums and playlists.

Different DMRs are compatible with different file formats. Most support music in the MP3 and video in the MPEG-3 format. However, many people have files in different formats (such as MP4) that might not play on any given DMR. Before buying a DMR, carefully review the device's capabilities and reviews from other users.

CHAPTER 16

Figure 16-2 Use the Devices charm to push music to a DLNA stereo across your network.

If your DMR does not support your file formats, you might be able to run DLNA server software with transcoding capabilities. Transcoding converts media files from their original format into a format supported by your DMR. Transcoding can happen on-the-fly, meaning you do not have to wait for a conversion to take place.

Some of the more popular DLNA servers are:

- Mezzmo, available at *http://www.conceiva.com/products/mezzmo/*.

- Nero MediaHome, available at *http://www.nero.com/enu/ mediahome4-introduction.html*.

- Wild Media Server, available at *http://www.wildmediaserver.com/*.

- Tversity, available at *http://tversity.com/*.

- Serviio, a free DLNA server, available at *http://www.serviio.org/*.

Televisions with built-in DMR capabilities are particularly useful for those of us with minimalist design tastes. For example, if you want to use an Xbox as a Media Center Extender, you obviously need to place an Xbox somewhere near your TV. Traditionally, people do this with an entertainment center. However, minimalists might prefer a TV mounted on the wall without an entertainment center. By streaming content to the TV directly across the network, you can access all the content on your network without any other devices, eliminating the need for an entertainment center.

Different DLNA-certified devices have different capabilities. Before you buy, make sure the device you're using supports music, videos, and pictures and that its user interface is friendly enough for your whole family to use.

Inside OUT
Streaming video performance

Streaming transfers music and videos across your home network to your Xbox while you play them. While streaming music is rarely a problem, and just about any home network can handle streaming standard-definition video, high-definition (HD) video can cause performance issues.

If you stream HD video, you'll soon discover that network performance isn't as consistent as you might think. For example, if you're in the middle of watching a movie in 1080p and try to copy a big file across your network, chances are good that the streaming will begin to fail. Unlike video streaming on the Internet, streaming to your Xbox doesn't dynamically reduce the video quality as network performance drops. Instead, the video just buffers until it can play again.

You might be able to stream HD video if either your PC or your Xbox is connected to your wireless network, but only if you're using the latest wireless technologies, such as 802.11n, and have a very good wireless signal. If both your Xbox and PC are connected to the wireless network, you'll actually be using twice the bandwidth, because your video will need to fly through the air from your PC to your wireless access point, and then from the wireless access point to your Xbox. Therefore, connecting one of the devices with an Ethernet cable effectively doubles your streaming bandwidth.

If at all possible, avoid using wireless networks for streaming. You'll get the most reliable performance by running Ethernet cables to both your PC and Xbox. Often, an electrician can run cables between rooms so that you don't have cables running on the floor.

In some houses, including my own, running new cables through the walls isn't an option. As an alternative, I've had very good experiences with the latest generation of powerline Ethernet adapters. Plug one adapter into a wall outlet near your router, and connect it with an Ethernet cable to your router. Plug other adapters into wall outlets near your PC, Xbox, or both, and connect the devices to your powerline adapter with an Ethernet cable. Performance varies depending on the wiring in your house, but I reliably get more than enough bandwidth for streaming HD video.

Smartphone

All modern smartphones allow you to synchronize music from your computer. Depending on the type of phone you have, you might need to use software provided with your phone. All the major streaming-media services offer apps for all the major smartphones, so if you use a streaming-media service on your computer, you should install its app to take that music with you.

Once you get your music on your phone, it's easy to play it just about anywhere. Of course, you can put on headphones and listen to music. As described in the next section, there are several different ways you can listen to it in your car. You can also connect your phone to your stereo if you don't have an Xbox 360—simply run a 3.5mm male/male cable from your phone's headphone jack to your stereo's 3.5mm aux-in port and turn up the volume on your phone.

Car

The easiest way to play your music in your car is to copy your songs onto your smartphone or other media player. Connecting your media player to your car can be done in many different ways, depending on the capabilities of your car's stereo. In order from most to least preferred, those techniques are:

- **Device-specific connector**   Many cars come with connectors for popular phones and media players. If your car doesn't have a connector, you can probably buy an adapter specific to the model of your car and your media player and install it (or have a professional install it). Device-specific connectors offer the best experience because they provide perfect digital audio quality and often allow you to use your car stereo's controls to skip songs or even browse your music.

- **Aux-in**   An auxiliary-in connector (also known as a line-in connector) allows you to connect a 3.5mm male/male cable directly from the headphone jack of your media player to your car, as shown in Figure 16-3. The sound quality isn't quite as good as using a device-specific connector, but you might never notice. Be sure to turn the volume up on your media player.

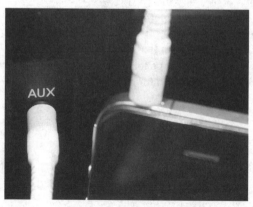

Figure 16-3 If your car has an aux-in port, connect it to your media player's headphone jack.

- **Cassette adapter** If your car has a cassette player, you can get a cassette adapter that connects to your media player's headphone jack. Push the cassette adapter into your stereo and turn your media player's volume up for a tape that never ends.

TROUBLESHOOTING

I have terrible sound quality when using an aux-in port

Aux-in ports aren't ideal for sound quality. Your device's headphone jack is designed to be used for headphones, not for connecting to other stereo equipment. Therefore, the sound quality will never be as good as when using a device-specific connector.

However, there are a few ways to improve the sound quality:

- Increase the volume on your device. Typically, I turn the volume all the way up.

- Decrease the volume on your device. I know I just told you to increase the volume, and most devices and audio files work well with the volume turned all the way up. If you hear popping or crackling, however, try turning the volume down until the distortion disappears.

- Use your stereo to control the volume. After you get your device's volume set to a point where it's as high as possible without crackling, don't touch the volume. Instead, use the volume controls on your stereo.

- Reencode the file with a higher volume. Some audio files are simply quiet. If you play one through your headphone jack, you'll have to turn your stereo's volume up very high to hear it, and increasing the volume will increase the prominence of any static in the connection. If some parts of the audio are loud and some are quiet, reencode the file using dynamic range compression (DRC). If all of the audio is quiet, reencode the file and increase the audio gain. For video files, you can use the free HandBrake desktop app, available at *http://handbrake.fr/*. Within HandBrake, select the Audio tab, click Advanced, and then specify the Audio Gain and Dynamic Range before reencoding the file. For audio files, use the free Audacity app, available at *http://audacity.sourceforge.net/*. Increase the gain and then save the audio file.

- Wiggle the connectors around. Sometimes headphone jacks and aux-in ports get loose. If that happens, you might get crackling sounds when the connector makes or loses contact. To determine whether that's the problem, try wiggling the connector around. If it crackles, your connector is too loose. You could try using a new cable. If that doesn't solve the problem, you might need to replace the headphone jack or aux-in port, which will require a soldering iron and some patience.

- **FM transmitter** If your car doesn't have an aux-in port, buy an FM transmitter and connect it to your media player, as shown in Figure 16-4. FM transmitters are like tiny radio stations that play your music. Connect the FM transmitter to the headphone jack of your media player, select a frequency that doesn't have an existing station broad-casting, and then set your car's radio to the same frequency. FM transmitters generally only broadcast strongly enough to be heard from within your car, the audio quality isn't always great, and you might need to change frequencies if you drive to a different area.

Figure 16-4 If your car lacks an aux-in port, use an FM transmitter.

If you don't have a smartphone or media player, burn a CD with Windows 8.1:

- **CD** Windows 8.1 can burn music CDs that play exactly like any other CD. For detailed instructions, read "Creating media" later in this chapter.

- **MP3 CD/WMA CD** Some car stereos support MP3 CDs or WMA CDs (there's usually a logo on the stereo). Instead of creating a CD with 10–12 songs, you can create a CD with about 200 songs, neatly organized into folders. MP3 CDs are like a more modern equiv-alent of a CD changer. For more information, read "Creating media" later in this chapter.

▶ **Playing your music in your car** Watch the video at *http://aka.ms/WinIO/car*.

Other computers

The easiest way to share media (or any file, for that matter) between computers in your home is by using a homegroup. Homegroups share the documents, music, videos, folders, printers, and backup drives (as shown earlier in Figure 16-1) that you choose to share across your home network using only a password.

Another option is to use shared folders, which allows you to limit access to specific users. Let's say you've used Windows Media Center to record some PG-13 movies. You want your older daughter to be able to watch the movies on the computer in her room, but you don't want your younger son to be able to watch them. You still want your younger son to be able to watch other videos, however.

A homegroup won't work for this. Any computer that participates in the homegroup can access any file shared to the homegroup. However, you can use folder sharing with different user permissions to control who can access which files and folders.

Either way, you should add the Music and Videos folders shared by other computers to your Music and Videos libraries on computers that will play the media. Figure 16-5 illustrates the Music library on a computer running Windows 8.1, containing several folders shared from other computers. The Music app can find and play any song in any of these folders, as long as the computer sharing them is turned on and connected to the local network. For more information about using libraries, refer to Chapter 9, "Organizing and protecting files."

Figure 16-5 Add shared folders to the Music and Videos libraries.

➤ **For more information about configuring homegroups and shared folders, refer to Chapter 24, "Sharing and managing files and printers."**

Music services

Music-streaming services come in two varieties: those that allow you to choose the specific songs and albums you want to listen to, and those that allow you to choose the type of music you want to hear but don't allow you to pick specific songs. Typically, you need to pay a subscription fee to use streaming services that allow you to choose specific songs.

Most free services don't allow you to pick exactly which song you listen to, but you can tell the service that you like jazz or rock or pop, and it'll play just that type of music for you. You can even identify specific artists that you like, and the service will play that artist's music along with music by similar artists.

The Store has many music services you might enjoy, and you can access others using a web browser. Some of the more popular music services include:

- Xbox Music

- Pandora

- MOG

- Rhapsody

- Slacker

- Spotify

- Rdio

- Last.fm

Windows 8.1 includes built-in support for Xbox Music. Xbox Music lets you download songs and albums, almost like a music store where everything is included in a subscription service. You get to pick the specific songs that you want to listen to.

I use Xbox Music when I want to listen to something specific, and I use free streaming-media music services (specifically, Pandora) when I just want to hear some music without having to think about it.

Video-streaming services

Online video streaming can give you much of what a cable or satellite TV company provides, but over the Internet and at much lower cost. The most popular are:

- Xbox Video (accessed using the Video app as described in Chapter 14, "Music and videos")

- Hulu

- Netflix

- Amazon Prime

- Roku

- iTunes and Apple TV

- Google TV

Right now, none of these services provide as complete a portfolio of TV and movies as traditional cable and satellite TV providers do. The video services need to negotiate with every single network, and often with individual TV show producers. So, they have enough TV shows and movies to keep you entertained, but they don't necessarily have everything you can get from cable or satellite TV.

In particular, live events such as sports have particularly poor coverage. Some services, such as Hulu, will provide live streaming for major events such as a popular New Year's Eve countdown. You probably won't be able to watch your favorite local sports team's games, however.

On the other hand, video-streaming services provide something beyond what cable TV offers: entire seasons of shows at your fingertips, TV shows and movies that might not be available elsewhere (such as indie and foreign-language TV shows and movies), and the ability to watch videos on a computer or mobile device.

If you stream video directly to your computer, you might want to connect your computer to your TV and stereo. For more information, refer to Chapter 17, "Creating a Home Theater PC." Some services, such as Apple TV, sell a dedicated hardware device that connects to the Internet and your TV.

CHAPTER 16

Creating media

At some point, you might be forced to share music or videos using antiquated equipment dating back to the beginning of the digital media era. This era, which we now refer to as "yesteryear," is a time period from the early 1980s to the late 1990s when our ancestors transferred data on shiny discs known as CDs and DVDs.

Believe it or not, some modern computers are still capable of saving data to physical media. Sure, it seems silly in the era of the Internet, but it's useful if you're driving a classic car with only a CD player or if you want to watch your videos in some place with only a DVD player when you're on a vacation.

CDs

Burning audio CDs is unchanged from Windows 7; you use the Burn tab of the Windows Media Player desktop app. To launch Windows Media Player, from the Start screen, type **Media**, and then select Windows Media Player.

In Windows Media Player, select the Burn tab. Then, simply drag items from your Music library to the Burn List in the right pane, as shown in Figure 16-6. If you add more music than can fit on a single disc, Windows Media Player automatically organizes the files into multiple discs. You can't burn music you've downloaded from Xbox Music.

Figure 16-6 Use Windows Media Player to burn audio CDs.

Drag a song to change the order. When you're satisfied, click Start Burn. The burning process takes a few minutes. Windows Media Player will eject the newly burned CD when it's done. Be sure to label it with a marker specifically designed for writing on CDs; if you use the wrong type of pen, you could damage the CD, making it unlistenable.

TROUBLESHOOTING

My CDs won't burn

Occasionally, a burn will fail, as shown in Figure 16-7. If that happens, just insert another CD and try again. CD media is neither perfect nor consistent, and sometimes you just get a bad CD. Before you buy CD-R media, be sure to check the reviews; some are better than others.

Figure 16-7 CD burning is an unreliable process.

If you have a large number of failed burns, you might improve your success rate by slowing down your CD burner. With the Burn tab selected in Windows Media Player, open the menu with the check mark near the upper-right corner and select More Burn Options. On the Burn tab, change the burn speed to Slow.

Some CD players are capable of playing MP3 CDs. These are not simply data CDs with MP3 files saved on them; MP3 CDs have a specific format that you must create. Windows 8.1 doesn't include software to burn MP3 CDs, but you can use Apple iTunes or Nero to create them.

DVDs

Windows 8.1 doesn't have a built-in way to create a DVD from a movie. However, you can download the free Windows Live Movie Maker tool and burn a DVD with just a few clicks.

First, download Movie Maker from *http://windows.microsoft.com/is-IS/windows-live/movie-maker-get-started*. The installer will prompt you to install other apps, but you don't need to install anything other than Movie Maker.

Movie Maker is a complete video editing app. If you're interested in learning how to edit videos, you should refer to Chapter 14. This chapter describes only how to create a DVD from a video file, which could be a video you recorded yourself, a video you downloaded, or even a slide show of your photographs.

CHAPTER 16

To create a DVD from a video, follow these steps:

1. Start Windows Movie Maker.

2. In the right pane, select Click Here To Browse For Photos And Videos. Select the video you want to burn as a DVD.

3. On the Project tab, select either Widescreen or Standard. Most videos today are widescreen.

4. On the Home tab, click Save Movie, and then click Burn A DVD, as shown in Figure 16-8.

Figure 16-8 Movie Maker, a free download, can burn a DVD from a downloaded video.

5. Save your video when prompted. You can delete this file after you burn your DVD.

6. On the Add Pictures And Video To The DVD page, click Options. On the DVD-Video tab, as shown in Figure 16-9, verify that the options are set correctly for your video.

Figure 16-9 Change the DVD options before burning.

7. Click OK to close the DVD Options dialog box, and then click Next.

8. When you see the Ready To Burn DVD page, insert a writable DVD (such as a DVD-R), and then click Burn.

After you burn the DVD, you'll be given the option to save your project. That's only necessary if you plan to burn another DVD. You can play the DVD in any modern DVD player, though some older DVD players might have problems with DVDs created by a computer. It's a good idea to test the DVD, just to be sure it burned properly, because DVD burning, like CD burning, can be an unreliable process.

CHAPTER 16

Creating a Home Theater PC

HTPC software 360
Media Center 362
Configuring HTPC software to start automatically 369
Choosing the hardware 371
Recording TV 382
Choosing a remote control 387

Chapter 14, "Music and videos," and Chapter 16, "Sharing and streaming digital media," each discussed different techniques for playing music and videos on your home TV and stereo. Those approaches, such as using an Xbox or a digital media receiver (DMR), are far less complex than connecting a Home Theater PC (HTPC). Additionally, your cable TV company will probably rent you a digital video recorder (DVR) with the most important HTPC features.

So why dedicate an entire chapter to the HTPC?

- **The apps**   You can run dozens of different apps to play your music and videos, and they can be infinitely customized. I'm not using hyperbole; people write custom scripts to accomplish anything they want to do with their HTPC.

- **The codecs**   DMRs can play music and videos using only a limited number of codecs. Because an HTPC is a full Windows PC, and Windows always has the latest codecs available, you'll never find a file you can't play back on your HTPC.

- **The capacity**   Large-capacity hard drives are relatively inexpensive, allowing you to store thousands of songs, movies, and TV shows for just a few hundred dollars. Most DMRs are not very easy to extend.

- **The online connection**   HTPCs can connect directly to online sources for streaming music and video, giving you entertainment options not available through your cable company.

- **The games**   Though PC games aren't typically designed to be played from your couch, many can be played with a wireless controller. MAME (Multiple Arcade Machine Emulator) is particularly popular, because it allows you to play retro games. To download MAME and some free games, visit *http://mamedev.org/roms/*.

- **The cost**   While many people build high-end HTPCs that cost thousands of dollars, you can also create an HTPC from a very inexpensive computer—even a 10-year-old computer is capable of being a useful HTPC. So, you can create an HTPC from a computer that you would otherwise throw away, and you can probably find a capable computer on eBay for less than US$100 (just make sure it can run Windows 8.1). Computers with slower processors might struggle with some HD codecs, but I personally use an old laptop with an Intel Core2 processor at a meager 2 GHz. Compared to renting a DVR from your cable company, an HTPC can even save you money.

Still, an HTPC is not for everyone. Fortunately, you don't have to go all out. Start by running free HTPC software on your computer and see if you like it. If you do, spend a few minutes connecting your PC to your TV so you can experience it the way it should be. Once you get a taste for the power of HTPC, you may never want to go back to a conventional DVR.

HTPC software

HTPC software manages your music, TV, and movies and lets you access everything from your couch with a remote control. Different apps have different features, but most HTPC software provides these basic capabilities:

- **Remote control**   Whereas most apps are designed to be controlled by a mouse, keyboard, or touch, HTPC apps are primarily controlled using an infrared remote control, just like your TV and stereo.

- **10-foot user interface**   Whereas tablet computers are accessed from a foot or two away, and desktop and laptops are usually within two or three feet, most people watch TV from across the room. The so-called 10-foot user interface (UI) is similar to a touch interface, with large text and icons.

- **Digital video recorder (DVR)**   Many HTPC apps can play and record live TV. This is known as time-shifting, and it requires specialized hardware known as a tuner card (discussed later in this chapter). DVR capabilities usually allow you to skip past commercials in recorded TV.

- **Converting recorded TV for mobile devices**   HTPC software, or add-ons such as MCEBuddy (discussed later in this chapter), can convert TV into formats you can play on your smartphone or media player, allowing you to take your shows with you.

- **Skipping commercials**   HTPC software makes it easy to skip through the commercials. Typically, you can simply fast-forward 30 seconds at a time until the commercials have passed. Some HTPC software even supports add-ons that can automatically remove commercials from recorded TV shows. This makes the shows more enjoyable and reduces their storage requirements by making the video files shorter and the file sizes smaller.

- **Photo slide shows**   HTPC software can show off your photos on the big screen, giving a much nicer presentation than a computer monitor.

- **Access to online streaming services**   HTPC software can allow you to connect to online streaming services such as Zune HD (previously known as Zune Internet TV, available to download from within Media Center), Hulu, Netflix, and YouTube without leaving the HTPC user interface. Basically, you can stream TV from these services by using your remote control.

- **Streaming to digital media receivers (DMRs)**   HTPC software often allows you to stream to other rooms in your house using a DMR. For example, Windows Media Center can stream content to an Xbox 360. For more information about streaming, refer to Chapter 16.

- **The ability to use your smartphone as a remote control**   Popular HTPC software has spawned mobile apps that allow you to use your phone as a remote control or even stream music and video directly to your phone. While non-techies will still prefer a traditional remote control, smartphones allow you to view detailed information about shows, see album art, and select the next show without interrupting playback on the TV.

Some of the more popular HTPC apps include:

- **Media Center**   Microsoft's official HTPC software, it's also the easiest to set up and has some of the best third-party add-ons available for it. Provides CableCARD support, allowing you to record TV shows from digital cable without using a cable box. Media Center is not as customizable as some of the other HTPC apps, however.

- **XBMC**   Free HTPC software with some amazing capabilities. It provides a richer user interface than Media Center by displaying artwork, cast information, and reviews for TV shows and movies. Setup is more challenging than for Media Center, however.

- **Boxee**   Based on XBMC, Boxee makes it very simple to install add-ons that give you access to many interesting Internet entertainment sources.

- **SageTV**   Not free, but extremely customizable HTPC software for the enthusiast.

If you're new to HTPCs, Media Center is a great place to start. If you learn to love your Media Center HTPC but wish the software was more customizable, you should explore XMBC, Boxee, and SageTV.

CHAPTER 17

Media Center

Windows Media Center, as shown in Figure 17-1, is Microsoft's own HTPC software. Technically, it's a desktop app. However, once you maximize the window, it very much feels like a native Windows 8.1 app, and works perfectly with touch.

Figure 17-1 Media Center is the official Microsoft HTPC app.

Some editions of Windows XP, Windows Vista, and Windows 7 included Media Center. With Windows 8.1, Media Center is an add-on. If you buy a new computer, you'll have to buy Media Center. If you upgrade from Windows 7, Media Center might be available as a free add-on by using the Add Features tool, which you can access by searching Settings for **add features** and then selecting Add Features To Windows 8.1.

▶ **Windows Media Center overview** Watch the video at *http://aka.ms/WinIO/mediacenter*.

Media Center settings

When using Media Center for a dedicated HTPC, there are some settings you should change. Adjust settings by selecting Settings from Tasks, as shown in Figure 17-2.

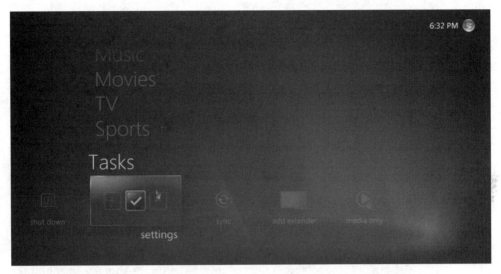

Figure 17-2 Adjust Media Center settings from the Tasks menu.

I won't bother describing all the settings, but there are some that you might want to adjust. First click Settings, then click through the menus as indicated to adjust the settings:

- **General, Startup And Window Behavior**   Clear the Show Taskbar Notifications setting to prevent annoying messages from appearing while you watch videos.

- **General, Windows Media Center Setup, Set Up TV Signal**   Use this wizard to configure Media Center with the information it needs to determine your TV schedule so that it can record TV shows for you. The section "Recording TV" later in this chapter describes the hardware requirements.

- **General, Windows Media Center Setup, Set Up Your Speakers**   Use this wizard to configure and optimize the sound through your speakers. You can select from common speaker setups including two speakers, 5.1 surround speakers, and 7.1 surround speakers. The wizard lets you test your speakers to make sure they are all working correctly and to verify that you haven't plugged any of the wires into the wrong connectors.

CHAPTER 17

Inside OUT
Understanding surround sound

With speakers, more is always better. 5.1 surround-sound setups have five speakers and one subwoofer. The first speaker is a center speaker directly under or over the TV, and it is primarily used for voices of people speaking. The second and third speakers are the left and right speakers, located near the TV. They provide stereo effects to make sound seem to come from different parts of the TV.

The fourth and fifth speakers are located behind the audience, to the left and right, and they typically provide ambient noise. The subwoofer provides all low sounds that the direction speakers are incapable of providing. You don't need subwoofers spread throughout your room to feel like the bass sounds are coming from all around; your ears simply can't tell the direction of lower sounds, but your brain kindly fills in the direction.

7.1 surround sound simply adds two speakers to the 5.1 speaker arrangement, placed directly to the left and right of the audience.

- **General, Windows Media Center Setup, Configure Your TV Or Monitor**   Use this wizard to configure display settings, such as whether you have a 4:3 (standard) or 16:9 (widescreen) TV, which of your multiple displays you should use, and the type of cable you use to connect to your TV. Figure 17-3 shows the wizard selecting a flat panel TV.

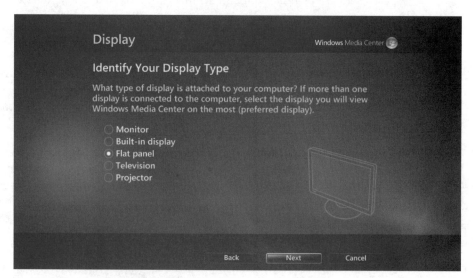

Figure 17-3 Use the Display wizard to optimize your video for your TV.

- **General, Windows Media Center Setup, Install PlayReady**   Installing the PlayReady component allows you to play some content encrypted using Digital Rights Management (DRM) and to copy content to portable devices.

- **General, Parental Controls**   Allows you to configure the TV and movie ratings so that you can block shows that might be inappropriate for your family. The first time you open these settings, you will be prompted to configure a four-digit PIN. This PIN is required to bypass the parental controls and to change the parental control settings. Navigate to General\Parental Controls\TV Ratings and then click Advanced to fine-tune the TV content that is allowed based on violence, dialogue, and other criteria, as shown in Figure 17-4.

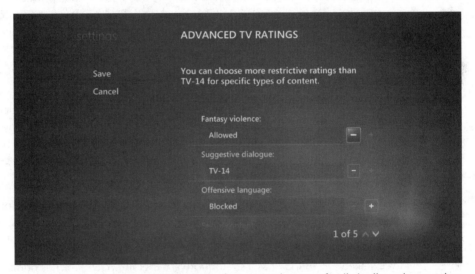

Figure 17-4 Use Advanced TV Ratings to fine-tune what your family is allowed to watch.

- **General, Optimization**   Select the Perform Optimization check box and choose a time when your HTPC will be turned on but you aren't likely to be using it.

- **TV, Closed Captioning**   Media Center records closed captioning when you record TV, and many videos and movies that you download include closed captioning information. By default, closed captioning is turned on only when you mute the sound.

- **Pictures**   Use these settings to turn on the slide show screen saver, which starts a slide show of your favorite photos when you're not using Media Center. Use the other settings within this section to choose exactly which pictures from your Pictures library Media Center shows as part of the default slide show. You can also specify a different folder, which is a good way to force Media Center to show specific pictures.

CHAPTER 17

- **Music**   Use these settings to choose the types of songs Media Center displays in your favorite music playlist. You can also start visualizations automatically and select which visualizations Media Center shows while music is playing.

- **Extenders**   Choose this option to configure an Xbox 360 to work with Media Center.

- **Media Libraries**   Choose this option to add Music, Pictures, Videos, Recorded TV, and Movies folders to your Media Center library. There's an easier way to do this, however: follow the instructions in Chapter 9, "Organizing and protecting files," to add the folder to the appropriate Windows 8.1 library using File Explorer. Then, Media Center will find the folder automatically, and you'll also be able to access the folder from the Music or Video app. The one exception to this is the Recorded TV library, which does not have an equivalent in Windows 8.1. If you have multiple PCs running Media Center, share the folder from each PC that records TV, and add it to every other Media Center PC so that you can watch recorded TV from any of your PCs.

Converting recorded shows

One of the great things about using an HTPC is that you can take your recorded shows with you by copying them to a mobile computer, your smartphone, or a media player. Media Center records TV in a very high-quality format that uses a great deal of disk space. Most smartphones and media players won't be able to play the format, and if they could, the large size of the files would quickly fill up their storage.

To solve these problems, convert your recorded shows into a different video format. My favorite tool for this is MCEBuddy, available at *http://mcebuddy2x.codeplex.com/*. When you install MCEBuddy, it will prompt you to install other required tools.

Once installed, MCEBuddy has a straightforward user interface, which is primarily used to monitor the conversion process. Change the Priority in the lower-right corner to Low (shown in Figure 17-5) to reduce the performance impact that converting videos has on other running apps.

MCEBuddy is designed to automatically find and convert new recordings. By default, it monitors your C:\Users\Public\Recorded TV\ folder, which is the folder Media Center uses to store new recordings, and stores converted files in your C:\Users\Videos folder. You can change these settings by launching the app and clicking Settings to open the MCEBuddy Settings dialog box, as shown in Figure 17-6.

Figure 17-5 MCEBuddy works automatically in the background but allows you to monitor progress.

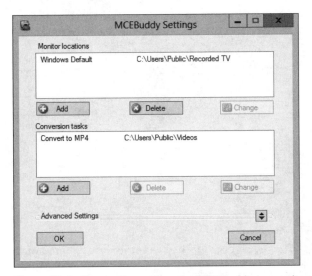

Figure 17-6 Change the settings for MCEBuddy to monitor different folders.

When you specify a new folder to monitor, you can specify a search pattern that will convert only files that match the pattern you specify. For example, if you don't want to convert every TV show you record, you can specify the names of the shows you want to convert as part of the search pattern. First, examine your Recorded TV folder to see how Media Center names the shows you want to convert. Then, specify a pattern that matches those names, using an asterisk for a wildcard and separating different names with a semicolon. For example, entering *HisShow*;*HerShow* will convert all files that have either HisShow or HerShow in the file name. For more information about creating search patterns, hover your pointer over the phrase "Search pattern" in the Monitor Location dialog box.

Converting videos will consume every bit of your computer's processor time. This has the potential to slow down other apps and might heat up your HTPC so much that the fan starts to make noise, disturbing your audio experience. Expand the Advanced Settings area at the bottom of the MCEBuddy Settings dialog box, as shown in Figure 17-7, to fine-tune the conversion schedule. For example, you could use these settings to perform all conversions when your family is asleep.

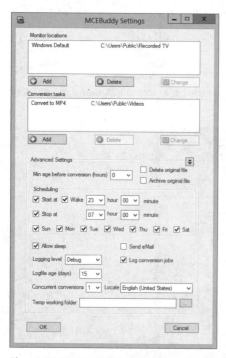

Figure 17-7 Use MCEBuddy Advanced Settings to schedule conversions for times when you are not using your HTPC.

MCEBuddy allows you to convert to several different formats. Naturally, you should choose the newest video format supported by the devices you plan to play the video on. When in doubt, choose the MP4 format, which is the default for MCEBuddy. MP4 provides great compression and quality and is supported by most video players, including iOS, Android, and Windows Phone devices.

As an added bonus, MCEBuddy can automatically remove commercials from recorded TV shows. Not only does this make the show more enjoyable to watch, but it reduces the file size, allowing you to fit more shows onto your media players.

Configuring HTPC software to start automatically

There are several settings you'll want to change to configure your PC as a dedicated HTPC.

First, configure your PC to log on automatically after you restart your computer. This saves you from having to type a password every time the computer restarts, which can happen when Windows automatically installs updates. This is only a good choice if you're not at all concerned about security.

To configure your PC to log on automatically, follow these steps:

1. At the Start screen, type **netplwiz** and then press Enter.

2. In the User Accounts dialog box, clear the Users Must Enter A User Name And Password To Use This Computer check box, as shown in Figure 17-8.

Figure 17-8 Clear the check box at the top of this dialog box to configure your PC to log on automatically.

CHAPTER 17

3. Click OK and type your password twice when prompted.

The next time you restart your PC, Windows will automatically log on with your account.

In previous versions of Windows, Media Center provided a simple check box to configure it to start automatically when you log on. Media Center in Windows 8.1 lacks that option, but you can still configure Media Center (or other HTPC software) to start automatically when you log on. Follow these steps:

1. Open the desktop by clicking the Desktop app from the Start screen or by pressing Windows+D.

2. Open File Explorer. Type the following path in the address bar and then press Enter: **%AppData%\Microsoft\Windows\Start Menu\Programs\Startup**.

3. Right-click in the Startup folder, click New, and then click Shortcut.

    The Create Shortcut wizard appears.

4. On the What Item Would You Like To Create A Shortcut For page, type **%WinDir%\ ehome\ehshell.exe**, as shown in Figure 17-9. Ehshell.exe is Media Center's executable file. If you use other HTPC software, select the app's executable file, which is probably located under C:\Program Files\. Click Next.

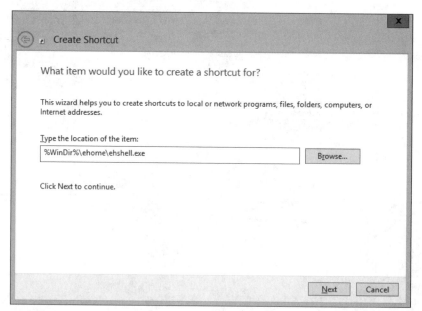

Figure 17-9 Create a shortcut for Media Center in the Startup folder to configure it to start automatically.

5. On the What Would You Like To Name The Shortcut page, type **Media Center** (or the name of your HTPC software), and then click Finish.

6. Right-click in the Startup folder, click New, and then click Shortcut.

    The Create Shortcut wizard appears.

7. On the What Item Would You Like To Create A Shortcut For page, type **explorer.exe shell:::{3080F90D-D7AD-11D9-BD95-0000947B0257}**. Running this command opens the Windows desktop, and creating a shortcut for it allows you to run the command automatically when Windows starts. If you were to automatically run Media Center or another desktop app at startup, it would start, but it would be hidden behind the Start screen. Opening the Windows desktop brings any running desktop app to the foreground. Click Next.

8. On the What Would You Like To Name The Shortcut page, type **Show Desktop**, and then click Finish.

The next time you log on, Media Center (or the HTPC software you selected) will start automatically a short time after the Start screen appears. If you also configure Windows to log you on automatically, then Media Center will appear each time your computer starts, making it always available to everyone in your family.

One last setting to verify: disable backups for your Recorded TV folder. Recorded TV takes up a great deal of drive space, and if you do lose your hard drive, it's probably easier for you to wait for your episode to air again. For more information, refer to Chapter 10, "Backing up and restoring files."

Choosing the hardware

You can turn almost any computer into an HTPC. This section describes the benefits of different types of hardware if you plan to buy a new PC or upgrade an existing PC, and gives you information about getting the best out of the hardware you already have.

For information about selecting a tuner card to record TV, refer to section "Recording TV" later in this chapter.

▶ **Home Theater PC hardware** Watch the video at *http://aka.ms/WinIO/hardware*.

Case

A computer's case determines its form factor. Large desktop computers offer plenty of room for internal adapters and drives, but they also take up more space in your entertainment center. Small form-factor cases are the most popular for HTPCs, but if you have room in your entertainment center, a full desktop case offers lower cost, easier upgrades, and more flexibility.

My favorite way to store an HTPC is to keep it with the audio/video (A/V) equipment in a closet or the basement and just run cables through the wall to the TV and speakers. I recommend that approach if it's an option because you can pick any size case, you won't have to see it from your living room, and fan noise will never be an issue.

If you do plan to keep your HTPC near your TV, choose an attractive case that fits in with your A/V equipment. Several vendors sell PC cases specifically for this purpose, or you can simply look for a case with a black front.

Fan

Here's an audiophile's nightmare: you spend thousands on a top-of-the-line digital amplifier and connect it to an amazing subwoofer and surround-sound speakers. You position your couch for absolutely perfect acoustics. Then, you play your first movie on your HTPC, and the fan buzzes the entire time, ruining the sound for you.

PC processors, power supplies, and memory get hot when you use them. Almost all PCs are air cooled; they have a couple of fans inside them that blow whenever the thermostat inside the computer determines that it's getting too hot. Unfortunately, those fans can be very noisy.

As I recommended in the previous section, one of the simplest solutions is to put your HTPC in a closet or another room. Then, the fan can buzz all it wants and you won't be bothered by it. If that's not an option, find a quiet PC. Many PCs are designed to stay as cool as possible and have particularly quiet fans, and some are so efficient they don't need a fan at all. They'll cost more than a more conventional PC, but the extra cost might be worth it if you get the most out of your sound system.

Other than specially designed quiet PCs, mobile computers tend to be quieter. They're designed to minimize power usage, which in turn minimizes heat and how fast the fan needs to run.

Many entertainment centers have doors that close. That door can minimize the sound that comes from your computer. It can also trap the heat in, causing your computer to overheat and run the fan even more. The point is: consider cooling when choosing an entertainment center for your HTPC.

Video card

Here's some great news: you don't need an expensive video card for playing music and videos. You only need an expensive video card if you plan to play 3-D games.

You do, however, need to make sure you can easily connect your video card to your TV and stereo. Most newer TVs support High-Definition Multimedia Interface (HDMI), so choose a video card that outputs both audio and video through HDMI. Figure 17-10 shows an HDMI connector.

Figure 17-10 HDMI provides perfect quality and simple wiring.

Typically, you can run an inexpensive HDMI cable from your HTPC to your stereo, and then run a second HDMI cable from your stereo to your TV. The stereo will play the audio and pass the video on to your TV. This makes for a very simple connection because you don't need to run a second cable for audio.

If you plan to use your TV's speakers, simply run an HDMI cable from your HTPC to your TV. Verify that your video card, your HDMI cable, and your TV all support both audio and video over HDMI. Figure 17-11 shows a video card with DVI, HDMI, and VGA outputs.

Figure 17-11 To simplify wiring, choose a video card that supports HDMI output.

If your TV doesn't support HDMI, check to see whether it supports VGA or DVI (Digital Visual Interface). Most new video cards support one or the other, and you can use an inexpensive adapter to convert between the formats. Figure 17-12 shows a VGA cable with an inexpensive DVI adapter connected to it.

Figure 17-12 Convert between VGA and DVI using an adapter.

If your TV doesn't support HDMI, VGA, or DVI, then choose a video card that supports TV out in the format your TV requires. For example, some early HDTVs require component input, while others support composite input. Video cards are available with both types of connections. Figure 17-13 shows a video card designed for connecting to analog TVs. From left-to-right, the video card has three outputs: composite, S-Video, and VGA.

Figure 17-13 To connect to an analog TV, buy a video card with analog outputs.

If you already have a video card you want to use and it isn't compatible with your TV, you can purchase an adapter. For example, you can buy an adapter that connects HD video to HDMI, as shown in Figure 17-14, allowing you to connect otherwise incompatible HD systems. These adapters tend to be more expensive than basic video cards, however.

Figure 17-14 Use an HDMI converter for devices that lack HDMI output.

Most new mobile computers include an HDMI, mini-HDMI, or micro-HDMI port. Use an HDMI cable with the appropriate connector type to connect directly to a TV. If you are using a mobile computer and your TV requires analog composite or S-Video connectors, purchase an adapter such as the one shown in Figure 17-15, along with the appropriate cables to connect to your TV.

CHAPTER 17

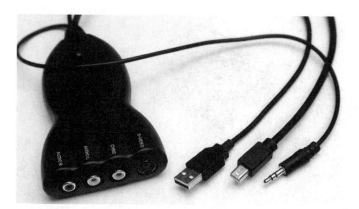

Figure 17-15 Use adapters to convert HDMI output to connect to analog TVs.

When I travel, I bring a PC running Windows 8.1 with Media Center installed, an HDMI cable, the adapter shown in Figure 17-15, a composite cable with audio support, and an S-Video cable (they don't take up as much room as you might think). Depending on the type of TV the hotel room has, I connect my mobile PC with either the HDMI cable or the adapter and watch TV shows and movies using Media Center. While I could watch them on the PC's screen, I much prefer watching them on the TV. This is particularly important when traveling to foreign countries/regions where I don't know the local language.

Inside OUT

HD video resolutions

Higher resolutions offer sharper images if your monitor or TV can display them in full resolution. For example, 1080p video looks fantastic on a 1080p display. However, many mobile PCs, especially tablets, have a display that is 768 pixels tall, which means they can't display the extra resolution. Rather than playing 1080p video, you should use 720p video, which almost perfectly suits a 768 pixel display.

If you record broadcast HDTV, it will almost always be 720p. Currently, 1080p HDTV is only available online or on Blu-ray DVDs.

Don't be too bummed out. In most households, people don't sit close enough to TVs to see the difference between 720p and 1080p, and 720p video files take up much less storage space, which means you have room to keep far more videos at your fingertips.

Processor

Playing videos doesn't require a particularly cutting-edge processor, but there's no specific formula I can give you; the processing requirements vary depending on the resolution of your video and the codec being used. For example, 1080p HD video requires much more processing capacity to play smoothly than does 480p video. With that said, modern, low-end mobile processors are very capable of playing 1080p video.

As an added benefit, lower-power processors use less power and generate less heat. Not only will that help keep your electricity bill down, but it will allow the HTPC's fan to run at lower speeds, keeping the HTPC quieter.

Encoding or transcoding video can be a different story. If you have remote DMRs connecting to your HTPC across the network and you run transcoding software (as described in Chapter 16), you should choose the fastest processor you can afford. Transcoding video in real time, especially HD video, can max out even higher-end systems.

Memory

Memory is another area where you can skimp with an HTPC. Even 1 gigabyte (GB) of RAM is sufficient for playing any video, including HD video. As with the processor, if you plan to transcode video, more memory can help. Additionally, other apps you run on your HTPC might require more memory, so refer to those apps' recommendations.

Storage

Even the slowest modern hard drives can play back 1080p video with no problem. Therefore, choose a low-RPM, low-power hard drive for your HTPC, as shown in Figure 17-16.

If you plan to stream video across the network, you need only enough storage for Windows 8.1 and any apps that you plan to run. Even the smallest modern hard drives will be more than sufficient.

If you plan to store movies and TV shows, you might need a very large hard drive, and you might even need to combine multiple drives. Table 17-1 lists typical file sizes for different media types, though file size can vary widely depending on the video quality and the compression algorithm being used. Multiply these sizes by the number you plan to store on your HTPC simultaneously to determine your storage requirements.

CHAPTER 17

Figure 17-16 Use high-capacity, inexpensive, low-power hard drives in HTPCs.

Table 17-1 Approximate storage required for different file types

File type	Approximate size
Medium-quality MP3 or WMA song	3 megabytes (MB)
High-quality MP3 or WMA song	5 MB
Lossless song	25 MB
480p, 30-minute TV show without commercials	200 MB
720p, 30-minute TV show without commercials	750 MB
1080p, 30-minute TV show without commercials	2 GB
480p, one-hour TV show without commercials	400 MB
720p, one-hour TV show without commercials	1.5 GB
1080p, one-hour TV show without commercials	4 GB
480p movie	700 MB
720p movie	2.5 GB
1080p movie	8 GB

If you need more capacity than a single drive can provide, combine your drives into a Storage Space so that you can access them as a single volume. For detailed information, refer to Chapter 12, "Managing storage."

Sound card

The type of sound card you need is determined by how you connect your HTPC to your stereo and TV:

- **HDMI or other digital connection (recommended)**   If you use HDMI for both audio and video, you don't need a sound card at all. Your computer will simply pass the digital audio signals directly across the HDMI cable with no additional processing. Your receiver or TV will be responsible for decoding the stereo and surround-sound signals.

- **Analog**   When you use an analog connection, your computer must perform the decoding of stereo and surround-sound signals. This isn't an extremely processor-intensive task, and many inexpensive sound cards (including sound cards built into most motherboards) are quite capable of this task. However, the quality of analog sound can vary widely because analog sounds are subject to interference from both other components within your computer and other wiring that the cables are near outside your computer. For best results, use an external USB sound card (which eliminates interference from internal components) and use shielded cabling that only crosses other wires perpendicularly.

Digital is always superior. If you're not sure whether your receiver or TV supports digital audio, just look at the connectors on the back of the receiver and choose a sound card with similar connectors. The most common digital connection types are HDMI, Toslink/SPDIF, and digital coaxial.

As a last resort, you can connect your amplifier or speakers to the headphone jack on your computer. While many stereos have a 3.5mm auxiliary port, many others require red and white RCA connectors. Figure 17-17 shows a specialized cable designed to connect any device with a headphone jack to a stereo that uses RCA connectors.

Figure 17-17 As a last resort, connect your headphone jack to your stereo.

CHAPTER 17

If you connect your computer's headphone jack to a stereo, turn the volume on the computer all the way up, and then adjust the volume using your amplifier. Sound quality might be noticeably bad, especially when playing back quiet recordings. If you hear crackling during the louder parts of the sound track, turn the volume on the computer down until the crackling disappears.

Network

If you plan to record all your TV and movies using a tuner card, your HTPC's network connection isn't terribly important. You'll still need some network connection so that the HTPC software can download show schedules and information, but any wired or wireless connection will be sufficient.

Similarly, streaming music across the network doesn't require much bandwidth. As long as your network connection is stable, you shouldn't have any problem streaming music.

If you plan to stream video, however, your bandwidth becomes very important. If you plan to stream HD video, especially 1080p video, getting sufficient bandwidth could be the most challenging aspect of setting up your HTPC.

If you plan to stream standard-definition video from the Internet, just about any broadband connection should be sufficient. On your local network, make sure that you consistently maintain at least 10 Mbps available bandwidth. The latest wireless networks are capable of that; in particular, look for equipment that supports 802.11n, and try to keep your HTPC as close to your wireless access point (WAP) as possible.

If you plan to stream HD video from the Internet, make sure your LAN speeds are at least as fast as your Internet connection. For example, if you have a 20 Mbps Internet connection, configure your LAN so that it has at least 20 Mbps throughput. Remember that wireless bandwidth estimates are wild exaggerations, and even the latest 802.11n networks can reach 20 Mbps only when the wireless access point is very close to the PC.

If you plan to stream 1080p HD video across your LAN, you're going to need as much bandwidth as possible. The precise amount of bandwidth varies depending on the compression level used in the video, but 100 Mbps throughput is a good value to strive for. Wireless networks will simply be inefficient. Instead, run wired Ethernet cables between the PC storing your videos and the HTPC or DMR playing the videos. If you can't run wired Ethernet, use the latest powerline networking adapters rated at 200 Mbps or 500 Mbps, as shown in Figure 17-18. In my experience, the 200 Mbps and 500 Mbps adapters have similar performance, so paying more for 500 Mbps might not be worth it.

Figure 17-18 Powerline networking can provide the consistent bandwidth you need for streaming HDTV.

Cables

When choosing connection types and cables, choose digital over analog whenever possible. You have several choices for digital connections, and the quality will be similar regardless of which you choose. However, for simplicity, you should choose HDMI for both audio and video when your equipment supports it.

Don't buy expensive digital cables. Digital signals don't degrade from interference like analog signals do; digital signals either work or they don't. Don't trust anyone who tells you that a more expensive digital cable will improve your sound or image quality. Really, you only need to spend a few dollars on cables.

TROUBLESHOOTING

How can I improve my sound quality?

If you have poor sound or video quality with an analog connection, it could be caused by several sources: interference at the cable, poor connections, poor-quality audio/video equipment, or poor-quality speakers. To troubleshoot the problem, use a different cable, preferably a short cable, even if you need to move your speaker or monitor closer to your HTPC.

If the problem goes away, it's the cable. If not, it's an internal component.

If your cable is to blame, try moving the cable away from any other cables. If the problem persists or you can't move the cable away from other cables (for example, if they are bundled together), replace the cable with a thicker cable featuring better shielding.

If you regularly remove and reconnect a cable, you should pay particular attention to how the connector is attached to the cable because that area tends to wear out quickly. However, if you simply plan to connect a cable once and leave it connected for years, even the most flimsy cable should work fine.

Speaker cables (the two-wire cables that connect your amplifier to your speakers) are analog. Therefore, proper shielding really can make a difference. Still, as long as you're not running them through the wall or alongside power cables (always cross power cables perpendicularly to minimize interference), you shouldn't notice a difference.

If you do run cables through the wall, be sure to get cables that meet your local building codes. Typically, this requires plenum cables that minimize the risk that fire will travel up a cable, thus reducing the risk that the cable will help spread a fire throughout your house.

Recording TV

If you want to use your computer to record TV, you'll need a tuner card. You can use a tuner card to connect your computer to your cable or satellite TV or to record broadcast transmissions. The four ways of connecting, in rough order of preference, are:

- Digital, by connecting your cable service directly to a tuner card and using a CableCARD with Media Center

- Digital, by connecting your cable service to a cable box, and then connecting the cable box to a tuner card

- Analog, by connecting your cable service directly to a tuner card

- Analog, by connecting an antenna directly to your tuner card

The sections that follow describe these four ways in more detail. Except for the discussion of CableCARD, references to cable TV also apply to satellite TV.

Inside OUT

Choosing a tuner card

Because some people still watch live TV, TV networks tend to air the best TV shows at the same time, but on different channels. Look for tuner cards that allow you to record two shows airing on different channels simultaneously. Look for a card with dual tuners that has a single incoming connection with an internal splitter, because it will minimize the number of cables that you need to run.

Encrypted digital cable with a CableCARD

The best way to record premium and encrypted digital channels is by using a CableCARD. If you had a laptop 15 years ago, you might remember Personal Computer Memory Card International Association (PCMCIA) cards, which were later known as PC cards. CableCARDs are PCMCIA cards that contain the technology to allow your computer to decrypt the digital cable signals that most consumers use a cable box to decrypt.

When you use a CableCARD, you do not have to use an infrared (IR) blaster (described later in the chapter), so you never have to worry about missed channels. Additionally, you can save some money by not having to rent a cable box from your cable provider. Modern CableCARDs allow your HTPC to record multiple channels simultaneously, so you typically need only a single CableCARD and a single connection to your HTPC.

CableCARDs came about as part of the Telecommunications Act of 1996. Among other purposes, CableCARDs free consumers from needing to use their cable company's cable box. By connecting a CableCARD to a DVR or an HTPC, your HTPC can receive all the basic and premium digital cable channels you receive with a cable box.

Your cable company should be able to provide a CableCARD at your request. Many people complain that their cable companies make this process as difficult as possible. This makes sense because the alternative to using a CableCARD in an HTPC is to rent a costly DVR from the cable company.

You'll also need a tuner card that supports the CableCARD standard. A single tuner card, CableCARD, and coaxial connection will allow you to record multiple channels simultaneously. At the time of this writing, some of the popular cards include:

- **The Ceton InfiniTV 4 card**   An internal card that can record four channels. Costs about US$200.

- **The SiliconDust HDHR3-CC HDHomeRun PRIME**   An external USB device that can record three channels. Costs about US$150.

- **The Hauppauge WinTV-DCR-2650**   An external USB device that can record two channels. Costs about US$110.

Finally, you'll need HTPC software that is compatible with the CableCARD standard. The cable companies define copy protection for shows recorded with a CableCARD, and software must be certified for use with the CableCARD; otherwise, it would be too easy to circumvent copy protection. Right now, only Media Center is certified for use with a CableCARD. For detailed information about CableCARD copy protection, read "Cable Provider Copy Protection, Switched Digital Video and Self-Install Status Master List" at *http://www.missingremote.com/ forums/cable-provider-copy-protection-switched-digital-video-and-self-install-status- master-list.*

Unfortunately, pay-per-view and on-demand services are not available when using a Cable-CARD. Therefore, you might need a separate cable box connected directly to your TV for those services.

Using a cable box or other device that connects to a TV

If your cable company won't provide a CableCARD, you can still record TV output from a cable box. For example, the Hauppauge Colossus PCI Express Internal HD-PVR has HDMI and component video (YCrCb) HD inputs, allowing it to record 1080i video from any device that would normally connect to an HDTV. This allows you to record from almost any source. To allow your HTPC to change the channel on your cable box, you need an IR blaster, which is included with most tuner cards.

If you want to record multiple channels simultaneously, you need multiple cable boxes, each separately connected to a video recording card in your HTPC. Naturally, you'll need to pay a rental fee to your cable company, making this a much more expensive option than using a tuner card that supports a CableCARD.

Higher-end tuner cards include a hardware encoder, whereas lower-end tuner cards require the processor in your HTPC to do the encoding. Choosing a tuner card with a hardware encoder will reduce your processor usage, but it might not be necessary if your computer has a powerful processor. If you have a low-end processor and you plan to record HDTV, choosing a tuner card with a hardware encoder can ensure trouble-free operation.

Analog and unencrypted digital cable

You can watch and record analog and unencrypted digital cable by connecting the coaxial cable directly to your tuner card (shown in Figure 17-19) and recording analog TV. Inexpensive TV tuners, such as those made by Hauppauge, can be used to record analog or unencrypted digital cable TV using quadrature amplitude modulation (QAM). QAM basically broadcasts over-the-air channels, including local HDTV, across cable TV unencrypted and for free.

Figure 17-19 Use a tuner card to record TV from analog cable.

Internal tuners tend to work better than USB tuners. However, if you are using a mobile computer, a USB tuner is your only option.

Typically, only basic cable channels are provided as analog and unencrypted digital cable. Premium channels such as HBO and Showtime are not available using this recording technique. This type of recording is the simplest because your computer can control the channel without communicating with any external device.

Some tuner cards can also receive FM radio when connected to an antenna. Most popular radio stations stream across the Internet, and that's how I prefer to listen to them on my HTPC. However, if you listen to FM radio and your favorite station doesn't stream, look for a card with an FM tuner.

CHAPTER 17

Over-the-air broadcasts

Though most tech-savvy people seem to use cable or satellite TV, there are some distinct advantages to recording over-the-air broadcasts:

- There are no monthly fees.

- You can receive high-quality HDTV.

- You can receive local news, which is often not available through a cable provider.

- Your HTPC can act as the tuner, so you do not need a separate cable box or IR blaster (discussed later in this chapter).

Most tuner cards that record directly from a coaxial cable can also record over-the-air broadcasts. Of course, most cable channels do not broadcast over the air, but you can receive your local TV for free by connecting a TV antenna to your tuner card. A significant advantage of recording over-the-air broadcasts is that you can record digital, HDTV without using a cable box.

To record over-the-air broadcasts, you need an HDTV antenna, which typically costs between US$35 and US$80.

Using IR blasters

HTPCs can use a device, known as an IR blaster, that transmits infrared (IR) signals to control other components of your entertainment system. These devices send the same IR signals you send with a remote control.

Most commonly, IR blasters are used to change the channel on the cable box, just like you do when you watch TV. In other words, if you use a cable box and you want to watch live TV on channel 36 on your HTPC, you'll use your HTPC's remote control to change the channel. The HTPC will then change the channel on your cable box and begin recording and playing back the video signal.

Some people also use IR blasters and HTPC software to turn their TV and receiver on or off and to make sure they are configured for the right input.

You should stick your IR blaster directly on the IR receiver of the device to be controlled. They tend to have an adhesive surface that allows you to fasten them semi-permanently to the device. If they fail to stick properly, you might need to tape them down.

Unfortunately, IR blasters can be unreliable, and they tend to be the weak link in an HTPC setup. For example, if your computer needs to tune your cable box to channel 36, the cable box might not receive the 6 and will tune to channel 3, causing your HTPC to record the wrong channel. How reliable your signals are depends on both your IR blaster and the cable box that you're controlling. While many people experience problems, others report never having a missed channel.

All IR signals are unreliable, but when you're changing the channel manually, you notice when a signal isn't received and push the button again. Your computer simply isn't that smart. As a result, if you must use IR blasters to control your cable box, be prepared for missed recordings at times.

Choosing a remote control

Most people want to be able to control their HTPC with an infrared remote control. An inexpensive USB IR receiver, as shown in Figure 17-20, provides that capability.

Figure 17-20 Use a USB IR receiver to control your computer with a remote control.

You'll probably need two remote controls for your HTPC: a full-featured wireless keyboard and mouse and a more conventional remote that your family can use.

While Media Center and other HTPC software is designed to be used with a traditional remote (that is, only requiring you to type numbers and use a direction pad), a keyboard/mouse is useful for installing updates, configuring Windows, and browsing the web. You might not think that's important, but when you have a few friends over and one of them says, "Hey! Did you see that video where the cat that looks like a dog eats bacon and then looks suspicious?" you'll be able to quickly pull it up on the big screen so everyone can watch it comfortably, instead of having people crowd around a tiny smartphone.

Those times are frequent enough that you'll want to manage them when you're comfortable, not while you're sitting cross-legged on the floor with the wired mouse and keyboard you've kept stored in the basement from a long-dead computer. The example shown in Figure 17-21 is an infrared keyboard with a pointing device in the upper-right corner that functions like a mouse.

Figure 17-21 Use a wireless keyboard with a built-in mouse when you need to set up your HTPC.

Bluetooth keyboards with a built-in trackball or trackpad work well for this purpose. Bluetooth's range of 30 feet is usually good enough, though it can be unreliable at a distance, and enclosing the HTPC in an entertainment center can substantially reduce that range.

You can download apps for your smartphone that control your HTPC across your wireless network, providing both a touchpad and a small keyboard. HippoRemote LITE for the iPhone or Valence for Android do this very well. Some remote-control apps even support Wake-on-LAN to wake your computer up across the network, which can save you the trouble of walking to your HTPC and pushing the power button.

Only use an IR keyboard or mouse if you use an IR relay system to send signals to your audio/video equipment in an enclosed room. While it's fairly easy to point a traditional remote at your computer, you typically use a keyboard while it's on your lap, and your attention is focused on typing rather than on keeping the keyboard pointed directly at the computer. IR keyboards tend to miss keystrokes, and using them can be a very laborious process.

For all scenarios that don't involve an IR relay system, choose an RF (radio frequency) keyboard and mouse combination. RF devices communicate more reliably and don't need to be pointed directly at a receiver.

Most of the time, you'll want a remote just to turn your gear on and off and select music, TV shows, and movies. Your TV and stereo probably require IR anyway, and if you don't want to teach everyone in your family to juggle three remotes, you're going to want to be able to control your HTPC with a universal IR remote. You'll still want an RF keyboard and mouse combo when you need the extra power.

Your family remote should be small and simple, because while you're clearly good with technology (you're reading this book, after all), you probably live with someone who simply wants to watch their show without dealing with an 80-button keyboard. The simplest way to control Media Center is to use a remote designed for Media Center, such as the remote shown in Figure 17-22.

Figure 17-22 Use a smaller remote for day-to-day tasks.

PART 4

Security and privacy

CHAPTER 18
Managing users and Family Safety 393

CHAPTER 19
Windows, application, and network
security 437

CHAPTER 20
Using Hyper-V 473

Managing users and Family Safety

Logon security 394

Configuring sign-on options 398

Password best practices. 405

Managing accounts 415

Family Safety 422

Each person in your home should have their own user account, and each time they use a PC, they should sign in to that account. Signing off or switching users takes a couple of clicks, literally: from the Start screen, click your picture and then click Sign Out or select a different account. That inconvenience is outweighed by many benefits:

- **Personalization** Each user account can use its own colors, Start screen arrangement, web bookmarks, and more.

- **Privacy** Each user's files, apps, browsing history, and bookmarks can be kept separate.

- **Security** The first account you create is an administrator account and is allowed to change system settings. Administrators can also mistakenly install malware, which is easy to do. By creating new accounts for other people in your house, you can let them do almost anything they want while limiting the potential damage they might accidentally cause.

- **Protection** Unless you're ready to reveal the entire Internet to your children, you probably want to restrict what they can do with a PC. By creating a separate account for your kids, you can use Family Safety to control their access without restricting your own.

- **Monitoring** Family Safety is also capable of monitoring PC and web activity. However, if everyone uses the same account, you can't know for sure who did what on a PC.

This chapter discusses how to create user accounts, how to assign them different privileges, and how to configure Family Safety to allow your children to use a PC while keeping them as safe as possible.

Logon security

By default, users sign on to Windows 8.1 using a Microsoft account, which is linked to Microsoft's online services. You can also sign on using a local account, which is how users have logged on to Windows 7 and earlier versions of Windows. The sections that follow describe the advantages of each account type.

Microsoft accounts

When you use a Microsoft account, you sign on with your email address and a password. Microsoft accounts authenticate with a Microsoft service across the Internet, though you don't always need an Internet connection to sign on. As part of using a Microsoft account, Windows 8.1 backs up important settings to servers on the Internet.

Because settings are stored on the Internet, you can sign on to multiple computers with the same credentials and have your settings automatically synchronized. For example, if you rearrange your Start screen tiles and change the Start screen color on your desktop PC, the next time you sign on to your laptop, Windows 8.1 will download and apply those same settings.

Signing on with a Microsoft account also allows you to manage your account with a web browser. If you forget your password, you can reset it from any computer by visiting *https://account.live.com/*, as shown in Figure 18-1.

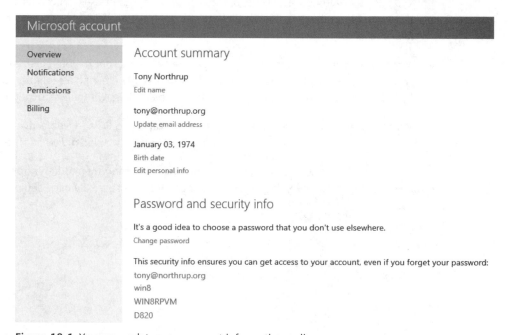

Figure 18-1 You can update your account information online.

If you were to forget your password for a local account, you might never be able to sign on again, and you would permanently lose access to all of your encrypted files. This happens more often than you think; someone changes their password, forgets it the next day, and then needs to reinstall Windows before they can use their computer again. So, being able to update your account information from a browser can save you a great deal of frustration—it's convenient, but it carries with it important security risks:

- Microsoft stores your password, so you have to trust Microsoft to keep it safe. I do.

- An attacker who gains access to your password can use the convenient online tools to change your password, possibly locking you out of your computer. To mitigate this, Microsoft allows you to change your password only from trusted computers. If you log in from a computer that isn't trusted, you have to verify the computer's trust using your email. If the password for your computer is the same as for your email, that won't slow down the attacker.

Windows prompts you to create a Microsoft account when you first set it up. If you don't already have a Microsoft account associated with your email address, Windows walks you through that process.

After you sign on with your account, you can create other accounts. Within PC Settings, select Users, and then select Add A User. Provide the user's email address. If a Microsoft account is already associated with that address, setup is complete. The user will need to sign on with their existing Microsoft account password, and the computer will need to connect to the Internet the first time they sign on. If that email address doesn't have a Microsoft account, you'll be prompted to create a password and provide other account information, including information to allow you to reset your password, as shown in Figure 18-2, your date of birth, and your gender.

As shown in Figure 18-3, the last step of setting up a new account is to confirm whether the account is for a child. Specifying that the account is for a child turns on Family Safety, which is discussed later in this chapter.

Figure 18-2 The Add Security Info page prompts you for information to allow you to reset your password.

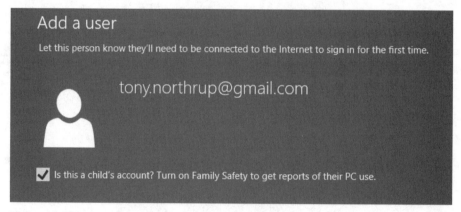

Figure 18-3 Turn on Family Safety for accounts that should be restricted.

Under the covers, Windows 8.1 creates two accounts: a Microsoft account and a local account. When you sign on with your Microsoft account, Windows 8.1 verifies your password with your online Microsoft account if you have Internet access. If you don't have Internet access, it verifies it against cached credentials. So, if you don't have an Internet connection, you can sign on using the same password you used for your previous sign on.

All local authorization occurs using a behind-the-scenes local account, which you can manage using the same tools described in the following section. The local account user name is the name you typed as the user's first name when creating the account. By default, additional Microsoft accounts are added to two local groups:

- **Users**   A group that grants access to run and install apps from the Windows Store, but not to change important system settings. Users can install most, but not all, desktop apps.

- **HomeUsers**   A group that grants access to your homegroup. Windows only creates this group membership if the PC has joined a homegroup.

Notice that additional Microsoft accounts are not added to the Administrators group. Only members of the Administrators group are allowed to change system settings and install desktop apps. By default, only the first account you create is a member of the Administrators group. To add an account to the Administrators group, follow the instructions in "Changing group memberships" later in this chapter.

▶ **Creating users** Watch the video at *http://aka.ms/WinIO/logon*.

Local accounts

As the name implies, local accounts are stored on your local computer. They don't automatically synchronize like Microsoft accounts do, and you can't reset your password from another computer. However, if none of the online features of Microsoft accounts are useful to you, you should use a local account because they've withstood the test of time; every earlier version of Windows used local accounts.

Windows prompts you to choose between a Microsoft account and a local account when you first create your password, but it's easy to overlook. Look for the Sign In Without A Microsoft Account link. If you change your mind and want to change account types, open the Accounts page of PC Settings, select Your Account, as shown in Figure 18-4, and then click Disconnect.

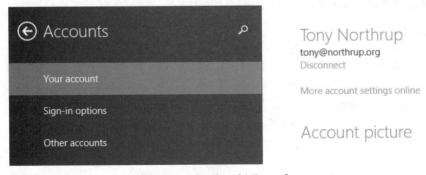

Figure 18-4 You can switch between local and Microsoft account types.

Configuring sign-on options

Windows 8.1 gives you two additional authentication options that Windows 7 and earlier versions of Windows didn't offer: picture passwords and PINs. Picture passwords are perfect for tablets, while PINs are useful anytime typing is difficult. Both reduce your computer's security, but that compromise might be worth it for you.

You can create a picture password or a PIN only when you're physically at your computer. In other words, you can't do it across the network when using Remote Desktop.

▶ **Passwords, picture passwords, and PINs** Watch the video at *http://aka.ms/WinIO/passwords*.

Using a picture password

Typing a password on a touch screen is a pain. As an alternative, Windows 8.1 supports using a picture password. When you enable the picture password feature, you tap, circle, and draw lines on the picture of your choosing.

To enable picture passwords, select Users in PC settings and click Create A Picture Password. Then, verify your credentials by retyping your existing password.

Select a picture to use for your picture password, and then select Open. The best pictures have multiple points of interest. A point of interest can be a person's eyes, the peak of a mountain, or the wingtip of a bird. Any place you can remember to touch the picture is a point of interest.

After you select your picture, you can drag it to position it. The left portion of the picture is going to be hidden when you enter your picture password, just as it is in Figure 18-5. Select Use This Picture.

Now you can specify your gestures. For every single point of interest on the picture, you can make five gestures:

- A tap
- A small clockwise circle

- A large clockwise circle

- A small counterclockwise circle

- A large counterclockwise circle

Figure 18-5 When entering a picture password, the left portion of the picture is hidden.

For every pair of points of interest on the picture, you can draw a line between them in either direction. Figure 18-6 shows three gestures:

- A large counterclockwise circle drawn around the ibis's right wingtip.

- A small counterclockwise circle drawn around the ibis's left wingtip.

- A line drawn from the ibis's eye to the tip of its bill.

CHAPTER 18

Figure 18-6 Tap, draw circles, and draw lines to create your picture password.

The next time you log on, Windows prompts you to enter your picture password.

Windows doesn't expect you to be precise with your touch; as long as the points you touch are relatively close to those you specified when you created your picture password, you won't have any problem logging on. If you do have problems, click Switch To Password to type your conventional password, as shown in Figure 18-7.

Picture passwords can be quite secure, and I discuss the math behind this later in this section. Of course, because Windows always gives you the option to sign on using your password, adding a picture password reduces your security by just a tiny amount by giving an attacker another option for breaking into your computer.

Figure 18-7 You can always switch to entering a conventional password.

Nonetheless, the convenience of tablet computers makes it worthwhile for me and many other users. To minimize the security risks of picture passwords, follow these best practices:

- Use a complicated picture with many different points of interest. For example, a group picture of five people is better to use than a portrait of a single person, because there are more possible points to circle, tap, or draw a line to.

- Don't pick the obvious gestures. If you choose a picture of three people, tapping each of the three faces would be very easy to guess.

- Go counterclockwise with your circles. Most people are inclined to draw clockwise circles, so a counterclockwise circle will be a bit more difficult to guess.

- Go right to left with your lines. Like using counterclockwise circles, going against the natural inclination improves security.

- Cover your screen. Don't let people see you enter your picture password. Be wary of cameras that might record you logging in.

- Leave your screen dirty. The worst thing you can do is to clean your touch screen and then log in, because the only smudges on the screen will be from your picture password. While those smudges wouldn't reveal the sequence or the direction of lines and circles, they might reveal the three actions that you performed. When you do clean your screen, clean it after you log on instead of before you log on. Figure 18-8 shows my tablet computer after I cleaned the screen and then logged in with my picture password. You can clearly see the three actions, but you don't know the sequence or the direction, so there are still 120 possible combinations. Windows stops you from guessing after five. Under these ideal circumstances, an attacker who gains physical access to my PC immediately after I clean the screen and log on still has only a 4 percent chance of guessing my picture password correctly.

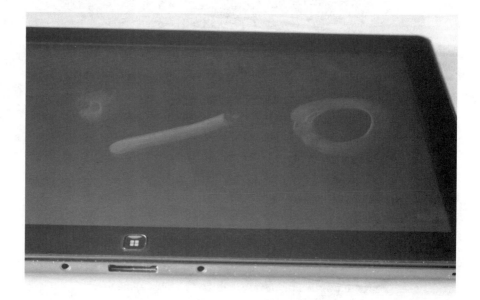

Figure 18-8 Smudges can reveal information about a picture password, but the security might still be strong enough for your needs.

- Don't use picture passwords. Really, if you're paranoid about someone guessing your picture password and breaking into your computer, you're better off using a complex and long conventional password. Picture passwords are a convenience, and they're better than nothing (and also better than a PIN), but they're simply not the most secure way to log on if you don't want other people using your account.

Consider the simplest scenario: a picture password composed of three taps on a picture with three points of interest. If the attacker knows you use only taps and don't tap in the same place twice, this results in six possible combinations, with the average attacker guessing it after three attempts. WIndows locks out users after five failed attempts to enter a picture pasword, so most attackers would be able to guess the password.

You can repeat yourself, however, raising the number of possible sequences to 27. The average attacker would need to guess 13 or 14 times to get it right, and by being locked out after five failed attempts, most attackers wouldn't be able to guess this very simple picture password even when given information they wouldn't normally have.

Consider a scenario where an attacker knows you hate drawing lines and large circles, and thus would only use taps and small circles (both clockwise and counterclockwise) on a picture with three points of interest. In that case, the number of possible combinations jumps to 729. Use only taps, small circles, and large circles, and the number of possible combinations is 3,375.

If the attacker doesn't know anything about your picture password, but your picture only has three points of interest, the attacker would also have to guess lines drawn in different directions. Add lines in different directions between the three points of interest, and now the attacker would need to guess 9,261 combinations. Because they're locked out after five guesses, the attacker would need an average of 926 separate sessions separated by a password sign on to guess the picture password (assuming they could precisely keep track of the different possibilities and what they previously guessed).

That's secure enough for most home users. If you use a picture password with more points of interest, the possible combinations skyrocket. A picture with 10 points of interest has 2,744,000 possible combinations. If you don't feel comfortable with the security of picture passwords, just keep typing a conventional password.

If you want to disable your picture password, open PC Settings, select Users, and then click Remove next to Change Picture Password.

Inside OUT

Unnecessary algebra

Each single point of interest can have one of five actions performed on it. Therefore, the number of possible actions is 5p, where p is the number of points of interest. Windows 8.1 requires a series of three actions and allows repetition. Therefore, the number of permutations is $(5p)^3$.

To calculate the number of combinations lines add, use the formula $p! / (p - 2)!$, where p is the number of points of interest. Therefore, a picture with two points of interest allows only two lines to be drawn. A picture with 10 points of interest allows 90 points to be drawn, and a picture with 20 points of interest allows 380 lines to be drawn.

Therefore, to calculate the total use the formula $(5p + (p! / (p - 2)!))^3$.

Using a PIN

You can sign on with a numeric personal identification number (PIN) instead of using a password. PINs aren't terribly secure, but they're easier to type.

Think of using a PIN as a compromise between typing an annoying password and not having any security at all. PINs are much easier to guess than a password, but if a password is annoying or difficult for you, a PIN is much better than nothing.

To enable signing on with a PIN, open PC Settings and select Users. Then select Create A PIN. Type your password to confirm your identity. As shown in Figure 18-9, you then need to type your new PIN twice and select Finish.

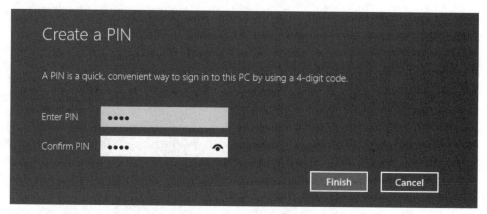

Figure 18-9 You can log on to Windows 8.1 using a four-digit numeric PIN.

The next time you sign on to your computer, Windows will prompt you to enter your PIN. If you are using touch, Windows displays a numeric keypad, which is much easier to type on than a full keyboard. To sign on with a conventional password or a picture password instead, select Sign-In Options.

The math behind an attacker guessing your PIN is much easier to calculate: there are always 10,000 possible combinations (0000–9999), so the odds of guessing your PIN (assuming you don't use your birth date or some other significant number) are 1 in 10,000. Like picture passwords, if you type the PIN incorrectly five times, Windows requires you to type your full password. So, the odds of an attacker guessing your PIN correctly in five attempts is 1 in 2,000.

If you want to disable your PIN, open PC Settings, select Users, and then click the Remove button beside Change PIN.

Password best practices

We rely on passwords to protect our privacy and our important data. If your passwords fall into the wrong hands, the results can be devastating:

- Your identity is stolen.

- Your credit card is used to buy things for other people.

- Your credit is ruined.

- Your private data is posted on the Internet.

- Justin Bieber is added to your Likes on Facebook.

You can greatly reduce the risk of your password being compromised, and the damage that can be done with a successful compromise, by following a few basic password best practices.

Password uniqueness

Every time you create an account on a website, you trust everyone involved in that website with your password. If anyone who manages the website isn't trustworthy, they might abuse your password. If you happen to use the same password on multiple websites, a single untrustworthy IT guy can log in as you on all of those websites. I worked in IT for many years. Most IT guys are very trustworthy, but some of them aren't.

Besides requiring you to trust everyone who manages the website with your password, you also trust the skills of their IT staff to protect the password database from outside intruders. If a website's password database gets hacked, that malicious person will definitely do terrible things with your identity. Websites and password databases get hacked all the time, and often the IT staff never even discovers it, so they can't notify you of the intrusion. Sometimes the IT staff does discover it and they don't notify anyone because they want to protect their reputation.

Password complexity

There are several ways attackers guess passwords:

- If an attacker knows you personally or they have access to your personal information (for example, using your Facebook profile), they'll attempt to guess your password using your favorite sports teams, your pets' names, the names of your children, the name of your spouse/partner, different dates that are important to you, and so on.

- If an attacker doesn't have personal information about you, they'll use a dictionary attack. A dictionary attack attempts to access your account using common passwords listed in a password dictionary. If your password is a common term or name, or a password used by other people, it'll be in the dictionary and your account will be compromised.

Inside OUT

Storing your passwords

Now, I don't know you personally, but I'd be willing to bet that you used the same password on two different websites. Almost everyone does. I don't, and I have over 400 different passwords. Considering I have the long-term memory of a fruit fly, you'd be right in guessing that I store my passwords somewhere, and it's not on sticky notes all over my desk.

I use a free tool called KeePass (Professional Edition), as shown in Figure 18-10. KeePass does a really good job of organizing your different passwords and keeping them as safe as they can be. You can synchronize KeePass databases between different computers and even your smartphone, giving you access to your passwords wherever you are.

Figure 18-10 Use KeePass to track all your passwords.

Besides tracking your passwords, KeePass can protect your passwords with a key file, remind you to change your passwords on a regular basis, and can generate random, complex passwords, as shown in Figure 18-11.

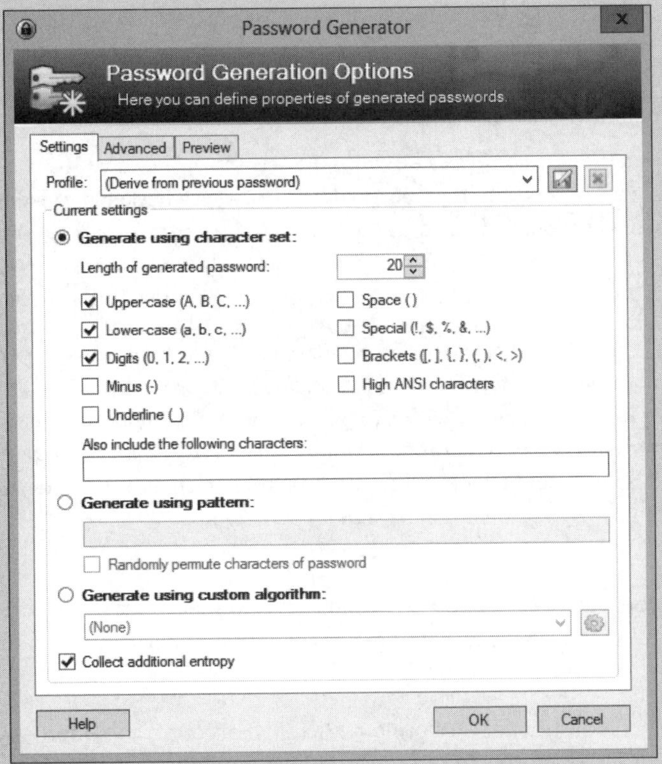

Figure 18-11 KeePass can generate very complex passwords.

Download the latest version of KeePass from *http://keepass.info/*.

The best way to keep your password from being guessed in these ways is to use a random, complex password, because that password won't contain any personal information and it won't appear in a password dictionary. Complex passwords mix uppercase and lowercase characters, numbers, and symbols. For example, "password" isn't complex and would be easily guessed, while "XC3m$U}L" is complex and would be very difficult to guess.

If you use a random, complex password, attackers might be forced to use a brute force attack, which guesses every combination of letters, numbers, and symbols. There are so many possible combinations, however, that a complex password of more than six characters would probably take far too long to guess.

Inside OUT

Complex but nonsecure passwords

Avoid using pseudo-complex passwords. For example, "P@ssw0rd" mixes uppercase and lowercase letters, numbers, and symbols. However, hackers have long since figured out that sort of character substitution, and dictionary attacks will automatically replace A for @, E for 3, S for $, O for 0, and more. They'll also add punctuation onto the end of other words, so don't think that adding a ! or ? to the end of your password helps.

To create the most secure password possible, use a random password generator. My favorite is at *http://www.thebitmill.com/tools/password.html*. That website uses JavaScript running in your browser to generate a random complex password that meets your requirements. Because it generates the password in your browser, your new password is never sent over the Internet. Nonetheless, I'm rather paranoid, so I always change at least one character in the random password.

Complex passwords are a very good way to improve your account security. They're also a very good way to make yourself crazy. Random passwords especially can be almost impossible to remember.

That's one of the biggest benefits of using a Microsoft account. If you forget your password, you can use your email address to reset it. Microsoft accounts do not require you to use complex passwords (though the website will warn you that you aren't using one when you change your password).

Inside OUT

Become a believer in complex passwords by cracking yourself

If you still have any doubt about the importance of complex passwords, download the Ophcrack live CD (the version for Windows Vista and Windows 7) and boot from it. If you can't boot from a CD, use the Unetbootin tool (available at *http://sourceforge.net/ projects/unetbootin/*) to create a bootable USB flash drive. In just a few minutes, the handy tool will display any passwords that aren't complex, as shown in Figure 18-12. Only your complex passwords will remain private.

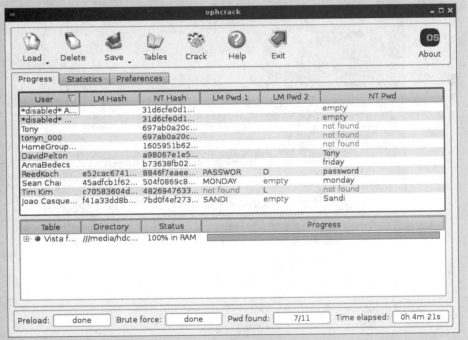

Figure 18-12 Use Ophcrack to identify weak passwords on your own PC.

Ophcrack is a great way to make sure other people on your PC are using complex passwords.

However, you can configure Windows 8.1 to require complex passwords when you change the password for your local account or your Microsoft account using the PC Settings tool, as shown in Figure 18-13. This doesn't stop you from changing your Microsoft account password online to something weak, but if you don't trust yourself not to break your own rules, who can you trust?

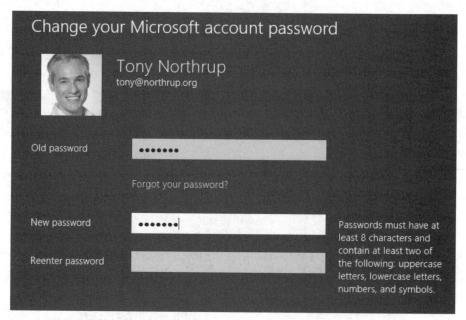

Figure 18-13 Windows 8.1 can require you to use complex passwords.

Follow these steps to require complex passwords for Windows 8.1:

1. At the Start screen, type **secpol.msc** and press Enter.

    Windows opens the Local Security Policy desktop app.

2. Select Security Settings\Account Policies\Password Policy.

3. Double-click Minimum Password Length, and choose a minimum length. As shown in Figure 18-14, eight characters is typically considered very secure. Click OK.

4. Double-click Password Must Meet Complexity Requirements. Select Enabled, and then click OK.

5. Close the Local Security Policy app.

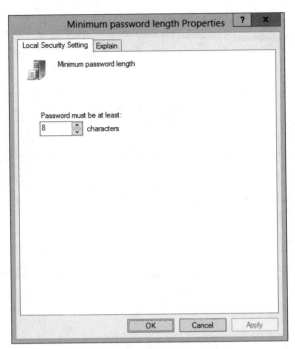

Figure 18-14 Use the Local Security Policy tool to require complex passwords for local accounts.

When you require complex passwords for a local account, Windows 8.1 requires that passwords:

- Not contain the user's account name or parts of the user's full name that exceed two consecutive characters

- Be at least six characters in length (though you can require more characters using the Minimum Password Length policy)

- Contain characters from three of the following four categories:
    - English uppercase characters (A through Z)
    - English lowercase characters (a through z)
    - Base 10 digits (0 through 9)
    - Nonalphabetic characters (for example, !, $, #, %)

CHAPTER 18

Regularly changing your password

You should regularly change your password. Changing your password protects you in a number of ways:

- If someone steals your old password, changing your password will prevent them from accessing your account in the future. Basically, it limits the damage a bad guy can do with your password.

- If someone is attempting to crack your password by guessing it, they'll have to start the entire process over.

- It makes it virtually impossible for someone to identify your password by examining fingerprints on a touchscreen or keyboard wear.

- It reduces the risk that you'll use the same password for multiple accounts.

Changing your password regularly has a few disadvantages important enough to cause Microsoft to not require users to change them by default:

- It's quite annoying.

- You're much more likely to forget a password you recently changed.

- If you're afraid of forgetting your password, you're much more likely to write it down somewhere.

- If someone sees your password written on a note stuck to your monitor (this really does happen often), they'll be able to log in as you, completely defeating the purpose of having a password.

- If a sophisticated attacker steals your password, they might use your credentials to create their own account, negating the first benefit in the previous list.

Weighing the benefits and costs, most businesses require their employees to regularly change their passwords. As a home user, though, the choice is up to you. I don't think most home users need to change their password on a regular basis. Instead, you should use a different password for logging on to Windows than you do for other websites, and change your password if you think someone might know it, if you break up with someone, or if someone you live with moves out.

If you use a Microsoft account, edit your account information online at *https://account.live.com/* and click the Change Password link. As shown in Figure 18-15, select the Make Me Change My Password Every 72 Days check box and then click Save.

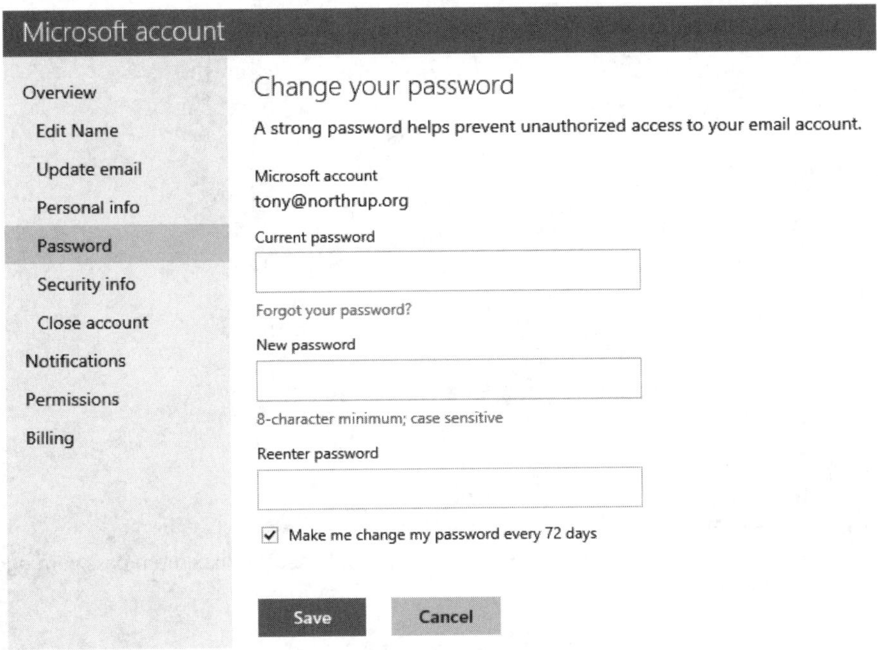

Figure 18-15 Select the option to be required to change a Microsoft account password regularly.

If you use a local account, follow these steps to require regular password changes:

1. At the Start screen, type **secpol.msc** and press Enter.

    Windows opens the Local Security Policy desktop app.

2. Select Security Settings\Account Policies\Password Policy.

3. Double-click Maximum Password Age, and choose a time span after which the user will be required to change their password, as shown in Figure 18-16. Windows will notify the user several days in advance that they need to change their password. Click OK.

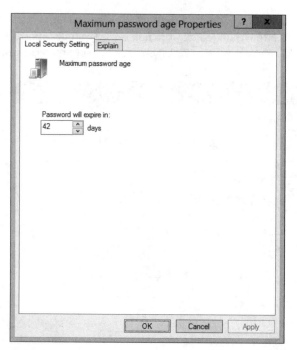

Figure 18-16 Use the Local Security Policy tool to set the maximum password age for local accounts.

4. Double-click Enforce Password History. Set the value to 10, and then click OK. This prevents users from choosing a password that they have recently used, which is a concern because many people simply alternate between passwords when required to change their password.

5. Double-click Minimum Password Age, and set it to 1 day and then click OK. Working with Enforce Password History, this setting prevents the user from changing their password to something new and then immediately changing it back.

6. Close the Local Security Policy app.

The next time you change the password on your local account, Windows 8.1 will require it to meet the complexity requirements.

Using passphrases

If you have a difficult time remembering long or complex passwords, there's a new approach: passphrases. Whereas a complex password might be *P@s5w0R>*, a passphrase might be *A little password is a dangerous thing.*

The extra length of a passphrase offers several security advantages:

- They're easier to remember than a complex password.

- Brute force cracking tools that guess passwords by attempting every combination will probably never guess the passphrase. These tools start with "a," "b," "c" and work their way to "zzzzzzzzzz," covering every combination of letters, numbers, and characters in between. Guessing a long passphrase would be impractical.

- Dictionary cracking tools guess passwords from a list of commonly used passwords. Because passphrases are not common, password dictionaries aren't likely to have them.

- Shoulder surfing (a process whereby someone learns your password by watching you type it) would be much more difficult.

They also have a couple of disadvantages:

- If you're using touch, or you're not a good typist, typing your passphrase will be time-consuming.

- Passphrases are a fairly new concept and haven't withstood the test of time. There could be some fundamental security flaw that simply hasn't been discovered yet.

- As passphrases become more popular, attackers will add common phrases to password dictionaries, making those passphrases easy to guess. For example, "We're not in Kansas anymore" and "Go ahead, make my day" will be as easily guessed as your dog's name.

In summary, use a passphrase if you have a hard time remembering complex passwords. Just don't use a common phrase, or a phrase that someone who knew you well might be able to guess. Instead, make up something ridiculous that you can remember but nobody else would ever be able to guess.

Managing accounts

You can do basic account management using the same Users tool in PC Settings that you use to manage Microsoft accounts, including changing your password and adding new users. Perform more complex actions, such as adding users to groups or disabling an account, using the Computer Management console.

The easiest way to open the Computer Management console is to select Computer Management from the WinX menu. You can open the WinX menu by pressing Windows+X on your keyboard or by right-clicking in the lower-left corner.

With touch, the easiest way to open the Computer Management console is to enable administrative tools on the Start screen. To do that, open the Start screen and touch the Settings charm. Under Settings, touch Tiles, and then set Show Administrative Tools to Yes. The console will then appear on the right side of the Start screen.

With the Computer Management console open, browse to System Tools\Local Users And Groups\Users, as shown in Figure 18-17. Some editions of Windows might not have the Local Users And Groups node.

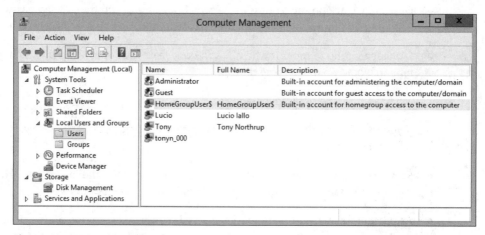

Figure 18-17 Use the Computer Management console for advanced user account management.

The sections that follow describe common account management tasks.

Creating accounts for guests

If you have a friend or family member who occasionally uses your computer (say, your parents when they visit on vacation), it's a good idea to create an account for them. This does a few things:

- It lets them rearrange things on their Start screen without messing up your settings.

- Assuming you don't add them to the Administrators group, it greatly reduces the risk that they'll install software or accidentally infect your computer with malware.

- It keeps your own files and browsing history private so you don't have to worry about them stumbling across something.

- It keeps their files and browsing history private, so you aren't scarred for life when you see what your parents are searching for.

If they already have a Microsoft account, just create an account for their email address, and their settings will be synchronized automatically. If they don't have a Microsoft account, create a local account for them.

Creating an account is easy enough. Here's the trick: when they leave and won't be using your computer for a while, you should disable their account. Disabling an account keeps the settings and files on your computer but prevents the user from logging on. That reduces your security risk, especially if your dad still uses your birth date for his password.

To disable an account, double-click the user in the Computer Management console. As shown in Figure 18-18, select the Account Is Disabled check box, and then click OK.

Figure 18-18 Disable user accounts when they won't be used for more than a week.

The next time they visit, simply repeat the process to clear the Account Is Disabled check box and they will be able to log on, with all their files and settings intact.

Deleting a user

If a person isn't ever going to use your computer again, you can just delete their account. From the Computer Management console, right-click an account and then click Delete. If you use the Computer Management console, you will also need to use File Explorer to delete their user profile, which is located in C:\Users\ by default.

A more user-friendly way to delete an account is to use Control Panel. To delete an account with Control Panel, search from the Start screen for **remove user** and then select Add, Delete, And Manage Other User Accounts. Select the account you want to delete. As shown in Figure 18-19, click Remove, and follow the prompts that appear to delete or keep their files.

If you delete a Microsoft account, the account still exists online, but that user will no longer be able to log on to your computer.

Figure 18-19 To improve security, permanently delete user accounts you no longer need.

Creating groups

You can create security groups, such as Parents, Kids, and Guests, add users to one or more groups, and then assign different permissions to each. This isn't usually necessary, however, even if you want to keep some files private, because encryption, sharing, and Family Safety are sufficient authorization for most home users. For more information about encryption, refer to Chapter 9, "Organizing and protecting files."

To create a security group, open the Computer Management console and select System Tools\Local Users And Groups\Groups. On the Action menu, select New Group. In the New Group dialog box (as shown in Figure 18-20), type the name of your group. Click the Add button to add members to the group by typing their user names. Then, click Create, and click Close.

Figure 18-20 Create new groups to assign specific permissions to multiple users.

Changing group memberships

You can also add users to existing groups. The easiest way is to select System Tools\Local Users And Groups\Users in the Computer Management console, double-click a user, select the Member Of tab, and then click Add (as shown in Figure 18-21). Then, type the name of the group and click OK.

Figure 18-21 Use the Member Of tab to add a user to groups.

CHAPTER 18

Default groups

Windows 8.1 includes 19 groups by default. Most of these groups are designed for use in business environments; they allow IT departments to delegate very specific responsibilities to different people within the organization. At home, of course, all PC management responsibilities typically fall on a single person, and since you're reading this book, that person is probably you. Some of these groups are used to assign privileges to services such as HomeGroup and Remote Desktop.

The groups built into Windows 8.1 are:

- **Access Control Assistance Operators**   Purely for professional use, members of this group can audit security settings to ensure computers comply with an organization's security requirements.

- **Administrators**   One of the two groups home users will access on a regular basis, Administrators can do just about anything on the computer, including installing apps, changing settings, and infecting a computer with malware (not that they'd do that deliberately). Administrators have all the rights described for the other groups listed. In other words, if you're a member of the Administrators group, you automatically have the privileges to run backups, administer Hyper-V, and so on. Therefore, members of the Administrators group don't need to be in the other groups.

- **Backup Operators**   As the name implies, members of this group can run backups on a computer. They can't change settings, but they can read every single file on a computer, so you really need to trust members of this group.

- **Cryptographic Operators**   Purely for large businesses with a public key infrastructure (PKI), members of this group can create certificates and perform other cryptography related tasks.

- **Distributed COM Users**   Distributed COM (DCOM) isn't used very often anymore because it was notorious for security vulnerabilities. This group is useful for restricting the users who can use it.

- **Event Log Readers**   For businesses that allow some members of the IT staff to monitor events on computers to identify potential problems.

- **Guests**   A very restricted group that allows users to do very little on a computer. Their privileges are enough to run many applications. If you need to create an account for a friend and you're worried they're going to do something bad to your computer, add their account to the Guests group and remove them from the Administrators, Users, and HomeUsers groups.

- **Hyper-V Administrators**   Members of this group can manage the Hyper-V virtual machine software, as described in Chapter 20, "Using Hyper-V."

- **IIS_IUSRS**   A group used only by the system to run Internet Information Services, a rarely used (in home environments) web server built into Windows.

- **Network Configuration Operators**   This group has privileges to configure network settings. In business environments, responsibilities within an IT department are often divided up so that individual personnel perform different tasks, and granting granular permissions using these groups limits security risks.

- **Performance Log Users**   Members of this group can monitor a computer's performance. If you're curious about the Windows 8.1 performance monitoring capabilities, run the app Performance Monitor by typing its name at the Start screen, select Monitoring Tools\Performance Monitor, and click the green plus symbol on the toolbar to add some interesting counters.

- **Power Users**   A now outdated group that grants more privileges than the Users group but fewer privileges than the Administrators group.

- **Remote Desktop Users**   Users who have the right to log on across the network by using Remote Desktop. Administrators have this right by default, but Users don't, so if you want a user with standard privileges to be able to connect across the network, you should add them to this group.

- **Remote Management Users**   There's not much purpose for this group in home environments. In enterprise environments, this allows administrators to run network management tools to monitor and configure remote computers.

- **Replicator**   A group that grants the necessary privileges for a service account to replicate files in an enterprise environment.

- **Users**   The most commonly used group, Users grants members of the group permission to perform day-to-day tasks within Windows, including saving files to their profile, browsing the web, and running apps.

- **HomeUsers**   A group that grants the necessary privileges for different computers to access files and other resources shared within a home network. Most privileges are assigned to individual users on a computer. HomeUsers assigns privileges to every user on a computer, allowing homegroups to be accessible to everyone on your home network, saving you the inconvenience of manually assigning per-user privileges. This group is only created when the PC joins a homegroup.

- **WinRMRemoteWMIUsers**   Like the Remote Management Users group, this group allows enterprises to assign permissions to remotely manage computers across the network.

Family Safety

Part of the beauty of PCs and the Internet is that they provide unlimited access to people and information anywhere around the world. If you're a parent, that potential can be very scary, however. Most parents want to supervise their children, and many parents want to do their best to protect their children from unpleasant outside influences.

Family Safety, a feature of Windows 7 and Windows 8.1, can help you do that. Family Safety is capable of monitoring your child's PC and web activity. It can also restrict what your child can do, where they can browse on the web, and how long they can do it.

You can manage Family Safety either locally (using Control Panel tools) or on the Family Safety website. The two tools provide similar capabilities. The website is handy if you need to make changes while you're away from home. For example, you can use the Family Safety website while you're at work to extend a child's PC time while they do homework.

The sections that follow describe best practices for using Family Safety and show you how to configure it.

Turning on Family Safety

You can use Control Panel to turn on Family Safety on a user-by-user basis. From the Start screen, search for **Family Safety**, and then select Family Safety. Control Panel opens and lists the users on your computer, as shown in Figure 18-22.

Figure 18-22 Use Control Panel to turn on Family Safety.

Select the user for whom you want to turn on Family Safety, and then select On, Enforce Current Settings, as shown in Figure 18-23. Once Family Safety is enabled, you need to customize it to your particular needs.

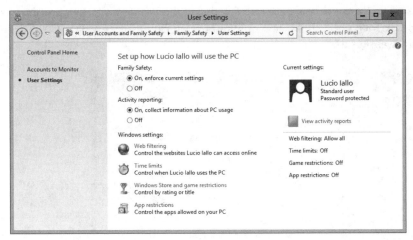

Figure 18-23 Once you turn on Family Safety, you'll be able to customize a large number of settings.

▶ **Using Family Safety** Watch the video at *http://aka.ms/WinIO/familysafety*.

The sections that follow discuss each of the settings in more detail.

Web filtering

Web filtering lets you control which websites users can visit. At a high level, there are three approaches to this:

- **Block all except**   Also known as whitelisting, this approach allows the user to visit only the sites that you specify. This is the most secure approach, but it can be a frustrating experience for the user, because many links simply won't work, and components of a webpage might not load correctly.

- **Allow all except**   Also known as blacklisting, this approach allows the user to visit any website except those that you specify. This is not at all a good way to protect your children from the dangers of the Internet, because there's no way to list every website that might be objectionable. However, it's an excellent way to stop someone from spending their time on Facebook instead of doing their homework.

- **Allow based on ratings**   This approach provides a compromise between the previous two approaches. You can specify the types of websites the user can visit. Internet Explorer will allow or block websites according to a rating system that you specify. This isn't perfect, but it's pretty good. If someone is determined, they can still find ways around the system. Likewise, there will be times when the rating system might block content that wouldn't be objectionable.

To use any of these options, click Web Filtering in the User Settings window (shown in Figure 18-23). Then select the second option shown in Figure 18-24, which allows the user to use only the websites that you specify.

Figure 18-24 Enable web filtering to restrict which websites a user can visit.

To allow a user to visit only the websites you specify, click Set Web Filtering Level, and select Allow List Only, as shown in Figure 18-25. Finally, select the Click Here To Change Allow List link, and specify the websites the user is allowed to visit.

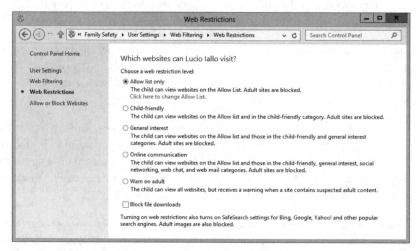

Figure 18-25 Select Allow List Only to limit a user to those websites you have reviewed and approved of.

To allow a user to visit any website except those you specify, simply click Allow Or Block Websites and add the websites you don't want the user to visit, as shown in Figure 18-26. You can block specific websites in addition to applying other web filtering options.

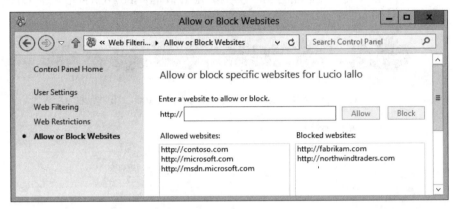

Figure 18-26 If there are particular websites that you don't want someone to visit, you can block them.

Blocking a website is far from foolproof. The user might be able to find a proxy server or gateway that will forward requests to the unauthorized website. Family Safety has thought of this, naturally, and blocks most such websites (including Anonymizer.com and translate.bing.com). However, it's possible to find one that hasn't been blocked.

Of course, you can't be expected to compile a list of every good or bad website on the Internet. Most of the work of filtering websites needs to be done by Family Safety, and the simplest way to do that is to select one of the predefined web filtering levels:

- **Designed For Children**   For little kids. This blocks just about the whole Internet, including search sites such as Bing.com and Google.com. Blocking search sites makes it more difficult for kids to find what they're looking for, but they can still type the URLs for family-friendly sites such as Disney.com, Microsoft.com, and Northrup.org. For best results, create bookmarks for the sites your kids can use, and show them how to use those bookmarks.

- **General Interest**   For older kids who might need to use the Internet for research, but who you don't want on Facebook or Twitter. This allows most of the Internet, including sites such as Wikipedia.com, Bing.com, and Google.com. Search sites will have filtering active, somewhat limiting what kids can search for. Kids can still craft searches that will return very objectionable content, however.

- **Online Communications**   This setting adds social networking sites such as Facebook and Twitter. Of course, the risks with these sites is that your kids will talk to people you wouldn't want them to talk to.

- **Warn On Adult** The least restrictive setting, this blocks no part of the web. However, Family Safety warns the user if they're visiting a site that might have adult content. The warnings work well if you rely on activity reporting to monitor your child's web activity. After all, forcing the child to click past the warning (shown in Figure 18-27) removes any possibility that your child might have accidentally stumbled onto a site.

Family Safety

! Your parent might not want you to visit this website.

Go back to previous page

If you're not sure this website would be OK with your parents, don't visit it.

It's OK. I want to visit this page.

Figure 18-27 If you don't want to restrict a child's browsing, you can enable warnings that reduce the risk of the child accidentally visiting an adult website.

- **Block File Downloads** You can select this option in addition to selecting any of the previous options to prevent the user from downloading files. It's generally a good idea to select this option.

When you enable Family Safety, the user is notified when they log on, as shown in Figure 18-28. Some people prefer to secretly monitor a user's web activity, but my personal philosophy is to always let the person know that they're being watched. For example, I might install a camera to monitor employees at work, but I would never install a hidden camera. I believe it's often important to monitor people, especially children, but I also believe that everyone has a right to privacy and to know when they're being watched. People get tense if they think people might be watching them at any particular moment.

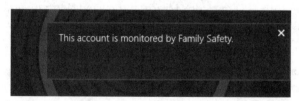

This account is monitored by Family Safety.

Figure 18-28 Family Safety notifies users that they are being monitored when they log on.

Inside OUT

Trust, but audit

My personal philosophy on web filtering comes from my IT security background: trust, but audit. Therefore, I don't rely on web filtering to block my daughter's web browsing. Instead, I rely on activity reporting to allow me to monitor her browsing, and I let her know that I'm monitoring how she uses her computer. She knows the types of activities she can and can't use her computer for, and if she breaks the rules, she knows she won't be allowed to use the computer anymore. Your children may vary, but it's been 100 percent effective with Madelyn.

In my opinion, this approach is more effective than filtering without activity monitoring. If you trust the filters to keep your child away from the darker parts of the Internet, a determined and tech-savvy child might eventually find a way to bypass those filters. Once they figure that out, they know they can continue to use the same technique without being caught. If you monitor their activity, they know they'll never get away with it, because as soon as you check the activity report, they'll be in trouble.

The biggest problem with filtering websites is that legitimate, safe content occasionally gets blocked. If a user attempts to visit a website that's blocked, Windows 8.1 notifies them, and if they click the notification, they are given the opportunity to bypass the block by having a parent type their password (click My Parent Is Here), as shown in Figure 18-29.

Figure 18-29 Family Safety makes it easy for parents to bypass web filtering when legitimate content cannot be accessed.

Activity reporting

Activity reporting records every website a user visits, every Internet search, and how long they use the PC and different apps (including both Windows 8.1 apps and desktop apps). It's a very precise way to find out what your children are doing on their computer. Figure 18-30 shows the Activity Reporting summary page, which you can view by visiting *https://familysafety.microsoft.com/*. Naturally, it will only have useful information if you've had it turned on for a user and that user has been at their PC.

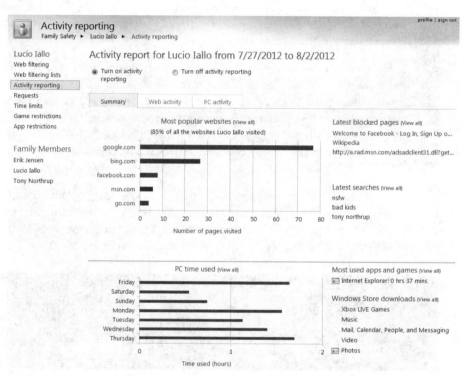

Figure 18-30 The Activity Reporting summary page provides a snapshot of a user's PC activity.

The Web Activity tab (Figure 18-31) shows a list of every website the user attempted to visit, even if Family Safety blocked the website for the user. You can expand each website to view specific pages the user visited (click a link to open it in your own browser). It also shows you how many visits the user made, though it doesn't show you how much time they spent on that website. In other words, if your child is playing a game at the same website all day, it will still show up as a single visit.

Figure 18-31 The Web Activity tab shows every website the user has visited.

The PC Activity tab, as shown in Figure 18-32, shows how long the user was signed in, which apps they downloaded, which apps they ran, and how long they used each app.

Combined, these reports are a perfect way to make sure your child is using a computer appropriately. For example, if you tell your child not to play any games, you can check the PC Activity tab to make sure they didn't launch any game apps, and check the Web Activity tab to make sure they didn't play an online game. If you tell your child they can only use the computer for an hour a night, you can make sure they're following your rule with the PC Activity tab (or allow Family Safety to forcibly limit their usage, as described in the next section). It wouldn't hurt to give them a few minutes of leeway, because Family Safety doesn't always detect precisely when a user steps away from the PC.

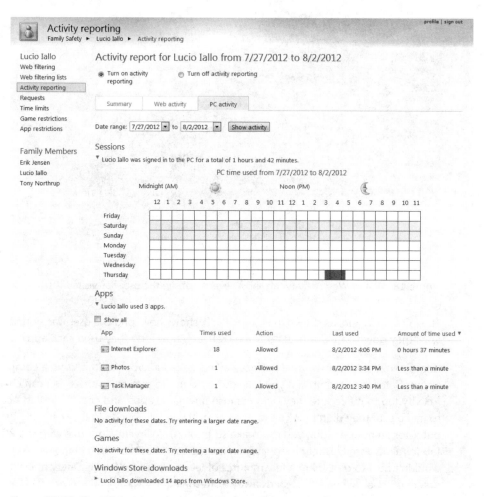

Figure 18-32 The PC Activity tab shows how long the user was signed in to their PC and which apps they ran.

If you enable Family Safety for a user before they log in for the first time, you'll see a large number of apps downloaded from the Windows Store. You can ignore this part of the report; it's Windows 8.1 installing the standard apps that are available for all users. It doesn't even need to download the apps from the Windows Store, because they're already on your local hard drive.

While you can view the Activity Report online at any time, Family Safety also sends you a weekly email for each user that contains the same information shown on each user's summary page.

Time limits

As shown in Figure 18-33, Family Safety can also limit how long a user is on a computer, making it easy to enforce rules like, "You can only use your PC for 45 minutes on weeknights."

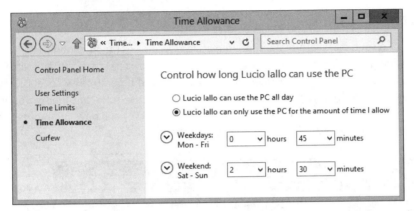

Figure 18-33 Use time limits to control how long your child uses a PC (but set the times carefully).

Keep in mind this is total PC usage. You can't, for example, allow your kid to play a game for 30 minutes and do their homework for as long as they need to. If your child is using Microsoft Word to finish an important report and their time allowance expires, you'll have to use the Get More Time button (as shown in Figure 18-34) to allow them to continue working. You can then choose exactly how much additional time they can have, in 15 minute increments.

Unfortunately, time limits aren't very flexible. For example, you might want the weekend schedule to apply to holidays, or you might want to give your child extra time on Fridays. Time Limits can't do that. If you don't want to bypass the time limit for those exceptions, you could set the time limit to the most amount of time you'd ever want your child to use the PC, and then use activity reporting to monitor your child's PC usage after the fact.

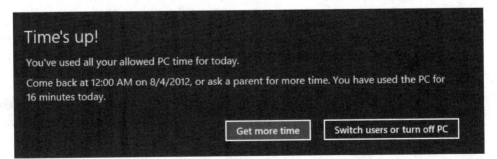

Figure 18-34 Click Get More Time to bypass the time limit.

If you have more than one child, clever children might start bartering PC time. For example, if your daughter runs out of time, your son might log on with his account and allow the daughter to use his time. There's no way around this type of trickery other than physically keeping an eye on your kids.

Curfew

You can also set a curfew to make sure your child doesn't use the PC when they're supposed to be sleeping or doing their homework. Figure 18-35 shows a schedule that limits PC use on weeknights to a few hours in the evening, but allows more time on the weekends. If you also set time limits, the child will be limited by the most restrictive rules. In other words, if you set the curfew to stop them from using the PC at 8 P.M., but they still have 30 minutes of their time limit left, the curfew will sign them off.

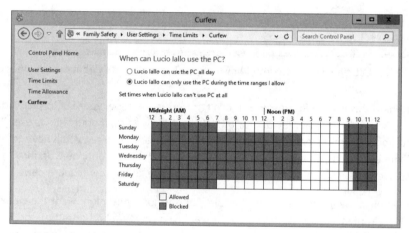

Figure 18-35 Use curfews to limit the times of day your child can use a PC.

App restrictions

App restrictions let you choose which apps users can run. This is important to configure along with web filtering, because many apps simply provide a user interface for a website. For example, if you block the Facebook.com website but allow the Facebook app, the user can still access Facebook.

You can configure app restrictions using the Family Safety Control Panel tool or by using the Family Safety website, as shown in Figure 18-36. Simply select which apps users can run.

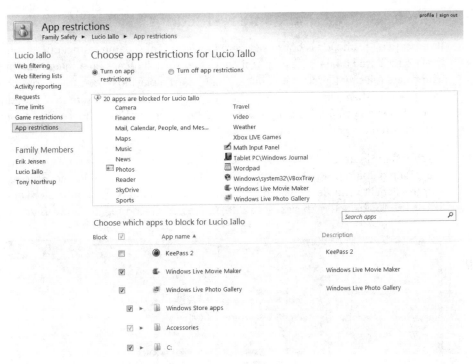

Figure 18-36 Use app restrictions to limit which apps users can run.

Family Safety shows the user a notification when apps are blocked, as shown in Figure 18-37, and when the user attempts to run a blocked app. Oddly, it doesn't remove the tiles for the apps the user can't run, so those tiles simply tease the user on the Start screen. It would be a good idea to unpin apps that you don't want the user to run.

Figure 18-37 Family Safety notifies users of app restrictions.

Windows Store and game restrictions

Whereas app restrictions control access to individual apps, game restrictions allow you to control access based on game ratings. This way, if you install games on a shared computer, you can create rules that limit your younger children from playing games that might be too scary or violent for them without limiting which games you can play. Be sure to always sign out of Windows when you finish a session at the PC, however, because all these rules are useless if your children use your account.

As shown in Figure 18-38, Windows Store and game restrictions use the Entertainment Software Rating Board (ESRB) rating system by default. You can use the Rating Systems page in Control Panel to choose a different game rating system, but games in the Store are rated according to age and map closely to ESRB ratings, so I recommend simply using the default.

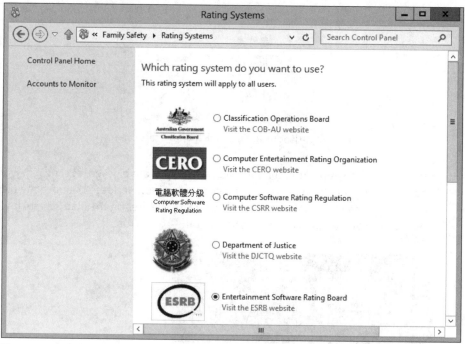

Figure 18-38 Select a rating system that meets your family's needs.

Figure 18-39 shows the Control Panel page used to select a game rating level when you use the ESRB rating system (different rating systems can have different levels). There are two very important options on the page: Allow Games With No Rating and Block Games With No Rating.

Choosing to allow unrated games means the user can run any game that hasn't been rated, but all the games in the Windows Store are rated, so choosing this option would only block desktop apps. Blocking unrated games improves security, but it prevents the user from running any app that doesn't have a rating and that you haven't specifically allowed by selecting Allow Or Block Games. My recommendation is to select Block Games With No Rating and make a point of allowing every desktop game you want your child to play. It's a nuisance, but it's better than allowing a scary game to slip past the filter.

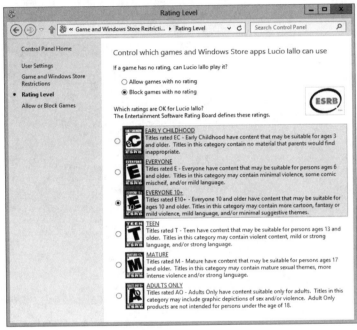

Figure 18-39 Use game restrictions to limit the games users can play to specific ratings.

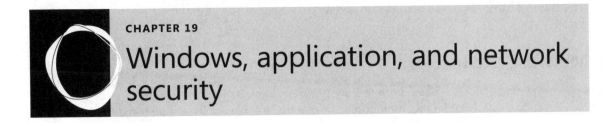

Windows, application, and network security

Malware protection 438

Protecting your privacy 447

Removing malware 449

Windows Firewall 457

Wireless security 468

Turning off security features 469

Microsoft designs all its software according to the "secure by default" security principle. This is a deep philosophy that has required completely changing the way developers create software. Put simply, Microsoft software is designed to leave fresh installs in a state that should protect them from common threats.

Note that I say common threats. Windows 8.1 can't possibly protect you from every threat. For example, someone might see you type your password by looking over your shoulder, or someone might break into your house and steal your PC.

Secure by default, like all practical security, involves a compromise between protection and convenience. Window 8 includes quite a few security features that are disabled by default because they would be inconvenient to more users than they would help protect. You should take a few minutes to understand these security features because your specific needs might warrant the extra protection (and inconvenience).

File encryption is one such example. File encryption can reduce performance and make data more difficult to recover, and it only protects users from attacks more sophisticated than most home users will ever encounter. File encryption is discussed in Chapter 9, "Organizing and protecting files," and Chapter 12, "Managing storage."

On the other hand, some default security settings might be annoying and inconvenient to you. For example, if you keep your PC physically secure and you're the only user, you might prefer to completely bypass the password prompt. Similarly, if you find yourself annoyed by the User Account Control (UAC) prompts, understand the security implications, and are willing to accept increased security risks, you can turn UAC off with just a few clicks. I don't recommend it, but I will show you how to do it.

This chapter will discuss security fundamentals and the most important security features of Windows 8.1, as well as how to configure those features. If you don't care about the security background information and you just want to streamline Windows 8.1 by disabling some security features, skip to "Turning off security features" at the end of this chapter.

Malware protection

Internet use was booming in the late 1990s and early 2000s. Many people connected their PCs to the Internet for the first time, and neither the user nor the PC was prepared for the dangers.

Criminal elements around the world began to seek out different ways to capitalize on the rapid growth and widespread security vulnerabilities. Many of those criminal elements created malicious software (commonly known as malware) that could earn a few cents when installed on a person's PC by showing them advertisements, reporting on their Internet usage, or stealing their credit card information.

Obviously, the more PCs these criminal developers could install their software on, the more money they could steal. Like much of organized crime, they approached the problem like business people and found many different ways to distribute their software:

- **Viruses**   Viruses spread by attaching themselves to an email message, a floppy disk, a flash drive, or some other method for transferring data. Early versions of Windows would run viruses attached to floppy drives automatically, but recent versions of Windows require the user to choose to run the virus. To trick the user into running the virus, they often have names that entice the user to open it, such as, "How to make that slow driver get out of the left lane.exe."

- **Worms**   Worms typically exploit a network vulnerability in a PC and then begin spreading to other PCs across the network. Operating systems with built-in firewalls, such as Windows Vista, Windows 7, and Windows 8.1, can block most worms and have greatly reduced their presence in recent years.

- **Browser exploits**   Up until the early-to-mid 2000s, many modern browsers had security vulnerabilities that would allow websites to run applications with administrative privileges without the user's knowledge. Simply by visiting a website, the PC could become infected with malware. Users didn't need to visit a questionable website because attackers exploited legitimate web servers to infect the website's code with malware that would spread to every user who visited the website.

- **Trojans**   Named for the famous Trojan horse that pretended to be a wonderful gift but was filled with uninvited and rather poorly mannered guests, Trojans pretend to be something you want, such as a game, but they actually install malware.

- **Bundling**   Sometimes, legitimate apps also install unwanted software. Legitimate apps always warn you about any other apps they might install, but many users click Next so quickly in the installer that they install the malware without noticing.

Inside OUT

How to avoid bundled apps

Bundled apps are not technically considered malware. If the installer warns you about a bundled app and allows you to choose not to install it, they're technically giving you the choice.

The installers are sneaky, though. They know that many people accept the default settings without reviewing them. Sometimes they require you to scroll to see a check box that needs to be cleared.

To avoid installing unwanted bundled software, never install an app using the recommended settings, and always review each page of the installer carefully.

Once a single malware app installed itself, it would often install many other malware apps. Each would monitor the PC and reinstall malware if the user successfully removed any of it. This could make it almost impossible to remove the malware from the PC (even with antimalware software), often requiring the user to restore their PC from a backup.

The malware itself takes many different forms:

- **Spyware**   Monitors the user's activity and private files, making money by reporting on their usage for demographics or stealing their credit card information. A subspecies of spyware, keyloggers, monitors your PC usage closely. Keyloggers are often installed by family members, ex-spouses/partners, and even law enforcement agencies to monitor another person's PC usage.

- **Adware**   Displays extra advertisements to the user, making fractions of a penny for each ad displayed or when users click on an ad.

- **Scareware**   These apps warn you that something bad will happen unless you buy a product or pay someone money. Many scareware apps pretend to be antimalware apps that detect malware on your PC and then offer to remove the malware if you purchase the software. Ironic, since the app itself is the malware. Other scareware apps threaten to expose private information on your PC unless you pay an extortion fee.

- **Browser add-ons**   These add an unwanted toolbar or other add-on to a browser. Browser toolbars have become such a nuisance that the touch version of Internet Explorer in Windows 8.1 does not support toolbars.

Inside OUT

How Internet Explorer protects you from unwanted add-ons

Windows 8.1 includes two versions of Internet Explorer: the touch version and the desktop version. The touch version doesn't allow any add-ons, so it should be completely immune to that type of malware. The desktop version does allow add-ons, but it never installs them by default. If an app attempts to install an add-on, Internet Explorer prompts you with the message, "Several add-ons are ready for use." If you then select Choose Add-Ons, you receive the prompt shown in Figure 19-1, allowing you to enable the add-ons.

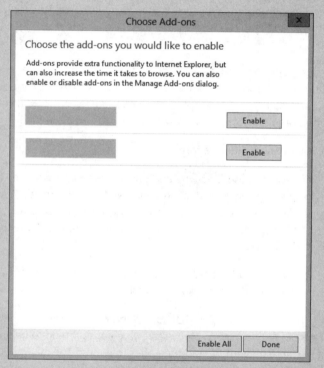

Figure 19-1 Internet Explorer 11 does not install add-ons by default.

This is just another example of how Windows 8.1 is secure by default.

- **Rootkits** Malware that installs itself between the PC's hardware and operating system, allowing it to perform any task on a PC while remaining almost undetectable.

● **Backdoors**   Malware that gives an attacker remote access to the PC. Backdoors have been installed on millions of PCs, which are then known as bots or zombies. Attackers have large networks of these PCs at their disposal, known as botnets. The attacker can then command the PCs in a botnet to perform different tasks, such as attacking websites or sharing illegal files.

Beyond all the nasty symptoms I've already described, the number one complaint about malware is that it slows down a person's PC. In summary, you don't want malware.

Fortunately, malware is much less of a risk now. Whereas you absolutely needed antimalware software with Windows 98 or Windows XP, more recent versions of Windows, including Windows Vista, Windows 7, and Windows 8.1, are much more resistant to malware. The default settings protect the average user from viruses, worms, and browser exploits.

However, software alone cannot protect users from Trojans and bundling, because those malware distribution methods rely on social engineering. Social engineering tricks the user into doing something that's bad for them, and as long as software gives users the freedom to choose their own software, their risks can't go away.

There are a few ways to reduce the risk of Trojans. Some publishers, such as Microsoft, Adobe, and Apple, have a reputation to protect, and they genuinely do their best to avoid malicious acts against the user. Digital signatures, a form of cryptography, allows these publishers to sign their applications with a private key. Software such as Windows 8.1 can examine and verify that digital signature, allowing the user to decide to trust publishers.

If you attempt to run an app from a publisher that can't be verified, Windows 8.1 warns you. The warning varies depending on where you run the app. Figure 19-2 shows the prompt that appears when you run an unverified app from across your local network.

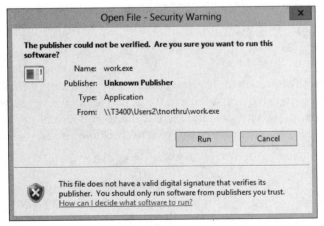

Figure 19-2 You really should read these warnings carefully.

User Account Control

Regardless of whether an app is signed by a verified publisher, Windows will warn you before it runs an app that requires administrative privileges. Only apps that need to change the system configuration require administrative privileges. Windows displays a User Account Control (UAC) prompt, as shown in Figure 19-3, every time you try to perform an administrative task with an app. If you don't completely trust the app, click No to prevent it from running. If you click Yes, the app can do anything to your system, including install malware.

Figure 19-3 User Account Control warns you before you do something that might change your system configuration.

The problem with UAC is summed up in every parent's favorite fable: "The Boy Who Cried Wolf." As users, we've been forced to bypass zillions of warnings when performing perfectly safe tasks, and as a result, most people now assume every one is a false alarm and simply bypass it.

If you find UAC annoying, you can disable it. I don't recommend that, though. For instructions on how to disable it, refer to "Turning off security features" later in this chapter.

SmartScreen

SmartScreen provides some protection for files you download from the web. If SmartScreen thinks a file might be dangerous, it blocks it for you. The option to run the app anyway is hidden by default. To run the app, select More Info. Then, as shown in Figure 19-4, you can select Run Anyway. You should only bypass SmartScreen if you're absolutely certain that the file is safe.

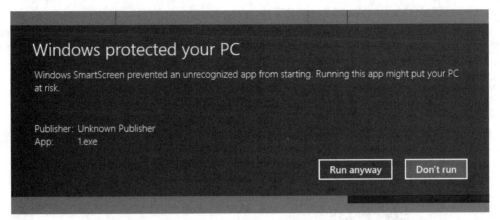

Figure 19-4 SmartScreen warns you about potentially dangerous files from the Internet.

SmartScreen also appears if you attempt to visit a website that might be dangerous. For example, a phishing site might pretend to be your bank to trick you into entering your credit card number. SmartScreen won't detect every phishing site, but it will warn you about many. If SmartScreen is annoying you, you can turn it off by following the instructions in the last section of this chapter.

Inside OUT

How to avoid phishing sites

Phishing sites are the con artists of the web. They pretend to be something they're not. Often, they pretend to be sites very important to you: Facebook, your online bank, your email, or even a law enforcement agency.

Phishing sites can be very convincing. It's easy to steal another website's layout, so a phishing site can look exactly like the site it's impersonating. Even experienced users wouldn't be able to tell the difference between a phishing site and the original site, so it's no wonder that so many users enter their user name, password, credit card number, or other private information into phishing sites.

Before a phishing site can steal your private information, it has to get you to visit the site. There are different ways to do this, but the most common is an email or instant message. The message will attempt to motivate you to click a link to the phishing site. Often, the messages show urgency.

The themes phishing sites use to trick you into clicking a link are the same themes social engineering hackers have been using for years to trick people over the phone or in person:

- Your bank account is overdrawn.

- Your package could not be delivered.

- A law enforcement agency has caught you doing something bad.

- Something personal of yours is available on the Internet.

- Someone is giving away something you want for free.

- Someone you know is in jail or has been hurt and needs your help.

- You've won some money or a prize.

Sometimes your bank account really is overdrawn or your package can't be delivered, so how can you tell the real messages from the fake? You can't always. Logos and writing style are easy to copy. The From address in an email message is completely meaningless, because anyone can send a message from any email address.

There's one easy way to avoid the tricks: never click a link in an email or instant message. Instead, type the URL directly into your web browser. For example, if your bank sends you a message saying your account is overdrawn, type the name of your bank's website into your browser instead of clicking a link in the message.

You should also use HTTPS instead of HTTP when accessing websites that have any sort of confidential information. That *S* means your communications are encrypted and the server is authenticated. To use HTTPS, simply type **https://** before the website name instead of the standard http://.

HTTPS authenticates the web server by verifying that the name you typed matches the server's certificate. Certificates are issued by certification authorities (CAs) that your browser trusts by default. Assuming these CAs are good at their jobs and only issue certificates to legitimate organizations, and assuming that your PC hasn't been previously compromised, it is almost impossible for a phishing site to impersonate a legitimate site if you type **HTTPS** and the website name into your address bar.

Don't simply look at the address bar to verify a URL after clicking a link. Phishing websites often use names that are easily confused with the original site. For example, instead of contoso.com, they might use comtoso.com, contoso.fabrikam.com, or contóso.com. Always type the name into the browser yourself.

Windows Defender

It's when you decide to ignore all the various operating system warnings and run potentially malicious software that an antimalware app takes over. If you do decide to run an app, antimalware can examine the app to determine if it's actually safe or not. Then, the antimalware app can attempt to remove traces of the malware, or at least the antimalware can give you a more stern warning to ignore.

Windows 8.1 includes antimalware software, commonly called antispyware or antivirus software: Windows Defender. Windows Defender, which is enabled by default, monitors files that you download or copy to your PC and checks them against a database to see if they might be dangerous.

If Windows Defender discovers a dangerous file, it automatically quarantines the file. When a file is quarantined, it's placed in a special location where it can't do any harm. To view quarantined files, open Windows Defender, select the History tab, select Quarantined Items, and then select View Details. Defender lists any files that have been quarantined.

You probably won't ever need to manually run Windows Defender. By default, Windows Defender runs in the background, automatically scanning any new files you save or download. However, if you turn Windows Defender off (as described in "Turning off security features" at the end of this chapter), or if you think your PC might have malware on it, you can manually initiate a scan.

To manually scan your PC with Windows Defender, type **defender** at the Start screen and then select Windows Defender. As shown in Figure 19-5, Windows Defender provides three types of scans:

- **Quick**   As the name implies, this scans just the most critical parts of your PC for potentially dangerous files. If you have real-time protection enabled, there's no good reason to do a quick scan.

- **Full**   Also appropriately named, the full scan checks every part of your PC. Run a full scan periodically just to double-check your PC's integrity, or run it whenever you think you might have malware on your PC.

- **Custom**   Use this scan to check specific folders. For example, if you download a new app or are installing software from a DVD and you want to check it for malware, select a custom scan and then specify the folder containing the software.

Like most antimalware apps, Windows Defender needs to regularly download new signatures to detect the latest threats. Microsoft delivers Windows Defender signatures using Windows Update, so Windows will automatically install them if you selected the default settings to automatically install all updates when you set up Windows.

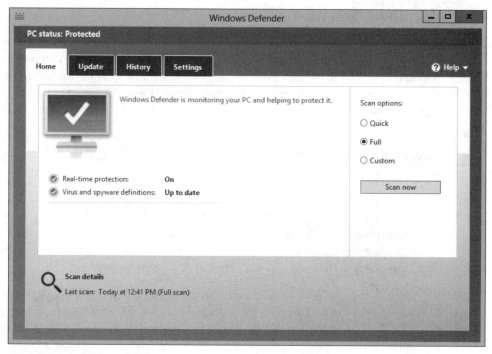

Figure 19-5 Windows Defender provides three types of scans.

▶ **Using Windows Defender** Watch the video at *http://aka.ms/WinIO/defender*.

Inside OUT

Do you really need antimalware?

Most of us have smartphones in our pockets that browse the web and install apps. Yet, unless you've hacked your phone, you've probably never installed an antimalware app, or had a problem with malware.

So, why does your PC need antimalware when your smartphone doesn't? Smartphone vendors limit the apps you can install to those approved by the vendor. During the approval process, they check the apps to make sure they won't do anything dangerous on your system. Additionally, smartphone operating systems are restricted so that apps don't have permission to do anything damaging to your smartphone.

Your PC, however, is much more flexible. Using the desktop, you can install random apps from the web and override the default permissions to allow those apps to make system configuration changes. That's what gives your PC the flexibility you need to run really powerful apps. It's also what introduces the risk of malware.

Protecting your privacy

Whether you're doing your taxes or shopping for your child's birthday present, there are times when you use the PC for tasks you'd rather keep private. Windows 8.1 supports privacy, but not by default. By default, just about everything you do on your PC is recorded in some way.

Privacy while browsing the web

First, let's discuss how to keep web browsing private. By default, web browsers record a history of every webpage you visit, store search terms and URLs for use with autocomplete, and store copies of pages on your local PC for faster retrieval should you visit the same page in the future. Those features are convenient until they spoil the surprise you had planned for your wife's anniversary by revealing the gift you just ordered for her.

Fortunately, all modern browsers include a private mode that doesn't record any part of your action. In Internet Explorer, this is known as InPrivate browsing. To start InPrivate browsing, open Internet Explorer from the Start screen, swipe up from the bottom or right-click the window, select the ellipses (...) near the upper-right corner, and then select New InPrivate Tab, as shown in Figure 19-6. Internet Explorer shows InPrivate near the address bar.

Figure 19-6 InPrivate browsing doesn't keep a record of webpages you visit.

Even if you don't browse in private mode, you can still delete your browsing history. In Internet Explorer, open the Settings charm, select Options, and then, under History, click Select. As shown in Figure 19-7, you can then select the parts of your history you want to delete.

InPrivate browsing is far from foolproof. There are many other ways people can monitor your actions on the web:

- Some network routers can log the webpages that PCs on the local network visit. This can be mitigated by using a virtual private network (VPN), as described in "Wireless security" later in this chapter.

- Someone with administrative privileges or physical access to your PC could install software that logs your keystrokes. This can be mitigated by using the touch keyboard.

- Someone with administrative privileges or physical access to your PC could install software that records the PC's display. This can only be circumvented by detecting and removing the software using antimalware, as described in "Removing malware" later in this chapter.

- Someone could look over your shoulder, either physically or by using a hidden camera. This can be mitigated by using a privacy filter on your screen or by securing your environment.

- Someone could read your thoughts. This can be mitigated by creating a hat made from tinfoil. I'm kidding, of course; the mind readers are everywhere and cannot be stopped.

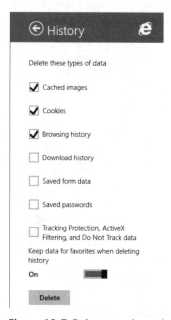

Figure 19-7 Delete your browsing history to reduce the risk of ruining a birthday surprise.

Privacy while using Windows

Windows records your app usage so that you can find recently opened apps. Imagine your daughter's sixteenth birthday is coming up and you're shopping for an affordable first car using the imaginary "Contoso Auto Shopper" app. If you left yourself signed in to your PC, she could easily stumble across this app and figure out your plan. Then you'd spend the next month listening to her dropping hints about how practical and safe yellow convertibles are.

You need to edit Group Policy settings to turn this functionality off. (Group Policy settings are available only in the Windows 8.1 Pro and Enterprise editions.) From the Start screen, type **gpedit.msc** and then press Enter. Then, open each of these settings, enable them, and sign off your PC:

- User Configuration\Administrative Templates\Windows Components\Edge UI\Turn Off Tracking Of App Usage

- User Configuration\Administrative Templates\Windows Components\Edge UI\Turn Off Switching Between Recent Apps

- User Configuration\Administrative Templates\Windows Components\IME\Turn Off History-Based Predictive Input

While you're at it, there's another Group Policy setting you might want to enable. Some apps track your location. If your PC doesn't leave your house or go anywhere you wouldn't want other people to know about, this isn't a problem. If you don't want your daughter to know that you brought your tablet along with you to the car dealership, you could enable the User Configuration\Administrative Templates\Windows Components\Location And Sensors\Turn Off Location setting.

Removing malware

If you do happen to get malware installed on your PC, you can almost always remove it. It's not always easy, though. The sections that follow walk you through the process step by step. Continue working through the steps as long as there is still some trace of the malicious software; you can stop at the point that the problem seems to be solved.

▶ **Removing malware** Watch the video at *http://aka.ms/WinIO/malware*.

Step 1: Uninstall apps

First, from the Start screen, search for **uninstall**, and then select Programs And Features. One by one, select every program you do not recognize, and then select Uninstall. This will allow you to remove any annoying software that is not technically considered malware. If they don't break a specific rule, such as providing an uninstall tool, apps can be rather malicious without technically being considered malware.

Step 2: Scan with Windows Defender

Second, launch Windows Defender and perform a full scan. Remove anything it suggests removing. If Windows Defender does remove something, restart your PC, and run Windows Defender again.

Windows Defender is convenient because it's included with Windows and installed by default. It's not the most thorough antimalware app available, though.

Step 3: Scan with third-party antimalware

Third, install third-party antimalware and run a full scan. Other apps, such as Malwarebytes Anti-Malware (my favorite, available at *http://www.malwarebytes.org*), can find and remove malware that Windows Defender doesn't detect. Figure 19-8 shows Malwarebytes identifying malware that Windows Defender failed to detect.

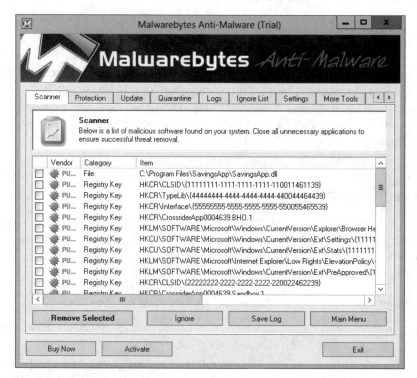

Figure 19-8 Third-party antimalware can be more effective than Windows Defender.

TROUBLESHOOTING

How can I remove malware that won't go away?

Often, when you remove malware, it simply reappears the next time you start your PC. This is extremely common, and it means that your antimalware app didn't detect every piece of malware. The remaining malware re-installed any components that the anti-malware successfully removed. To troubleshoot this problem, perform a system restore, as described in the following section.

Step 4: Perform a system restore

If your PC continues to show symptoms of malware, you can perform a system restore. System Restore returns your PC's state to an earlier date, hopefully before it became infected with malware.

System Restore doesn't remove any of your personal files. However, it can impact the integrity of apps. In other words, legitimate apps that you have installed or updated since the restore point might no longer work.

To restore your system, open PC Settings, select Update And Recovery, select the Recovery page, and then select Restart Now under Advanced Startup. On the Choose An Option page, as shown in Figure 19-9, select Troubleshoot.

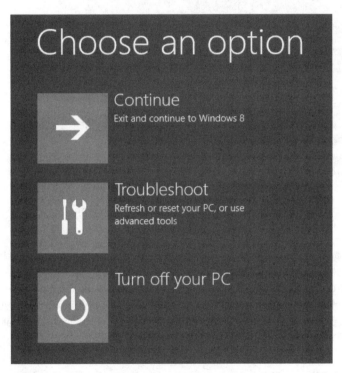

Figure 19-9 Advanced Startup provides troubleshooting tools helpful for removing malware.

On the Troubleshoot page, as shown in Figure 19-10, select Advanced Options.

Figure 19-10 Select Advanced Options within the troubleshooting tools to perform a system restore.

On the Advanced Options page, as shown in Figure 19-11, select System Restore. Windows will restart and begin the system restore process.

On the System Restore page, select your account and then type your password. Click Next on the first page of the System Restore wizard. On the Restore Your PC To The State It Was In Before The Selected Event page (shown in Figure 19-12), choose a restore point from before your PC became infected with malware. Windows creates a restore point when it installs updates and new apps. If you're in doubt, choose a more recent time, and if the malware persists, repeat this process and select an earlier date until the problems disappear.

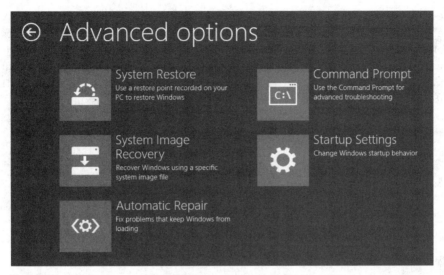

Figure 19-11 Start by performing a system restore, and then perform a system image recovery if necessary.

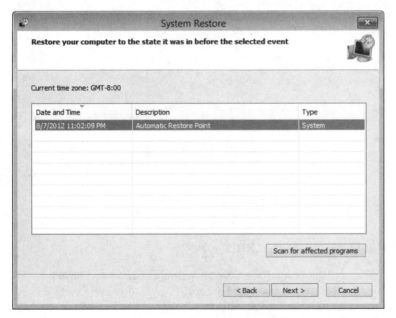

Figure 19-12 Select the most recent system restore point from before your malware symptoms appeared.

Click Scan For Affected Programs. As shown in Figure 19-13, System Restore shows you a list of applications that have been installed since the restore point was created. These apps won't run after you return to the restore point, and that's why this process is useful for removing malware—because the malware will also be removed. If any of these apps are important to you, make note of them so you can reinstall them after you return to the restore point. The older the restore point is, the more likely you are to experience problems running apps.

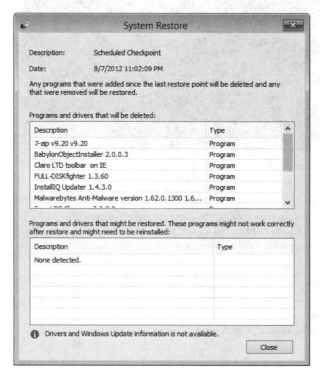

Figure 19-13 System Restore can break any apps installed after the restore point was created.

Click Close, click Next, and then click Finish to start the system restore process.

Step 5: Restore from backup

System Restore should allow you to remove all malware. If you don't have a system restore point available from before the malware infection, but you do have a system image backup, you can use that instead.

Before you restore from the system image, back up all your files and settings. Unlike recovering a restore point, recovering a system image removes all files created since the system image was created.

To recover your PC from a system image, follow the steps described in "Step 4, perform a system restore," until you reach the Advanced Options page. On the Advanced Options page, select System Image Recovery, and then follow the prompts that appear.

For detailed information about creating different types of backups and restoring a system image, refer to Chapter 10, "Backing up and restoring files."

Step 6: Refresh your system

If nothing else works, or you don't have a recent backup, you can refresh your system. Refreshing your system reinstalls Windows but keeps your files and apps from the Store (which aren't likely to be malware). You will need to reinstall any desktop apps, however, so make a list of the desktop apps you need and any licenses or product keys required to reinstall them.

To refresh your system, open the Update And Recovery page of PC Settings, click the Recovery tab, and then select Get Started. Then, simply follow the steps that appear. Windows will restart and refresh your PC without prompting you, as shown in Figure 19-14. After the refresh is complete, your PC should be in a clean and malware-free state, and all your files will be intact.

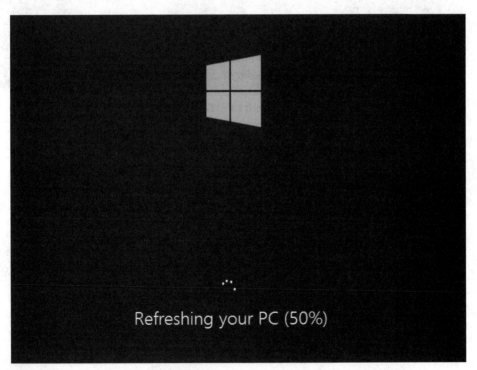

Figure 19-14 Refreshing your PC is a very reliable way to remove malware.

You can encounter a few problems as you attempt to refresh your system. If the Windows setup files aren't available on your PC, you need to insert the Windows 8.1 setup DVD. Hardware manufacturers should include those files, so this is typically only a problem for users who installed Windows 8.1 themselves, in which case, you probably have the Windows 8.1 DVD somewhere.

Another common problem is not having sufficient free space, as shown in Figure 19-15. If you have a way to back up your files, do so, and then delete your files and repeat this process. Alternatively, you can back up your files, return to the General page of PC Settings, and then choose Remove Everything And Reinstall Windows. Either way, you need to restore your files after the process is complete.

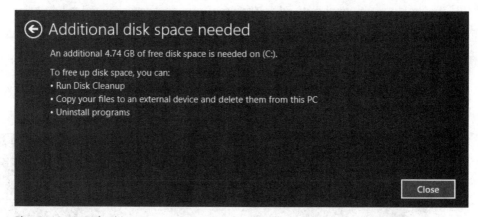

Figure 19-15 Refreshing your system requires about 5 gigabytes of free disk space.

Step 7: Removing rootkits

While antimalware tools can detect and even remove some rootkits, it's possible for rootkits to be entirely undetectable and unremovable from within Windows. That undetectable aspect of rootkits is particularly worrisome, because you might have a rootkit installed and never know it. For that reason, prevention by using malware protection is particularly important.

If you think you might have a rootkit installed on your PC, run the GMer app, available at *http://www.gmer.net/*. It can detect and remove many different rootkits, but not all of them.

To be more certain about removing a rootkit, make sure you have your files backed up, and then start your PC from the Windows 8.1 setup DVD. When prompted, delete all existing partitions, and then install Windows on the blank drive. Repartitioning a drive is an effective way to remove most hidden rootkits.

Some rootkits, such as Mebromi and Niwa!mem, install themselves into the PC's BIOS and cannot be removed even by repartitioning a hard drive. If you think you have malware in your

BIOS, contact your PC manufacturer to see if they might have a removal tool. If you assembled the PC yourself, contact your motherboard or BIOS manufacturer.

Ultimately, it can be impossible to remove a rootkit from a PC's BIOS, and your only certain option for removal is to replace the PC's motherboard.

Windows Firewall

Network communications can be two-way, just like phone calls. Most of the time, your PC makes outgoing connections. As long as you don't connect to a malicious server, the security risks of outgoing connections are pretty minimal.

However, most PCs also listen for some incoming connections, like waiting to receive a phone call. For example, if you share files on your home network, your PC is actually waiting for another PC to contact it.

These incoming connections are a potential security vulnerability. In the early days of Windows networks, millions of PCs were compromised by worms because of security vulnerabilities created by listening for incoming connections. Most of the time, the PC's owner didn't do anything wrong; a vulnerability in Windows allowed anyone who could connect to the PC to take control over it.

Windows network security is much stronger now. One of the key parts of this security is Windows Firewall. Windows Firewall monitors both incoming and outgoing connections and does its best to block any unwanted and potentially dangerous connections.

When you connect to a public network, Windows Firewall blocks most incoming connections, making your PC almost impervious to network attacks. That's why Windows prompts you to choose whether a new network is a home, work, or public network. If you choose public network, or don't choose anything at all, Windows Firewall vigilantly blocks most incoming connections.

If you want to share files and printers on your home network, Windows has to allow some incoming connections. However, Windows Firewall allows only those connections from other PCs on your home network. For that reason, it's really important to allow only people and devices that you trust to connect to your home network. In other words, protect your wireless network with a password that's not easy to guess, and don't give your wireless password to people you don't trust.

Typically, Windows Firewall configuration happens automatically. If you install a new app that needs to listen for incoming connections, the app configures Windows Firewall to allow those connections. If an app attempts to listen for connections without configuring Windows Firewall, Windows prompts you to allow the connection.

You can manually configure Windows Firewall, too. The sections that follow describe the most common configuration tasks.

Allowing an app to listen for incoming connections

Some apps need to listen for incoming connections. For example, instant messaging apps often listen for incoming connections to allow users to transfer pictures or files between their computers without sending them through a server on the Internet.

Windows Firewall blocks all incoming connections by default. Therefore, to allow apps that require incoming connections to work properly, Windows Firewall needs to be configured with an inbound rule that allows that type of traffic through the firewall.

Normally, the app installer does this for you automatically. If not, you can manually configure it. First, search Settings for **firewall**, and then select Allow An App Through Windows Firewall. In the Allowed Apps window, select Change Settings. As shown in Figure 19-16, select the app that needs to accept incoming connections.

Figure 19-16 If an app's network functionality doesn't work, you can manually allow it through Windows Firewall.

Typically, you should select only the Private check box for the app. If you absolutely need the app to work while you're connected to public networks, also select the Public check box. However, be aware that you are slightly increasing the risk of an attacker gaining access to your PC while you are connected to the public network.

If your app is not shown in the Allowed Apps And Features list, click Allow Another App. As shown in Figure 19-17, select the app that you want to allow through from the Apps list. If the app isn't shown in this list either, click the Browse button and select the path to the executable file.

Figure 19-17 Use Add An App to specify apps that Windows Firewall does not list by default.

▶ **Allowing an app through Windows Firewall** Watch the video at *http://aka.ms/WinIO/ firewall*.

Inside OUT

How to find an app's executable file

To find the path to an executable file, launch the app. Then start Task Manager. In Task Manager, right-click the app and then click Properties. Select the Security tab. As shown in Figure 19-18, the Object Name field at the top of the dialog box shows the full path to the app's executable file.

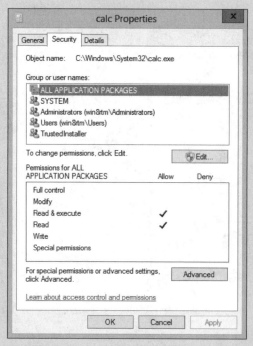

Figure 19-18 Use Task Manager and an app's properties to find the executable file.

Preventing an app from listening for incoming connections

To prevent an app from listening for incoming connections, follow the steps in the previous section and then simply clear the associated check box.

Be careful which apps you disable, though. Many apps need to listen for incoming connections for specific functionality to work. So, blocking an app or a Windows feature might cause a feature to stop working. If you've forgotten that you changed the firewall rules, troubleshooting that broken feature could be really time-consuming.

If you think firewall rules might be the cause of an app problem, you can temporarily disable Windows Firewall to determine whether the problem persists. For detailed instructions, refer to "Temporarily disabling Windows Firewall" later in this chapter.

Manually configuring firewall rules

Some apps might require you to manually configure firewall rules. To do this, it helps to understand a bit about how network communications work.

When two PCs connect to each other across a network, they use two pieces of information to identify the sender and recipient:

- **IP address**   The IP address, such as 192.168.2.25 (for a traditional IPv4 network) or fe80::95aa:b974:daac:9df9%13 (for a more modern IPv6 network), identifies a single PC on your network. Just like a mailing address includes a home's city and state, the IP address has the network's location on the Internet encoded within it.

- **Port number**   The port number, such as TCP port 80 or UDP port 53, identifies a specific application on a PC. Ports can range from 1 to 65535 and are either TCP (most common) or UDP (used for streaming and low-latency communications).

The first step in manually configuring firewall rules is to determine the port numbers your app requires. A quick Internet search for "*<app_name>* port number" usually returns the information you need, but you might need to refer to your app's instructions or contact the app developer's technical support.

As an example, imagine that you want to configure a firewall rule to run web server software on your PC. Web server software uses TCP port 80 by default.

Now that you know the port number you need to configure, you can manually allow the connection through Windows Firewall. Search Settings for **firewall** and then select Windows Firewall. Then, in the left pane, select Advanced Settings. As shown in Figure 19-19, Windows Firewall With Advanced Security appears.

Select Inbound Rules, which configures connections for other network devices connecting to your PC. You rarely need to configure outbound rules because Windows Firewall does not block outbound communications by default.

On the Action menu, select New Rule. The New Inbound Rule Wizard appears. Select Port, as shown in Figure 19-20, and then click Next.

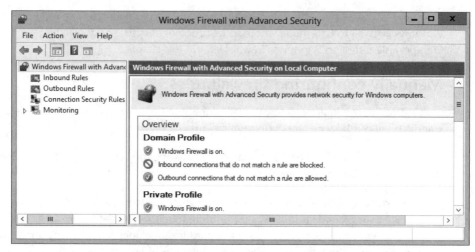

Figure 19-19 Use Windows Firewall With Advanced Security to manually configure your firewall.

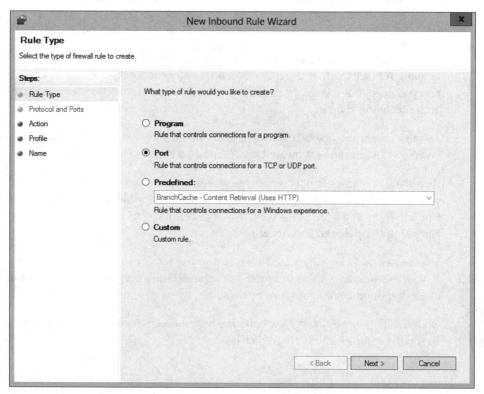

Figure 19-20 The New Inbound Rule Wizard allows you to specify port numbers and IP addresses for firewall rules.

On the Protocols And Ports page, select either TCP or UDP, and type the port numbers that you need in the Specific Local Ports box, as shown in Figure 19-21. If an app requires multiple port numbers, separate the numbers by using commas. You can't mix TCP and UDP ports. If an app requires both TCP and UDP ports, create one rule for the TCP ports and a second rule for the UDP ports. Click Next.

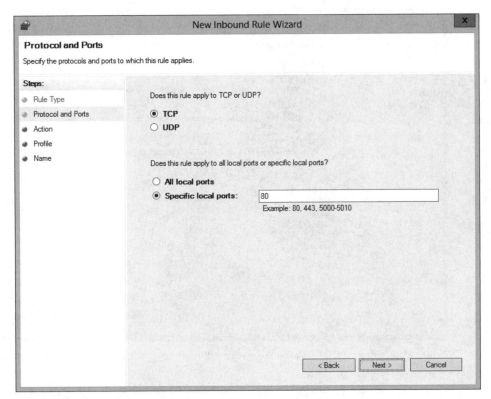

Figure 19-21 When manually configuring firewall rules, you must know the port number (or numbers) and whether the ports are TCP or UDP.

On the Action page, accept the default setting (Allow The Connection) and click Next.

On the Profile page, as shown in Figure 19-22, you must choose the types of networks that will allow the inbound connection. Typically, you should leave Domain and Private selected and clear the check box for Public. Domain networks are used only in business environments that have an Active Directory domain controller, so if you connect your PC to a domain at work and you don't want to use the app on that network, you should also clear the Domain check box. Your home network is considered a private network. Public networks are untrusted networks such as hotspots at coffee shops. For information about configuring which type of network you're connected to, read "Switching between public and private networks" later in this chapter.

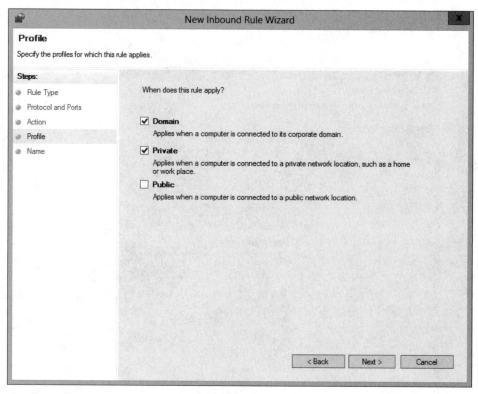

Figure 19-22 Typically, you should create firewall rules only for domain and private networks.

Finally, on the Name page, type a descriptive name and click Finish. The name is important because you want to understand every firewall rule on your PC, and you're likely to forget why you created any given rule.

To see your rule, select Inbound Rules, click the Name column heading, and find it in the list. You can disable the rule by right-clicking it and then clicking Disable Rule.

To change the settings later, select Inbound Rules, right-click your rule, and then click Properties. Use the Scope tab (shown in Figure 19-23) and the Remote IP Address list to limit inbound connections to specific PCs on your network or specific IP addresses on the Internet. This can reduce your security risks, but only if you know which IP addresses will be connecting to your PC.

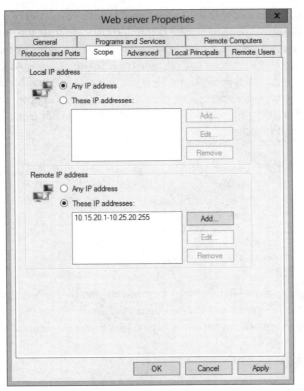

Figure 19-23 Limit the scope to specific remote IP addresses to reduce your security risks.

Temporarily disabling Windows Firewall

If Windows Firewall is incorrectly configured, network features of Windows 8.1 or specific apps might not work properly. If you think Windows Firewall might be the cause of the problem, you can temporarily disable it, test the problem to see if it goes away, and then reenable Windows Firewall.

If disabling Windows Firewall does solve the problem, you should reenable Windows Firewall and then create a firewall rule for your app.

First, connect your PC to a network you trust, such as your home network. Your PC will be vulnerable to attacks across the network while your firewall is disabled, so it's important that you minimize the security risks.

Next, make sure your current network is configured as a private network instead of a public network. Windows Firewall blocks most incoming connections for public networks. If your current network is configured as public, apps that require incoming network connections probably won't work properly, and rather than change the Windows Firewall configuration, you should simply configure the network as private (assuming that you trust the network). To verify that your current network is private, open Network And Sharing Center by searching Settings for **network sharing** and then selecting Network And Sharing Center. As shown in Figure 19-24, verify that the network type is Private Network. If it shows Public Network, follow the steps in "Switching between public and private networks" later in this chapter to switch it to a private network, and then test your app again. If your app still does not work, continue working through the steps in this section.

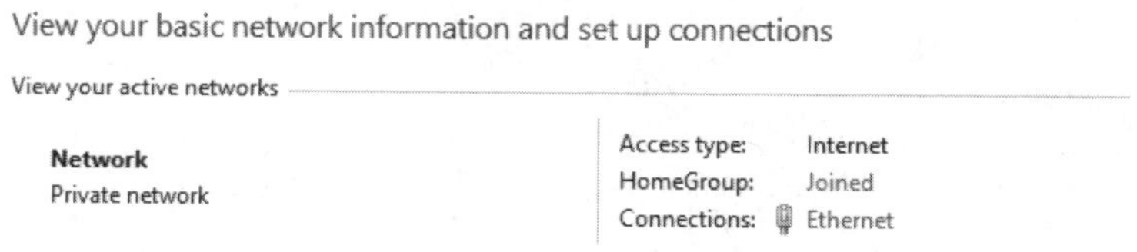

View your basic network information and set up connections

View your active networks

Network
Private network

Access type: Internet
HomeGroup: Joined
Connections: Ethernet

Figure 19-24 Verify that your network is configured as private.

When you feel your network is safe, search Settings for **firewall**, and then select Check Firewall Status. In the left pane, select Turn Windows Firewall On Or Off. Under Private Network Settings, select Turn Off Windows Firewall, as shown in Figure 19-25, and then click OK.

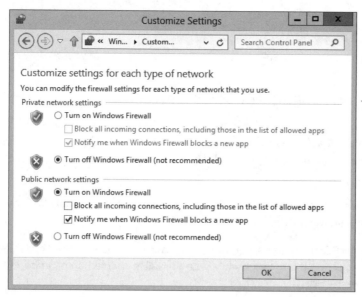

Figure 19-25 Turn off Windows Firewall only briefly for troubleshooting purposes.

With the firewall disabled, test your app. Whether it works properly or not, quickly repeat the steps in the previous paragraph and turn Windows Firewall back on.

If your app worked while Windows Firewall was disabled, Windows Firewall is probably the problem. Follow the instructions in "Allowing an app to listen for incoming connections" earlier in this chapter to set up a rule to allow the app through the firewall. If that doesn't solve the problem, search the Internet for "*<app_name>* firewall" to see if other people have had the same problem and found a solution. Or, just contact the app developer's technical support for help. Some apps work with a separate service that might require manual firewall configuration. To manually configure Windows Firewall to allow communications for specific ports, follow the steps in "Manually configuring firewall rules" earlier in this chapter.

If your app didn't work while Windows Firewall was disabled, Windows Firewall isn't to blame. However, if you are trying to communicate across the Internet, the problem could be caused by your router's firewall settings (described later in this section). On most home networks, routers block all incoming connections that have not been explicitly allowed.

Verify that your router supports Universal Plug and Play (UPnP) and that the option is turned on. Windows uses UPnP to tell your router which types of incoming connections to allow from the Internet.

If UPnP is enabled and the app is still not working, you might have to configure port forwarding on your router, also known as creating a virtual server. Refer to your router's manual for specific instructions.

Switching between public and private networks

Windows 8.1 supports two types of networks:

- **Public** The default network type, Windows 8.1 blocks most incoming traffic from public networks, improving your security.

- **Private** Suitable for home and work networks where you trust the network infrastructure and the other PCs connected to the network, Windows 8.1 allows many types of incoming connections on private networks (also known as home or work networks) to allow sharing and support some network apps.

Windows 8.1 does a good job of managing this automatically. If you want to switch between the network types, select the Network, Connections page from PC Settings, and then select your network. Turn on Find Devices And Content for private networks (shown in Figure 19-26), or turn it off for public networks.

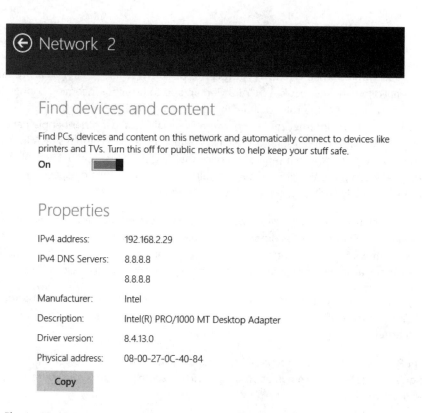

Figure 19-26 Use HomeGroup settings to configure a network as public or private.

Wireless security

One of the greatest modern security risks is unencrypted Wi-Fi and wireless hotspots. Wireless hotspots, such as those at coffee shops, airports, and hotels, are tremendously useful. They can also be a tremendous security risk.

The greatest risk is unencrypted Wi-Fi. Windows 8.1 warns you when you connect to an unencrypted wireless network, and for a good reason—all your network communications are visible to any savvy hacker close enough to receive your wireless signals, which can be a radius of several hundred feet. Those people can see every website you visit and everything you type into a form. Depending on whether your email client is configured to use encryption, they might even be able to read any email you download.

Don't believe me? Check out WireShark, a free tool available at *http://wireshark.org*.

Sometimes you don't have a choice but to connect to an unprotected wireless network, such as when you're travelling. If you must take this security risk, don't do anything on your PC you wouldn't want other people to see. Whenever possible, connect to websites using HTTPS instead of HTTP. Websites such as Facebook now require you to use HTTPS specifically because people's account information was being intercepted across unprotected wireless networks.

Another option is to use a virtual private network (VPN). VPNs encrypt all of your communications and send them to a server on the Internet somewhere. That server then decrypts your communications and sends them to the final destination. You'll have to pay for a VPN service, but if you're serious about your data confidentiality, it can be worth it. Some popular VPN services include VyprVPN, WiTopia, and StrongVPN.

Your data can be compromised when connecting to any untrusted network, including encrypted wireless networks. Anyone with access to the wireless access point or router can intercept any communications that aren't encrypted by HTTPS or a VPN. Therefore, you should only connect to networks that you trust—and you shouldn't be so quick to trust hotspots at coffee shops, hotels, and airports.

Turning off security features

Windows 8.1 is designed to be secure by default. That means that many different security features are enabled when you install Windows.

That's a great choice on Microsoft's part. Microsoft knows that the average PC user doesn't have an in-depth knowledge of PC security risks such as malware, and those security features can save the average user an incredible number of headaches.

For security-savvy power users, however, some of these features are more annoying than useful. If you're confident in your security skills and would rather accept some additional security risk than deal with various prompts, you can turn these features off (at your own risk).

The sections that follow describe how to disable some security features. For instructions on bypassing the login screen, refer to Chapter 17, "Creating a Home Theater PC."

UAC

To turn off UAC, from the Start screen search for **uac** and then select Change User Account Control Settings. In the User Account Control Settings dialog box, drag the slider all the way down. Figure 19-27 shows UAC being disabled.

To watch a video showing how to turn UAC on and off, visit *http://windows.microsoft.com/ en-US/windows7/turn-user-account-control-on-or-off*.

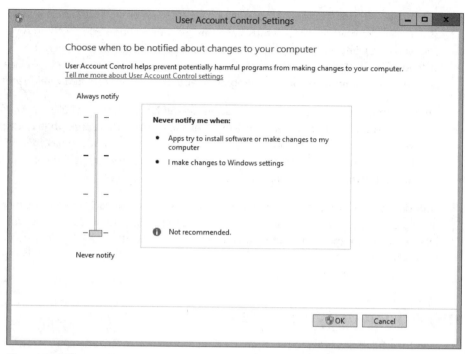

Figure 19-27 Turn off UAC only if you understand the security implications.

SmartScreen

To turn off SmartScreen, from the Start screen search for **smartscreen**, select Change Smart-Screen Settings, and then select Change Windows SmartScreen Settings. You can then choose between three options, as shown in Figure 19-28.

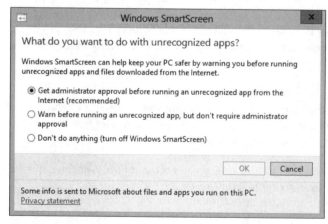

Figure 19-28 Turn off SmartScreen at your own risk.

Windows Defender

Windows Defender's real-time protection scans files as you update them. You really should leave it on, but if you install another antimalware app, or if you're concerned about any performance impact Windows Defender might cause, you can disable real-time monitoring.

Start Windows Defender, select the Settings tab, select Real-Time Protection, and then clear the Turn On Real-Time Protection check box, as shown in Figure 19-29. Finally, select Save Changes.

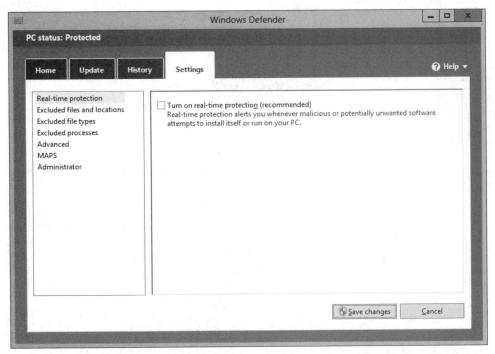

Figure 19-29 Turn off real-time protection to increase your performance, and your security risk.

You'll immediately see a warning from the Action Center about not having antimalware software running. Select it and then select Open Action Center. As shown in Figure 19-30, you can disable the resulting messages by selecting Turn Off Messages About Spyware And Unwanted Software Protection and Turn Off Messages About Virus Protection.

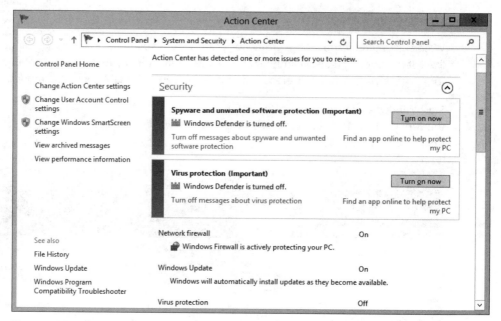

Figure 19-30 If you're receiving unnecessary alerts, you can disable Action Center messages.

If you turn off real-time protection, you can still run Windows Defender on demand to check for malware, and you still benefit from other security features such as User Account Control and SmartScreen.

Using Hyper-V

Hyper-V requirements 474

Installing Hyper-V. 475

Creating your first virtual switch 476

Configuring VM settings. 484

Starting a VM 495

Using snapshots 495

Managing virtual disks 496

Hyper-V tips and tricks 499

When not to use a VM. 500

Using VirtualBox. 501

Hyper-V is virtual machine (VM) software. A VM is a software-based PC that runs within Windows. It's basically an entire PC, including an operating system, all within a window on your desktop.

I know what you're thinking: "I heard you like PCs, so we put a PC inside your PC so you can compute while you compute." VMs really are useful, however.

Most importantly, you can run an entirely different operating system within the VM. So, while you run Windows 8.1 on your PC, you could run Windows XP within a VM if you had an application that required Windows XP. You could even run non-Microsoft operating systems, including many varieties of Linux (shown in Figure 20-1) and FreeBSD.

VMs are terrifically useful for those of us who test software. I've used more than half-a-dozen different VMs while writing this book. I really needed to run Windows 8.1 through some serious testing, and sometimes that testing left Windows 8.1 not working properly. I wouldn't want to do that on the PC I was using to write this book, so I did it within a VM.

What happens in the VM stays in the VM. For example, when writing about malware for Chapter 19, "Windows, application, and network security," I had to visit some dark corners of the Internet to see how Windows Defender would handle malware. Before I did that, I captured a snapshot of my Windows 8.1 VM. The snapshot records the VM's state so that it can be restored later. Then, I got my hands dirty and installed some malware. That malware could have devastated my primary PC. Within a VM, though, I simply restored the snapshot and returned the VM to the exact state it was in before I installed the malware.

Those are the two biggest reasons to use VMs: compatibility and isolation. Those words aren't as much fun as music and videos, but to the hardcore geeks among us, they're equally exciting.

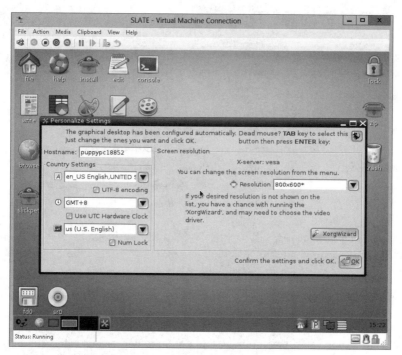

Figure 20-1 Use Hyper-V to run another operating system in a window.

Hyper-V requirements

Running Hyper-V requires that your PC:

- Run a 64-bit version of Windows 8.1, rather than a 32-bit version. Once Hyper-V is running, you can create both 32-bit and 64-bit VMs.

- Run Windows 8.1 Pro or Windows 8.1 Enterprise.

- Have at least 4 gigabytes (GB) of RAM.

- Support Second Level Address Translation (SLAT) hardware virtualization. Many PCs have SLAT hardware virtualization turned off by default.

To turn on hardware virtualization, restart your computer and edit the computer's BIOS settings. Unfortunately, every computer has different BIOS settings, so if you can't find the option, refer to your computer's manual. Look for options indicating virtualization, SLAT, Extended Page Tables (EPT), or Rapid Virtualization Indexing (RVI).

If your PC doesn't support hardware virtualization, you can use the free VirtualBox desktop app instead. For more information, refer to "Using VirtualBox" at the end of this chapter.

Installing Hyper-V

To install Hyper-V, from the Start screen, search for **windows features**. Then, select Turn Windows Features On Or Off.

In the Windows Features dialog box, as shown in Figure 20-2, select Hyper-V and then click OK.

After installation, launch Hyper-V Manager from the Start screen. If you don't see your PC's name listed under Hyper-V Manager in the left pane, then your PC didn't meet one or more of the Hyper-V requirements. It's too bad you're not warned about this during setup.

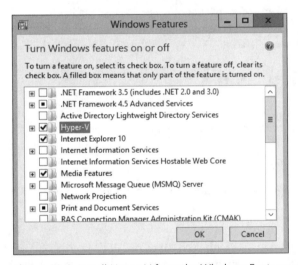

Figure 20-2 Install Hyper-V from the Windows Features dialog box.

Inside OUT

Understanding Hyper-V terminology

The PC running Hyper-V is called the host. The host has direct access to your PC hardware. All VMs are called guests. The guests run in a virtual environment on the host. Guests cannot directly access PC hardware. Instead, guests communicate with the virtual environment created by Hyper-V, which pretends to be a physical PC.

Inside OUT
Using Hyper-V to test your website in different browsers

If you do any web development, you know how difficult it can be to make sure your website works in different browsers. Sure, you can install all the common browsers on your PC, but how will it look in earlier versions of Internet Explorer, and in different versions of Windows?

Microsoft provides virtual hard disks (VHDs) for earlier versions of Windows and Internet Explorer. Download the VHDs you need, load them into Hyper-V, and you can quickly start a VM to see exactly how that version of Windows and Internet Explorer will render your website. As an added benefit, it's easy to change the screen resolution on a VM.

To download the Internet Explorer application compatibility images, visit *http://www.microsoft.com/download/details.aspx?id=11575*.

Creating your first virtual switch

Hyper-V uses virtual switches to connect VMs to networks, including your local area network (LAN) and the Internet. In network terminology, a switch is a network hardware device that connects multiple computers together within a network, so the Hyper-V virtual switch does exactly that without requiring you to buy any hardware.

▶ **Creating a virtual machine in Hyper-V** Watch the video at *http://aka.ms/WinIO/hyperv*.

You can choose from three types of virtual network switches:

- **Private** Guests can communicate with each other, but not with the host or the Internet. Private networks are ideal if you need to isolate your VMs, which would be the case if you were testing potentially malicious software.

- **Internal** Guests can communicate with each other and the host, but cannot communicate on the Internet. If a VM has malware, the malware could potentially spread to the host computer across the network.

- **External** Guests and the host can all communicate with each other and with the Internet. This is important if your VM needs to download updates or drivers from the Internet. If a VM has malware, however, using an external switch could allow the malware to spread to other computers on your local network or even to computers on the Internet. When you use external networking, Hyper-V creates a virtual network switch that all guests and your host computer use to communicate. This virtual network switch has the potential to impact other apps on your host computer. In practice, though, the impact is minimal.

If you don't create a virtual switch, none of your VMs can connect to the network. Therefore, you should create a virtual switch before creating your first VM. In Hyper-V Manager (which you can open from the Start screen), open the Action menu and then select Virtual Switch Manager. In the Create Virtual Switch group, select the type of virtual switch you want to create and then click Create Virtual Switch. Figure 20-3 shows how to create an external virtual switch, which is the type most home users will need.

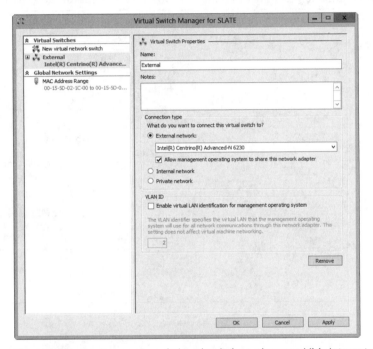

Figure 20-3 Create an external virtual switch to give your VMs Internet access.

To create your first VM, launch Hyper-V Manager from the Start screen. Select your computer name in the left pane. On the Action menu, select New and then select Virtual Machine. The New Virtual Machine Wizard appears.

TROUBLESHOOTING

Why is Hyper-V Manager empty?

If Hyper-V Manager doesn't show your computer name in the window, your PC doesn't have hardware virtualization enabled. It might not support it at all, or it might simply be disabled in the BIOS. Refer to the section "Hyper-V requirements" earlier in this chapter for more information.

Most of the settings are self-explanatory. A few of the settings require some consideration, however, as the sections that follow describe.

Startup memory

Just like your PC has RAM, your VM has startup memory. You must specify at least the guest operating system's minimum required memory, as shown in Table 20-1. Specifying more memory will improve the VM's performance, but might decrease the host's performance.

Table 20-1 Minimum and recommended memory for common operating systems

Operating system	Minimum memory	Recommended memory
Windows 98	16 megabytes (MB)	24 MB
Windows XP	64 MB	128 MB
Windows Vista	512 MB	1 GB
Windows 7	1 GB (32-bit) or 2 GB (64-bit)	1 GB (32-bit) or 2 GB (64-bit)
Windows 8.1	1 GB (32-bit) or 2 GB (64-bit)	1 GB (32-bit) or 2 GB (64-bit)
Ubuntu Linux	64 MB	512 MB (with a desktop environment)
Linux Mint	512 MB	2 GB
Arch Linux	192 MB	512 MB (with a desktop environment)
Debian	64 MB	512 MB (with a desktop environment)
Fedora	512 MB	1 GB
FreeBSD	64 MB	512 MB (with a desktop environment)

Inside OUT

Determining optimal startup memory

When determining how much memory to assign to VMs, factor in the total RAM in your host PC, how much the host PC needs for its operating system and apps other than Hyper-V, and the number of VMs you plan to run simultaneously.

In Task Manager, select More Details (if you need to). Select the Performance tab and then select Memory, as shown in Figure 20-4. The available memory is the maximum total amount you would want to assign to your VMs. In the case shown in Figure 20-4, that amount is 2.8 GB.

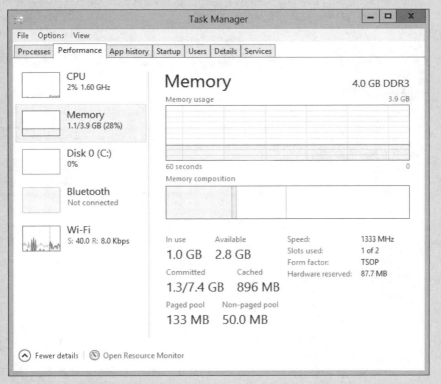

Figure 20-4 Select Memory in Task Manager to determine the maximum you can assign to VMs.

You should leave a bit of extra memory available to your host operating system. So, with 2.8 GB of memory available, you could assign a VM 2 GB of memory and have great performance. If you wanted to run two VMs simultaneously, you could assign them both 1 GB of memory.

The amount of memory available on the host varies with the apps you currently have running. Therefore, it's a good idea to close any desktop apps before starting a VM.

Dynamic memory

By default, VMs continue to use the amount of memory you specify for their startup memory as long as they are running. If you enable dynamic memory by selecting the Use Dynamic Memory For This Virtual Machine option, as shown in Figure 20-5, Hyper-V might reduce the amount of memory used by the VM if it doesn't need it after startup. This can allow you to run more VMs in less memory.

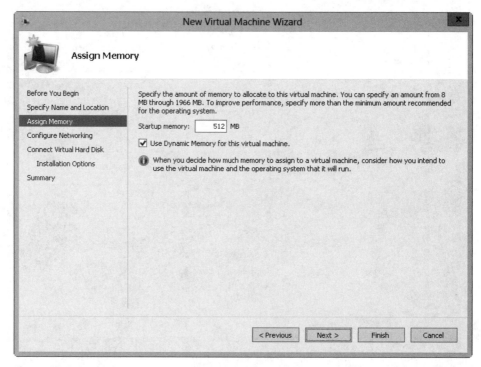

Figure 20-5 Dynamic memory can grow or shrink a VM's memory.

Dynamic memory can also increase the memory allocated to a VM if it needs more after startup. For example, if you launch Adobe Photoshop within a VM, the app might allocate several gigabytes of additional RAM. Dynamic memory can adjust for that on an on-demand basis.

Dynamic memory is very important in business environments where Hyper-V is used to host dozens of VMs simultaneously. In most home and small business scenarios, however, it's not necessary.

You can adjust the minimum and maximum memory assigned by dynamic memory after you create the VM. For more information, see "Configuring VM settings" later in this chapter.

Connection

As shown in Figure 20-6, select the virtual switch that you want the VM to be connected to. You must create these virtual switches ahead of time. For more information, refer to "Creating your first virtual switch" earlier in this chapter.

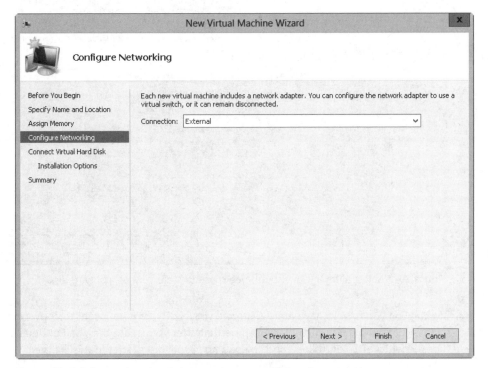

Figure 20-6 Select a virtual switch to connect your VM to the network.

Virtual hard disk size and location

Use this page, as shown in Figure 20-7, to specify where you want Hyper-V to store the VM's virtual hard disk. The virtual hard disk is the VM's storage for the operating system, apps, and app data. Virtual disks grow automatically in size, so be sure the drive you select has several gigabytes of free space. The faster the physical drive, the better your VM will perform.

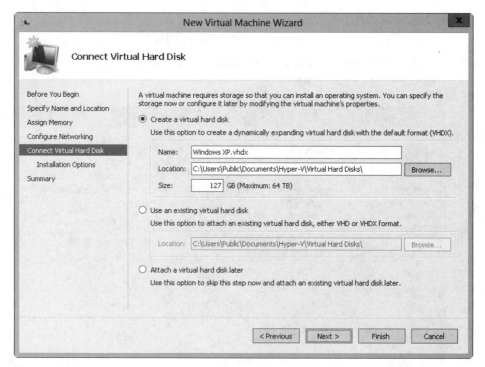

Figure 20-7 Select a drive with enough free space to store your virtual hard disk.

If you want your VM to have more than one virtual disk, or if you want to copy the contents of a physical disk to a virtual disk, you can do that after you create the VM. For detailed instructions, refer to "IDE controllers" and "Managing virtual disks" later in this chapter.

Operating system

VMs don't have an operating system such as Windows; they're basically a PC without any software whatsoever. So, your first task is always to install an operating system. If you have a Windows setup CD or DVD, you can insert it into your computer and then select Physical CD/DVD Drive. If you don't have a CD/DVD drive, you can download an ISO (or image) file and select it, as shown in Figure 20-8.

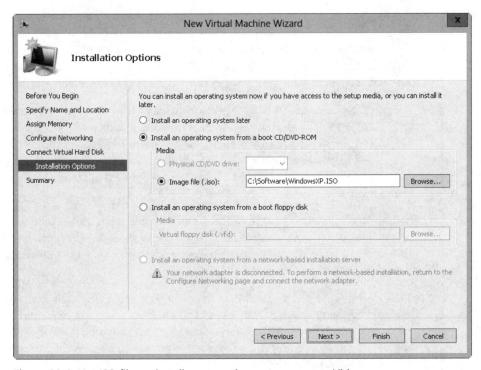

Figure 20-8 Use ISO files to install an operating system on your VM.

Inside OUT

Virtual SANs

Hyper-V has an amazing feature that I'm not going to describe in this chapter: virtual Fibre-Channel storage area networks (SANs). With a SAN, PCs are connected to their drives across a very high-speed network, allowing multiple PCs to share storage efficiently.

For example, you could configure ten 2-terabyte (TB) drives into 20 TB of storage. You could then connect 30 different PCs to that storage, and each would use only the storage it needed. If most PCs needed just 20 GB of storage, they would consume only that 20 GB. If you had to put a 2-TB drive in each PC, most of that storage would be wasted.

Because SANs centralize storage, they can also reduce the number of duplicated files. Each of those 30 PCs probably has Windows installed, and therefore has about 10 GB of system files. Some SANs are smart enough to store only one copy of each file, and then share it between the different PCs. Therefore, those 30 PCs could access the same 10 GB of system files, rather than keep a separate copy for each of them. That's a savings of about 290 GB.

Besides efficiently using storage, SANs allow you to add more storage without opening up a PC's case or even turning the PC off. So, if one of those PCs suddenly needed 5 TB instead of just 20 GB, it could allocate the extra storage automatically. SANs also make it easier to back up and maintain storage.

SANs are awesome, but here's why I'm not describing how to use them with Hyper-V: you probably don't have a SAN in your house. SANs are pretty expensive and almost exclusively used by enterprises in server data centers. I'm writing this book for consumers and small businesses, so as much as I like SANs, they're out of scope. For more information, read "Hyper-V Virtual Fibre Channel Overview" at *http://technet.microsoft.com/en-US/hh831413.aspx*.

Configuring VM settings

The New Virtual Machine Wizard collects just the basic information about your VM's configuration. You can change these settings and configure many other options from the Settings dialog box. You don't necessarily need to, however. The default settings work fine for most home environments.

The sections that follow describe only the most important settings.

Add hardware

Use these settings to add SCSI, network, and Fibre-Channel adapters to your computer. For example, if you're testing Network Address Translation (NAT) software within a VM, you could add two network adapters and connect each of them to different virtual switches.

BIOS

Configure BIOS settings to change the VM's boot order. Just like a physical computer, VMs look in several different places to find their operating system. By default (as shown in Figure 20-9), Hyper-V VMs look for a bootable CD and then check for a hard drive with Windows or another operating system installed. If those options aren't available, then they connect to the network and look for a service such as Windows Deployment Services (WDS) that can provide an operating system across the network. Finally, they attempt to start from a floppy drive.

Figure 20-9 Use the BIOS settings to change the boot order.

You might want to change these settings if, for example, you leave a bootable CD connected to a VM but you want it to start from the hard drive. If a VM already has an operating system installed and you want it to install a new version of Windows from WDS, you should change the boot order so that Legacy Network Adapter comes before IDE.

Memory

Use the Memory settings to configure how much RAM the VM has available. If you enable dynamic memory, you can also configure the minimum and maximum RAM that dynamic memory will assign the VM while it is running. Figure 20-10 shows the VM memory settings dialog box.

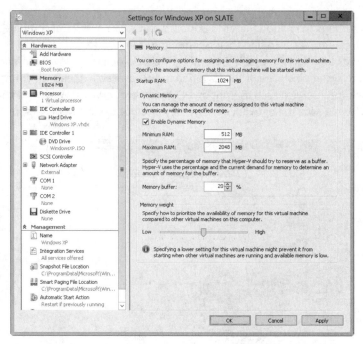

Figure 20-10 Use the Memory settings to configure dynamic memory.

If you select the Enable Dynamic Memory check box, Hyper-V might adjust the memory assigned to the VM as low as the minimum or as high as the maximum. Hyper-V is smart about it, naturally, and tries to assign only as much RAM as the VM is actually using. By using RAM efficiently, you have more RAM available for other VMs or apps running on your PC.

Besides defining the minimum and maximum settings, you can adjust the settings for Memory Buffer and Memory Weight, both of which impact how dynamic memory allocates RAM to VMs. Most consumers won't even need to adjust these settings, however. Set a lower value for Memory Buffer to save a bit of memory. On your most important VMs, choose a higher value for Memory Weight to make sure the VMs get the RAM they need if you run multiple VMs simultaneously and your PC starts to run out of memory.

Processor

By default, Hyper-V assigns each VM a single processor. However, most modern PCs have multiple processors. Therefore, increasing the number of virtual processors can increase the VM's performance. In most home scenarios, you should set Number Of Virtual Processors to the maximum allowed (which corresponds to the number of logical processors your PC has), as shown in Figure 20-11.

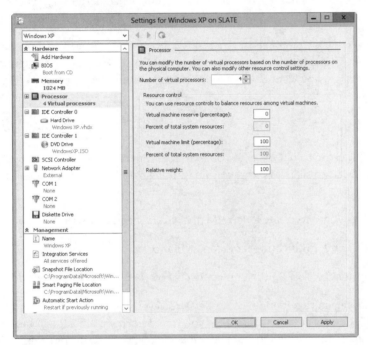

Figure 20-11 Use the Processor settings to configure the number of virtual processors and to reserve processor time.

You can use the remaining settings to prioritize processor time between multiple VMs. Doing so is relevant only if you run multiple VMs simultaneously, however:

- **Virtual Machine Reserve**   The percentage of processing time that is reserved just for this VM. Reserving processing time isn't usually required in home environments. In business environments, you can do this to guarantee a VM receives a specific amount of processing time.

- **Percent Of Total System Resources**   This box simply displays the percentage of the total processing time reserved for this VM, based on the VM reserve and the number of virtual processors assigned.

- **Virtual Machine Limit**   Use this box to limit the amount of processor time the VM can consume. For example, if you limit it to 50 percent, the VM will never use more than half your PC's processing time. If you perform a long-running, processor-intensive task such as rendering video within a VM, this setting allows your PC and other VMs to continue working normally.

- **Percent Of Total System Resources**   This box simply displays the percentage of the total processing time this VM is allowed to consume when performing a processor-intensive task, based on the VM limit and the number of virtual processors assigned.

- **Relative Weight**   Compared to other VMs, a VM with a higher relative weight will receive more of the PC's processing time when processing time is limiting performance. In other words, if you want one VM to be faster than the others, assign it a higher relative weight.

IDE controllers

Many physical PCs use IDE controllers to communicate with hard drives and CD or DVD drives. VMs use virtual IDE controllers to communicate with their virtual hard drive and virtual CD or DVD drives.

When you use the wizard to create a new VM, the wizard creates two IDE controllers:

- **IDE Controller 0**   This controller is connected to your virtual hard drive.

- **IDE Controller 1**   This controller is connected to your virtual CD or DVD drive.

You won't typically need to add more controllers. However, you might want to add more virtual drives to IDE Controller 0. For example, if you want to experiment with Storage Spaces (as described in Chapter 12, "Managing storage"), you could add multiple virtual drives to a VM. In fact, that's exactly what I did when I was writing the chapter.

To add an extra virtual drive to a VM, select IDE Controller 0, select Hard Drive, and then click Add. This adds a slot to your IDE controller. Select Virtual Hard Disk, and then click New to run the New Virtual Hard Disk Wizard. Figure 20-12 shows a VM configured with two hard drives connected to IDE Controller 0.

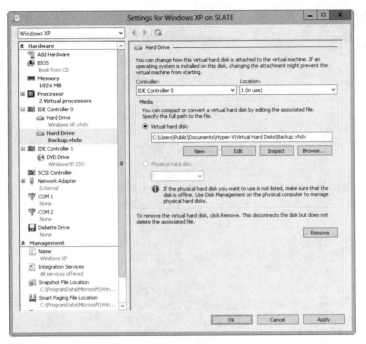

Figure 20-12 Use IDE controllers to add multiple virtual hard drives.

For more information about how to configure the virtual disk, refer to "Managing virtual disks" later in this chapter.

SCSI controllers

SCSI controllers perform the same function as IDE controllers. In the world of physical PCs, SCSI controllers provide much better performance than IDE controllers. However, in the world of VMs, SCSI controllers and IDE controllers provide identical performance.

IDE controllers tend to be more widely supported by different operating systems, however. Because of that benefit, you should simply use IDE controllers and disregard the support for SCSI controllers.

Network adapter

Use the Network Adapter page of VM settings to enable bandwidth management, as shown in Figure 20-13.

Figure 20-13 Use bandwidth management to limit the bandwidth a VM uses.

In most home scenarios, the Maximum Bandwidth setting is the only useful setting. This limits the amount of bandwidth the VM can consume. You might want to specify a maximum bandwidth if you're doing large file transfers between your VM and another computer on your LAN or on the Internet and you don't want to impact the network performance of other computers.

For example, if you're downloading a large file from the Internet to a VM, the VM will use every bit of bandwidth available on your Internet connection, slowing other PCs on your home network to a crawl. If you have a 20 Mbps connection, you could set Maximum Bandwidth for the VM to 10 Mbps, allowing it to use only half of your Internet connection. The other half of the connection would be available to other PCs on your network.

The same scenario is useful with wireless networks. If you are running a VM on a host connected with a wireless network and transferring files between other PCs on your LAN, the VM might use all the bandwidth available on the wireless network, slowing the performance of your other PCs. Limit the maximum bandwidth to a fraction of that available on your wireless LAN to allow other PCs to get their fair share.

Inside OUT

Limiting the bandwidth of physical PCs

Limiting network bandwidth is so useful that you might want to use the functionality for a physical PC. One way to do that is with NetBalancer Free, available at *http://seriousbit.com/netbalancer/*. As shown in Figure 20-14, NetBalancer can limit the bandwidth used on a per-process basis, which basically means it limits specific apps.

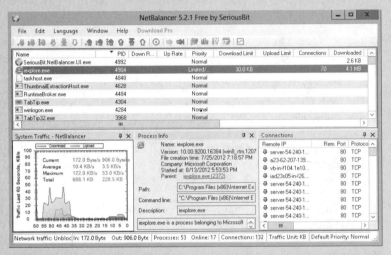

Figure 20-14 Use NetBalancer Free to limit the network bandwidth of individual processes within Windows.

The Minimum Bandwidth setting takes effect only when your host or VMs running on your host are consuming all available bandwidth. When the bandwidth is completely consumed, Hyper-V will split the available bandwidth between the different VMs. If you want each VM to be guaranteed a specific amount (up to the total amount of bandwidth available), set the Minimum Bandwidth setting to that amount. You can simply leave this value at 0 to not guarantee the VM any specific share of the available bandwidth.

Integration services

Integration services connect your host PC to the VM more closely than they would otherwise be connected. Without integration services, your only connections to a VM are your keyboard, mouse, and network. Even the mouse can be rather difficult to use, because the VM can capture the mouse and you need to press a special key (Ctrl+Alt+Left Arrow by default) to release it from the VM window.

With integration services, you can work with VMs much more easily and accomplish the following:

- Shut down the guest operating system. This helps protect the integrity of the guest VM by allowing you to easily shut it down instead of simply turning off the VM by unplugging it.

- Copy and paste between the host PC and the VM. This is particularly helpful when activating Windows and other software in the VM. Instead of typing the entire key, you can copy and paste it from your host.

- Move the mouse freely in and out of the VM without pressing a special key.

- Synchronize the time between the host PC and the VM. This helps keep your operating systems synchronized. Most modern operating systems synchronize their time with services on the Internet. However, this is useful if you connect the VM to a private or internal virtual switch.

- Data exchange services move small values to and from a VM. For exchanging files, simply connect the VM to a virtual network switch and then connect to shared folders across the network.

- Heartbeat services verify that the VM is still responding. This allows Hyper-V to determine when a VM has crashed.

- Backup services allow you to more efficiently back up and restore VMs.

After a VM is up and running with an operating system, connect to it, open the Action menu, and then select Insert Integration Services Setup Disk. This swaps the CD you had selected for the VM with a virtual CD containing the guest integration services software. Within your VM, navigate to the CD and run the setup software. Most operating systems will automatically prompt you to run software contained on a newly inserted CD, as shown in Figure 20-15, which is Windows 7 running within a Hyper-V VM.

Figure 20-15 Install integration services to better control your VMs.

Because integration services must run within the guest operating system, they won't work with every operating system. Integration services are available for:

- Windows XP

- Windows 2000

- Windows 2000 Server

- Windows Server 2003

- Windows Server 2008

- Windows Vista

- Windows 7

- Windows 8.1

- CentOS 5.2–6.1

- Red Hat Enterprise Linux 5.5–6.1

- SUSE Linux Enterprise Server 10 and 11

Other versions of Linux might work as well. Download Linux Integration Services Version 3.3 for Hyper-V at *http://www.microsoft.com/en-us/download/details.aspx?id=29991*. Better yet, search the Microsoft Download Center for a newer version.

Automatic stop action

As shown in Figure 20-16, Hyper-V provides three options for the automatic stop action.

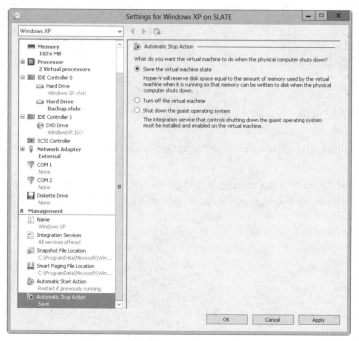

Figure 20-16 Configure the automatic stop action to determine how Hyper-V handles VMs that you close.

Each of these three options is useful for different scenarios:

- **Save The Virtual Machine State**   The default choice, this stores the VM's memory to a file when you close it. The next time you open the VM, it is restored to the exact moment that you closed it, without restarting the operating system in the VM. This requires Hyper-V to save a file equal to the amount of memory used by the VM. In other words, if the VM has 2 GB of memory, using this option will consume an extra 2 GB of your drive space. Use this option if you like to leave apps running within the VM.

- **Turn Off The Virtual Machine**   This unplugs the VM, immediately stopping it. Turning off VMs can cause problems with the guest operating system, such as data inconsistency. You should only use this option if you're in a hurry and don't care about the VM.

- **Shut Down The Guest Operating System**   This sends a signal to the guest operating system to go through its normal shutdown procedure. This is the best choice for most home scenarios.

Starting a VM

After you create a VM, you can start it by right-clicking it and then selecting Connect. This opens the Virtual Machine Connection window. Next, click the green Start button on the toolbar. You can also start a VM in the background by right-clicking the VM and clicking Start. If you want to control it, right-click it again and select Connect.

Using snapshots

Imagine if you could quickly and reliably turn back time on your PC. Install an app you hate? Turn back time. Want to experiment with different settings without messing up your PC? Turn back time. Accidentally install some malware? You know what to do.

You can use snapshots to turn back time within a VM. Before you do anything crazy with the VM, create a snapshot. A snapshot remembers the VM's state at that point in time, including the contents of its memory. Later, you can easily restore the snapshot and return the VM to the exact state it was in at the time you took the snapshot.

Figure 20-17 shows a VM with two snapshots in the Hyper-V Manager.

Figure 20-17 Snapshots capture a VM's state at a particular moment in time.

To create a snapshot, right-click the VM and then click Snapshot. You can also click the Snapshot button on the Virtual Machine Connection toolbar.

To restore a snapshot, right-click the snapshot and then click Apply. You can also click the Revert button on the Virtual Machine Connection toolbar.

If you don't need to return to a snapshot later, right-click the snapshot in the Hyper-V Manager and then select Delete Snapshot. Deleting a snapshot saves disk space and does not affect a VM.

▶ **Using snapshots in Hyper-V** Watch the video at *http://aka.ms/WinIO/snapshots*.

Managing virtual disks

The contents of a virtual disk are stored in a virtual disk file. Hyper-V gives you several options for the virtual disk format and type. The settings you choose can drastically impact the size of the virtual disks and the performance of your VM.

Virtual disk formats

Hyper-V supports two different formats for virtual disks. Their file extensions are:

- **.vhd**   The older virtual disk format, .vhd files are limited to 2 TB.

- **.vhdx**   Supports file sizes up to 64 TB and helps protect the VM from being corrupted if the host PC loses power. There are some other minor improvements, as well.

Besides the lack of backward compatibility, there's no disadvantage to using the VHDX format, so that's always the better choice. You can even boot Windows 8.1 from either type of file. For more information, refer to Chapter 3, "Buying and installing Windows 8.1."

You also have the option of connecting a VM to a physical disk connected to your host PC. This option dedicates that disk to the VM, so it cannot be accessed by the host PC. Physical disks run within the VM at about the same speed they run within your PC, so there's no performance penalty for connecting a physical disk to a VM.

Virtual disk types

As shown in Figure 20-18, Hyper-V supports three different types of virtual disks.

The three types of virtual disks are:

- **Fixed size**   When you create a fixed size virtual disk, Hyper-V immediately creates a huge file of the virtual disk's maximum size. This provides the best performance, because Hyper-V will never have to dynamically expand the disk. In fact, fixed size disks are the fastest type, and are typically only about 6 percent slower than the underlying physical drive. Fixed size disks waste a great deal of space on your PC's physical drive, however.

- **Dynamically expanding**   Dynamically expanding disks start out very small and grow only as the VM writes data to the disk. Because Hyper-V needs to expand this type of disk as the VM writes new data, the performance is 10–35 percent slower when writing new data. The overall performance impact depends on how you use the VM, but you can expect it to run 5–10 percent more slowly. Additionally, if the virtual disk expands too much, it's possible for the host PC to run out of free space. Dynamically expanding disks are smart enough to not expand when sections of the disk are filled with all zeros, which can happen when the disk is formatted. Therefore, you can format a dynamically expanding disk from within the guest OS and the virtual disk file will not need to grow.

- **Differencing**   Differencing disks track changes from an original disk. This can save a great deal of disk space. For example, if you need to run three different VMs with Windows 8.1 installed, you could first install Windows 8.1 on a single VM with a dynamically expanding disk. Then you could create three new VMs, each with their own differencing disk based on the original Windows 8.1 virtual disk. Because the Windows system files would need to be stored only on the original disk, the total storage required would be much smaller than if you created three different Windows 8.1 VMs, each with a dynamically expanding disk.

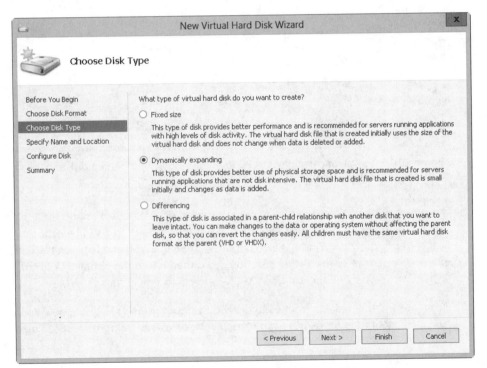

Figure 20-18 Most virtual hard disks should be dynamically expanding.

Migrating physical disks

When creating a new virtual disk, you have the option to copy the contents of a physical disk, as shown in Figure 20-19. This is useful for migrating a physical computer to a VM.

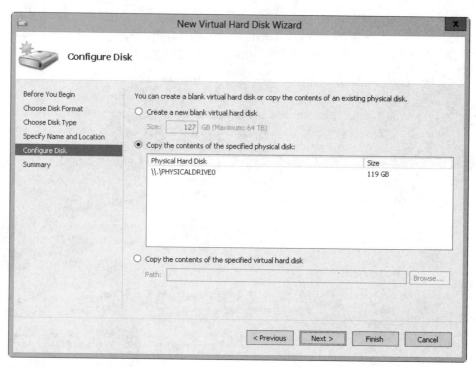

Figure 20-19 You can move a physical PC to a VM by attaching its hard disk and then copying the contents to a virtual hard disk.

Imagine you had an old desktop running Windows XP that had an important app you couldn't run on Windows 8.1. You could migrate that entire computer to a VM by connecting the physical hard drive to your Windows 8.1 computer, creating a VM, and copying the contents of the physical hard drive to the virtual disk. You could then return the virtual disk to the original PC. Whenever you needed the Windows XP PC, you could simply start the VM.

To create a virtual disk file from a physical disk without running Hyper-V, download the free Disk2VHD tool from *http://technet.microsoft.com/en-us/sysinternals/ee656415.aspx*.

Using Hyper-V for forensics

The process of copying a physical hard drive to a virtual disk is very similar to how many law enforcement agencies handle PCs that become evidence. The law enforcement agency can't simply start up the PC, because the process of starting the PC would change the state of the PC, possibly limiting their ability to submit it as evidence.

For example, some criminals configure computers to self-destruct. If a user doesn't type a particular sequence or perform a particular action, often without prompting, the computer will destroy the data on the disk.

By copying the contents of the PC's hard disk to a virtual drive, the law enforcement agency is free to browse the contents of the drive. By taking a snapshot of its original state, they could even start the operating system while keeping an exact copy of the state that it was in when seized as evidence.

Hyper-V tips and tricks

Integration services allow you to copy and paste within a VM. However, you often need to type an operating system product key during the operating system setup, which means you have to do it before integration services are installed.

To avoid that typing (and retyping when you inevitably make a typo), copy the product key to the Clipboard of your host PC. Connect to the VM, and from the Clipboard menu, select Type Clipboard Text. Hyper-V will paste the contents of the Clipboard using the virtual keyboard.

If you frequently use keyboard shortcuts like Alt+Tab and Ctrl+Alt+Del, you probably want the VM to receive those keystrokes. By default, the VM will only receive keystrokes like Alt+Tab or the Windows key when you have it running full screen. To configure the VM to receive all special keystrokes while the window is active, select the Hyper-V Manager window and select your PC name in the left pane. Open the Action menu and then select Hyper-V Settings. In the left pane, select Keyboard and then select Use On The Virtual Machine, as shown in Figure 20-20.

If you're not using integration services on a VM, you need to press Ctrl+Alt+Left Arrow to free your pointer from the VM. That's a rather difficult sequence to press because it requires two hands. In the Hyper-V Settings dialog box, select Mouse Release Key, and then select Ctrl+Alt+Spacebar or Ctrl+Alt+Shift, either of which can be typed with one hand.

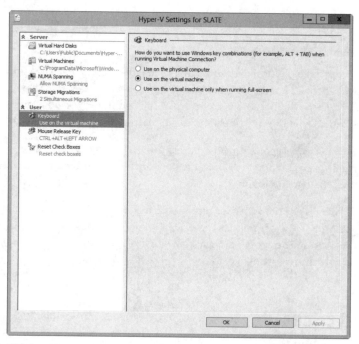

Figure 20-20 Configure Hyper-V options to change how it handles special keystrokes

For the best performance, start a VM and then connect to it with Remote Desktop. Remote Desktop can offer better performance than interacting directly with the VM by using Hyper-V.

When not to use a VM

VMs can't be used for everything. Some of the scenarios that VMs aren't useful for include:

- Action games, especially 3-D games.

- Any app that relies on the graphics processing unit (GPU) for processing.

- BitLocker and Measured Boot.

- Apps that rely on timers of less than 10 ms, such as live music mixing apps.

- Testing hardware accessories (although VirtualBox, described in the next section, can connect to USB devices).

- Testing mobile features, because the VMs will not be able to detect the battery status or distinguish between wired and wireless networks.

Using VirtualBox

VirtualBox is an alternative to Hyper-V that can be downloaded for free from *http://virtualbox.org*. Figure 20-21 shows the main VirtualBox window.

Figure 20-21 VirtualBox provides some consumer features that Hyper-V lacks.

VirtualBox does most of what Hyper-V does, and it also includes several features useful in home environments:

- **Audio**   VirtualBox provides a virtual sound card for VMs, allowing them to play sounds. Hyper-V doesn't support audio.

- **USB devices**   You can connect USB devices to VMs. For example, you could connect a USB webcam to a VM with VirtualBox, but you would not be able to do that with a Hyper-V VM.

- **Shared folders**   Share folders between your host PC and a VM without connecting it to the network.

- **2-D and 3-D acceleration**   VirtualBox supports 2-D and 3-D acceleration, which can improve video performance and allow you to play 3-D games (such as first person shooters) within a VM.

- **Multiple monitors**   VirtualBox can simulate multiple monitors, which can be very useful if your host PC has multiple monitors. With Hyper-V, you could simulate this for VMs running Windows by using Remote Desktop.

VirtualBox lacks Hyper-V's powerful resource prioritization capabilities, however. While you can set the maximum amount of processor time a VirtualBox VM will consume, Hyper-V provides much more control over network resources and allows you to guarantee different VMs a specific amount of processing time.

PART 5

Networking

CHAPTER 21

Setting up a home or small office network **505**

CHAPTER 22

Setting up ad hoc, Bluetooth, and mobile networks **547**

CHAPTER 23

Troubleshooting your network **563**

CHAPTER 24

Sharing and managing files and printers . . . **583**

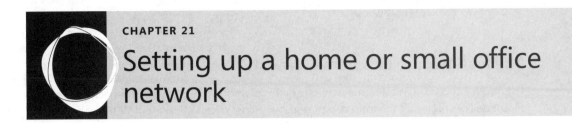

Setting up a home or small office network

Network technology overview. 505

Choosing an ISP 513

Connecting Windows 8.1 to your network 515

Manually configuring Windows 8.1 networking. 517

Fine-tuning wireless settings 518

Routers. 521

Choosing home networking technologies. 525

Designing a wireless network. 530

Web applications 541

Without an Internet connection, a PC is nothing more than an expensive brick. Getting connected to the Internet can be a very simple task, but getting everything you can out of your home network can be a very complex task.

This chapter provides an overview of networking technologies and describes how to select an Internet service provider (ISP), how to configure Windows 8.1 networking, how to choose a router and wireless access point, how to get the best performance out of your home network, and how to configure common network services such as email, file hosting, and web hosting.

➤ For information about sharing files and printers, including how to use homegroups, read Chapter 24, "Sharing and managing files and printers."

➤ For information about configuring firewalls and port filtering on your home office network, including how to switch a network between public and private or public and work/home, refer to Chapter 19, "Windows, application, and network security."

➤ For information about Bluetooth and mobile networks (such as 3G networks), refer to Chapter 22, "Setting up ad hoc, Bluetooth, and mobile networks."

➤ For information about troubleshooting network problems, including performance problems, refer to Chapter 23, "Troubleshooting your network."

Network technology overview

To configure Windows 8.1 and optimize a home network, you need to understand just the basics of home networking, including typical home network architectures and common technologies, such as IP addressing, NAT, DHCP, and DNS. The sections that follow provide that overview.

The architecture of a home network

Figure 21-1 shows a typical home network. In this diagram, the solid lines connecting the different devices represent Ethernet cables, and the wireless signals represent Wi-Fi.

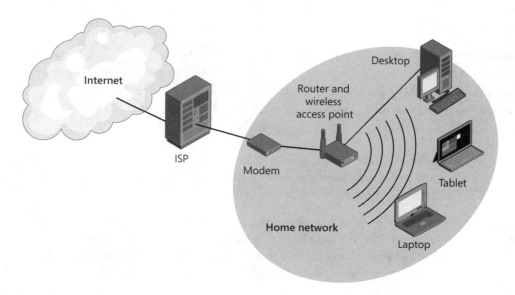

Figure 21-1 Several elements are included in a typical home network architecture.

Here's a description of the most important components of a home network:

- **Internet**   The Internet is really a group of thousands of companies, universities, and individuals who have agreed to connect their networks to each other using routers, cables, and computers. Your home network becomes part of the Internet once you connect to it.

- **Internet service provider (ISP)**   As mentioned in the previous bullet point, the Internet is a bunch of organizations that have agreed to connect to each other. The biggest organizations, known as Tier 1 ISPs, usually connect to each other and exchange data for free. Unless you've spent billions to run cables across continents and oceans, the Tier1 ISPs probably won't want to connect you to their network for free. Instead, you have to pay a business that already has an Internet connection to borrow their network. This business is your Internet service provider (ISP). Today, the biggest ISPs are cable, phone, and satellite companies. Other types of ISPs exist, but the big ISPs are used most often because they already had connections to people's homes and knew how to sell them services when the Internet became popular.

- **Modem**   Short for MOdulator DEModulator, a modem sends Internet communications across whatever type of Internet connection you have. Typically modems have two network connectors: one specific to your connection with your ISP (such as a coaxial connection for a cable provider or a phone connection for a DSL provider) and a wired Ethernet connection. You usually rent your modem from your ISP. Figure 21-2 shows a cable modem's connectors. Today, many modems have routers and wireless access points built into a single device.

Figure 21-2 A cable modem sends your network communications across a cable TV provider's network.

- **Router**   While you can connect a PC directly to your modem's Ethernet connection, nowadays most people have multiple PCs on their home network that need Internet access. A router's job is to combine the communications from every network device in your home and forward them to your ISP. Routers always have at least two Ethernet ports: one to connect to the modem, and one to connect to a PC. Routers usually provide Network Address Translation (NAT) and Dynamic Host Configuration Protocol (DHCP) services, described later in this chapter, and firewall services, described in Chapter 19. Most ISPs will rent you a router; however, if you're technically savvy, you can save yourself some money by buying your own. Routers are also called gateways.

- **Wireless access point** Wireless access points connect Wi-Fi devices, such as laptops, tablets, and smartphones, to your router. Many routers include a wireless access point, or you can buy a separate wireless access point. Wireless access points are described in more detail in "Designing a wireless network" later in this chapter.

- **Wired Ethernet clients** For the best performance, you can connect desktop PCs and other stationary devices, such as an Xbox 360, to your router with an Ethernet cable.

- **Wireless clients** Wireless clients never connect to the network as fast as wired clients. However, wireless clients aren't tethered with a cable, which allows you to move around your house and even your yard with a moderately fast Internet connection. Often, wireless networking is fast enough for your purposes. Particularly if you have a strong wireless signal, wireless networks can offer satisfactory performance for tasks such as browsing the web and online gaming.

IP addresses

Just like every home has a mailing address and every phone has a phone number, every device connected to the Internet has an IP address. Standard IP addresses, known as IPv4 addresses, use a sequence such as 192.168.4.20.

There are about 4 billion possible IP addresses. That's a big number, but it's not nearly big enough, because billions of devices are already connected to the Internet, and we haven't done a very good job of efficiently assigning the 4 billion addresses we do have. So, if every device needs its own IP address and we don't have enough addresses, what do we do?

The long-term answer is to implement an entirely new addressing scheme: IPv6. There are about 340,000,000,000,000,000,000,000,000,000,000,000,000 IPv6 addresses, which should last us a while. IPv6 addresses use a sequence such as fe80::95aa:b974:daac:9df9%13. Unfortunately, using the new IPv6 addressing scheme requires a major overhaul of the Internet, and the Internet is a big place, so that overhaul isn't happening quickly.

NAT

The short-term answer to the lack of IPv4 addresses is Network Address Translation (NAT). NAT lets multiple devices share a single Internet connection, and it's the way the vast majority of devices connect to the Internet today.

You don't need to be an expert in NAT to set up your home network, but what you should understand is that your ISP is going to give you one valid IP address, known as a public IP address. Your router is going to use that IP address. Every other device on your network is going to use a private IP address.

Private IP addresses have been set aside for use on home and business networks. You can't access them directly from the Internet, but you can access them across a local area network. These private IP addresses will be 192.168.*something.something*, 10.*something.something.something*, or 172.16-31.*something.something*. Figure 21-3 shows how a router with NAT connects the Internet's public IP addresses to your network's private IP addresses.

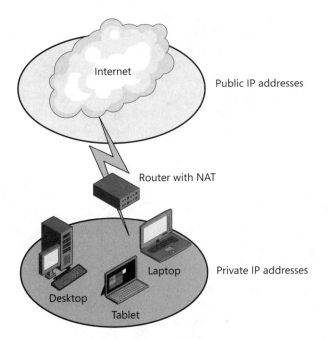

Figure 21-3 Routers use NAT to allow many devices to share a single public IP address.

If you're curious what your IP addresses are, open the Command Prompt desktop app. At the command prompt, type **ipconfig** and press Enter. There's way too much information in there, but just look for the IPv4 Address line:

```
Windows IP Configuration

Ethernet adapter Local Area Connection 1:
   Connection-specific DNS Suffix  . :
   Link-local IPv6 Address . . . . . : fe80::95aa:b974:daac:9df9%13
   IPv4 Address. . . . . . . . . . . : 192.168.2.7
   Subnet Mask . . . . . . . . . . . : 255.255.255.0
   Default Gateway . . . . . . . . . : 192.168.2.1
```

That's your private IP address, and it's assigned by your NAT device. It's the address your device uses to communicate with other devices on your home network.

If you want to know your public IP address, visit *http://ipchicken.com*. You'll see the address your ISP has assigned to your router. However, since your router is using NAT, it's the address every device on the Internet sees when you communicate.

DHCP

Odds are that you've never manually assigned an IP address to a device. Your ISP uses Dynamic Host Configuration Protocol (DHCP) to assign a public address to your router. In turn, your router uses DHCP to assign private addresses to devices on your home network.

When a network device wakes up, it sends out a message to its local network looking for a DHCP server, and the DHCP server responds with an IP address the device can use. If you don't have a DHCP server on your network, the device will either completely fail to connect or use APIPA to make up an IP address that looks like 169.254.*something.something*.

Inside OUT

Understanding Automatic Private IP Addressing (APIPA)

That 169.254.*something.something* address is an APIPA address. APIPA assigns PCs a random address on the 169.254 network if the PC is configured for automatic IP addressing but no DHCP server is available.

Nobody would ever intentionally use APIPA. APIPA doesn't use a router, and therefore, PCs with an APIPA address can't get to the Internet. Without being able to communicate on the Internet, your supply of bacon jokes and cat memes is reduced, rendering your computer useless.

APIPA is designed to let people share files and folders across an ad hoc network. Basically, if you don't know anything about networking, APIPA at least lets you communicate with other PCs in the same location. Without APIPA, the PCs wouldn't be able to communicate on the network at all.

During my years of working at ISPs, I had to learn everything there is to know about DHCP. I don't want you to waste the brain space, but do try to remember these points:

- Computers and devices try to retrieve DHCP addresses when they start. Therefore, restarting everything (possibly including your modem and router) often fixes DHCP problems.

- Your ISP probably uses DHCP to assign an IP address to your router. If your router complains that it can't contact a DHCP server, make sure your modem is connected and working. Then call your ISP.

- Your router assigns IP addresses to devices on your home network. If a device on your network complains that it could not contact a DHCP server, make sure your router is connected and working.

- If a PC has an APIPA IP address like 169.254.*something.something*, it couldn't contact the DHCP server. Check your router.

- Because each component of your network receives an address from DHCP when it starts, it's important to restart devices in the following sequence: modem, router and wireless access point, and finally PCs and other devices. Wait about a minute after restarting each device before restarting the next.

DNS

Every computer, including server computers that host websites, has its own IP address, yet you've probably never typed an IP address into your web browser. Instead, you type a more friendly name, such as contoso.com.

Domain Name Service (DNS) converts names such as contoso.com to one or more IP addresses. To see it in action, open the Command Prompt desktop app and run the command **nslookup contoso.com**. You'll see output that resembles the following, which shows the IP address associated with the name contoso.com in bold:

```
Server:  dns.fabrikam.com
Address:  10.8.8.8

Non-authoritative answer:
Name:    contoso.com
Addresses:  64.4.6.100
```

Many names associated with websites have more than one IP address because the website uses more than one computer to return webpages.

To resolve names to IP addresses, your computer sends queries to its DNS server. DHCP configures the DNS server at the same time it configures your computer's IP address.

If your DNS server fails, the experience is almost like completely losing your Internet connection. Basically, it's like borrowing someone else's phone; it would work just fine if you memorized everyone's phone number, but it's not 1995 anymore, and you're probably accustomed to looking up people by their name.

As with DHCP, there's a great deal to know about DNS. All you really need to know is:

- DNS translates names to IP addresses.

- DHCP automatically configures PCs with the IP address of a DNS server.

CHAPTER 21

TROUBLESHOOTING

I can't connect to the Internet

If you're like me, you get a bit frantic when you lose your Internet connection. Most of the time, I just tell people to relax and do something that doesn't require the Internet, like staring at their useless PC, or frantically refreshing their web browser while shaking their fist at their ISP.

If your Internet seems to be offline, it's possible that it's just your DNS server. To test that theory, open a command prompt and type **ping 8.8.8.8**. If you see "Request timed out," your Internet really is offline. However, if you see "Reply from 8.8.8.8," your DNS server is simply offline.

Your ISP typically uses DHCP to configure your computers to connect to the ISP's closest DNS servers, and that's usually the best choice. If they're offline, though, you can configure your PC to connect to a public DNS server to work around the problem. Follow these high-level steps:

1.   Open the Network And Sharing Center.
2.   Click Change Adapter Settings.
3.   Right-click your adapter, and then click Properties.
4.   Click Internet Protocol Version 4, as shown in Figure 21-4, and then click Properties.

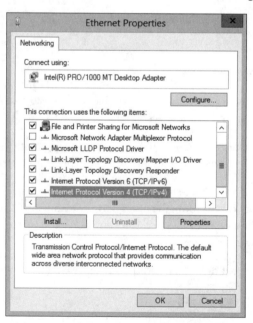

Figure 21-4 Manually configure IP settings by using the adapter's Properties dialog box.

5. Select Use The Following DNS Server Addresses. In the Preferred DNS Server and Alternate DNS Server boxes, type 8.8.8.8 and 8.8.4.4, as shown in Figure 21-5. Click OK. These two addresses are public DNS servers provided by Google, and I chose them only because the numbers are easy to remember. You can find other public DNS servers at *http://pcsupport.about.com/od/tipstricks/a/free-public-dns-servers.htm*.

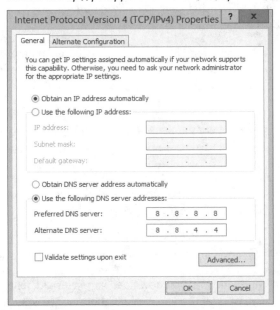

Figure 21-5 Use 8.8.8.8 and 8.8.4.4 if your ISP's DNS servers are unavailable.

6. Click Close.

If DNS really was your only problem, you should now be able to access the Internet.

Choosing an ISP

There are many different types of ISPs out there. If you live in a big city, you might have a dozen different options for Internet access. If you live in a rural area, you might have only one or two.

In order from most to least preferred, my personal preference for Internet connection types are:

● **Fiber optic**   Incredibly high-speed fiber optic connections are currently available only in limited areas because the ISP has to physically drag expensive cable out to everyone's house. However, the performance is unmatched. In the United States, Verizon and Google are currently offering fiber optic Internet services in limited locations.

- **Cable**　Cable ISPs send Internet communications across the same wiring used for cable TV services. Performance can be very good, but ultimately it depends on the ISP. Most cable TV providers also offer Internet access.

- **DSL**　DSL ISPs send Internet communications across dedicated phone circuits. The performance is much slower than offered by fiber optic or cable connections. Local phone companies usually offer DSL-based Internet access.

- **Wireless**　Some urban areas have ISPs that offer home Internet access using wireless connections. These can be based on Wi-Fi or they might use the same mobile wireless networks used by your phones.

- **Satellite**　Satellite Internet connections advertise high bandwidth, but it takes so long to bounce a signal from your house into orbit and then back down to Earth that the connections suffer from high latency. If you live in a rural area without other offerings, it's better than nothing.

While I recommend starting at the top of the list and working your way down, not all ISPs are created equal. There are many different factors to consider:

- **Pricing**　Cost is important for most of us. Your television or phone provider will often bundle Internet access in with other services, allowing you to save some money.

- **Downstream bandwidth**　If you download large files or stream video, downstream bandwidth is very important to you. Besides choosing the Internet connection with the fastest advertised rates, do some online research to determine how your ISP performs in the real world. Especially during peak hours (typically after working hours), your actual available bandwidth is likely to be much lower than the advertised service rate.

- **Upstream bandwidth**　Upstream bandwidth is the speed at which you can upload files to the Internet, and if you play online games or upload videos, it's very important to you. ISPs usually give you more downstream bandwidth than upstream bandwidth, because most people's web usage is like having a conversation with an eight year old— you ask a short question and you receive an extremely verbose response that includes a story about turtles and four knock-knock jokes.

- **Reliability and customer service**　In the last few years, ISPs have gotten to be almost as reliable as television and phone services. However, some ISPs have more failures than others. Online research and talking to people in your neighborhood are the two best ways to evaluate an ISP's reliability.

• **Business services**   If you run a business, you might need business services. These services tend to include priority customer service, higher bandwidth, static IP addresses (as opposed to DHCP-assigned IP addresses), and permission to host web servers on your premises. Business services often cost much more than personal services.

Connecting Windows 8.1 to your network

Windows 8.1 makes it very easy to connect to your network. If you use a wired Ethernet connection, simply plug in the cable, and Windows will take care of the rest automatically (in most cases). If your PC doesn't have an Ethernet port, you can connect a USB Ethernet adapter, as shown in Figure 21-6.

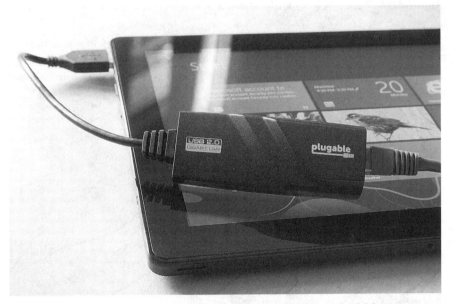

Figure 21-6 Use a USB Ethernet adapter to connect PCs without wired Ethernet ports.

If you use a wireless network, you'll need to choose the network to connect to and type a password. Open the Settings charm. If Windows is not currently connected to a network but one is available, the network icon will display Available, as shown in Figure 21-7.

Figure 21-7 The Settings charm displays Available when it can connect to a wireless network.

Select the network icon. Windows 8.1 lists every wireless network that it can connect to. Select the name of your wireless network. If this is your home network, select Connect Automatically, as shown in Figure 21-8. Then select Connect. When prompted, type your wireless network password.

Figure 21-8 Windows 8.1 displays all available wireless networks.

Manually configuring Windows 8.1 networking

For most networks, DHCP will automatically configure your computer's settings. Some ISPs require you to manually configure IP settings. If you connect to a network that does not use DHCP, ask the network administrator to assign you an IP address and provide you the subnet mask, default gateway, and DNS servers.

Windows 8.1 (and earlier versions of Windows as well) support an alternate configuration. With an alternate configuration, Windows attempts to retrieve an IP configuration from DHCP, but if it can't find one, it uses the static IP settings you specify as the alternate configuration.

This type of configuration is useful for mobile computers that sometimes connect to networks with a DHCP server but at other times connect to a single network with static IP addressing. For example, your home network almost certainly uses DHCP. However, some business networks still use static IP addressing. If you attempt to connect your PC to your work's network, it won't be able to find a DHCP server, and therefore won't be able to connect to the network.

If you specify an alternate configuration, the PC's default configuration will still be to use DHCP when you connect to your home network or to hotspots. However, when no DHCP server is available, Windows will apply the alternate configuration. Therefore, if you specify the IP settings required for your static network as the alternate configuration, you will be able to use your PC on both networks without changing any configuration settings each time you connect.

Follow these steps to set up an alternate configuration:

1. Open the Network And Sharing Center.

2. Click Change Adapter Settings.

3. Right-click your adapter, and then click Properties.

4. Click Internet Protocol Version 4, and then click Properties.

5. Select the Alternate Configuration tab and fill in the required fields with the information provided by your ISP or network administrator. The alternate configuration applies static IP settings when a DHCP server isn't available. You could configure your static IP settings using the General tab, but your PC would use those settings for every network it connected to, preventing it from connecting to most networks that do use DHCP.

    Figure 21-9 shows a completed alternate configuration.

CHAPTER 21

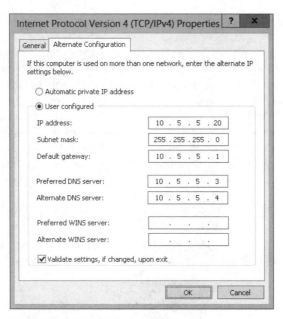

Figure 21-9 Use an alternate configuration when you roam between multiple networks and one uses static IP settings.

6. Click OK.

7. Click Close.

If you need to configure IP settings on a desktop computer that only ever connects to a single network, use the General tab of the Internet Protocol Version 4 Properties dialog box to configure the settings. This prevents the computer from connecting to networks that use DHCP, but it can slightly speed up your networking.

Fine-tuning wireless settings

From the Start screen, search for **power options**, and then select Power Options. As shown in Figure 21-10, Windows displays the power plans available, with the currently selected plan shown in bold.

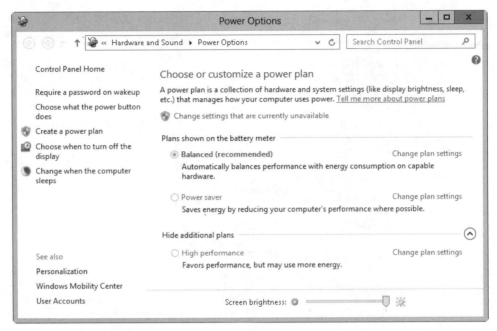

Figure 21-10 Power options have a profound effect on your wireless network performance.

Select Change Plan Settings next to your current power plan. Near the bottom of the window, select Change Advanced Power Settings. In the Power Options dialog box, select Change Settings That Are Currently Unavailable. Then expand Wireless Adapter Settings and Power Saving Mode, and set On Battery and Plugged In to the performance level of your choice (as shown in Figure 21-11). Naturally, Maximum Performance gives you the best performance but drains your battery the fastest. At times, however, you might not be able to connect to a wireless network unless you set the Power Saving Mode to Maximum Performance.

Many wireless adapters have settings that you can modify from the adapter properties dialog box. To edit these, from the Start screen, search for **network connections**. Then select View Network Connections. Right-click your wireless adapter, select Properties, and then click the Configure button to view the adapter's properties dialog box. The Advanced tab, as shown in Figure 21-12, has settings that are specific to your wireless adapter. These vary too much for me to describe all the settings for you, but if you have unusual circumstances and a solid understanding of wireless networking, you can fine-tune them to improve your wireless performance.

Figure 21-11 The advanced power options control how much power your wireless adapter receives.

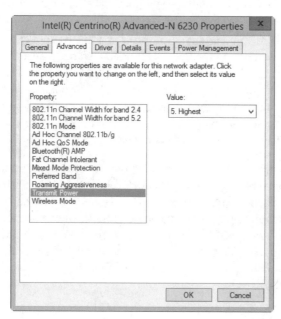

Figure 21-12 Adapter driver settings often have useful configuration options.

Routers

Routers are a key component of your network. They connect your PCs both to the Internet and to each other. You can choose from hundreds of different routers, each with different performance, price, security, and usability.

The sections that follow describe how to choose a router and perform the initial configuration.

Choosing a router

Most people can purchase a router that will suit their needs for less than US$30 (and often, you can spend less than US$20). As with all electronic equipment, I recommend shopping online and choosing products that are well reviewed.

Even the most basic routers offer these features:

- Password-protected management by using a web browser.

- DHCP services to automatically assign IP addresses to PCs and other devices on your home network.

- NAT to allow multiple devices to share a single public IP address.

- Port forwarding or virtual servers to allow you to host a server on your home network.

- Universal Plug and Play (UPnP) to allow apps, such as online games and instant messaging apps, to automatically configure the router to receive incoming connections.

Those features are enough for most users. Some higher-end routers also offer the following features, which might be important to some users:

- **Wireless networking**   Some, if not most, new routers include a wireless access point. You can buy a separate router and wireless access point, but you might as well save yourself some setup time and buy a router with wireless networking built in. Look for routers that support Wireless N.

- **Printer sharing**   Many routers allow you to connect a USB printer directly to them, and then print from any PC on your network. This feature is very important if you have a USB printer that cannot directly connect to the network and your printer isn't connected to a desktop PC. If your printer is connected to a desktop PC, you can simply share the printer, as described in Chapter 24.

- **External drive sharing**   Some routers allow you to connect an external hard drive (such as a USB hard drive) and share it across the network. Called *network attached storage* (NAS), this feature can be useful for sharing files between PCs and providing a destination for backing up files when all your PCs are mobile.

- **Web monitoring and filtering**   Some routers can record the URLs that devices on the internal network visit or only allow devices to visit an approved list of websites. The monitoring and filtering can be circumvented if one of the devices uses a VPN (unless you also disable VPNs), but it's harder to bypass than features like Family Safety in Windows 8.1.

- **Dynamic DNS**   Updates DNS servers if your IP address changes. This allows you to assign a DNS name to your home network, such as home.conotoso.com, and have the name automatically updated if your ISP assigns you a new IP address (which they might do from time to time).

- **Quality of Service (QoS)**   Prioritizes outgoing traffic based on the computer or app sending it. This is useful for ensuring that a game or server is responsive to other people on the Internet. It typically isn't useful for prioritizing incoming traffic, so you can't use it to keep a file transfer from slowing down video streaming, for example.

- **Multiple Internet connections**   Some routers, such as the Duolinks SW24 2 Port Dual WAN Load Balancing Router that I use (about US$170), can connect to two different Internet connections and then distribute traffic across both connections for better performance, or automatically switch between the connections when one fails. This can allow you to combine cable and DSL connections, for example, to keep you connected to the Internet if one fails. Figure 21-13 illustrates this scenario. If your ISP is unreliable, or you can't afford to be without an Internet connection (for example, if you often work from home), multiple links can be very important. Be sure to connect your router and modems to an uninterruptable power supply (UPS) so they don't go offline if you lose power.

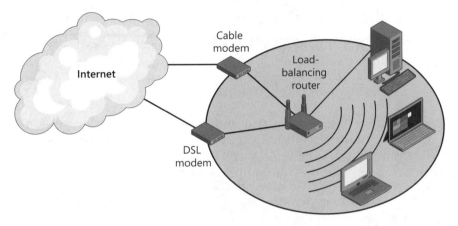

Figure 21-13 Some routers allow you to combine multiple Internet connections for speed and resiliency.

- **Virtual private networking (VPN)**   Some routers support connecting with a VPN, as shown in Figure 21-14. You can use a VPN to connect to resources on your home network while travelling. VPN capabilities can also securely connect two remote networks without configuring the PCs on those networks. For example, if you have separate networks at home and at a small business that you run, you could connect the networks with a VPN and access resources on each as if they were all in the same building.

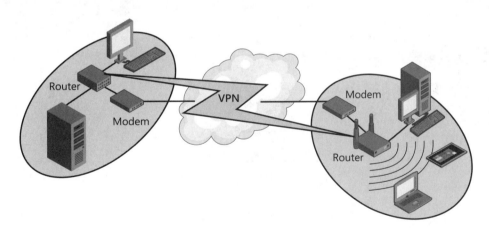

Figure 21-14 VPNs extend your network across the Internet.

Configuring a router or wireless access point

Sometimes, you can simply plug in your router and have everything work automatically. At other times, you need to configure your router to your ISP's specifications. If your router supports Wi-Fi, you must configure your router to specify a unique SSID (the name of your wireless network) and to create a network password.

Refer to your router's manual for instructions on how to configure it. Some routers include a software tool that you need to run, while others simply have you open your browser and visit a local IP address such as *https://192.168.1.1*.

Windows 8.1 does have a tool capable of configuring some routers. To try it, open the Network And Sharing Center and then click Set Up A New Connection Or Network. In the wizard, select Set Up A New Network, as shown in Figure 21-15.

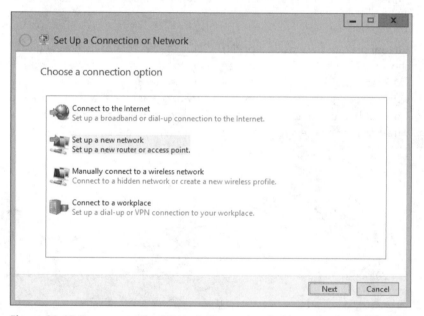

Figure 21-15 You can use the Set Up A Connection Or Network wizard to configure a new router.

Then follow the prompts that appear. Windows 8.1 will prompt you for a network name, security key, security level, and encryption type. For detailed information about different Wi-Fi encryption technologies, refer to "Designing a wireless network" later in this chapter.

After you buy a router and get it connected to your network, you should immediately check to see whether the router manufacturer has released any firmware updates for the router. Most routers do not automatically update their firmware. However, router firmware updates often contain critical security updates to fix serious vulnerabilities that might allow uninvited guests into your home network.

Choosing home networking technologies

There are many ways you can connect your PCs and other network devices (such as your smartphone) to your home network. Most people simply need to set up a router with a built-in wireless access point and then connect every device to the wireless network.

Some of us, however, have more demanding needs. For example, if you stream HD video across your network (as described in Chapter 16, "Sharing and streaming digital media"), a wireless network might not be fast enough. If you transfer large files between PCs on your network, you might find wireless networks take an annoyingly long time to copy files.

The sections that follow describe different home networking types.

Wireless Ethernet

If a PC or network device doesn't support wireless networking, you can connect it in a couple of different ways:

- **USB wireless adapters**   To connect a desktop PC to a wireless network, connect a USB wireless adapter, which you can buy for less than US$20.

- **Wireless bridges**   If a device does not support USB network adapters, such as older gaming systems and digital video recorders (DVRs), but it does have a wired Ethernet connection, use a wireless bridge. Wireless bridges connect to your Wi-Fi network like any wireless client, but they also include a wired Ethernet port. Use an Ethernet cable to connect your device to your wireless bridge, and then configure the wireless bridge to connect to your wireless network. Wireless bridges typically cost between US$40 and $100. For best results, choose a wireless bridge made by the same manufacturer that produced your wireless access point.

➤ For more information about setting up Wi-Fi, refer to "Designing a wireless network" later in this chapter.

Wired Ethernet

Wired Ethernet always provides the best performance. The downside, of course, is the wire. However, for stationary network devices such as desktop PCs, DVRs, Home Theater PCs, and game consoles, wired Ethernet provides the consistent high performance you need.

▶ **Creating a wired home network**   Watch the video at *http://aka.ms/WinIO/wired*.

To connect wired Ethernet devices, use an Ethernet switch, as shown in Figure 21-16. Most routers come with a four-port Ethernet switch built in. If you need more ports, you can purchase inexpensive switches to expand your network. With most modern switches, you can simply connect an Ethernet cable from your router to the new switch. With older switches, you might need to use a special crossover Ethernet cable. Either way, remember that the cable you use to connect your router and your switch will consume one port on each device, so purchase a switch with more ports than you need.

Figure 21-16 Use an Ethernet switch to connect computers across a wired network.

There are several wired Ethernet standards: 10 Mbps, 100 Mbps, and 1000 Mbps (also known as gigabit). Faster is always better, so look for switches and adapters that support 1000 Mbps. Faster speeds are backward compatible, so they will work fine with devices designed for 10 Mbps or 100 Mbps networks.

When purchasing Ethernet cables, look for Category 6 Ethernet, commonly called "Cat6." Category 7 cables are beginning to appear, but they require special connectors that are not yet commonly supported.

What if your home is too large to easily run Ethernet cables to every device? I know, first-world problems, right? There are a few ways you can lay Ethernet cables to connect hard-to-reach places:

- **Within walls**   You can run cables through your basement or attic and then raise them or drop them through the hollow spaces in your walls. If you didn't already know this, I strongly suggest hiring an electrician or alarm company to run your cabling. Be sure to use plenum cable rated for use inside walls and to follow your local building codes to minimize the risk of fire.

- **Under carpeting**   You can purchase flat Ethernet cables that can be run under carpeting without making a noticeable bump. For best results, avoid high-traffic areas. Prolonged walking over a cable might damage it, even when protected by carpeting.

- **Along baseboards and doorframes**   You can run Ethernet cables along baseboards and doorframes so people don't trip over them. They can be ugly, however. Purchase far more Ethernet cable than you think you need; many people underestimate the length of cable they need to follow walls and doors.

These are the best solutions. Unfortunately, they're also quite difficult. Powerline networking, HPNA, and coaxial networking provide much easier ways to extend your wired Ethernet network, but they don't offer the same high level of performance.

Ethernet over coax

With the proper adapter, you can use existing cable TV wires for Ethernet networking within homes. This is perfect if you have cable TV jacks in the rooms where you want to connect your wired Ethernet device.

Basically, you need to purchase a pair of Ethernet over coax adapters. Each adapter has two ports: a coax port and an Ethernet port. Connect one adapter's Ethernet port to your router and its coax port to a coax connection in your home. Connect the second adapter's Ethernet port to your wired network device and its coax port to another coax connection in your home. Assuming the two coax ports are connected within your walls, you should be able to use the coax as a reliable and moderately high-speed network extension.

Many homes are prewired for cable TV. However, that doesn't mean that every single coax connection is plugged in. Often, the coax wires run to a single point in your home (usually near your circuit breaker or fuse box), and only those cables that are currently connected to

TVs are plugged in. If your Ethernet over coax adapters can't communicate, make sure the other end of the cable is connected.

Ethernet over phoneline

Though phone cable and Ethernet cable look similar, Ethernet cabling uses eight wires, while telephones use only two wires (though telephone cable might have more wires). Unfortunately, telephone cable simply hasn't proven to be reliable enough for home networking. At the least, performance doesn't match options such as wireless networking and home power-line networking.

However, if you need to connect two buildings that have a dedicated phone connection, you can purchase an Ethernet extender kit that works with single-pair wire such as a telephone connection. StarTech makes several products for both single-pair and coaxial cabling. For more information, visit *http://www.startech.com/Networking-IO/Media-Converters/ Ethernet-Extenders.*

Powerline networking

Besides cable TV and phone connections, most modern homes have power connectors in every room. While these cables aren't designed for network communications, they do closely resemble a wired network: they're made from copper, distributed throughout your house, well shielded, and all connect to a single hub—your circuit breaker or fuse box.

Unfortunately, they also have dangerously high network current flowing through them, dozens of different non-network devices using them, and links often have fuses, circuit breakers, and other less-than-ideal connectors.

Nonetheless, several companies make powerline networking adapters. As for Ethernet over coax adapters, you always use powerline networking adapters in pairs: one at your router, and the other at the network device you are connecting.

As shown in Figure 21-17, the adapters have two connectors: a wired Ethernet connector and a power plug. Plug it directly into your wall (don't plug it into a power strip), and then connect the Ethernet adapter to your router or PC. When a pair is active, they automatically connect and allow networking. If you need to connect multiple network devices in one location, you can purchase powerline adapters with multiple Ethernet ports.

Figure 21-17 Powerline adapters turn your home's power grid into an Ethernet network.

Figure 21-18 shows the powerline network adapters in my own home and their current per-formance (as rated by the adapter vendor's tools). Different homes have different levels of performance. In general, the newer your home is and the better quality the wiring, the better performance you will get. However, I've used powerline adapters with success in homes that predate electricity, using retrofit electrical wiring from the 1920s.

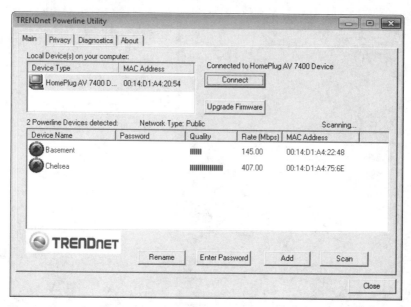

Figure 21-18 Powerline networking performance varies, but it is almost always faster than wireless.

Designing a wireless network

Setting up your wireless network doesn't have to be complicated; often, your ISP will plug in a wireless access point for you, and all you have to do is type your password.

On the other hand, the setup is often not that simple. Many of us have more demanding network requirements than any standard wireless access point can provide. We need better performance, a bigger range, and better security.

The sections that follow provide detailed information about setting up wireless networks for a variety of different household scenarios.

▶ **Creating a wireless home network** Watch the video at *http://aka.ms/WinIO/wireless*.

Choosing a wireless network standard

Wireless networks are extremely popular, and wireless network vendors are constantly releasing new wireless standards that offer better range and performance. Fortunately, these wireless standards are backward-compatible, making choosing a standard easy: always buy equipment for the latest standard.

From newest to oldest, and best to worst, common wireless standards include:

- **802.11n** From 2009, 802.11n offers bandwidth up to about 80 Mbps (though performance of all wireless networks drops with distance and interference). To improve performance, set the channel bandwidth to 20/40 MHz. 802.11n is backward-compatible with 802.11g, 802.11b, and 802.11a. However, performance drops dramatically when an 802.11n wireless access point must communicate with clients using older standards. For best performance, upgrade all of your clients to 802.11n and then set the wireless access point to 802.11n-only mode.

- **802.11g** From 2003, 802.11g offers bandwidth up to about 30 Mbps. 802.11g is backward-compatible with 802.11b devices; however, like 802.11n, 802.11g performs best in 802.11g-only mode.

- **802.11b** From 1999, 802.11b offers bandwidth of about 5 Mbps.

- **802.11a** Technically faster than 802.11b, 802.11a isn't compatible with most wireless access points and wireless devices, and for that reason should be avoided.

Basically, buy 802.11n gear whenever possible, and know that your older wireless gear will connect to it just fine.

Choosing a wireless access point

Like routers, wireless access points (and the wireless access points built into many routers) have a variety of features. You probably don't need any of these features, but you should be aware of them so that if one of them sounds particularly useful, you can seek out a wireless access point that supports that feature.

- **Guest access** Some wireless access points (particularly those designed for businesses) provide support for a second Wi-Fi network to be used by guests. These guest networks are often unencrypted so that guests do not have to know a password. The wireless access point often requires the user to confirm a usage agreement before accessing the Internet, and may limit the amount of time they use the network connection. In home environments, most people provide their guests access by just telling them the Wi-Fi password, but maybe you don't trust your friends that much.

- **Weatherproofing** If you frequently use Wi-Fi outdoors, you might want to purchase a wireless access point that you can mount outdoors. Such wireless access points are ruggedized to withstand the weather.

CHAPTER 21

- **Proprietary speed improvements**   While all wireless access points support some basic standard, such as 802.11g or 802.11n, some also support proprietary modes that advertise performance increases when you use wireless network adapters from the same brand. These really can offer speed improvements, but you won't benefit when using the wireless adapters built into your mobile devices.

- **Wireless bridging**   Some wireless access points can also function as bridges. Rather than being a wireless access point, they act as a Wi-Fi client, and their wired Ethernet ports allow wired clients to connect to your network across the wireless network. For more information, refer to "Choosing home networking technologies" earlier in this chapter.

- **Scheduling**   Even the most serious geeks among us sleep at some point. Some wireless access points support scheduling (as shown in Figure 21-19), so they shut their radio off at specific times of day or on some days of the week. Not only does this reduce the risk that your network will be abused, but it can save power.

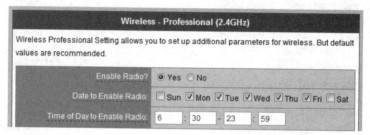

Figure 21-19 Some wireless access points support scheduling, which can reduce abuse and save power.

- **Replaceable antennas**   Many modern wireless access points have internal antennas for a clean appearance. However, they might not give you ideal reception. If you have a particularly large area to cover or you want to send wireless signals in a specific direction, choose a wireless access point with replaceable antennas, as shown in Figure 21-20. Most include an omnidirectional antenna that transmits evenly in all directions. You can also install directional antennas that transmit in a specific direction.

Figure 21-20 Swap out the antennas on a wireless access point to control your signal direction.

Figure 21-21 compares omnidirectional and directional antennas.

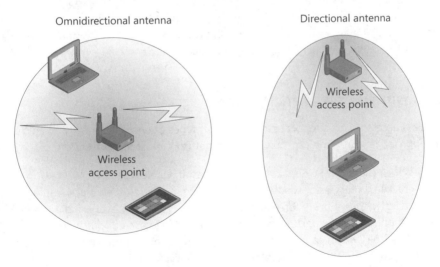

Omnidirectional antenna

Directional antenna

Wireless access point

Wireless access point

Figure 21-21 Omnidirectional antennas send signals in all directions, while directional antennas focus the output in one direction.

Inside OUT

Understanding Wi-Fi performance

Here are a few facts that will be helpful when you're optimizing your Wi-Fi performance:

- Directional antennas don't increase power output, they simply focus it in one direction. Therefore, if you replace an omnidirectional antenna with a directional antenna, you're adding power in one direction while taking power away in every other direction. To reinforce this important point: no antenna can increase your router's power output.

- No antenna is perfectly omnidirectional; most transmit power in a relatively flat circle rather than a sphere. Therefore, you might get better performance between any two points by tilting or turning your wireless access point. Have someone with a mobile PC stand where you hope to get more signal, and then make minor adjustments to the wireless access point to optimize the signal at that location.

- Wi-Fi requires two-way communications. If your wireless access point can transmit two miles but your laptop can only transmit 100 feet, your wireless range is still going to be limited to 100 feet.

You can get directional antennas for PCs. Look for USB Wi-Fi adapters that support external antennas. Some stick to the back of a laptop and allow you to point them to a nearby wireless access point. They won't work well if you're constantly moving around, but if you're stationary, they can greatly extend your range.

Choosing wireless encryption

Wireless access points support several different types of encryption. Only a handful of them are appropriate for home use, however. In order from most to least preferred, they are:

- **WPA2 (Personal)**   The latest and greatest in wireless security, WPA2 isn't easily cracked. In fact, as of the time of this writing, no widespread crack would be any more effective than a brute force attack, which requires trying every single password combination. Security experts seem to agree that as long as your password isn't easily guessed, WPA2 passwords cannot be cracked by current computing hardware. Most recent Wi-Fi devices support WPA2, but older wireless devices might not.

- **WEP (128-bit)**   The WEP protocol has some cryptographic flaws that make it much easier to crack. Under ideal circumstances, it can be cracked by a skilled attacker in a few minutes. There's a great deal of information on the Internet talking about how secure

128-bit WEP is, and I even wrote some of it. That information is now outdated; the hackers won, and no version of WEP is secure.

- **WPA (Personal)**   The original version of WPA, this version has flaws that make it easily cracked.

- **WEP (64-bit)**   Never a good choice for wireless security, 64-bit WEP can often be cracked in a few seconds.

Your wireless access point probably also supports enterprise authentication modes, which might be labeled WPA2-Enterprise, RADIUS, or 802.1X. These modes require an authentication infrastructure that most home environments will not have.

If you're interested in wireless encryption cracking techniques, check out AirCrack-NG (at *http://www.aircrack-ng.org/*) and the BackTrack Linux live CD (at *http://www.backtrack-linux.org/*). It's important to understand threats to your security so you can protect yourself, but you should never use your skills to attack. I learned that from Mr. Miyagi.

Note that each of these wireless encryption standards authorizes devices using a password. That's a good choice for home use, but it's a terrible choice for all but the smallest of businesses. The problem with passwords is that you can't revoke someone's access to your wireless network without changing the password, and changing the password requires you to update every wireless device. It's a nuisance, but if you give someone your wireless network password and you no longer trust them, you'll need to change the password on your wireless access point and then reconfigure every single wireless device. Yes, it's one more reason not to break up with your girlfriend.

CHAPTER 21

Inside OUT

Wireless MAC filtering

Wireless access points support MAC address filtering. MAC addresses are hardware addresses that uniquely identify every network adapter. Whereas an IP address identifies a host on the Internet, a MAC address identifies a host only on the local network.

You can see the MAC address of your PC by opening a command prompt and then running the command **ipconfig /all**. Look for the Physical Address line, as the following output demonstrates:

```
C:\>ipconfig /all
Ethernet adapter Local Area Connection 1:

   Connection-specific DNS Suffix  . :
   Description . . . . . . . . . . . : RTL8168D/8111D Gigabit Ethernet
   Physical Address. . . . . . . . . : F0-4D-A2-3A-C7-9D
   DHCP Enabled. . . . . . . . . . . : Yes
   Autoconfiguration Enabled . . . . : Yes
```

With MAC filtering, you look up the MAC address of every wireless adapter on your network and type them into your wireless access point, as shown in Figure 21-22. Then, you can enable MAC filtering, and your wireless access point will ignore requests from any other adapter.

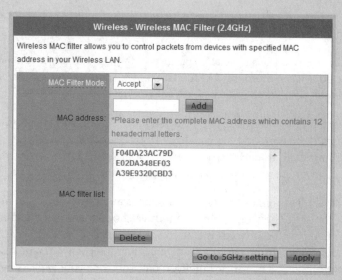

Figure 21-22 Wireless MAC filtering doesn't improve security enough to justify the inconvenience.

In theory, this means that only clients with the network adapters you approve can connect to your wireless network. This would provide near-perfect wireless authentication without requiring a password, except for one critical flaw: MAC addresses are broadcast unencrypted. Therefore, any moderately sophisticated attacker could identify valid MAC addresses and impersonate them.

With that said, MAC address filtering can theoretically improve security by making it more difficult to connect to your wireless access point. However, it's a nuisance that isn't typically worth the effort. After all, every time you get a new computer, replace a network adapter, or have a friend over, you have to look up the 12-digit hexadecimal MAC address and configure your wireless access point before they can connect. Security is always a compromise between protection and convenience, and in the case of MAC filtering, the trade-off isn't typically worth it.

Inside OUT

What is a honeypot?

In network security, a honeypot is a trap. It's like a geeky version of those stings and undercover operations you see in police shows.

For example, a security engineer might set up a honeypot on their network. The honeypot looks exactly like a real computer to other users connected to the network. However, nobody knows about it, and it serves no useful function to legitimate users.

The honeypot records every detail of incoming network requests. If anyone attempts to connect to the honeypot, the security engineer knows they're up to no good, because there's no legitimate reason to be connecting to this computer. While the security engineer could monitor any computer on the network for attacks, it's particularly easy to monitor a honeypot because the security engineer doesn't have to filter out legitimate requests from potentially malicious requests—every connection request (except his own) is unwanted.

Honeypots can often be configured to impersonate vulnerable computer systems. For example, they might appear to be a PC running Windows XP without important security updates. An attacker would see this as tempting and attempt to break into it. Meanwhile, the honeypot is recording the attacker's every action, allowing the security engineer to identify the techniques the attacker is using, gather evidence that might be admissible in court, and possibly even personally identify the attacker so that a law enforcement agency could take action.

Wireless honeypots exist, and they're a bit scary. They appear to be a wireless access point, and they might even give people who connect to them Internet access. If someone connects to the honeypot, they're obviously an uninvited guest, since nobody would ever invite anyone to use a honeypot. Once the uninvited guest connects to the honeypot, it's possible for the security engineer to use special equipment to track the client's wireless signal back to the origin, which is the attacker who is physically within range of the honeypot's wireless signal. It's one of the few cases in network security where you can physically confront an attacker.

You wouldn't ever set a honeypot's SSID to "Honeypot," because then an attacker would know it was a trap. However, by naming a legitimate Wi-Fi network Honeypot, you might scare away potential attackers who think it's a trap. Anyway, I'm breaking my own personal rule by explaining a joke, but honeypots are too much fun to not talk about.

Choosing a SSID

The SSID is the name of your wireless network. It appears when you browse networks, but it has no impact on security. Wireless access points allow you to hide a SSID, but there's no security benefit, and a hidden SSID is more difficult to connect to.

Choosing a proper SSID is very important, however, because all your neighbors can see it. Some suggestions include:

- TurnYourMusicDown

- PartyFriday8pmBringBeer

- PickUpAfterUrDog

- Honeypot

- PrettyFly4AWiFi

- iH8uChet

You get the idea (and so does my neighbor, Chet, who never brings beer).

Providing wireless access throughout your house

Oh, the burdens of the first-world lifestyle: your house is so large that Wi-Fi doesn't work well, or at all, in some places. Until some philanthropist finally takes pity on us and founds a charitable organization to offer relief to those of us with subsatisfactory Wi-Fi performance, we'll have to get our hands dirty to get the coverage we need.

The first step to getting coverage throughout your house is choosing the right location for your wireless access point. Your ISP probably plugged it in next to your router, which might be in your basement or some other infrequently used part of your house. You should move it to a central part of your house. If you can't run an Ethernet cable from your modem to where you would like your wireless access point, then use powerline networking or Ethernet over coax, as described earlier in this chapter.

Try to position your wireless access point away from interfering objects. The worst interferers are large metal objects such as filing cabinets and refrigerators. Power cords are bad, too.

If you want to use your PC outside (which is a great idea; I'm writing this on my patio), be aware that window screens completely scramble wireless signals. To get coverage in your backyard, position your wireless access point near an outside wall or window, but not near any screens. Screens have this really confusing effect on wireless signals: your PC will show that it has a strong connection to the wireless network, but your performance will be terrible or unreliable.

Using two wireless access points

If you followed the advice in the previous section but still don't have coverage, you can add a second wireless access point in a different part of your house and connect it to your router using powerline networking or Ethernet over coax.

If you set up a second wireless access point using a different SSID, your house will have two wireless networks. That's not great, though. Not only will you need to configure devices to connect to both networks, but your wireless devices won't always connect to the strongest network in the house; they'll connect to the network they were most recently connected to. So, you might have a connection with five bars available, but Windows will stay connected to the distant Wi-Fi network with just one bar. You could manually switch networks as you moved around your house, but that's a nuisance.

Here's a better way to configure that second wireless access point:

- Change its IP address to something other than the IP address of your first wireless access point or your router, but keep it on the same network. For example, if your first wireless access point has the IP address 192.168.1.1, change the IP address for the second wireless access point to 192.168.1.2 or 192.168.1.3. As long as you change just the last number, you should be okay. Don't use the same IP address as any other device on your network, however.

- Turn off DHCP on the second wireless access point. Wireless clients will still get their IP addresses from your router.

- Set the second wireless access point to a different channel. In the United States, we use channels 1, 6, and 11. So, you could set your first wireless access point to 11, and your second to 1 or 6. If a neighbor has a wireless access point that might interfere, it would be good to avoid that channel, too.

- Choose the same security settings, including the key.

- Set the SSID to the same name as your first wireless network.

Use inSSIDer, available at *http://www.metageek.net/products/inssider/*, to analyze the performance of your Wi-Fi networks and to determine the channels your neighbors are using. As shown in Figure 21-23, inSSIDer displays the relative signal strength of different visible Wi-Fi networks. If you are attempting to improve the wireless strength at a specific location, this app is a great way to determine how signal strength changes as you move or tilt the wireless access point.

CHAPTER 21

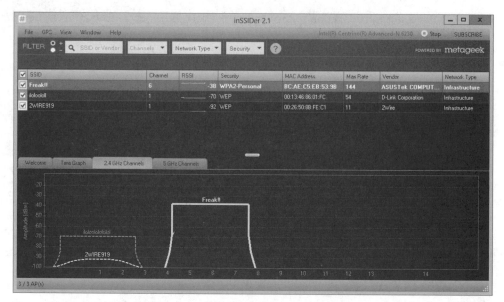

Figure 21-23 Use inSSIDer to analyze wireless networks around you.

Managing wireless networks

Windows 8.1 provides basic network management through the PC Settings, Network, Connections page. To change the settings for a connected network, simply select the network on this page. As shown in Figure 21-24, Windows 8.1 displays detailed information about the network connection and allows you to change several important settings.

The settings available depend on the type of network. Some networks will have these options:

- **Find Devices And Content**   Turning on this option sets the network type to private, enabling file sharing and homegroups.

- **Show My Estimated Data Use In The Networks List**   Turning on this option causes Windows 8.1 to track the network usage, which can increase processing time.

- **Set As Metered Connection**   Turn on this option for wireless broadband connections without unlimited bandwidth, or for any other connection that requires you to pay for usage. Windows 8.1 is more conservative with your bandwidth for metered connections, disabling features such as automatic update downloads.

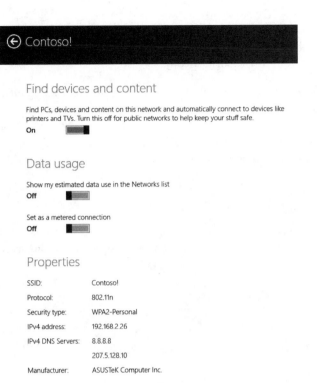

Figure 21-24 Right-click networks to access additional settings.

Web applications

Most individuals and small businesses need a few different web services beyond simply browsing the web. The sections that follow discuss the most important web services.

Email

Everyone needs email, and there are dozens of different companies quite excited to provide an email address for you. Microsoft is one such company, and millions of people use the free Hotmail service (also known as Outlook.com). Since you probably already have an account, Facebook also allows you to receive email by sending messages in the format *<username>*@facebook.com.

However, I don't recommend any service that requires you to use its domain name. Using Hotmail as an example, you'll be required to use an email address such as *<yourname>*@hotmail.com. If you ever discover a better email service, you then have to tell all your friends about your new address, and that's a nuisance.

I recommend getting your own domain name so that you aren't tied to another organization. For example, even though you could contact me at tony.northrup@facebook.com, the email address on my business card is tony@northrup.org.

Getting my last name as a domain name isn't that hard. It requires registering a custom domain name, which costs about $10 a month. Dozens of different domain name registrars, such as godaddy.com, will register a domain name for you and even host your email. Then, you simply need to configure the Mail client in Windows 8.1 with the email server settings the registrar provides. Your domain name registrar will probably charge you for email services, however.

Configuring Mail

The first time you launch Mail, it prompts you for information it needs to connect to your mail server. At a minimum, Mail needs to gather your email address and password, as shown in Figure 21-25.

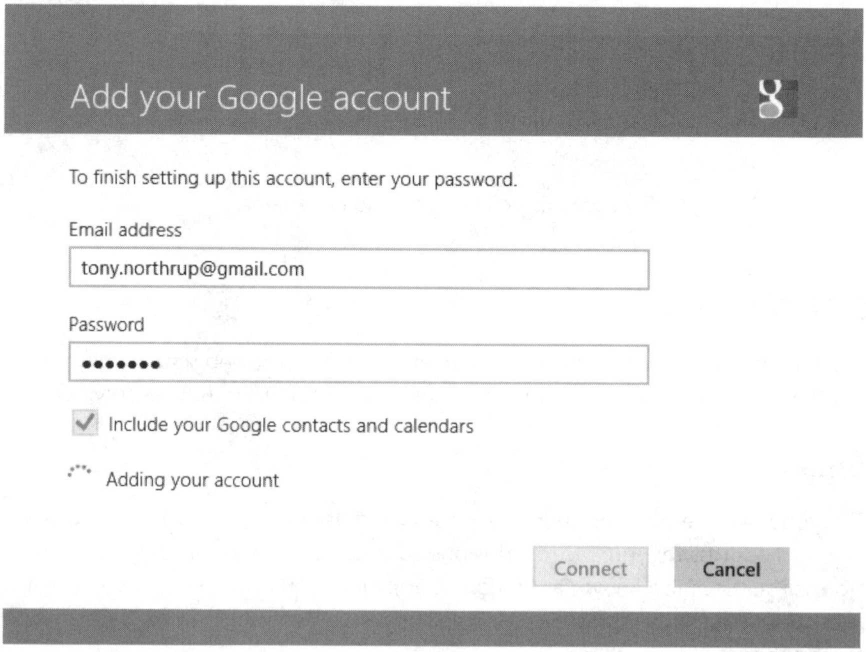

Add your Google account

To finish setting up this account, enter your password.

Email address

tony.northrup@gmail.com

Password

••••••••

☑ Include your Google contacts and calendars

⋯ Adding your account

Connect   Cancel

Figure 21-25 Mail can usually connect using just your email address and password.

Mail actually needs much more information to connect to your account, including your user name, your IMAP server address, and your SMTP server address. It's pretty smart, though, and can usually figure out those details without making you look them up. If Mail is unable to determine your settings, it will prompt you, as shown in Figure 21-26. Ask your system administrator for the missing details, or simply search the Internet for "*<mail service>* IMAP SMTP server."

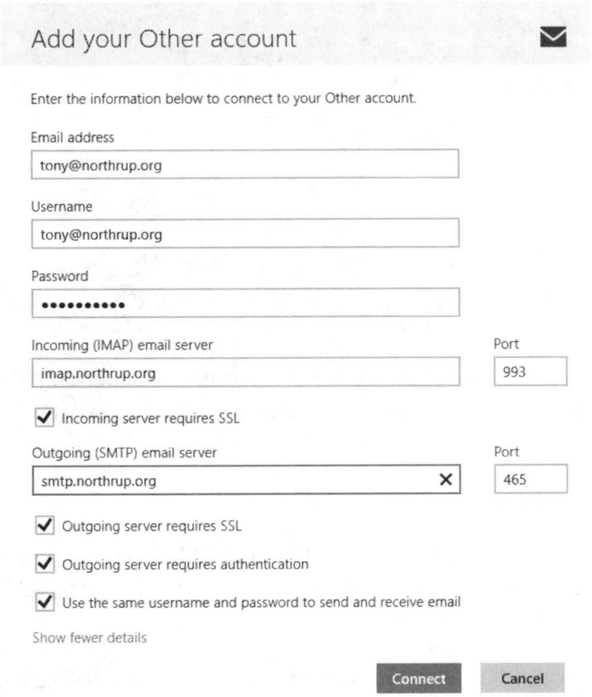

Figure 21-26 Mail might need to prompt you for additional information.

Adding extra mail accounts

Mail can download your email from all your different accounts. Though Mail prompts you to configure your first email account, you need to use the Settings charm to add more accounts. After opening the Settings charm with Mail open, select Accounts, select Add An Account, and then select your account type, as shown in Figure 21-27. Use the Hotmail link for Live and MSN mail. Use the Outlook link if you use Outlook.com or Office 365, or you're connecting to a business's email system and it uses Microsoft Exchange Server for email. If you use Gmail or Google Apps, select the Google link. If none of these apply, or you're not sure, select Other Account.

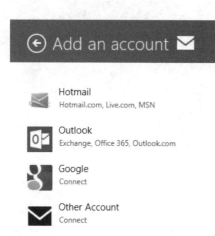

Figure 21-27 Mail can access all of your email accounts.

Rather than configuring Mail with more than one account, consider forwarding all your mail to a single account. For more information, read "Centralizing your email services" later in this chapter.

Learning to live without POP

Mail in Windows 8.1 can download your messages using only IMAP. That's different from the mail clients included with earlier versions of Windows, which supported both IMAP and POP (also called POP3).

You're not missing much, because POP is an outdated protocol that isn't well suited to the modern world. POP downloads messages from the server to the local computer, creating a copy of the message. Most POP clients also remove the message from the server. Creating a local copy of every email message creates a couple of challenges:

- It fills up your PC's drive. Over time, mail storage can consume many, many gigabytes of free space (especially if you don't regularly clean your spam folder).

- It takes longer to download. When you use IMAP, mail doesn't download attachments until after you view the message. When you use POP, mail has to download the entire message, including all attachments. You'll discover how frustrating this is the first time you're waiting for an important message and someone sends you a 10 megabyte (MB) picture of their cat that you have to watch download for several minutes.

- It doesn't allow you to synchronize messages across multiple devices. Most people check their email from several places, including their smartphone and their PC. If you use POP, Mail will remove the messages from the server, preventing you from reading them from your phone.

Centralizing your email services

Now that you hate POP as much as I do, what can you do if your mail server doesn't support IMAP? That should be an extremely rare situation, but if that's the case for you, you can use an email service that downloads messages from your POP server.

This is also useful if you regularly check more than one email account. Instead of separately logging in to each email account, forward all your messages to a single account.

For example, you can configure Windows Live Hotmail or Outlook online to download messages from your POP server. Then, you can configure Mail (and your other email clients) to connect to Hotmail or Outlook online. To do this, open your account settings and then select Sending/Receiving Email From Other Accounts. As shown in Figure 21-28, you can add accounts to check email and use different accounts to send email.

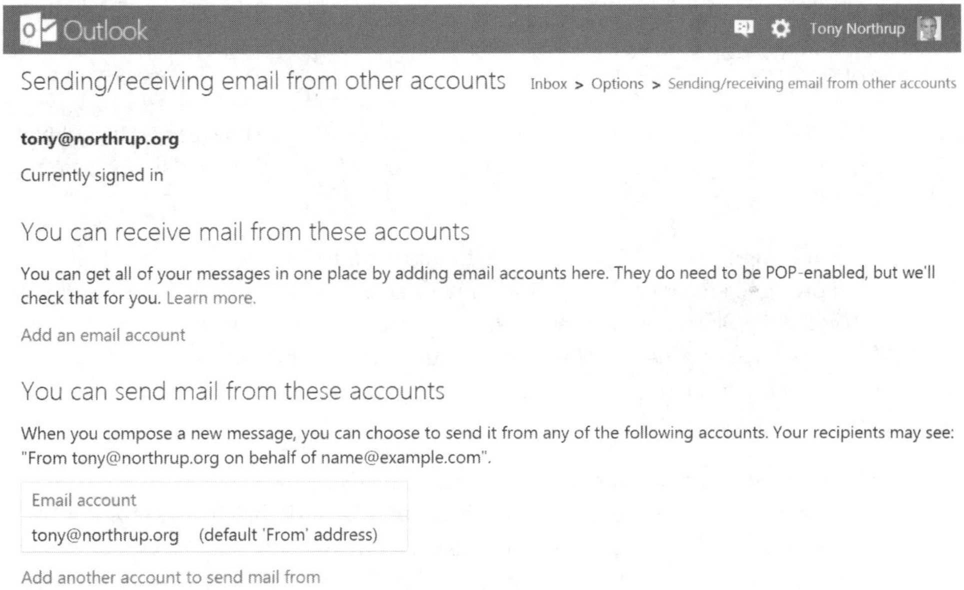

Figure 21-28 Hotmail, Outlook, and other email services can move messages from all your accounts to a single server.

Other email services, including Office 365, Gmail, and Google Apps, support downloading email from other services.

File hosting

Email attachments have size limits, and those size limits depend on both the sender and the recipient's email servers. So, there's no single size limit.

Most email services can send messages with attachments up to 8 MB in size. Some allow larger files, while some only allow smaller files.

When you need to send larger files, you'll need file hosting. The Microsoft solution to this is SkyDrive, as discussed in Chapter 13, "Using SkyDrive." SkyDrive is integrated throughout Windows 8.1, making it simple to share large files across the Internet. Chapter 13 also discusses third-party file-hosting alternatives.

Web hosting

Many small businesses also need web hosting. Individuals often needed web hosting in the past, but today, sites like Facebook.com and YouTube.com take care of most people's hosting needs.

If you also run a small business, you might still need to host a website. If you're not familiar with setting up a website, hire a website designer from a site such as *elance.com*. They can handle everything for you.

If you're familiar with HTML and CSS, or you want to be, you can simply find a web hosting provider. I recommend most small businesses seek out a WordPress hosting provider. WordPress is a very popular and free web hosting application that supports thousands of different plug-ins that add features to your website. WordPress is perfect for making mostly static websites, but it also has amazing blogging capabilities if you plan to regularly add new content to your website.

Naturally, you should purchase your own domain name (as discussed in the section "Email" earlier in this chapter) for your business website. Your domain name registrar will try very hard to sell you web hosting services, but they're rarely the best value. You can host your website with any provider, and although the steps you take to configure your site are outside the scope of this book, your web designer should have no problem setting it up.

Setting up ad hoc, Bluetooth, and mobile networks

Ad hoc networking. 547   3G/4G mobile broadband. 559

Bluetooth. 554

Chapter 21, "Setting up a home or small office network," described the types of home networking we rely on every day to keep our PCs connected to the Internet, including connecting to wireless hotspots. This chapter, on the other hand, covers less frequently used networking technologies:

- **Ad hoc networking**   Connect two PCs to each other wirelessly. This is good for sharing files between PCs when you travel.

- **Bluetooth**   Connect your PC to wireless accessories such as keyboards, mouse devices, and headphones. You can even use Bluetooth to transfer files between PCs and devices.

- **3G/4G mobile broadband**   Along with a service agreement with a wireless broadband provider, keep your mobile PC connected wherever you go (within range of a wireless signal).

Ad hoc networking

PCs connect to wireless access points most of the time. You probably don't travel with a wireless access point, however. If you need to connect two PCs together when there isn't a wireless access point around, you can use ad hoc networking. You can also use that same ad hoc network to share an Internet connection, which is incredibly useful in hotels where you might otherwise have to pay separately for each device connected to their network.

▶ **Creating an ad hoc network**   Watch the video at *http://aka.ms/WinIO/adhoc*.

Creating an ad hoc wireless network

Not all wireless devices support ad hoc networking, but most seem to. To determine whether your PC supports ad hoc networks, open a command prompt with administrative privileges, which you can do by selecting Command Prompt (Admin) from the WinX menu, and then run the command **netsh wlan show drivers**. If the Hosted Network Supported line shows Yes, then your PC supports creating an ad hoc network. The following shows the output.

```
C:\>netsh wlan show drivers

Interface name: Wi-Fi
    Driver                 : Intel(R) Centrino(R) Advanced-N 6230
    Vendor                 : Intel Corporation
    Provider               : Microsoft
    Date                   : 10/7/2011
    Version                : 14.2.1.3
    INF file               : C:\WINDOWS\INF\netwns64.inf
    Files                  : 2 total
                             C:\WINDOWS\system32\DRIVERS\NETwNs64.sys
                             C:\WINDOWS\system32\drivers\vwifibus.sys
    Type                   : Native Wi-Fi Driver
    Radio types supported  : 802.11a 802.11b 802.11g
    FIPS 140-2 mode supported : Yes
    802.11w Management Frame Protection supported : No
    Hosted network supported  : Yes
```

Inside OUT

Quickly opening an administrative command prompt

If you're a keyboard jockey like I am, you can get much more done if you learn keyboard shortcuts for common tasks. To quickly open an administrative command prompt in Windows 8.1, press the following keys: Windows+X, A, Alt+Y. If you disable User Access Control (UAC), you don't need the final Alt+Y.

Windows 7 provided graphical tools to create ad hoc networks. However, with Windows 8.1, you need to run commands at a command prompt with administrative privileges. Open the command prompt and run these commands, replacing *<name>* and *<password>*:

```
netsh wlan set hostednetwork mode=allow ssid=<name> key=<password>

netsh wlan start hostednetwork
```

For example, you might run the following command:

```
C:\>netsh wlan set hostednetwork mode=allow ssid=QuickNet key=mG9s5Unx
The hosted network mode has been set to allow.
The SSID of the hosted network has been successfully changed.
The user key passphrase of the hosted network has been successfully changed.

C:\>netsh wlan start hostednetwork
The hosted network started.
```

TROUBLESHOOTING

When I set up an ad hoc network, I get the message, "The hosted network couldn't be started"

If you see this error message, run the command **devmgmt.msc** at the command prompt to open Device Manager. You can access Device Manager from the Computer Management console, too.

With Device Manager open, right-click Network Adapters and then click Scan For Hardware Changes.

Now return to your administrative command prompt and rerun the command **netsh wlan start hostednetwork**.

As shown in Figure 22-1, the new (QuickNet) network appears in the Network And Sharing Center.

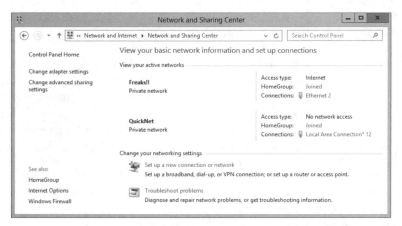

Figure 22-1 Use ad hoc networking to turn your PC into a wireless access point.

Now you'll be able to connect to the network from other wireless devices using the SSID and password that you specified, just as if it were a wireless access point. Once connected, you should be able to connect to other Windows PCs by name and by using homegroups.

When you no longer need the network, run the following command at the administrative command prompt to stop it: **netsh wlan stop hostednetwork**.

CHAPTER 22

TROUBLESHOOTING

I can't find the other computer on my ad hoc network

If you manage to connect to the ad hoc network but can't find shared files or printers, try connecting by using the IP address. From the computer sharing the resources, open a command prompt and run the command **ipconfig**. Make a note of the IPv4 address.

On the computer that you want to use to access the shared resources, open File Explorer. In the address bar, type \\<*ip_address*> and press Enter. You should be able to see the shared resources.

Specifying two backslashes and the IP address bypasses the name resolution process, which can be a bit unreliable on networks without a DNS server.

Sharing an Internet connection

You can also use an ad hoc network to share an Internet connection. This is useful when you're at a hotel that only supports a single Internet connection per room, but you have up to 20 devices that need to share the connection.

I know it might sound silly that you'd travel with multiple wireless devices, but for me, I typically travel with a mobile PC and a smartphone that supports wireless, and then each person in my family has a wireless device that they want to use to access the Internet. Particularly when in foreign countries/regions, I can save quite a bit in data roaming fees if I set up my own ad hoc wireless network in the hotel room to share the hotel's Internet connection instead of having each person's smartphone connect to the Internet via a mobile data provider.

First, connect one computer to the Internet with a wired or wireless connection. You can use a single wireless adapter to both connect to the Internet and create an ad hoc network to share the connection. Then, follow the instructions in the section "Creating an ad hoc wireless network." Finally, share the Internet connection by following these steps:

1. In Network And Sharing Center, click Change Adapter Settings.

2. In the Network Connections window, make note of the name of your ad hoc network adapter name. It shows the SSID you specified, and it's not the name of your normal Wi-Fi adapter. For example, in Figure 22-2, it's Local Area Connection* 12. Don't do anything with it, just remember the name for the next steps.

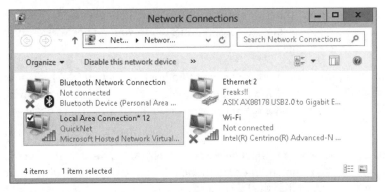

Figure 22-2 You must identify the adapter name Windows assigns to your ad hoc wireless network.

3. Right-click your Internet connection (Ethernet 2 in Figure 22-2), and then click Properties.

4. Select the Sharing tab in the Ethernet 2 Properties dialog box. As shown in Figure 22-3, select Allow Other Network Users To Connect Through This Computer's Internet Connection. In the Home Networking Connection list, select the network adapter you identified in step 2, and then click OK.

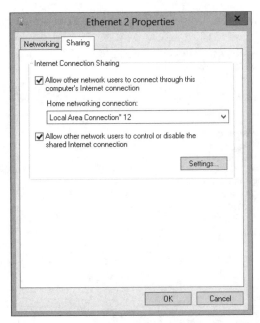

Figure 22-3 Use Internet Connection Sharing to share your Internet access.

CHAPTER 22

You can now connect other wireless devices to your ad hoc network and access the Internet. If any wireless devices were previously connected to your ad hoc wireless network, disconnect them and then reconnect them.

This process turns your PC into a Network Address Translation (NAT) server and DHCP server, as described in Chapter 21, "Setting up a home or small office network." In many cases, even the PC's wired Internet adapter will have a private IP address. That's okay; you can have NAT within NAT.

If you're curious about the inner workings of Internet Connection Sharing (ICS), run **ipconfig /all** at a command prompt on the PC sharing the Internet connection and then on the clients. You'll find that the PC sharing the Internet connection has separate IP addresses for the Internet and private links. The private link will always be 192.168.137.1. Any computers connecting to the Internet will have an IP address in the range 192.168.137.127 to 192.168.137.255 and will have 192.168.137.1 as their default gateway and DNS server.

You might want to change these IP addresses if you are replacing an existing router and don't want to renumber the clients. You can change these IP addresses by modifying several registry entries on the Windows 8.1 PC that will be sharing the connection. Modifying registry entries isn't common in Windows 8.1; most settings are now defined using Group Policy. However, if you're an old-school Windows user like I am, you probably already know the registry well, and you probably hate it, too.

To modify a registry entry, launch the Registry Editor. From the Start screen, type **regedit** and then press Enter. Next, browse to HKEY_LOCAL_MACHINE\SYSTEM\CurrentControlSet\ Services\SharedAccess\Parameters, as shown in Figure 22-4.

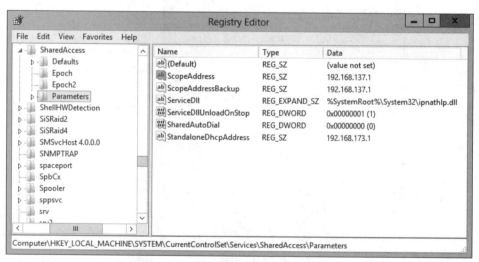

Figure 22-4 Use the Registry Editor to change the IP address that ICS uses.

To change the IP address ICS uses, modify the following values by double-clicking them:

- **ScopeAddress**   Set this to the private IP address that you want the PC sharing the Internet connection to have on your ad hoc network.

- **StandaloneDhcpAddress**   Set this to the same IP address.

Windows 8.1 automatically figures out the IP addresses to assign to clients and the subnet mask based on the IP address you choose. In other words, if you set the ScopeAddress to 10.1.1.1, ICS will assign clients addresses on the 10.1.1.0 network with a subnet mask of 255.255.255.0. ICS always uses a subnet mask of 255.255.255.0.

Easier ways to share an Internet connection

The previous sections described how to share an Internet connection using nothing but a wireless PC running Windows 8.1. The steps are rather complicated, though: you need to open an administrative command prompt, type a bunch of commands (which won't be easy on a tablet), modify adapter properties to share a connection, and finally connect to the wireless network.

There are a couple of easier ways. Still using only Windows 8.1, you can run the Connectify Hotspot desktop app, available at *http://www.connectify.me/*. As shown in Figure 22-5, the free version works great. When prompted, be sure to allow Connectify Hotspot to communicate through Windows Firewall. After installation, you can start Connectify Hotspot from the Start screen and manage it from the desktop.

You can also bring a router with you. You could simply unplug your home router and bring it with you when you travel, though it might take up more room in your suitcase than you're willing to sacrifice. As an alternative, you can buy a travel router for US$12–$50. Either way, just plug your router into your hotel's Internet connection and then connect your devices to your router to share the connection.

CHAPTER 22

Figure 22-5 Use Connectify Hotspot to simplify sharing an Internet connection.

Bluetooth

Bluetooth is a low-power, low-speed, and short-range (about 30 feet) networking technology. The low power makes it ideal for mobile devices because it doesn't drain too much of their battery power. The low speed and short range limit the use of the technology to short network communications. As a result, Bluetooth is primarily used to connect wireless accessories such as keyboards and mouse devices to mobile PCs.

PCs and Bluetooth accessories connect via the pairing process. Pairing a PC and a Bluetooth device is an authentication process. Basically, the pairing process prevents the guy sitting next to you at the café from controlling your PC with his mouse (accidentally or deliberately).

Pairing can occur only when both the Bluetooth device and the PC are in discoverable mode. Discoverable mode causes Bluetooth to actively look for other devices in discoverable mode. Bluetooth ignores any devices that aren't in discoverable mode.

▶ **Pairing Bluetooth accessories** Watch the video at *http://aka.ms/WinIO/bluetooth*.

Pairing Bluetooth accessories

To add a Bluetooth accessory, first put the accessory in discoverable mode. Check the accessory's manual for specific instructions, but typically there's a button you need to press. Sometimes, you need to press and hold the button. On smartphones, you should find the Bluetooth section of the settings.

On your PC, select PC & Devices from PC Settings, select Devices, and then select Add A Device. As shown in Figure 22-6, Windows will display any nearby Bluetooth devices that are in discoverable mode. Select a device to connect to it.

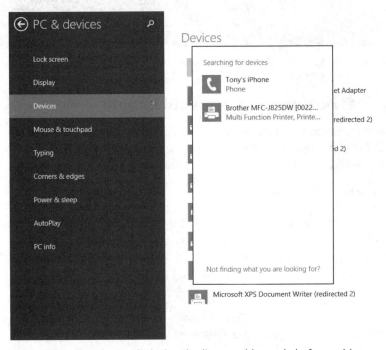

Figure 22-6 Put Bluetooth devices in discoverable mode before pairing.

Next, Windows 8.1 might ask you to perform some sort of authentication. This might involve typing a code into a keyboard or, as shown in Figure 22-7, confirming that two codes match. This authentication process helps prevent a sneaky person within a few feet of you from intercepting your connection.

You don't need to remove a Bluetooth device when you're done with it. Simply leave it configured, and it'll be available the next time you want to use it. If you do want to remove a Bluetooth pairing, select PC & Devices from PC Settings, select Devices, select the device, and then select the – symbol in the upper-right corner.

Figure 22-7 Windows 8.1 often needs to authenticate Bluetooth pairings.

Sending files between PCs across Bluetooth

You can use Bluetooth to send files between two PCs. This is a clumsy and slow process (a maximum of 721 Kbps), but it's an effective way to send a file or two when other forms of networking aren't available and you don't have a USB flash drive to exchange files.

The process involves five high-level steps:

1. **Enable discovery on one of the PCs**   To pair the two PCs, you need to make one of them discoverable. From the Start screen, search for **bluetooth** and then select Change Bluetooth Settings. In the Bluetooth Settings dialog box, select Allow Bluetooth Devices To Find This Computer, as shown in Figure 22-8. Click OK.

2. **Pair the two PCs**   On the other PC, select PC & Devices from PC Settings, select Devices, and then select Add A Device. Choose the other PC. Then, type the passcode provided, as shown in Figure 22-9. Click Next to complete the pairing.

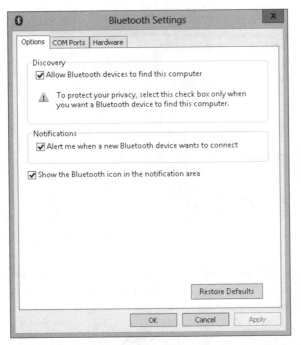

Figure 22-8 To pair two PCs, you must make one of them discoverable.

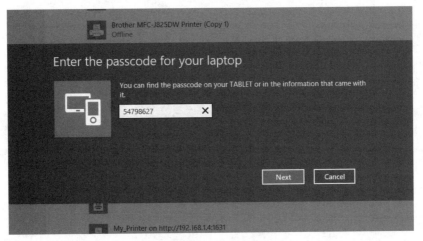

Figure 22-9 Type the passcode to pair two PCs.

3. **Start receiving a file on one PC**   On the receiving PC, open the desktop. Expand the
    system tray icon next to the clock. Click the Bluetooth icon, and then select Receive A
    File, as shown in Figure 22-10. Windows opens the Bluetooth File Transfer wizard to the
    Waiting For A Connection page.

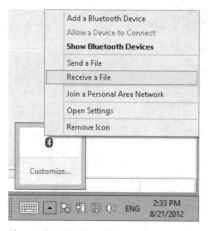

Figure 22-10 Click the Bluetooth icon and then select Receive A File.

4. **Send the file from the other PC** On the sending PC, click the Bluetooth icon in the system tray and then click Send A File. As shown in Figure 22-11, select the PC to send the file to and then click Next. Then, select the file you want to transfer.

Figure 22-11 You can use Bluetooth to transfer files . . . slowly.

5. **Save the file**   On the receiving PC, choose where you want to save the file and click Finish, as shown in Figure 22-12.

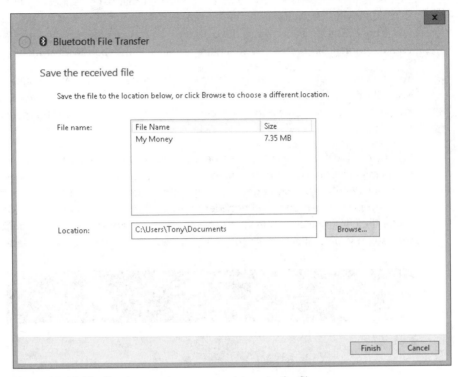

Figure 22-12 Finally, choose where you want to save the file.

If you need to send multiple files, compress them into a ZIP archive before transferring them. You can use the same process for transferring files to other devices, including smartphones. You might need to run a special app to transfer files to your smartphone, however.

3G/4G mobile broadband

Windows 8.1 has built-in support for 3G and 4G wireless broadband. Of course, your mobile computer needs to have a mobile broadband radio and a SIM card, and you'll need a service agreement from a mobile broadband provider such as AT&T or Verizon Wireless.

Windows 8.1 automatically detects the hardware and, if the mobile broadband adapter was designed for Windows 8.1, will even automatically download your service provider's app from the Store. With that capability, you'll be able to click View My Account under your mobile broadband network and open the mobile broadband provider's app.

Windows 8.1 apps can be made aware of whether your current connection might charge you for data. They can then make intelligent choices to minimize the bandwidth usage. For example, if you're connected to a metered mobile broadband connection and run an app that downloads video from the Internet, the app could choose to stream a lower quality (and thus lower bandwidth) version of the video. When you connect to a nonmetered Wi-Fi network, it could automatically switch you to a higher quality, higher bandwidth video stream.

You manage mobile broadband connections alongside standard Wi-Fi connections. For example, if you enable airplane mode, Windows 8.1 also turns off your mobile broadband connection. The Wi-Fi network overview in Chapter 21 applies to most aspects of using mobile broadband.

Windows 8.1 will configure mobile broadband connections as metered connections by default, which minimizes the amount of unnecessary communications sent across the connection. For example, Windows 8.1 won't download updates while you're connected to a metered connection. If your mobile broadband provider doesn't charge you for data usage (or if you're always under the amount included in your service), open PC Settings, Network, Connections, and then select your connection. As shown in Figure 22-13, turn off Set As A Metered Connection.

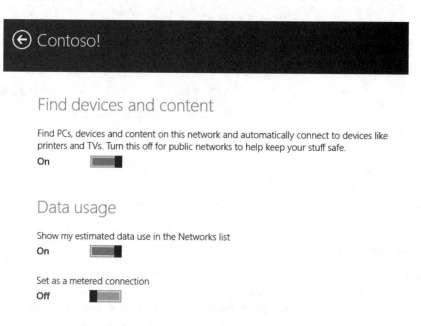

Figure 22-13 Change a mobile broadband connection to nonmetered if you are not charged for data.

When multiple network connections are available, Windows 8.1 intelligently chooses which network to send data across. For example, if you have a nonmetered Wi-Fi connection available, Windows 8.1 will use that connection instead of sending data across your metered mobile broadband network. If you move out of range of the Wi-Fi network, Windows 8.1 will automatically use the mobile broadband network, providing you seamless connectivity while minimizing your cost.

You can monitor the amount of data a connection is using by expanding a mobile broadband network from the networks panel. To view how much metered bandwidth individual apps are using, launch Task Manager, select More Details, and then select the App History tab. As shown in Figure 22-14, clicking the Metered Network column heading sorts the apps from most to least bandwidth used.

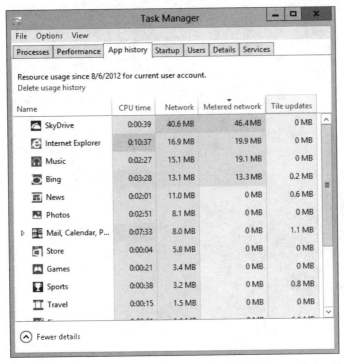

Figure 22-14 Use the App History tab of Task Manager to determine which apps use the most mobile bandwidth.

If your PC doesn't include built-in mobile broadband, you can purchase a USB mobile broadband adapter. Most smartphones also support tethering, which allows your PC to use your smartphone's Internet connection. Tethering connects the PC to the smartphone by using a USB cable, Wi-Fi, or Bluetooth. You might need to pay extra for tethering support.

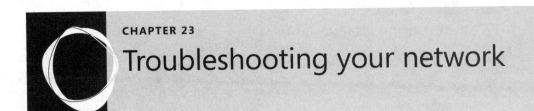

Troubleshooting your network

Troubleshooting tools 563   Troubleshooting network performance problems 579

The home network troubleshooting process 577

All communications with the outside world have been cut off. Your children are crying. Your spouse/partner is screaming. Even the family dog seems unsettled.

The start of a horror movie? No, it's even scarier. The Internet is down, and nobody knows why.

How will you know what your high school friend ate for breakfast? What will your son destroy without Xbox Live to keep him busy? Will you be the last person on earth to see that hilarious new meme with the dog talking on the telephone?

Fortunately, a powerful hero has risen to restore the Internet: you. Using some basic networking knowledge and the troubleshooting techniques described in this chapter, you can diagnose the cause of network problems (including complete outages and performance issues). In many cases, you might be able to solve them yourself. When you can't, you'll know who to call, and you can skip past the worst part of the tech support guy's script.

Troubleshooting tools

This section describes the most important tools for troubleshooting networks, in roughly the order you should use them. Windows has dozens of other network tools built in, but I'm only going to describe the few that you really need to know how to use. After I describe the tools, I'll give you a step-by-step process you can follow for troubleshooting most home network problems.

Restarting

"Have you tried turning it off and on again?"

That's a quote from *The IT Crowd*, a fantastic British comedy. The main characters work in the technical support department, and they greet every phone call with that line.

It's actually pretty sound advice. Restarting completes several tasks that can solve problems:

- It stops all running software, including software that might be running in the background and misbehaving.

- It unloads memory, temporarily solving memory leaks.

- It resets all network connections, curing intermittent problems caused by software or network conditions that might overload buffers.

- It reacquires network settings from the DHCP server, potentially retrieving updated settings.

- For modems, it causes them to redownload settings from your ISP and reassess signal levels, and that updated information might improve the reliability of the connection.

Restarting obviously won't solve recurring issues, but it should always be the first step you take to get yourself back online. If you later call tech support, it's going to be the first thing they make you do, anyway.

Restart your equipment in the following order:

1. Modem

2. Router

3. Wireless access points, switches, and bridges (if separate from your router)

4. PCs or other network devices

Network And Sharing Center

Windows 8.1 includes automated tools that can diagnose and fix many types of problems. Yes, the tools do more than tell you to turn everything off and on (though they really will tell you to do that).

If you're having a network problem, your first step in diagnosis is to open the Settings charm and check the network icon. If it shows a yellow triangle, as shown in Figure 23-1, that means Windows can't communicate with the Internet.

Now, from the Start screen, search for **network sharing center** and select Network And Sharing Center. Within Network And Sharing Center, the Access Type field shows your current connection level. In Figure 23-2, it is No Network Access.

Figure 23-1 A yellow icon means Windows doesn't have an Internet connection.

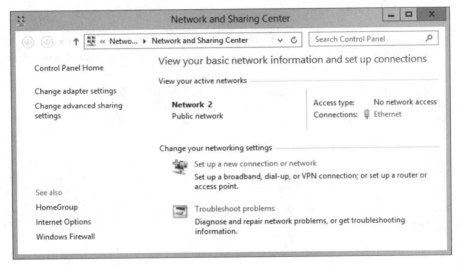

Figure 23-2 Access Type within Network And Sharing Center shows whether you can reach the local network or the Internet.

Access Type can have one of several different results:

- **No network access**   Windows can't access any network resources, including those on your local network. This means the problem is probably a PC configuration problem or a problem with your home network, including your wireless access point, router, or switch.

- **No Internet access**   Windows can communicate on your local network, but it can't reach the Internet. The problem could be with your PC's network configuration, your wireless access point or router, or with your ISP. You'll have to do some more trouble-shooting to determine the exact source of the problem.

- **Internet** Everything is working, and Windows can communicate on the Internet. If you're having a problem connecting to a website or some other network service, it's probably that specific website or service. Contact them directly if you can think of a way to communicate with someone other than over the Internet.

Note that it might take several minutes for Network And Sharing Center to determine that you have lost Internet access or reconnected to the Internet, so if your network status changes, give it a few minutes. You can use Ping to more quickly check your Internet access, as described later in this chapter.

That narrows the problem down, but it doesn't fix it, or even really tell you who to call. Your next step should be to use Network Diagnostics.

Network Diagnostics

You can open Network Diagnostics by clicking the Troubleshoot Problems link in the Network And Sharing Center. You'll see the prompt shown in Figure 23-3. Click Internet Connections.

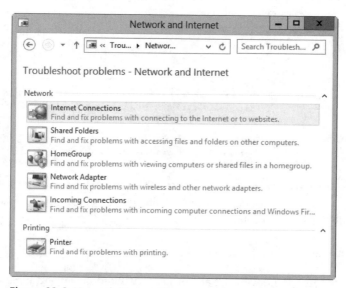

Figure 23-3 Network Diagnostics can solve many types of connection problems.

Click Next. Network Diagnostics will then give you a choice of how to diagnose the problem, as shown in Figure 23-4. If you're having general Internet problems, select the first option. If your problem is with a specific website, select the second option.

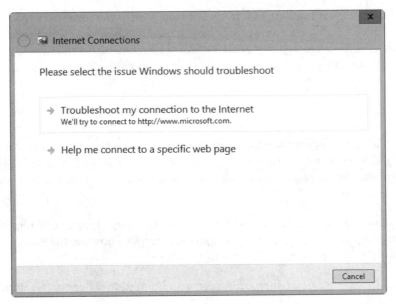

Figure 23-4 Network Diagnostics will attempt to connect to Microsoft.com.

Network Diagnostics will spend a few minutes trying different things. Eventually, it will show you the results, as shown in Figure 23-5. Naturally, you might see different results depending on the nature of your problem.

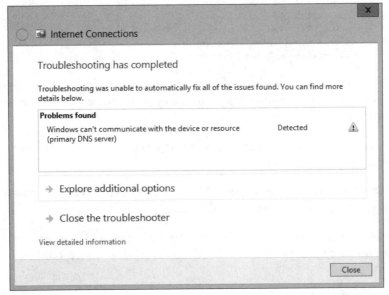

Figure 23-5 Network Diagnostics identified a problem connecting to the Internet.

Network Diagnostics isn't perfect. In fact, it's not even great. It will correctly diagnose a small portion of network problems, and it's really easy to use, so I do recommend that people try it after they've restarted everything. However, most of the time, you'll still have to do some manual troubleshooting to isolate your problem. The sections that follow describe some useful tools.

Ping

Ping is such a commonly used troubleshooting tool that it's become part of the modern vocabulary, at least among the somewhat geeky people I hang around. As a verb, ping means to quickly make contact—for example, "I'll ping you before I leave." Ping has even made it into the Urban Dictionary.

Ping is a command-line tool, so you need to open the Command Prompt desktop app to use it. As a reminder, you can quickly open a command prompt by opening the WinX menu and then clicking Command Prompt.

Use Ping by specifying a destination address on your home network or on the Internet. For example:

```
ping northrup.org
Pinging northrup.org [74.125.228.3] with 32 bytes of data:
Reply from 74.125.228.3: bytes=32 time=122ms TTL=52
Reply from 74.125.228.3: bytes=32 time=83ms TTL=52
Reply from 74.125.228.3: bytes=32 time=688ms TTL=52
Reply from 74.125.228.3: bytes=32 time=39ms TTL=52

Ping statistics for 74.125.228.3:
    Packets: Sent = 4, Received = 4, Lost = 0 (0% loss),
Approximate round trip times in milli-seconds:
    Minimum = 39ms, Maximum = 688ms, Average = 233ms
```

By default, Ping sends four messages to the destination. In the previous output, you can see that Ping got responses to all four messages, meaning the PC can successfully communicate with the destination.

Besides the fact that you can communicate with a single host, the Ping output tells you quite a bit about your network conditions:

- Your DNS server is properly configured and working, because Ping was able to resolve northrup.org to the IP address 74.125.228.3.

- All four pings succeeded, meaning packets are being sent and received reliably. At times, some packets might be dropped, indicating an unreliable connection.

- Your PC's network adapter, your home network, and your ISP's network are all working properly (at least for basic communications).

- The round trip time (RTT) between the PC and the northrup.org server averages 233 milliseconds (ms). That's a measure of the network latency, which measures the time it takes for communications to travel between two locations. In this example, the latency is moderately high.

- The quickest RTT was 39 ms and the longest 688 ms. That's a 1,700 percent difference, which means the network connection has very high jitter. Jitter is a measure of how much the latency varies.

That's quite a bit of information to extract from one command. The other common results you might get from Ping are Request Timed Out and Destination Host Unreachable (which usually mean the same thing), as the following example demonstrates:

```
ping microsoft.com
Pinging microsoft.com [64.4.11.37] with 32 bytes of data:
Request timed out.
Request timed out.
Request timed out.
Request timed out.

Ping statistics for 64.4.11.37:
    Packets: Sent = 4, Received = 0, Lost = 4 (100% loss),
```

These results could indicate one of several different conditions:

- You've completely messed up your home network.

- Your ISP is on a lunch break.

- Your neighbor with the backhoe didn't call the electric company before digging and has broken through a very important underground cable.

- The Internet has seen one too many cat photos and taken a much deserved vacation.

- Microsoft.com is offline.

- Microsoft.com doesn't reply to pings.

As you can see, you can tell a great deal from a successful ping, but almost nothing from a failed ping. In this example, the last condition is the true one, and there's no problem whatsoever. You simply can't ping Microsoft.com, because their server ignores the requests.

CHAPTER 23

For that reason, it's good to remember a destination that does return pings. I tend to use northrup.org, google.com, and yahoo.com because they reply to pings, they have servers everywhere, and they've never been offline when I've tested them.

Ping has several options, and you can view them all by running **ping –?** at a command prompt. The only one I use on a regular basis is –t, which keeps pinging a destination forever until you stop it by pressing Ctrl+C. For example, you can run the following command:

```
ping -t 8.8.8.8
```

The constant stream of pings is a good way to temporarily monitor your Internet connection and latency. For example, if you're waiting for your Internet connection to come back online, run that command and wait. Once you start seeing replies, your connection is back online. If you're having latency problems, you can run that command and see when the latency increases or decreases.

PathPing

Windows 8.1 includes a more powerful, if not as famous, tool: PathPing. PathPing sends separate ping requests to every router between your PC and the destination you specify, and it does this for several minutes to give you a better understanding of your current network conditions. PathPing, and network geeks, call the interconnected routers that forward communications between two points "hops."

Take a look at this example:

```
pathping microsoft.com

Tracing route to microsoft.com [64.4.11.37]
over a maximum of 30 hops:
  0  Win8Rules [192.168.2.7]
  1  192.168.2.1
  2  10.112.192.1
  3  static-206-53-95-130.cpe.contoso.com [206.53.95.130]
  4  static-206-53-95-3.cpe.contoso.com [206.53.95.3]
  5  ten10-4.ur1.rochester.nh.contoso.com [65.175.142.201]
  6  TBD-65-175-128-2.contoso.com [65.175.128.2]
  7  te0-6-0-2.ccr21.bos01.atlas.fabrikam.com [38.122.126.73]
  8  te0-0-0-3.mpd21.jfk02.atlas.fabrikam.com [154.54.6.2]
  9  te0-5-0-1.ccr21.jfk07.atlas.fabrikam.com [154.54.80.182]
 10     *        *        *
Computing statistics for 225 seconds...
```

Line 0 indicates that PathPing was able to communicate with my own PC, named Win8Rules. While it's a bad sign if you talk to yourself, it's a good sign when your PC is able to.

Line 1, 192.168.2.1, is my router, also known as my default gateway. The first hop outside your own PC is always your default gateway. If that responds correctly, you know your home network is working properly, and any problems you're having are either between your house and your ISP or on the Internet.

Line 2, 10.112.192.1, is the router my ISP uses to connect my home to their network. The second hop outside your own PC should always belong to your ISP. If that's the first hop that fails, then your ISP is having a problem, and you should call them.

The last hop in this output, line 10, has three asterisks (*). This indicates that the three requests PathPing sent to it didn't get returned. As we learned earlier, Microsoft.com doesn't reply to pings. However, because lines 0-9 worked, we know our Internet connection is working properly.

After a few minutes, PathPing will compute performance statistics and display them to you:

```
                Source to Here   This Node/Link
Hop   RTT       Lost/Sent = Pct  Lost/Sent = Pct  Address
 0                                                 Win8Rules [192.168.2.7]
                                  0/ 100 =   0%    |
 1    3ms       0/ 100 =   0%     0/ 100 =   0%    192.168.2.1
                                  0/ 100 =   0%    |
 2    20ms      0/ 100 =   0%     0/ 100 =   0%    10.112.192.1
                                  0/ 100 =   0%    |
 3    31ms      0/ 100 =   0%     0/ 100 =   0%    static-206-53-95-130.cpe.contoso.com
[206.53.95.130]
                                  0/ 100 =   0%    |
 4    27ms      0/ 100 =   0%     0/ 100 =   0%    static-206-53-95-3.cpe.contoso.com
[206.53.95.3]
                                  0/ 100 =   0%    |
 5    39ms      0/ 100 =   0%     0/ 100 =   0%    ten10-4.ur1.rochester.nh.contoso.com
[65.175.142.201]
                                  0/ 100 =   0%    |
 6    37ms      0/ 100 =   0%     0/ 100 =   0%    TBD-65-175-128-2.contoso.com
[65.175.128.2]
                                  0/ 100 =   0%    |
 7    27ms      0/ 100 =   0%     0/ 100 =   0%    te0-6-0-2.ccr21.fabrikam.com
[38.122.126.73]
                                  0/ 100 =   0%    |
 8    41ms      0/ 100 =   0%     0/ 100 =   0%    te0-0-0-3.atlas.fabrikam.com [154.54.6.2]
                                  0/ 100 =   0%    |
 9    41ms      0/ 100 =   0%     0/ 100 =   0%    te0-5-0-1.atlas.fabrikam.com
[154.54.80.182]
Trace complete.
```

The performance output is more difficult to read. Each numbered hop corresponds to the hops listed in the previous output.

The second column, RTT, is the average round trip time, which measures the latency. This gives you a tremendous amount of information about the performance of the network between you and the destination. You can tell roughly how much latency each hop is adding to your total round trip time. In this case, my home router is adding 3 ms of latency, and most of the rest of the latency is occurring in the second and third hops—on my ISP's own network. The latency is still fairly small, however. If that RTT number were more than 250 ms, I might call to complain.

Notice that the RTT for hop 7 is actually lower than for hop 6. The RTTs aren't particularly accurate; they're only useful as a general gauge. Latency varies quite a bit on every network. Additionally, some routers don't respond to pings immediately, which can make their RTT higher than the true latency.

If your local network is working but your Internet connection is down, PathPing output will resemble the following:

```
Tracing route to microsoft.com [64.4.11.37]
over a maximum of 30 hops:
  0  Win8Rules [192.168.2.7]
  1  192.168.2.1 reports: Destination host unreachable
```

As you can see, PathPing was able to communicate with the local PC and your local router, but it couldn't get past your router. The problem could be your router configuration, but it's probably your ISP. Go ahead and give your ISP a call. If you're the patient type, you might just wait for them to detect the problem and fix it—they probably already know about the issue, because most ISPs monitor that type of problem very closely.

PortQry

Both Ping and PathPing have a serious weakness: not every host replies to pings. For example, Ping isn't a good way to determine if www.microsoft.com is working because www.microsoft.com never responds to pings, whether it's working or not.

PortQry is a better way to determine whether a specific server on the Internet is working. Unfortunately, it's not included with Windows. However, you can download PortQry from *http://www.microsoft.com/en-us/download/confirmation.aspx?id=17148* and save it to a folder on your local computer.

Like Ping and PathPing, PortQry is a command-line tool. Before you can run the command, you should change the command prompt's current folder by running the command CD. For example, if you extracted the tool to its default folder of C:\PortQryV2, you would run the command **cd \PortQryV2**.

Once you've switched to the appropriate folder, run the command using the –n parameter to specify a name in the format **portqry –n <hostname>**.

The following example shows that the server at Microsoft.com is responding:

```
portqry -n microsoft.com

Querying target system called:

 microsoft.com

Attempting to resolve name to IP address...


Name resolved to 65.55.58.201

querying...

TCP port 80 (http service): LISTENING
```

We know the web server is responding because the last line shows LISTENING, which indicates that it's listening for incoming connections. That doesn't tell us that the web server software is working properly, but the operating system is listening for connections.

If you only specify a name, PortQry assumes you want to check for a working web server. There are other types of servers on the Internet, such as mail servers. You can add the –e parameter to PortQry to check a different port number.

For example, if you want to check whether a mail server is running, use TCP port 25 (for an SMTP server). The following command verifies that the Microsoft SMTP server is listening for connections on port 25, and even shows you the message the server sends upon an initial connection:

```
portqry -n mail.messaging.microsoft.com -e 25

Querying target system called:

 mail.messaging.microsoft.com

Attempting to resolve name to IP address...


Name resolved to 216.32.180.22

querying...

TCP port 25 (smtp service): LISTENING

Data returned from port:
220 VA3EHSMHS031.bigfish.com Microsoft ESMTP MAIL Service ready at Wed, 22 Aug 2012
20:07:24 +0000
```

CHAPTER 23

Inside OUT
Finding mail servers

You can use Nslookup to find the names of an organization's mail servers. At a command prompt, run the command **nslookup –type=mx** *<domain_name>*. For example, to find the name of Microsoft's mail server, I ran this command. Your output won't match mine; this is just an example:

```
nslookup -type=mx microsoft.com
Server:  mydnsserver.contoso.com
Address:  10.15.3.12

Non-authoritative answer:
microsoft.com  MX preference = 10, mail exchanger = mail.messaging.microsoft.com
```

The last line reveals the name of the mail server: mail.messaging.microsoft.com.

Mail servers use this technique to find each other on the Internet. In other words, when you send a message to tony@northrup.org, your mail server needs to communicate directly with the northrup.org mail server. To do that, it performs a DNS lookup for a special type of DNS record, the MX record, which stands for Mail Exchange. Every MX record in a domain points to an SMTP server that is ready to receive messages for anyone at that domain.

Network Monitor

While tools like Ping, PathPing, and PortQry are useful for troubleshooting network connectivity problems, many network problems impact only a single application. When network problems occur at the application layer, you can analyze and isolate the problem with Network Monitor.

Network Monitor is a protocol analyzer, which is a tool network administrators use to examine individual network packets. Besides being a useful troubleshooting tool, it's really fun to peer inside your network to see how different apps communicate.

You can install Network Monitor for free from Microsoft.com. The current version is 3.4 and is available at *http://www.microsoft.com/en-us/download/details.aspx?id=4865*, but the program is updated regularly, so search the Internet for "download network monitor" to be sure you get the latest version.

Once you install Network Monitor, you need to log out and then log in before you can start it. After starting Network Monitor, begin recording by clicking the New Capture button and then clicking Start. As shown in Figure 23-6, you'll discover that Windows is constantly communicating on the network even when you don't have any apps running.

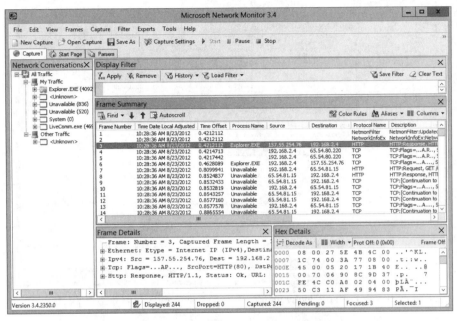

Figure 23-6 Use Network Monitor to capture and analyze network communications.

To use Network Monitor to analyze an app's communications, start a capture and then perform an action in an app. Then, return to Network Monitor and click Stop.

With the capture made, you can take your time and analyze the communications that occurred while you were recording. In the left pane, select the process name that you want to analyze. This isn't the same as the app name, but it's usually pretty obvious. For example, Internet Explorer is IExplore.exe.

Select individual frames in the Frame Summary pane, and view their details in the Frame Details pane. You can close the Hex Details and Display Filter panes to save screen space.

Figure 23-7 shows Network Monitor analyzing HTTP communications from Internet Explorer retrieving the default page of Microsoft.com. As you can see, Internet Explorer sent the HTTP command GET /en-us/default.aspx. The Frame Details pane also reveals the source and destination IP addresses and port numbers.

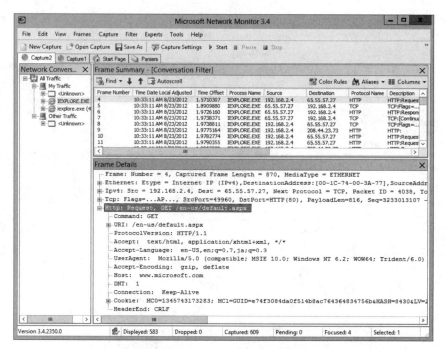

Figure 23-7 You can use Network Monitor to analyze individual web requests.

Figure 23-8 shows the response from the Microsoft.com web server, an HTTP Ok message, along with the compressed contents of the webpage. Examining the frames recorded by Network Monitor, you can see that retrieving the webpage required dozens of individual requests to several different locations on the Internet, which is typical of modern webpages.

This example shows a healthy web request. In a troubleshooting scenario, you'd probably be examining an app that wasn't working properly. Examining individual packets can reveal that the app attempts to communicate with a server that isn't responding, that the client's request is failing an authentication attempt, or that the server requires the client to be upgraded.

Network Monitor is not a simple tool to use. However, when an app is experiencing problems communicating across a network, it's the best way to examine every detail of the communications.

CHAPTER 23

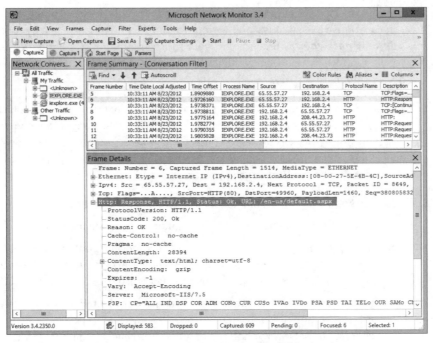

Figure 23-8 Network Monitor reveals the details of individual web responses.

The home network troubleshooting process

There's no one process that you can follow to troubleshoot all network problems. However, this straightforward process can isolate or solve most common home networking issues. After each step, test to see if your network is working again, and stop if your problem is solved.

▶ **Troubleshooting a failed Internet connection** Watch the video at *http://aka.ms/WinIO/ homenetwork*.

1. Restart your modem, router, switches, wireless access points, and PCs in that order.

2. Test the Internet from different PCs or network devices. If the network is offline for all of them, continue with the next step. If some devices can connect and others cannot, jump to step 6.

3. Open a command prompt and run **ipconfig**. Identify the default gateway. Then, run the command **ping <*default_gateway*>**. For example, you might run **ping 192.168.1.1**. If you receive replies, the problem is probably with your modem or your ISP's network. Call your ISP for technical support and stop working through this process. If you do not receive replies from ping, continue on to the next step.

4. If you performed the previous step from a wireless PC, connect it to a wired network if you can, or use a PC that is wired to your router. Then, repeat the test by running **ping** **<*default_gateway*>**. If it fails again, your router is either misconfigured or failed; if you've recently changed the configuration, change it back. If you receive replies to your ping, continue to the next step.

5. You now know that your problem is specific to your wireless network. If you've recently changed the configuration, change it back. If you haven't changed the configuration and it previously worked properly, contact your wireless access point's technical support or seek help from the Internet, as described in Chapter 8, "Obtaining help and support." You can stop working through this process.

6. You now know that the problem is specific to a single PC. Follow these steps:

   a. If you've recently changed that PC's configuration, change it back.

   b. If the problem persists, verify that the IP settings are configured to Obtain An IP Address Automatically and Obtain DNS Server Address Automatically, as described in Chapter 21, "Setting up a home or small office network."

   c. If the problem persists, run Device Manager from Settings, expand Network Adapters, right-click your network adapter, and then click Properties. If available, click Roll Back Driver. If not, use another PC to check the Internet for an updated driver and install it. You can use a USB flash drive or memory card to transfer it to the PC without an Internet connection.

   d. If the problem persists, it's likely that your network adapter has failed. Attempt to connect a different network adapter to the computer, such as a USB network adapter. If that solves the problem, you've confirmed that the network adapter has failed. Contact your PC's technical support to have it replaced if it's under warranty.

   e. If the problem persists, there is an incompatibility between your PC and your router or wireless access point. For example, the router or wireless access point might be configured to block communications from that PC. Reset your router or wireless access point to its default settings (in particular, turn off any vendor-specific performance enhancements) and attempt to reconnect.

   f. If the problem persists, seek help for additional troubleshooting, as described in Chapter 21.

Troubleshooting network performance problems

At times, your network won't completely fail. Instead, it will slowly limp along. Pages will seem to take forever to load, file transfers will take longer than they should, or video streaming will repeatedly pause while it buffers.

Network performance problems can be introduced in two places: your Internet connection (which your ISP manages) or your home network (which you manage). The sections that follow describe how to measure and optimize the performance of both parts of your Internet connection.

Measuring and optimizing Internet performance

Measuring Internet performance is simple; visit *http://speedtest.net/*. As shown in Figure 23-9, the website measures your performance by sending data to and from your PC. In my experience, it's quick and accurate.

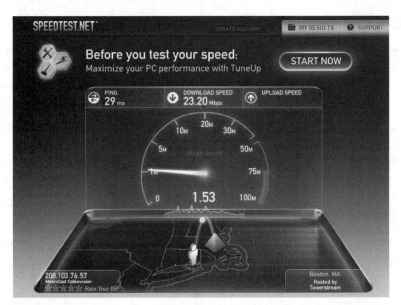

Figure 23-9 Many websites offer free Internet speed tests.

Of course, unless you have your PC connected directly to your modem, it's not really measuring just your Internet performance. Instead, it's measuring the combined performance of both your home network and your Internet connection, and whichever is slower will limit your performance. In the IT world, we refer to this as the performance bottleneck.

To really test your Internet connection, connect a PC directly to your router with wired Ethernet. If the performance while connected to wired Ethernet is significantly better than the performance while connected to your wireless network, then your wireless network is limiting the connection of your Internet. For tips on getting the best performance out of your wireless network, read Chapter 21.

Your Internet performance is likely to vary throughout the day. Typically, after work hours on weekdays are the busiest times for residential ISPs, and as a result, you'll see the lowest speeds at those times. Unfortunately, those are also the times you're likely to be downloading files and streaming video.

There's probably nothing you personally can do to improve the performance of your Internet connection. You can try restarting your modem and router, but it probably won't help. Other than that, you can call your ISP to complain that your network performance doesn't match what they advertise, but they'll probably just tell you that your contract states that your performance will vary.

Measuring and optimizing local network performance

Most home users won't ever need to worry about the performance of their local network, because all their communications travel between their PC and the Internet. Local network performance is only important to those of us who transfer large files between two computers or who use tools such as Remote Desktop to remotely control a PC on their home network.

If you do care about local network performance and your network seems to be slow, the first step is to measure the network performance so you can determine whether the network is performing like it's supposed to. In other words, if your 100 Mbps wired network seems slow, but it's actually performing near the practical limit of 60 Mbps, then your network is doing the best it can, and there's nothing you can do to troubleshoot it. Instead, you would need to upgrade your network. Network design is discussed in Chapter 21.

If you have two PCs connected to your network, install LAN Speed Test v1.1.7 (the free version, available at *http://www.totusoft.com/lanspeed.html*) on the PC that seems slow. Click the button next to Folder Or Server IP field, and browse to a folder on a remote computer (for example, within Homegroup). Then, click Start Test and click OK.

Figure 23-10 shows the results on my home network, across both wired Ethernet and powerline network adapters. The only field you need to look at is Mbps. In Figure 23-10, the writing speed is 497 Mbps, and the reading speed is 576 Mbps.

Now that you know how fast your local network is, how can you determine whether it's performing as it should be, or whether there's a problem? Table 23-1 shows typical throughputs for different types of home networks. These aren't the stated bandwidth, or even the theoretical maximums, but rather the practical throughput that you can expect in a real-world

environment. With wireless networks, of course, distance, obstacles, and interference can drastically reduce the maximum throughput.

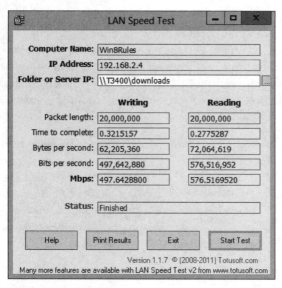

Figure 23-10 Use LAN Speed Test to determine the speed of your local network.

Table 23-1 Practical speeds of different home networks

Network type	Speed
802.11a	25 Mbps
802.11b	5 Mbps
802.11g (with 802.11b compatibility)	18 Mbps
802.11g (native mode)	25 Mbps
802.11n (with 802.11b/g compatibility)	80 Mbps
802.11n (native mode)	125 Mbps
100 Mbps wired Ethernet	65 Mbps
1000 Mbps (gigabit) wired Ethernet	650 Mbps
Powerline networking rated 85 Mbps	.5-10 Mbps
Powerline networking rated 200 Mbps	5-150 Mbps
Powerline networking rated 500 Mbps	30-200 Mbps

To optimize your network, follow the network design guidelines described in Chapter 21.

CHAPTER 23

Inside OUT

The wrong ways to test network performance

I've talked to many people confused about network performance because they used invalid metrics. It seems like you could trust the network hardware manufacturers, or even Windows, but you have to completely disregard the stated maximum speed of a link, especially with wireless connections. That includes the description Windows provides you. Just because Windows says your network link is 100 Mbps doesn't mean it's actually achievable.

Second, transferring large files isn't a good way to measure network performance. You can copy files between computers, and Windows will show you the transfer speed. For example, Figure 23-11 shows a transfer speed of 9.1 MB/s. Since there are 8 megabits (Mb) in one megabyte (MB), this transfer speed converts to about 73 Mbps. That might be the maximum throughput of the network, but it also might be the maximum read speed of the source's hard drive, or the maximum write speed of the destination's hard drive, factoring out any competing input/output from other apps.

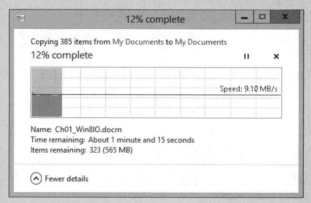

Figure 23-11 Copying files across a network doesn't necessarily measure your maximum network performance.

Sharing and managing files and printers

Using a homegroup. 583

Using folder sharing. 588

Granting permissions to files 592

Using shared printers. 593

If you have multiple PCs, you can share files and printers between them across your local network. This allows you to access the same resources no matter which PC you pick up or where you hang out in your house.

This chapter describes how to share files and printers. I'll cover using homegroups as well as how you can manually share files and printers. I'll also cover how to share your printer if you don't have a desktop PC you can connect it to.

Using a homegroup

The easiest way to share media (or any file, for that matter) between computers in your home is by using a homegroup. Homegroups share the documents, music, videos, folders, printers, and backup drives that you choose to share across your home network using only a password. With a homegroup, it doesn't matter who is logged on to a PC. As long as the PC is part of the homegroup, any logged-on user can access your shared network resources.

▶ **Sharing files in a homegroup** Watch the video at *http://aka.ms/WinIO/homegroup*.

Creating a homegroup

You can create only a single homegroup on your network. Therefore, you create a homegroup on one PC and then join that homegroup from every other PC. To create a homegroup, open PC Settings, select Network, and then select HomeGroup. Select which file types and resources you want to share, as shown in Figure 24-1. After creating the homegroup, open this same window to change the sharing settings.

To make browsing for shared files on other computers easier, don't share file types that you don't plan to store on that computer. For example, if you store all your music and videos on your desktop computer, share music and videos from only that computer and turn off sharing for music and videos on mobile computers that might connect only to those shared resources.

If you turn on sharing for Media Devices, digital media receivers (DMRs) will be able to play resources on your computer.

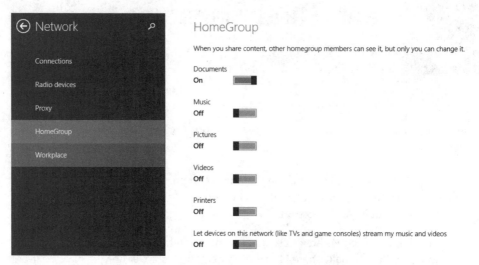

Figure 24-1 A homegroup gives you control over which resources you share.

At the bottom of the HomeGroup settings page, as shown in Figure 24-2, is a password that you must type when you join another computer to the homegroup. You don't need to memorize it; you can simply look it up on the settings page of any computer connected to the homegroup.

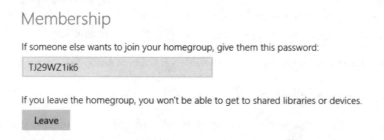

Figure 24-2 Type the password to allow other computers to join your homegroup.

Joining a homegroup

Only computers running Windows 7 or Windows 8.1 can participate in a homegroup. Earlier releases of Windows do not support homegroups.

To join a homegroup from a PC running Windows 8.1, just access the HomeGroup page of PC Settings, type the password, and click Join (as shown in Figure 24-3).

Figure 24-3 Other PCs will detect the existing homegroup and prompt you to join it.

To join a homegroup from a PC running Windows 7 (or from the Windows 8.1 desktop), start the Network And Sharing Center and then click HomeGroup in the lower-left corner. As shown in Figure 24-4, click Join Now.

Figure 24-4 Windows 7 computers can join a homegroup.

TROUBLESHOOTING

Why can't I connect to a homegroup?

If the HomeGroup page in PC Settings prompts you to create a new homegroup instead of joining an existing one, but you've already created a homegroup on a different PC, verify that the PC that created the homegroup is connected to the network. You might need to wait a few minutes for Windows to detect the existing homegroup. If that doesn't work, from the Start screen search for **fix homegroup** and select Find And Fix Problems With Homegroup. The HomeGroup troubleshooter, as shown in Figure 24-5, will attempt to diagnose your problem, and it might even fix it for you.

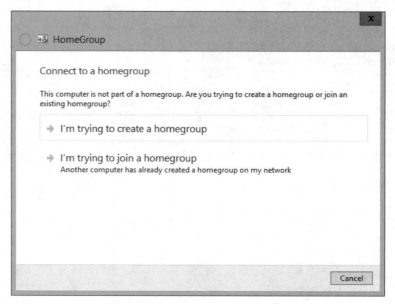

Figure 24-5 Use the HomeGroup troubleshooter to solve problems connecting to a homegroup.

Accessing shared files

Accessing shared files hasn't changed from Windows 7. Open File Explorer and navigate to Homegroup, as shown in Figure 24-6. Within Homegroup, files are organized by users, file types, and then individual folders. If a user has multiple folders within a single library (for example, three folders within their Documents folder), each will be listed separately.

If you regularly use a mobile PC to access folders shared from a desktop PC, consider adding the shared folders to the appropriate library on the mobile PC. For example, if you keep your pictures on your desktop PC but want to be able to browse them from your tablet, add the Pictures folder from the desktop PC to the Pictures library on the tablet. For detailed instructions, refer to Chapter 9, "Organizing and protecting files."

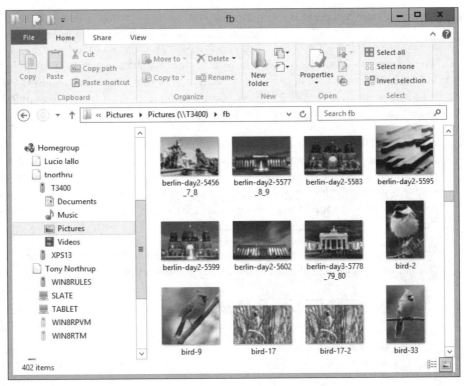

Figure 24-6 Use File Explorer to access homegroup files.

Inside OUT

Limiting access to files in a homegroup

Let's say you've used Windows Media Center to record some PG-13 movies. You want your older daughter to be able to watch the movies on the computer in her room, but you don't want your younger son to be able to watch them. You still want your younger son to be able to watch other videos, however.

Homegroups don't limit access to files based on individual user. Any computer that participates in the homegroup can access any file shared to the homegroup. However, you can use file permissions to limit which files different users can access. For detailed information, refer to "Using file sharing" and "Granting permissions to files" later in this chapter, as well as the section "Protecting files" in Chapter 9.

Using folder sharing

Windows Vista and earlier versions of Windows can't participate in homegroups. However, when you create a homegroup, Windows automatically shares your Users folder in a way that lets other PCs connect to it. In earlier versions of Windows, simply use Windows Explorer to map a network drive to \\<PC_name>\Users. Be sure to grant the user file permissions as described in "Granting permissions to files" later in this chapter.

For most people, homegroups make sharing folders and printers much simpler than in Windows Vista and earlier versions of Windows, which required you to share individual folders and printers. However, you might still want to manually share an individual folder and then map it as a network drive if you access it frequently. For example, it's much easier to access my E:\ drive that's mapped to a shared folder than it is to browse to Homegroup\Tony\Win8\ Documents\My Documents\Windows 8.1 Inside Out\.

To manually share a folder, right-click it in File Explorer and then click Properties. Select the Sharing tab, as shown in Figure 24-7, and click the Advanced Sharing button.

Figure 24-7 Use the Properties dialog box to share individual folders.

In the Advanced Sharing dialog box, select the Share This Folder check box as shown in Figure 24-8.

Figure 24-8 Advanced Sharing provides more control of shared folders than homegroups do.

Then, click the Permissions button. Here, you need to specify the users who have access to the shared folder and what level of access they have when accessing the share. The default settings allow everyone to connect to the shared folder with nothing more than Read access. If you want users to be able to edit any file or folder for which they also have sufficient file permissions, grant Change access to Everyone. Full Control also allows users to change permissions when accessing the shared folder.

Whereas homegroups automatically allow users to access both shares and the files contained within, when you manually share folders, you must separately configure both share permissions and file permissions. Sharing a folder and granting share permissions does not grant users any permission to the files within the shared folder. Therefore, while everyone will have access to connect to the share by default, file permissions can restrict them from accessing any of the contents in the share.

Share permissions simply define the greatest permissions users can have to the contents of the share. For example, if you grant Read access to the Everyone group, nobody will be able to update a file within the share, even if they have full control over the file permissions.

Inside OUT

Setting share permissions

I recommend simply granting Change or Full Control permissions to everyone. That seems like a remarkably unsecure way to assign permissions, but as I describe in "Granting permissions to files," it's only one of two levels of protection, and one level of protection is enough for most people.

However, there's a concept in security known as *belt and suspenders*. If you're under 85, you might not be familiar with suspenders, but they're shoulder straps for your pants. They do the same job as a belt, and it would be silly to wear both a belt and suspenders unless you didn't trust your belt or you really didn't want your pants to fall off.

Business environments rely heavily on the belt and suspenders approach because they understand that humans often make mistakes. For example, imagine that you're in tech support and a user on the local computer can't update a file. One of the ways you might troubleshoot the problem is to temporarily give everyone access to update the file. It solves the problem, and you go back to browsing the web. However, you've left the file open to everyone, creating a huge security vulnerability.

If you used the belt and suspenders approach to security, the shared folder permissions would still restrict other users from updating the folder across the network. The additional layer of security provided some protection even though another layer was accidentally removed.

If you really don't want to be caught with your pants down, you can specify more restrictive share permissions than the default settings that allow everyone to read files. From the Permissions dialog box, select Everyone and then click Remove. Then, click Add. You'll see the remarkably confusing Select Users Or Groups dialog box. This dialog box is designed for use in enterprises that have thousands of users, and as such, it's quite inefficient in a home environment. Type the name of the user you want to share with in the box and then click OK. Returning to the Permissions dialog box, select the user and choose which permissions they should have (Figure 24-9). Then, click OK.

Now, your folder is shared with the share permissions you specified. Your next step is to connect to it from the remote PC. In File Explorer, select the Home tab, click Easy Access (in the New group), and then click Map As Drive.

The Map Network Drive wizard appears. Make note of the drive letter at the top of the wizard; you'll use this drive letter to access the folder in the future. Click Browse to select the shared folder, or type the name of the shared folder in the format \\<*PC_name*>\<*folder_name*>. If you're logged on using an account that doesn't exist on the sharing PC, or that doesn't have sufficient permissions to the shared folder and files, then select the Connect Using Different Credentials check box as shown in Figure 24-10. Finally, click Finish.

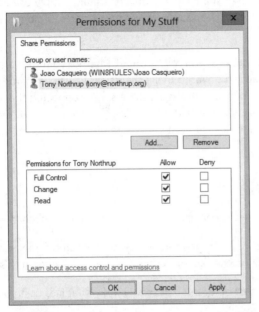

Figure 24-9 Use the Permissions dialog box to specify share permissions.

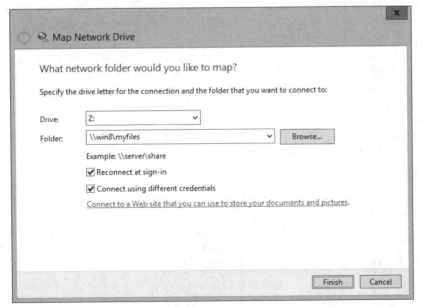

Figure 24-10 Map a drive to a shared folder to make access to the folder easier.

You can also map drives to folders within a shared folder by browsing to a subfolder or specifying the folder name using the format \\<*PC_name*>\<*folder_name*>\<*subfolder*>\ <*subfolder*>. That way, you don't have to share each folder separately. Simply use the Users folder that homegroups automatically share and map drives to specific subfolders within it for your own convenience.

If you switch between computers frequently, you might forget whether your files are stored in the Documents folder or on a mapped drive. To make things easier, use the same drive letters on each of your PCs to connect to the same shared folders. I've connected the W drive on each of my PCs to the Windows 8.1 Inside Out folder I'm using to write this book. I've even done that on the PC that stores the files locally. That way, no matter which PC I'm using, I can open the W drive and find my files.

Granting permissions to files

If you aren't using homegroups, you must configure two different security mechanisms:

- **Share permissions**   The user must be granted access to the shared folder, which can be done manually as described in the section "Using file sharing" earlier in this chapter.

- **File permissions**   The user must be granted access to individual files using NTFS file permissions.

Users can access a file across the network only if they have both share and file permissions. Think of it like a bank vault with locked safe deposit boxes within it. Use share permissions to decide who can enter the bank vault. Use file permissions to grant access to the individual safe deposit boxes, which represent folders and files. Homegroups grant both share permissions and file permissions to everyone in the homegroup, essentially allowing everyone into the bank vault and then into the safe deposit boxes. When you manually share folders, you have separate locks for the bank vault and safe deposit boxes, and you need to separately define both share and file permissions.

To set permissions to share a folder or file with another user, right-click the file or folder in File Explorer and then click Properties. Select the Sharing tab and click the Share button. The File Sharing dialog box appears.

On the Choose People To Share With page, select the users who you want to share the folder or file with and whether you want them to have Read or Read/Write permissions (Figure 24-11). If you're sharing the folder with other users, you must create an account for them on the PC sharing the folder, and the user name and password must match their credentials on the PC they're connecting from. Click Share.

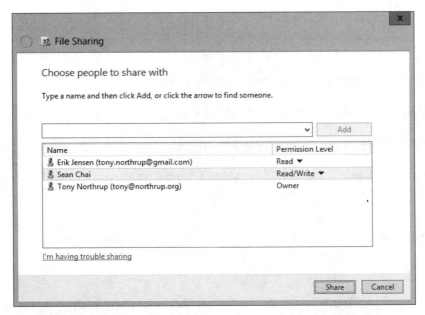

Figure 24-11 Sharing individual folders requires specifying share permissions.

File permissions apply to users who access files and folders both across the network and when logged on locally to the computer. To set file permissions for a user, right-click the file or folder and click Properties. Then, select the Security tab. Click the Edit button to modify permissions for the file or folder. If you edit a folder's permissions, the permissions you specify will be applied to all files and folders contained within the folder.

➤ **For more information about file permissions, refer to "Protecting files" in Chapter 9.**

Using shared printers

Occasionally, you need to take something from the digital world and bring it into the physical world by spraying some ink on mushed up trees. It seems like a rather antiquated process, and I avoid it whenever possible, but we still need to print.

Printing has actually become more complex in recent years, because PCs became mobile and printers will always be stationary. In the days when everyone had a desktop PC, they plugged their printer into the PC's USB port (or the parallel port, if you're as old as I am)—connecting to a printer was as easy as connecting your mouse or keyboard. If you have a Wi-Fi network, however, your printer needs to become a network device.

CHAPTER 24

There are several ways to share your printer across your network. The sections that follow describe each option in more detail and then describe how to connect to shared printers from client PCs.

▶ **Sharing printers**   Watch the video at *http://aka.ms/WinIO/shareprinters*.

Sharing a printer with a desktop PC and a homegroup

If you happen to have a desktop PC, connect your printer to your desktop PC and then have that PC join your homegroup, as described earlier in this chapter. Any other PC that participates in the homegroup will be able to connect to the printer as long as the PC sharing the printer is turned on and connected to the network.

Depending on how often you print, you might want to change your desktop PCs power settings so that it stays turned on during the hours when you might want to use the printer. For more information, refer to the section "Power settings" in Chapter 5, "Personalizing Windows 8.1."

Sharing a printer with a desktop PC without using a homegroup

Even if you have PCs that can't connect to your homegroup, such as a PC running Windows XP or Windows Vista, you can still connect to a printer that's shared using homegroups.

If you prefer not to use a homegroup (for example, if you prefer to grant access to shared resources on a user-by-user basis), you can manually share a printer.

From the Start screen, search for **printers**, and then select View Devices And Printers. Right-click the printer and select Printer Properties. On the Sharing tab, as shown in Figure 24-12, select Share This Printer.

Windows is available for both 32-bit (x86) and 64-bit (x64) processors. By default, Windows automatically installs a driver only for clients with the same processor type. If you have both 32-bit and 64-bit versions of Windows Vista, Windows 7, or Windows 8.1 in your home, click the Additional Drivers button and select the other processor type, as shown in Figure 24-13. Windows will prompt you to select the printer driver, so you'll need to download the appropriate version from the printer manufacturer's website and extract the files to a folder on your computer.

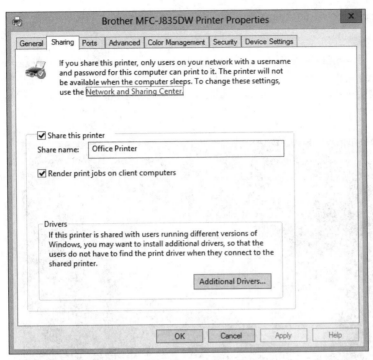

Figure 24-12 Manually share a printer using the Sharing tab of the Printer Properties dialog box.

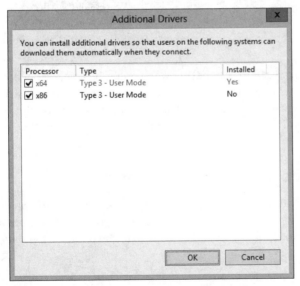

Figure 24-13 If you have both 32-bit and 64-bit versions of Windows, install both drivers.

Sharing printers without a PC

Printers are rather stationary devices, whereas many new PCs are extremely mobile. Even if all of your PCs are mobile devices, you can still print from anywhere in your house by using a printer that connects directly to your wired or wireless network without using a PC. As shown in Figure 24-14, you might need to retrieve the printer's IP address directly from the printer to connect to it.

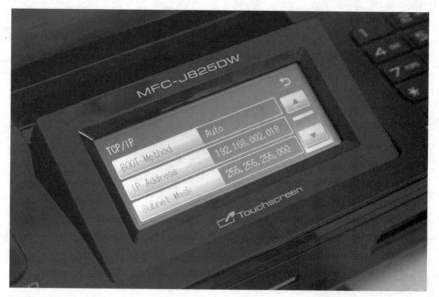

Figure 24-14 When you buy a new printer, look for models that connect directly to your network.

If your printer can't connect directly to your network, you might be able to connect it to your router or wireless access point. Some routers and wireless access points support sharing a USB printer across the network, instantly converting any printer into a network printer. For more information about routers and wireless access points, refer to Chapter 21, "Setting up a home or small office network."

Automatically connecting to shared printers

Whereas File Explorer automatically connects you to every shared folder in your homegroup, you must manually connect to printers shared in your homegroup. No matter how your printer is shared on the network, the process of connecting to the printer is the same: from the

Start screen, search for **printer** and then select Add Printer. Windows will prompt you to connect to any printers that it can find on the local network, as shown in Figure 24-15, including any shared by homegroups.

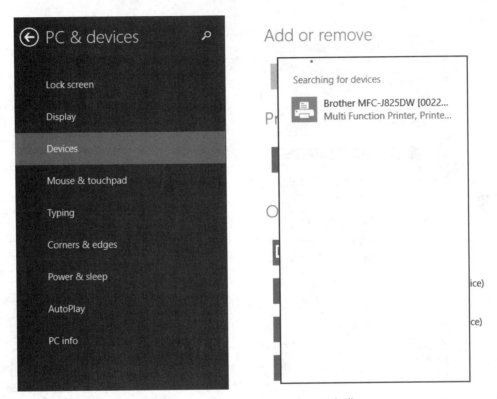

Figure 24-15 Windows will find most network printers automatically.

Although this technique is supposed to find shared printers, it doesn't always succeed. The desktop provides a more reliable approach. From the Start screen, search for **printer** and then select Devices And Printers. Then, click Add A Printer. As shown in Figure 24-16, the Add Printer wizard more reliably finds network printers. Select a printer, click Next, and follow any prompts that appear.

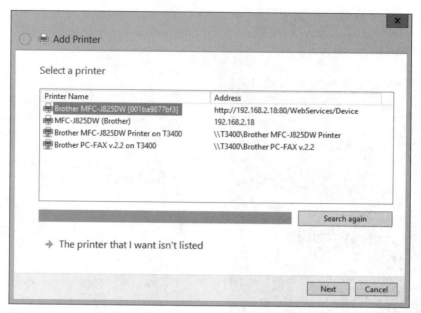

Figure 24-16 Use the desktop to reliably connect to printers.

Inside OUT
Different ways to share a printer

In Figure 24-16, notice that the Select A Printer page of the Add Printer wizard shows four different printers. I have only one printer, but it's shared four different ways.

Because it's a network printer, it connects directly to the network and shares itself by using printer sharing standards. The first two items in the list show the ways that the printer shares itself on the network: using HTTP and using IP. I could connect to either item and print equally well.

The third item on the list is the same printer shared from my desktop PC, T3400. The only benefit to also sharing the printer through my PC is that clients can automatically download the printer driver from my PC. If they connect directly to the printer, the user needs to select the printer driver. Plus, it doesn't hurt anything to have multiple paths to a resource. And if the printer has a network issue, I can still access it through my PC, and if the PC is turned off, I can still print using the direct network connection.

The last item on the list is the printer's fax feature. I haven't had a conventional phone line in my house in about five years, so the fax feature isn't even connected. Windows automatically shared it.

As shown in Figure 24-17, Windows might prompt you to install a driver by downloading it from the PC sharing the printer. It's technically possible (though highly unlikely) that the driver might not be trustworthy, so installing the driver requires administrative privileges. If the printer driver needs to install software, you might get a second confirmation prompt.

Figure 24-17 Installing a driver downloaded from the PC sharing the printer requires administrative privileges.

As shown in Figure 24-18, Windows might instead prompt you to select a driver. It will only do this if it can't automatically download the driver, which will happen if you're running a version of Windows with incompatible drivers or if you connect directly to the printer. These drivers are approved by Microsoft, so you can trust them, at least to the extent you trust other Microsoft-approved software. Click Windows Update to get the latest list of printer drivers.

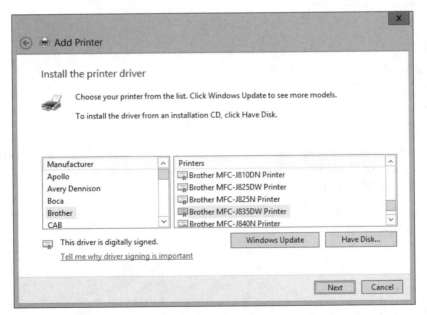

Figure 24-18 You might have to manually select the driver for the printer.

CHAPTER 24

If you still don't see your printer, download the latest version of the driver from your printer manufacturer's website and click Have Disk to select it (or just install it using the printer manufacturer's software). If you do click Have Disk, be prepared to take a trip down memory lane. By default, the wizard selects the A drive. Apparently, the Windows developers at Microsoft haven't updated this dialog box since people used to install printer drivers from floppy disk drives, which were typically named A and B.

Manually connecting to a printer shared from a PC

If the Add Printer wizard doesn't find your printer (which does happen regularly), you might have to identify the printer's name on the network and connect to it manually.

If your printer is connected directly to another PC on the network (for example, using a USB cable), go to the PC sharing the printer and open a command prompt. First, run the command **hostname**, which displays the PC's hostname, which is Win8PC in the following example.

```
C:\>hostname
Win8PC
```

While you're at it, run the command **ipconfig** and make note of the IPv4 address, which is 192.168.2.7 in the following example. You probably won't need this, but you might:

```
C:\>ipconfig

Windows IP Configuration


Ethernet adapter Local Area Connection 1:

   Connection-specific DNS Suffix  . :
   Link-local IPv6 Address . . . . . : fe80::95aa:b974:daac:9df9%13
   IPv4 Address. . . . . . . . . . . : 192.168.2.7
   Subnet Mask . . . . . . . . . . . : 255.255.255.0
   Default Gateway . . . . . . . . . : 192.168.2.1
```

Now, run one more command at the command prompt: **net share**. Net Share lists every shared resource on the PC. In the following example, the resource you're looking for is Brother MFC-J825DW Printer. Make note of the exact name.

```
C:\>net share

Share name    Resource                         Remark

-------------------------------------------------------------------------------
ADMIN$        C:\Windows                       Remote Admin
Q$            Q:\                              Default share
print$        C:\Windows\system32\spool\drivers
                                               Printer Drivers
C$            C:\                              Default share
IPC$                                           Remote IPC
Brother MFC-J825DW Printer
              USB002               Spooled   MFC-J825DW
Brother PC-FAX v.2.2
              USB002               Spooled   MFC-J825DW
The command completed successfully.
```

Now you have all the information you might possibly need to connect to the shared printer. Return to the PC that you want to print from and open the Add Printer wizard. This time, click The Printer That I Want Isn't Listed. Windows gives you several different options. Choose Select A Shared Printer By Name and type **\\\<*hostname*>\\<*printer name*>** as shown in Figure 24-19. Click Next and complete the wizard.

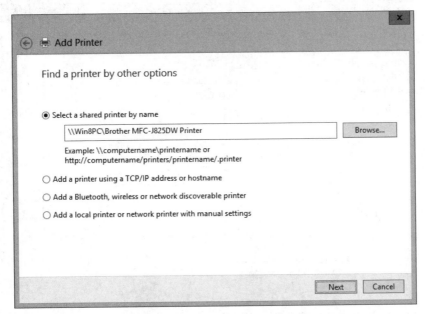

Figure 24-19 If you can't automatically connect to a printer, you can identify its name and connect manually.

If you still can't connect, attempt to connect to the printer again. This time, type the name **\\<*ip_address*>\\<*printer name*>**. Specifying the IP address bypasses the name resolution process, and resolving names on the local network is a notoriously unreliable process.

TROUBLESHOOTING

Why can't I connect to my printer?

If you've tried connecting to a shared printer manually and still receive an error, restart both PCs. You knew I was going to say that, didn't you?

On the PC sharing the printer, follow the instructions in "Switching between public and private networks" in Chapter 19, "Windows, application, and network security," to configure the local network as a private (home) network and verify that sharing is turned on.

Next, while still on the PC sharing the printer, search Settings for **sharing** and then select Manage Advanced Sharing Settings. As shown in Figure 24-20, verify that Turn On Network Discovery, Turn On Automatic Setup Of Network Connected Devices, and Turn On File And Printer Sharing are selected.

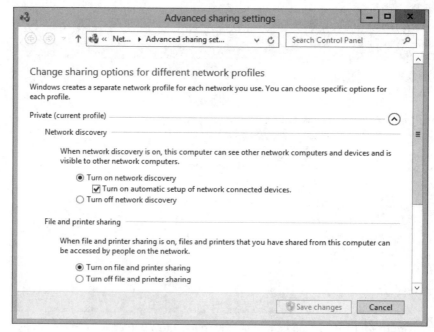

Figure 24-20 Network Discovery and File And Printer Sharing should be enabled on the PC sharing the printer.

With that done, there's another setting to verify: Windows Firewall. Windows Firewall can block incoming communications, including those sent by the PC sharing the printer. Search Settings for **Firewall** and select Windows Firewall. Then, select Advanced Settings. In the Windows Firewall With Advanced Security window, verify that the following inbound rules are enabled for the Private profile only:

- File And Printer Sharing (Echo Request – ICMPv4-In)

- File And Printer Sharing (Echo Request – ICMPv6-In)

- File And Printer Sharing (LLMNR-UDP-In)

- File And Printer Sharing (NB-Datagram-In)

- File And Printer Sharing (NB-Name-In)

- File And Printer Sharing (NB-Session-In)

- File And Printer Sharing (SMB-In)

- File And Printer Sharing (Spooler Service-RPC)

➤ For more information about using Windows Firewall, refer to Chapter 19.

If it still doesn't work, open a command prompt (without administrative privileges) on the PC connecting to the printer. Run the command **ping** *<ip_address>*, where *<ip_address>* is the IP address of the server sharing the printer. If you see replies, then your PC is able to communicate with the PC sharing the printer. At the command prompt, type **net use **<*ip_address*>. You might be prompted for your user name and password.

```
C:\>net use \\Win8PC
The password or user name is invalid for \\Win8PC.

Enter the user name for 'Win8PC': tony@northrup.org
Enter the password for Win8PC:
The command completed successfully.
```

This step establishes a connection to the PC sharing the printer and authenticates your account to the printer. This connection is used for all shared file and printer communications, so you shouldn't have any problems connecting to the PC until you restart.

With that connection established, you should be able to browse for the printer using the steps in "Automatically connecting to shared printers" earlier in this chapter.

If you don't see replies when you ping the PC sharing the printer, you have a network problem. Refer to Chapter 23, "Troubleshooting your network."

CHAPTER 24

TROUBLESHOOTING

Why can't I print anymore?

If you were able to print and suddenly you can't, there are a few things that could cause this. Go through these steps to identify the problem:

1. Make sure the correct printer is selected as the default. In Devices And Printers in Control Panel, the printer should have a green check mark. If not, right-click it and select Set As Default Printer.

2. Is the printer OK? Check the ink or toner, make sure it has paper and isn't jammed. Most printers are smart enough to display some sort of error message.

3. Does Windows know what the problem is? Go to the Devices page of PC Settings. Beneath your printer, Windows will display the status if it has detected a problem, as shown in Figure 24-21. If the status is Offline, then your computer can't connect to the printer. Check the USB cable or verify the printer's connection to the network.

Brother MFC-J825DW Printer
Toner/ink low

Figure 24-21 Windows can often tell you the problem with your printer.

4. Restart the printer, restart whatever it's connected to (your PC or router), and restart the PC that's trying to print. I know, it's not an elegant solution, but it often works.

5. If you're trying to print to a printer connected by a USB cable, unplug the printer and then remove it from Devices And Printers in Control Panel. Then, reconnect the printer and turn it on. Windows 8.1 should detect it automatically, which will probably solve your problem. If Windows 8.1 doesn't detect it, try a different USB port, and try replacing the USB cable. If Windows 8.1 still will not detect it, try connecting the printer to a different computer. If another computer can connect to the printer, the problem is with the first computer. If neither computer can connect to the printer, then the problem is with the printer.

6. If you're trying to print across the network and the printer is shared from a PC, try to print from the PC sharing the printer. If it can't print, return to the previous step. If the PC can print directly to the local printer, then the problem is network related. Verify that the PCs can connect to shared folders. Try removing the printer from both PCs, and then reinstall it and share it again. If you run into problems reconnecting to the shared printer, follow the instructions in the troubleshooting tip, "Why can't I connect to my printer?"

Manually connecting to a network printer

If Windows doesn't display the name of a network printer, you can manually connect to it. Start by looking up your printer's IP address. If your printer has an LCD display, there will be a menu option to display the current IP address. If not, there will be a command to print the network settings. Refer to your printer's manual for more information.

On your Windows 8.1 PC, search from the Start screen for **printer** and then select Devices And Printers. Then, click Add A Printer, just as you would when automatically connecting to a printer. This time, click The Printer That I Want Isn't Listed. On the Find A Printer By Other Options page, select Add A Printer Using A TCP/IP Address Or Hostname, and then click Next. On the Type A Printer Hostname Or IP Address page, do as it requests and type the IP address, as shown in Figure 24-22. When you click Next, Windows should connect to the printer.

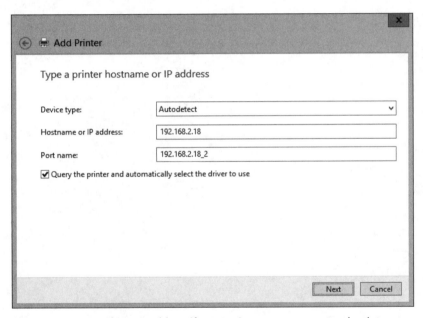

Figure 24-22 Specify an IP address if you can't connect to a network printer.

If you continue to have problems, check the printer manufacturer's website to see if it has any software for Windows Vista, Windows 7, or Windows 8.1 that you can download and install. Any of them should work.

CHAPTER 24

PART 6

Maintaining, tuning, and troubleshooting

CHAPTER 25

Maintaining your PC 609

CHAPTER 26

Monitoring, measuring, and tuning performance 621

CHAPTER 27

Troubleshooting startup problems, crashes, and corruption 653

Maintaining your PC

Updates 609

Backups 617

Uninstalling apps 617

Disk integrity. 618

Disk space 618

Maintaining your batteries 618

Earlier versions of Windows required regular maintenance to keep them running smoothly: defragmenting your hard disk, checking your hard disk for errors, cleaning up temporary files, and removing apps that started automatically. Windows 8.1 has automated most maintenance tasks for you, and even an unmaintained PC should perform well after years of use.

However, you can do several things to keep your PC running quickly and reliably. This chapter covers the most important maintenance tasks.

Updates

One of the most powerful qualities of software is the ability of the developer to release updates after its initial release. Updates can fix problems, block security vulnerabilities, and add new features.

Updates can also be quite a nuisance. Windows and many individual apps regularly remind you to install some updates, and many of those updates require you to restart your computer.

Updates are a nuisance, but they're important. The philosophy of "If it ain't broke, don't fix it" simply doesn't apply in the world of software. A PC can be functioning just fine, but a newly discovered security vulnerability could threaten your data privacy and integrity if you don't install a newly released security update. Similarly, updates might fix a relatively uncommon bug that will impact you at some point in the future, even if you haven't yet noticed the bug.

The sections that follow discuss the different types of updates you should plan to install on your PC and how to retrieve those updates.

▶ **Maintaining Windows 8.1** Watch the video at *http://aka.ms/WinIO/maintenance*.

Windows updates

Microsoft will release updates to Windows 8.1 on a regular basis. Microsoft releases several types of updates:

- **Security updates**   An update that is intended to protect your computer from a newly discovered security vulnerability.

- **Critical updates**   An important update that isn't security related. Often, critical updates solve problems related to reliability or data integrity.

- **Windows Defender definitions**   An update to Windows Defender definitions, which Windows Defender uses to detect the latest malware. For more information about Windows Defender, refer to Chapter 19, "Windows, application, and network security."

- **Service packs**   A large update that contains dozens or even hundreds of smaller updates. Service packs occasionally contain new features as well. Basically, a service pack contains all the minor updates Microsoft has released up to that point in time.

You should install each of these updates as soon as possible. I realize that installing updates that require you to restart your computer is a bit of a nuisance, especially if you're like me and tend to keep many different apps open. Nonetheless, the few minutes of computing time you lose while restarting your computer can save you the hours or days of time that you would lose if a vulnerability on your PC is exploited or if a reliability problem causes issues with your PC.

Microsoft might release updates at any time, but Microsoft releases the most updates on "Patch Tuesday," which is the second Tuesday of every month.

Inside OUT

Exploit Wednesday

How important is it to install updates? Well, the day after Patch Tuesday is known as "Exploit Wednesday." Attackers reverse engineer Microsoft's update to determine the nature of a vulnerability and then create software to exploit it.

Having a vulnerability is like leaving your door unlocked; it's only a problem if there's a criminal who wants to break in. Exploits are that criminal. Therefore, if you don't install the update, not only will your PC have a vulnerability, but it will have a vulnerability for which there is an active exploit.

Configuring automatic updates

When you first set up your PC, Windows prompts you to configure automatic updates. If you later want to change how updates are installed, from the Start screen search for **updates** and select Choose Whether To Automatically Install Windows Updates from the search results.

On the Choose How Updates Get Installed page, shown in Figure 25-1, select your preferences. I prefer allowing updates to install automatically, but if you find the update reminders annoying, select Download Updates But Let Me Choose Whether To Install Them. Click Apply to save your setting.

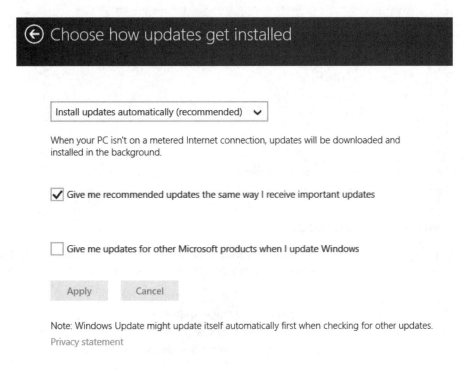

Figure 25-1 Change your update settings to prevent Windows from reminding you about updates.

By default, Windows installs your updates at 2 A.M. Presumably, you're asleep at 2 A.M., so the updates won't bother you. Here's the problem with that schedule: your computer is probably also asleep. So, when you wake up and start your PC, that update will be waiting to interrupt your work.

You can configure automatic updates to install updates at a different time or to wake up your PC so that the updates can be installed while you're sleeping. Open Control Panel on the desktop, and browse to System And Security, Windows Update, Change Settings. Then, click Updates Will Be Automatically Installed During The Maintenance Window. In the Automatic Maintenance window, pick the time to install the updates, as shown in Figure 25-2, and select the Allow Scheduled Maintenance To Wake Up My Computer At The Scheduled Time check box.

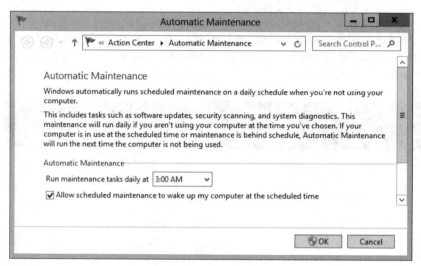

Figure 25-2 Select the time that you want Windows to install updates.

Installing optional updates

Optional updates include language packs and driver updates, and they're never installed automatically. However, there will occasionally be optional updates that are important to you, so you should check for them regularly.

To install optional updates, open Control Panel on the desktop, and browse to System And Security, Windows Update. If necessary, click Check For Updates. If any optional updates are available, click the Optional Update Is Available link, as shown in Figure 25-3.

Now you can view the optional updates that are available. You don't necessarily want to install them all, but you probably do want to install any updates for your PC's hardware. Click Install to download and install the selected updates. Windows might prompt you to restart your PC to complete the installation.

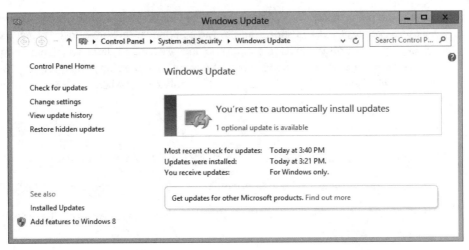

Figure 25-3 Use optional updates to install drivers.

Manually downloading updates

To manually install updates, select Windows Update in PC Settings. Click Check Now even if Windows already shows that some updates are available, because Windows might not have detected newly available updates, and you might as well install everything all at once.

The Windows life cycle

Although it's never an issue for those among us who love to be the first to upgrade to the latest version, Windows has a life cycle. Microsoft releases a new version of Windows, and it remains current for a few years. Then, Microsoft releases a newer version of Windows, and continues to release updates for and support both the current and previous versions.

At some point, though, Microsoft has to stop supporting older versions of Windows. You're welcome to continue running that version of Windows, but it's probably not a great idea, because without that version being updated regularly, some attacker is going to discover a vulnerability, and they'll be able to compromise your computer.

Compare it to the world of cars. The 1967 Chevrolet Camaro SS is one of my favorite cars of all time. If you were wise enough to buy one in 1967, you wouldn't expect Chevy to keep it up to date by installing airbags or stability control. It's simply impractical; at some point, Chevy needs to release a new model that incorporates those features. In fact, if you liked the 1967 Camaro, you probably wouldn't even want those newer features.

Microsoft has to handle Windows in the same way. Windows 95 wasn't designed for touch screens or the threats of the modern Internet, and it's simply not practical to keep it up to date indefinitely.

So, at some point, Windows 8.1 is going to become outdated, and Microsoft is going to stop releasing updates for it and supporting it. The company hasn't announced exactly when that will be, but Microsoft commits to supporting and releasing updates for "a minimum of 5 years from the date of a product's general availability, or for 2 years after the successor product is released, whichever is longer." Based on that, I would expect Microsoft to support Windows 8.1 until at least October, 2017.

Here are a couple of examples:

- Windows XP was released on December 31, 2001, and supported until April 14, 2009.

- Windows Vista was released on January 30, 2007, and supported until April 10, 2012.

For a complete description of the Windows life cycle, read the "Windows lifecycle fact sheet" at *http://windows.microsoft.com/en-US/windows/products/lifecycle*.

Windows 8.1 app updates

If you download an app using the Store, you also update it using the Store. As shown in Figure 25-4, the Store tile shows the number of updates available in the lower-right corner.

Figure 25-4 The Store notifies you when app updates are available.

To install updates, open the Store and then click Updates in the upper-right corner. If you don't see a link there, it means the Store hasn't found any updates. You can manually check for updates by opening the Settings charm and then clicking App Updates.

Desktop app updates

Updating desktop apps is nowhere near as straightforward. There's no single process, but the following are common approaches:

- Desktop apps automatically check for updates when you run the app, notify you when one is available, and prompt you to download and install it.

- Desktop apps have a separate app that checks for updates and notifies you when they're available, even if you don't run the app. I don't want to single anyone out, Java, but these notifications can become really annoying.

- Desktop apps include a menu item that allows you to manually check for updates. For example, the Help menu often has a menu item such as Check For Updates.

- Microsoft desktop apps, such as Office, might distribute updates automatically using Windows Update. These updates will be installed the same way as updates to Windows 8.1.

- Desktop apps might not be capable of checking for updates, but updates might be available on the software developer's website. Visit the website to download the update. For best results, bookmark each app's page, and add a reminder to your calendar to check for app updates monthly.

Because desktop apps install updates differently, people have a tendency to overlook them, leaving installed apps without the benefit of any new improvements. That's one of the greatest improvements to the Windows 8.1 app infrastructure.

Driver and firmware updates

Almost every piece of hardware in your computer, including components hidden inside your computer, has a driver. A driver is a small piece of software that allow Windows to talk to your hardware.

Driver updates are extremely important because they can fix serious security, reliability, and data integrity problems. Microsoft distributes updates for signed drivers through Windows Update, so you receive some driver updates automatically.

However, the process of having Microsoft approve and sign a driver can take some time. As a result, hardware vendors often release driver updates directly through their websites. If you're having a problem with a particular piece of hardware, first check Windows Update for a new driver. If you don't find an update there, visit the hardware manufacturer's website.

Often, hardware vendors have a different driver for every model that they make. So, it is important to know the exact model of your hardware. To determine the model of your hardware, from the Start screen search for **Device Manager** and run the app.

As shown in Figure 25-5, Device Manager lists every device in your PC. Browse the list to find the name of the device for which you want to update the driver, and then search the Internet for an update. For example, in Figure 25-5, the network adapter is the Intel Centrino Advanced-N 6230, the Kernel adapter will be updated only with Windows updates, and Bluetooth isn't used for traditional network communications. Only download updated drivers from trusted sources.

Figure 25-5 Use Device Manager to find the names of devices in your PC.

Besides driver updates, some hardware manufacturers release firmware updates. Firmware updates actually update the low-level software that runs within the device itself. Firmware updates are infrequent, and most devices will never have a firmware update.

Inside OUT

The importance of driver and firmware updates

While updates to Windows are particularly critical, driver and firmware updates tend to be less important. Typically, I recommend seeking out updated drivers only when something's not working right with your PC.

Video driver updates can be an exception to that rule. Updated video drivers often improve the performance of your PC, particularly for playing games. If you're a big PC gamer, check for updates to your video card driver regularly. Often, the video card manufacturer will release updates to improve the performance of a specific game. If you can get higher frames per second from a game for free, why wouldn't you want the update?

BIOS updates

Your PC has a BIOS, which is low-level firmware that resides on a chip on your motherboard and runs before Windows starts. Occasionally, PC and motherboard manufacturers will release an updated BIOS to solve newly discovered problems and to support new hardware or software introduced after the motherboard was released.

Installing the latest BIOS can solve a wide variety of reliability and compatibility problems. It's particularly important to check for BIOS updates in the first six months after a PC is released and in the first six months after upgrading to a new operating system. In other words, if you recently bought your PC or you just upgraded to Windows 8.1, you should check for BIOS updates.

If you bought a prebuilt computer, visit your PC manufacturer's website and find the support page for your specific model of PC. If you built your own PC, visit your motherboard manufacturer's website.

If you have a mobile PC, be sure the power is plugged in before installing a BIOS update. BIOS updates have the potential to damage your PC (though I've never had a problem), so you don't want your PC to run out of battery power in the middle of a BIOS update.

Backups

If you store important files on your PC, daily backups are a critical part of your PC maintenance. Without backups, you will lose your files at some point, because all PCs fail at some point. For detailed information about backing up your PC, refer to Chapter 10, "Backing up and restoring files."

Uninstalling apps

Finding new apps is fun. Often, though, you use an app only once or twice. If you aren't using an app, you should remove it to free up disk space and save yourself the trouble of installing updates. This is particularly true of desktop apps that run at startup.

You can remove Windows 8.1 apps by selecting them from the Start screen and then clicking Uninstall. To remove desktop apps, from the Start screen search for **uninstall**, select Uninstall A Program, and use Programs And Features to remove the app.

Disk integrity

Disks aren't perfect. Power outages, power fluctuations, running out of battery power unexpectedly, passing through magnetic fields, and even solar flares can cause data on your disk to become corrupted. These corruptions can damage your files. If Windows system files become corrupted, Windows might become unreliable, or you might not be able to start Windows at all.

Windows 8.1 checks for data corruption and will often fix it automatically. Therefore, you might never have to manually fix problems, but it never hurts to check your disk for errors.

For detailed information, refer to the section "Fixing errors" in Chapter 12, "Managing storage."

Disk space

You can never have enough storage. Especially if you take a lot of pictures or record videos, you're bound to fill up your disk at some point. When you run out of disk space, you'll be unable to save new files.

If your PC uses a conventional magnetic hard disk, your PC can actually slow down as your disk starts to fill up. For that reason, it's especially important to delete any unnecessary files on a regular basis.

For detailed instructions, refer to the section "Freeing up disk space" in Chapter 9, "Organizing and protecting files." For information about expanding your storage space by adding a new disk, refer to Chapter 12.

Maintaining your batteries

Rechargeable batteries lose capacity over time. If you can get nine hours of battery life when your PC is new, you might be down to five hours of battery life after two years. After five years, your battery might be completely unusable.

There are a few things you can do to improve the lifespan of your battery:

- Use software from your hardware manufacturer to intelligently charge your battery. Some hardware manufacturers offer settings that charge your battery more slowly above 50 percent, which can increase your battery's lifespan. This feature might be called "desktop mode."

- Store your batteries at 40 percent charge and keep them in a cool place. If you're not going to be using your mobile PC for a few days or more, allow the battery to discharge to a little less than half before powering it down. Don't store your PC in a hot car.

- Every two or three weeks, run the battery down to empty. Batteries work better when they go through a full cycle on a regular basis. If you often run your PC without being plugged in, this shouldn't be a problem. If your PC is constantly plugged in, however, it's a good idea to unplug it once in a while and wait until the battery is almost empty before plugging it back in.

Inside OUT

Replacing your battery

With current technology, decreased battery capacity is simply a fact of life. If you're the type who wants to get many years of use out of a mobile PC, you'll want to replace your battery at some point.

Unfortunately, replacement batteries can be shockingly expensive. My Dell D820 is at least six years old (but still useful), and I've gone through three different batteries. New batteries from Dell, however, cost US$136. That same laptop sells used for about US$180 now, which means a new battery is worth almost as much as the PC itself.

I can buy a generic battery for as little as US$15, but in my experience, you get what you pay for. The generic batteries often have lower capacity and might work properly only for a month or two. So, buyer beware.

Some mobile PCs (especially tablets) might have batteries that can't be easily replaced. Search the Internet for advice about replacing the battery if you find that you can no longer achieve the battery life you need. Often, the best choice is to send the PC to a specialty repair shop to have the battery professionally replaced.

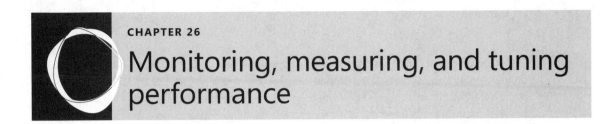

CHAPTER 26

Monitoring, measuring, and tuning performance

Benchmarking your computer 621

Finding and controlling a troublesome app 625

Setting priority and affinity when starting an app 627

Speeding up startup 630

Using Task Manager 634

Using Performance Monitor 644

Everyone would like their PC to be faster. Good news: Windows 8.1 is faster, and it does a great job of keeping your PC running smoothly. The casual user should never need to think about their PC's performance.

Some of us, however, are a bit obsessed. We strive to get the best performance possible out of our PC's hardware. We obsess over processor, memory, and disk usage, and we scrutinize apps and services that might be slowing down our PC. This chapter is for those obsessed readers; it's a practical guide to making your PC faster without spending a penny.

First, I'll discuss how to use benchmarking tools to assess your PC's performance. Then, I'll cover some common performance troubleshooting scenarios, including finding and stopping troublesome apps. Next, I'll describe how to tune your PC to start as fast as possible. Finally, I'll describe two important performance tools: Task Manager and Performance Monitor.

Benchmarking your computer

Benchmarking tools give you a sense for your computer's overall performance. It's a great way to see how much faster your new computer is than your old one or how much of a difference upgrading a hard disk, processor, or your computer's memory made.

Windows 8 (as well as many earlier versions of Windows) included the Windows Experience Index tool. This tool has been removed from Windows 8.1. Fortunately, you can still use the third-party PassMark PerformanceTest tool to benchmark your PC. You can download a free trial at *http://www.passmark.com/products/pt.htm*.

PerformanceTest runs a series of tests on your PC and calculates individual scores for different components and a composite score that summarizes your PC's speed. Figure 26-1 shows PerformanceTest's analysis of my tablet PC's processor performance. The top number is the most important: 2565.

This score isn't unlike WEI, but PerformanceTest has a really useful feature that WEI lacks: online comparisons. With online comparisons, you can see how your PC compares to other people's, allowing you to determine whether your PC is performing like it should, which components might benefit the most from an upgrade, and how other people are putting together their PCs to get better performance.

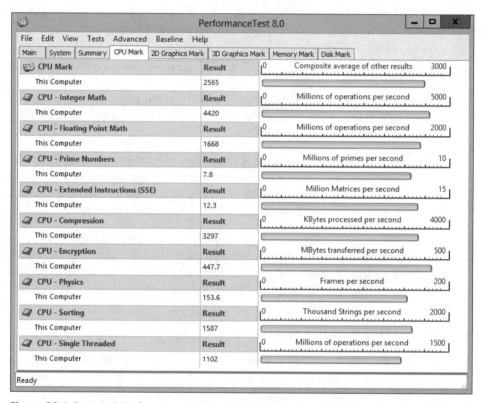

Figure 26-1 PassMark PerformanceTest provides a detailed analysis of your PC's hardware performance.

For example, by visiting *http://www.cpubenchmark.net/high_end_cpus.html* (shown in Figure 26-2) or by clicking View Online Comparison Charts on the PerformanceTest Baseline menu, I can see that the fastest of the high-performance desktop CPUs has a rating of 16,629. By comparison, my tablet PC's performance of 2565 seems pitiful. Of course, I'm confident nobody with the high-end processor is lounging on their couch with their PC in their lap.

To upload your own PC's benchmarks, choose Upload Baseline To Web from the Baseline menu.

Perhaps it's fun to see how fast other people's PCs are, but I generally find it a bit torturous to know that my video rendering could be happening faster if only I was willing to spend $5,000 on a new PC. However, these benchmarks do have a very practical purpose: verifying that your PC components are performing as expected.

For example, if your hard disk seems slow, it's entirely possible that it's in the process of failing. In the past, I've seen hard disks that continue to function, but simply do a worse job of it. With PerformanceTest, you could test the performance of your hard disk and then look up how the same hard disk performs in other people's computers.

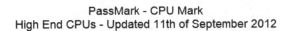

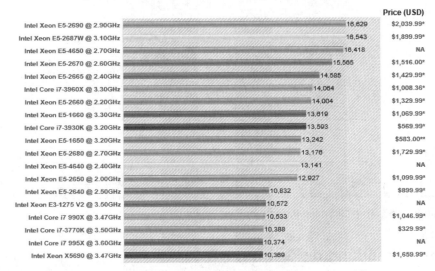

Figure 26-2 Because PassMark is a popular test, it's easy to compare different components of your PC with those of other people around the world.

To look up how your disk performs in benchmarks, first run PerformanceTest. Then, click the View menu and click Disk Read Graph. As shown in Figure 26-3, the graph shows the number of megabytes (MB) your PC could read from the disk in a second (my tablet averaged 191 MB/sec). In the upper-right corner, you'll find your hard disk model. In my case, it's the Samsung MZMPA128HMFU. You can also view information about all system components on the System tab of the main PerformanceTest window.

With that information, click Close, click the Baseline menu, and then click View Online Comparison Charts. At the PassMark website, select the Hard Drive Benchmarks tab. Then, click Search For Your Hard Disk Drive and type your model number. If your performance doesn't match up with what you see on the website, it doesn't necessarily indicate a problem; it could just be that your PC has a slower bus speed. However, if a benchmark drops over time, that probably does indicate a problem.

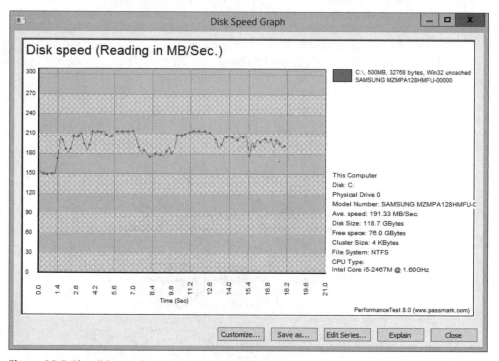

Figure 26-3 The disk speed graph shows your hard disk model number.

Benchmarking disks using HD Tune

HD Tune is a free app for benchmarking your disk performance. Whereas WEI gives you a single and rather vague number to summarize your disk performance, HD Tune can measure the exact read and write speeds, as well as the disk latency.

For more information about HD Tune and disk performance, read "Choosing a new drive" in Chapter 12, "Managing storage."

Benchmarking network performance

WEI makes no mention of network performance, which I think is odd because that's the most important performance factor for those of us who spend time on websites, use cloud services like SkyDrive, connect to other PCs with Remote Desktop, stream video, or transfer large files between PCs.

For detailed information about benchmarking your network's performance, including your Internet connection, and improving that performance, refer to Chapter 21, "Setting up a home or small office network."

Finding and controlling a troublesome app

Often, there's a single app on your computer that's doing something processor intensive. While Windows is quite good at sharing processor time between multiple apps, a single busy app can slow down every other app on your PC.

A busy app can have other bad side effects, too. It can drastically reduce your mobile PC's battery life. It can also increase the temperature of your PC, possibly causing your PC to slow the processor down, further reducing your PC's performance.

Use Task Manager to find a busy app. Launch Task Manager, click More Details (if you need to), and then select the Processes tab. Click the CPU column heading to display the busiest apps at the top of the list. As shown in Figure 26-4, Task Manager shows you which app is using your processor time the heaviest.

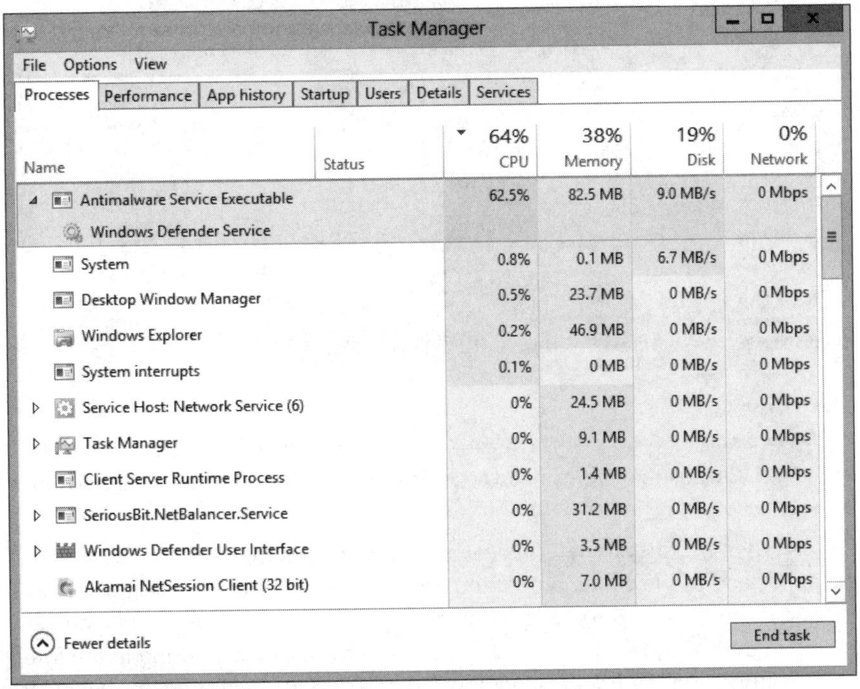

Figure 26-4 Use Task Manager to find the app consuming the most processor time.

You can stop the app by right-clicking and then clicking either End Task or Stop. Don't be too hasty, though. First, you should stop the app by closing the window if you can; ending a task from Task Manager doesn't allow the app to save its data. Second, the app might be doing something important. In Figure 26-4, the app is Windows Defender performing a scan for malware.

If you want to allow the app to continue running, you can minimize the impact it has on your PC's performance by lowering its priority. On the Processes tab, right-click the app and then click Go To Details. This selects the app on the Details tab. Now, right-click the process name (which might be different from the name displayed on the Processes tab), select Set Priority, and click Below Normal or Low, as shown in Figure 26-5.

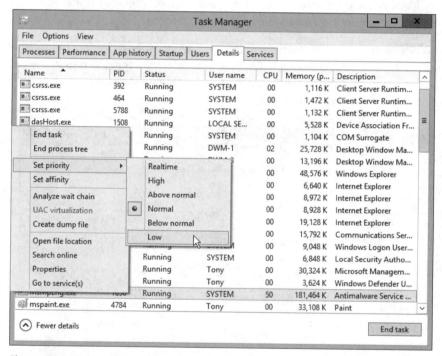

Figure 26-5 Change the priority of an app to reduce its impact on your PC's performance.

Windows uses priorities to determine which apps receive the most processor time when multiple apps need to use all the processing time available. If you have a single app using your processor time, changing the priority won't impact that at all. However, if you have an app running in the background and it's slowing down the app you're using in the foreground, lowering the priority of the background app can make your foreground app seem faster.

If you want to prevent an app from using 100 percent of your processor time, even if it's the only app running, you can adjust the processor affinity. Follow the series of steps described earlier to find the process on the Details tab. Then, right-click the process and select Set Affinity. As shown in Figure 26-6, use the Processor Affinity dialog box to specify which processors the app is allowed to use. To limit an app to half your total processing time, select only half of your processors.

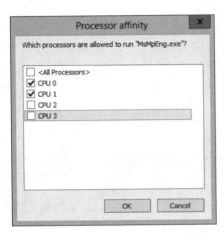

Figure 26-6 Change a process's affinity to limit its processor utilization.

Setting priority and affinity when starting an app

Windows doesn't remember your priority or affinity settings after you close an app. The next time you start it, Windows will run the app at normal priority on all processors. To manually set the priority or affinity for an app, use the Start command-line tool. For example, to start Notepad with low priority and allow it to run on only one processor, you would run the following command at a command prompt:

```
start /low /affinity 0x1 %windir%\System32\Notepad.exe
```

To have Notepad run with below normal priority on two processors, you would run the following command:

```
start /belownormal /affinity 0x3 %windir%\System32\Notepad.exe
```

You can see full instructions by running the command **start /?** at a command prompt. The only tricky part about using Start is setting the affinity, which requires a binary mask that needs to be specified in hexadecimal format. Rather than teaching you Boolean and base-16 mathematics, I'll just tell you the codes to use to enable different numbers of processors (Table 26-1).

Table 26-1 Affinity codes for different processor quantities

Number of processors	Affinity code
1	0x1
2	0x3
3	0x7
4	0xF
5	0x1F
6	0x3F
7	0x7F
8	0xFF

Understanding processors

Different PCs have different numbers of processors, but most newer PCs have more than one (though each "processor" is probably just a different core on a single processor or a virtual processor created using a technique called hyper-threading).

If you regularly start an app with a manually defined priority or affinity, create a shortcut for it. From your command prompt, press the Up Arrow key to recall the last command you ran. Then, press the Home key to move the cursor to the beginning of the line. Type **echo** and add a space before the command. Then, press the End key, and type **> slowapp.bat**. Press Enter. Your command should resemble the following:

```
echo start /belownormal /affinity 0x3 %windir%\System32\Notepad.exe > slowapp.bat
```

The Echo command simply echoes whatever you write. If you were to run the command **echo hello world**, the command prompt would repeat "hello world" back to you. However, adding the > symbol to the end of the command redirects the output to the file specified. So, that command writes a batch file named slowapp.bat with your previous command. Now, you can run the entire command by running slowapp.bat from your current folder, and you can use that batch file to create a shortcut.

To create a shortcut to your new batch file and run your app with your specified priority and affinity, right-click your desktop, click New, and then click Shortcut. Click Browse and select the batch file you created, as shown in Figure 26-7. If you didn't change your current folder at the command prompt, it's probably in your Users folder.

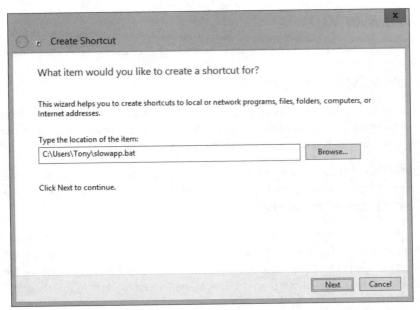

Figure 26-7 Create a shortcut using a batch file and the Start command to easily start an app with a custom priority and affinity.

Finish the remaining steps in the wizard, and you'll have a shortcut you can run from the desktop. From the Start screen, type the name of your shortcut (such as **slowapp**) to run it.

TROUBLESHOOTING

Why is my hard drive making so much noise?

If you find that your hard drive is making a great deal of noise, and you'd like to know which app is causing it, launch Task Manager, click More Details (if you need to), and then select the Processes tab. Click the Disk column heading to display the busiest apps at the top of the list. Unlike with processor priority and affinity, there's no way to limit how much a process can access your drive.

If no app is using your disk heavily, you might have a failing disk. Failing disks often begin making terrible sounds before they crash completely. Make sure you have a recent backup, as described in Chapter 10, "Backing up and restoring files." For information about troubleshooting and replacing a failing drive, refer to Chapter 12.

CHAPTER 26

Speeding up startup

The sections that follow describe several different ways to make your PC start faster.

Removing startup apps

Previous versions of Windows struggled with long startup times after users had installed a few apps. In earlier versions of Windows, apps often created agents that started automatically and slowed down the startup process even if the user never accessed the app.

The style of app designed for Windows 8.1, described in Chapter 2, "Using Windows 8.1 apps," does a great job of reducing the impact apps have on startup time. Basically, very few (if any) Windows 8.1 apps will increase your startup time.

You might still have desktop apps that start automatically. To view those apps, launch Task Manager, click More Details, and then select the Startup tab. If you understand what an app does and you don't want it to start automatically, select it and then click Disable. For more information, refer to "Startup tab" in the Task Manager section later in this chapter.

It doesn't hurt to simply uninstall any apps you aren't using. You can remove Windows 8.1 apps by selecting them on the Start screen and then clicking Uninstall. To remove a desktop app, search from the Start screen for **programs and features**, select that tool, and then use it to remove the desktop app.

Delaying automatic services

Services are apps that run in the background without a user interface. Many services start automatically so they can do important things in the background while you use your computer. For example, the Windows Search service indexes new files that you save to your PC, and the Print Spooler service waits for you to print something. These services start automatically, and they need to use your processor, memory, and disk a bit when they start, which can slow down your PC a little as you try to launch your first app.

Therefore, if your startup speed is slow, you might check your services to see if there are any services you don't need to start automatically. To view the services on your PC, open the Computer Management console by running **compmgmt.msc** from the Start screen or by using the WinX menu. In Computer Management, select Services And Applications\Services, as shown in Figure 26-8.

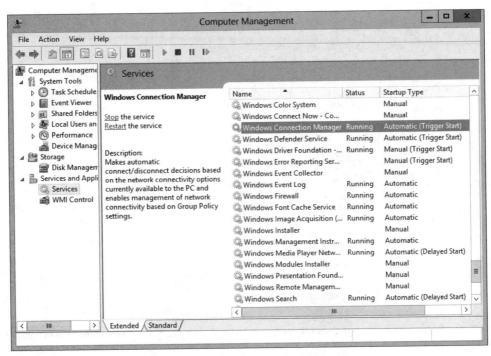

Figure 26-8 Use the Computer Management console to configure services.

The only services that will impact your startup time are those that have Startup Type set to Automatic. Services that have a startup type of Automatic (Trigger Start) or Manual start only when they're needed, and services that have a startup type of Automatic (Delayed Start) start after you've had a chance to open your first app.

To prevent a service from starting automatically, double-click it and change Startup Type to Manual, as shown in Figure 26-9, or Automatic (Delayed Start). The next time you restart your computer, the service won't start automatically.

Choose Manual if you don't want the service to run automatically; you'll be able to start it manually whenever you need it. Choose Automatic (Delayed Start) to allow the service to start shortly after startup so that it won't impact your startup time but will still be available when you need it—as long as you don't need it immediately after logging on to your PC.

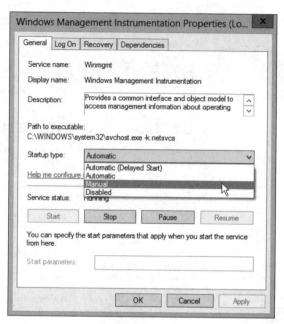

Figure 26-9 Change the startup type of a service to prevent it from slowing down your PC's startup time.

Please don't change the startup type for services if you don't understand what they do. Windows 8.1 already minimizes the number of services that start automatically. For your reference, Windows 8.1 comes preconfigured to start the following services automatically. If you change their startup type, something won't work right:

- Background Tasks Infrastructure Service

- Base Filtering Engine

- COM+ Event System

- Cryptographic Services

- DCOM Server Process Launcher

- DHCP Client

- Diagnostic Policy Service

- Distributed Link Tracking Client

- IP Helper

- Local Session Manager

- Multimedia Class Scheduler

- Network Location Awareness

- Network Store Interface Service

- Power

- Print Spooler

- Program Compatibility Assistant Service

- Remote Procedure Call (RPC)

- RPC Endpoint Mapper

- Security Accounts Manager

- Server

- Shell Hardware Detection

- Superfetch

- System Event Notification Service

- Task Scheduler

- Themes

- User Profile Service

- Windows Audio

- Windows Audio Endpoint Builder

- Windows Event Log

- Windows Firewall

- Windows Font Cache Service

- Windows Image Acquisition (WIA)

- Windows Management Instrumentation

- Windows Modules Installer

- WLAN AutoConfig

- Workstation

Additionally, Windows will configure other built-in services to start automatically if you add or configure different features. For example, if you share a network connection as described in Chapter 22, "Setting up ad hoc, Bluetooth, and mobile networks," Windows will set the Internet Connection Sharing (ICS) service to start automatically.

To summarize, services with Startup Type set to Automatic contribute to a longer startup time. However, most automatic services are important, and you shouldn't change their startup type. Some desktop apps will install services that start automatically but aren't necessarily required for how you use your PC, such as services that check for app updates. Therefore, by carefully choosing apps and services and changing their startup type, you can speed up your startup time without losing important functionality.

Disabling unused hardware

When Windows starts, it loads software drivers that allow it to communicate with every hardware component in your PC. If your PC has hardware components you never use, disabling them in Device Manager can improve your startup time, if only by a few milliseconds.

To disable a hardware device, launch Device Manager by running **devmgmt.msc** at the Start screen. Then, right-click your device and click Disable, as shown in Figure 26-10. To use it again, right-click it and then click Enable.

CHAPTER 26

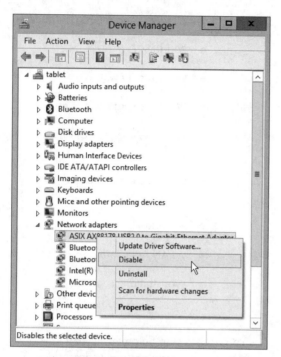

Figure 26-10 Disable unused hardware to decrease your startup time.

Upgrading your hard drive

One last suggestion for speeding up PC startup times: upgrade to a new solid state drive (SSD). For more information, refer to Chapter 12.

Using Task Manager

Task Manager gives you detailed insight into the inner workings of your computer and the power to prioritize and stop processes. The redesigned Windows 8.1 Task Manager is both easier to use and more powerful.

Task Manager is a quick way to answer 90 percent of the performance-related questions you might have about your PC, including:

- Why is my PC so slow right now?

- What exactly is my PC doing instead of what I asked it to do?

- Is anything using the network now?

- What's using my network connection now, and how much bandwidth is it using?

- Which app is to blame for that data usage bill I just got?

- Which desktop apps are making my PC so slow at startup?

- Which services are running right now?

▶ **Monitoring Windows 8.1 with Task Manager** Watch the video at *http://aka.ms/WinIO/taskmanager*.

You can open Task Manager by pressing Ctrl+Shift+Esc on a keyboard or Windows+Power on a tablet and then clicking Task Manager. You can also open Task Manager from the WinX menu.

Inside OUT

Stopping a desktop app that won't close

It happens: you click the red X and a window just won't close. Though it's possible for an app to disregard your request to close (this happens when you attempt to close the app and it prompts you to save your work first), the most common problem is that an app is busy doing something and was written as a single-threaded app, which allows the app to do only one thing at a time.

Most often, if an app isn't responding for more than a few minutes, it's because the app has frozen. Apps freeze for different reasons, but one of the most common is that there's a resource locking conflict.

Imagine two apps: AppOne and AppTwo. AppOne needs to access both FileOne and FileTwo, in that order. Under normal conditions, AppOne might read from FileOne, write to FileTwo, and then close both files so other apps can access them.

However, today, AppTwo needs to access FileTwo and FileOne in that order. AppOne first locks FileOne to start its work. Then AppTwo locks FileTwo to start its work. AppOne tries to open FileTwo, but discovers that it's in use by AppTwo, so it waits patiently, keeping FileOne locked while it waits. AppTwo tries to open FileOne, but it's locked by AppOne, so AppTwo waits for AppOne to close FileOne.

But AppOne can't close FileOne, so the two processes just wait patiently forever.

Odds are, you aren't patient enough to wait forever. That's when you should pull up Task Manager and kill the unresponsive app (either AppOne or AppTwo in this case). Just click the app or process, and then click End Task. Sometimes, you might need to do it twice.

Windows 8.1 starts Task Manager with a simplified interface, as shown in Figure 26-11, that displays a list of applications and the End Task button. This interface (which replaces the Applications tab in earlier versions of Task Manager) is ideal for casual users, but it does not allow the user to stop the Explorer task and lacks the level of detail that power users might have become accustomed to in earlier versions of Windows.

Figure 26-11 The simplified view of Task Manager lets you close running applications.

Click the More Details link to view expanded information about running applications and the operating system's state. This view of Task Manager displays seven tabs, as described in the following sections.

Inside OUT

Resource Monitor

If you liked Resource Monitor in Windows 7, you can still open it by selecting the Performance tab in Task Manager and then clicking Open Resource Monitor. However, just about everything you love about Resource Monitor is available in the Windows 8.1 Task Manager.

Processes tab

All apps and many different components of Windows run in a process. A process is the container Windows uses for an app that's running. Processes have a set of instructions to run (the app's code), a block of memory, and privileges to other system components, such as storage, network, and hardware devices.

Some apps use multiple processes, but typically, each app has a single process. There are quite a few processes running in Windows that aren't for apps you started, however. For example, every background service (such as the Print Spooler, which manages print jobs) runs within a process. You'll see many different processes that you don't recognize, but they're probably OK, and you definitely shouldn't start ending processes without understanding what they are.

You can view every process running on your PC by clicking the More Details link in Task Manager and then selecting the Processes tab. Windows 8.1 introduces the option to organize apps into groups such as Apps, Background Processes, and Windows Processes when processes are sorted by name. Switch between grouping or a simple list by clicking the View menu and then selecting Group By Type.

If a single application or service runs multiple processes and you have Group By Type selected, Task Manager groups those processes together, as shown in Figure 26-12. Task Manager also displays the status of an application if it is not responding. To end a process, select the process and then click End Task.

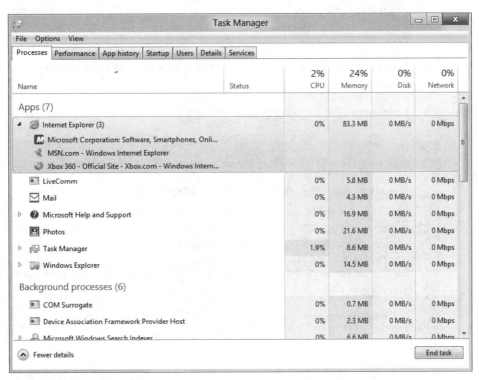

Figure 26-12 The Processes tab groups processes to make them easier to find.

There's another option you should enable: click the View menu, select Status Values, and then select Show Suspended Status. This shows which Windows 8.1 apps you've opened but are suspended. Suspended apps won't consume any processor time and consume very little memory. For more information about suspended apps, refer to Chapter 2.

The Processes tab is useful for identifying which process is slowing down a computer. To identify which processes are using the most resources, click each of the column headings to sort the list so that the processes consuming the most CPU, memory, disk, or network resources appear at the top of the list.

To view more information about each process, right-click the column heading and select one of the following columns:

- **Type** Indicates whether a process is an app, a background process, or a Windows process. If you sort by name, Task Manager groups processes according to the type, making this column unnecessary.

- **Publisher** The publisher that signed the executable running within the process.

- **PID** The process ID, which uniquely identifies a specific process.

- **Process Name** The name assigned to the process, which is typically based on the executable file name.

- **Command Line** The command line used to run the process, including any parameters.

Inside OUT

Starting an app when you can't open the Start screen

If you can't open the Start screen for some reason (this used to happen regularly in earlier versions of Windows, but I've never seen it happen with Windows 8.1), you can always use Task Manager to start a new app.

On the File menu, click Run New Task. You can then type the name of the executable you want to start.

If the desktop isn't responding, use Task Manager to view the processes and end the Explorer.exe process. Then use Task Manager to run Explorer.exe.

The Processes tab is also useful for finding more information about a specific process. To find a process's executable file, right-click it and then click Open File Location. Often, the name of the folder an app is located in gives you more detail about the app itself.

Performance tab

The Performance tab, as shown in Figure 26-13, gives you an overview of the amount of CPU, memory, disk, and network resources that Windows 8.1 and your applications are currently using. By checking this tab, you can determine which resources are limiting your computer's performance and use that information to identify the best way to upgrade your computer. For example, if memory utilization is consistently above 75 percent when your computer seems slow, adding more memory might improve the performance.

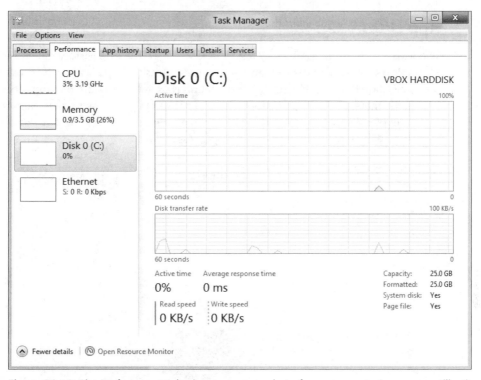

Figure 26-13 The Performance tab gives you a snapshot of your computer's resource utilization.

The Performance tab combines information from both the Performance and Networking tabs of the Windows 7 Task Manager. It also adds detailed information about disk utilization, including the average response time, read speed, and write speed. If you determine that one of the resources is near peak utilization, switch to the Processes tab and click a column heading to determine which processes are using the most of that resource. If you no longer need a process, you can then close the associated application or end the task to free up those resources.

> **More Info**
>
> The Performance tab measures disk utilization and current performance, but you should not use it to assess your computer's performance capabilities. Instead, use a tool such as HD Tune. For more information about assessing disk performance, read "How to Test (and Understand) Hard Disk Drive Performance" at *http://www.vistaclues.com/how-to-test-and-understand-hard-disk-drive-performance/*.

App History tab

Windows 8.1 adds the App History tab to Task Manager. The App History tab, as shown in Figure 26-14, shows you the CPU and network resources that applications have used, even if the application has been closed. This information is useful for troubleshooting problems users had earlier that can no longer be reproduced. For example, if someone complains that their computer often runs slow, but it is not currently running slow, check the App History tab to determine if an application used excessive processor time.

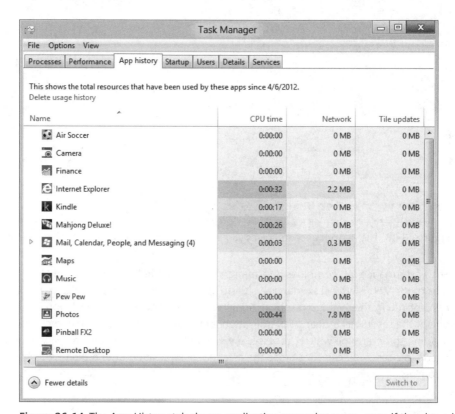

Figure 26-14 The App History tab shows applications users have run, even if they have been closed.

In addition to viewing the standard columns, you can right-click a column heading to add columns for non-metered network utilization, bytes downloaded, and bytes uploaded.

For privacy, click Delete Usage History to clear the history.

Startup tab

Desktop apps can start automatically when Windows starts, which makes them instantly available. However, each app that starts automatically also slows down the PC and increases the time it takes to manually start your own apps. Therefore, you want as few apps as possible to start automatically.

You can use the Startup tab (as shown in Figure 26-15) to control which applications start automatically. To remove a startup application, select it and then click Disable.

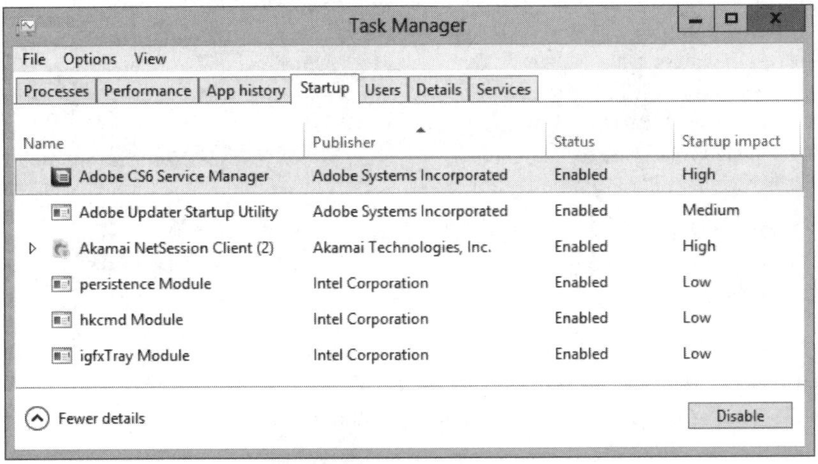

Figure 26-15 The Startup tab allows you to view and stop applications that start automatically.

If you're not sure what an app does, you shouldn't simply disable it, because you could cause an app or hardware accessory to not work properly the next time you start your computer. Spend a few moments to research what the startup app does. Task Manager makes this easy; simply right-click the app and then click Search Online.

To create a startup task, open Task Scheduler, create a basic task, and specify the trigger as When The Computer Starts. For more information about configuring startup apps, refer to Chapter 6, "Adding, removing, and managing apps." For information about starting desktop apps automatically, read "Configuring HTPC software to start automatically" in Chapter 17, "Creating a Home Theater PC."

CHAPTER 26

Users tab

The Users tab, shown in Figure 26-16, displays running and suspended applications for each logged-in user. You can use this tab to sign off other users or close their applications, freeing any resources they might be using, which can potentially improve your computer's performance. Most of the time, it's easier to simply restart your PC, however.

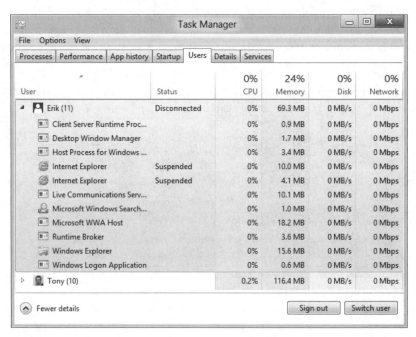

Figure 26-16 The Users tab allows you to log off other users and close their applications.

To log off a user, select the user and then click Sign Out. To close a process, select the process on the Processes tab and then click End Task.

To create users, open the Users tool within PC Settings. To switch users, click the currently logged-in user in the upper-right corner of the Start screen, and then click the user you prefer to log in as. For more information about users, refer to Chapter 18, "Managing users and Family Safety."

Details tab

The Details tab, shown in Figure 26-17, displays in-depth information about every process running on the computer, similar to the information provided by the Processes tab in the Windows 7 Task Manager. Click a column heading to sort the processes by that column. To view other information about each process, right-click the column heading and then click Select Columns.

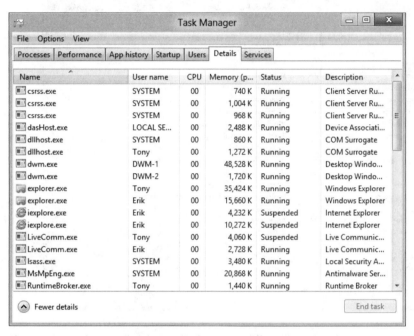

Figure 26-17 The Details tab can display many different metrics about every running process.

In practice, the Processes tab displays the most commonly accessed information about each process. However, if you have a detailed understanding about operating system resources, you can use the Details tab to understand each process's utilization.

Services tab

Services are processes that run in the background without a user interface. In typical usage, you will never need to interact directly with a service. The Services tab, shown in Figure 26-18, displays all services installed in Windows, whether or not they are running. You can start and stop services by right-clicking them.

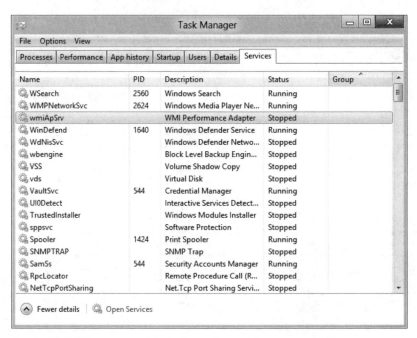

Figure 26-18 The Services tab displays all services.

To better manage services, click Open Services at the bottom of the Services tab.

Using Performance Monitor

Task Manager shows you just about everything you might want to know about your PC's performance. However, if you have a solid understanding of the inner workings of an operating system and you want even more detail, or if you want to log performance data over time, you can use the Performance Monitor tool.

▶ **Monitoring Windows 8.1 with Performance Monitor** Watch the video at *http://aka.ms/ WinIO/performance.*

Monitoring performance in real time

To start Performance Monitor, type **perfmon** at the Start screen and then press Enter. In the Performance Monitor window, select Performance\Monitoring Tools\Performance Monitor. Figure 26-19 shows the Performance Monitor graph after adding counters.

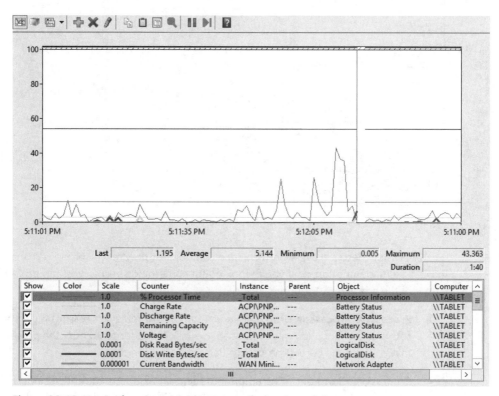

Figure 26-19 Use Performance Monitor to graph data in real time.

By default, Performance Monitor simply charts the PC's processor usage, which you can see more easily by using Task Manager. However, you can add hundreds of different counters to the Performance Monitor chart and even log the data to a file for later analysis.

To add counters to the chart, click the green Add button on the toolbar. You'll see the Add Counters dialog box, as shown in Figure 26-20. Select the Show Description check box to view information about each counter. Then, select a counter, select an instance of the counter (if available), and click Add. Repeat the process until you have added all the counters you want to monitor.

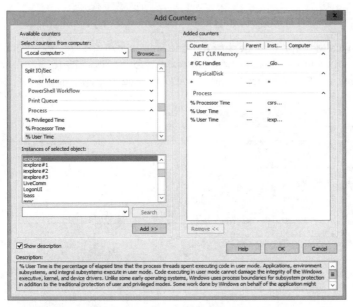

Figure 26-20 Add counters to Performance Monitor to watch your PC's performance in real time.

I can't possibly describe every performance counter, but they're well organized and they each have a useful description, so if you're looking for something specific, you can probably find it. Some of the more useful counters include:

- **Process\% Processor Time** An indication of how much processor time a specific process is consuming. You might want to use Task Manager to identify the process name so that you add the correct process to Performance Monitor.

- **Process\Working Set** The amount of memory an app is currently using. Use this to reveal apps that use the most memory. If you chart a desktop app over a long period of time and it has a gradually increasing memory set, the app might have a memory leak, which is a problem the developers should be able to solve.

- **Processor Performance\% of Maximum Frequency** To reduce heat and power usage, processors do not always run at full speed. This shows how fast your processor is currently running. The busier your PC is, the faster the processor will run, and the more power it will consume.

- **Battery Status**   These counters provide detailed information about your battery, including how fast it is charging or discharging and the estimated time left on the battery (in seconds). It might take several minutes after disconnecting or reconnecting power for you to see the counters updating.

- **Power Meter\Power**   For mobile PCs, this shows the power consumption in milliwatts.

- **Logical Disk\% Disk Time**   Shows how busy the selected disk is.

- **Logical Disk\% Free Space**   Shows how much of a disk is occupied.

- **Logical Disk\Disk Read Bytes/sec and Disk Write Bytes/sec**   Shows the number of bytes per second currently being read from or written to the disk.

- **Network Adapter\Bytes Received/sec and Bytes Sent/sec**   Shows the number of bytes per second currently being read from or written to the network adapter. Note that this is bytes per second, whereas bandwidth is usually measured in bits per second. To determine the number of bits per second, multiply this value by eight.

- **Paging File\% Usage**   The amount of the paging file currently in use. Windows uses the paging file to store data from the memory in the hard disk. Though the paging file is used even under ideal situations, high paging file usage can indicate that the PC is running more apps than it has memory for, and a memory upgrade would benefit the PC.

- **Server\Bytes Transmitted/sec**   Shows the number of bytes per second currently being sent using shared folders or homegroups. To determine the number of bits per second, multiply this value by eight.

By default, Performance Monitor updates the counters every second and displays 100 seconds of data in the graph. Though each counter can have a different behavior, the value displayed for each one-second sample is usually the average value of that counter over that time.

Updating the graph every second can lead to very spikey charts, limiting the usefulness of the maximum and minimum values. If you want to see the graph updated less frequently (resulting in smoother charts), you can edit Performance Monitor properties to update the graph less frequently. Figure 26-21 shows Performance Monitor configured to update the graph every minute and display the last hour of data. To edit Performance Monitor properties, click the Action menu and then click Properties.

CHAPTER 26

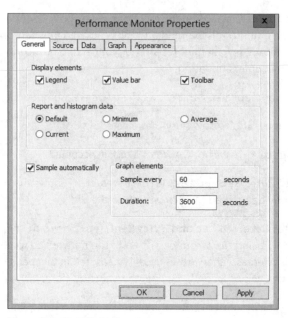

Figure 26-21 Edit Performance Monitor properties to change the time span of the chart.

Logging performance data

When you add counters to Performance Monitor, you can view the data in real time. If you want to view the data over a long period of time, you can decrease the sample frequency so that all the data shows on the chart at once.

There's a better way, though: logging the performance data to the disk and then analyzing it in Performance Monitor. This allows you to collect as much data as you'd like, over a long period of time, and then analyze it at your convenience. Logging performance data is the right choice for any scenario where you don't plan to be staring at the graph the entire time the PC is on.

To log performance data, start Performance Monitor and then right-click Performance\Data Collector Sets\User Defined, click New, and then click Data Collector Set. On the first page of the Create New Data Collector Set wizard, select Create Manually, and then click Next.

On the What Type Of Data Do You Want To Include page, as shown in Figure 26-22, select the Performance Counter check box and then click Next (but don't click Finish). Note the Performance Counter Alert option, which is useful if you want to be notified when a performance counter goes above or below a threshold.

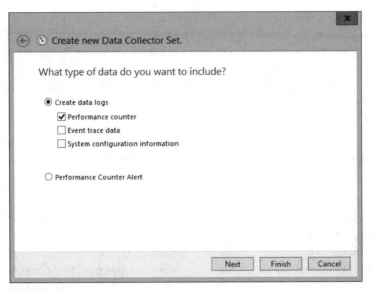

Figure 26-22 Log performance counter data for later analysis.

On the Which Performance Counters Would You Like To Log page, click the Add button and add the counters you want to monitor, as shown in Figure 26-23. The counters are the same as those you use with Performance Monitor in real time. Also set the sample interval. Use the longest sample interval you're comfortable with to reduce the amount of storage space required for logging. Click Next.

Figure 26-23 Specify the counters to log data for.

The rest of the wizard is self-explanatory. On the last page, you can leave Run As set to the default; this just specifies the user account the data collector set should use to gather the data. You can also choose to start the data collector set immediately or save it for later use.

If you don't start your data collector set immediately, you can start it later by selecting it within Performance\Data Collector Sets\User Defined and then clicking the Start The Data Collector Set button.

When you're done gathering data and want to analyze it, click the Stop The Data Collector Set button. Then, select Performance\Monitoring Tools\Performance Monitor and click View Log Data on the toolbar (or press Ctrl+L). Select Log Files, click Add, and then select your log data file. By default, it will be buried a few folders deep within the Admin folder.

As shown in Figure 26-24, click the Time Range button and set the time period you want to analyze if you want to see data from a specific period of time. That's useful if you're trouble-shooting a performance problem that seems to appear randomly; create and start a data collector set, and once the problem occurs, analyze just the data from that time period to determine the source. You can also adjust the time range after you click OK by dragging the bar beneath the graph.

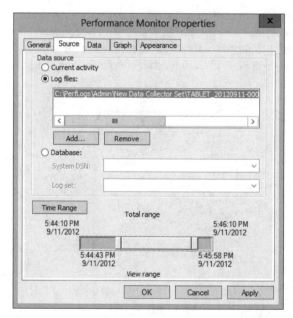

Figure 26-24 Configure a time range to analyze only a portion of your logged data.

Now, you can analyze the logged data within Performance Monitor. To examine data from a specific time range, simply drag your pointer across the chart to select that time period. Note the Average, Minimum, Maximum, and Duration fields below the graph, which provide detailed information about the counter selected at the bottom of the window.

Creating performance reports

If your PC seems slow and you want to track down the source of the problem, create a System Performance report. A System Performance report includes detailed information about your PC's current state that you can analyze at a later time. The information includes:

- Number of processors

- Processor utilization overview

- Interrupts per second

- Which processors were the highest utilized

- Speed at which different processors were running

- Which services and apps used the most processor time

- Disk utilization

- Which files are accessed the most

- Which disks are used the most

- Memory utilization

- Processes using the most memory

- Network utilization

- Top IP addresses sending and receiving network data

- Amount of network data sent and received

- Number of active and failed connections

To run the report from Performance Monitor, select Performance\Data Collector Sets\System\ System Performance. Then, click the Start The Data Collector Set button on the toolbar.

The test takes one minute to run. After a minute, select Performance\Reports\System\System Performance\<*computer name*> to view the report. The report, as shown in Figure 26-25, contains a great deal of information about your PC.

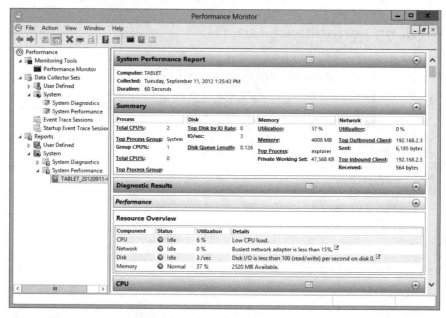

Figure 26-25 The System Performance report summarizes your PC's performance over a single minute.

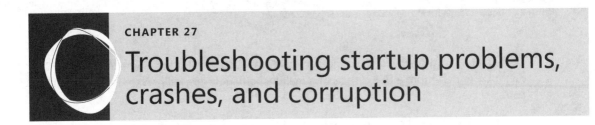

Troubleshooting startup problems, crashes, and corruption

Troubleshooting startup problems 653

Troubleshooting corruption and intermittent failures . 661

Refreshing your PC 671

Resetting your PC 674

PCs are complex devices, and complex devices always, eventually, encounter problems. This chapter is designed to help you solve a variety of Windows problems, including startup problems, intermittent crashing, and data corruption.

If Windows won't start, read the first section, "Troubleshooting startup problems." If you're experiencing corruption or Windows is randomly crashing, read "Troubleshooting corruption and intermittent failures" later in this chapter.

At the end of the chapter I describe two techniques that are useful for solving a variety of problems: refreshing your PC and resetting your PC. Refreshing your PC reinstalls Windows while keeping your files and Windows 8.1 apps intact. Resetting your PC cleans your PC completely and reinstalls Windows.

For information about troubleshooting performance problems, refer to Chapter 26, "Monitoring, measuring, and tuning performance." Also refer to the book *Troubleshoot and Optimize Windows 8.1 Inside Out* from Microsoft Press.

Troubleshooting startup problems

Windows won't start. It's a scary moment, but take a deep breath, because it's often easily solved. In this section, I'll walk you through a straightforward troubleshooting process that's designed to solve most startup problems that people encounter. I can't attempt to cover every problem that might occur, but I think this process will identify most problems.

First, unplug your PC and let it sit for about five minutes. If you have a mobile PC, remove the battery if you can. Now, plug it back in.

In my experience, that simple process gets Windows to start about 25 percent of the time. Of course, 75 percent of the time, I need to do more troubleshooting.

If Windows prompts you to repair your PC, allow it to do so. That often helps, but not always. If Windows doesn't prompt you, start your PC from the Windows 8.1 DVD.

Next, unplug any USB devices and memory cards that you aren't using. Sometimes, your PC might try to boot from a USB device, or a malfunctioning device will prevent it from starting correctly.

If you have a desktop PC, open the case and remove any expansion cards that aren't required for startup. Sometimes, a malfunctioning expansion card can prevent your PC from starting. While you're in there, spend a few minutes and reseat every card and cable. Reseating cards and cables is the process of unplugging them and then plugging them back in, just to make sure they have a good connection.

If you've recently added or replaced a hard drive, upgraded Windows, or run another operating system on your PC, that is probably the source of your problem. The steps described in the sections that follow will probably fix your problem, but there is one thing you should try first. Within your PC's BIOS settings, make sure that the correct hard drive is configured for startup. Hard drives are usually identified by their serial numbers, which might not make any sense to you. Therefore, you might need to use trial and error to select the correct boot hard drive to start Windows.

▶ **Troubleshooting startup problems** Watch the video at *http://aka.ms/WinIO/startup*.

Using Windows Recovery Environment

You can use Windows Recovery Environment (Windows RE) to solve many startup problems. To start Windows Recovery Environment, insert your Windows 8.1 DVD. When you restart your computer, your PC will boot from your recovery drive. If the Windows DVD prompts you to Press Any Key To Boot From CD Or DVD, do what it tells you to do: press a key. If your PC does not attempt to start from the DVD or flash drive, edit your PC's BIOS settings to configure it to boot from the DVD or flash drive first.

If you're starting from the Windows 8.1 DVD, click Repair Your Computer. Regardless of which media you use, on the Choose An Option page, as shown in Figure 27-1, click Troubleshoot.

On the Troubleshoot page, select Advanced Options. Then, on the Advanced Options page, as shown in Figure 27-2, select Automatic Repair. If the Automatic Repair page allows you to select Windows 8.1 as an option, that's a really good sign, because that means Windows recovery can still communicate with your hard disk and can probably fix your problem automatically. Select your Windows installation.

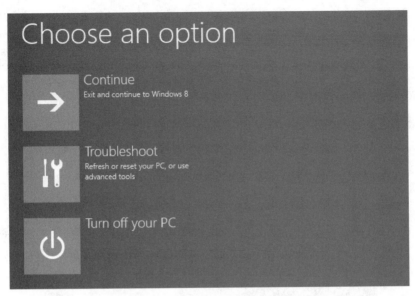

Figure 27-1 Windows 8.1 provides a touch friendly recovery interface.

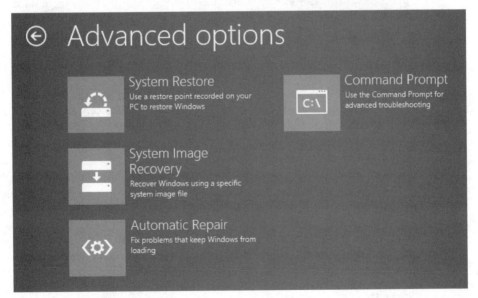

Figure 27-2 Advanced Options provides access to the tools you need to troubleshoot startup problems.

Troubleshooting startup from a command prompt

If Automatic Repair reports that it can't repair your PC, click Advanced Options, Troubleshoot, Advanced Options (again), and then Command Prompt. From the command prompt, run the command **wmic logicaldisk get name**. This command lists all the drives that are visible to Windows, as shown in this example output:

```
wmic logicaldisk get name
Name
C:
D:
E:
X:
```

Normally, your system drive is your C drive. However, the drive lettering can change when you start Windows recovery. To find your system drive, run the command **dir <*drive_letter*>:** for each drive letter until you find the one that contains the Windows folder. For example, you might run **dir C:**, **dir D:**, and **dir E:**.

What to do if you can see your system drive

If one of the drives contains a Users folder and a Windows folder, that's great news, because it means that your system drive is still readable.

If you have a recent system image and your files are backed up, you should attempt to restore the system image and your files. For information about restoring a system image and files from a backup, refer to Chapter 10.

I've been at this point in the troubleshooting process without a recent backup, too. It happens to all of us. After seeing that my files are still accessible, my first thought is usually, "Oh my goodness, glory be, my files live!" OK, I don't actually think in the dialect of a character from *Gone with the Wind*, but I swear a lot when I'm emotional, and my actual thoughts wouldn't be appropriate for print. Anyway, the first thing I always do is use the command prompt to copy my files to another drive so I can be sure I don't lose them. After all, if Windows won't start, it's probably because your drive is failing, and when drives start to fail, data begins to disappear.

To copy your files to another drive, connect a USB drive to your PC and rerun the command **wmic logicaldisk get name** to determine its drive letter. If it doesn't appear, then restart your computer and return to the command prompt from the Advanced Options page.

Now, run this command to copy your user profiles to the external drive: **xcopy <*system_drive*>:\users\ <*backup_drive*>:\backup /E /C /Y**. For example, if your backup drive is F and your system drive is D, you might run the command **xcopy D:\users\ F:\backup /E /C /Y**. If you have files stored outside your user profile, use the same command to copy those folders.

Unplug your backup drive and breathe a sigh of relief, because at least you have a copy of the files that were still readable. With your files safe, it's time to move on to getting Windows to start. First, fix any errors that might be present on the disk by using the ChkDsk tool: **chkdsk <*system_drive*>: /f /r**. This command might just fix all your problems. If your drive is close to total failure, it might be enough to cause it to completely fail, which is why I wanted you to back up your files first.

It's possible that ChkDsk did a good enough job of fixing your hard disk that you can now restart the automatic repair process and it will succeed. If it doesn't, restart Windows recovery and select Refresh Your PC from the Troubleshoot page, as shown in Figure 27-3.

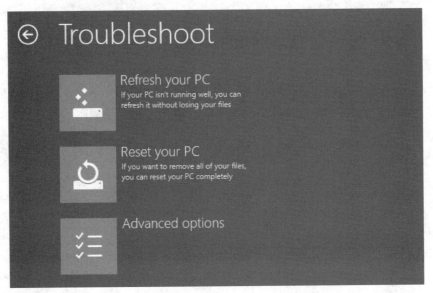

Figure 27-3 Refreshing your PC reinstalls Windows while keeping your files intact.

Inside OUT

Troubleshooting startup with a live CD

I love Windows recovery, but it's not perfect, and I've encountered many different startup problems that automatic repair couldn't fix but could be easily fixed by starting free third-party tools. However, these tools aren't supported, and they're not especially easy to use. Still, they might just work.

My favorite tool for troubleshooting startup is Hiren's BootCD, available at *http://www.hirensbootcd.org/*. After unzipping the ISO file, insert a blank CD into your computer, right-click the ISO file in File Explorer on the desktop, and then click Burn Disk Image. If you can't boot from a CD, use the Unetbootin tool (available at *http://sourceforge.net/projects/unetbootin/*) to create a bootable USB flash drive.

Start your PC from the CD or flash drive, and you'll see the menu shown in Figure 27-4.

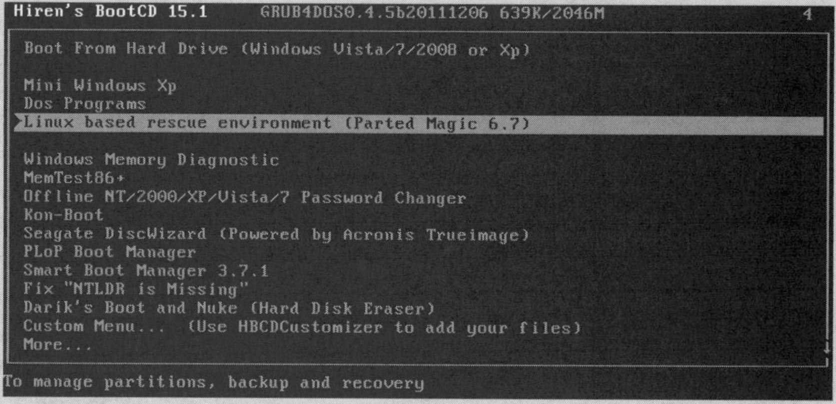

```
Hiren's BootCD 15.1      GRUB4DOS0.4.5b20111206 639K/2046M                    4

Boot From Hard Drive (Windows Vista/7/2008 or Xp)

Mini Windows Xp
Dos Programs
Linux based rescue environment (Parted Magic 6.7)

Windows Memory Diagnostic
MemTest86+
Offline NT/2000/XP/Vista/7 Password Changer
Kon-Boot
Seagate DiscWizard (Powered by Acronis Trueimage)
PLoP Boot Manager
Smart Boot Manager 3.7.1
Fix "NTLDR is Missing"
Darik's Boot and Nuke (Hard Disk Eraser)
Custom Menu... (Use HBCDCustomizer to add your files)
More...

To manage partitions, backup and recovery
```

Figure 27-4 Hiren's BootCD can fix some problems that Windows recovery cannot.

From here, you have a few choices for troubleshooting:

- If your primary concern is rescuing your data from your drive, launch the Linux Based Rescue Environment and start File Manager from the desktop. If you can see your files, copy them to another drive. If you can't see your files, start Partition Editor from the desktop to launch GParted, select your drive, open the Device menu, and then select Attempt Data Rescue. If this succeeds, you'll be able to copy your files to another drive, such as an external USB drive, using File Manager on the desktop.

- If your primary concern is getting Windows started as quickly as possible, start the PLoP Boot Manager and select the partition containing Windows. Selecting the right partition might require some trial and error, but it's probably HDA Partition 1. If that fails, try the Fix NTLDR Is Missing option on the main menu of Hiren's BootCD and work through each of the options in sequence. If you're able to start Windows correctly, it means your disk is intact, but the boot sector has been modified. Automatic repair should be able to fix this problem, but if it doesn't, refreshing your PC should solve it. If none of the partitions start correctly, your drive is probably corrupted.

- If your primary concern is permanently solving the startup problem, launch the Linux Based Rescue Environment and start Partition Editor from the desktop to launch GParted. Right-click your boot drive (which is usually the first drive listed with a size of 350 MB) and select Flags. Select the Boot flag, as shown in Figure 27-5, and click Close. If your boot sector was corrupted, or if installing another operating system changed your boot sector, this will fix the problem.

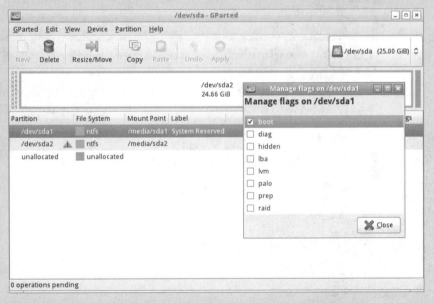

Figure 27-5 Use GParted to repair your boot sector.

If refreshing your PC doesn't work, start your PC from the Windows 8.1 installation media and reinstall Windows using the Custom option shown in Figure 27-6. On the Where Do You Want To Install Windows page, select your primary drive, not the smaller drive labeled System Reserved.

CHAPTER 27

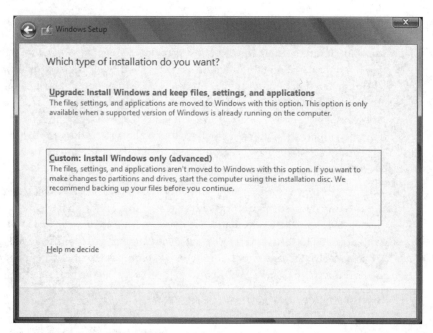

Figure 27-6 Reinstalling Windows 8.1 is almost a last resort to get Windows to start.

If reinstalling Windows fails, your hard drive is probably too corrupted to be usable. Follow the steps in the next section, "What to do if you can't see your system drive," to replace your drive and reinstall Windows.

What to do if you can't see your system drive

If you can't read your system drive, that could mean several different things:

- Your hard drive has completely failed.

- The cable attaching your hard drive to your PC has failed.

- The power cable attached to your hard drive has failed.

- The port on your motherboard that connects to your hard drive has failed.

If your PC is under warranty, now is a good time to contact your hardware manufacturer's technical support. If your PC isn't under warranty, you're not comfortable digging inside your computer, and you think your PC might be less expensive to repair than replace, you might want to hire a repair technician. For more information about technical support services, refer to Chapter 8, "Obtaining help and support."

Of the different components that might have failed, the hardest to fix is a failed hard drive. Therefore, I suggest taking an optimistic approach to the testing by starting with the easiest components to replace. After each step, attempt to start Windows:

1. Replace the cable that connects your hard drive to your PC.

2. Connect a different power cable to your hard drive.

3. Connect your hard drive to a different port on your PC's motherboard.

If Windows still won't start and you've replaced all of these components, your hard drive has probably completely failed. However, it's worth repeating the steps in "Troubleshooting startup from a command prompt" earlier in this chapter to determine whether your drive might be readable.

If you determine that your hard drive has completely failed, replace your drive, which your hardware manufacturer will probably do for free if you are still under warranty. Then, install Windows on the new drive and restore your files. For information about replacing a hard drive, refer to Chapter 12, "Managing storage." For information about installing Windows, refer to Chapter 3, "Buying and installing Windows 8.1." For information about restoring files from a backup, refer to Chapter 10.

Troubleshooting corruption and intermittent failures

The most challenging problems to troubleshoot are those that are intermittent. Your PC might work great for days, weeks, or even months, and then it will unexpectedly crash. Or, even worse, you might experience data corruption issues—files that won't open, weird sounds in audio files, jaggedness in videos, or unexpected blocks of color in image files, as shown in Figure 27-7.

Intermittent problems are usually caused by failing hardware. Sometimes, the cause of the problem is simply a loose connection. Start by unplugging and reconnecting every external adapter. If the problem persists, unplug your PC, open it, remove every card and connector, and then firmly reconnect them.

If that doesn't solve the problem, a component of your PC might be failing. If you can identify the failing component, you can replace it and restore your PC's reliability. The more frequently the problem occurs, the easier it will be to identify the source of your problem. The sections that follow describe different ways to test your PC for hardware problems.

CHAPTER 27

Figure 27-7 A corrupted picture could be caused by a faulty disk or memory chip.

Identifying system changes and error details

Sometimes, intermittent problems are related to a change on your PC, such as updating a driver or installing a new hardware component. Wouldn't it be nice if you kept track of every change you made to your PC and every problem you had so you could look back and see what changed right before you started having problems?

Windows actually does that for you, and you can browse the data using Reliability Monitor, as shown in Figure 27-8. To start Reliability Monitor, search from the Start screen for **reliability** and then click View Reliability History.

Selecting a day on the calendar shows you the events that occurred on that day, including application failures, Windows failures, warnings, and informational events such as updating drivers.

Often, Reliability Monitor will display exactly what's wrong. For example, Figure 27-9 shows an important critical event: Video Hardware Error. This can indicate that the video driver needs to be updated or that the video adapter is failing.

▶ **Troubleshooting blue screens** Watch the video at *http://aka.ms/WinIO/bluescreen*.

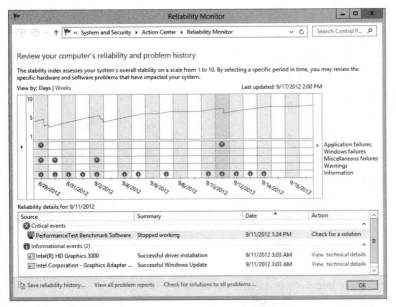

Figure 27-8 Reliability Monitor displays system changes and errors.

Reliability details for: week of 7/29/2012

Source	Summary	Date	Action
⊗ Critical events (2)			⌃
Windows Explorer	**Stopped responding and was closed**	**7/30/2012 1:51 PM**	Check for a solut...
Windows	Video hardware error	8/3/2012 8:31 PM	Check for a soluti...

Figure 27-9 Reliability Monitor lists critical events that can identify failing hardware.

If you experience a Stop error, more commonly known as a blue screen, you'll see a Windows critical event labeled Shut Down Unexpectedly or Windows Stopped Working. Double-click it to view the details, and then identify the error code. In Figure 27-10, the error code is 27 (it's labeled BCCode). Now, search the Internet for "stop error *<error_code>*" for clues about likely causes.

I dedicated entire chapters in the *Windows Vista Resource Kit* and *Windows 7 Resource Kit* to troubleshooting blue screens, and little has changed in Windows 8.1. However, most blue screens are caused by hardware and driver problems, and the other techniques described in this chapter should be sufficient for you to identify the source of those failures. If you really want to get your hands dirty and analyze the cause of your blue screen, read "Windows Bugcheck Analysis" at *http://social.technet.microsoft.com/wiki/contents/articles/6302.windows-bugcheck-analysis-en-us.aspx.*

CHAPTER 27

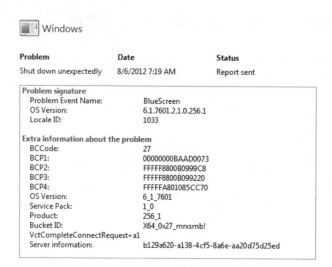

Figure 27-10 After a blue screen, use Reliability Monitor to identify the error code, and then search the Internet for more information about the code.

To use Reliability Monitor to identify the source of a less obvious problem, look through the calendar for the red icons that indicate some type of error. Find when the errors started, and then look for informational events that occurred that same day or just prior.

If you updated a driver a few days before your PC started crashing randomly, there's a good chance that the driver is the cause of your problems. Visit the hardware manufacturer's website to see if an updated driver is available. If you have the latest version of the driver, you might be able to solve your problem by rolling back the driver to the previous version. Run Device Manager from Settings, right-click the problem device, and then click Properties. If available, click Roll Back Driver.

If you installed new hardware before the problems started, check the hardware manufacturer's website for a newer version of the driver. If one is available, install it and see if that solves your problem. If a newer driver isn't available, or if it doesn't solve your problem, try disconnecting the new hardware to see if your problems stop. If your problems go away when you remove the hardware, the hardware was the source of your problem.

Testing your hard drive

A failing hard drive can read data from or write data to the disk incorrectly. This can lead to corrupted files. If Windows 8.1 attempts to read in data from different parts of the system, such as a system file or the page file, that corrupted data might cause Windows to display a Stop error, commonly known as a blue screen.

The easiest way to test your disk for errors is to open a command prompt and run **chkdsk c:**. If the output contains the phrase "Windows found problems with the file system," shown in bold among the other ChkDsk output in the following example, your disk has some corruption.

```
The type of the file system is NTFS.
Volume label is OS.

WARNING!  F parameter not specified.
Running CHKDSK in read-only mode.

CHKDSK is verifying files (stage 1 of 3)...
  808960 file records processed.
File verification completed.
  3805 large file records processed.
  0 bad file records processed.
  0 EA records processed.
  123 reparse records processed.
CHKDSK is verifying indexes (stage 2 of 3)...
  988174 index entries processed.
Index verification completed.
  0 unindexed files scanned.
  0 unindexed files recovered.
CHKDSK is verifying security descriptors (stage 3 of 3)...
  808960 file SDs/SIDs processed.
Security descriptor verification completed.
  89608 data files processed.
CHKDSK is verifying Usn Journal...
  35799856 USN bytes processed.
Usn Journal verification completed.
The Volume Bitmap is incorrect.
Windows found problems with the file system.
Run CHKDSK with the /F (fix) option to correct these.

  468847615 KB total disk space.
  439772332 KB in 444431 files.
     327964 KB in 89609 indexes.
          0 KB in bad sectors.
     929763 KB in use by the system.
      65536 KB occupied by the log file.
   27817556 KB available on disk.

       4096 bytes in each allocation unit.
  117211903 total allocation units on disk.
    6954389 allocation units available on disk.
```

If ChkDsk finds any errors, your disk might be in the process of failing. However, because errors can be caused by power fluctuations, power failures, and unexpected shutdowns, your disk might also be healthy. Run **chkdsk c: /f /r** at a command prompt and restart your computer to fix the errors on your C drive (a process that can take minutes or hours). In a few days or a week, run **chkdsk c:** again. If more errors have appeared, that's a sign that your disk is failing, and you should replace it, as described in Chapter 12.

Either way, please make sure you have a recent backup, as described in Chapter 10.

Testing your memory

Memory failures can cause intermittent, unpredictable crashes and data corruption. In fact, memory errors can show the same symptoms as a failing hard drive.

If you're experiencing those symptoms, you should run memory-testing software to diagnose it. Windows 8.1 has memory-testing software built in. To run the memory-testing software, search from the Start screen for **memory** and select Windows Memory Diagnostic. Then, click Restart Now And Check For Problems, as shown in Figure 27-11.

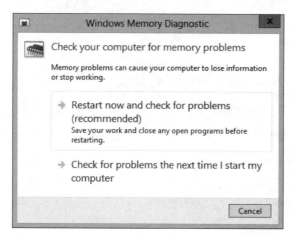

Figure 27-11 Use Windows Memory Diagnostics to test your memory.

Windows shuts down and launches the Windows Memory Diagnostics Tool within Windows Recovery Environment (RE), as shown in Figure 27-12. It's not a touch friendly app, but you don't really need to interact with it; just wait a few minutes for it to finish. Windows will restart and notify you whether Windows Memory Diagnostics found any problems.

▶ **Testing your memory** Watch the video at *http://aka.ms/WinIO/memory*.

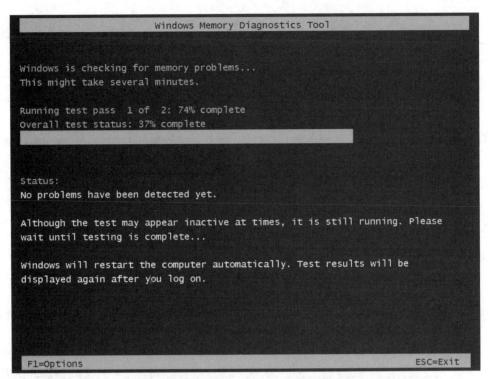

```
                        Windows Memory Diagnostics Tool

Windows is checking for memory problems...
This might take several minutes.

Running test pass  1 of  2: 74% complete
Overall test status: 37% complete



Status:
No problems have been detected yet.

Although the test may appear inactive at times, it is still running. Please
wait until testing is complete...

Windows will restart the computer automatically. Test results will be
displayed again after you log on.




 F1=Options                                                      ESC=Exit
```

Figure 27-12 The Windows Memory Diagnostics Tool runs within Windows RE.

Windows Memory Diagnostics tells you of the results in a notification on the desktop, but that's easy to miss. To look up the results in Event Viewer, run **compmgmt.msc** from the Start screen. Select System Tools\Event Viewer\Windows Logs\System. Then, look through the results for an event with a source of MemoryDiagnostics-Results. Select it, as shown in Figure 27-13, and view the results on the General tab of the lower pane.

If Windows Memory Diagnostics finds a problem, you definitely have failing memory. If it doesn't find a problem, you might still have failing memory, because Windows Memory Diagnostics isn't the most thorough testing software. I recommend getting a second opinion by running the free Memtest86+ tool.

Download the Memtest86+ Auto-installer for USB Key from *http://www.memtest.org/#downiso* and use it to create a bootable flash drive. If you prefer to boot from a CD, download the Pre-Compiled Bootable ISO (.zip). Extract the ISO file from the ZIP file, and then burn it to a CD. Restart your PC and boot from the flash drive or CD. Memtest86+ automatically runs its exhaustive testing, as shown in Figure 27-14, which might take an hour depending on how much memory your PC has.

CHAPTER 27

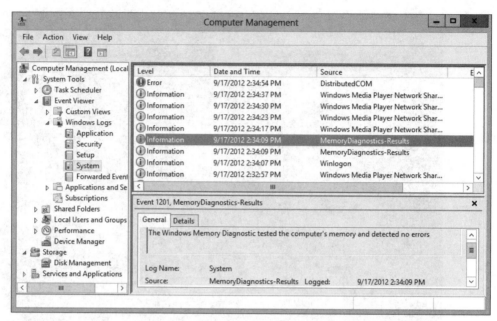

Figure 27-13 View Windows Memory Diagnostics results in Event Viewer.

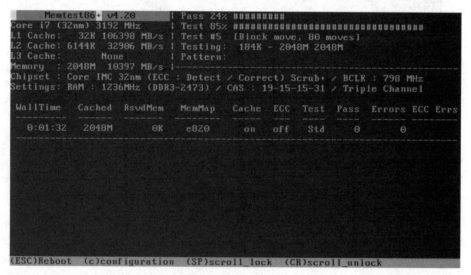

Figure 27-14 Memtest86+ provides more exhaustive testing than Windows Memory Diagnostics.

Memtest86+ displays errors in bright red messages in the bottom half of the screen, and if your memory is faulty, it'll find the problem. Memtest86+ typically does a good job of displaying precisely which memory chip is failing. However, it can be difficult to determine which of several chips is failing. If you're not sure which chip is the problem, replace one chip and repeat the test. If you see errors again, you replaced the wrong chip. Swap the next memory chip until the errors stop.

If your PC is still under warranty, contact your hardware manufacturer's support so they can repair your PC. If your PC isn't under warranty, don't worry: replacing memory is one of the more inexpensive and straightforward PC repair tasks.

On a desktop PC, memory chips are relatively easy to replace. Buy a new memory chip exactly like your original chip, shut down and unplug your PC, open the case, touch the case to discharge any static electricity in your body, and then replace the chip. Your problem should be solved.

On mobile PCs, it might be just as easy. Many mobile PCs, especially larger mobile PCs, have memory that users can replace or upgrade. More compact mobile PCs, especially netbooks, ultrabooks, and tablets, often have memory that is permanently attached to the motherboard and therefore cannot be easily replaced. Contact your hardware manufacturer or a skilled repair technician to perform the repair.

Testing other hardware components

You can use Ultimate Boot CD, available at *http://www.ultimatebootcd.com*, to test your memory and hard disk, as well as just about every other hardware component, including your processor, video memory, and monitor pixels. Figure 27-15 shows the startup menu.

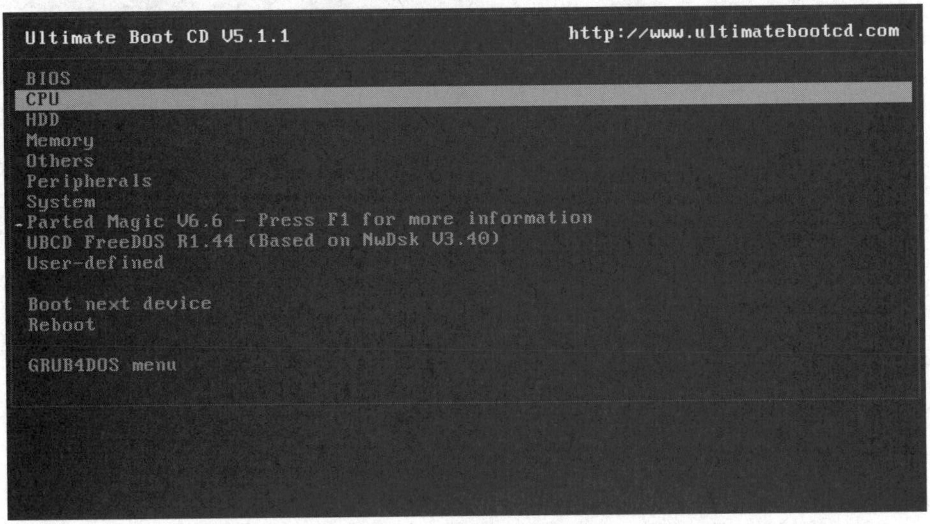

Figure 27-15 The self-proclaimed Ultimate Boot CD includes a variety of useful tools for testing your PC's hardware.

As the not-so-humble name suggests, the Ultimate Boot CD really is quite comprehensive. In fact, it has a few too many tools for me to describe them all. The categories of tools include:

- **CPU**   A variety of tools to give your processor an extreme workout. If your processor is overclocked or overheating, this will cause a failure. Verify that your processor fan is working properly, clean the dust out of your PC, and if you overclocked your processor, set it back to the default speed.

- **HDD, Diagnostics**   A variety of tools for testing and diagnosing your hard drives.

- **Memory**   Test your PC's memory. Among other tools, this includes Memtest86+, discussed in the previous section.

- **Peripherals, Video Memory Stress Test**   Tests the memory in your video card for errors, as shown in Figure 27-16.

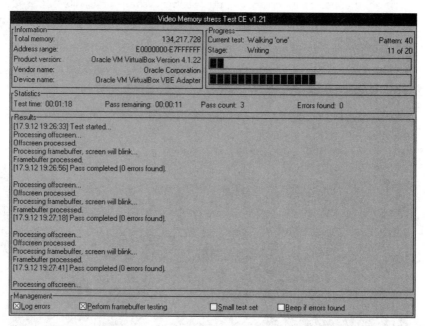

Figure 27-16 Use Video Memory Stress Test to determine whether your video adapter has faulty memory.

Refreshing your PC

With earlier versions of Windows, many people followed a two-step troubleshooting process for all problems: first, they restarted their PC. If that didn't fix the problem, they reinstalled Windows.

That's a rather unsophisticated approach, but it does have merit. Restarting the PC clears the memory and solves most temporary software issues. Reinstalling Windows cleans the slate completely, and usually solves all problems that aren't hardware related.

As powerful as it is to reinstall Windows, it's also really time-consuming. You need to reinstall every application that you use and reconfigure all your settings. The entire task can take a full day.

Windows 8.1 has a new feature: refreshing your PC. When you choose to refresh your PC, Windows 8.1 follows this process:

1. Starts Windows RE.

2. Saves user settings and files to a location on the same disk.

3. Reinstalls a fresh copy of Windows 8.1.

4. Restores user files and settings.

5. Restarts the new installation of Windows 8.1.

Windows does not restore all system settings when you refresh your PC. Refreshing does restore those settings that have little impact on system stability, including:

- Windows 8.1 applications

- Desktop wallpaper and other personalization settings

- Wireless network connections

- Mobile broadband connections

- Drive letter assignments

- BitLocker and BitLocker To Go settings

Other settings are not retained because they might have an impact on system stability and usability. These include:

- Desktop applications

- File type associations

- Display settings

- Windows Firewall settings

Before beginning the refresh process, take the time to identify any desktop applications that you will need to reinstall afterward. If necessary, locate the installation media and determine any product keys that will be required. Some applications, such as iTunes, might need to be deauthorized before refreshing your PC.

To refresh your PC, click Update And Recovery in PC Settings and then click Recovery. Under Refresh Your PC Without Affecting Your Files, click Get Started. You might be prompted to insert your Windows 8.1 installation media. After a few minutes, Windows 8.1 will restart and refresh your PC, as shown in Figure 27-17.

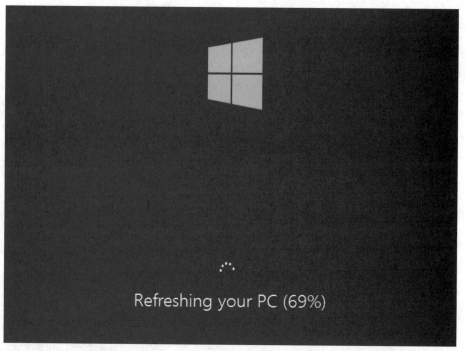

Figure 27-17 Refreshing your PC reinstalls Windows while keeping your documents and most of your settings.

If there were any desktop applications installed prior to the refresh, they will not be available. However, Windows 8.1 will have created an HTML file named Removed Apps on your desktop. View this file in Internet Explorer to see a list of applications that were previously installed.

Inside OUT

Creating a custom refresh image

By default, when you refresh your PC, Windows restores an image created by your PC manufacturer, if it's available, or the default image from the Windows installation media. That image won't include any desktop apps you've installed, however.

Once you get your PC set up and running smoothly, it's a great idea to create a custom refresh image that you can restore in the event something goes wrong in the future, such as a malware infection. Refreshing with that custom image can save you many hours of reinstalling apps and reconfiguring Windows. Custom refresh images are also useful in many business scenarios, such as PCs that are used in classrooms, as kiosks, or by temporary staff.

To capture your PC's current state as the refresh image, open an administrative command prompt (most easily done from the WinX menu) and then run the command **recimg /createimage** *<directory>*, where *<directory>* is a folder that's not in your user profile. If the folder doesn't yet exist, RecImg creates it automatically.

Here's a sample command and output:

```
recimg /createimage C:\RecoveryImage
Source OS location: C:
Recovery image path: C:\RecoveryImage\CustomRefresh.wim
Creating recovery image. Press [ESC] to cancel.
Initializing
100%
Creating snapshot
100%
Writing image (this may take a while)
100%
Registering image
100%

Recovery image creation and registration completed successfully.
```

The next time you refresh your PC, Windows 8.1 will restore that image rather than the default image. If you'd rather not use your custom image, open an administrative command prompt and run the command **recimg /deregister**. You can also simply delete the CustomRefresh.wim file that RecImg creates.

You can also create multiple custom images and refresh your PC to different states. This might be useful if you use your PC for teaching; you could have custom images for different classes or labs. To create multiple images, simply use the **recimg /createimage** *<directory>* command and specify a different folder. Then, run **recimg /setcurrent** *<directory>* to specify the image to use for the next refresh.

Resetting your PC

If refreshing your PC does not solve your problems, you can reset your PC. This process removes all your applications, files, and settings. This allows Windows to fix any software-related problems, but you need to have a backup of your data available to restore and be ready to reinstall any applications and drivers. Be sure to have any media and product keys required to reinstall applications.

When you choose to reset your PC, Windows 8.1:

1. Starts Windows RE.

2. Formats the system drive.

3. Reinstalls a fresh copy of Windows 8.1.

4. Restarts the new installation of Windows 8.1.

To reset your PC, click Update And Recovery in PC Settings, and then click Recovery. Under Remove Everything And Reinstall Windows, click Get Started.

When prompted to fully clean your drive, select Just Remove My Files if you are going to continue to use your PC. If you're giving your PC to someone else, select Fully Clean The Drive to help protect your privacy. You might be prompted to insert your Windows 8.1 installation media. After you click Reset, Windows 8.1 will restart and reset your PC.

Inside OUT

Reset your PC before selling it or giving it away

Before you give your PC away or sell it, you should be sure you completely remove all your apps and files. Resetting your PC is the perfect way to do this. On the Do You Want To Fully Clean Your Drive page, as shown in Figure 27-18, select Fully Clean The Drive.

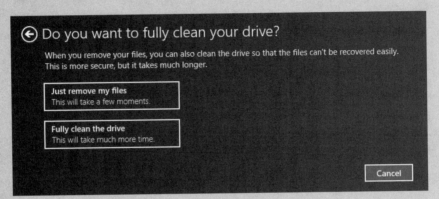

Figure 27-18 Select Fully Clean The Drive before giving your PC to someone you don't trust.

If you select Just Remove My Files, your PC's next owner could get to your data quite easily. When you select Fully Clean The Drive, Windows writes random patterns over your data to reduce the risk of someone recovering your personal files. While this provides sufficient confidentiality for most users, you might need special software to meet regulatory requirements or to protect your data from sophisticated computer forensics.

If you really want to do everything you can to erase the contents of your hard disk, download Darik's Boot And Nuke and create a bootable CD or flash drive from the ISO file. After downloading the ISO file, insert a blank CD into your computer, right-click the ISO file in File Explorer on the desktop, and then click Burn Disk Image. If you can't boot from a CD, use the Unetbootin tool (available at *http://www.blancco.com/us/frontpage/*) to create a bootable USB flash drive. Start your PC from the CD or flash drive, and type **autonuke** at the prompt. Darik's Boot And Nuke is free software, and doesn't offer any guarantees, and neither can I. However, my experience has been that your data will be about as gone as it's going to get. Darik's Boot And Nuke writes over your data multiple times using cryptographic techniques, going beyond what Windows does.

If you need to remove your data in a way that complies with regulatory requirements, or you want software that really does offer a guarantee, check out Blancco, available for a fee at *http://www.blancco.com/us/frontpage*.

Index to troubleshooting topics

Topic	Description	Page
Audio	I have terrible sound quality when using an aux-in port	349
	My CDs won't burn	355
	How can I improve my sound quality?	382
AutoPlay	How can I fix what Windows does with a memory card?	329
Backups	How do I recover app-specific backups?	235
	My backups aren't working	239
BitLocker	Windows says I don't have a TPM	281
Disk management	Why can't I shrink my drive more?	102
File management	Where did my app data go?	121
Hardware	Why is my hard drive making so much noise?	629
Hyper-V	Why is Hyper-V Manager empty?	477
Malware	How can I remove malware that won't go away?	450
Networking	I have trouble watching videos. Is my Internet connection fast enough?	318
	I can't connect to the Internet	512
	When I set up an ad hoc network, I get the message, "The hosted network couldn't be started"	549
	I can't find the other computer on my ad hoc network	550
	Why can't I connect to a homegroup?	586
	Why can't I connect to my printer?	602
Printing	Why can't I print anymore?	604
Search	My search is not working correctly	251

Topic	Description	Page
Start screen	One of my apps is missing from the Start screen	125
Startup	Why isn't my PC booting from the DVD or flash drive?	93
	How do I fix Windows when it won't start?	243

Index

Symbols and Numbers

* (asterisk) wildcard, 225–226
... (ellipses), 308
+ (Plus sign), Music app, 311
3-D printer support, 46
3G/4G. *See* mobile broadband
7-Zip tool, 218
32-bit vs. 64-bit upgrades to Windows 8.1, 113
802.11 Wi-Fi standards, 530–531

A

accelerometers, 21–22
Access Control Assistance Operators group, 420
access control lists (ACLs), 219
accessibility
  app guidelines for, 173
  apps, zooming, 176
  Braille support, 186
  configuration wizard for, 174–175
  desktop size settings, 176
  dyslexia, 173, 192–193
  FilterKeys, 188–189
  hardware for, 174
  high contrast mode for, 177
  keyboard shortcuts for, 188–189
  keyboard-only input, 187–189
  MAGic Screen Magnification, 183
  Magnifier, 174, 177–182
  Make Everything On Your Screen Bigger option,
    175–176
  monitor size recommendation, 174
  mouse only access, 189
  mouse sticks, 174
  new features of Windows 8.1, 18
  On-Screen Keyboard, 189
  passwords, 187
  pointer settings, 186–187
  purpose of features for, 173
  speech recognition, 190–191
  Sticky Keys, 187
  tabbing for element access, 187
  touch screen keyboard, activate key on lift option, 192
  visual, 175–183
  voice recognition feature for, 174
accounts
  assigned access to apps, 46
  Computer Management console, opening, 415–416
  deleting, 417–418
  disabling, 417
  guests, creation for, 416–417
  local user. *See* local user accounts
  Microsoft. *See* Microsoft accounts
  setting up during installation, 100
  SYSTEM account, 219–220
  user. *See* user accounts
ACLs (access control lists), 219
Action Center warnings, 471–472
active areas of screens, 4
Active Directory, 91
Active Protection Service, 99
activity reporting feature, Family Safety, 428–430
ad hoc networking
  creating hosted networks, 547–549
  error messages, 549
  ICS settings, 552–553
  IP addresses, connecting by, 550
  IP addresses, editing, 552–553
  name resolution issues, 550
  sharing Internet connections with, 550–553
  situations used for, 547
  SSIDs for, 549
  stopping, 549
adapters. *See* network adapters
adaptive brightness, 21, 138
administrative tools on Start screen, 126, 416

administrators
　command prompts run as, 548
　group for. *See* Administrators group
　privileges, UAC warnings, 442
　running apps as, 143–144
　taking ownership of folders as, 163
Administrators group
　additional accounts not added to, 397
　permissions held by, 219–220
　rights of, 420
Adobe Flash support, 45
Adobe Lightroom, 79
Adobe Photoshop Lightroom, 341
Adobe Premiere, 323
Advanced Query Syntax (AQS), 16
advanced searching with File Explorer, 225–227
adware, 439
affinity, processor, 627–629
AirCrack-NG, 535
airplane mode, 28, 560
All Apps page, 125–126
ALS (ambient light sensors), 21
Alt+Tab command, 5
Amazon Prime, 353
ambient light sensors (ALS), 21
analyzing disk space, 229
Android devices, accessing SkyDrive from, 292–294
Anonymizer.com, 425
Answer Desk, 196
answerdesk.com, 195
antennas, Wi-Fi, 533–534
antimalware apps
　third-party, scanning with, 450
　Windows Defender, 445–446
antivirus apps, 445–446
APIPA (Automatic Private IP Addressing), 510
App History tab, Task Manager, 34
app searches
　adding folders to search indexes, 251
　disabling indexing for files or folders, 252–254
　file type filter issues, 256
　history, clearing, 250
　managing file indexing, 251–260
　managing search suggestions, 250
　managing searchable files and folders, 251–254
　recording of, 250
　Search charm for, 249
appearance. *See* personalization
Apple TV, 353

apps. *See also specific apps*
　accessibility guidelines, 173
　activity reporting feature of Family Safety, 429–430
　adding to Start screen, 125
　administrator, running as an, 143–144
　affinity settings, processor, 627–629
　All Apps screen, 43
　as an architectural layer, 197
　assigned access to, 46
　background apps, 51
　background tasks, 63–64
　backups specific to, 235
　booting to, 38–40
　busy, finding, 625–627
　charms for, 13–14. *See also* charms
　closing by sliding, 6, 59
　commands, keyboard shortcut to view, 8
　commands, swiping to view, 5
　commands, toolbar, 58
　common features of, 52–54
　compatibility settings for, 165–167
　configuration settings for, 162
　desktop. *See* desktop apps
　desktop, compared to, 160
　developers of, determining, 198
　Devices app with, 53
　digital signatures of, 161, 162
　displaying multiple, 37–38
　docking by sliding, 6
　event monitoring, 170–171
　executable files of, finding paths for, 460
　file associations for, 64–67
　file locations of components of, 162
　flicking to select to change settings, 6
　grouping on Start screen, 124
　help specific to, 196–197, 199–200
　history, viewing in Task Manager, 640–641
　HTML5 style, 160–162
　icons of, file location for, 124
　incoming connections for, allowing or denying, 458–465
　installing, 55–56, 147–148
　internal mechanics of, 160–165
　isolation of, 62
　launching from the desktop, 132–133
　line-of-business (LOB) apps, 55–56
　listing apps installed since last restore point, 454
　live tiles of, 59–61. *See also* tiles
　lock screen, displaying data on the, 61
　lock screen notifications, enabling, 130–131

manifests, 164–165
multiple on a screen, 58–59. *See also* snapping apps
network packet examination of, 574–577
new user default apps, 168
notifications from. *See* notifications
package management, 168–170
paying for, 55
performance requirements for, 63
permissions for, 158–159
persistence through PC refreshes, 51
Pin To Start option, 61, 125
pinning to the Start screen, 120
preventing users from uninstalling, 149
priority, setting, 626–629
publishers of, viewing, 638
recently used, viewing, 5–7
resource access, configuring, 52
restricting with Family Safety, 432–433
resuming, 54
running, keyboard shortcut for, 8
sandboxing of, 62
saving data during upgrades to Windows 8.1, 121–122
Search charm with, 52, 249
searching the Store for, 52
searching within. *See* app searches
Settings charm with, 52, 53
Share charm with, 53. *See also* Share charm
sideloading, 55–56
single user rule, 160, 168
SmartScreen filter warnings about, 24
snapping, 58–59
snapping with a mouse, 7
snapping with shortcuts, 8
standardization for Windows 8.1, 147
Start screen, adding to, 125
starting, special settings for, 627–629
starting with Task Manager, 638
startup, launching during. *See* startup apps
Steps Recorder, 157
stopping with Task Manager, 626
suspended, viewing, 638
suspension of, automatic, 62–63
switching, 8
System Performance reports, 651–652
tiles for. *See* tiles
transferring during upgrades, 114–116
troubleshooting, 157
uninstalling, 148–149, 228, 449, 617
updates for, 56–57, 614
users, listing by, 642

Windows 8.1–specific features of, 51
Windows Firewall, disabling to test, 465–467
Windows Store apps vs. desktop apps, 8
XAML style, 160–161
AQS (Advanced Query Syntax), 16
Arch Linux, 478
architecture of Windows 8.1
basic layers of, 197
networking architecture, 505–508
ARM processors
support for apps, 51
Windows 8.1 RT, support for, 22
assistance. *See* **Remote Assistance**
associating files with apps, 64–67
asterisk (*) wildcard, 225–226
Audacity, 349
audio
analog output of, 379
file format issues with DMRs, 345
MP3 format, 313
music. *See* music; Music app
sound cards for, 379–380
sound quality, 381–382
stereos, Xbox Music service with, 343–344
support for VMs, 502
surround sound, 364
transcoding media files, 346
volume, increasing by reencoding files, 349
WMA (Windows Media Audio) format, 312–313
authentication. *See also* **login screen**
Bluetooth device, 555–556
cached credentials for, 27
autocorrection of words, 15, 68
Automatic Private IP Addressing (APIPA), 510
Automatic Repair option for startup problems, 654–655
**Automatic Setup Of Network Connected Devices
setting, 602**
automatic stop action for VMs, 494
AutoPlay
configuring, 151–152
memory card settings, 329
aux-in ports, 348, 349

B
backdoors, 441
background apps, 51
background tasks, 63–64
backgrounds of Start screen, 39, 125
BackTrack Linux, 535
Backup Operators group, 420

backups
app-specific, 235
connecting to external disks, 235–236
connecting to internal disks, 236–238
desktop apps, of, 243
different disk backups, 234
disaster scenarios, 246–247
disk capacity recommendation, 238
File History for, 239–241
frequency of, 240–241
homegroup drive specification, 241
logs of, 239
loss scenarios, 233–234
Macrium Reflect Free, 243
Microsoft accounts for, 243
multiple versions of files, settings for, 240–241
off-site backups, 234–235
online backup services, 246
RAID with, 235
resiliency compared to, 267
restoring files, 241–242
same disk backups, 234
SkyDrive, excluding from, 300
strategies for, basic, 234–235
system image, 243
techniques matched to loss scenarios, 235
testing, 242
travel, disks for, 238–239
troubleshooting, 239
backward compatibility
drivers, of, 3
with earlier versions of Windows, 3
Hyper-V for running other OSs. *See* Hyper-V
settings for apps, 165–167
Windows RT lack of, 22
Balanced power plan, 136–137
bandwidth issues
ISP upstream vs. downstream, 514
limiting bandwidth per process, 491
video quality issues from, 318
VM settings for, 489–491
banking online, dangers of, 443–444
batch files, 628–629
batteries
counter for, 647
efficiency improvements to extend life of, 22
maintaining, 618–619
power plans for, 136–137
preventing indexing while running on, 258

replacing, 619
warning settings, 138
BCDEdit tool
Safe Mode, addition with, 19
startup timer control with, 109
belt and suspenders concept, 590
benchmarking. *See also* **performance**
hard disk drives, 623–624
HD Tune, 624
online comparisons of PCs, 622
PerformanceTest tool, 621–622
Windows Experience Index discontinued, 621
Bing
News, 83
settings, 135
translate.bing.com, 425
BIOS (basic input/output system)
adding disk drives, boot settings for, 237
boot order settings, 93
DEP (Data Execution Prevention), 112
hard drive for booting, selecting, 654
Hyper-V settings, 474
rootkits in, 456–457
TPM settings, 280–281
UEFI support, 18
updating to Windows 8.1, 111
VM settings configuration, 485
BitLocker
automatic unlock mode, 271
Back Up Recovery Key command, 279
benefits of, 268
data drives with, 270–271
data loss and recovery issue, 269–270
deleted file security issue, 269
drawbacks of, 269–270
enabling, 279–280
encryption role of, 26
error-free drive requirement, 279
Full Volume encryption advantage, 269
identification modes for decryption, 271–273
improvements in, 268
keys, 269–270
locking computer when not in use recommendation, 273
Microsoft accounts with, 277–278
offloading feature, 268
performance impact of, 269
recovery keys, 276–279
removable drives with, 281–283

standard edition, added to, 46
startup, encryption limited to, 273
suspending, 275–276
system drives with, 270
TPM chips with, 269–273, 280–281
TPM, using without a, 274–275
troubleshooting failed enabling of, 281
turning off, 275
USB flash drives as keys, 271, 276–279
Use Disk Space Only encryption feature, 268–269
VM incompatibility with, 500
Windows 8.1 Pro, as a feature of, 91
Blancco, 675
Blocked By Family Safety warning, 433
blue screens of death, 663–665
Bluetooth
adding devices, 555–556
capabilities of, 554
discoverable mode, 554–556
keyboards, 388
pairing process, 554–557
sending files between PCs, 556–559
tethering, 561
bookmarks. *See* **Favorites**
bootable flash drives
making, 92–93
Puppy Linux, 220–221
UNetbootin tool, 92, 221
booting VMs, 485
booting Windows 8.1
advanced options of, 20
BIOS boot order settings, 93
boot sector corruption, fixing, 659
change defaults option, 19–20
to the desktop, 38–40
dual operating systems. *See* dual-booting
live CDs for, 220–221
Safe Mode, 19
Secured Boot, 22
startup after boot sequence. *See* startups
TPM (Trusted Platform Module), 26
UEFI support, 18
VHD (virtual hard disk) booting, 91
botnets, 441
bottom edge of screen, swiping from, 5
Boxee, 361
Braille support, 186
brightness
adaptive brightness, 21, 138

power settings, relation to, 136–138
browsers, Internet
add-on malware, 439–440
default. *See* Internet Explorer 11
exploitation of by malware, 438, 441
legacy, testing in Hyper-V, 476
private browsing, 447–448
SkyDrive with, 294–295
buffer overflow attacks, 45
built-in apps
ability to work together, 67
Calendar. *See* Calendar app
Camera. *See* Camera app
default apps for new users, 168
File Explorer. *See* File Explorer
Finance, 80–81
Food And Drink, 85
Games, 77
Health And Fitness, 85–86
Help + Tips app, 86–87
Internet Explorer 11. *See* Internet Explorer 11
Mail. *See* Mail app
Maps, 82
Music. *See* Music app
News, 83
People. *See* People app
Photos. *See* Photos app
Reader, 81
Reading List, 87
Scan app, 87
Sound Recorder app, 87
Sports, 84
Travel, 84
Video. *See* Video app
Weather, 80
bundled malware, 438–439
BYOD (Bring Your Own Device) support, 47

C

cable Internet connections, 514, 581
cable TV service with HTPCs, 382–387
CableCARD, 383–384
cabling
building codes for, 382
Ethernet, 527
HDMI, 373, 375–376
HTPCs with TVs, 373–376, 381–382
intermittent failures, as a source of, 661
speaker cables, 382
caches, Internet Explorer, 229

Calendar app
editing events in, 75
live tiles of, 75
notifications by, 60
as part of larger app, 149
Camera app
as a default new user app, 168
taking pictures with, 82
cameras
access to while in lock screen, 42
AutoPlay with, 151–152
importing photos from, 326–330
JPG files, 332–333
manufacturers' websites for codecs, 334
RAW files, 79, 332–334
wireless networking of, 327
Carbonite, 246
cars, playing music from portable devices, 348–350
CAs (certification authorities), 444
cases, 371–372
cassette adapters, 349
Category 6 cables, 527
cd command, 572
CDs
AutoPlay, 151–152
burning, 354–355
MP3 format on, 350, 355
ripping songs from, 308, 313–315
CEIP (Customer Experience Improvement Program), 97–99
cellular networks. *See* mobile broadband
CentOS integration services, 491–493
certificates
Certificate Export Wizard, 223–224
Certmgr, 224–225
HTTPS use of, 444
Ceton InfiniTV4 card, 384
Change access, 589–590
charms
Devices. *See* Devices charm
keyboard shortcut for displaying, 8
purpose of, 13–14
Search. *See* Search charm
Settings. *See* Settings charm
Share. *See* Share charm
standard set of, 13
Start, 10, 13
swiping to view, 5
viewing with mouse controls, 7

children
protecting. *See* Family Safety
user accounts, specifying as, 395–396
chkdsk command, 284–285, 657, 665–666
circles, selection, 4
ClearType, 178
Clipboard with Hyper-V, 499
closed captioning, 365
closing apps, 6, 59
cloud services
connection speed issues, 245
costs of, 245
Microsoft accounts enabling of integration with, 26–27
as new feature of Windows 8.1, 3
storage. *See* SkyDrive
coax cables for Ethernet, 527–528
codecs
Home Theater PCs, availability for, 359
Movie Maker limitations without, 320
collaboration, 302–304
Collection command, Music app, 307, 310–311
command prompts
administrators, running as, 548
as boot option, 20
Shift+F10 to open, 105
commands
app toolbar commands, 58
app-specific, swiping to view, 5
command line. *See* command prompts
keyboard. *See* keyboard shortcuts
speech-based, 190–191
Start screen, running from, 10
compatibility
drivers, backward, 3
with earlier versions of Windows, 3
Hyper-V for running other OSs. *See* Hyper-V
settings for apps, 165–167
Windows RT lack of backward, 22
complex passwords, 406–411, 414
composite TV connections, 374–376
compression
compressed attribute, 214
compressing drives, 228
zipping folders, 218
Computer Management console
adding users to existing groups, 419
delaying starting automatic services, 630–633
deleting accounts, 417–418
disabling accounts, 417
groups, creating custom, 418–419

guests, account creation for, 416–417
indexing settings, 258–259
launching, 101
Local Users And Groups node, 416
opening, 415–416
Connectify Hotspot app, 553–554
context menus
vs. app toolbar commands, 58
displaying with hold gesture, 5
opening with a mouse device, 7
contrast, high mode for accessibility, 177
Control Panel
deleting user accounts, 418
PC Settings as partial replacement for, 14–15
Rating Systems page, 434–435
copy protection of music, 312–313
copying
files to a new PC, 116–119
files with File Explorer, 72–74
corruption issues
examples of, 661–662
testing hard disk drives, 664–666
testing memory, 666–669
Ultimate Boot CD, 669–670
counters, performance
data collector sets, 648–652
graphing, 645–646
list of, 646–647
CPUs. *See* processors
Cryptographic Operators group, 420
CSS3 support, 69, 162
Ctrl+H command, 53
Ctrl+Shift+Esc, 635
Curfew feature, Family Safety, 432
Customer Experience Improvement Program (CEIP),
    97–99

D

Darik's Boot And Nuke, 675
data collector sets, Performance Monitor, 648–652
Data Execution Prevention (DEP), 112
data loss scenarios, 233–235
data storage. *See* storage
dates, sorting files by, 226–227
Debian, VM memory requirements for, 478
default apps for new users, 168
default gateways
configuring, 517–518
pinging, 570–571, 577–578
default programs, setting, 64–67, 149–151

delaying automatic services, 630–633
DEP (Data Execution Prevention), 112
desktop
applications running on. *See* desktop apps
backward compatibility function of, 132
booting directly to, 38–40
launching apps from, 132–133
listing apps of first, 40
opening, 8
peek preview, 141
personalization of, 132–135
pinning apps to taskbar, 132–133
Recycle Bin, 134–135
Run dialog box, 10
shortcuts, creating for apps, 133
Start button, 40
Start menu, adding to, 12, 132
switching with Start screen, 10
text size settings, 176
wallpaper selection for, 44
desktop apps
administrative privileges for, 165–167
affinity settings, processor, 627–629
automatic startup, setting for, 370–371
busy, finding, 625–627
closing frozen, 635
compatibility settings for, 165–167
defaults file types for, setting, 149–151
legacy apps, options for running, 116
pinning to Start screen, 134
pinning to taskbar, 133
priority, setting, 626–629
removing startup apps, 630
saving data during upgrades to Windows 8.1, 121–122
security dangers of, 446. *See also* malware
starting, special settings for, 627–629
startup apps, 153–154
superior control of app windows with, 59
transferring during upgrades, 114–116
updates for, 614–615
Windows Store apps, difference from, 9, 160
Device Manager
disabling unused hardware, 633–634
hardware models, determining, 615–616
Network Adapters settings, 578
Devices charm
capabilities of, 13
commonality to touch apps, 53
printing from, 330–331
streaming to stereos with, 345–346

DHCP (Dynamic Host Configuration Protocol)
address assignment by, 510–511
alternate configuration, 517–518
DNS configuration by, 511–512
IP address settings, 578
router provision of, 507
sharing Internet connections from one device, 552
dictionary attacks, 406
diet app, 85–86
Digital Living Network Alliance (DLNA) devices, 345–346
digital media
music. *See* Music app
video. *See* Video app
digital media receivers (DMRs), 345–347
digital signatures
apps, for, 161, 162
malware prevention with, 441
Digital Video Recorders (DVRs), 360
disabling accounts, 417
disaster scenarios, 246–247
Disk Cleanup tool
deletion of unnecessary files with, 228
removing previous Windows installations, 121–122
Disk Management console
initializing disk drives, 237–238
shrinking partitions, 101–104
VHD creation, 104–108
disk space, freeing up, 228–230
Disk2VHD, 498
DiskPart command, 106
Dism, 168–170
displays
accessibility options, 175–183
adaptive brightness, 21
automatic screen rotation, 21–22
brightness settings, 136–138
high contrast mode for accessibility, 177
Media Center settings for, 364
multiple monitor support, 33, 139–140
multitasking apps, 37–38
power settings, 136–138
resolution requirements, 21
Distributed COM Users group, 420
.dll files, 161, 162
DLNA (Digital Living Network Alliance) devices, 345–346
DMRs (digital media receivers)
homegroups, setting sharing for, 583
HTPCs streaming to, 361
processor requirements for HTPCs with, 377
video and music, configuring to stream, 345–347

DNS (Domain Name Service)
Dynamic DNS, 522
mail server lookups, 574
manually configuring, 517–518
mechanics of, 511
pinging to test servers, 568
public DNS server addresses, 513
troubleshooting, 512–513
Do Not Track IE setting, 98
docking apps, 5–6
documents, editing online with SkyDrive, 302–304
Documents library, 215–216
Domain Name Service. *See* DNS (Domain Name Service)
domain names, registering for, 542, 546
Domain network type, 463–464
dragging objects, gesture for, 5–6
Dragon voice recognition, 174, 191
drive letters
mapping network drives, 590–592
pools, Storage Space, associated with, 262
relation to partitions, 101
drivers
32-bit vs. 64-bit driver printer issues, 594–595
as an architectural layer, 197
backward compatibility of, 3
as interface between Windows and hardware, 198
optional updates including, 612–613
printer, downloading from PC sharing, 598–599
Reliability Monitor to diagnose problems with, 662–664
updated, as cause of errors, 664
updates for, 615–616
Windows XP compatibility issues, 165–166
drives. *See also* storage
choosing new, 286–287
error correction, 283–285
hard disk. *See* hard disk drives
removable. *See* removable drives
solid state drives. *See* SSDs (solid state drives)
USB. *See* USB flash drives
DRM (Digital Rights Management), 365
Dropbox, 245, 289
DSL Internet connections, 514
dual-booting
benefits of, 100
configuring boot options for, 108–110
separate partition method, 101–104
VHD method for, 104–108
VHD vs. partition method for, 101
DVDs
AutoPlay, 151–152

burning movie DVDs, 355–357
codecs for movie playback not included, 47
DVI, 373–374
DVRs (Digital Video Recorders), 360
Dynamic Host Configuration Protocol. *See* DHCP
    (Dynamic Host Configuration Protocol)
dyslexia, 173, 192–193
Dyslexie, 193

E

Ease Of Access page, PC Settings
high contrast mode option, 177
Magnifier options, 177–182
Make Everything On Your Screen Bigger option,
    175–176
Narrator for, 183–184
Ease Of Access wizard, 174–175
Easy Connect, 204, 206
EasyBCD, 109–110
echo command, 628
edge of screen, swiping from, 5
editing video, 319–323
editions of Windows 8.1
Enterprise edition, 4, 89, 90
list of, 87
Pro edition, 30, 90–91
RT edition, 22
EFS (Encrypting File System), 91, 222–224
elance.com, 546
ellipses (...), 308
email
app for. *See* Mail app
centralizing multiple accounts, 545
cloud storage of, 245
domain names, obtaining for, 542
Hotmail, 541, 543–544
mail servers, 76, 573–574
notifications on lock screen, 130
phishing, 442–444
POP service, 544–545
sharing photos with, 334–335
Windows Live Hotmail, 545
emoticons, 76
encryption
7-Zip tool, 218
backing up keys, 223–224
BitLocker for. *See* BitLocker
encrypted attribute, 214
Encrypting File System (EFS), 91, 222–224
encrypting files and folders, 222–224

hashes, 145
keys, 222–224
recovering files, 224–225
salts, 145
searches, indexing to allow with, 254–255
Wi-Fi standards for, 534–535
Enhanced Protected Mode (EPM), 45–46
Enterprise edition, Windows 8.1, 4, 89, 90
Entertainment Software Rating Board (ESRB), 434–435
environment variables, 163
EPM (Enhanced Protected Mode), 45–46
error correction, drives, 283–285
error messages, 199
ESRB (Entertainment Software Rating Board), 434–435
Ethernet. *See also* networking
coax cables for, 527–528
USB adapters for, 515
wired clients, 508, 526–530
wireless. *See* Wi-Fi
Event Log Readers group, 420
Event Viewer
backup logs, 239
logs for monitoring apps, 170–171
memory diagnostics results, 666–669
Everyone group
access settings for, 589
permissions associated with, 219
Exchange Server, 543
.exe (executable) files
as an XAML file type, 161
finding paths for apps, 460
exercise tracking app, 85–86
Exploit Wednesday, 610
Explore command, Music app, 307
extensions, file name
associating apps with, 64–67
viewing, 213–214
external disks, connecting to, 235–236
Eye-Fi SD cards, 327

F

Facebook
email, 245, 541
Online Communications level, Family Safety, 425
People app integration of, 74
publishing video to, 322–323
Family Safety
activity reporting feature, 428–430
allow all except method, 423
allow based on ratings method, 423–424

Family Safety, *continued*
Allow List Only option, 424
Allow Or Block Websites command, 425
app restrictions, 432–433
Ask A Parent For Permission option, 427
block all except method, 423
Block File Downloads option, 426
capabilities of, 422
children's accounts, option to turn on when creating, 395–396
Curfew feature, 432
Designed For Children level, 425
emailed Activity Reports, 430
evading, 425
General Interest level, 425
Get More Time button, 432
monitoring advice, 426–427
notification on login, 426
Online Communications level, 425
opening, 422
restricting games with, 434–435
Set Web Filtering Level command, 424
Time Allowances, 431–432
turning on, 423
user accounts with, 393
viewing blocked sites with parent's password, 427
Warn On Adult level, 426
web filtering options, 423–427
Your Parent ... warning, 426
fans, 372, 377
favorites
File Explorer, 231
Internet Explorer 11, 70
faxing, 598
Fedora, VM memory requirements for, 478
fiber optic Internet connections, 513
File Explorer
advanced searching with, 225–227
asterisk (*) wildcard, 225–226
batch workflow recommendation, 338–339
context-sensitive tabs, 72
copying files with, 72–74
creating custom libraries, 217
dates, sorting files by, 226–227
default apps for file types, setting, 149–151
desktop app nature of, 71
disabling content indexing for a folder, 253–254
enabling thumbnails by default, 336–337
encryption with, 222–224
extensions of file names, 213–214
favorites, 231
file associations, setting, 65
file permissions, setting, 592–593
finding specific photos, 339
folder sharing, 588–592
homegroups, accessing shared files of, 586–587
mapping network drives, 590–592
modifying file and folder attributes, 214–215
music metadata, editing, 315–316
Open With command, 150–151
opening, 212
organizing photos with, 337–340
permissions, viewing, 219–222
Picture Tools tab, 72
Program Compatibility Troubleshooter, 166–167
rating photos, 337–339
RAW files with, 334
ribbon, 71–72
Scan Drive command, 283–284
searches, non-indexed, 259–260
SkyDrive with, 295–302
taking ownership of folders as an administrator, 163
viewing hidden folders, 163
zipping folders, 218
File History
backups with, 239–241
restoring backed-up files, 241–242
file hosting, web, 546. *See also* SkyDrive
file system
app-first nature of, 211–212
attributes of files and folders, 214
compressed attribute, 214
encrypted attribute, 214
extensions of file names, 213–214
folder hierarchy of, 212–213
hidden attribute, 214
names of files, 213–214
NTFS, 212
read-only attribute, 214
files
accessing remotely with SkyDrive, 300–302
app-first management in Windows 8.1, 211–212
associations with apps, 64–67
attributes, finding by, 16
attributes of, 214
compressed attribute, 214
copying with File Explorer, 72–74
corruption of, 234, 235

dates, sorting by, 226–227
default programs for, setting, 149–151
deleting accidentally, 233, 235
disabling indexing for, 252–254
do not delete files, list of, 230
encrypted attribute, 214
encrypting, 222–224
extensions of file names, 213–214
hidden attribute, 214, 226
names of, 213–214
organization of, tips for, 230–231
permissions for, 219–222, 592–593
read-only attribute, 214
saving, 230
searching for, 16
sending between PCs with Bluetooth, 556–559
sharing. *See* homegroups; sharing
storing. *See* storage
System Performance reports, 651–652
transfer speeds, 582
Turn On File And Printer Sharing setting, 602
versioning issues, 298–300
filtering, adult content settings, 135
FilterKeys, 188–189
Finance app, 80–81, 168
fingerprint scanners, 46
Firewall, Windows. *See* Windows Firewall
firmware updates, 615–616
flash drives
solid state drives. *See* SSDs (solid state drives)
USB. *See* USB flash drives
Flash (Adobe) support, 45
flicking, 6
Flickr, 322–323
FM radio via tuner cards, 385
FM transmitters for streaming, 349–350
folders
attributes of, 214
compressed attribute, 214
counter for data transfers, 647
disabling indexing for, 252–254
encrypting, 222–224
hidden attribute, 214, 226
hidden, viewing, 163
hierarchy of, 212–213
homegroup, adding to another device's library, 586
libraries as collections of, 215. *See also* libraries
mapping network drives to, 590–592
naming strategies for, 231
organization of, tips for, 230–231

permissions for, 219–222
permissions for sharing, 350–351, 589–592
public, 220
read-only attribute, 214
searching within, 225
sharing. *See* homegroups; sharing
sharing manually, 588–592
sharing media with varied permissions, 350–351
taking ownership of as an administrator, 163
zipping, 218
fonts, 193
Food And Drink app, 85
forums, Internet, as sources of help, 198–201
FreeBSD, 478
freeing up disk space, 228–230
Full Control access, 589–590
full-screen immersion design goal, 4

G

games
activity reporting feature of Family Safety, 429–430
Games app, 77, 168
limitations of using with Hyper-V, 500
restricting with Family Safety, 434–435
surround sound, 364
VirtualBox support for, 501
gestures, touch, 4–6
Gimp, 341
Gmail, 245, 542–544
GMer app, 457
godaddy.com, 542
Google
Docs, 245
Drive, 289
Drive cloud storage, 245
Gmail, 245, 542–544
People app integration of, 74–75
public DNS server addresses, 513
TV, 353
GOP (Graphics Output Protocol), 18
GParted tool, 102–104
gpedit.msc. *See also* Group Policy
automatic startup of apps, 153
disabling updates for apps, 57
disabling Windows Store, 56
GPT (GUID Partition Table), 238
GPUs not good with VMs, 500
**graphics hardware requirements, 21. *See also* video
cards**
Graphics Output Protocol (GOP), 18

Group Policy
privacy settings, 449
startup apps, setting with, 153
groups
Administrators group, 219–220
built-in, 420–421
creating custom, 418–419
Everyone group, 219
HomeUsers group, 397
Select Users Or Groups dialog box, 590
Users group, 397
guests
account creation for, 416–417
Guests group, 420
Hyper-V, 475
GUID Partition Table (GPT), 238
gyro sensors, 21–22

H

HandBrake, 349
hard disk drives
access times of, 286
analyzing disk space, 229
benchmarking, 623–624
BitLocker with. *See* BitLocker
booting from, BIOS settings for, 654
cables for, 236–237
cabling problems, 660–661
chkdsk command, 284–285, 657, 665–666
choosing new, 286–287
combining into a single drive letter. *See* Storage Spaces
compressing drives, 228
connecting to external disks, 235–236
counters for, 647
disaster scenarios, 246–247
disk integrity, 618
erasing completely, 674–675
errors in, fixing, 283–285
failures of, 234–235, 263, 623, 629, 660–661, 665–666
fixing errors with chkdsk, 665–666
freeing up disk space, 228–230
HD Tune, 286, 624
IDE controllers, VM settings for, 488–489
initializing, 237–238
internal, connecting to, 236–238
mapping network drives, 590–592
MTTF (Mean Time to Failure), 264
NAS (network attached storage), 522
noisy, 629

performance measurement of, 287, 623–624
preparing PCs for ownership transfer, 674–675
recovery tools, 246–247
speed reduced by utilization of space, 618
splitting into multiple partitions, 101
Storage Spaces, 31–32
System Performance reports, 651–652
testing, 664–666
troubleshooting, 660–661
Ultimate Boot CD test of, 670
virtual, for VMs, 482
wmic logicaldisk get name command, 656
hardware
accessibility, specifically for, 174
as an architectural layer, 197
breadth of devices supported by Windows 8.1, 20
cases, 371–372
corrupted. *See* corruption issues
display resolution requirements, 20, 21
driver updates for, 615–616
fans, 372, 377
firmware updates for, 615–616
graphics support requirements, 21
headsets, speech recognition, 190–191
HTPCs, recommendations for, 371–382
intermittent problems with. *See* intermittent failures
minimum requirements, 21
photo editing recommendations, 340
Reliability Monitor, 662–664
sensor support, 21–22
testing after upgrades and migrations, 120–121
touch hardware requirements, 21
tuner cards, 382–387
unused, disabling, 633–634
virtualization with SLAT, 37, 474–475
hashes for WinX, 145
Hauppauge Colossus PCI Express Internal HD-PVR, 384
Hauppauge WinTV-DCR-2650, 384
HD Tune, 624, 640
HD (high-definition) video issues, 347, 380
HD video resolutions, 376
HDDs. *See* hard disk drives
HDMI
as preferred HTPC cabling, 381
as preferred video card to TV cabling, 373, 375–376
sound cards not needed with, 379
headphone jacks, 379–380
headsets, speech recognition, 190–191
Health And Fitness app, 85–86

HEIP (Help Experience Improvement Program), 98, 99
help. *See also* support
    answerdesk.com, 195
    describing problems in detail, 200–201
    F1 key no longer invokes, 196
    forums as sources of, 198–201
    Help command, Settings charm, 196
    Help system, 196–197
    Internet searches to solve problems, 198–201
    Microsoft Answer Desk, 196
    Microsoft Stores, 196
    Microsoft Support searches, 199
    remote assistance for. *See* Remote Assistance
    Steps Recorder, 206–207
    steps to take before asking for, 199
    Windows Community, 200
Help + Tips app, 86–87
Help Experience Improvement Program (HEIP), 98, 99
hidden attribute, 214, 226
High Performance power plan, 136–137
Hiren's BootCD, 657–658
history
    app, turning off, 448–449
    app, viewing in Task Manager, 640–641
    clearing, 135, 447
    InPrivate browsing, 447–448
holding a finger on an object, 5
Home Theater PCs. *See* HTPCs (Home Theater PCs)
homegroups
    accessing shared files, 586–587
    advantages of, 583
    backup specification for, 241
    counter for data transfers, 647
    creating, 583–584
    file types to share, selecting, 583–584
    HomeGroup streaming settings, 345
    joining from a PC, 584–586
    limited backward compatibility of, 584
    limiting file access, 587
    Media Devices, setting for sharing, 584
    passwords for, 584
    printer sharing with, 594
    sharing media using, 350–351
    troubleshooting, 586
HomeUsers group, 397, 421
honeypots, 537
hosted networks. *See* ad hoc networking
hostname command, 600
hosts, Hyper-V, 475
Hotmail, 245, 541, 543–544

hotspots app, 553–554
hovering, gesture equivalent of, 5
HTML
    embedding files in, from SkyDrive, 295–296
    .html files, 161
    HTML5 based apps, 160–162
    HTML5 support, 69
HTPCs (Home Theater PCs)
    advantages of, 359–360
    app availability for, 359
    automatic startup settings, 369–371
    Boxee, 361
    broadcast TV with, 386
    cable service with, 382–387
    CableCARD, 383–384
    cabling for, 373–376, 381–382
    capacity advantage, 359
    cases, 371–372
    codecs, 359
    commercial skipping capabilities, 360
    conversion of TV to mobile device formats, 360,
        366–368
    cost advantage, 359–360
    DMRs with, 361
    DVD playback not included in Windows 8.1, 47
    DVR capabilities, 360, 366–369
    fans, 372
    games on, 359
    hardware for, 371–382
    HD video resolutions, 376
    HDMI, 373, 375–376, 379, 381
    IR blasters, 386–387
    IR receivers, 387–389
    keyboards for, 387–389
    MAME, 359
    MCEBuddy, 360, 366–369
    Media Center, adding, 48
    Media Center, advantages of, 361
    Media Center, settings for, 363–366
    memory requirements, 377
    networking considerations, 380
    processor requirements, 377
    recording TV, 360, 366–369, 382–387
    remote control capability, 360, 361
    remote controls for, 387–389
    SageTV, 361
    slide shows, 361
    smartphones as remote controls, 361, 388
    software capabilities, typical, 360–361
    sound cards, 379–380

HTPCs, *continued*
sound quality, 381–382
storage recommendations, 377–378
streaming media capabilities, 361
temperature regulation for, 372, 377
tuner cards, 380, 382–387
user interface, 10-foot, 360
XMBC, 49, 361
HTTP vs. HTTPS, 444
HTTPS, 444, 469
Hulu, 353
Hyper-V
add hardware settings for VMs, 485
alternative to, VirtualBox, 37, 501–502
automatic stop action, 494
BIOS settings for VMs, 485
capabilities of, 36–37
Clipboard with, 499
compatibility capabilities of, 473
differencing disks, 497
dynamic memory option, 480–481, 486
external virtual switches, 476–477
forensics with, 499
guests, 475
hardware accessory issues, 500
hosts, 475
Hyper-V Administrators group, 420
IDE controller settings for VMs, 488–489
included in Windows 8.1 Pro, 91
installing, 475
integration services for VMs, 491–493
internal virtual switches, 476
isolation capabilities of, 473
limitations of VMs, 500
memory settings for VMs, 486
memory, specifying, 478–481
migrating physical disk contents to virtual disks,
    497–499
Mouse Release Key setting, 500
network adapter settings for VMs, 489–491
OS installation, 483
private virtual switches, 476
processor settings for VMs, 487–488
product keys for OS installs, 499
requirements, 474–475
SCSI controller support, 489
snapshots, 495
starting VMs, 495
troubleshooting, 477
virtual disk management, 496–497

virtual hard disk configuration, 482
virtual machine capabilities of, 473
virtual SANs, 484
virtual switch creation, 476–478
virtual switch selection, 481

I

iCloud, 245, 289
ICS (Internet Connection Sharing), 552–553, 633
IDE controllers, VM settings for, 488–489
IIS_IUSRS group, 421
images
built-in app for. *See* Photos app
desktop app for viewing, 336
editing programs for, 341
importing, 326–330
JPG files, 332–333
memory cards, importing from, 327–330
naming, 329
online printing services for, 332
organizing, 337–341
raw camera files, editing, 79
RAW files, 332–334
SkyDrive synchronization options for, 296
wireless imports of, 327
IMAP, 544–545
indexes
adding folders to search indexes, 251
batteries, preventing indexing while running on, 258
capabilities of Windows 8.1, 249
content indexing, disabling, 253–254
diacritics, differentiating, 255
Disable Indexer Backoff setting, 258
disabling indexing of specific files or folders, 252–254
disabling indexing permanently, 258–259
disabling indexing temporarily, 258
encrypted file contents, allowing for, 254–255
file type filter issues, 256
location of, 252, 255
managing file indexing, 251–260
managing searchable files and folders, 251–254
performance issues, 255, 257–258
settings for, 254–255
InPrivate browsing, 447–448
inSSIDer, 539–540
installing applications
apps from the Store, 55
Hyper-V, 475
sideloading apps, 55–56

installing Windows 8.1
  bootable flash drive creation, 92–93
  color scheme selection during, 96–97
  custom settings, selecting, 98–100
  express settings, using, 97–98
  license terms, 94
  naming the PC during, 96–97
  online solutions, setting for, 98, 99
  partition configuration, 96
  product keys, 94–95
  sharing settings, 98
  starting, 93
  troubleshooting failed boots, 93
  upgrading from a prior version. *See* upgrading to
    Windows 8.1
  Where Do You Want To Install page, 96
  Which Type Of Installation options, 94–95
  Windows Setup options, 93–94
instant messaging
  incoming connections, 458
  malware in, 443–444
integration services for VMs, 491–493
interface, user. *See* user interface
intermittent failures
  cabling as a source of, 661
  difficulty of diagnosing, 661
  identifying system changes leading to, 661–662
  refreshing PCs to fix, 671–673
  Reliability Monitor for diagnosing, 662–664
  resetting PCs to fix, 674–675
  Shut Down Unexpectedly events, 663–664
  testing hard disk drives, 664–666
  testing memory, 666–669
  Ultimate Boot CD, 669–670
  Windows Stopped Working events, 663
Internet
  activity reporting feature of Family Safety, 428–430
  browser, built-in. *See* Internet Explorer 11
  connections. *See* Internet connections
  definition of, 506
  filtering options, Family Safety, 423–427
  name service for. *See* DNS (Domain Name Service)
  pages. *See* webpages
  service providers. *See* ISPs (Internet Service Providers)
Internet connections
  Access Type field, Network And Sharing Center, 564–566
  bandwidth issues, 514
  bandwidth testing, 318
  Connectify Hotspot app, 553–554
  DNS failures, 511–513
  firewalls to protect. *See* Windows Firewall

  ICS (Internet Connection Sharing), 552–553
  ISP connection types, 513–515
  latency issue, 514
  Microsoft Internet Connectivity Evaluation Tool, 206
  multiple with one router, 522–523
  NAT for multiple devices on, 508–510
  Network Diagnostics tool, 566–568
  networking architecture, place in, 506–507
  PathPing indication of failure, 572
  performance measurement, 579–580
  permissions for apps to access, 158–159
  process for troubleshooting, recommended, 577–578
  QoS (Quality of Service), 522
  restarting devices to fix problems, 563–564
  Settings charm, network icon status indication, 564, 565
  sharing through ad hoc networks, 550–553
  troubleshooting, 512–513. *See also* network
    troubleshooting
Internet Explorer 11
  autocorrect feature, 68
  cache size reduction, 229
  Compatibility Lists, setting for, 98
  compatibility mode, 70
  CSS3 support, 69
  displaying buttons and tabs, 68
  Do Not Track, 98
  Enhanced Protected Mode, 45–46
  Favorites, 70
  font options for, 193
  graphics acceleration, 69
  HTML5 support, 69
  improvements from earlier versions, 68–69
  InPrivate browsing, 447–448
  malware add-ons, protection from, 439–440
  multiwindow capability, 69
  Narrator for, 183
  new features supported by, 45–46
  packet examination, 574–577
  panning and zooming capability, 69
  Pin To Start, 68
  pinning pages to Start screen, 70
  Reading List app, 87
  SkyDrive with, 294–295
  spelling checker feature, 68
  star icon, 70
  synchronization between devices, 70
  tabs, 70
  touch gestures with, 68
  touch vs. desktop versions of, 67–68
  uninstalling not allowed, 149
  Wrench command, 68

Internet Explorer legacy compatibility images, 476
interrupts per second reports, 651–652
invitations, Remote Assistance, 203–205
IP addresses
  APIPA, 510
  assignment by DHCP, 510–511
  conversion to names. *See* DNS (Domain Name Service)
  IPv4 vs. IPv6, 508
  NAT extension to local networks, 508–510
  pinging, 568–572
  of printers, 605
  private, 508–510
  registry, changing in, 552–553
  static, manually configuring, 517–518
  viewing local, 509–510
  Windows Firewall settings for, 461, 464–465
iPads
  accessing SkyDrive from, 292–294
  WMA incompatibility, 312
ipconfig command
  /all for ICS addresses, 552
  default gateway identification, 577
  IP address determination with, 509
  MAC addresses, viewing, 535–536
iPhones
  accessing SkyDrive from, 292–294
  WMA incompatibility, 312
IR blasters, 386–387
IR receivers, 387–389
ISO files
  Hyper-V OS installation from, 483
  Puppy Linux, 220–221
  Windows 8.1, 92–93
isolation of apps, 62–63
ISPs (Internet Service Providers)
  bandwidth issues with, 318, 514
  business services from, 515
  choosing, 513–515
  customer service quality, 514
  DHCP use by, 510
  IP addresses provided by, 508
  performance measurement of, 579–580
  pinging routers of, 571
  pricing by, 514
  role of, 506
  troubleshooting connections to, 512–513
iTunes
  streaming video service, 353
  WMA incompatibility, 312

J
JavaScript
  apps written in, 54
  .js files, 161
JAWS, 186
jitter, 569
JPG files, 332–333
.js files, 161

K
KeePass, 406–407
keyboard shortcuts
  accessibility related, 188–189
  Ctrl+Shift+Esc for Task Manager, 635
  Magnifier shortcuts, 181–182
  Narrator shortcuts, 184–185
  Start screen, opening with, 10
  table of Windows+ shortcuts, 8
  VMs, allowing for, 499–500
  Windows+Power, 635
  Windows+X, 548
keyboards
  backward compatibility with, 3
  Bluetooth, 388
  keyboard-only input accessibility, 187–189
  mouse-only input with, 189
  on-screen. *See* On-Screen Keyboard
  Sticky Keys, 187
  touch screen, activate key on lift option, 192
  wireless for HTPCs, 387–389
keys, encryption
  BitLocker recovery keys, 276–279
  EFS with File Explorer, 222–224
keystroke loggers, 448
K-Lite Codec Pack, 320

L
LAN (local area network). *See also* **networking**
  bandwidth availability, 318
  LAN Speed Test, 580
  video streaming bandwidth requirements, 380
landscape mode, 16
languages
  adding multiple, 142–143
  language packs, 17–18
  optional updates including packs, 612–613
  selecting during installation of Windows 8.1, 93–94
laptop lid closing, power options, 138
Last.fm, 352

latency
  pinging to determine, 568–569, 572
  satellite Internet issues with, 514
left edge of screen, swiping from, 5
legacy apps. *See* **desktop apps**
Lexia Readable, 193
libraries
  adding folders to, 217–218
  adding shared folders from other devices, 586
  advantages of, 216–217
  custom, creating, 217
  data files of, 216
  definition of, 215
  extending to new drives, 216–217
  Media Center, setup for, 366
  permissions for apps to access, 158–159
  private folders, 215–216
  public folders, 215–216
license terms, 94
lid closing, laptop, power options, 138
life cycles, Windows, 613–614
line-of-business (LOB) apps, 55–56
LinkedIn, People app integration of, 74–75
Linux
  integration services for VMs running, 491–493
  Puppy Linux, 220–221
  VM memory requirements, 478
live CDs, 220–221, 247
live tiles. *See* **tiles**
LOB (line-of-business) apps, 55–56
Local Group Policy Editor
  clearing tile notifications, 129
  disabling lock screens, 131–132
  disabling the Windows Store, 56
  disabling updates for apps, 57
  opening, 10
  preventing users from uninstalling apps, 149
local groups, 397
Local Security Policy password policy settings, 413–414
local user accounts
  advantages of, 393
  creating on first sign in, 397
  deleting, 417–418
  disabling accounts, 417
  guest accounts, 416–417
  logging off from Task Manager, 642
  lost passwords, need to reinstall Windows, 395
  PINs for, 404
  requiring regular password changes for, 413–414

location information
  permissions for apps to access, 158
  setting for, 135
  turning off tracking, 449
lock screens
  accessing login screen from, 8
  app resource allocations by, 64
  apps displaying data on, 61
  camera access with, 42
  disabling, 131–132
  features of, 9
  image for, setting in Photos app, 78
  notifications, enabling for apps, 130–131
  personalizing, 131–132
  picture for, setting, 130
  slide shows, adding to, 41–42
  turning off, 10
logging performance data, 648–651
login screen
  accessing, 8
  automating logins, 369–370
  biometric logins, 46
  bypassing for accessibility, 191
  Microsoft accounts for, 26–27
  picture passwords, 23–24, 398–403
  PIN logins, 24, 404
lower-left corner of screen, 7

M

MAC address filtering, 535–536
Macrium Reflect Free, 243
Macs, SkyDrive with, 294–295
MAGic Screen Magnification, 183
magnetometers, 21–22
Magnifier, 174, 177–182
Mail app
  attachments, 544
  centralizing multiple accounts, 545
  configuring on initial use of, 542–543
  Gmail setup, 542–544
  Hotmail, 541, 543–544
  IMAP, 544–545
  mail server security issues, 76
  multiple account setup with Settings charm, 543–544
  Outlook email, 543–545
  as part of larger app, 149
  Photos app with, 334–335
  POP service issues, 544–546
  sending email with, 75–76

Mail app, *continued*
Share charm with, 53
SMTP servers, 543
Windows Live Hotmail for POP, 545
mail servers, 76, 573–574
maintaining PCs
backups, 617. *See also* backups
batteries, 618–619
BIOS updates, 617
disk integrity, 618. *See also* hard disk drives
disk space, 618. *See also* storage
uninstalling apps, 617
updates. *See* updates for apps; updates for Windows 8.1
malware
adware, 439
backdoors, 441
botnets, 441
browser add-ons, 439–440
browser exploits, 438, 441
buffer overflow attacks, 45
bundling, 438–439
digital signatures, prevention with, 441
Exploit Wednesday, 610
honeypots for, 537
keystroke loggers, 189, 448
Malwarebytes Anti-Malware, 450
phishing, 442–444
Program Compatibility Troubleshooter enabling of, 167
quarantined files, 445
reappearance of, 450
refreshing PCs to remove, 455–456, 671–673
removal methods, 449–457
resetting PCs to fix, 674–675
restoring from backup to remove, 454–455
rootkits, 25, 26, 268, 440, 456–457
scanning for, 445
scareware, 439
signatures of, 446
SmartScreen filter, 442–444
social engineering of, 441
spyware, 439
System Restore as antimalware, 451–454
third-party antimalware apps, 450
Trojans, 438, 441
types of, 438–439
viruses, 438, 441
VMs for testing, 473
warning notices of, 441
Windows 8.1 resistance to, 441

worms, 438, 441
zombies, 441
MAME, 359
manifests, 164–165
mapping network drives, 590–592
Maps app, 82, 168
MBR (Master Boot Record), 238
MCEBuddy, 360, 366–369
meal planning, app for, 85
Measured Boot, 500
Media Center, Windows
adding to Windows 8.1, 362
automatic startup, setting for, 370–371
CableCARD certified status, 384
closed captioning with, 365
display settings, 364
extenders setting, 366
HTPC app, as a, 361
included in Windows 8.1 Pro, 91
library setup, 366
music settings, 366
notifications, clearing setting for, 363
parental controls settings, 365
Perform Optimization setting, 365
Pictures settings, 365
PlayReady, 365
purchasing, 48
remote controls for, 388–389
replaced by Music app, 307
settings for HTPC, 363–366
slide shows, 365
speaker setup, 363
TV signal setup, 363
Xbox 360 streaming with, 344, 366
medical app, 85–86
memory
available, determining, 479
Details tab, Task Manager, 643
HTPC requirements for, 377
Memtest86+, 667–669
photo editing recommendations, 340
replacing, 669
requirements, 21, 112
System Performance reports, 651–652
testing, 666–669
Ultimate Boot CD test of, 670
utilization, viewing with Task Manager, 639–640
VMs, specifying for, 478–481
Windows Memory Diagnostics tool, 666–669

memory cards
AutoPlay with, 151–152, 329
interfering with Windows startup, 654
readers for, 327–330
Memtest86+, 667–669
Messaging app
as default app for new users, 168
as part of larger app, 149
messaging services, 245
metadata
music, editing, 315–316
searching files by, 227
metered connections, 540, 560–561
Mezzmo, 346
Microsoft accounts
adding multiple users to a PC, 395
Administrators group, adding to, 397
backups by Microsoft, 243
BitLocker recovery keys using, 277–278
children's, specifying as, 395
creating during installation, 100
deleting locally, effect of, 418
groups added to, 397
guest accounts with, 417
local account creation with, 396–397
logging into Windows 8.1 with, 26–27
passwords, resetting, 26–27, 413
resetting passwords for, 394–395
roaming of settings, 52
security information requested with, 395–396
upgrades, using for logins, 116
user accounts, for, 394–397
Xbox Music with, 343–344
Microsoft Active Protection Service, 99
Microsoft Answer Desk, 196
Microsoft Exchange Server, 543
Microsoft Office 365. *See* Office 365
Microsoft Office 2010. *See* Office 2010
Microsoft OneNote, SkyDrive with, 294
Microsoft Points, 319
Microsoft Store (apps). *See* Windows Store
Microsoft Stores (physical retail), 196
Microsoft Support, 199
Microsoft.com pings, 569
migrating to a Windows 8.1 PC
app configuration, 120–122
apps require reinstallation, 117
Windows Easy Transfer for, 116–119
mirroring disks, 31, 263, 266–267

mobile broadband
airplane mode, 28, 560
app metering, 560
hardware detection for, 559
ISP connections using, 514
metered connection settings, 560–561
monitoring bandwidth use, 561
service provider apps, 559
settings for, 27–28
support for, 559
tethering, 47, 561
USB adapters for, 561
mobile devices, SkyDrive with, 292–294
modems
restart order for devices, recommended, 511, 564
role within home networks, 507
MOG, 352
monitors. *See also* displays
accessibility, large size recommended, 174
accessibility options, 175–183
high contrast mode for accessibility, 177
multiple monitor support, 33, 139–140
multitasking apps, 37–38
photo editing recommendations, 340
motion accents, 44
mounting a VHD file as a drive, 106
mouse devices
backward compatibility with, 3
charms, viewing with, 7
head mouse devices, 174
mouse only accessibility, 189
Mouse Release Key setting, Hyper-V, 500
new mouse controls in Windows 8.1, 7
releasing from VMs, 491–492
right-clicking to view menus, 7
mouse sticks, 174
Movie Maker
burning movie DVDs, 355–357
editing with, 320–322
installing, 319–320
sharing from, 322–323
movies. *See also* video
Adobe Premiere for editing, 323
burning movie DVDs, 355–357
editing. *See* Movie Maker
purchasing in Video app, 317–319
storage requirements, by resolution and time, 378
MozyHome, 246

MP3 format
music CDs in, 350, 355
song file sizes, 378
stereos, pushing songs to, 345
WMA compared to, 313
MP3Tag, 316
MP4 format, 368
MPEG-3 format, 345
mpix.com, 332
MSConfig, 155
MTTF (Mean Time to Failure), 264
multiple monitor support
dual background images, 33
photo editing recommendations, 340
setting up, 139–140
taskbar setup, 140–141
taskbar spanning, 33
VirtualBox for simulating, 502
multiple operating systems on a single device. *See* dual-
booting; Hyper-V
multiple processors
affinity settings for apps, 627–629
VM settings for, 487–488
multitasking
improvements with Windows 8.1 update, 37–38
minimum display resolution for, 21
music
advantages of Internet for, 307
analog output of, 379
app for. *See* Music app
AutoPlay, 151–152
aux-in ports for transferring, 348
burning CDs, 354–355
buying downloads of, 313
cassette adapters, 349
copy protection of, 312–313
HTPCs for listening to. *See* HTPCs (Home Theater PCs)
library for. *See* Music library
metadata, editing, 315–316
MP3s. *See* MP3 format
Music command, Search charm, 52
power settings for mobile, 138
ripping songs from CDs, 308, 313–315
song file sizes, 378
sound quality, 381–382
streaming services, 352
volume, increasing by reencoding files, 349
Xbox Music app, 308, 312–313
Zune accounts, 312

Music app
Add To Now Playing command, 309–310
capabilities of, 77–78
Collection command, 307, 310–311
default app for new users, 168
docking, 309
ellipses (...), 308
Explore command, 307
listening methods with, 308–309
Music library, scanning of, 308
Now Playing list, 309–310
one album at a time method, 308
one song at a time method, 308
By options, Collection, 310
Play button, 309–310
Play On Xbox button, 343
playlists, 309
Plus button, 309–310
Plus sign (+), 311
Radio command, 307
repeating, 308
stereos, pushing songs to, 345–346
streaming to stereos, 343–346
volume control, 309
Music library
adding existing music to, 308
adding Music folders from other computers, 351
burning CDs from, 354–355
scanning by Music app, 308

N
name resolution. *See* DNS (Domain Name Service)
names of files, 213–214
names of PCs
hostname command, 600
selecting during installation, 96–97
Narrator
dyslexic users, advantages for, 173, 192
improvements for Windows 8.1, 18
keyboard shortcuts for, 184–185
keystroke reading by, 190
settings for, 183–184
touch keyboard options, 192
NAS (network attached storage), 522
NAT (Network Address Translation)
IP addresses, relation to, 508–510
router provision of, 507
sharing Internet connections from one device, 552
Navigation tab, Taskbar And Navigation Properties
dialog box, 39–40

near field communications (NFC) tap-to-print, 47
Nero MediaHome, 346
.NET Framework, 159–160
NetBalancer Free, 491
Netflix, 353
network adapters
  automatic setup of wired connections, 515
  counters for, 647
  drivers, updating, 578
  failures of, 578
  manually configuring, 512–513, 517–518
  VM settings for, 489–491
Network Address Translation. *See* **NAT (Network Address**
    Translation)
Network And Sharing Center
  Access Type field, 564–566
  ad hoc networks, viewing, 549
  manually configuring IP settings, 512–513, 517–518
  Network Diagnostics tool, 566–568
  opening, 564
  private network configuration, 466–468
  sharing Internet connections, 550–553
  Troubleshoot Problems link, 566
Network Configuration Operators group, 421
network connections
  automatic setup of wired connections, 515
  diagnostic tools for. *See* network troubleshooting
  file transfer speeds, 582
  firewalls to protect. *See* Windows Firewall
  LAN Speed Test, 580
  performance measurement, 579–582
  Set As Metered Connection option, 540
  sharing Internet connections, 550–553
  System Performance reports, 651–652
  utilization, viewing with Task Manager, 639–640
  Wi-Fi power options for, 519–520
Network Diagnostics tool, 566–568
Network Discovery setting, 602
Network Monitor, 574–577
network printers
  automatic connections to, 596–597
  manual connections to, 605
network troubleshooting
  Access Type field, Network And Sharing Center, 564–566
  app issues, 574–577
  file transfer speeds, 582
  LAN Speed Test, 580
  latency, determining, 568–569, 572
  mail servers, testing, 573–574
  network adapter drivers, updating, 578

Network And Sharing Center, 564–566
Network Diagnostics tool, 566–568
Network Monitor, 574–577
packet examination, 574–577
PathPing, 570–572
performance measurement, 579–582
performance, typical by type of network, 581
ping, 568–572, 577–578
PortQry, 572–573
process for, recommended, 577–578
restarting devices, 563–564
Settings charm, network icon status, 564, 565
speedtest.net, 579–580
networking
  ad hoc, 547–554
  alternate configuration, 517–518
  architecture, components of, 505–508
  automatic setup of wired connections, 515
  bandwidth availability, 318
  home network architecture, typical, 506
  HTPC requirements, 380
  limiting bandwidth per process, 491
  Microsoft Internet Connectivity Evaluation Tool, 206
  mobile broadband, 27–28
  new features of Windows 8.1 for, 27–28
  packet examination, 574–577
  performance measurement, 579–582
  permissions for apps to access, 159
  powerline Ethernet adapters, 347, 380–381
  printer connection troubleshooting, 602–603
  private network configuration, 466–468
  restart order for devices, recommended, 511, 563–564
  Set Up A New Network option, 524
  speed standards, 526
  System Performance reports, 651–652
  troubleshooting. *See* network troubleshooting
  video streaming requirements, 380
  VPNs, 469, 523
  Wi-Fi capabilities, 28
  wired Ethernet methods, 526–530
  wired LAN recommended for HD streaming, 347
new features of Windows 8.1
  3-D printer support, 46
  accessibility features, 18
  autocorrect, 15
  biometric logins, 46
  booting to the desktop, 38–40
  charms, 13–14
  cloud integration, 3
  hardware capabilities and requirements, 20–22

new features of Windows 8.1, *continued*
Hyper-V, 36–37
language packs, 17–18
lock screens, 9–10, 41–42
mouse controls, 7
multiple monitor support, 33
networking features, 27–28
overall design, 3–4
PC Settings, 14–15
personalization options, 44
picture passwords, 23–24
PIN logins, 24
productivity features, 33–37
provided by the October 2013 update. *See* Windows 8.1
update features
refresh and reset options, 35–36
remote data removal feature, 46
search capabilities, 15–17
security features, 22–27
security improvements, 46
SkyDrive, 29–31
SmartScreen filter, 24
social networking integration, 3
Start button, 40
Start screen, 10–13
Storage Spaces, 31–32
Task Manager, 33–35
tethering, 47
touch controls, 4–7
touch screens, design for, 3
user interface features, 8–20
viewing modes, 16–17
WinX menu, 10–11, 41
New Technology File System (NTFS), 212
new user default apps, 168
News app, 83
NFC (near field communications) tap-to-print, 47
notifications
disabling briefly, 130
lock screens, on, 130–132
Media Center, clearing setting for, 363
standard vs. detailed, 131
turning off, 129–130
Nslookup, 574
NTFS (New Technology File System), 212
NVDA (NonVisual Desktop Access) screen reader, 185

O
**objects, touch gesture for displaying information
about, 5**
Office 365
cloud nature of, 245
collaboration with, 302–304
email setup, 543–544
Office 2010
collaborating on documents simultaneously, 303–304
editing documents in browsers with SkyDrive, 294–295
SkyDrive, opening documents in, 292
OneNote, SkyDrive with, 294
online backup services, 246
online services in general. *See* cloud services
online solutions, setting for, 98–99
On-Screen Keyboard
large displays helpful with, 174
mouse-only use of, 189
touch, activating keys on finger lift option, 192
Open command, 64–65
opening apps, 4, 7
opening files, 150–151
Ophcrack, 409
optional updates, 612–613
Outlook email, 543–545

P
packages, app, 168–170
paging file counter, 647
Pandora, 352
parental controls
app for. *See* Family Safety
Media Center settings for, 365
parity, Storage Spaces use of, 32, 263, 267
partitions
choosing during Windows 8.1 installation, 96
MBR vs. GPT, 238
rootkit removal by repartitioning, 457
separate partition method for dual-booting, 101–104
splitting a drive into multiple, 101
passphrases, 414–415
passwords
accessibility, 187
age of, limiting, 412–414
best practices for, 405–415
changing regularly, 412–414
complex but accessible, 187

complex, settings for requiring, 409–410, 414
complexity guideline, 406–411
cracking, 409
fingerprint scanners, 46
guessing, 406–407
homegroup, 584
importance of, 405
KeePass, 406–407
lockouts after failed attempts, 403
Microsoft accounts, resetting for, 26–27
On-Screen Keyboard for, 189
Ophcrack, 409
phrases for, 414–415
picture passwords, 23–24, 398–403
PIN logins, 24, 404
pseudo-complex, 408
random, 407–408
Require A Password On Wakeup option, 137
resetting for Microsoft accounts, 394–395
skipping logins, 369–370
for SkyDrive, 301
storing, 406
uniqueness guideline, 405
Wi-Fi, 535
Wi-Fi, entering, 516
zipped folders, for, 218
Patch Tuesday, 610. See also updates for Windows 8.1
PathPing, 570–572
paths
  cd command to change, 572
  finding paths for apps, 460
PC names, 96–97, 600
PC Settings
  accessing, 14
  complex passwords, requiring, 409–410
  Ease Of Access page, 175–176
  Fully Clean The Drive option, 674–675
  HomeGroup settings, 583–585
  lock screen settings, 41–42
  picture passwords, 23–24, 398–403
  PIN logins, 24
  Refresh Your PC option, 35–36, 455–456, 672
  Region & Language page, 17–18
  Remove Everything And Reinstall Windows command,
    674–675
  Reset Your PC option, 36
  streaming settings, 345
  System Restore, steps to open, 451–453

Update & Recovery command, 239
  Wi-Fi settings, 540–541
PCMCIA cards, 383
PDF files, Reader app for, 81
peek preview, 141
People app
  contact list for Mail app, as, 75
  Facebook integration, 74
  as part of larger app, 149
  Share charm with, 53
  Twitter integration, 74–75
perfmon command, 645. See also Performance Monitor
performance. See also Performance Monitor
  affinity settings, 627–629
  apps, requirements for, 63
  backup disk considerations, 238
  benchmarking tools, 621–624
  BitLocker impact on, 269
  counters, list of, 646–647
  hard disk drive, 623–624
  HD Tune, 640
  indexes, search, 255, 257–258
  logging data with Performance Monitor, 648–651
  network, measuring, 579–582
  network, typical by type of, 581
  Performance tab, Task Manager, 34, 639–640
  PerformanceTest tool, 621–622
  priority settings for apps, 626–629
  SkyDrive issues with, 297–298
  Smooth Edges Of Screen Fonts option, 178
  Storage Spaces issues, 263
  streaming video, 347
  System Performance reports, 651–652
  Wi-Fi, 534, 539–540
Performance Log Users group, 421
Performance Monitor
  counters, list of, 646–647
  data collector sets, 648–652
  graphing counters, 645–646
  logging data with, 648–651
  perfmon command to start, 645
  property settings, 647–648
  purpose of, 645
  SkyDrive processor utilization, 297
  System Performance reports, 651–652
  time intervals, setting, 647–648
Performance reports, System, 651–652
PerformanceTest tool, 621–622

permissions
access control lists (ACLs), 219
access types, 589
apps, of, 158–159
belt and suspenders concept, 590
bypassing using a different OS, 221–222
Change permission, 589–590
file, 592–593
file and folder, 219–222
file vs. folder, 589, 592
folder sharing with, 589–592
Full Control permission, 589–590
legacy desktop app issues with, 165–167
Read permission, 589, 592–593
user folder, 219

personalization
across devices, Microsoft accounts for, 394–397
AutoPlay, 151–152
Bing, 135
default programs, setting, 149–151
desktop, 132–135
filtering adult content settings, 135
language settings, 142–143
lock screens, 131–132
multiple monitor settings, 139–140
new options in Windows 8.1, 44
power settings, 136–139
search, 135
Start screen. *See* Start screen
user accounts for, 393
WinX menu, 143–145

phishing
avoiding phishing sites, 443–444
detection by SmartScreen, 442–443

phone lines for Ethernet, 528

Photo Gallery. *See* **Windows Photo Gallery**

Photo Viewer, Windows, 336

PhotoRec, 247

photos
batch workflow recommendation, 338–339
built-in app for viewing. *See* Photos app
desktop app for viewing, 336
editing programs for, 341
organizing, 337–341
rating, 337–339
RAW files, 79, 332–334

Photos app
batch workflow recommendation, 338–339
capabilities of, 78–80
default app for new users, 168

desktop alternative to, 336
ease of use of, 325
editing capabilities, 78–79
emailing from, 334–335
finding specific photos, 339
importing images, 326–330
live tile of, 325–326
lock screen image, setting, 78
naming imported images, 329
printing from, 330–332
Share charm with, 79
sharing from, 334–335
SkyDrive with, 291
Windows 8.1 changes from Windows 8, 78–79
wireless imports, 327

Picasa, 79

picture passwords, 23–24, 398–403

Picture Tools tab, 72

pictures. *See* **images; photos**

PIDs (process IDs), 638

PIN logins, 24, 404

Pin To Start command for apps, 125

pinching, 6

ping, 568–572, 577–578

playlists
creating, 309, 311–312
streaming to stereo devices, 345–346

PlayReady, 365

Plus sign (+), Music app, 311

pointers, accessibility settings for, 186–187

Points, Microsoft, 319

pools, Storage Space, 262–268

POP service, 544–545

portrait mode, 16

ports
forwarding, 521
mail server, testing, 573–574
PortQry, 572–573
Windows Firewall settings for, 461–465

power
Advanced settings, 137–139
Balanced power plan, 136–137
counter for, 647
CPU management options, 137–138
efficiency improvements, 22
fans to reduce heat from, 372, 377
High Performance plan, 136–137
laptop lid, options on closing, 138
multimedia settings, 138
Power Saver plan, 136–137

PowerCfg command-line tool, 139
Require A Password On Wakeup option, 137
Settings charm access to settings, 136
settings for, 136–139
shutdowns and restarts with Power command, 127
UPSs (uninterruptable power supplies), 234
Wi-Fi, options for, 518–520
wireless adapter settings, 137
Power Users group, 421
powerline Ethernet adapters
installing, 528–530
network performance, typical by type of network, 581
streaming video over, 347, 380–381
preparing PCs for ownership transfer, 674–675
printers
3-D printer support, 46
32-bit vs. 64-bit driver issues, 594–595
adding to a device, 596–598
default, checking for, 604
drivers, downloading from manufacturers, 600
drivers, downloading from PC sharing, 598–599
faxing capability, 598
help from forums, 199–200
homegroups for sharing, 594
IP addresses of, 596, 602, 603, 605
mobile devices with, 596
names of, using to connect to, 600–601
network, manual connections to, 605
network problems, testing for, 603
one showing as multiple selections, 598
printing from. See printing
routers, connecting to, 596
Share This Printer option, 594
shared, manual connections to, 600–605
sharing, 593–605
status of, checking, 604
troubleshooting connections to, 602–603
troubleshooting steps, 604
Turn On File And Printer Sharing setting, 602
unlisted, connecting to, 600–602
USB connections to routers, 521
USB, detection of, 604
Windows Firewall settings to allow, 603
printing
3-D printer support, 46
adding a shared printer to a device, 596–598
Devices charm for, 13, 53
devices for. See printers
ink, status of, 604
isolating problems with, 197–198
from mobile devices, 596
NFC tap-to-print, 47
online services for, 332
Photo app, from, 330–331
Print Spooler service, 630, 632
to shared printers, 593–605
troubleshooting steps, 604
USB connection problems, 604
Windows Firewall settings to allow, 603
priority, setting for apps, 626–629
privacy
app usage recording, turning off, 448–449
Group Policy settings for, 449
InPrivate browsing, 447–448
keystroke loggers, 448
logging of webpages visited, by routers, 447
permissions for. See permissions
preparing PCs for ownership transfer, 674–675
user accounts for, 393
private folders of libraries, 215–216
private networks
configuration, 466–468
Find Devices And Content option, 540–541
Pro version of Windows 8.1
features not available in standard edition, 90–91
Hyper-V capabilities of, 37, 91
processes
busy apps, spotting, 625–627
command lines to run, 638
composition of, 636
counters for, 646
Details tab, Task Manager, 643
ending, 637
executable files of, finding, 638
groups, organization by, 637
limiting bandwidth per process, 491
names of, 638
PIDs, 638
priority, setting for apps, 626–629
Processes tab, Task Manager, 34–35, 636–638
resource consumption by, 638
services, of, 637
suspended apps, 638
System Performance reports, 651–652
type of, 638
processors
busy apps, finding, 625–627
counters for, 646
Details tab, Task Manager, 643
history of app use of, 640–641

processors, *continued*
HTPC recommendations, 377
overclocked, 670
PerformanceTest tool, 621–622
photo editing recommendations, 340
power management options, 137–138
priorities for apps, 626–629
requirements, Windows 8.1, 21, 22
System Performance reports, 651–652
testing, 670
utilization, viewing with Performance Monitor, 645
utilization, viewing with Task Manager, 639–640
VMs, assignment to, 487–488
product keys
installation, entering during, 94–95
for OS installs in Hyper-V, 499
upgrades requiring, 113–114
profiles, user
copying to another drive, 657
deleting, 417–418
folders for, 162–163
Program Compatibility Troubleshooter, 166–167
programs
legacy desktop style. *See* desktop apps
saving data during upgrades to Windows 8.1, 121–122
Windows 8.1 touch-enabled. *See* apps
protecting files. *See* encryption; permissions
public folders
of libraries, 215–216
sharing using, 220
public networks
allowing incoming connections from, 459, 463–464
switching to or from private networks, 467–468
Windows Firewall blocking of incoming connections, 457
publisher verification warnings, 441
publishers of apps, viewing, 638
Puppy Linux, 220–221
.px7 files, 161, 162

Q
QAM (quadrature amplitude modulation), 385
quarantined files, 445
Quick Launch toolbar, 134–135
quick links, 7, 8

R
Radio command, Music app, 307
radio, tuner cards with, 385

RAID (redundant array of independent disks)
purpose of, 235
Storage Spaces as alternative for, 261, 262
Rapid Virtualization Indexing, 37
rating photos, 337–339
RAW files, 79, 332–334
RCA connectors, 379
Rdio, 352
RDP (Remote Desktop Protocol), 202
Read access, 589
Read permissions, 592–593
Reading List app, 87
read-only attribute, 214
Read/Write permissions, 592–593
recently used apps, viewing, 5–6, 7
recimg /createimage command, 673
recipes, app for, 85
recording sounds, 87
recording TV, 382–387
recovering data with non-Windows tools, 246–247
recovering encrypted files, 224–225
recovery of Windows 8.1
Automatic Repair option, 654–655
booting from, BIOS settings for, 654
Hiren's BootCD to repair, 657–658
recovery environment, launching during startup, 244
refreshing for. *See* refreshing
Repair Your Computer option, 654–655
system drives, copying to another drive, 656–657
unplugging PCs before retrying, 653
Update And Recovery page, PC Settings, 455
Windows Recovery Environment (WinRE), 654–660
wmic logicaldisk get name command, 656
Recycle Bin, 134–135, 230, 233
Red Hat Enterprise Linux, 491–493
redundancy, Storage Spaces for, 261, 263
redundant array of independent disks. *See* RAID
(redundant array of independent disks)
refreshing
advantages over reinstalling the OS, 35–36
custom refresh images, 673
initiating, 672
process during, 671
Refresh Your PC command, 657
Removed Apps list, 672
removing malware by, 455–456
settings restored by, 671
startup problems, resolving with, 657, 659
Region & Language page, 17–18

registry
    IP addresses, modifying, 552–553
    startup app settings in, 153–154
reinstalling Windows 8.1
    fixing startup problems by, 659–660
    options for, 35–36
    refreshing alternative. *See* refreshing
    resetting alternative, 35–36, 674–675
Reliability Monitor, 662–664
remote access, SkyDrive for, 300–302
Remote Assistance
    bandwidth settings, 205
    confirming control requests, 205
    connecting to provide, 204–205
    connectivity issues, 206
    Easy Connect, 204, 206
    enabling and disabling, 202–203
    invitations, 203–205
    purpose of, 202
    Request Control command, 205
    technology behind, 202
    viewing without controlling option, 203
    wizard for, 203–204
remote controls, 387–389
remote data removal feature, 46
Remote Desktop
    host, 90
    uninstalling host not allowed, 149
    VMs (virtual machines), controlling, 500
Remote Desktop Protocol (RDP), 202
Remote Desktop Users group, 421
Remote Management Users group, 421
removable drives
    BitLocker with, 271, 281–283
    USB 2.0 speed limit, 286
Replicator group, 421
requirements
    Hyper-V, 474–475
    Windows 8.1, 112
Rescue Remix, 247
resetting, 35–36, 674–675
resiliency, Storage Spaces, 262, 263, 266–268
.resjson files, 162
Resource Manager, 636
restarting
    Automatic Repair option, 654–655
    fixing networking problems with, 510
    hardware to fix network problems, 563–564
    printers to solve problems, 604
    Repair Your Computer option, 654–655
    restart command, adding to Start screen, 127

    as a troubleshooting technique, 199, 653
    unplugging PCs before, 653
    Windows Recovery Environment options for, 654–655
restore points, selecting in System Restore, 452–453
restoring
    from backups to remove malware, 454–455
    file backups, 241–242
    testing, 242
resuming apps, 54
Rhapsody, 352
right edge of screen, swiping from, 5
ripping songs from CDs, 308, 313–315
Roku, 353
rootkits
    definition of, 440
    nature of, 268
    removing, 456–457
    Secured Boot defense against, 26
    Windows Defender defense against, 25
rotation between portrait and landscape mode, 16,
        21–22
rotation gesture, 6–7
routers
    basic features of, 521
    choosing, 521–523
    configuring, 524–525
    Dynamic DNS with, 522
    external drive sharing feature, 522
    firmware updates, 525
    hops, 570–572
    IP address assignment by DHCP, 510–511
    logging of webpage visits, 447
    multiple Internet connections, 522–523
    NAT, provision by, 509
    PathPing, 570–572
    port forwarding, 521
    printer sharing with USB, 521
    printers, connecting to, 596
    Quality of Service feature, 522
    resetting to defaults to troubleshoot, 578
    restart order for devices, recommended, 511, 564
    role within home networks, 507
    switches, built-in, 526
    traveling with, 553
    UPnP (Universal Plug and Play) requirement for, 467,
        521
    VPN support, 523
    web monitoring and filtering features, 522
    wireless access points in, 521
RT, Windows 8.1, 22
Run dialog box, 10

S

Safe Mode, 19, 244
SafeSearch, 135
SageTV, 361
salts, 145
SANs (storage area networks), virtual, 484
SATA
    cables, 236–237
    connection speeds, 286
satellite Internet connections, 514
satellite TV, 382–387
saving
    default save location, 215, 216
    files, 230
Scan app, 87
Scanner tool (disk space analyzer), 229
scanning for malware, 445
scareware, 439
scheduled tasks, 153, 155–156
screen readers. See text-to-speech
screens
    accessibility options, 175–183
    automatic rotation of, 21–22
    brightness settings, 136–138
    high contrast mode for accessibility, 177
    multiple monitor support, 33
    multitasking apps, 37–38
    power settings, 136–138
    resolution requirements, 21
scrolling, slide gesture for, 5–6
SCSI controllers, Hyper-V support for, 489
Search charm
    app selection after opening, 52
    asterisk (*) wildcard, 225–226
    changing search settings, 135
    commonality to all touch apps, 52–53
    configuring apps to appear on bar, 53
    default programs, setting, 149–151
    disabling service for, 258–259
    file searches, 249
    finding apps with from Start screen, 125
    history, clearing, 250
    keyboard shortcut for opening, 13, 52
    managing file indexing, 251–260
    Music, searching in, 13, 52
    Store, searching in, 52
searching
    adding folders to search indexes, 251
    advanced, 225–227

all files from Apps view option, 39
apps, within. See app searches
AQS for, 16
asterisk (*) wildcard, 225–226
Bing search settings, 135
changing settings, 135
content searches, disabling, 253–254
by dates of files, 226–227
details, hovering to view, 17
diacritics, differentiating, 255
disabling indexing for files or folders, 252–254
everywhere searches, 249
file management, as a technique for, 212
file type filter issues, 256
files, 16
files and folders, 249
filtering adult content settings, 135
within folders, 225
help for computer problems, 198–201
history, clearing, 135, 250
indexes for, 249
keyboard shortcuts for, 8
location-based, options for, 135
managing file indexing, 251–260
by metadata, 227
new paradigm vs. Windows 7, 135
non-indexed, 259–260
organization of results of, 16
SafeSearch, 135
Settings, 16
within settings, 249
types of Windows 8.1 searches, 249
Windows 8.1 update improvements for, 44–45
Windows Search service, 630
Windows+F shortcut, 13, 52
Second Level Address Translation (SLAT), 37
Secured Boot, 22, 25, 26
security
    belt and suspenders concept, 590
    BitLocker for encryption. See BitLocker
    bypassing permissions using a different OS, 221–222
    Exploit Wednesday, 610
    honeypots, 537
    HTTPS, 444
    local vs. Microsoft user accounts, 395
    MAC filtering, 535–536
    malware as threat to. See malware
    new features of Windows 8.1 for, 22–27
    passwords for. See passwords
    permissions for. See permissions

picture passwords, 23–24, 398–403
PIN logins, 24, 404
preparing PCs for ownership transfer, 674–675
protection vs. convenience tradeoff, 437
rootkit dangers. *See* rootkits
secure by default principle, 437, 469
Secured Boot, 22, 25–26
SmartScreen filter, 24
turning off features of, 469–472
updates, 610. *See also* updates for Windows 8.1
user accounts for, 393
Windows 8.1 update improvements in, 46
Windows Defender, 25

selecting
files in SkyDrive, 64
objects by flicking, 6
text by tapping, 4

sensor support, 21–22

service packs, 610

services
delaying automatic, 630–633
do not change startup type, list of, 632–633
manual startup type, 631–632
processes corresponding to, 637
shell service objects, 154
starting, 644
as startup apps, 153
stopping, 644
System Performance reports, 651–652
Task Manager Services tab, 644
viewing with Task Manager, 34

Serviio, 346

settings
keyboard shortcuts for, 8
migrating to a new PC, 116–119
sharing between devices, 26–27
transferring during upgrades, 114–116

Settings charm
About command, 198
app configuration settings, 162
commonality to all touch apps, 52, 53
Help command, 196
Lock Screen settings, 130–131
Mail app account setup, 543–544
Make Everything On Your Screen Bigger option, 175–176
multiple language support, 142–143
network icon, status from, 564, 565
notifications, disabling or turning off, 129–130
opening, 13

PC Settings access, 14–15
personalization options, new with 8.1, 44
Photos app live tile options, 325–326
power settings, 136–138
roaming of settings, 52
screen brightness, 136–137
searching within, 16
Show Administrative Tools option, 416
shutdowns and restarts with Power command, 127
Start screen background options, 125
touch interface improvements, 44–45
Wi-Fi connection setup, 515–516

Share charm
commonality to touch apps, 53
Ctrl+H command, 53
opening, 13
Photos app with, 334–335
Reading List app, 87
SkyDrive, copying files to, 30–31
SkyDrive, sharing links to files in, 292

sharing
with apps, setting for, 100
belt and suspenders concept, 590
file permissions for, 592–593
folders, sharing manually, 588–592
folders with a VM, 501
folders with another user, 220
homegroups for. *See* homegroups
Internet connections through ad hoc networks, 550–553
mapping network drives, 590–592
media among home computers, 350–351
printers, 593–605
setting during installation, 98
settings between devices, 26–27
Turn On File And Printer Sharing setting, 602

shell service objects, 154

shopping lists, app for, 85

shortcuts for app startup batch files, 628–629

shrinking partitions, 101–104

Shut Down Unexpectedly events, 663–664

shutdown command, 127

sideloading apps, 55–56

SiliconDust HDHR3-CC HDHomeRun PRIME, 384

SkyDrive
access to local computer files by, 30
adding files to with browsers, 295
advantages of, 289–290
alternative cloud storage services, 289
apps, accessing from, 291
backups, excluding from, 300

SkyDrive, *continued*
bandwidth issues, 298
browser access to, 294–295
cloud basis of, 289, 292
collaboration with, 302–304
commands for, 290–291
as a default app for new users, 168
desktop, File Explorer for, 295–302
desktop settings, 301–302
device compatibility of, 29–30
downloading files to local devices, 295
editing documents with, 302–304
embedding files in HTML from, 295–296
file associations of, 64–67
free storage limitation, 31
installing, 30
lazy synchronization, 298
Metered Connections settings, 296
Microsoft OneNote with, 294
mobile access to PC computer files, 300–302
mobile devices, accessing from, 292–294
mobile devices, insufficient storage issue, 296
Office documents, opening with, 292
online storage competitors, 245
passwords with, 301
performance issues, 297–298
publishing video to, 322–323
selecting files in, 64
Share charm with, 30–31
sharing files, 292
sharing files to social networks, 295
synchronization, 289–290, 292, 296, 298
version histories for files, 295–296
versioning issues, 298–300
viewing documents in, 30
Slacker, 352
SLAT (Second Level Address Translation), 37, 474–475
slide gesture, 5–6
slide shows
HTPC capability for, 361
lock screens, displaying with, 41–42
Media Center, 365
smartphones
cars, playing on systems of, 348–350
iPhones. *See* iPhones
malware, relative lack of, 446
music on, 347–348
remote control of HTPCs with, 361, 388
SkyDrive with, 292–296, 300–302
tethering, 47, 561

SmartScreen filter
Run Anyway option, 442–443
turning off, 470
turning on during installation, 98
warnings from, 24
SMTP mail servers, 573
snapping apps
display options, 58–59
gesture for, 7
minimum display resolution for, 21
snapshots of VMs, 495
social engineering of malware, 441
social networking integration
as new feature of Windows 8.1, 3
SkyDrive, 295
solid state drives. *See* SSDs (solid state drives)
songs. *See* music; Music app
sound cards, 379–380
Sound Recorder app, 87
speakers
cabling for, 382
RCA connectors, 379
settings in Media Center, 363
surround sound, 364
speech recognition
accessibility, as a feature for, 174
Dragon for, 191
dyslexic readers, as aid to, 193
setting up, 190–191
speed of computation. *See* benchmarking
speedtest.net, 579–580
spelling
autocorrection of words, 15
checking in Internet Explorer 11, 68
Sports app, 84
sports, lack of Internet video coverage of, 353
Spotify, 352
spyware, 439, 445–446
SSDs (solid state drives)
advantages of, 286
errors in, fixing, 283–285
for increasing speed of startups, 634
performance measurement of, 287
photo editing recommendations, 340
SSIDs, 524, 538, 539–540, 549
star system for ratings, 339
Start button, 40
Start charm, 10, 13
start command-line tool, 627–629

Start menu. *See also* **Start screen**
discontinued, 3
emulation by apps, 12, 132
Start screen
accessing at startup, 8
administrative tools, adding to, 126
apps not displayed by, finding, 10
Apps view on startup option, 39
backgrounds, setting for, 39, 125
boot to desktop option, 38–40
colors for, selecting, 44
commands, running from, 10
features of, 10–12
grouping apps, 124
keyboard shortcut for displaying, 8
motion accents, 44
multiple display options for, 39
opening from an app, 10
opening with a mouse device, 7
personalization, advantages of, 123
pinning webpages to, 68, 70
restarts, adding links for, 127–128
scrolling, 10
searching from, 44–45
shutdowns, adding links for, 127–128
tiles organization, 13, 42–43, 124. *See also* tiles
zooming, 10
Start8, 12, 40
StartKiller app, 40
startup apps
adding, 155–156
creating, 641
examining, 154–155
Group Policy settings for, 153
issues with, 152
Magnifier, setting to be, 177
methods for setting up, 153–154
registry settings for, 153–154
removing, 155, 630
scheduled tasks, 153
services as, 153
shell service objects, 154
Task Manager, Startup tab, 34, 641
Windows 8.1 improvements for, 153
Startup Repair as boot option, 20
Startup Settings as boot option, 20
Startup tab, Task Manager, 34, 641
startups
apps auto launching during. *See* startup apps
Automatic Repair option, 654–655

boot process preceding. *See* booting Windows 8.1
chkdsk command, 657
delaying automatic services, 630–633
failures, troubleshooting, 243
hard disk drive troubleshooting, 660–661
Hiren's BootCD to repair, 657–658
PC internals and cables, checking for problems, 654
recent changes, problems caused by, 654
recovery environment, launching, 244
Refresh Your PC command, 657
reinstalling Windows 8.1 to fix, 659–660
removing startup apps, 630
Repair Your Computer option, 654–655
Safe Mode, 244
Settings page, 244
speeding up, 630–634
SSDs for increasing speed of, 634
start menu, always showing, 244
troubleshooting, 653–661
unplugging PCs before retrying, 653
USB and other devices interference with, 654
WinRE for solving problems with, 654–660
wmic logicaldisk get name command, 656
static IP addresses, configuring, 517–518
Steps Recorder, 157, 206–207
stereos
aux-in ports for, 348–349
car stereos, 348–350
FM transmitters for, 349–350
HDMI cabling for, 373, 379
RCA connectors, 379
from smartphones, 348–349
streaming music to, 343–346
Sticky Keys, 187
stock market news, 80–81
Stop errors, 663–665
storage
analyzing disk space, 229
app for managing. *See* Storage Spaces
BitLocker encryption of. *See* BitLocker
cloud services for, 244–245
compressing drives, 228
connecting to external disks, 235–236
data loss scenarios, 233–235
freeing up disk space, 228–230
HDDs for. *See* hard disk drives
HTPC recommendations, 377–378
NAS (network attached storage), 522
photo editing recommendations, 340
resiliency options for, 31–32

storage, *continued*
SkyDrive for. *See* SkyDrive
Storage Spaces for. *See* Storage Spaces
System Performance reports, 651–652
utilization, viewing with Task Manager, 639–640
storage area networks (SANs), virtual, 484
Storage Spaces
advantages of, 261
block sizes, 262
capabilities of, 31–32
configuring, 264–268
Control Panel tool for managing, 264–265
creating new pools, 264–265
drive failure effects, 263
drive selection, 264–265
format, file system, 262
lack of portability to older computers, 262
mirroring with, 263, 266–267
parity, 263, 267
performance issues, 263
pools, 262–268
portability issues of, 262–263
RAID, as alternative to, 261, 263
redundancy benefit, 261, 263
resiliency benefit, 262, 263
resiliency configuration, 266–268
system drive not allowed in, 262
Store, Windows. *See* **Windows Store**
streaming
FM transmitters for, 348–350
homegroup option for, 584
HTPC capabilities for, 361
music services for, 352
music to stereos and TVs, 343–346
performance issues, 347
video services for, 353
stretching, 6
subnet masks, configuring, 517–518, 553
support. *See also* **help**
90 days of free premium phone support, 195
answerdesk.com, 195
determining who to contact for, 197–198
manufacturer-provided, 195
Microsoft Answer Desk, 196
Microsoft Stores, 196
Microsoft Support searches, 199
paid, non-Microsoft, 196
remote assistance for. *See* Remote Assistance
Steps Recorder, 206–207
Windows Community, 200

SUSE Linux Enterprise Server, 491–493
suspension of apps, 62–63
S-Video TV connections, 374–376
swiping
accessing login screen with, 8
actions performed by, 5
switches, Ethernet, 526, 564
SYSTEM account, 219–220
System Configuration, 155
system drives
BitLocker encryption of, 270
copying to another drive, 656–657
not allowed in Storage Spaces pools, 262
troubleshooting, 656–657, 660–661
wmic logicaldisk get name command, 656
system files
corrupted by drive errors, 283
saving of old during upgrades to Windows 8.1, 121–122
system folders, permissions for, 219
system images
backups of, 243
System Image Recovery, 454–455
System Image Recovery boot option, 20
System Information tool, 154–155
System Performance reports, 651–652
System Restore
as an antimalware option, 451–454
apps, effect on, 451
as boot option, 20
listing apps installed since last restore point, 454
restore point selection, 452–453
SystemRescueCD, 247

T
tapping gesture, 4
Task Manager
affinity, setting, 627
App History tab, 60, 640–641
apps, researching online, 641
available memory, determining, 479
capabilities of, 634–635
closing apps with, 635–636
command lines to run processes, 638
CPU utilization of apps, viewing, 625–627
Delete Usage History command, 641
detailed interface for, 34–35
Details tab, 643
End Task command, 635–637
executable files, finding, 638
groups, processes organized by, 637

More Details link, 637
noisy hard disk drives, 629
opening, 635
Performance tab, 639–640
PIDs, 638
priority, setting, 626
Process Name, 638
Processes tab, 636–638
publisher of process, viewing, 638
removing startup apps, 155
Resource Manager functionality in, 636
Run New Task command, 638
Search Indexer performance, 257–258
Services tab, 644
simple interface for, 33–34
starting apps with, 638
startup apps, examining, 154
Startup tab, 641
stopping apps from, 626
types of processes, viewing, 638
Users tab, 642
Task Scheduler, 153, 155–156, 641
taskbar, desktop
multiple monitor options for, 33, 140–141
pinning apps to, 132–133
Recycle Bin, adding to, 134–135
TCP ports, 461–463
television. *See* **TV**
temp folder, 230
TestDisk, 247
testing
apps after upgrades and migrations, 120–121
memory, 666–669
tethering, 47, 561
text
adjusting selections with circles, 4
ClearType, 178
Magnifier with, 177–182
typing, autocorrection of words during, 15
text-to-speech
Narrator, 18, 173, 183–185
third-party software, 185–186
***The IT Crowd*, 563**
thumbnails, File Explorer, enabling by default, 336–337
Thunder, 185
tiles
bandwidth used by, viewing, 60
clearing data from, 128–129
disabling live updates, 128
grouping on Start screen, 124

icons of, file location for, 124
live, 59–60, 128
organizing, 13, 42–43, 124
overriding defaults for, 60
Photos app, 325–326
Pin To Start option, 61
resizing, 124
settings, 128–129
updating of data displayed, 59–61
Time Allowances, Family Safety, 431–432
Time's Up warning, Family Safety, 432
toolbar, Quick Launch, 134–135
top edge of screen, swiping from, 5
touch controls
active areas of screen, 4
flicking, 6
holding a finger on an object, 5
Internet Explorer 11, for, 68
pinching, 6
rotation gesture, 6–7
slide gesture, 5–6
stretching, 6
swiping, 5
tapping, 4
Windows 8.1 designed for, 3
touch gestures, 4–6
touch hardware requirements, 21
TPM (Trusted Platform Module), 26, 269–273, 280–281
transcoding media files, 346
transferring files to a new Windows 8.1 PC, 116–119
translate.bing.com, 425
travel
backup disks for, 238–239
Travel app, 84
Trinity Rescue Kit, 247
Trojans, 438, 441
troubleshooting networks. *See* **network troubleshooting**
Trusted Platform Module (TPM), 26, 269–273, 280–281
tuner cards, 380, 382–387
Turn On File And Printer Sharing setting, 602
TV. *See also* **video**
Apple TV, 353
broadcast TV with HTPCs, 386
cable service for, 382–387
cabling for HTPCs with, 373–376
closed captioning, 365
conversion to mobile device formats, 360
Google TV, 353
HD video resolutions, 376
HDMI cabling to, 373, 375–376, 379

TV, *continued*
   HTPCs for watching. *See* HTPCs (Home Theater PCs)
   MCEBuddy for converting, 366–369
   purchasing in Video app, 317–319
   recording, 382–387
   satellite, recording, 382–387
   sets, streaming to, 345–347
   storage requirements, by resolution and time, 378
   televisions, streaming to, 345–347
   video-streaming services, 353
Tversity, 346
Twitter
   Online Communications level, Family Safety, 425
   People app integration of, 74–75
typing, autocorrection of words during, 15

U

UAC (User Account Control)
   turning off, 469–470
   warnings by, 442
Ubuntu Linux, 478
Ubuntu Rescue Remix, 247
UDP ports, 461–463
UEFI (Unified Extensible Firmware Interface), 18, 25, 26
Ultimate Boot CD, 247, 669–670
UNetbootin tool, 92–93, 221
Unified Extensible Firmware Interface (UEFI), 18, 25, 26
uninstalling apps, 148–149, 228, 449, 617
uninstalling Windows 8.1, 122
uninterruptable power supplies (UPSs), 234
unique passwords guideline, 405
Universal Plug and Play (UPnP) routers, 467, 521
Update & Recovery, File History command, 239
updates
   BIOS, 617
   legacy OS, 613–614
updates for apps
   automatic downloads with notifications, 56–57
   desktop app, 614–615
   installing, 614–615
   as troubleshooting technique, 199
updates for Windows 8.1
   automatic, setting during installation, 98
   configuring, 611–612
   critical updates, 610
   importance of, 609
   manual downloads of, 613
   optional updates, 612–613
   Patch Tuesday, 610

   restarts required by, 609, 610
   router firmware, 525
   scheduling, 611–612
   security updates, 610
   service packs, 610
   as a troubleshooting technique, 199
   types of, 610
   updating to Windows 8.1, 111
   waking up for option, 611–612
   Windows Defender definitions, 610
   Windows life cycles, 613–614
upgrading to Windows 8.1
   32-bit vs. 64-bit, 113
   app configuration, 120–122
   backup recommended, 111
   BIOS and firmware requirements, 111
   choosing what to keep options, 114–116
   configuring apps, 120
   DEP requirement, 112
   disk space requirement, 112
   features provided by. *See* Windows 8.1 update features
   freeing up disk space after, 121–122
   hardware issues, 116
   limited licenses, deactivating, 112
   memory requirements, 112
   Microsoft accounts for logins, 116
   migration alternative. *See* migrating to a
     Windows 8.1 PC
   preparations for, 111–112
   product keys for, 113–114
   Program Files folder, saving of old, 121–122
   Setup, starting Windows 8.1, 113
   system files, saving of old, 121–122
   testing, 120–121
   uninstalling unwanted apps, 112
   user profiles, saving of old, 121–122
   versions of Windows that can be upgraded, 111
   Vista, from, 112–113
   Windows 8, from, 111
   XP, from, 112–113
UPnP (Universal Plug and Play), 467
upper-left screen corner, 5, 7
UPSs (uninterruptable power supplies), 234
usage information, sending to Microsoft, 97–99
USB flash drives
   AutoPlay with, 151–152
   as BitLocker keys, 271, 276–279
   bootable, 92–93, 220–221

USB ports
2.0 speed limit, 286
3.0, photo editing recommendation for, 340
cables, importing photos from cameras with, 326–327
devices interfering with Windows startup, 654
Ethernet adapters, 515
flash drives. *See* USB flash drives
mobile broadband adapters, 561
version 3.0, 22
wireless adapters, 525
User Account Control (UAC), 442
user accounts
adding to groups, 419
advantages of, 393
children's, specifying as, 395–396
deleting, 417–418
disabling accounts, 417
Family Safety with, 393
guest accounts, 416–417
local. *See* local user accounts
logging off from Task Manager, 642
lost local passwords, need to reinstall Windows, 395
Microsoft accounts as, 394–397
PINs for, 404
requiring regular password changes for, 413–414
resetting passwords for, 394–395
setting to skip logins, 369
user interface. *See also specific components*
design theme of, 8
desktop. *See* desktop
full-screen apps with, 51
new features of Windows 8.1, 3, 8–20
Start screen. *See* Start screen
touch gestures, 4–6
%UserProfile%, 162–163
users
accounts for. *See* user accounts
adding to existing groups, 419
permissions for sharing folders, 589–592
permissions for user folders, 219
profile of. *See* profiles, user
Select Users Or Groups dialog box, 590
Task Manager, Users tab, 642
users folder, 230
viewing with Task Manager, 34
Users folder, sharing of, 588–592
Users group, 397, 421
utilization of resources
Details tab, Task Manager, 643
viewing with Task Manager, 639–640

V
VGA, 373–374
VHDs (virtual hard disks)
booting, 91, 104–108
legacy Windows OSs on, 476
video
advantages of Internet for, 307
animations for, 321
AutoPlay, 151–152
built-in app for. *See* Video app
burning movie DVDs, 355–357
codecs, 320
DVD playback not included, 47
editing, 319–323
file format issues with DMRs, 345
graphics cards for. *See* video cards
HandBrake to increase audio volume, 349
HD (high-definition) issues, 347
HD resolutions, 376
HTPCs for watching. *See* HTPCs (Home Theater PCs)
library for, 308, 316–317, 351
MCEBuddy for converting, 366–369
MP4 format, 368
MPEG-3 format, 345
power settings for mobile, 138
publishing, 322–323
recording TV, 382–387
Reliability Monitor detection of problems with, 662–664
SkyDrive synchronization options for, 296
still photos, adding, 322
storage requirements, by resolution and time, 378
streaming, network requirements for, 380
streaming performance, 347
streaming services, 353
surround sound with, 364
transcoding media files, 346, 377
TV shows. *See* TV
visual effects, adding, 321
Video app
capabilities of, 78
controls for, 316–317
default installs for new users, 168
Free TV, 319
Microsoft Points, 319
Personal Videos category, 316
Play vs. Download option for purchases, 319
purchasing with, 317–319
streaming videos, 316–317
troubleshooting, 318

Video app, *continued*
  Video library, choosing from, 316
  watching with, 316–317
video cards
  driver updates, 616
  for HTPCs, 373–376
  for photo editing, 340
  Reliability Monitor detection of problems with, 662–664
  Ultimate Boot CD test of, 670
Videos library
  adding Video folders from other computers, 351
  scanning by Music app, 308
  Video app with, 316–317
virtual disks
  adding to VMs, 488–489
  formats available for, 496
  migrating physical disk contents to, 497–499
  types of, 496–497
virtual hard disk (VHD) booting, 91, 104–108
virtual machines. *See* VMs (virtual machines)
Virtual Network Computing (VNC), 202
virtual SANs, 484
virtual switch creation, Hyper-V, 476–478
VirtualBox, 37, 501–502
virtualization
  Hyper-V for. *See* Hyper-V
  VirtualBox, 37, 501–502
  VMs. *See* VMs (virtual machines)
viruses. *See also* malware
  default protections from, 441
  methods of spreading, 438
  signatures of, 446
  Windows Defender antivirus software, 445–446
Vista. *See* Windows Vista
ViStart, 12
visual accessibility, 175–183
VMs (virtual machines)
  add hardware setings, 485
  audio support for, 502
  automatic stop action, 494
  backup services for, 492
  bandwidth settings, 489–491
  BIOS setings for, 485
  Clipboard with, 499
  closing, handling of, 494
  creating new, 477–483
  cutting and pasting to or from the host, 492
  data exchange services for, 492
  differencing disks, 497

  dynamic memory option, 480–481, 486
  dynamically expanding virtual disks, 496–497
  hardware accessory issues, 500
  heartbeat services for, 492
  Hyper-V for running. *See* Hyper-V
  IDE controller settings for, 488–489
  integration services for, 491–493
  isolation capabilities of, 473
  keyboard shortcuts with, 499–500
  limitations of, 500
  malware testing with, 473
  memory settings, 486
  memory, specifying, 478–481
  migrating physical disk contents to virtual disks, 497–499
  mobile feature issues, 500
  mouse release from, 491–492, 500
  network adapter settings, 489–491
  Percent Of Total System Resources settings, 487, 488
  processor settings, 487–488
  Relative Weight setting, 488
  Remote Desktop control of, 500
  SCSI controller support, 489
  shutting down, 492, 494
  snapshots of, 495
  starting, 495
  state of, saving, 494
  time synchronization with host, 492
  virtual disk management, 496–497
  virtual drives, adding extra, 488–489
  virtual hard disk configuration, 482
  Virtual Machine Limit setting, 488
  Virtual Machine Reserve setting, 487
  virtual switch selection, 481
VNC (Virtual Network Computing), 202
voice recognition. *See* speech recognition
volumes
  naming, 238
  shrinking, 101–104
VPNs (virtual private networks)
  router support for, 523
  Wi-Fi with, 469

W
waking up, requiring password on, 137
Weather app, 80, 168
web hosting, 546
WebAnywhere, 186
webcam permissions, 158

webpages
embedding files in, from SkyDrive, 295–296
InPrivate browsing, 447–448
websites
activity reporting feature of Family Safety, 428–430
filtering options, Family Safety, 423–427
pinging, 568–572
testing on varied browsers, 476
testing servers with PortQry, 572–573
WEI (Windows Experience Index), 621
WEP, 534, 535
Wi-Fi
802.11 standards, choosing from, 530–531
access points for. *See* wireless access points
ad hoc networking, 547–554
adapter driver settings, 519–520
airplane mode, 28, 560
antennas, 533–534
bandwidth availability, 318
channels, setting, 539
client devices, 508
Connectify Hotspot app, 553–554
device adapters for, 525
encryption standards, 534–535
Eye-Fi SD cards, 327
Find Devices And Content option, 540–541
firewall for. *See* Windows Firewall
hacking software, 535
home network architecture, typical, 506
HTTPS with, 469
improvements in Windows 8.1 for, 28
inSSIDer, 539–540
interference, objects causing, 538–539
ISP connections using, 514
laptop range, limited by, 534
MAC address filtering, 535–536
multiple access points, adding coverage with, 539
passwords, 535
passwords, transferring during upgrades, 112
performance issues, 534, 580
performance monitoring, 539–540
performance, typical by type of network, 581
physical coverage, extending, 538–540
power options for, 518–520
power settings, 137
printers connected to, 596
revoking access to, 535
router configuration for, 524–525
security for, 469–470

Set As Metered Connection option, 540
setting up, 515–516
Show My Estimated Data Use option, 540
SSIDs, 524, 538, 539–540
streaming performance issues, 347
tethering, 47, 561
troubleshooting process, 577–578. *See also* network troubleshooting
two PCs, connecting without an access point. *See* ad hoc networking
unencrypted, dangers of, 469–470
video streaming requirements, 380
VPNs with, 469
WEP, 534, 535
wireless access points for. *See* wireless access points
WPA, 535
WPA2, 534
Wild Media Server, 346
wildcards, 225–226
Windows 7
integration services for VMs running, 491–493
migrating to a Windows 8.1 PC, 116–119
version of, viewing, 90
VM memory requirements, 478
Windows 8.1 Enterprise, 4, 89, 90
Windows 8.1 Pro, 37, 90–91
Windows 8.1 RT, 22
Windows 8.1 update features
3-D printer support, 46
All Apps screen, 43
booting to the desktop options, 38–40
camera access while locked, 42
lock screen slide shows, 41–42
multitasking improvements, 37–38
personalization options, 44
remote data removal feature, 46
search improvements with, 44–45
security improvements, 46
Start button, 40
Start screen tiles organization, 42–43
WinX menu improvements, 41
Windows 98 VM memory requirements, 478
Windows 2000, 491–493
Windows Community, 200
Windows Defender
local network monitoring by, 46
new features in Windows 8.1, 25
scanning for malware, 445–446, 449–450
turning off, 471–472

sfer
...er 715

...–446
... 149
..., 610
...er, 116–119
...porting, 98, 99
...rience Index discontinued, 621
...plorer
...le management approach of, 211
...dows 8.1 replacement for. *See* File Explorer
...dows Features dialog box, Hyper-V option, 475
Windows Firewall
  allowing apps to listen for incoming connections,
    458–459
  blocking incoming connections for apps, 460–461
  capabilities of, 457
  disabling rules, 464
  disabling temporarily, 465–467
  IP addresses, 461, 464–465
  manual rule configuration, 461–465
  naming rules, 464
  network types, selecting, 457, 459, 463–464
  port number settings, 461–465
  printer sharing, settings to allow, 603
  Scope tab, 464–465
Windows Home Server Drive Extender, 32
Windows key keyboard shortcuts
  Start screen, opening, 10
  table of, 8
  Windows+F shortcut, 13, 52
  Windows+I, 13, 14
  Windows+K, 13
  Windows+Plus Sign, 181–182
  Windows+Power, 635
  Windows+R, 10
  Windows+X, 10, 548
Windows life cycles, 613–614
Windows Live Essentials
  Movie Maker, 319–323, 355–357
  Windows Photo Gallery, 341
Windows Live Hotmail, 545
Windows Media Audio format. *See* WMA (Windows
  Media Audio) format
Windows Media Center. *See* Media Center, Windows
Windows Media Player
  burning CDs, 354–355
  replaced by Music app, 307
  ripping CDs with, 313–315
Windows Memory Diagnostics tool, 666–669

Windows Phones
  accessing SkyDrive from, 292–294
  Xbox Music compatibility, 313
Windows Photo Gallery
  editing capabilities of, 341
  RAW files with, 334
Windows Photo Viewer, 336
Windows Push Notification Services (WNS), 59–60
Windows Recovery Environment (WinRE)
  booting to, 20
  troubleshooting with, 654–660
  Windows Memory Diagnostics tool, 666–669
Windows Search service, 630
Windows Server integration services, 491–493
Windows Setup
  custom settings, selecting, 98–100
  express settings, using, 97–98
  license terms, 94
  online solutions, setting for, 98, 99
  options, 93–94
  Personalize screen, 96
  product key entry, 94–95, 113–114
  sharing settings, 98
  upgrading to 8.1 with, 113–116
  user account setup, 100
  Where Do You Want To Install page, 96
  Which Type Of Installation options, 94–95
Windows Stopped Working events, 663–664
Windows Store
  app packages, 168–170
  apps vs. desktop apps, 8
  disabling, 56
  game restrictions with Family Safety, 434–435
  installing apps from, 55–56, 147–148
  permissions for apps, viewing, 158
  quality safeguards, 148
  Search charm with, 55
  searching for apps in, 52
  services and processes used by, 54
  uninstalling apps, 148–149
  uninstalling of not allowed, 149
Windows Update. *See* updates for Windows 8.1
Windows Vista
  folder sharing, 588
  integration services for VMs running, 491–493
  migrating to a Windows 8.1 PC, 116–119
  updates no longer available, 614
  updating to Windows 8.1, 112–113
  VM memory requirements, 478

Windows XP
folder sharing, 588
integration services for VMs running, 491–493
migrating to a Windows 8.1 PC, 116–119
updates no longer available, 614
updating to Windows 8.1, 112–113
VM memory requirements, 478
Windows+F shortcut, 13, 52
Windows+I shortcut, 13, 14
Windows+K shortcut, 13
Windows+Plus Sign, 181–182
Windows+Power (Task Manager), 635
Windows+R shortcut, 10
Windows+Volume Up, 183
Windows+W shortcut, 16
Windows+X shortcut, 10, 143, 548
.winmd files, 161, 162
WinRE. *See* **Windows Recovery Environment (WinRE)**
WinRMRemoteWMIUsers group, 421
WinX menu
adding items to, 144
administrative command prompt from, 548
Computer Management, opening from, 415
Editor tool, 144
improvements in, 41
mechanism of, 145
opening, 10–11
personalization of, 143–145
shortcut to, 10, 143, 548
wiping data remotely, 46
wired Ethernet clients
cabling for, 527
coax cables for, 527–528
network performance, typical by type of network, 581
performance advantages of, 508, 526
phone lines for, 528
place in network architecture, 508
powerline Ethernet adapters, 528–530
speed standards, 526
switches, 526
wireless access points
antennas, 533–534
bridging feature, 532
channels, setting, 539
configuration, 524–525
encryption standards, 534–535
guest access feature, 531
interference, objects causing, 538–539
locating for maximum coverage, 538
MAC address filtering, 535–536

multiple, adding coverage with, 539
performance issues, 534
performance monitoring, 539–540
printers, connecting to, 596
proprietary improvements in, 532
purpose of, 508
resetting to defaults to troubleshoot, 578
restart order for devices, recommended, 564
routers, as part of, 521
scheduling support, 532
SSIDs, 524, 538–540
weatherproofed, 531
wireless bridges, 525, 532
wireless networks. *See* **Wi-Fi; wireless access points**
WireShark, 469–470
WMA (Windows Media Audio) format
car stereo support for, 350
song file sizes, 378
Xbox Music's use of, 312–313
wmic logicaldisk get name command, 656
WNS (Windows Push Notification Services), 59–60
WordPress, 546
work folder synchronization with BYOD, 47
worms, 438, 441
WPA, 535
WPA2, 534
WWAHost.exe, 54

X

XAML based apps, 160–161
XBMC, 361
Xbox 360
Music app with, 343–344
Music Player app of, 344
streaming performance issues, 347
Video Player app of, 344
Windows Media Center with, 344
Xbox Companion app, 343–344
Xbox Live login required to stream music, 343
Xbox Music app, 308, 312–313
Xbox Music service
determining if songs are available in, 343
format and copy protection, 312–313
stereos, outputting to, 343–344
subscription nature of, 352
Xbox Video, 353
xcopy command, 657
.xml files, 161
XPS files, 81

video to

les 717

322–323

zooming
  as an accessibility option for apps, 176
  Magnifier for, 177–182
  touch controls for, 6
Zune accounts, 312

About the author

Tony Northrup, MCPD, MCITP, MCSE, and CISSP, is an author and photographer. He lives in Waterford, Connecticut. Tony's love of PCs started as a child in 1981, when his dad built a Sinclair ZX81, one of the first affordable home computers. Thirty years later, Tony has played with every version of Windows and created more than 30 books and several video training courses about his favorite operating system. Tony is the coauthor of *Windows Vista Resource Kit* and *Windows 7 Resource Kit* and the author of *Windows 8 Inside Out*, among other titles. You can friend Tony on Facebook at *http://www.facebook.com/tony.northrup* or follow his photo blog at *http://www.facebook.com/NorthrupPhotography*.

a-